Laura Lemay
Rogers Cadenhead

SAMS

Teach Yourself

Java™ 2

PLATFORM

in 21 Days

PROFESSIONAL REFERENCE EDITION

SAMS

201 West 103rd St., Indianapolis, Indiana, 46290

Copyright © 1999 by Sams Publishing

International Standard Book Number: 0-672-31438-X

Library of Congress Catalog Card Number: 97-80859

Printed in the United States of America

First Printing: December 1998

00   99   98   4   3   2   1

Trademarks

Executive Editor
Mark Taber

Development Editor
Scott D. Meyers

Managing Editor
Patrick Kanouse

Project Editor
Carol Bowers

Copy Editors
Sean Medlock
Tonya Maddox

Proofreader
Kim Cofer

Indexer
Erika Millen

Technical Editor
Eric Wolf

Layout Technician
Brian Borders

Cover Designer
Aren Howell

Book Designer
Gary Adair

Overview

Introduction

Contents

Dedication

To Eric, for all the usual reasons (moral support, stupid questions, comfort in dark times, brewing big pots of coffee).—LL

To my grandfather Bill Craker, for always being the first relative to find my writing in the newspaper; and uncle George Craker, for the gut-to-gut hugs that made it look like a sumo match had broken out at the family Christmas gathering. You're both missed.—Rogers

Acknowledgments

From Laura Lemay:

To Sun's Java team, for all their hard work on Java, the language, and on the browser, and particularly to Jim Graham, who demonstrated Java and HotJava to me on very short notice in May 1995 and planted the idea for this book.

To everyone who bought my previous books and liked them: Buy this one, too.

From Rogers Cadenhead:

I'm one of those people who plans his Oscar acceptance speech years in advance, even though I have never worked on any project that could possibly lead to winning an Academy Award. If this book were eligible for an Oscar, my speech would start with profuse thanks to the folks at Macmillan who've contributed greatly to the quality of this book, including Mark Taber, Scott Meyers, Carol Bowers, Sean Medlock, Erika Millen, and Kim Cofer. Next, I would thank my former agent Brian Gill and my current agent David Rogelberg, and I would blow a kiss to my wife Mary and my son Max, who would be in the audience. After the kiss, I would throw out the names of personal acquaintances and relatives whom I owe either thanks or money—Wade DuChene, Jonathan Bourne, Mark Winner, Phil Weinstock, Eric Manuel, Chad Cadenhead, Kelly Cadenhead, Mom, Dad, Clint Moewe, Marie Moewe, Industrial Light and Magic, James Cameron, the Academy, Mike Rhyner, the Anti-Defamation League of B'nai Brith, Andrew Borokove, Greg Williams, Walker Texas Ranger, the Dewey Decimal System, and radio station KTCK/Dallas-Fort Worth. Finally, I would finish with a plea for all people to live together in harmony and peace, and for the immediate abolishment of the designated hitter.

I'd also like to thank readers who have sent helpful comments about corrections, typos, and suggested improvements to the prior edition of the book. The list includes, but is probably not limited to, the following people: Lawrence Chang, Jim DeVries, Ryan Esposto, Bruce Franz, Owen Gailar, Ben Hensley, Jon Hereng, Drew Huber, Stephen Loscialpo, Brad Kaenel, Chris McGuire, Chip Pursell, Luke Shulenburger, Joseph Walsh, Chen Yan, Kyu Hwang Yeon, and J-F. Zurcher.

About the Authors

Laura Lemay is a technical writer and a nerd. After spending six years writing software documentation for various computer companies in Silicon Valley, she decided that writing books would be much more fun. In her spare time she collects computers, email addresses, interesting hair colors, and non-running motorcycles. She is also the perpetrator of *Sams Teach Yourself Web Publishing with HTML in a Week*, *The Official Marimba Guide to Castanet*, and *Laura Lemay's Teach Yourself Perl in 21 Days*.

Rogers Cadenhead is a serial author who will write again unless he is stopped. He is the author of three of the following four books: *Sams Teach Yourself Java 1.2 in 24 Hours*, *Sams Teach Yourself to Create a Home Page in 24 Hours*, *Sams Teach Yourself SunSoft Java WorkShop in 21 Days*, and *Sams Teach Yourself to Erase Incriminating Audiotape in 17 Minutes*. He also writes a question-and-answer trivia column for the *Fort Worth Star-Telegram*, Knight-Ridder News Service, and *New York Times* News Syndicate. He maintains this book's official World Wide Web site at http://www.prefect.com/java21pre.

Tell Us What You Think!

As a reader, you are the most important critic of and commentator on our books. We value your opinion and want to know what we're doing right, what we could do better, what areas you'd like to see us publish in, and any other words of wisdom you're willing to pass our way. You can help us make strong books that meet your needs and give you the computer guidance you require.

As the executive editor for the Web development team at Macmillan Computer Publishing, I welcome your comments. You can fax, email, or write me directly to let me know what you did or didn't like about this book, as well as what we can do to make our books stronger.

Fax: 317-817-7070
Email: webdev@mcp.com
Mail: Mark Taber
           Executive Editor, Web Development
           Macmillan Computer Publishing
           201 W. 103rd Street
           Indianapolis, IN 46290

Introduction

Four years ago, the word *java* conjured up images of either an Indonesian island or a hot cup of coffee. Today, anyone who has seen a Web page, computer magazine, or newspaper business section knows about another kind of Java—the programming language introduced by Sun Microsystems.

There are movie stars, athletes on crime sprees, and misbehaving politicians who receive less hype and attention than Java. The language is becoming as much a part of software development as the beverage of the same name. One kind of java keeps programmers up nights. The other enables programmers to rest easier after they develop software.

The Java programming language rose to prominence in late 1995 after Netscape licensed it for use in their Navigator browser. Today there are several options for adding interactive programs to Web pages, including Macromedia Shockwave and Microsoft ActiveX. When Java was introduced, it revolutionized the nature of Web pages. Java applets— small programs that run inside the browser as part of a page—are used for games, multimedia, animation, and other special effects. According to the AltaVista search engine, more than one million pages on the World Wide Web include Java applets.

With the release of Java 2, Java has fully extended its reach beyond the Web. The language that's so popular on the Internet can be used for general-purpose software development as well.

You might be familiar with Java programming tools such as Symantec Visual Café and SunSoft Java WorkShop. These programs make it possible to develop functional Java programs, but the best way to learn the full scope of the language is to work directly with it via Sun's Java Development Kit or JDK. The JDK, which is available for free on the Web at http://java.sun.com, is a set of command-line tools for writing, compiling, and testing Java programs.

This is where *Sams Teach Yourself Java 2 in 21 Days, Professional Reference Edition* comes in. You'll be introduced to all aspects of Java software development, using the most current version of the language and the best available techniques. By the time you're done, you'll know why Java has become the most talked-about programming language of the past decade, and why it might be the most popular language of the next decade.

How This Book Is Organized

Sams Teach Yourself Java 2 in 21 Days, Professional Reference Edition covers the Java language and its class libraries in 21 days, organized into three separate weeks. Each week covers a different, broad area of Java applet and application development. There's also a bonus week that covers the most advanced and sophisticated elements of the language, exploring topics such as JavaBeans, Remote Method Invocation, and Java Database Connectivity.

In the first week you'll learn about the Java language itself:

- Day 1 is the basic introduction: what Java is, why it's cool, and how to get the software needed to create Java programs. You'll also create your first Java application.
- On Day 2, you'll explore basic object-oriented programming concepts as they apply to Java.
- On Day 3, you'll start getting down to details with the basic Java building blocks—data types, variables, and expressions such as arithmetic and comparisons.
- Day 4 goes into detail about how to deal with objects in Java—how to create them, how to access their variables and call their methods, and how to compare and copy them. You'll also get your first glance at the Java class libraries.
- On Day 5, you'll learn more about Java with arrays, conditional statements, and loops.
- Day 6 fully explores the creation of classes (the basic building blocks of any Java program) and how to put together a Java application (a program that can run on its own without a Web browser).
- Day 7 builds on what you learned on Day 6. You'll learn more about how to create and use methods, including overriding and overloading methods and creating constructors.

Week 2 is dedicated primarily to applets and graphical programming techniques such as animation and image handling:

- Day 8 provides the basics of applets—how they differ from applications, how to create them, and the most important parts of an applet's life cycle. You'll also learn how to create HTML pages that contain Java applets.
- On Day 9, you'll learn about the Java classes for drawing shapes and characters on the screen, including coverage of the new Java2D classes introduced in Java 2.
- On Day 10, you'll create multimedia programs that use images, sound, and animation sequences. You'll also get your first experience with multithreading—a way to get your programs to handle multiple tasks at the same time.
- Day 11 begins a four-day exploration of visual programming. You'll learn how to create a graphical user interface for applets using the Abstract Windowing Toolkit (AWT), a set of classes introduced in Java 1.02.

- Day 12 covers how to make a user interface look good using layout managers, a set of classes that determine how components on an interface will be arranged.
- Day 13 continues the coverage of the AWT with event-handling classes, which enable a program to respond to mouse clicks and other user interactions.
- On Day 14, you'll round out your knowledge of the AWT by learning how to develop pop-up windows, menus, and standalone applications.

Week 3 includes advanced topics and an introduction to Swing, the new visual programming expansion of the Abstract Windowing Toolkit:

- On Day 15, you'll learn more about interfaces and packages (which are useful for grouping classes and organizing a class hierarchy), as well as other advanced aspects of the core language itself.
- Day 16 covers exceptions—errors, warnings, and other abnormal conditions—generated in your programs by either you or the system.
- Day 17 covers input and output using streams, a set of classes that enable file access, network access, and other sophisticated data handling.
- On Day 18, you'll extend your knowledge of streams to write programs that communicate with the Internet, including socket programming and URL handling.
- Day 19 begins a three-day introduction to Swing, the remarkable new set of classes that are part of Java 2. You use these classes to create the user interface for an application, making use of such features as a variable look and feel.
- On Day 20, you'll turn a graphical user interface into a functioning application that can respond to user events.
- On Day 21, you'll round out your knowledge of Swing by learning about new interface components such as docktable toolbars, sliders, and scrolling panels. You'll also create a working Swing applet that can be used to view and rescale graphics files.

The bonus week, included only with the *Professional Reference Edition* of this book, covers the most advanced topics in Java 2:

- On Day 22, you'll get more experience with the JDK's tools, including several new ones such as the jdb debugging tool and the javadoc documentation-creation tool.
- Day 23 covers an element of Java Foundation Classes called the Accessibility classes. These classes enable you to create Java programs that work in conjunction with assistive technology such as screen readers and Braille terminals. They also make programs more usable for everyone running them.

- On Day 24, you'll learn how to create digitally signed applets that can bypass the normal security measures in place for Java programs that run over the Web.

- On Day 25, you'll be introduced to a third type of input/output stream: object streams. These can be used to save and restore objects from disk. You'll also learn how to use Remote Method Invocation (RMI) to call an object's methods over a computer network.

- Day 26 covers the new data structures that are part of the `java.util` package, including enumerations, stacks, bit sets, and vectors. You'll also create your own implementation of a linked list.

- The component model of programming is extended on Day 27. You'll learn how to create JavaBeans, self-contained classes that enable rapid application development. The JavaBean Development Kit (BDK) is used to work with existing beans and create relationships between them.

- Your fourth week of Java 2 tutelage concludes on Day 28 with Java Database Connectivity (JDBC), which enables you to use relational databases in your Java programs. You'll also use ODBC, a similar database connectivity solution.

About This Book

This book teaches you all about the Java language and how to use it to create applets for both the World Wide Web and for standalone applications. By the time you finish *Sams Teach Yourself Java 2 in 21 Days, Professional Reference Edition*, you'll know enough about Java and the Java class libraries to do just about anything—inside an applet or out.

Who Should Read This Book

This book teaches the Java language to three groups:

- Novices who are relatively new to programming.
- People who have been introduced to Java 1.1 or 1.02.
- Experienced developers in other languages, such as Visual C++, Visual Basic, or Delphi.

You'll learn how to develop applets, interactive Java programs that run as part of a Web page, and applications, programs that run anywhere else. When you finish *Sams Teach Yourself Java 2 in 21 Days, Professional Reference Edition*, you'll be comfortable enough with Java to dive into your own ambitious programming projects—on the Web or off.

If you're still reasonably new to programming or haven't even written a program before, you might be wondering if this is the right book for you. It is. All of the concepts in this book are illustrated with working programs, so you'll be able to work your way through them no matter your experience level. If you understand what variables, loops, and functions are, you'll benefit from this book.

If any of the following rings true, this book is for you:

- You're a real whiz at HTML, understand CGI programming in Perl, Visual Basic, or some other language, and want to move on to the next level in Web page design.
- You had some BASIC or Pascal in school, you have a grasp of what programming is, and you've heard Java is powerful, easy to learn, and cool.
- You've programmed in C and C++ for a few years, keep hearing accolades about Java, and want to see if it lives up to the hype.
- You've heard that Java is great for Web programming and want to see how well it can be used for other software development.

If you've never been introduced to object-oriented programming, the style used by Java, you don't have to worry. This book assumes no background in object-oriented design, so you'll get a chance to learn this groundbreaking development strategy as you're learning Java.

If you're a complete beginner, the book might move a little fast. Java is a good language to start with, though, and if you take it slow and work through all the examples, you can still pick up Java and start creating your own applets.

How This Book Is Structured

This book is intended to be read and absorbed over the course of three weeks. During each week you'll read seven chapters that present concepts related to the Java language and the creation of applets and applications.

Conventions

A Note presents interesting, sometimes technical pieces of information related to the surrounding discussion.

A Tip offers advice or an easier way to do something.

Caution | A Caution advises you of potential problems and helps you steer clear of disaster.

 NEW TERM New terms are accompanied by New Term boxes, with the new term in *italics*.

TYPE A Type icon identifies some new Java code that you can type in yourself. You can also get the code from the book's companion Web site.

INPUT An Input icon accompanies command prompts.

OUTPUT An Output icon shows the output from a Java program.

Text that you type and text that should appear on your screen is presented in monospace type:

```
It will look like this
```

This font mimics the way text looks on your screen. Placeholders for variables and expressions appear in monospace *italic*.

The end of each chapter offers common questions asked about that day's subject matter, with answers from the authors.

WEEK 1

Getting Started with Java Programming

1

2

3

4

5

6

7

DAY **1**

A Fistful of Java

This represents the end result of nearly 15 years of trying to come up with a better programming language and environment for building simpler and more reliable software.

—Sun Microsystems cofounder Bill Joy

Crazy bellringer was right. There's money to be made in a place like this.

—The Man with No Name, *A Fistful of Dollars*

When the Java programming language was first released publicly in November 1995, it was a lot like a Clint Eastwood gunfighter moseying into a surly Western town.

Like Clint, Java was something the townsfolk hadn't seen before. It was a programming language that could run on a World Wide Web page, making a name for itself amongst the graphics, text, audio, and ubiquitous "under construction" signs. People came from miles around—mostly over Internet connections, but sometimes in person to Silicon Valley—to take a gander at the language.

The legend of Java sometimes outdistanced the reality a bit:

- "Java programs run flawlessly on different computer platforms without modification!"
- "Java ends Microsoft's hegemony over operating systems!"
- "Java turns computer book authors into internationally beloved celebrities!"

In a similar way, legend quickly attached itself to Clint's cinematic gunfighters:

- "He eats bullets for breakfast!"
- "He hits so hard your grandfather gets a bruise!"
- "He can kill a man simply by squinting!"

However, during the past three years Java has lived up to much of its initial hype. The release of Java 2 is a testament to the continuing success and growth of the programming language.

Starting today, you learn about the Java language and why it shot so quickly to prominence in the computer industry. You use Java 2—the most current version at the time of this writing—to create applications that run on your personal computer and can run over a network such as the Internet. You also create programs that run on Web pages using Java 1.0, the version that first became popular and is still supported by the largest number of Web browsers.

When you reach the end of the book, it is hoped that you'll realize another way in which Java is like Clint Eastwood…Java is cool.

Not cool in the just-came-out-of-the-shower-where-the-heck-is-my-towel sense, or cool in the "Jonathan Taylor Thomas is so money and he doesn't even know it" sense, or cool in the "I'm a rap star and I can mumble 75 derogatory remarks about women in a minute" sense.

Java is cool because it's a remarkable language that makes it easier for many programmers to accomplish remarkable things. Java is cool because it makes mind-altering concepts like object-oriented programming more understandable.

Like the word "salsa," Java is cool because it's fun to say out loud. The experience of pronunciation is much more satisfying than exclaiming "Visual Basic," "C plus plus," "Algol," or "Mumps."

If you work your way through the 21 days of this book, you'll become an expert in the full range of Java's capabilities, including graphics, file input and output, user-interface design, event handling, and animation. You will write programs that run on Web pages and others that run on your PC.

1

Today's goals are reasonably modest. You'll learn about the following topics:

- What Java is like today and how it got there
- Why Java is worth learning, and why it's a worthy competitor to other programming languages
- What you need to start writing Java programs—the software, the skills, and some basic terminology
- How to create your first Java program

What Java Is

Based on the enormous amount of press Java has received over the past several years and the huge number of books about Java (1,186 according to the most recent *JavaWorld* count), you might have an inflated impression of what Java is capable of doing.

Java is a programming language that's well-suited to designing software that works in conjunction with the Internet. It's also an object-oriented programming language making use of a methodology that is becoming increasingly useful in the world of software design. Additionally, it's a cross-platform language, which means its programs can be designed to run the same way on Microsoft Windows, Apple Macintosh, and most versions of UNIX, including Solaris. Java extends beyond desktops to run on devices such as televisions, wristwatches, and cellular phones. JavaStation, Sun's network computer, runs the JavaOS operating system and is optimized for the language.

Java is closer to popular programming languages such as C, C++, Visual Basic, and Delphi than it is to a page-description language such as HTML or a simple scripting language such as JavaScript.

Born to Run...on the Web

Java is best known for its capability to run on World Wide Web pages. The Netscape Navigator and Microsoft Internet Explorer browsers can download a Java program from a Web page and run it locally on the Web user's system.

These programs, which are called *applets*, appear in a Web page in a similar fashion to images. Unlike images, applets can be interactive—taking user input, responding to it, and presenting ever-changing content.

Applets can be used to create animation, figures, games, forms that immediately respond to input from the reader, or other interactive effects on the same Web pages among the text and graphics. Figure 1.1 shows an applet running in Netscape Navigator 4.04. Java enables a person to play against three computer opponents in a game of dominos.

FIGURE 1.1.

A Java applet running on Netscape Navigator 4.04.

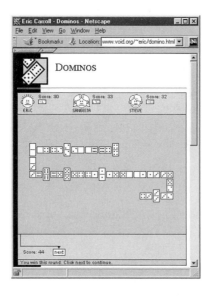

 Note

The Dominos applet was written by Eric Carroll, a Java programmer, cartoonist, and the spike-headed computer opponent in Figure 1.1. You can find Dominos and Eric's home page by visiting http://www.void.org/~eric/domino.html.

Applets are downloaded over the World Wide Web just like HTML pages, graphics, or any other Web site element. On a browser that is equipped to handle Java, the applet will begin running when it finishes downloading.

Applets are written with the Java language, compiled into a form that can be run as a program, and placed on a Web server. Most servers can deliver Java files without any changes to their configuration.

 Note

Almost all applets today are written using Java 1.0, the first popular version of the language, because the leading browser companies have been slow to add support for Java 1.1 and Java 2 applets. At the time of this writing, Netscape has released a software patch that adds partial 1.1 support to Navigator 4.04, and Microsoft has not announced plans to support 1.1 fully in Internet Explorer 4.

1

Web users with a browser that doesn't support Java may see text, a graphic, or nothing—it depends on whether the page designer offers an alternative to the Java applet. You learn more about how applets, browsers, and the World Wide Web work together throughout this book.

Although applets are probably the most popular use of Java, they're just one way in which the language can be used. Like Visual C++, Visual Basic, and Delphi, Java is a robust language that can be used to develop a wide range of software, supporting graphical user interfaces, networking, database connectivity, and other sophisticated functionality. To differentiate from applets, Java programs that don't run within a Web browser are called *applications*.

The Unauthorized Biography

The Java language was developed at Sun Microsystems in 1991 as part of the Green project, a research group working to develop software to control consumer electronics devices. The researchers were hoping to develop the programming language that would run the smart appliances of the future—interactive TVs, interactive toasters, interactive track lighting (sensing a theme here?). Sun's researchers also wanted these devices to communicate with each other, so the lawnmower could tell the blender to let you know that the neighbors had returned from college and were sunbathing again.

To put their research into action, the Green researchers developed a prototype device called the Star7, a remote control-like gadget that could communicate with others of its own kind. The original idea was to develop the Star7 operating system in C++, the hugely popular object-oriented programming language developed by Bjarne Stroustrup. However, Green project member James Gosling became fed up with how C++ was performing on the task, so he barricaded himself in his office and wrote a new language to better handle the Star7. The language was named Oak, in honor of a tree Gosling could see out his office window.

Note

Sun later found out that the name Oak was already in use, but it didn't use Gosling's look-out-the-window method when renaming the language. If it had, you might be adding one of the following language names to your résumé in 21 days:

- Shrubbery
- OfficeBuildingNextDoor
- LightPole
- WindowWasher

- SecretaryLeavingForLunch
- WeirdSecurityGuard
- FatGuyMowing

Because it was designed with appliances in mind rather than state-of-the-art PCs, Java had to be small, efficient, and easily portable to a wide range of hardware devices. It also had to be reliable. People have learned to live with the occasional system crash or glitch in a software application that takes up 5 MB of disk space. It's not as easy to overlook a misprogrammed toaster with an unpleasant habit of bursting into flame.

Although Java didn't originally work out as an appliance- and interactive TV–development tool, the things that made it good for the Star7 turned out to be good for the World Wide Web:

- Java is small—Makes programs faster to download off of a page
- Java is secure—Prevents hackers from writing programs that wreak havoc on browser users' systems
- Java is portable—Allows it to run on Windows, Macintosh, and other platforms without modification

Additionally, Java could be used as a general-purpose programming language for developing software that can run on different platforms.

In order to demonstrate Java's potential and to save its research project from being shelved, a Web browser that could run Java applets was created in 1994. The browser demonstrated two things about Java: what it offered the World Wide Web, and what kind of program Java could create. Programmers Patrick Naughton and Jonathan Payne used Java to create the browser, originally named WebRunner, but rechristened HotJava.

Although Java and the HotJava browser received a lot of attention in the Web community, the language really took off after Netscape became the first company to license the language in August 1995. Netscape executive and boy millionaire Marc Andreesen was one of the first outside Sun to see the appeal of Java, and he gave it a glowing endorsement at the JavaOne conference in May 1996. "Java is a huge opportunity for all of us," he told attendees. Shortly after Java's first public release, Sun spun off its Java development efforts and added hundreds of employees to continue expanding the language.

Versions of the Language

Sun's Java Division has released three major versions of the Java language:

- Java 1.0—Still the most widely supported by Web browsers
- Java 1.1—A spring 1997 release with improvements to the user interface, event handling, and more consistency across the language
- Java 2—The new version, released for public beta-testing first in December 1997 as JDK 1.2 and finalized in December 1998 as "Java 2."

The version numbers of the Java language usually correspond to Sun's primary Java development software—the Java Development Kit. Commonly referred to as the JDK, the kit is currently available in 1.0, 1.1, and 1.2 versions. At press time, JDK 1.2 is still the version of the JDK that's used in what Sun calls the Java 2 platform.

The JDK has always been available at no cost from Sun's Java Web site at http://java.sun.com, and this availability is one of the factors behind the language's rapid growth. It is the first development tool that supports new versions of Java when they're released, often six months or more ahead of other Java development software.

In addition to the JDK, there are more than a dozen Java commercial development tools available for Java programmers. These include the following:

- Symantec Visual Café
- Borland JBuilder
- SuperCede
- Rogue Wave JFactory
- Natural Intelligence Roaster
- MetroWerks CodeWarrior
- SunSoft Java WorkShop

If you are going to use something other than Sun's JDK 1.2 to create Java 2 programs, you need to make sure that it supports Java 2. At the time of this writing, the JDK is still the only tool that has full support for version 2 of the language.

Caution

The programs in this book were tested with JDK 1.2, the most current version of the Development Kit at press time. If you're using something other than the JDK as you work through this book, you should make sure first that it has full JDK 1.2/Java 2 support.

Tell Me, Tell Me, Crystal Ball

Anyone who can precisely define the future of Java should be going after venture capital instead of writing a book. The technology firm Kleiner, Perkins, Caufield and Byers (KPCB) has offered $100 million to support start-up companies doing Java-related work.

However, the enhancements included with Java 2 bode well for its future as a multipurpose, sophisticated language. Early versions of Java were better suited to small Web-based software rather than full-scale applications like group collaboration software, productivity suites, and networked multiplayer games.

That no longer can be said of Java circa 2. Some of the advanced features introduced with the current version include the following:

- Swing—New features for creating a graphical user interface, either in the style of a specific operating system or a new Java "look-and-feel" called Metal
- Drag-and-drop—The capability to interactively transfer information across different applications, and from one part of a program's interface to another
- Complete revision to Java's audio features, bringing them more in line with the sound capabilities of other languages

You get a chance to work with these and other new features in the next three weeks.

Why Are You Here?

It used to be a lot easier to figure out why people were picking up a book of this kind. Most readers wanted to use Java to create applets.

Today it's not as clear. Each new version of Java introduces features that extend it beyond its roots as an interesting Web technology.

However, Java's strengths remain its platform-independent, object-oriented nature, as well as it ease of learning.

Java Is Platform Independent

Platform independence—the capability of the same program to run on different platforms and operating systems—is one of the most significant advantages that Java has over other programming languages.

When you compile a program written in C or most other languages, the compiler translates your source file into *machine code*—instructions that are specific to the processor your computer is running. If you compile your code on an Intel-based system, the resulting program will run on other Intel-based systems but wouldn't work at all on

Macintoshes, Commodore VIC-20s, or other machines. If you want to use the same program on another platform, you must transfer your source code to the new platform and recompile it to produce machine code specific to that system. In many cases, changes to the source will be required before it will compile on the new machine, due to differences in their processors and other factors.

Figure 1.2 shows the result of a platform-dependent system: Multiple executable programs must be produced for multiple systems.

FIGURE 1.2.

Traditional compiled programs.

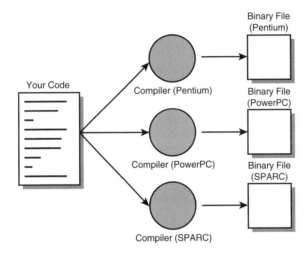

Your Code

Compiler (Pentium)

Compiler (PowerPC)

Compiler (SPARC)

Binary File (Pentium)

Binary File (PowerPC)

Binary File (SPARC)

Java programs achieve this independence by the use of a virtual machine—a sort of computer-within-a-computer. The *virtual machine* takes compiled Java programs and converts their instructions into commands that an operating system can handle. The same compiled program, which exists in a format called bytecode, can run on any platform and operating system that has a Java virtual machine.

NEW TERM   *Bytecode* is the Java virtual machine's version of machine code, the instructions it directly understands.

The virtual machine also is known as the *Java interpreter* or *Java runtime*.

If you're having trouble figuring out the role of the virtual machine, think of the device on the original *Star Trek* that converts English into whatever language the aliens are speaking to the crew of the starship *Enterprise*. Captain James T. Kirk doesn't have to learn a new language each time he lands on a planet, because the universal translator turns his words into whatever the aliens comprehend. In the same way, Java programmers don't have to create different versions of their programs for each platform they land on, because the virtual machine handles the necessary translation. (Of course, Kirk used the translator to meet otherworldly women. We offer no guarantees express nor implied that Java will get you dates.)

Java also is platform independent at the source level. Java programs are saved as text files before they are compiled, and these files can be created on any platform that supports Java. For example, you could write a Java program on a Macintosh and compile it into bytecode on a Windows 95 machine.

NEW TERM *Source*, also called *source code*, is the set of programming statements a programmer enters into a text editor when creating a program. Source code is compiled into bytecode so that it can be run by a Java virtual machine.

Bytecode is similar to the machine code produced by other languages, but it isn't specific to any one processor. It adds a level between source and machine code, as shown in Figure 1.3.

FIGURE 1.3.

Java's multiplatform programs.

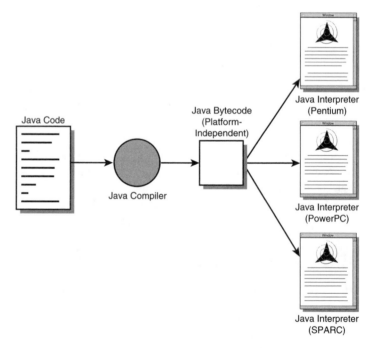

The Java virtual machine can be found in several places. For applets, the virtual machine is either built into a Java-enabled browser or installed separately for the browser's use. Applet programmers don't have to worry about whether it exists on a user's system.

> **Caution**
>
> This isn't worry-free, however. You must concern yourself with the Java virtual machine supported by the browser. If you create an applet that uses new Java 2 features, its bytecode won't work on browsers that only contain the Java 1.0 virtual machine. Java Plug-in, a browser enhancement under development by Sun, enables developers to specify a different virtual machine than the one included with Netscape Navigator or Microsoft Internet Explorer. This would enable Java 1.1 and 2 applets to work as long as their corresponding virtual machine was specified. Details on the Java Plug-in are available from the following Web page:
>
> `http://java.sun.com/products/plugin/`

Java applications, on the other hand, can only run on a system where the corresponding Java virtual machine has been installed. If you want to run Java 2 applications on your desktop system, you must first install the virtual machine.

If you're used to the way languages like Visual Basic and Delphi create platform-specific code, you might think the bytecode interpreter adds an unnecessary layer between your source and the compiled machine code.

This does cause some performance issues—Java programs execute more slowly than platform-dependent compiled languages such as C, and the speed difference is the primary knock against Java. Some Java development tools include just-in-time compilers, which can execute Java bytecode at greater speed.

The capability of a single bytecode file to run across platforms is crucial to what makes Java work on the World Wide Web, because the Web itself is platform-independent. Just as HTML files can be read on any platform, applets can be executed on any platform with a Java-enabled browser.

For many basic Java programs, speed may not be an issue. If you write programs that require more execution speed than the virtual machine can provide, you have solutions available to you:

- Using calls to system-specific machine code in your Java program, which makes it platform-dependent
- Using just-in-time compilers, which convert Java bytecodes into system-specific code

By using either of these solutions, you gain speed at the expense of Java's portability. A Java application that uses Windows calls for its disk access would not work on a Macintosh without modification.

Java Is Object-Oriented

If you're not yet familiar with object-oriented programming, you get plenty of chances to become so during the next six days.

Object-oriented programming—also called *OOP*—is a way of conceptualizing a computer program as a set of interacting objects. To some it is merely a way to organize programs, and any language can be used to create object-oriented programs.

However, you achieve the most benefits from object-oriented programming when you use a language designed for it. Java inherits many of its OOP concepts from C++, the language Java is strongly based upon. Java borrows concepts from other object-oriented languages as well.

You learn more about object-oriented programming and Java during Day 2, "A Taste of Object-Oriented Programming."

Java Is Easy to Learn

In addition to its portability and object orientation, Java is smaller and simpler than comparable languages. This stems from the original goal for Java to be a language that requires less computing muscle to run—nobody's going to drop $3000 on a Pentium II toaster oven with MMX technology.

Java was intended to be easier to write, compile, debug, and learn. The language was modeled strongly after C++, and much of the syntax and object-oriented structure comes straight from that language. If you're a C++ programmer, you'll be able to learn Java much more quickly, and can probably skim through some of the material in this book's first week.

Despite Java's similarities to C++, the most complex and error-prone aspects of that language have been excluded from Java. You won't find pointers or pointer arithmetic in Java, because those features are easy to mess up in a program and even harder to fix. Strings and arrays are objects in Java, and memory management is handled automatically rather than requiring the programmer to keep track of it. Experienced programmers might miss these features as they start to use Java, but others will learn Java more quickly because of their absence.

Although Java is easier to learn than many other programming languages, a person with no programming experience at all will be greatly challenged by Java. It is more complicated than working in something such as HTML or JavaScript, but definitely something a beginner can accomplish.

> **Note**
> Sams publishes another line of Java tutorials aimed directly at beginning programmers. *Sams Teach Yourself Java in 24 Hours* by Rogers Cadenhead, one of this book's coauthors, is also available.

Diving into Java Programming

All history lessons will be set aside for the second half of today's work. You get a chance to see Java in action by creating your first Java program—an application.

Before you can get started, you need to install a Java 2 development tool on your system.

Selecting a Java Development Tool

Writing Java programs requires some kind of Java programming software. If your system can already run applets when you surf the Web, you might think it already is set up for development. This isn't the case—you need a programming tool in order to create and run your own Java programs.

In order to use this book to its fullest, you must use a development tool that fully supports Java 2. At the time of this writing, the only choice is the JDK. The JDK is always the first tool that supports a new version of Java.

The JDK is a set of command-line programs, text-based utilities that don't make use of a graphical user interface. Programmers run each of the JDK's utilities by typing commands at a prompt, such as the following:

```
java GetFunky.class
```

This command tells the `java` program—the bytecode interpreter—to run a bytecode file called `GetFunky.class`. (As you see later today, compiled Java programs all have the `.class` file extension.)

Windows 95 users must use the MS-DOS Prompt command (Start | Programs | MS-DOS Prompt from the taskbar) to open a window where commands can be typed.

This is a far cry from most modern programming tools, which make use of graphical user interfaces, debuggers, programming editors, and many other niceties. People who are comfortable with MS-DOS and DOS-like operating systems will be at home with the JDK.

If you have another Java development tool and you're certain it supports Java 2, you can use it to create the programs throughout this book. Otherwise, JDK 1.2 should be used.

Installing the Java Development Kit

Version 1.2 of the Java Development Kit is currently available for the following platforms:

- Windows 95
- Windows NT
- Solaris SPARC
- Solaris x86

The JDK for these platforms is available on this book's CD-ROM, or from Sun's Java Web site, which is found at the following address:

```
http://java.sun.com
```

The Web site's Products & APIs section offers links to the different versions of the JDK and other Sun products.

For Sun's official Windows and Solaris versions of the JDK, the current direct address is the following Web page:

```
http://java.sun.com/products/JDK/1.2/index.html
```

This page contains installation instructions and a link to download the JDK for your platform. Use this link to download the JDK and save it to a folder on your system.

 Caution

> Choose the most current version of the JDK , whether it's 1.2, 2.0, or something along those lines. Sun periodically issues bug-fix releases that add an extra digit to the number, as when Java 1.1 was followed by 1.1.1, 1.1.2, and so on. You should download the most current version of the JDK available for your platform.

If you're using another platform, such as the Apple Macintosh, you can check to see if it has a 1.2-compliant JDK by visiting Sun's official Java site at

```
http://java.sun.com
```

The current page, which lists all known JDK versions for different platforms, has the following address:

`http://java.sun.com:80/cgi-bin/java-ports.cgi`

You should make sure that the entire file was received after downloading the it. Sun's installation instructions on the Web list the size for the current version of the JDK on your platform.

To check the size in Windows 95, 98 or NT, go to the folder that contains the JDK installation archive and right-click the file. A drop-down menu appears, and you can select the Properties command to see the file's size in bytes, along with other pertinent information.

Windows Installation

Before installing the JDK on your system, you should make sure that no other Java development tools are installed. Having more than one Java programming tool on your system will probably cause configuration problems when you try to use the JDK.

To install the JDK on Windows, double-click the installation archive file or use the Start | Run command from the Windows taskbar to find and run the file.

After you see a dialog box asking whether you want to install JDK 1.2, the JDK Setup Wizard is displayed (see Figure 1.4). You can use this window to configure how the JDK is installed on your system.

FIGURE 1.4.

The JDK Setup Wizard.

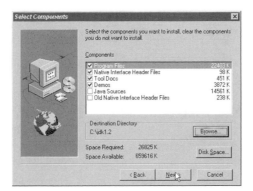

The default settings for this wizard should be fine for most users. The JDK is installed in a new folder with a name based on the version you're downloading (such as `\jdk1.2`), unless you use the Browse button to select a different folder on your system.

Tip

Any configuration problems you might have with the JDK will be easier to fix if you make sure it is installed in the folder \jdk1.2, which may be the default.

The wizard will install the following JDK components:

- Program files—The executable programs needed to create, compile, and test your Java projects.
- Native Interface header files—Files used only by programmers who are making calls to native code from their Java programs. You can omit these for the tutorials in this book.
- tooldocs—Help Files for the programming tools that comprise the JDK.
- Demo files—Java 1.2 programs, with versions you can run and source files you can examine to learn more about the language.

If you accept the default installation, you need 26 MB of free hard disk space. Omitting everything but the program files saves 4 MB, in case you're trying to squeeze the JDK onto a crowded drive.

You can also choose to install source files—the source of the Java language itself is publicly available. However, these files take up more than 14 MB of disk space and aren't needed for any of the material in this book.

Solaris Installation

Sun's Solaris version of the JDK can be installed on the following platforms:

- SPARC systems running Solaris 2.4 or higher
- x86 systems running Solaris 2.5 or higher

The JDK installation archive should be unpacked into a directory that does not already have a subdirectory called jdk1.2; if you do, you may overwrite some existing files on your system.

If you downloaded the installation file, you should make sure you can access the file correctly by using `chmod a+x` shell command on the filename.

For example, SPARC users would use the following command:

```
% chmod a+x jdk12-solaris2-sparc.bin
```

To install the JDK after making the `chmod` change, use a shell window to enter the command `./` followed by the archive filename. The following is an example:

```
% ./jdk12 -solaris2-sparc.bin
```

Testing the Installation

In an ideal world, the JDK should work correctly upon installation. In addition, cheese should be fat-free, presidents should be virtuous, and Jimmy Johnson should still be the coach of the Dallas Cowboys.

The most common problems made when learning Java result from errors setting up the JDK.

Windows users can test their JDK installation by using the MS-DOS Prompt command (Start | Programs | MS-DOS Prompt on most systems). This brings up a window in which you can enter commands in MS-DOS, the operating system that preceded Windows.

The MS-DOS prompt also is called a *command prompt* because you can use it to type commands that the operating system carries out.

Tip

MS-DOS can be intimidating for people accustomed to the graphical point-and-click style of Windows 95. However, you can't use the JDK without learning a little MS-DOS. This book offers some tips to enable you to learn as little MS-DOS as humanly possible.

Type the following at a command prompt to test whether your system can find the right version of the JDK on it:

INPUT `java -version`

If you're using JDK 1.2, you should see the following message in response:

OUTPUT `java version "1.2"`

The version number shown is specific, so if you have downloaded a subsequent bug release with a number like 1.2.1, it should be indicated by the `java -version` command.

If you see the wrong version number or a `"Bad command or file name"` error, your system can't find the right version of `java.exe`, the file that runs Java programs. This must be corrected before you can start writing Java programs. See Appendix B, "Configuring the Java Development Kit," for more information.

Your First Java Application

Now actually get to work. Start by creating a simple Java application: a program that displays one of the strangest things ever yelled at a celebrity by a member of the public— "What's the frequency, Kenneth?"

 Note

> On October 4, 1986, a man screamed "What's the frequency, Kenneth?" at television anchorman Dan Rather shortly before beating him up on a New York City street. For years no one understood the motive for the attack, and the group R.E.M. immortalized the remark in a song. The man was later arrested after gunning down an NBC technician in 1994, and he told a psychiatrist the TV networks were out to get him.

Java applications are standalone Java programs that do not require a Web browser to run. They're more like the programs that you use most often on your system—you run them locally with your mouse or by typing the program name at a command line.

Although a Java program can be designed to be both an applet and an application, almost all programs you encounter will be one or the other.

Throughout this first week, you write mostly applications as you learn the Java language. This knowledge will be extended into applet programming during Week 2, "Moving into Advanced Java." If you're one of those readers who is primarily interested in applet development, don't try to skip ahead to the second week. Everything that you learn while you're creating simple Java applications applies to creating applets, and starting with the basics is best. You create plenty of applets in Day 8, "Putting Interactive Programs on the Web," through Day 14, "Developing Advanced User Interfaces with the AWT."

Creating the Source File

As with most programming languages, your Java source files are saved as plain text files. You can create them with any text editor or word processor that can save plain text, a format that's also called ASCII text or DOS text. Windows users can write Java programs with Notepad, DOS Edit, and Write, as well as Microsoft Word if you're careful to save the file as text rather than in Word's proprietary format. UNIX users can author programs with emacs, pico, and vi, and Macintosh users have SimpleText for Java source file creation.

The Java Development Kit does not include a text editor, but almost all other Java development tools come with their own editor for creating source code files.

If you're using Windows 95, 98, or NT, a text editor such as Notepad may add an extra .txt file extension to the filename of any Java source files you save (which turns a name like GetFunky.java into GetFunky.java.txt). The Java compiler will only handle source files with the .java file extension. To avoid this problem, place quotation marks around the filename when you're saving a source file. Figure 1.5 shows this technique being used to save the source file Craps.java from Windows Notepad.

FIGURE 1.5.

Saving a source file.

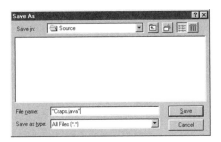

Tip

A better solution is to use Windows Explorer to permanently associate .java files with the text editor you'll be using. This enables you to open a source file for editing by double-clicking the file in a Windows folder. To learn how to set this up, see Appendix C, "Using a Text Editor with the JDK."

Writing the Program Fire up your editor of choice and enter the Java program shown in Listing 1.1. Be careful that all the parentheses, braces, and quotation marks in the listing are entered correctly, and use the correct capitalization of uppercase and lowercase letters. If your editor requires a filename before you start entering anything, use HelloDan.java.

TYPE **LISTING 1.1.** THE HelloDan APPLICATION SOURCE CODE.

```
1: class HelloDan {
2:     public static void main (String[] arguments) {
3:         System.out.println("What's the frequency, Kenneth?");
4:     }
5: }
```

The line numbers and colons along Listing 1.1's left side are not part of the program—they're included so you can refer to specific lines by number in a program. If you're ever unsure about the source code of a program in this book, you can compare it to a copy on the book's official World Wide Web site at the following address:

```
http://www.prefect.com/java21pre
```

After you finish typing in the program, save the file somewhere on your drive with the name **HelloDan.java**.

Tip

> If you're a Windows JDK user trying to learn as little MS-DOS as possible, open the root folder on your system and create a new subfolder called **J21work**. Save HelloDan.java and all other Java source files from this book into that folder. You'll see why soon.

Java source files must be saved with the extension .java. Java source files are compiled into bytecode with the .class file extension. In some ways, the term *class* in Java is synonymous with the term *program*. (You learn more about classes in the next three days.)

Line 1 of Listing 1.1 identifies that the Java program is the class HelloDan, so the filename must be HelloDan.java. If you name your source file something else (even something like hellodan.java or Hellodan.java), you won't be able to compile it.

Compiling and Running the Program Under Windows

Now you're ready to compile the file. If you're using a development tool other than the JDK, you should consult that software's documentation for details on how to compile Java programs. It is probably a reasonably simple operation, such as a button click or pull-down menu command.

With the JDK, you need to use the command-line tool javac, the Java compiler. The compiler reads a .java source file and creates one or more .class files that can be run by the Java virtual machine.

Windows users should load an MS-DOS prompt window using Start | Programs | MS-DOS Prompt, and change folders to the one containing HelloDan.java.

If you saved the file into a newly created J21work folder off the root folder on your system, the MS-DOS command would be the following:

```
cd \J21work
```

cd is an abbreviation of "change directory"; the terms folder and directory are synonymous.

When you are in the right folder, you can compile HelloDan.java by entering the following at a command prompt:

INPUT   `javac HelloDan.java`

Note

If you use the `dir` command to list all files in a folder under MS-DOS, you might notice that a file has two filenames—the one you gave it, such as HelloDan.java, and an abbreviated version, such as HELLOD~1.JAV. The abbreviated form is an offshoot of how Windows manages filenames with more than eight character names and three character file extensions. When using the JDK utilities at a command prompt, always use the filename you gave to a file, not the abbreviation.

Figure 1.6 shows the MS-DOS commands used to switch to the \J21work folder, list the files in the folder, and compile HelloDan.java.

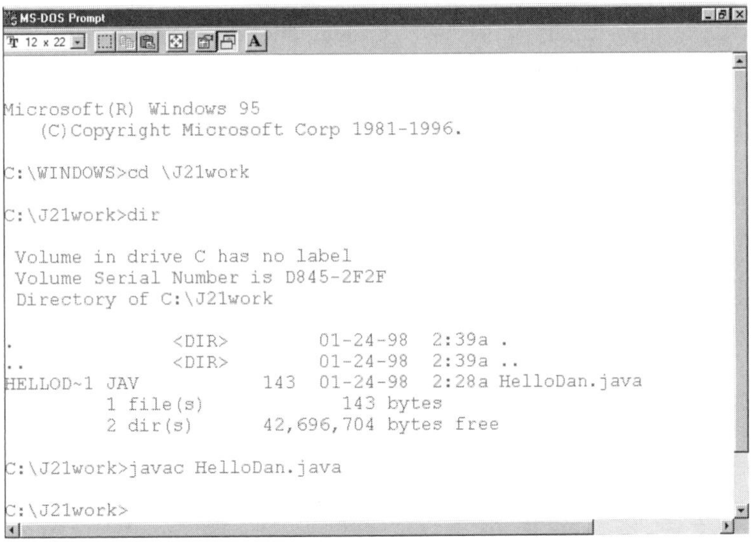

FIGURE 1.6.

Compiling Java programs in an MS-DOS window.

```
MS-DOS Prompt
T 12 x 22

Microsoft(R) Windows 95
    (C)Copyright Microsoft Corp 1981-1996.

C:\WINDOWS>cd \J21work

C:\J21work>dir

 Volume in drive C has no label
 Volume Serial Number is D845-2F2F
 Directory of C:\J21work

.              <DIR>         01-24-98   2:39a .
..             <DIR>         01-24-98   2:39a ..
HELLOD~1 JAV            143  01-24-98   2:28a HelloDan.java
        1 file(s)              143 bytes
        2 dir(s)        42,696,704 bytes free

C:\J21work>javac HelloDan.java

C:\J21work>
```

The JDK compiler does not display any message if the program compiles successfully. If the program compiled without any errors, a file called HelloDan.class is found in the same folder that contains `HelloDan.java`. This `.class` file is the Java bytecode that can be executed by the virtual machine. If you get any errors, go back to your original source file and make sure you typed it exactly as it appears in Listing 1.1.

Once you have a class file, you can run that file using the bytecode interpreter. The JDK's version of the interpreter is called `java`, and it also is run from the MS-DOS prompt under Windows. Run `HelloDan` by switching to the folder containing `HelloDan.class` and entering the following:

 `java HelloDan`

If your program was typed and compiled correctly, you should see the phrase `What's the frequency, Kenneth?` displayed onscreen in your MS-DOS Prompt window.

Note

> Make sure to leave off the `.class` extension when running a Java program with the `java` tool—entering `java HelloDan.class` will result in an error. In addition, if you see a `"Class Not Found"` error message—even though you're in the same folder as `HelloDan.class`—you might need to change another setting in your `autoexec.bat` file. See Appendix B.

Figure 1.7 shows the successful output of the `HelloDan` application along with the MS-DOS commands used to get to that point.

FIGURE 1.7.

Running Java applications in an MS-DOS window.

```
MS-DOS Prompt
T 12 x 22
Microsoft(R) Windows 95
    (C)Copyright Microsoft Corp 1981-1996.

C:\WINDOWS>cd \J21work

C:\J21work>dir

 Volume in drive C has no label
 Volume Serial Number is D845-2F2F
 Directory of C:\J21work

.              <DIR>        01-24-98  2:39a .
..             <DIR>        01-24-98  2:39a ..
HELLOD~1 JAV          143   01-24-98  2:28a HelloDan.java
HELLOD~1 CLA          486   01-24-98  2:49a HelloDan.class
         2 file(s)              629 bytes
         2 dir(s)       39,419,904 bytes free

C:\J21work>java HelloDan
What's the frequency, Kenneth?

C:\J21work>
```

1

Compiling and Running the Program Under Solaris

Use the command-line Java compiler that comes with the JDK to compile the Java source file on a Solaris system. From a UNIX command line, cd to the directory containing the Java source file HelloDan.java. If you used the J21work directory recommended to Windows users, this command would be used:

```
cd ~/J21work
```

After you're in the right directory, use the javac command with the name of the file, like this:

javac HelloDan.java

Barring any errors, you will end up with a file called HelloDan.class. This is the Java bytecode file that can be executed by the virtual machine. If you get any errors, go back to your original source file and make sure you typed it exactly as it appears in Listing 1.1.

Once you have a class file, you can run that file using the bytecode interpreter.

The JDK's version of the Java interpreter is called java, and it also is run from the command line. Run HelloDan by switching to the directory containing HelloDan.class and entering the following:

java HelloDan

If your program is typed and compiled correctly, you should see the phrase What's the frequency, Kenneth? displayed onscreen.

Note

> If you see a "Class Not Found" error message even though you're in the same folder HelloDan.class is in, you might need to change how your system is set up to find the JDK. See Appendix B.

Summary

Now that you have set up a Java development tool and used it to write your first Java program, you can add the title "Java programmer" to your résumé.

It's not an untruth, after all. Not only did you create a working Java application, you took a day trip through the history, strengths, weaknesses, and future of the language.

Java is an object-oriented programming language inspired by C++. It was designed to be simpler, less error-prone, and easier to learn than C++. It is platform-independent and small, two features that make it ideal for running on World Wide Web pages.

Applets are Java programs that run on the Web, and applications are all other software that can be written with Java.

That's a lot to cover, but you should now have the foundation to create more complex applications and your first applets. Add a blank line to that résumé. Tomorrow you'll be able to pencil in "Object-oriented programmer."

Q&A

Q What's the relationship between JavaScript and Java?

A They have the same first four letters.

A common misconception in the Web world is that Java and JavaScript have more in common than they actually do. Java is the general-purpose programming language that you learn about in this book; you use it to create applets. JavaScript is a Netscape-invented scripting language that looks sort of like Java; with it you can do various nifty things in Web pages. They are independent languages used for different purposes. If you're interested in JavaScript programming, you'll want to pick up another book, such as *Sams Teach Yourself JavaScript in a Week* or *Laura Lemay's Web Workshop: JavaScript*, both also available from Sams Publishing.

Q Where can I learn more about Java and find applets and applications to play with?

A You can read the rest of this book! Here are some other places to look for Java information and Java applets:

- The Java home page at `http://www.java.sun.com/` is the official source for Java information, including information about the JDK, about the upcoming 1.2 release, and about developer tools such as the Java Workshop, as well as extensive documentation.

- Gamelan, at `http://www.gamelan.com/`, is a repository of applets and Java information organized into categories. If you want to play with applets or applications, you should look here.

- For Java discussion, check out the `comp.lang.java` newsgroups, including `comp.lang.java.programmer`, `comp.lang.java.tech`, `comp.lang.java.advocacy`, and so on. (You'll need a Usenet newsreader to access these newsgroups.)

Q **I thought Sun's Java Development Kits were always free, so how come the license for 1.2 is only for 90 days? Don't you think this should be mentioned in a book about java programming?**

A Sun has always been strongly commited to giving the JDK away for free, and there has been nothing from the company indicating a change in that policy. perhaps the 90-day license is associated with the beta release, because it is only intended for use until a newer version becomes available.

DAY 2

A Taste of Object-Oriented Programming

Object-oriented programming is a lot like beer.

Most people who take a drink of the malted beverage for the first time don't like it, and may question the sanity of those who sing its praises. "What have I ever done to you," they exclaim, "that you would make me imbibe this?"

Over a period of time, however, an appreciation of beer can be cultivated in those who continue to drink it. (For many people, this period of time is called college.)

Object-oriented programming, like beer, is an acquired taste. It's one of the most remarkable programming ideas to be introduced in recent years, and also the source of great consternation for programmers unfamiliar with it.

In some ways, the reputation is deserved. Object-oriented programming, also called *OOP*, is a subject that can be studied and practiced for years. However, the central idea is simple: Organize your programs in a way that mirrors the way objects are organized in the real world.

Today you get your first taste of how Java embodies the principles of object-oriented programming. The following topics are covered:

- Organizing programs into elements called classes, and how these classes are used to create objects

- Defining a class by two aspects of its structure: how it should behave and what its attributes are

- Connecting classes to each other in a way that one class inherits functionality from another class

- Linking classes together through packages and interfaces

If you already are familiar with object-oriented programming, much of today's lesson will be a review for you. Even if you skim over the introductory material, you should create the sample program to get some experience developing your first Java applet.

Thinking in Terms of Objects

Object-oriented programming is, at its root, a way to conceptualize a computer program. You may think of a program as a list of instructions that tells a computer what to do, or a bunch of small programs that respond to specific events initiated by user input.

The OOP way to look at a program is as a set of objects that work together in predefined ways to accomplish tasks. Consider the example of LEGO building bricks.

LEGO bricks, for those of you without children or an inner child to keep occupied, are small plastic blocks sold in various colors and sizes. These bricks have small round studs on one side, and they fit snugly into holes on other bricks. These brick combinations create larger shapes, and there are many different LEGO pieces, such as wheels, engines, hinges, and pulleys, to use.

By using LEGO bricks you can make all kinds of things: castles, automobiles, doublewide trailers, braces, sportswear—just about anything you can imagine. Each LEGO piece is an object that fits together with other objects in specific ways to create a larger object.

Consider another example. With a little experience and some help, you can walk into a computer store and assemble an entire personal computer system from various components: a motherboard, CPU chip, video card, hard disk, keyboard, and so on. Ideally, when you finish assembling the various self-contained units, you have a system in which all the units work together to create a larger system. You can use this larger system to solve the problems you bought the computer for in the first place.

Internally, each of those components might be extremely complicated and engineered by different companies using different methods of design. However, you don't need to know how each component works, what every chip on the board does, or how an "A" gets sent to your computer when you press the A key on your keyboard. Each component you use is a self-contained unit, and as the assembler of the overall system, you only are interested in how the units interact with each other:

- Will this video card fit into a slot on the motherboard?
- Will this monitor work with this video card?
- Will each component speak the right commands to the other components it interacts with, so that each part of the computer is understood by every other part?

Once you know about the interactions between the components and can match those interactions, putting together the overall system is easy.

Object-oriented programming is a lot like building structures from LEGO bricks or assembling a PC. Using OOP, your overall program is made up of different components called objects.

NEW TERM An *object* is a self-contained element of a computer program that represents a related group of features and is designed to accomplish specific tasks. Objects also are called *instances*.

Each object has a specific role in a program, and all objects can work with other objects in defined ways.

Objects and Classes

Object-oriented programming is modeled on the observation that in the real world, objects are made up of many kinds of smaller objects. However, the capability to combine objects is only a general aspect of object-oriented programming. It also includes concepts and features that make the creation and use of objects easier and more flexible. The most important of these features is the class.

NEW TERM A *class* is a template used to create multiple objects with similar features.

Classes embody all features of a particular set of objects. When you write a program in an object-oriented language, you don't define individual objects. Instead, you define classes of objects.

For example, you might have a Tree class that describes the features of all trees:

- Has leaves and roots
- Grows
- Creates chlorophyll

The Tree class serves as an abstract model for the concept of a tree. To actually have an object that you can manipulate in a program, you must have a concrete instance of the Tree class.

Classes are used to create objects, and you work with the objects directly in a program. A Tree class can be used to create lots of different Tree objects, and each could have different features:

- Short or tall
- Bushy or sparse
- Fruit-bearing or not

Although these objects differ from each other, they still have enough in common to be immediately recognizable as related objects. Figure 2.1 shows a Tree class and several objects created from that template.

An Example of Class Design

In an example closer to something you might do using Java, you could create a class for a command button, an item for use on windows, dialog boxes, and other interactive programs. When the CommandButton class is developed, it could define a button's following features:

- The text that identifies the button's purpose
- The size of the button
- Aspects of its appearance, such as whether it has a 3D shadow

The CommandButton class also could define how a button behaves:

- Whether the button needs a single click or a double-click to use
- Whether it should ignore mouse clicks entirely
- What it does when successfully clicked

Once you define the CommandButton class, you can create instances of that button—in other words, CommandButton objects. The objects all take on the basic features of a command button as defined by the class, but each one could have different appearances and behavior based on what a particular button can do. By creating a CommandButton class, you don't have to keep rewriting the code for each command button that you want to use in your programs. In addition, you can reuse the `CommandButton` class to create different kinds of buttons as you need them, both in this program and in others.

FIGURE 2.1.

The Tree *class and several* Tree *objects.*

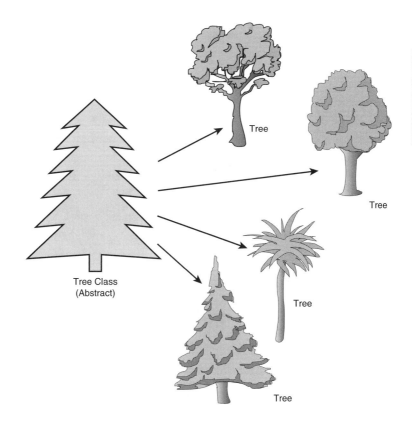

Tree

Tree

Tree Class
(Abstract)

Tree

Tree

2

> **Note**
>
> One of Java's standard classes, `java.awt.Button`, encompasses all of the functionality of this hypothetical `CommandButton` example and more. You get a chance to work with it during Day 11, "Building Simple User Interfaces for Applets."

When you write a Java program, you design and construct a set of classes. When your program runs, objects are created from those classes and used as needed. Your task as a Java programmer is to create the right set of classes to accomplish what your program needs to accomplish.

Fortunately, you don't have to start from scratch. Each version of the Java language includes a group of classes that implement most of the basic functionality you will need. These groupings are called libraries.

NEW TERM   A *class library* is a group of classes designed to be used with other programs. The standard Java class library contains dozens of classes.

When you're talking about using the Java language, you're actually talking about using the Java class library and some keywords and operators that are recognized by a Java compiler.

Java's standard library handles numerous tasks, such as mathematical functions, text handling, graphics, sound, user interaction, and networking. In many cases, the Java class libraries will be sufficient for your needs. Your job in such a circumstance would be to create a single class that is used to create objects from the standard Java classes and handle their interaction.

For complicated Java programs, you might create a whole set of new classes with defined interactions between them. These could be used to form your own class library, for use later in other programs.

Reuse is one of the fundamental benefits of object-oriented programming.

Attributes and Behavior

Generally, every class you write in Java is made up of two components: attributes and behavior. In this section you learn about each component as it applies to a theoretical class called Jabberwock. To complete this section, you create a Java class that implements a representation of a jabberwock—a dragonlike monster from the Lewis Carroll poem *Jabberwocky*.

Attributes of a Class of Objects

Attributes are the individual things that differentiate one class of objects from another and determine the appearance, state, and other qualities of that class. Think about how a theoretical class called Jabberwock could be created. The attributes of a jabberwock might include the following:

- Color `orange`, `raw umber`, `lemon yellow`, `maize`
- Sex `male`, `female`, `mind-your-own-business`
- Appetite `full`, `hungry`

Attributes of a class of objects also can include information about an object's state. For example, you could have features for the jabberwock's disposition (enraged or calm), health status (alive or dead), and voting tendencies (conservative, independent, soccer mom).

In a class, attributes are defined by variables. You can consider them analogous to global variables for each object of that class. Each object can have different values for its variables, and these are called instance variables.

NEW TERM   An *instance variable* is an item of information that defines an attribute of one particular object. The object's class defines what kind of attribute it is, and each instance stores its own value for that attribute. Instance variables also are called *object variables*.

Each class attribute has a single corresponding variable; you change that attribute in an object by changing the value of the variable. In the program that you create later today, the following statement is used to indicate that a Jabberwock object represented by j is no longer hungry:

```
j.hungry = false;
```

Instance variables can be given a value when an object is created and stay constant throughout the life of the object, or they can be given different values as the object is used in a running program.

Another type of attribute is used to describe a whole class of objects instead of specific objects from the class. These are called class variables.

NEW TERM   A *class variable* is an item of information that defines an attribute of an entire class. The variable applies to the class itself and to all of its instances, so only one value is stored, no matter how many objects of the class have been created.

For a good example of a class variable, consider a variable that keeps track of the exact number of Jabberwock objects living in a community. If an instance variable were created for the count in the Jabberwock class, each of the objects could have a different count, which wouldn't be accurate. A class variable would be used in order for only one value to be stored, and each Jabberwock object would have access to that variable.

Behavior of a Class of Objects

Behavior is the way that a class of objects can do anything to themselves or to other objects. The behavior of a class determines what objects of that class do to change their attributes, and also what they do when other objects ask them to do something. The behavior of a Jabberwock object might include the following:

- Get angry
- Calm down
- Eat a peasant
- Skip dinner
- Recuperate

Behavior for a class of objects is done by using methods.

NEW TERM   *Methods* are groups of related statements in a class of objects that act on themselves and on other classes and objects. They are used to accomplish specific tasks, in the same way that functions are used in other programming languages.

Objects communicate with each other using methods. A class or an object can call methods in another class or object for many reasons, including the following:

- To report a change to another object
- To tell the other object to change something about itself
- To ask another object to do something

For example, consider the swordsman in the poem *Jabberwocky*. He attacks the jabberwock with his vorpal blade; here's the play-by-play of what happened from poet Lewis Carroll:

"One, two! One, two! And through and through

The vorpal blade went snicker-snack!

He left it dead, and with its head

He went galumphing back."

In Java, the swordsman could be created as a `Knight` object, using the `Knight` class as the template for what a `Knight` object should be like. When the swordsman chops the head off the jabberwock, this definitely causes a change in the jabberwock's internal state. To note this change, the `Knight` object would use a method to tell the `Jabberwock` object "Hey! I chopped your head off. You're dead."

Just as there are instance and class variables, there are also instance and class methods. *Instance methods*, which are so common they're usually just called *methods*, apply to an object of the class. If the method makes a change to an individual object, it must be an instance method. *Class methods* apply to a class itself.

Creating a Class

Now that the basic terminology of object-oriented programming has been introduced, things may become clearer with a more concrete example. You create a working example of the Jabberwock class, so that you can see how instance variables and methods are defined in a class. You also create a Java applet that creates a new object using the Jabberwock class, modifies its instance variables, and takes action based on their values.

2

Note

This example's actual syntax is not covered in great detail here. Use it as an introduction to object-oriented programming rather than a lesson on Java programming syntax, which you dive into during Day 3, "The ABCs of Java."

Open the text editor you're using to create Java programs, so that you can begin creating a Java source file. Instead of entering an entire program, you enter some statements while learning about their usage. You get a chance to double-check your work at the end to make sure it's correct.

The place to start is a basic class definition. Enter the following:

```
class Jabberwock {
}
```

You have created a class. It doesn't do much at the moment, but the two lines are an example of a Java class at its simplest.

To make Jabberwock more sophisticated, create three instance variables for this class. Just below the class Jabberwock { line, insert the following three lines:

```
String color;
String sex;
boolean hungry;
```

These lines create three instance variables. Two, color and sex, can contain String objects. A *string* is a general term meaning a group of characters, but a String object in Java is created using one of the standard classes in the Java class library. The String class is used for text storage and many text-manipulation functions.

The third object, hungry, is a boolean variable that can store only one of two values: true or false. This object is used to keep track of whether the jabberwock is hungry (true) or full (false).

Note

> Booleans are a special type of variable that can only hold the value `true` or `false`. Unlike other languages, Booleans in Java do not have numeric values where 1 is equivalent to `true` and 0 is equivalent to `false`. Booleans are named for George Boole, an Irish mathematician who lived from 1815 to 1864. His other namesake is Boolean algebra, which is fundamental to computer programming, digital electronics, and logic.

You can add some behavior to the Jabberwock class by adding methods. There are all kinds of things a jabberwock can do (claws that bite, jaws that catch, and so on), but to keep things short, two are added—one to feed the monster and another to check on the monster's attributes.

To begin, add the following lines directly below the three instance variables in your class definition:

```
void feedJabberwock() {
    if (hungry == true) {
        System.out.println("Yum -- a peasant.");
        hungry = false;
    } else
        System.out.println("No, thanks -- already ate.");
}
// more to come
```

Tip

> The last line, `// more to come`, is a comment line. Comments are used for the benefit of someone looking at source code to figure out what it's doing. Computers have no interest in them at all—everything from the initial `//` to the end of the line is ignored by a Java compiler. In the Jabberwock class, the comment is being used as a placeholder. You replace it soon.

The feedJabberwock() method tests to see whether a Jabberwock object is hungry (in the line `if (hungry == true)`). If it is hungry, the object is fed (much to its delight), and the state of `hungry` is changed to `false`. If the object is not hungry, a message is displayed that the monster already ate. Here's what your program should look like so far:

TYPE   **LISTING 2.1.** THE CURRENT TEXT OF JABBERWOCK.JAVA.

```
1: class Jabberwock {
2:     String color;
3:     String sex;
4:     boolean hungry;
```

```
 5:
 6:    void feedJabberwock() {
 7:        if (hungry == true) {
 8:            System.out.println("Yum -- a peasant!");
 9:            hungry = false;
10:        } else
11:            System.out.println("No, thanks -- already ate.");
12:    }
13:
14:    // more to come
15:}
```

Tip

> The indentation and blank lines used to provide spacing in the source file are disregarded by a Java compiler. Like comments, they're included for the benefit of programmers, so the logic of the program is easier to follow. The indentation and spacing used here, with blank lines between methods and indented variables and methods, is used throughout this book. The Java class library uses a similar indentation. You can choose any indentation style that you prefer.

Before you compile this class, you need to add one more method. The showAttributes() method displays the current values of the instance variables in an instance of your Jabberwock class.

In the program, delete the comment line // more to come and replace it with the following:

```
void showAttributes() {
    System.out.println("This is a " + sex + " " + color + " jabberwock.");
    if (hungry == true)
        System.out.println("The jabberwock is hungry.");
    else
        System.out.println("The jabberwock is full.");
}
```

The showAttributes() method displays two lines onscreen: the sex and color of the Jabberwock object and whether it is hungry. Save the source file in your text editor, making sure to name it Jabberwock.java, so that the filename matches the class name.

At this point, you have a Jabberwock class with instance variables and instance methods that can be used to display and modify those variables.

Use one of the following procedures to compile the program, depending on the system you're using.

WINDOWS Change to the folder containing your Java source file using the `cd` command from an MS-DOS prompt, and use the `javac` command to compile it:

INPUT `javac Jabberwock.java`

SOLARIS From a command line, change to the directory containing your Java source file using the `cd` command, and use the `javac` command to compile it:

`javac Jabberwock.java`

If you encounter any problems compiling the program, check it for typos against Listing 2.2.

TYPE **LISTING 2.2.** THE CURRENT TEXT OF JABBERWOCK.JAVA.

```
 1: class Jabberwock {
 2:     String color;
 3:     String sex;
 4:     boolean hungry;
 5:
 6:     void feedJabberwock() {
 7:         if (hungry == true) {
 8:             System.out.println("Yum -- a peasant!");
 9:             hungry = false;
10:         } else
11:             System.out.println("No, thanks -- already ate.");
12:     }
13:
14:     void showAttributes() {
15:         System.out.println("This is a " + sex + " " + color + "
            jabberwock.");
16:         if (hungry == true)
17:             System.out.println("The jabberwock is hungry.");
18:         else
19:             System.out.println("The jabberwock is full.");
20:     }
21: }
```

Running the Program

If you run the `Jabberwock.class` file with a command-line tool such as the Java interpreter, you get an error such as the following:

```
Exception inthread "main" java.lang.NoSuchMethodError: main
```

This error occurs because the Java interpreter assumes that the program is an application when you try to run it at the command line. When an application is run, the starting point of the program is its `main()` method. Because the `Jabberwock` class doesn't have a `main()` method, the interpreter doesn't know what to do with it.

There are two ways to use the Jabberwock class:

- Create a separate Java applet or application that uses this class.
- Add a main() method to the Jabberwock class, so it can be run directly.

The latter is done for this exercise. Load Jabberwock.java into a text editor and insert a blank line directly above the last line of the program (Line 21 in Listing 2.2).

At this line, insert the following:

```
public static void main (String arguments[]) {
    Jabberwock j = new Jabberwock();
    j.color = "orange";
    j.sex = "male";
    j.hungry = true;
    System.out.println("Calling showAttributes ...");
    j.showAttributes();
    System.out.println("-----");
    System.out.println("Feeding the jabberwock ...");
    j.feedJabberwock();
    System.out.println("-----");
    System.out.println("Calling showAttributes ...");
    j.showAttributes();
    System.out.println("-----");
    System.out.println("Feeding the jabberwock ...");
    j.feedJabberwock();
}
```

With the main() method in place, the Jabberwock class can now be used as an application. Save and compile the file.

Listing 2.3 shows the final Jabberwock.java source file, in case you have trouble compiling it.

 Tip

> If you encounter problems with any program in this book, you can find a copy of the source file and other related files on the book's official Web site at http://www.prefect.com/java21pre.

TYPE **LISTING 2.3.** THE FINAL VERSION OF JABBERWOCK.JAVA.

```
1: class Jabberwock {
2:     String color;
3:     String sex;
4:     boolean hungry;
```

continues

LISTING 2.3. CONTINUED

```
 5:
 6:     void feedJabberwock() {
 7:         if (hungry == true) {
 8:             System.out.println("Yum -- a peasant!");
 9:             hungry = false;
10:         } else
11:             System.out.println("No, thanks -- already ate.");
12:     }
13:
14:     void showAttributes() {
15:         System.out.println("This is a " + sex + " " + color + "
            jabberwock.");
16:         if (hungry == true)
17:             System.out.println("The jabberwock is hungry.");
18:         else
19:             System.out.println("The jabberwock is full.");
20:     }
21:
22:     public static void main (String arguments[]) {
23:         Jabberwock j = new Jabberwock();
24:         j.color = "orange";
25:         j.sex = "male";
26:         j.hungry = true;
27:         System.out.println("Calling showAttributes ...");
28:         j.showAttributes();
29:         System.out.println("-----");
30:         System.out.println("Feeding the jabberwock ...");
31:         j.feedJabberwock();
32:         System.out.println("-----");
33:         System.out.println("Calling showAttributes ...");
34:         j.showAttributes();
35:         System.out.println("-----");
36:         System.out.println("Feeding the jabberwock ...");
37:         j.feedJabberwock();
38:     }
39: }
```

The Jabberwock application can be run using one of the following platform-specific procedures.

WINDOWS From an MS-DOS prompt, change to the folder containing the Jabberwock.class file using the cd command. Use the java command to run it with the interpreter, as follows:

```
java Jabberwock
```

SOLARIS From a command line, change to the directory containing the `Jabberwock.class` file using the `cd` command. Use the `java` command to run it with the interpreter, as follows:

```
java Jabberwock
```

When you run the `Jabberwock` class, the output should be the following:

OUTPUT
```
Calling showAttributes ...
This is a male orange jabberwock.
The jabberwock is hungry.
- - - - -
Feeding the jabberwock ...
Yum -- a peasant!
- - - - -
Calling showAttributes ...
This is a male orange jabberwock.
The jabberwock is full.
- - - - -
Feeding the jabberwock ...
No, thanks -- already ate.
```

Using Listing 2.3 as a guide, the following things take place in the `main()` method:

- Line 22—The `main()` method is declared. The first line of the `main()` method always looks like this, and you learn about each element of this statement later this week.

- Line 23, `Jabberwock j = new Jabberwock();`—Creates a new object of the `Jabberwock` class and stores a reference to it in a new variable named `j`. As you have learned, you usually don't operate directly on classes in your Java programs. Instead, you create objects from those classes and call methods of those objects to operate on them.

- Lines 24–26—The instance variables `color`, `sex`, and `hungry` are set for the `Jabberwock` object created in line 2. The `color` is `orange`, the `sex` is `male`, and the `hungry` variable is given the Boolean value of `true`. This indicates that the `Jabberwock` object is hungry.

- Line 27—On this line and several others that follow, a `System.out.println()` statement is used to display information to the screen. Everything between the parentheses is displayed.

- Line 28—The `showAttributes()` method, defined in the `Jabberwock` object, is called. This prompts the `Jabberwock` object to indicate the values of its instance variables: `color`, `sex`, and `hungry`.

- Line 31—The feedJabberwock() method of the Jabberwock object is called, which changes the value of the hungry variable from true to false and displays an appreciative remark from the Jabberwock object: "Yum -- a peasant!".
- Line 33—The showAttributes() method is called again to display the values of the Jabberwock object's instance variables. This time, the output should reflect that the jabberwock is full (because hungry has the value false).
- Line 36—The feedJabberwock() method is called again in an attempt to feed the jabberwock. Because the jabberwock is already full, it declines to eat with a polite "No thanks -- already ate.".

> **Note**
>
> At this point it is assumed that you know how to compile and run a Java application successfully. Review Day 1, "A Fistful of Java," and your Java development tool's documentation for more guidance if needed.

Organizing Classes and Class Behavior

An introductory sampling of object-oriented programming in Java isn't complete without a first look at three concepts: inheritance, interfaces, and packages.

These three things all are mechanisms for organizing classes and class behavior. The Java class library uses these concepts, and the classes you create for your own programs also need them.

Inheritance

Inheritance is one of the most crucial concepts in object-oriented programming, and it has a direct effect on how you design and write your own Java classes.

 Inheritance is a mechanism that enables one class to inherit all of the behavior and attributes of another class.

Through inheritance, a class immediately has all the functionality of an existing class. Because of this, the new class can be created by indicating only how it is different from an existing class.

With inheritance, all classes are arranged in a strict hierarchy—those you create and those from the Java class library and other libraries.

NEW TERM A class that inherits from another class is called a *subclass*, and the class that gives the inheritance is called a *superclass*.

A class can have only one superclass, but each class can have an unlimited number of subclasses. Subclasses inherit all the attributes and behavior of their superclasses.

In practical terms, this means that if the superclass has behavior and attributes that your class needs, you don't have to redefine it or copy that code to have the same behavior and attributes. Your class automatically receives these things from its superclass, the superclass gets them from its superclass, and so on, all the way up the hierarchy. Your class becomes a combination of all the features of the classes above it in the hierarchy, as well as its own features.

The situation is pretty comparable to the way you inherited all kinds of things from your parents, such as height, hair color, love of ska music, and a reluctance to ask for directions. They inherited some of these things from their parents, who inherited from theirs, and backward through time to the Garden of Eden, Big Bang, or *insert personal cosmological belief here*.

Figure 2.2 shows the way a hierarchy of classes is arranged.

FIGURE 2.2.

A class hierarchy.

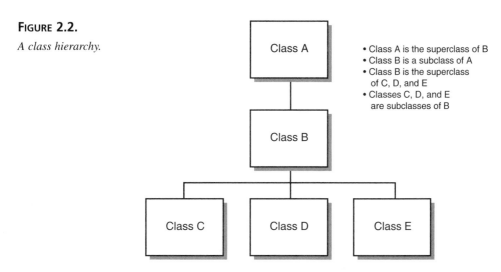

- Class A is the superclass of B
- Class B is a subclass of A
- Class B is the superclass of C, D, and E
- Classes C, D, and E are subclasses of B

At the top of the Java class hierarchy is the class Object—all classes inherit from this one superclass. Object is the most general class in the hierarchy, and it defines behavior and attributes inherited by all the classes in the Java class library. Each class further down the hierarchy becomes more tailored to a specific purpose. A class hierarchy defines abstract concepts at the top of the hierarchy. Those concepts become more concrete further down the line of subclasses.

Often when you create a new class in Java, you will want all the functionality of an existing class with some modifications of your own creation. For example, you might want a version of a CommandButton that makes an ear-deafening, explosive sound when clicked. (Neither the authors of this book nor Sams Publishing suggest that this is a good idea, nor will be held legally responsible in the case such sound is unappreciated by those who are unexpectedly deafened by it.)

To receive all of the CommandButton functionality without doing any work to re-create it, you can define your class as a subclass of CommandButton. Your class then would automatically inherit behavior and attributes defined in CommandButton and behavior and attributes defined in the superclasses of CommandButton. All you have to worry about are the things that make your new class different from CommandButton itself. Subclassing is the mechanism for defining new classes as the differences between those classes and their superclass.

NEW TERM *Subclassing* is the creation of a new class that inherits from an existing class. The only task in the subclass is to indicate the differences in behavior and attributes between it and the superclass.

If your class defines entirely new behavior and isn't a subclass of another class, you can inherit directly from the Object class. This allows it to fit neatly into the Java class hierarchy. In fact, if you create a class definition that doesn't indicate a superclass, Java assumes that the new class is inheriting directly from Object. The Jabberwock class you created inherits from the Object class.

Creating a Class Hierarchy

If you're creating a large set of classes, it makes sense for your classes to inherit from the existing class hierarchy and to make up a hierarchy themselves. Organizing your classes this way takes significant planning, but the advantages include the following:

- Functionality that is common to multiple classes can be put into superclasses, which enables it to be used repeatedly in all classes below it in the hierarchy.
- Changes to a superclass automatically are reflected in all of its subclasses, their subclasses, and so on. There is no need to change or recompile any of the lower classes; they receive the new information through inheritance.

For example, imagine that you have created a Java class to implement all the features of a jabberwock. (This shouldn't take much imagination if you didn't skip ahead to this point of the day.)

The Jabberwock class is completed, works successfully, and everything is copacetic. Now you want to create a Java class called Dragon.

Dragons and jabberwocks have many similar features—both are large monsters that eat peasants. Both have sharp claws, powerful teeth, and type-A personalities. Your first impulse might be to open up the Jabberwock.java source file and copy a lot of it into a new source file called Dragon.java.

A better plan is to figure out the common functionality of Dragon and Jabberwock and organize it into a more general class hierarchy. This might be a lot of work just for the classes Jabberwock and Dragon, but what if you also want to add Medusa, Yeti, Sasquatch, Grue, and DustBunny? Placing common behavior into one or more reusable superclasses significantly reduces the overall amount of work that must be done.

To design a class hierarchy that might serve this purpose, start at the top with the class Object, the pinnacle of all Java classes. The most general class to which a jabberwock and a dragon both belong might be called Monster. A monster, generally, could be defined as a ferocious creature of some kind that terrorizes people and lowers property values. In the Monster class, you define only the behavior that qualifies something to be ferocious, terrifying, and bad for the neighborhood.

There could be two classes below Monster: FlyingMonster and WalkingMonster. The obvious thing that differentiates these classes is that one can fly and one can't. The behavior of flying monsters might include swooping down on prey, carrying peasants off into the sky, dropping them from great heights, and so on. Walking monsters would behave differently and be much more susceptible to fallen arches. Figure 2.3 shows what you have so far.

FIGURE 2.3.

The basic Monster
hierarchy.

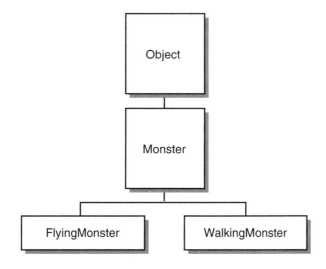

Now, the hierarchy can become even more specific. With FlyingMonster, you might have several classes: Mammal, Reptile, Amphibian, and so on. As an alternative, you could factor out still more functionality and have intermediate classes for TwoLegged and FourLegged monsters, with different behaviors for each (see Figure 2.4).

FIGURE 2.4.

Two-legged and four-legged flying monsters.

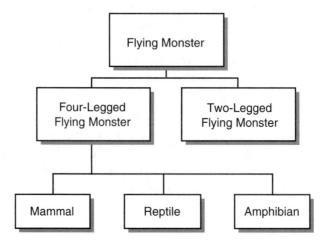

Finally, the hierarchy is done, and you have a place for Jabberwock. It can be a subclass of reptile, four-legged, flying monsters. (Actually, going all the way up the class hierarchy, Jabberwock would be a subclass of reptile, four-legged, flying monster, monster objects—because FlyingMonster is a subclass of Monster, and Monster is a subclass of Object.)

Where do qualities such as sex, color, or appetite come in? They come in at the place they fit into the class hierarchy most naturally. You can define sex and color as instance variables in Monster, and all subclasses have those variables as well. Remember that you need to define a behavior or attribute only once in the hierarchy, and it automatically is inherited by each subclass.

Note

Designing an effective class hierarchy involves a lot of planning and revision. As you attempt to put attributes and behavior into a hierarchy, you're likely to find reasons to move some classes to different spots in the hierarchy. The goal is to reduce the number of repetitive features that are needed. If you were designing a hierarchy of monsters, you might want to put Mammal, Reptile, and Amphibian immediately below Monster, if that better describes the functionality you're using classes to embody.

Inheritance in Action

Inheritance in Java works much more simply than it does in the real world. There are no executors, judges, or courts of any kind required in Java.

When you create a new object, Java keeps track of each variable defined for that object and each variable defined for each superclass of the object. In this way, all of the classes combine to form a template for the current object, and each object fills in the information appropriate to its situation.

Methods operate similarly: New objects have access to all method names of its class and superclass. This is determined dynamically when a method is used in a running program. If you call a method of a particular object, the Java interpreter first checks the object's class for that method. If the method isn't found, the interpreter looks for it in the superclass of that class, and so on, until the method definition is found. This is illustrated in Figure 2.5.

FIGURE 2.5.

How methods are located in a class hierarchy.

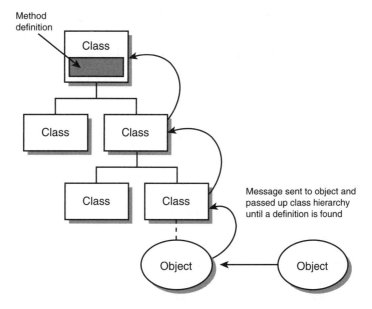

Things get complicated when a subclass defines a method that has the same name, return type, and arguments that a method defined in a superclass has. In this case, the method definition that is found first (starting at the bottom of the hierarchy and working upward) is the one that is used. Because of this, you can create a method in a subclass that prevents a method in a superclass from being used. To do this, you give the method with the same name, return type, and arguments as the method in the superclass. This procedure is called *overriding* (see Figure 2.6).

FIGURE 2.6.

Overriding methods.

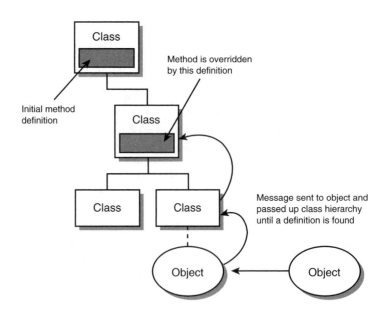

Single and Multiple Inheritance

Java's form of inheritance is called *single inheritance* because each Java class can have only one superclass (although any given superclass can have multiple subclasses).

In other object-oriented programming languages such as C++, classes can have more than one superclass, and they inherit combined variables and methods from all those superclasses. This is called *multiple inheritance*, and it provides the means to create classes that encompass just about any imaginable behavior. However, it significantly complicates class definitions and the code needed to produce them. Java makes inheritance simpler by allowing only single inheritance.

Interfaces

Single inheritance makes the relationship between classes and the functionality those classes implement easier to understand and to design. However, it also can be restrictive—especially when you have similar behavior that needs to be duplicated across different branches of a class hierarchy. Java solves the problem of shared behavior by using interfaces.

NEW TERM   An *interface* is a collection of methods that indicate a class has some behavior in addition to what it inherits from its superclasses.

Interfaces are a topic better explored after you've had some time to work with object-oriented programming and Java. You explore them fully during Day 15, "Class Roles: Packages, Interfaces, and Other Features."

Packages

Packages in Java are a way of grouping related classes and interfaces. Packages enable groups of classes to be available only if they are needed, and they eliminate potential conflicts between class names in different groups of classes.

For now, there are only a few things you need to know:

- *The class libraries in Java are contained in a package called* java. The classes in the java package are guaranteed to be available in any Java implementation and are the only classes guaranteed to be available across different implementations. The java package contains smaller packages that define specific subsets of the Java language's functionality, such as standard features, file handling, multimedia, and many other things. Classes in other packages such as sun and netscape packages often are available only in specific implementations.

- *By default, your Java classes have access to only the classes in* java.lang *(basic language features)*. To use classes from any other package, you have to refer to them explicitly by package name or import them in your source file.

- *To refer to a class within a package, you must list all packages the class is contained in followed by the class name, with each element separated by periods (.).* For example, consider the Color class. It is contained in the awt package, which in turn is contained in the java package. To refer to the Color class in your programs, the notation java.awt.Color can be used.

Creating a Subclass

As a final project today, you create a subclass of another class and override some methods. You also get a better feel for how packages work.

When you start programming in Java, the most common use of subclassing is when applets are created. Creating applets is different than creating applications. Java applets run as part of a Web page, and therefore have special rules for how they behave. Because of these special rules for applets, creating a simple applet is more complicated than creating a simple application.

All applets are subclasses of the class Applet (which is part of the java.applet package). By creating a subclass of Applet, you automatically receive all behavior and attributes that enable a Java program to run as part of a Web page.

In this example you create an applet similar to yesterday's `HelloDan` application. To start this example, first construct the class definition itself. Load your text editor and enter the following statements:

```
public class Palindrome extends java.applet.Applet {
    // more to come
}
```

This defines a class called `Palindrome`. The statements are similar to the way you created the `HelloDan` class during Day 1. One new addition is the text `extends java.applet.Applet`.

The `extends` clause is the way to declare that one class is a subclass of another. The `Palindrome` class is a subclass of the `Applet` class, which is part of the `java.applet` package. To indicate this in a program, the clause `extends java.applet.Applet` is used to define the relationship between the two classes.

Note

Because the `Applet` class is contained in the `java.applet` package, you don't have automatic access to that class, so you have to refer to it explicitly by package and class name. The only classes that you can refer to without considering the package name are those in the `java.lang` package.

Another new element in the `class` statement is the `public` keyword. This keyword indicates that your class is accessible to other classes that might need to use it. Ordinarily, you only need to make a class `public` if you want it to be usable by other classes in your Java program. However, all applets must be `public`.

A class definition with nothing in it but the comment statement `// more to come` doesn't have much of a point—it doesn't add anything new or override methods or variables from its superclass. To make the `Palindrome` class different from its superclass, delete the comment line `// more to come` and begin adding new statements to the program, starting with this statement:

```
Font f = new Font("TimesRoman", Font.BOLD, 36);
```

This statement accomplishes two things:

- A `Font` object called `f` is created. `Font`, part of the `java.awt` package, is used to represent a screen font. It is used to display a different font and font style than the default normally used in an applet.

- The `Font` object is given the value of a 36-point Times Roman boldface font. The `new` statement creates a new `Font` object with the values specified within parentheses, and this new object is assigned to `f`.

By creating an instance variable to hold this `Font` object, you make it available to all the methods in your class. The next step in the `Palindrome` project is to create a method that uses it.

When you write applets, there are several methods defined in the `Applet` superclass that you commonly override in your applet. These include methods to set up the applet before it runs, to start the applet, to respond to mouse input, and to clean up when the applet stops running.

One of these methods is `paint()`, which handles everything that should take place when the applet is displayed on a Web page. The `paint()` method inherited by `Palindrome` doesn't do anything—it's an empty method. By overriding `paint()`, you indicate what should be drawn on the applet window whenever it needs to be displayed as the program runs. Add a blank line below the `Font` statement, and enter the following to override the `paint()` method:

```
public void paint(Graphics screen) {
    screen.setFont(f);
    screen.setColor(Color.red);
    screen.drawString("Go hang a salami, I'm a lasagna hog.", 5, 40);
}
```

The `paint()` method is declared `public`, like the applet itself, but for a different reason. In this case, `paint()` must be public because the method it is overriding also is public. A superclass method that is public only can be overridden by a public method, or the Java program won't compile successfully.

The `paint()` method takes a single argument: an instance of the `Graphics` class called `screen`. The `Graphics` class provides the behavior to render fonts and colors and draw lines and other shapes. You learn more about the `Graphics` class during Week 2, "Web-Based and Graphical Programs," when you create more applets.

You've done three things inside your `paint()` method:

- You've told the `Graphics` object that the font to use when displaying text is the one contained in the instance variable `f`.
- You've told the `Graphics` object that the color to use on text and other drawing operations is an instance of the `Color` class for the color `red`.
- Finally, you've drawn the text `"Go hang a salami, I'm a lasagna hog!"` on-screen, at the x,y coordinate of `5, 40`. The string will be rendered in the font and color indicated.

Here's what the applet looks like so far:

```
public class Palindrome extends java.applet.Applet {
    Font f = new Font("TimesRoman", Font.BOLD, 36);

    public void paint(Graphics screen) {
        screen.setFont(f);
        screen.setColor(Color.red);
        screen.drawString("Go hang a salami, I'm a lasagna hog.",
        5, 40);
    }
}
```

You might have noticed that something is missing from the example up to this point. If you saved the file and tried to compile it, you would see a bunch of errors such as the following:

```
Palindrome.java:2: Class Font not found in type declaration.
```

These errors are occurring because the classes `Graphics`, `Font`, and `Color` are part of the `java.awt` package, and it isn't available by default. You referred to the `Applet` class in the first line of the class definition by referring to its full package name (`java.applet.Applet`). In the rest of the program, you referred to other classes without using their package names.

There are two ways to solve this problem:

- Refer to all external classes by full package name, such as `java.awt.Graphics`, `java.awt.Font`, and `java.awt.Color`.

- Use an `import` statement at the beginning of the program to make one or more packages and classes available in the program.

Which one you choose is mostly a matter of personal preference, but if you refer to a class in another package numerous times, you might want to use `import` to cut down on the amount of typing.

In this example, the latter will be used.

To import these classes, add the following three statements above the `public class Palindrome` statement:

```
import java.awt.Graphics;
import java.awt.Font;
import java.awt.Color;
```

> **Tip**
>
> You also can import an entire package by using an asterisk (*) in place of a specific class name. For example, you can use this statement to import all of the classes in the java.awt package:
>
> ```
> import java.awt.*;
> ```

Now, with the proper classes imported into your program, `Palindrome.java` should compile cleanly to a class file. Listing 2.4 shows the final version to double-check.

TYPE   **LISTING 2.4.** THE FINAL VERSION OF PALINDROME.JAVA.

```
 1: import java.awt.Graphics;
 2: import java.awt.Font;
 3: import java.awt.Color;
 4:
 5: public class Palindrome extends java.applet.Applet {
 6:     Font f = new Font("TimesRoman", Font.BOLD, 36);
 7:
 8:     public void paint(Graphics screen) {
 9:         screen.setFont(f);
10:         screen.setColor(Color.red);
11:         screen.drawString("Go hang a salami, I'm a lasagna hog.", 5,
            40);
12:     }
13: }
```

Save this file as **Palindrome.java**. Because this source file contains a public class, `Palindrome`, the filename must match the name of the public class in order for it to compile successfully. Capitalization is important here as well, so the upper- and lowercase letters must be identical.

This source file can be compiled the same way as the Java applications you have created up to this point. In order to run it, however, you have to create a Web page to put it on.

Many Web page development programs such as Claris Home Page and Macromedia Dreamweaver enable a Java applet to be put onto a Web page.

If you don't have one of these tools, you can create a simple Web page using the Java-related features of the HTML page-description language.

Tip

> Although some HTML features will be described in this book as they relate
> to Java, it's beyond the scope of the book to teach HTML and Web page
> development. This book's coauthors have each written books on the subject,
> including *Sams Teach Yourself Web Publishing with HTML 4 in 21 Days* by
> Laura Lemay and *Sams Teach Yourself to Create a Home Page in 24 Hours* by
> Rogers Cadenhead.

To create a new HTML page that can contain the `Palindrome` applet, load the same text
editor you're using to create Java programs and start a new document.

Enter Listing 2.5 and save the file as **`Palindrome.html`** in the same folder that contains
`Palindrome.java` and `Palindrome.class`. If you're using Windows, put quotation marks
around the filename to make sure that the `.txt` file extension isn't added.

TYPE   **LISTING 2.5.** THE WEB PAGE PALINDROME.HTML.

```
1: <APPLET CODE="Palindrome.class" WIDTH=600 HEIGHT=100>
2: </APPLET>
```

You learn more about the HTML `<APPLET>` tag later in this book, but here are two things
to note:

- The `CODE` attribute indicates the name of the class that contains the applet—
  `Palindrome.class` in this example.
- The `WIDTH` and `HEIGHT` attributes determine how large the applet window will be
  on a Web page, in pixels. In this example, the window will be 600 pixels wide and
  100 pixels tall.

In order to see this applet, you need a Web browser that can run Java applets or the
`appletviewer` tool included with the JDK.

Note

> All of the applets in this book only use Java 1.0 features unless otherwise
> noted, so that the applets can be viewed with any browser that supports
> Java. Applications use Java 2, because those can be run directly with a Java 2
> interpreter.

2

To open the `Palindrome.html` Web page using a Web browser, use a pull-down menu command in the browser to open local files instead of Web pages. In Netscape Navigator 4.04, the command is File | Open Page | Choose File.

To open the page with the JDK's `appletviewer` tool, go to a command-line prompt in the same folder that contains `Palindrome.html`, and enter the following command:

INPUT   `appletviewer Palindrome.html`

Unlike a Web browser, the `appletviewer` tool only displays the applet (or applets) that are included on the Web page. It does not handle anything else contained on the page.

Figure 2.7 shows the applet viewed with Netscape Navigator.

FIGURE 2.7.

The Palindrome applet running in Netscape Navigator.

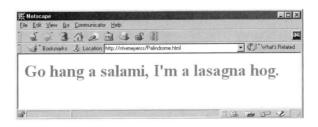

Go hang a salami, I'm a lasagna hog.

Tip

If you're still unfamiliar with what a palindrome is, take a look at Figure 2.7 and read the sentence "Go hang a salami, I'm a lasagna hog" backwards. Palindromes are words and phrases that read the same in either direction, if you disregard all spaces and punctuation. "Dennis and Edna sinned" is a palindrome, as are "Ah, Satan sees Natasha" and "To Idi Amin: I'm a idiot." The last three palindromes all came from Neil/Fred's Gigantic List of Palindromes at the following Web address:

`http://www.tsoft.net/~derf/palindrome.html`

Summary

If this is your first encounter with object-oriented programming, you might have discovered another way in which it is similar to beer.

Object-oriented program also is capable of making you dizzy, disoriented, and perhaps a bit nauseated.

If today's material seems theoretical and overwhelming at this point, don't be alarmed. You will be using object-oriented techniques for the rest of this book, and it will become familiar as you gain more experience using it.

One of the biggest hurdles of object-oriented programming is not necessarily the concepts—instead, it's the names. OOP has more jargon and vaguely ominous technical language than an episode of *The X-Files*.

To summarize today's material, here's a glossary of terms and concepts that were covered:

Class   A template for an object that contains variables to describe the object and methods to describe how the object behaves. Classes can inherit variables and methods from other classes.

Object   An instance of a class. Multiple objects that are instances of the same class have access to the same methods, but often have different values for their instance variables.

Instance   The same thing as an object. Each object is an instance of some class.

Method   A group of statements in a class that defines how the class' objects will behave. Methods are analogous to functions in other languages, but must always be located inside a class.

Class method   A method that operates on a class itself rather than on specific instances of a class.

Instance method   A method that operates on instances of that class rather than on the class itself. Because instance methods are much more common than class methods, they often are just called methods.

Class variable   A variable that describes an attribute of a class instead of specific instances of the class.

Instance variable   A variable that describes an attribute of an instance of a class instead of the class itself.

Interface   A specification of abstract behavior that individual classes can then implement.

Package   A collection of classes and interfaces. Classes from packages other than `java.lang` must be explicitly imported or referred to by their full package and class name.

Subclass   A class further down the class hierarchy than another class, its superclass. Creating a new class that inherits from an existing one is often called subclassing. A class can have as many subclasses as necessary.

Superclass   A class further up the class hierarchy than another class, its subclass. A class only can have one superclass immediately above it, but that class also can have a superclass, and so on.

Q&A

Q **In effect, methods are functions that are defined inside classes. If they look like functions and act like functions, why aren't they called functions?**

A Some object-oriented programming languages do call them functions (C++ calls them *member functions*). Other object-oriented languages differentiate between functions inside and outside a body of a class or object, because in those languages the use of the separate terms is important to understanding how each function works. Because the difference is relevant in other languages, and because the term *method* is now in common use in object-oriented terminology, Java uses the term as well.

Q **What's the distinction between instance variables and methods and their counterparts, class variables and methods?**

A Almost everything you do in a Java program will involve instances (also called objects) rather than classes. However, some behavior and attributes make more sense if stored in the class itself rather than in the object. For example, to create a new instance of a class, you need a method that is defined and available for the class itself. Otherwise, you run into a chicken-and-egg dilemma—you can't create a baby object without an existing momma object that has a baby-making method, and no momma object can exist without having been a baby first.

WEEK 1

DAY 3

The ABCs of Java

As you have learned, a Java program is made up of classes and objects, which in turn are made up of methods and variables. Methods are made up of statements and expressions, which are made up of operators.

At this point, you might be afraid that Java is like the Russian nesting dolls called Matryoshka. Every one of those dolls seems to have a smaller doll inside it, which is as intricate and detailed as its larger companion.

Relax, babushka—this chapter clears away the big dolls to reveal the smallest elements of Java programming. You'll leave classes, objects, and methods alone for a day and examine the basic things you can do in a single line of Java code.

The following subjects are covered:

- Java statements and expressions
- Variables and data types
- Comments
- Literals
- Arithmetic
- Comparisons
- Logical operators

Note

> Because of Java's ties to C and C++, much of the material in this chapter will look familiar to programmers who are well-versed in those single-letter languages. When necessary, technical notes such as this one describe specific differences between Java and other languages.

Statements and Expressions

All tasks that you want to accomplish in a Java program can be broken down into a series of statements.

 NEW TERM   A *statement* is a simple command written in a programming language that causes something to happen.

Statements represent a single action that is taken in a Java program. All of the following are simple Java statements:

```
int age = 31;

import java.awt.dnd;

System.out.println("You're not the boss of me!");

player.score = 41367;
```

Some statements produce a value, such as when you add two numbers together in a program. These statements are called expressions.

NEW TERM   An *expression* is a statement that results in a value being produced. The value can be stored for later use in the program, used immediately in another statement, or disregarded. The value produced by a statement is called its *return value*.

Some expressions produce a numerical return value, as in the example of adding two numbers together. Others produce a Boolean value—true or false—or can even produce a Java object. They are discussed later today.

Although many Java programs list one statement per line, this is a formatting decision that does not determine where one statement ends and another one begins. Each statement in Java is terminated with a semicolon character (;). A programmer can put more than one statement on a line and it will compile successfully:

```
j.color = "lemon yellow";
j.hungry = false;
```

Statements in Java are grouped using the opening curly brace ({) and closing curly brace (}). A group of statements organized between these characters is called a *block* or *block statement*, and you learn more about them during Day 5, "Lists, Logic, and Loops."

Variables and Data Types

In the Jabberwock application you created during Day 2, "A Taste of Object-Oriented Programming," you used variables to keep track of information.

 Variables are a place where information can be stored while a program is running. The value can be changed at any point in the program—hence the name.

In order to create a variable, you must give it a name and identify what type of information it will store. You also can give a variable an initial value at the same time you create it.

There are three kinds of variables in Java: instance variables, class variables, and local variables.

Instance variables, as you learned yesterday, are used to define an object's attributes. *Class variables* define the attributes of an entire class of objects, and apply to all instances of it.

Local variables are used inside method definitions, or even smaller blocks of statements within a method. They only can be used while the method or block is being executed by the Java interpreter, and they cease to exist afterward.

Although all three kinds of variables are created in much the same way, class and instance variables are used in a different manner than local variables. You learn about local variables today and cover instance and class variables during Day 4, "Object Lessons."

 Note

Unlike other languages, Java does not have *global variables* (variables that can be used in all parts of a program). Instance and class variables are used to communicate information from one object to another, and these replace the need for global variables.

Creating Variables

Before you can use a variable in a Java program, you must create the variable by declaring its name and the type of information it will store. The type of information is listed first, followed by the name of the variable. The following are all examples of variable declarations:

```
int highScore;
```

```
String username;
```

```
boolean gameOver;
```

 Note

> You learn about variable types later today, but you might be familiar with the types used in this example. The `int` type represents integers, `boolean` is used for `true`/`false` values, and `String` is a special variable type used to store text.

Local variables can be declared at any place inside a method, just like any other Java statement, but they must be declared before they can be used. The normal place for variable declarations is immediately after the statement that names and identifies the method.

In the following example, three variables are declared at the top of a program's `main()` method:

```
public static void main (String arguments[] ) {
    int total;
    String reportTitle;
    boolean active;
}
```

If you are creating several variables of the same type, you can declare all of them in the same statement by separating the variable names with commas. The following statement creates three `String` variables named `street`, `city`, and `state`:

```
String street, city, state;
```

Variables can be assigned a value when they are created by using an equal sign (=) followed by the value. The following statements create new variables and give them initial values:

```
int zipcode = 90210;
```

```
String name = "Brandon";
```

```
boolean cheatedOnKelly = true;
```

```
int age = 28, height = 70, weight = 140;
```

As the last statement indicates, you can assign values to multiple variables of the same type by using commas to separate them.

Local variables must be given values before they are used in a program, or the program won't compile successfully. For this reason, it is good practice to give initial values to all local variables.

Instance and class variable definitions are given an initial value depending on the type of information they hold:

- Numeric variables   `0`
- Characters   `'\0'`
- Booleans   `false`
- Objects   `null`

Naming Variables

Variable names in Java must start with a letter, an underscore character (_), or a dollar sign ($). They cannot start with a number. After the first character, variable names can include any combination of letters or numbers.

 Note

> In addition, the Java language uses the Unicode character set, which includes the standard character set plus thousands of others to represent international alphabets. Accented characters and other symbols can be used in variable names as long as they have a Unicode character number.

When naming a variable and using it in a program, it's important to remember that Java is case-sensitive—the capitalization of letters must be consistent. Because of this, a program can have a variable named X and another named x—and a `rose` is not a `Rose` is not a `ROSE`.

In programs in this book and elsewhere, Java variables are given meaningful names that include several words joined together. To make it easier to spot the words, the following rule of thumb is used:

- The first letter of the variable name is lowercase.
- Each successive word in the variable name begins with a capital letter.
- All other letters are lowercase.

The following variable declarations follow this rule of naming:

```
Button loadFile;
```

```
int areaCode;
```

```
boolean playerSetNewHighScore;
```

Variable Types

In addition to a name, a variable declaration must include the type of information being stored. The type can be any of the following:

- One of the basic data types
- The name of a class or interface
- An array

You learn how to declare and use array variables on Day 5. This lesson focuses on the other variable types.

Data Types

There are eight basic variable types for the storage of integers, floating-point numbers, characters, and Boolean values. These often are called *primitive types* because they are built-in parts of the Java language rather than being objects, which makes them more efficient to use. These data types have the same size and characteristics no matter what operating system and platform you're on, unlike some data types in other programming languages.

There are four data types that can be used to store integers. The one to use depends on the size of the integer, as indicated in Table 3.1.

TABLE 3.1. INTEGER TYPES.

Type	Size	Values That Can Be Stored
byte	8 bits	-128 to 127
short	16 bits	-32,768 to 32,767
int	32 bits	-2,147,483,648 to 2,147,483,647
long	64 bits	-9,223,372,036,854,775,808 to 9,223,372,036,854,775,807

All of these types are signed, which means that they can hold either positive or negative numbers. The type used for a variable depends on the range of values it might need to hold. None of these integer variables can reliably store a value that is too large or too small for its designated variable type, so you should take care when designating the type.

NEW TERM Another type of number that can be stored is a floating-point number, which has the type `float` or `double`. *Floating-point numbers* represent numbers with a decimal part. The `float` type should be sufficient for most uses, since it can handle any number from `1.4E-45` to `3.4E+38`. If not, the `double` type can be used for more precise numbers ranging from `4.9E-324` to `1.7E+308`.

The `char` type is used for individual characters such as letters, numbers, punctuation, and other symbols.

The last of the eight basic data types is `boolean`. As you have learned, Boolean values hold either `true` or `false` in Java.

All these variable types are listed in lowercase, and you must use them as such in programs. There are classes with the same name as some of these data types but different capitalization—for example, `Boolean` and `Char`. These have different functionality in a Java program, so you can't use them interchangeably. You see how these special classes are used tomorrow.

Class Types

In addition to the eight basic data types, a variable can have a class as its type, as in the following examples:

```
String lastName = "Walsh";

Color hair;

Jabberwock firstMonster;
```

When a variable has a class as its type, the variable refers to an object of that class or one of its subclasses.

The last of the examples in the preceding list, `Jabberwock firstMonster;` creates a variable named `firstMonster` that refers to a `Jabberwock` object.

Referring to a superclass as a variable type is useful when the variable might be one of several different subclasses. For example, consider a class hierarchy with a `Fruit` superclass and three subclasses: `Apple`, `Pear`, and `Strawberry`. If you create a `Fruit` variable called `favoriteFruit`, it could be used to refer to an `Apple`, `Pear`, or `Strawberry` object.

Declaring a variable of type `Object` means that it can hold any object.

Note

> Java does not have anything comparable to the `typedef` statement from C and C++. To declare new types in Java, a new class is declared and variables can use that class as their type.

Assigning Values to Variables

Once a variable has been declared, a value can be assigned to it with the assignment operator—an equal sign (=). The following are examples of assignment statements:

```
idCode = 8675309;
```

```
snappyDresser = false;
```

Comments

One of the most important ways to improve the readability of your program is to use comments.

NEW TERM   *Comments* are information included in a program strictly for the benefit of humans trying to figure out what's going on in the program. The Java compiler ignores comments entirely when preparing a runnable version of a Java source file.

There are three different kinds of comments you can use in Java programs, and you can use each of them at your discretion.

The first way to add a comment to a program is to precede it with two slash characters (/ /). Everything from the slashes to the end of the line is considered a comment, as in the following statement:

```
int creditHours = 3; // set up credit hours for course
```

In this example, everything from the / / to the end of the line is a comment and is disregarded by a Java compiler.

If you need to make a comment that takes up more than one line, you can begin it with the text /* and end it with the text */. Everything between these two delimiters is considered a comment, as in the following:

```
/* This program was written late at night under the
influence of expired antihistamine medicine and
generic supermarket soda. I offer no warranties
express nor implied that it works for any useful
purpose whatsoever. */
```

The final type of comment is meant to be computer-readable as well as human-readable. If you begin a comment with the text /** (instead of /*) and end it with */, the comment is interpreted to be official documentation on how the class and its public methods work.

This kind of comment then can be read by utilities such as the javadoc tool included with the JDK. The javadoc program uses official comments to create a set of Web pages that document the program, its class hierarchy and methods.

All of the official documentation on Java's class library comes from javadoc-style comments. You can view Java 2 documentation on the Web at the following page:

```
http://java.sun.com/docs
```

Literals

In addition to variables, you will also use a literal in a Java statement.

3

NEW TERM *Literals* are any numbers, text, or other information that directly represent a value.

Literal is a programming term that essentially means that what you type is what you get. The following assignment statement uses a literal:

```
int year = 1998;
```

The literal is 1998, because it directly represents the integer value 1998. Numbers, characters, and strings all are examples of literals.

Although the meaning and usage of literals will seem intuitive most of the time, Java has some special types of literals that represent different kinds of numbers, characters, strings, and Boolean values.

Number Literals

Java has several integer literals. The number 4, for example, is an integer literal of the int variable type. It also can be assigned to byte and short variables because the number is small enough to fit into those integer types. An integer literal larger than an int can hold is automatically considered to be of the type long. You also can indicate that a literal should be a long integer by adding the letter L (L or l) to the number. For example, the following statement stores the value 4 to a long integer:

```
long pennyTotal = 4L;
```

To represent a negative number as a literal, prepend a minus sign (-) to the literal, as in -45.

Note

Octal and hexadecimal numbering systems are convenient for many advanced programming uses, but unlikely to be needed by beginners. *Octal numbers* are a base-8 numbering system, which means they can only represent the values 0 through 7 as a single digit. The eighth number in octal is 10 (or 010 as a Java literal).

Hexadecimal is a base-16 numbering system, and it can represent 16 numbers as a single digit. The letters A through F represent the last six digits, so the first 16 numbers are 0, 1, 2, 3, 4, 5, 6, 7, 8, 9, A, B, C, D, E, F.

The octal and hexadecimal systems are better suited for certain tasks in programming than the normal decimal system is. If you have ever used HTML to set a Web page's background color, you have used hexadecimal numbers.

If you need to use a literal integer with octal numbering, prepend a 0 to the number. For example, the octal number 777 would be the literal 0777. Hexadecimal integers are used as literals by prepending the number with 0x, as in 0x12 or 0xFF.

Floating-point literals use a period character (.) for the decimal point, as you would expect. The following statement uses a literal to set up a double variable:

```
double myGPA = 2.25;
```

All floating-point literals are considered the double variable type instead of float. To specify a literal of float, add the letter F (F or f) to the literal, as in the following example:

```
float piValue = 3.1415927F;
```

You can use exponents in floating-point literals by using the letter e or E followed by the exponent, which can be a negative number. The following statements use exponential notation:

```
double x = 12e22;
```

```
double y = 19E-95;
```

Boolean Literals

The Boolean values true and false also are literals. These are the only two values you can use when assigning a value to a boolean variable type or using a Boolean in a statement in other ways.

If you have used other languages such as C, you might expect that a value of 1 is equivalent to `true` and `0` is equivalent to `false`. This isn't the case in Java—you must use the values `true` or `false` to represent Boolean values. The following statement sets a `boolean` variable:

```
boolean toThineOwnSelf = true;
```

Note that the literal `true` does not have quotation marks around it. If it did, the Java compiler would assume that it was a string of characters.

Character Literals

Character literals are expressed by a single character surrounded by single quotation marks, such as `'a'`, `'#'`, and `'3'`. You might be familiar with the ASCII character set, which includes 128 characters including letters, numerals, punctuation, and other characters useful in computing. Java supports thousands of additional characters through the 16-bit Unicode standard.

Some character literals represent characters that are not readily printable or accessible through a keyboard. Table 3.2 lists the special codes that can represent these special characters as well as characters from the Unicode character set. The letter *d* in the octal, hex, and Unicode escape codes represents a number or a hexadecimal digit (a–f or A–F).

TABLE 3.2. CHARACTER ESCAPE CODES.

Escape	Meaning
\n	New line
\t	Tab
\b	Backspace
\r	Carriage return
\f	Formfeed
\\	Backslash
\'	Single quotation mark
\"	Double quotation mark
d	Octal
\x*d*	Hexadecimal
\u*d*	Unicode character

3

> **Note**
>
> C and C++ programmers should note that Java does not include character codes for \a (bell) or \v (vertical tab).

String Literals

The final literal that you can use in a Java program represents strings of characters. A string in Java is an object rather than being a basic data type, and strings are not stored in arrays as they are in languages such as C.

Because string objects are real objects in Java, methods are available to combine strings, modify strings, and determine whether two strings have the same value.

String literals consist of a series of characters inside double quotation marks, as in the following statements:

```
String coAuthor = "Laura Lemay, killer of trees";

String password = "swordfish";
```

Strings can include the character escape codes listed in Table 3.2 previously, as shown here:

```
String example = "Socrates asked, \"Hemlock is poison?\"";

System.out.println("Bob Kemp\nOne on One Sports\n2 a.m. to 6 a.m.");

String title = "Sams Teach Yourself Java in a 3-Day Weekend\u2122"
```

In the last example here, the Unicode code sequence \u2122 produces a ™ symbol on systems that have been configured to support Unicode.

> **Caution**
>
> Most users in English-speaking countries aren't likely to see Unicode characters when they run Java programs. Although Java supports the transmission of Unicode characters, the user's system also must support it for the characters to be displayed. Unicode support provides a way to encode its characters for systems that support the standard. Although Java 1.02 only supported the Latin subset of Unicode, Java 1.1 and 2 support the display of any Unicode character that can be represented by a host font.
>
> For more information about Unicode, visit the Unicode Consortium Web site at http://www.unicode.org/.

Although string literals are used in a manner similar to other literals in a program, they are handled differently behind the scenes.

When a string literal is used, Java stores that value as a `String` object. You don't have to explicitly create a new object, as you must do when working with other objects, so they are as easy to work with as basic data types. Strings are unusual in this respect—none of the basic types is stored as an object when used. You learn more about strings and the `String` class today and tomorrow.

Expressions and Operators

An *expression* is a statement that produces a value. Some of the most common expressions are mathematical, such as in the following source code example:

```
int x = 3;
int y = 4;
int z = x * y;
```

The last statement in this example is an expression. The multiplication operator `*` is used to multiply the x and y integers, and the expression produces the result of the multiplication. This result is stored in the z integer.

The value produced by an expression is called a return value, as you have learned. This value can be assigned to a variable and used in many other ways in your Java programs.

Most of the expressions in Java use operators like `*`.

 Operators are special symbols used for mathematical functions, some types of assignment statements, and logical comparisons.

Arithmetic

There are five operators used to accomplish basic arithmetic in Java. These are shown in Table 3.3.

TABLE 3.3. ARITHMETIC OPERATORS.

Operator	Meaning	Example
+	Addition	3 + 4
-	Subtraction	5 - 7
*	Multiplication	5 * 5
/	Division	14 / 7
%	Modulus	20 % 7

Each operator takes two operands, one on either side of the operator. The subtraction operator also can be used to negate a single operand—which is equivalent to multiplying that operand by -1.

One thing to be mindful of when using division is the kind of numbers you're dealing with. If you store a division operation into an integer, the result will be rounded off to a whole number because the int data type can't handle floating-point numbers. As an example, the expression 31 / 9 results in 3 if stored as an integer.

Modulus division, which uses the % operator, produces the remainder of a division operation. Using 31 % 9 results in 4 because 31 divided by 9 leaves a remainder of 4.

Note that most arithmetic operations involving integers produce an int regardless of the original type of the operands. If you're working with other numbers, such as floating-point numbers or long integers, you should make sure that the operands have the same type you're trying to end up with.

Listing 3.1 is an example of simple arithmetic in Java.

TYPE   **LISTING 3.1.** THE SOURCE FILE AMOEBAMATH.JAVA .

```
 1: class AmoebaMath {
 2:     public static void main (String arguments[]) {
 3:         int x = 6;
 4:         short y = 4;
 5:         float a = .12f;
 6:
 7:         System.out.println("You start with " + x + " pet amoebas.");
 8:         System.out.println("\tTwo get married and their spouses move
            in.");
 9:         x = x + 2;
10:         System.out.println("You now have " + x);
11:
12:         System.out.println("\tMitosis occurs, doubling the number of
            amoebas.");
13:         x = x * 2;
14:         System.out.println("You now have " + x);
15:
16:         System.out.println("\tThere's a fight. " + y + " amoebas move
            out.");
17:         x = x - y;
18:         System.out.println("You now have " + x);
19:
20:         System.out.println("\tParamecia attack! You lose one-third of
            the colony.");
21:         x = x - (x / 3);
22:         System.out.println("You end up with " + x + " pet amoebas.");
```

```
23:            System.out.println("Daily upkeep cost per amoeba: $" + a);
24:            System.out.println("Total daily cost: $" + (a * x));
25:    }
26: }
```

If you run this Java application, it produces the following output:

OUTPUT

```
You start with 6 pet amoebas.
    Two get married and their spouses move in.
You now have 8
    Mitosis occurs, doubling the number of amoebas.
You now have 16
    There's a fight. 4 amoebas move out.
You now have 12
    Paramecia attack! You lose one-third of the colony.
You end up with 8 pet amoebas.
Daily upkeep cost per amoeba: $0.12
Total daily cost: $0.96
```

In this simple Java application, three variables are created with initial values in lines 3–5: the integer x, the short integer y, and the floating-point number a. Because the default type for floating-point numbers is double, an f is appended to the literal .12 to indicate that it is of type float.

The rest of the program uses arithmetic operators to track the population of an amoeba colony. (No amoebas were harmed during the making of this chapter.)

This program also makes use of System.out.println() in several statements. The System.out.println() method is used in an application to display strings and other information to the standard output device, which usually is the screen.

System.out.println() takes a single argument within its parentheses: a string. In order to present more than one variable or literal as the argument to println(), you can use the + operator to combine these elements into a single string.

You learn more about this use of the + operator later today.

More About Assignment

Assigning a value to a variable is an expression, because it produces a value. Because of this feature, you can string assignment statements together the following way:

```
x = y = z = 7;
```

In this statement, all three variables end up with the value of 7.

The right side of an assignment expression always is calculated before the assignment takes place. This makes it possible to use an expression statement as in the following code example:

```
int x = 5;
x = x + 2;
```

In the expression x = x + 2, the first thing that happens is that x + 2 is calculated. The result of this calculation, 7, is then assigned to x.

Using an expression to change a variable's value is an extremely common task in programming. There are several operators used strictly in these cases.

Table 3.4 shows these assignment operators and the expressions they are functionally equivalent to.

TABLE 3.4. ASSIGNMENT OPERATORS.

Expression	Meaning
x += y	x = x + y
x -= y	x = x - y
x *= y	x = x * y
x /= y	x = x / y

Caution

These shorthand assignment operators are functionally equivalent to the longer assignment statements for which they substitute. However, if either side of your assignment statement is part of a complex expression, there are cases where the operators are not equivalent. For example, if x equals 20 and y equals 5, the following two statements do not produce the same value:

```
x = x / y + 5;
x /= y + 5;
```

When in doubt, simplify an expression using multiple assignment statements and don't use the shorthand operators.

Incrementing and Decrementing

Another common task is to add or subtract 1 from an integer variable. There are special operators for these expressions, which are called increment and decrement operations.

NEW TERM   *Incrementing* a variable means to add 1 to its value, and *decrementing* a variable means to subtract 1 from its value.

The increment operator is ++ and the decrement operator is - -. These operators are placed immediately after or immediately before a variable name, as in the following code example:

```
int x = 7;
x = x++;
```

In this example, the statement x = x++ increments the x variable from 7 to 8.

These increment and decrement operators can be placed before or after a variable name, and this affects the value of expressions that involve these operators.

NEW TERM   Increment and decrement operators are called *prefix* operators if listed before a variable name, and *postfix* operators if listed after a name.

In a simple expression such as standards - -;, using a prefix or postfix operator doesn't change the result. When increment and decrement operations are part of a larger expression, however, the choice between prefix and postfix operators is important.

Consider the following two expressions:

```
int x, y, z;
x = 42;
y = x++;
z = ++x;
```

These two expressions yield very different results because of the difference between prefix and postfix operations. When you use postfix operators as in y = x++, y receives the value of x before it is incremented by 1. When using prefix operators as in z = ++x, x is incremented by 1 before the value is assigned to z. The end result of this example is that y equals 42, z equals 44, and x equals 44.

If you're still having some trouble figuring this out, here's the example again with comments describing each step:

```
int x, y, z; // x, y, and z are all declared
x = 42;      // x is given the value of 42
y = x++;     // y is given x's value (42) before it is incremented
             // and x is then incremented to 43
z = ++x;     // x is incremented to 44, and z is given x's value
```

Caution As with shorthand operators, increment and decrement operators can produce results you might not have expected when used in extremely complex expressions. The concept of "assigning x to y before x is incremented" isn't precisely right, because Java evaluates everything on the right side of an expression before assigning its value to the left side. Java stores some values before handling an expression in order to make postfix work the way it has been described in this section. When you're not getting the results you expect from a complex expression that includes prefix and postfix operators, try to break the expression into multiple statements to simplify it.

Comparisons

Java has several operators that are used when making comparisons between variables, variables and literals, or other types of information in a program.

These operators are used in expressions that return Boolean values of `true` or `false`, depending on whether the comparison being made is true or not. Table 3.5 shows the comparison operators.

TABLE 3.5. COMPARISON OPERATORS.

Operator	Meaning	Example
==	Equal	x == 3
!=	Not equal	x != 3
<	Less than	x < 3
>	Greater than	x > 3
<=	Less than or equal to	x <= 3
>=	Greater than or equal to	x >= 3

The following example shows a comparison operator in use:

```
boolean hip;
int age = 31;
hip = age < 25;
```

The expression age < 25 produces a result of either `true` or `false`, depending on the value of the integer age. Because age is 31 in this example (which is not less than 25), `hip` is given the boolean value `false`.

Logical Operators

Expressions that result in Boolean values such as comparison operations can be combined to form more complex expressions. This is handled through logical operators. These operators are used for the logical combinations AND, OR, XOR, and logical NOT.

For AND combinations, the & or && logical operators are used. When two Boolean expressions are linked by the & or && operators, the combined expression returns a true value only if both Boolean expressions are true.

Consider this example, taken directly from the film *Harold & Maude*:

```
boolean unusual = (age < 21) & (girlfriendAge > 78);
```

This expression combines two comparison expressions: age < 21 and girlfriendAge > 78. If both of these expressions are true, the value true is assigned to the variable unusual. In any other circumstance, the value false is assigned to unusual.

The difference between & and && lies in how much work Java does on the combined expression. If & is used, the expressions on either side of the & are evaluated no matter what. If && is used and the left side of the && is false, the expression on the right side of the && never is evaluated.

For OR combinations, the ¦ or ¦¦ logical operators are used. These combined expressions return a true value if either Boolean expression is true.

Consider this *Harold & Maude*-inspired example:

```
boolean unusual = (grimThoughts > 10) ¦¦ (girlfriendAge > 78);
```

This expression combines two comparison expressions: grimThoughts > 10 and girlfriendAge > 78. If either of these expressions is true, the value true is assigned to the variable unusual. Only if both of these expressions is false will the value false be assigned to unusual.

Note the use of ¦¦ instead of ¦. Because of this usage, if grimThoughts > 10 is true, unusual is set to true and the second expression never is evaluated.

The XOR combination has one logical operator, ^. This results in a true value only if both Boolean expressions it combines have opposite values. If both are true or both are false, the ^ operator produces a false value.

The NOT combination uses the ! logical operator followed by a single expression. It reverses the value of a Boolean expression the same way that a minus symbol reverses the positive or negative sign on a number.

For example, if age < 30 returns a true value, !(age < 30) returns a false value.

These logical operators can seem completely illogical when encountered for the first time. You get plenty of chances to work with them in subsequent chapters, especially on Day 5.

Operator Precedence

When more than one operator is used in an expression, Java has an established precedence to determine the order in which operators are evaluated. In many cases, this precedence determines the overall value of the expression.

For example, consider the following expression:

```
y = 6 + 4 / 2;
```

The y variable receives the value 5 or the value 8, depending on which arithmetic operation is handled first. If the 6 + 4 expression comes first, y has the value of 5. Otherwise, y equals 8.

In general, the order from first to last is the following:

- Increment and decrement operations
- Arithmetic operations
- Comparisons
- Logical operations
- Assignment expressions

If two operations have the same precedence, the one on the left in the actual expression is handled before the one on the right. Table 3.7 shows the specific precedence of the various operators in Java. Operators farther up the table are evaluated first.

TABLE 3.7. OPERATOR PRECEDENCE.

Operator	Notes
. [] ()	Parentheses (()) are used to group expressions; period (.) is used for access to methods and variables within objects and classes (discussed tomorrow); square brackets ([]) are used for arrays. (This operator is discussed later in the week.)
++ -- ! ~ instanceof	The instanceof operator returns true or false based on whether the object is an instance of the named class or any of that class's subclasses (discussed tomorrow).

Operator	Notes
new (type)expression	The new operator is used for creating new instances of classes; () in this case is for casting a value to another type. (You learn about both of these tomorrow.)
* / %	Multiplication, division, modulus.
+ -	Addition, subtraction.
<< >> >>>	Bitwise left and right shift.
< > <= >=	Relational comparison tests.
== !=	Equality.
&	AND
^	XOR
¦	OR
&&	Logical AND
¦¦	Logical OR
? :	Shorthand for if...then...else (discussed on Day 5).
= += -= *= /= %= ^=	Various assignments.
&= ¦= <<= >>= >>>=	More assignments.

Returning to the expression y = 6 + 4 / 2, Table 3.7 shows that division is evaluated before addition, so the value of y will be 8.

To change the order in which expressions are evaluated, place parentheses around the expressions that should be evaluated first. You can nest one set of parentheses inside another to make sure that expressions evaluate in the desired order—the innermost parenthetic expression is evaluated first.

The following expression results in a value of 5:

y = (6 + 4) / 2

The value of 5 is the result because 6 + 4 is calculated before the result, 10, is divided by 2.

Parentheses also can be useful to improve the readability of an expression. If the precedence of an expression isn't immediately clear to you, adding parentheses to impose the desired precedence can make the statement easier to understand.

String Arithmetic

As stated earlier today, the + operator has a double life outside the world of mathematics. It can be used to concatenate two or more strings.

NEW TERM *Concatenate* means to link two things together. For reasons unknown, it is the verb of choice when describing the act of combining two strings—winning out over paste, glue, affix, combine, link, and conjoin.

In several examples, you have seen statements that look something like this:

```
String firstName = "Raymond";
System.out.println("Everybody loves " + firstName);
```

These two lines result in the following text being displayed:

```
Everybody loves Raymond
```

The + operator combines strings, other objects, and variables to form a single string. In the preceding example, the literal Everybody loves is concatenated to the value of the String object firstName.

Working with the concatenation operator is easier in Java because of the way it can handle any variable type and object value as if it were a string. If any part of a concatenation operation is a String or String literal, all elements of the operation will be treated as if they were strings:

```
System.out.println(4 + " score and " + 7 + " years ago.");
```

This produces the output text 4 score and 7 years ago., as if the integer literals 4 and 7 were strings.

There also is a shorthand += operator to add something to the end of a string. For example, consider the following expression:

```
myName += " Jr.";
```

This expression is equivalent to the following:

```
myName = myName + " Jr.";
```

In this example, it changes the value of myName (which might be something like Efrem Zimbalist) by adding Jr. at the end (Efrem Zimbalist Jr.).

Summary

Anyone who pops open a set of Matryoska dolls has to be a bit disappointed to reach the smallest doll in the group. Ideally, advances in microengineering should enable Russian artisans to create ever-smaller and smaller dolls, until someone reaches the subatomic threshold and is declared the winner.

You have reached Java's smallest nesting doll today, but it shouldn't be a letdown. Using statements and expressions enables you to begin building effective methods, which make effective objects and classes possible.

Today you learned about creating variables and assigning values to them; using literals to represent numeric, character, and string values; and working with operators. Tomorrow you put these skills to use as you develop objects for Java programs.

To summarize today's material, Table 3.8 lists the operators you learned about. Be a doll and look them over carefully.

TABLE 3.8. OPERATOR SUMMARY.

Operator	Meaning
+	Addition
-	Subtraction
*	Multiplication
/	Division
%	Modulus
<	Less than
>	Greater than
<=	Less than or equal to
>=	Greater than or equal to
==	Equal
!=	Not equal
&&	Logical AND
¦¦	Logical OR
!	Logical NOT
&	AND

continues

TABLE 3.8. CONTINUED

Operator	Meaning
¦	OR
^	XOR
=	Assignment
++	Increment
- -	Decrement
+=	Add and assign
-=	Subtract and assign
*=	Multiply and assign
/=	Divide and assign
%=	Modulus and assign

Q&A

Q What happens if you assign an integer value to a variable that is too large for that variable to hold?

A Logically, you might think that the variable is converted to the next larger type, but this isn't what happens. Instead, an *overflow* occurs—a situation in which the number wraps around from one size extreme to the other. An example overflow would be a byte variable that goes from 127 (acceptable value) to 128 (unacceptable). It would wrap around to the lowest acceptable value, which is -128, and start counting upward from there. Overflow isn't something you can readily deal with in a program, so you should be sure to give your variables plenty of living space in their chosen data type.

Q Why does Java have all these shorthand operators for arithmetic and assignment? It's really hard to read that way.

A Java's syntax is based on C++, which is based on C (more Russian nesting doll behavior). C is an expert language that values programming power over readability, and the shorthand operators are one of the legacies of that design priority. Using them in a program isn't required because effective substitutes are available, so you can avoid them in your own programming if you prefer.

DAY **4**

Object Lessons

Two days ago, object-oriented programming was compared to beer because it's an acquired taste that might lead to disorientation, nausea, and an altered worldview.

Today's chapter offers a refill. You become reacquainted with this type of programming as you work with objects in Java.

Most of the things you do in the language are done with objects. You create objects, modify them, move them around, change their variables, call their methods, and combine them with other objects. You develop classes, create objects out of those classes, and use them with other classes and objects.

You work extensively with objects on this day. The following topics are covered:

- Creating objects (also called *instances*)
- Testing and modifying class and instance variables in those objects
- Calling an object's methods
- Converting objects and other types of data from one class to another

Creating New Objects

When you write a Java program, you define a set of classes. As you learned on Day 2, "A Taste of Object-Oriented Programming," classes are templates for objects; for the most part you merely use the class to create instances and then work with those instances. In this section, therefore, you learn how to create a new object from any given class.

Remember strings from yesterday? You learned that using a *string literal* (a series of characters enclosed in double quotation marks) creates a new instance of the class String with the value of that string.

The String class is unusual in that respect. Although it's a class, there's an easy way to create instances of that class using a literal. The other classes don't have that shortcut; to create instances of those classes you have to do so explicitly by using the new operator.

Note

> What about the literals for numbers and characters—don't they create objects, too? Actually, they don't. The primitive data types for numbers and characters create numbers and characters, but for efficiency, they actually aren't objects. You can put object wrappers around them if you need to treat them like objects (which you learn to do later in this book).

Using new

To create a new object, you use the new operator with the name of the class you want to create an instance of, followed by parentheses:

```
String teamName = new String();
Random randInfo = new Random();
Jabberwock j = new Jabberwock();
```

The parentheses are important; don't leave them off. The parentheses can be empty, in which case the most simple, basic object is created, or the parentheses can contain arguments that determine the initial values of instance variables or other initial qualities of that object.

The following examples show objects being created with arguments:

```
GregorianCalendar date = new GregorianCalendar(64, 6, 6, 7, 30);

Point pt = new Point(0,0);
```

The number and type of arguments you can use inside the parentheses with new are defined by the class itself using a special method called a *constructor.* (You learn more about constructors later today.) If you try to create a new instance of a class with the wrong number or type of arguments (or if you give it no arguments and it needs some), you get an error when you try to compile your Java program.

Here's an example of creating several different types of objects using different numbers and types of arguments: The Random class, part of the java.util package, creates objects that are used to generate random numbers in a program. These objects are called *random number generators*, and they range in decimal value from 0.0 to 1.0. Random numbers are useful in games and other programs in which an element of unpredictability is needed.

The Random object doesn't actually generate numbers randomly. Instead, it uses takes one number from an extremely long sequence of numbers. This is called *pseudo-random number generation*, and is used in many different programming languages. In order to take a different number from the random-number sequence, the Random() object must be given a seed value. This seed can be sent when the object is constructed.

Listing 4.1 is a Java program that creates Random objects using new in two different ways.

4

TYPE **LISTING 4.1.** THE FULL TEXT OF RANDOMNUMBERS.JAVA.

```
 1: import java.util.Random;
 2:
 3: class RandomNumbers {
 4:
 5:     public static void main(String arguments[]) {
 6:         Random r1, r2;
 7:
 8:         r1 = new Random();
 9:         System.out.println("Random value 1: " + r1.nextDouble());
10:
11:         r2 = new Random(8675309);
12:         System.out.println("Random value 2: " + r2.nextDouble());
13:     }
14: }
```

When you compile and run the program, the output should resemble the following:

OUTPUT
```
Random value 1: 0.3125961341023068
Random value 2: 0.754788115099576
```

In this example, two different Random objects are created using different arguments to the class listed after new. The first instance (line 8) uses new Random() with no arguments, which creates a Random object seeded with the current time. Your value for the first line of the output depends on the time you run the program, because the random value reflects the change in time.

For this reason, most Random objects default to using the time as the seed.

Calling the nextDouble() method of the Random() object in lines 9 and 12 returns the next number in the pseudo-random sequence of numbers.

The second Random object in this example has an integer argument when it is constructed in line 11. The second line of output should be the same each time it is run, showing a value of 0.754788115099576. When you use a literal as the seed, the random number sequence is always the same. This might be useful in testing purposes.

Note

> You might be having trouble figuring out why a long decimal number like 0.754788115099576 could be used to generate a random number. If you multiply this random value by an integer, the product is a random number between 0 and that integer. For example, the following statements multiply a random number by 12 and save the product as an integer:
>
> ```
> Random r1 = new Random();
> int number = (int)(r1.nextDouble() * 12);
> ```
>
> The integer in number will be a random number from 0 to 11.

What new Does

Several things happen when you use the new operator: The new instance of the given class is created, memory is allocated for it, and a special method defined in the given class is called. This special method is called a constructor.

NEW TERM   *Constructors* are special methods for creating and initializing new instances of classes. Constructors initialize the new object and its variables, create any other objects that the object needs, and perform any other operations that the object needs to initialize itself.

Multiple constructor definitions in a class each can have a different number or type of argument. When you use new, you can specify different arguments in the argument list, and the right constructor for those arguments will be called. Multiple constructor definitions are what enabled the Random() class in the previous example to accomplish different things with the different versions of the new statement. When you create your own classes, you can define as many constructors as you need to implement the behavior of the class.

A Note on Memory Management

If you are familiar with other object-oriented programming languages, you might wonder whether the new statement has an opposite that destroys an object when it is no longer needed.

Memory management in Java is dynamic and automatic. When you create a new object, Java automatically allocates the right amount of memory for that object. You don't have to allocate any memory for objects explicitly. Java does it for you.

Because Java memory management is automatic, you do not need to deallocate the memory that object uses when you're finished with an object. When you are finished with an object, the object no longer has any live references to it (it won't be assigned to any variables you still are using, or stored in any arrays). Java has a garbage collector that looks for unused objects and reclaims the memory that the objects are using. You don't have to explicitly free the memory—you just have to make sure you're not still holding onto an object you want to get rid of.

Accessing and Setting Class and Instance Variables

At this point, you could create your own object with class and instance variables defined in it—but how do you work with those variables? Easy! Class and instance variables behave the same ways the local variables you learned about yesterday behave. You just refer to them slightly differently than you refer to regular variables in your code.

Getting Values

To get to the value of an instance variable, you use dot notation. With dot notation, an instance or class variable name has two parts: the object on the left side of the dot and the variable on the right side of the dot.

 Dot notation is a way to refer to an object's instance variables and methods using a dot (.) operator.

For example, if you have an object assigned to the variable myCustomer and that object has a variable called orderTotal, you refer to that variable's value like this:

```
myCustomer.orderTotal;
```

This form of accessing variables is an expression (that is, it returns a value), and both sides of the dot also are expressions. This means that you can nest instance variable access. If the orderTotal instance variable itself holds an object and that object has its own instance variable called layaway, you could refer to it like this:

```
myCustomer.orderTotal.layaway;
```

Dot expressions are evaluated from left to right, so you start with myCustomer's variable orderTotal, which points to another object with the variable layaway. You end up with the value of that layaway variable.

Changing Values

Assigning a value to that variable is equally easy—just tack an assignment operator on the right side of the expression:

```
myCustomer.orderTotal.layaway = true;
```

This example sets the value of the layaway variable to true.

Listing 4.2 is an example of a program that tests and modifies the instance variables in a Point object. Point is part of the java.awt package and refers to a coordinate point with x and y values.

TYPE **LISTING 4.2.** THE FULL TEXT OF SETPOINTS.JAVA.

```
 1: import java.awt.Point;
 2:
 3: class SetPoints {
 4:
 5: public static void main(String arguments[]) {
 6:     Point location = new Point(4, 13);
 7:
 8:     System.out.println("Starting location:");
 9:     System.out.println("X equals " + location.x);
10:     System.out.println("Y equals " + location.y);
11:
12:     System.out.println("\nMoving to (7, 6)");
13:     location.x = 7;
14:     location.y = 6;
15:
16:     System.out.println("\nEnding location:");
17:     System.out.println("X equals " + location.x);
18:     System.out.println("Y equals " + location.y);
19:     }
20: }
```

When you run this application, the output should be the following:

OUTPUT
```
Starting location:
X equals 4
Y equals 13

Moving to (7, 6)
```

```
Ending location:
X equals 7
Y equals 6
```

In this example, you first create an instance of Point where x equals 4 and y equals 13 (line 6). Lines 9 and 10 display these individual values using dot notation. Lines 13 and 14 change the values of x to 7 and y to 6, respectively. Finally, lines 17 and 18 display the values of x and y again to show how they have changed.

Class Variables

Class variables, as you learned, are variables that are defined and stored in the class itself. Their values apply to the class and all of its instances.

With instance variables, each new instance of the class gets a new copy of the instance variables that the class defines. Each instance then can change the values of those instance variables without affecting any other instances. With class variables, only one copy of that variable exists. Changing the value of that variable changes it for all instances of that class.

You define class variables by including the static keyword before the variable itself. For example, take the following partial class definition:

```
class FamilyMember {
    static String surname = "Igwebuike";
    String name;
    int age;
}
```

Instances of the class FamilyMember each have their own values for name and age—but the class variable surname has only one value for all family members: "Igwebuike". Change the value of surname and all instances of FamilyMember are affected.

Note

> Calling these static variables refers to one of the meanings for the word *static*: fixed in one place. If a class has a static variable, every object of that class has the same value for that variable.

To access class variables, you use the same dot notation used with instance variables. To retrieve or change the value of the class variable, you can use either the instance or the name of the class on the left side of the dot. Both lines of output in this example display the same value:

```
FamilyMember dad = new FamilyMember();
System.out.println("Family's surname is: " + dad.surname);
System.out.println("Family's surname is: " + FamilyMember.surname);
```

Because you can use an instance to change the value of a class variable, it's easy to become confused about class variables and where their values are coming from—remember that the value of a class variable affects all of its instances. For this reason, it's a good idea to use the name of the class when you refer to a class variable. It makes your code easier to read and makes strange results easier to debug.

Calling Methods

Calling a method in an object is similar to referring to its instance variables: Dot notation is used. The object whose method you're calling is on the left side of the dot, and the name of the method and its arguments are on the right side of the dot:

```
myCustomer.addToOrder(itemNumber, price, quantity);
```

Note that all methods must have parentheses after them, even if the method takes no arguments:

```
myCustomer.cancelAllOrders();
```

If the method called returns an object that itself has methods, you can nest methods as you would variables. This next example calls the talkToManager() method, which is defined in the object returned by the cancelAllOrders() method, which was defined in myCustomer:

```
myCustomer.cancelAllOrders().talkToManager();
```

You can combine nested method calls and instance variable references as well. In the next example, the putOnLayaway() method is defined in the object stored by the orderTotal instance variable, which itself is part of the myCustomer object:

```
myCustomer.orderTotal.putOnLayaway(itemNumber, price, quantity);
```

System.out.println(), the method you've been using in all program examples to display information, is an example of nesting variables and methods. The System class, part of the java.lang package, describes behavior specific to the system Java is running on. System.out is a class variable that contains an instance of the class PrintStream. This PrintStream object represents the standard output of the system, which is normally the screen but can be redirected to a monitor or diskfile. PrintStream objects have a println() method that sends a string to that output stream.

Listing 4.3 shows an example of calling some methods defined in the String class. Strings include methods for string tests and modification, similar to what you would expect in a string library in other languages.

TYPE | **LISTING 4.3.** THE FULL TEXT OF CHECKSTRING.JAVA.

```
 1: class CheckString {
 2:
 3:     public static void main(String arguments[]) {
 4:         String str = "In my next life, I will believe in
               reincarnation";
 5:         System.out.println("The string is: " + str);
 6:         System.out.println("Length of this string: "
 7:             + str.length());
 8:         System.out.println("The character at position 7: "
 9:             + str.charAt(7));
10:         System.out.println("The substring from 24 to 31: "
11:             + str.substring(24, 31));
12:         System.out.println("The index of the character x: "
13:             + str.indexOf('x'));
14:         System.out.println("The index of the beginning of the "
15:             + "substring \"will\": " + str.indexOf("will"));
16:         System.out.println("The string in upper case: "
17:             + str.toUpperCase());
18:     }
19: }
```

The following is displayed on your system's standard output device when you run the program:

OUTPUT
```
The string is: In my next life, I will believe in reincarnation
Length of this string: 48
The character at position 7: e
The substring from 24 to 31: believe
The index of the character x: 8
The index of the beginning of the substring "will": 19
The string in upper case: IN MY NEXT LIFE, I WILL BELIEVE IN
REINCARNATION
```

In line 4 you create a new instance of String by using a string literal. (This way is easier than using new and putting the characters in individually.) The remainder of the program simply calls different string methods to do different operations on that string:

- Line 5 prints the value of the string you created in line 4: "In my next life, I will believe in reincarnation".

- Line 7 calls the length() method in the new String object. This string has 48 characters.

- Line 9 calls the charAt() method, which returns the character at the given position in the string. Note that string positions start at position 0 rather than 1, so the character at position 7 is e.

- Line 11 calls the `substring()` method, which takes two integers indicating a range and returns the substring with those starting and ending points. The `substring()` method also can be called with only one argument, which returns the substring from that position to the end of the string.

- Line 13 calls the `indexOf()` method, which returns the position of the first instance of the given character (here, `'x'`). Character literals are surrounded by single quotation marks—if double quotation marks surrounded the x in line 13, the literal would be considered a `String`.

- Line 15 shows a different use of the `indexOf()` method, which takes a string argument and returns the index of the beginning of that string.

- Line 17 uses the `toUpperCase()` method to return a copy of the string in all upper-case.

Class Methods

Class methods, like class variables, apply to the class as a whole and not to its instances. Class methods commonly are used for general utility methods that might not operate directly on an instance of that class but fit with that class conceptually. For example, the `String` class contains a class method called `valueOf()` that can take one of many different types of arguments (integers, Booleans, other objects, and so on). The `valueOf()` method then returns a new instance of `String` containing the string value of the argument. This method doesn't operate directly on an existing instance of `String`, but getting a string from another object or data type is definitely a `String`-like operation, and it makes sense to define it in the `String` class.

Class methods also can be useful for gathering general methods together in one place (the class). For example, the `Math` class, defined in the `java.lang` package, contains a large set of mathematical operations as class methods—there are no instances of the class `Math`, but you still can use its methods with numeric or Boolean arguments. For example, the class method `Math.max()` takes two arguments and returns the larger of the two. You don't need to create a new instance of `Math`—it can be called anywhere you need it, as in the following:

`int maximumPrice = Math.max(firstPrice, secondPrice);` dot notation is used to call a class method. As with class variables, you can use either an instance of the class or the class itself on the left side of the dot. However, for the same reasons noted in the discussion on class variables, using the name of the class makes your code easier to read. The last two lines in this example produce the same result—the string 5:

```
String s, s2;
s = "item";
s2 = s.valueOf(5);
s2 = String.valueOf(5);
```

References to Objects

As you work with objects, an important thing to understand is the use of references.

NEW TERM   A *reference* is a type of pointer used to indicate an object's value.

You aren't actually using objects when you assign an object to a variable or pass an object to a method as an argument. You aren't even using copies of the objects. Instead, you're using references to those objects.

To better illustrate the difference, Listing 4.4 shows how references work.

TYPE   **LISTING 4.4.** THE FULL TEXT OF REFERENCESTEST.JAVA.

```
 1: import java.awt.Point;
 2:
 3: class ReferencesTest {
 4:     public static void main (String arguments[]) {
 5:         Point pt1, pt2;
 6:         pt1 = new Point(100, 100);
 7:         pt2 = pt1;
 8:
 9:         pt1.x = 200;
10:         pt1.y = 200;
11:         System.out.println("Point1: " + pt1.x + ", " + pt1.y);
12:         System.out.println("Point2: " + pt2.x + ", " + pt2.y);
13:     }
14: }
```

4

The following is this program's output:

OUTPUT   Point1: 200, 200
Point2: 200, 200

The following takes place in the first part of this program:

- Line 5   Two Point variables are created.
- Line 6   A new Point object is assigned to pt1.
- Line 7   The value of pt1 is assigned to pt2.

Lines 9–12 are the tricky part. The x and y variables of pt1 are both set to 200, and then all variables of pt1 and pt2 are displayed onscreen.

You might expect pt1 and pt2 to have different values. However, the output shows this is not the case. As you can see, the x and y variables of pt2 also were changed, even though nothing in the program explicitly changes them.

This happens because line 7 creates a reference from pt2 to pt1, instead of creating pt2 as a new object copied from pt1.

pt2 is a reference to the same object as pt1; this is shown in Figure 4.1. Either variable can be used to refer to the object or to change its variables.

FIGURE 4.1.

References to objects.

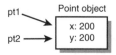

If you wanted pt1 and pt2 to refer to separate objects, separate new Point() statements could be used on lines 6 and 7 to create separate objects, as shown in the following:

```
pt1 = new Point(100, 100);
pt2 = new Point(100, 100);
```

The use of references in Java becomes particularly important when arguments are passed to methods. You learn more about this later today.

 Note

There are no explicit pointers or pointer arithmetic in Java as there are in C and C++. However, by using references and Java arrays, most pointer capabilities are duplicated without as many of their drawbacks.

Casting and Converting Objects and Primitive Types

One thing you discover quickly about Java is how finicky it is about the information it will handle. Like Morris, the perpetually dissatisfied cat on the 9 Lives cat food commercials, Java expects things to be a certain way and won't put up with alternatives.

When you are sending arguments to methods or using variables in expressions, you must use variables of the right data types. If a method requires an int, the Java compiler responds with an error if you try to send a float value to the method. Likewise, if you're setting up one variable with the value of another, they must be of the same type.

Note

There is one area where Java's compiler is decidedly un-Morrislike: Strings. String handling in println() methods, assignment statements, and method arguments is simplified with the use of the concatenation operator (+). If any variable in a group of concatenated variables is a string, Java treats the whole thing as a String. This makes the following possible:

```
float gpa = 2.25F;
System.out.println("Honest, dad, my GPA is a " + (gpa+1.5));
```

Sometimes you'll have a value in your Java program that isn't the right type for what you need. It might be the wrong class, or the wrong data type—such as a `float` when you need an `int`.

You use casting to convert a value from one type to another.

NEW TERM *Casting* is the process of producing a new value that has a different type than its source. The meaning is similar to acting, where a character on a TV show can be recast with another actor after a salary dispute or an unfortunate public lewdness arrest.

You don't change the value of a variable when it's cast. Instead, you create a new variable of the desired type.

Although the concept of casting is reasonably simple, the usage is complicated by the fact that Java has both primitive types (such as `int`, `float`, and `boolean`), and object types (`String`, `Point`, `ZipFile`, and the like). There are three forms of casts and conversions to talk about in this section:

- Casting between primitive types, such as `int` to `float` or `float` to `double`
- Casting from an instance of a class to an instance of another class
- Converting primitive types to objects and then extracting primitive values from those objects

When discussing casting, it can be easier to think in terms of sources and destinations. The source is the variable being cast into another type. The destination is the result.

Casting Primitive Types

Casting between primitive types allows you to convert the value of one type to another primitive type. It most commonly occurs with the numeric types, and there's one primitive type that can never be used in a cast. Boolean values must be either `true` or `false` and cannot be used in a casting operation.

In many casts between primitive types, the destination can hold larger values than the source, so the value is converted easily. An example would be casting a `byte` into an `int`. Because a `byte` holds values from –128 to 127 and an `int` holds from –2.1 million to 2.1 million, there's more than enough room to cast a `byte` to an `int`.

You can often automatically use a `byte` or a `char` as an `int`; you can use an `int` as a `long`, an `int` as a `float`, or anything as a `double`. In most cases, because the larger type provides more precision than the smaller, no loss of information occurs as a result. The exception is casting integers to floating-point values—casting an `int` or a `long` to a `float`, or a `long` to a `double` can cause some loss of precision.

Note A character can be used as an int because each character has a corresponding numeric code that represents its position in the character set. If the variable i has the value 65, the cast (char)i produces the character value 'A'. The numeric code associated with a capital A is 65, according to the ASCII character set, and this was adopted by Java as part of its character support.

You must use an explicit cast to convert a large value to smaller type because converting that value might result in a loss of precision. Explicit casts take the following form:

```
(typename)value
```

In the preceding, *typename* is the name of the data type you're converting to, such as short, int, and float. value is an expression that results in the value of the source type. For example, the value of x is divided by the value of y and the result is cast to an int in the following expression:

```
(int)(x / y);
```

Note that because the precedence of casting is higher than that of arithmetic, you have to use parentheses here—otherwise, the value of x would be cast to an int first and then divided by y, which could easily produce a different result.

Casting Objects

Instances of classes also can be cast to instances of other classes, with one restriction: The source and destination classes must be related by inheritance. One class must be a subclass of the other.

Analogous to converting a primitive value to a larger type, some objects might not need to be cast explicitly. In particular, because subclasses contain all the same information as their superclass, you can use an instance of a subclass anywhere a superclass is expected.

For example, consider a method that takes two arguments: one of type Object and another of type Window. You can pass an instance of any class for the Object argument because all Java classes are subclasses of Object. For the Window argument, you can pass in its subclasses such as Dialog, FileDialog, and Frame.

This is true anywhere in a program—not just inside method calls. If you had a variable defined as class Window, you could assign objects of that class or any of its subclasses to that variable without casting.

This is true in the reverse, and you can use a superclass when a subclass is expected. There is a catch, however: Because subclasses contain more behavior than their superclasses, there's a loss in precision involved. Those superclass objects might not have all of the behavior needed to act in place of a subclass object. For example, if you have an operation that calls methods in objects of the class Integer, using an object of class Number won't include many methods specified in Integer. Errors occur if you try to call methods that the destination object doesn't have.

To use superclass objects where subclass objects are expected, you must cast it explicitly. You won't lose any information in the cast, but you gain all the methods and variables the subclass defines. To cast an object to another class, you use the same operation that you used for base types:

```
(classname)object
```

In this case, *classname* is the name of the destination class and *object* is a reference to the source object. Note that casting creates a reference to the old object of the type classname; the old object still continues to exist as it did before.

The following example casts an instance of the class VicePresident to an instance of the class Employee; VicePresident is a subclass of Employee with more information to define that the VicePresident has executive washroom privileges:

```
Employee emp = new Employee();
VicePresident veep = new VicePresident();
emp = veep; // no cast needed for upward use
veep = (VicePresident)emp; // must cast explicitly
```

Casting one object is necessary whenever you use the new 2D graphics drawing operations introduced in Java 1.2. You must cast a Graphics object to a Graphics2D object before you can draw onscreen. The following example uses a Graphics object called screen to create a new Graphics2D object called screen2D:

```
Graphics2D screen2D = (Graphics2D)screen;
```

Graphics2D is a subclass of Graphics, and both are in the java.awt package. You explore the subject fully during Day 9, "Making Programs Look Good with Graphics, Fonts, and Color."

In addition to casting objects to classes, you also can cast objects to interfaces—but only if that object's class or one of its superclasses actually implements the interface. Casting an object to an interface means that you can call one of that interface's methods even if that object's class does not actually implement that interface.

Converting Primitive Types to Objects and Vice Versa

One thing you can't do under any circumstance is cast from an object to a primitive data type, or vice versa. Primitive types and objects are very different things in Java and you can't automatically cast between the two or use them interchangeably.

As an alternative, the `java.lang` package includes classes that correspond to each primitive data type: `Integer`, `Float`, `boolean`, and so on. Note that the class names have an initial capital letter and the primitive types have lowercase names. Java treats the data types and their class versions very differently, and a program won't compile successfully if you use one when the other is expected.

Using class methods defined in these classes, you can create an object for each of the primitive types using a `new` statement. The following statement creates an instance of the `Integer` class with the value `4403`:

```
Integer dataCount = new Integer(4403);
```

Once you have an object created in this manner, you can use it as you would any object. When you want to use that value again as a primitive value, there are methods for that as well. For example, if you wanted to get an `int` value from a `dataCount` object, the following statement would be used:

```
int newCount = dataCount.intValue(); // returns 4403
```

A common translation you need in programs is converting a `String` to a numeric type, such as an integer. When you need an `int` as the result, this can be done by using the `parseInt()` method of the `Integer` class. The `String` to convert is the only argument sent to the method, as in the following example:

```
String pennsylvania = "65000";
int penn = Integer.parseInt(pennsylvania);
```

The Java API documentation includes details on these classes. You can find these HTML pages in the Documentation section of Sun's Java Web site:

```
http://java.sun.com
```

 Note

There are special type classes for `boolean`, `Byte`, `Character`, `Double`, `Float`, `Integer`, `Long`, `Short`, and `Void`.

Comparing Object Values and Classes

In addition to casting, there are operations you can perform on objects:

- Comparing objects
- Finding out the class of any given object
- Testing to see whether an object is an instance of a given class

Comparing Objects

Yesterday you learned about operators for comparing values: equal, not equal, less than, and so on. Most of these operators work only on primitive types, not on objects. If you try to use other values as operands, the Java compiler produces errors.

The exception to this rule are the operators for equality: == (equal) and != (not equal). When used with objects, these operators don't do what you might first expect. Instead of checking whether one object has the same value as the other object, they determine whether the objects are the same object.

In order to compare instances of a class and have meaningful results, you must implement special methods in your class and call those methods.

A good example of this is the String class. It is possible to have two different String objects that contain the same values. If you used the == operator to compare these objects, however, they would be considered inequal. Although their contents match, they are not the same object.

In order to see whether two String objects have matching values, a method of the class called equals() is used. The method tests each character in the string and returns true if the two strings have the same values. Listing 4.5 illustrates this.

TYPE   **LISTING 4.5.** THE FULL TEXT OF EQUALSTEST.JAVA.

```
 1: class EqualsTest {
 2:     public static void main(String args[]) {
 3:         String str1, str2;
 4:         str1 = "Free the bound periodicals.";
 5:         str2 = str1;
 6:
 7:         System.out.println("String1: " + str1);
 8:         System.out.println("String2: " + str2);
 9:         System.out.println("Same object? " + (str1 == str2));
10:
11:         str2 = new String(str1);
12:
13:         System.out.println("String1: " + str1);
14:         System.out.println("String2: " + str2);
15:         System.out.println("Same object? " + (str1 == str2));
16:         System.out.println("Same value? " + str1.equals(str2));
17:     }
18: }
```

4

This program's output is as follows:

```
String1: Free the bound periodicals.
String2: Free the bound periodicals.
Same object? true
String1: Free the bound periodicals.
String2: Free the bound periodicals.
Same object? false
Same value? true
```

The first part of this program (lines 3–5) declares two variables (str1 and str2), assigns the literal Free the bound periodicals. to str1, and then assigns that value to str2. As you learned earlier, str1 and str2 now point to the same object, and the equality test at line 9 proves that.

In the second part you create a new String object with the same value as str1 and assign str2 to that new String object. Now you have two different string objects in str1 and str2, both with the same value. Testing them to see whether they're the same object by using the == operator (line 15) returns the expected answer (false—they are not the same object in memory). Testing them using the equals() method in line 16 also returns the expected answer (true—they have the same values).

Note

> Why can't you just use another literal when you change str2, rather than using new? String literals are optimized in Java—if you create a string using a literal and then use another literal with the same characters, Java knows enough to give you the first String object back. Both strings are the same objects—you have to go out of your way to create two separate objects.

Determining the Class of an Object

Want to find out what an object's class is? Here's the way to do it for an object assigned to the variable obj:

```
String name = obj.getClass().getName();
```

What does this do? The getClass() method is defined in the Object class, and as such is available for all objects. The result of that method is a Class object (where Class is itself a class), which has a method called getName(). getName() returns a string representing the name of the class.

Another test that might be useful is the instanceof operator. instanceof has two operands: an object on the left and a class name on the right. The expression returns true or false based on whether the object is an instance of the named class or any of that class's subclasses:

```
"swordfish" instanceof String // true
Point pt = new Point(10, 10);
pt instanceof String // false
```

The `instanceof` operator can also be used for interfaces; if an object implements an interface, the `instanceof` operator with that interface name on the right side returns `true`.

Inspecting Classes and Methods with Reflection

One of the improvements made to the Java language after Java 1.0 was the introduction of reflection, which also is called *introspection*. Under any name, *reflection* enables one Java class—such as a program you write—to learn details about any other class.

Through reflection, a Java program can load a class it knows nothing about, find that class' variables, methods, and constructors, and work with them.

This might make more sense if you see an example of it right off the bat. Listing 4.6 is a short Java application named `SeeMethods`.

TYPE   **LISTING 4.6.** THE FULL TEXT OF SEEMETHODS.JAVA.

```
 1: import java.lang.reflect.*;
 2: import java.util.Random;
 3:
 4: class SeeMethods {
 5:     public static void main(String[] arguments)  {
 6:         Random rd = new Random();
 7:         Class className = rd.getClass();
 8:         Method[] methods = className.getMethods();
 9:         for (int i = 0; i < methods.length; i++) {
10:             System.out.println("Method: " + methods[i]);
11:         }
12:     }
13: }
```

This program uses the `java.lang.reflect.*` group of classes, which provide information about the attributes, methods, and constructor methods of any class.

The `SeeMethods` application creates a `Random` object in line 6 and then uses reflection to display all of the public methods that are a part of the class. Listing 4.7 shows the application's output.

LISTING 4.7. THE OUTPUT OF THE SEEMETHODS APPLICATION.

```
 1: Method: public final native java.lang.Class
java.lang.Object.getClass()
 2: Method: public native int java.lang.Object.hashCode()
 3: Method: public boolean java.lang.Object.equals(java.lang.Object)
 4: Method: public java.lang.String java.lang.Object.toString()
 5: Method: public final native void java.lang.Object.notify()
 6: Method: public final native void java.lang.Object.notifyAll()
 7: Method: public final native void java.lang.Object.wait(long) throws
java.lang.InterruptedException
 8: Method: public final void java.lang.Object.wait(long,int) throws
java.lang.InterruptedException
 9: Method: public final void java.lang.Object.wait() throws
java.lang.InterruptedException
10: Method: public synchronized void java.util.Random.setSeed(long)
11: Method: public void java.util.Random.nextBytes(byte[])
12: Method: public int java.util.Random.nextInt()
13: Method: public long java.util.Random.nextLong()
14: Method: public float java.util.Random.nextFloat()
15: Method: public double java.util.Random.nextDouble()
16: Method: public synchronized double java.util.Random.nextGaussian()
```

By using reflection, the SeeMethods application can learn every method of the Random class and all methods that it inherited from superclasses Random. Each line of the listing shows the following information about a method:

- Whether it's public
- What type of object or variable the method returns
- Whether the method is from the current class or one of its superclasses
- The name of the method
- The type of objects and variables used as arguments when calling the method

The SeeMethods application could be done with any class of objects. Change line 6 of SeeMethods.java to create a different object and take a look at its innards.

Reflection is most commonly used by tools such as class browsers and debuggers as a way to learn more about the class of objects being browsed or debugged. It also is needed with JavaBeans, where the capability for one object to query another object about what it can do (and then ask it to do something) is useful when building larger applications. You learn more about JavaBeans during Day 27, "JavaBeans."

The `java.lang.reflect` package includes the following classes:

- `Field`   Manages and finds information about class and instance variables
- `Method`   Manages class and instance methods
- `Constructor`   Manages the special methods for creating new instances of classes
- `Array`   Manages arrays
- `Modifier`   Decodes modifier information about classes, variables, and methods (which are described on Day 15, "Class Roles: Packages, Interfaces, and Other Features").

In addition, there will be a number of new methods available in a class of objects called `Class` that helps tie together the various reflection classes.

Reflection is an advanced feature that you might not be readily using in your programs. It becomes most useful when you're working on object serialization, JavaBeans, and other, more sophisticated Java programming.

Summary

Now that you have drank deeply from the implementation of object-oriented programming in Java, you're in a better position to decide how useful it can be in your own programming.

If you are a "glass is half empty" person, object-oriented programming is a level of abstraction that gets in the way of what you're trying to use a programming language for. You learn more about why OOP is thoroughly engrained in Java in the coming chapters.

If you are a "glass is half full" person, object-oriented programming is worth using because of the benefits it offers: improved reliability, reusability, and maintenance.

Today you learned how to deal with objects: creating them, reading their values and changing them, and calling their methods. You also learned how to convert objects from one class to another, or from a data type to a class.

Finally, you took a first look at reflection, a way to make an object reveal details about itself.

At this point, you possess the skills to handle most simple tasks in the Java language. All that remains are arrays, conditionals, and loops (which are covered tomorrow), and how to define and use classes (on Day 6, "Creating Classes").

Q&A

Q **I'm confused about the differences between objects and the primitive data types, such as `int` and `boolean`.**

A The primitive types in the language (`byte`, `short`, `int`, `long`, `float`, `double`, `boolean`, and `char`) represent the smallest things in the language. They are not objects, although in many ways they can be handled like objects: They can be assigned to variables and passed in and out of methods. Most of the operations that work exclusively on objects, however, will not work with primitive types.

Objects are instances of classes, and as such are usually much more complex data types than simple numbers and characters, often containing numbers and characters as instance or class variables.

Q **No pointers in Java? If you don't have pointers, how am I supposed to do something like linked lists, where I have a pointer from one node to another so I can traverse them?**

A It's untrue to say Java has no pointers at all—it has no explicit pointers. Object references are, effectively, pointers. To create something like a linked list, you would create a class called `Node`, which would have an instance variable also of type `Node`. To link together node objects, assign a node object to the instance variable of the object immediately before it in the list. Because object references are pointers, linked lists set up this way behave as you would expect them to.

Q **In your book, you use so many methods, such as `lenth()`, `charAt()`, `indexOf()` and so on. How do we find these useful methods if we are beginners and don't know what methods exist?**

A The book covers a wide cross-section of the most useful methods in the Java class libraries, but you sometimes will need to expand beyond these when developing your own programs. Sun offers full Java 2 documentation on its Java site for all standard Java classes, the JDK, and many other Java-related subjects. Visit the Web site `http://java.sun.com` to browse through the documentation for Java 2.

DAY 5

Lists, Logic, and Loops

If you wrote a Java program with what you know so far, it would likely be a little dull. If you wrote a Java program with what you know so far, it would likely be a little dull. That last sentence isn't repeated twice because of an editorial mistake. It is a demonstration of how easy computers make it to repeat the same thing over and over. You learn today how to make part of a Java program repeat itself by using loops.

Additionally, you learn how to make a program decide whether to do something based on logic. (Perhaps a computer would decide it isn't logical to repeat the same sentence twice in a row in a book.)

You also learn how to organize groups of the same class or data type into lists called arrays.

First up on today's list is arrays. First up on today's list is arrays.

Arrays

At this point you only have dealt with a few variables in each Java program. It's manageable to use individual variables to store information in some cases.

However, what if you had 20 items of related information to keep track of? You could create 20 different variables and set up their initial values, but that becomes more unwieldy the more information you're working with. What if there were 100 items, or even 1,000?

Arrays are a way to store a list of items that have the same primitive data type or class. Each item on the list goes into its own slot, which is numbered, so you can access the information easily.

Arrays can contain any type of information that is stored in a variable, but once the array is created you only can use it for that information type. For example, you can have an array of integers, an array of `String` objects, or an array of arrays, but you can't have an array that contains both strings and integers.

Java implements arrays differently than some other languages do—as objects that can be treated just like other objects.

Do the following to create an array in Java:

1. Declare a variable to hold the array.
2. Create a new array object and assign it to the array variable.
3. Store information in that array.

Declaring Array Variables

The first step in array creation is to declare a variable that will hold the array. Array variables indicate the object or data type the array will hold and the name of the array. To differentiate from regular variable declarations, a pair of empty brackets ([ ]) is added to the object or data type, or to the variable name.

The following statements are examples of array variable declarations:

```
String difficultWords[];
```

```
Point hits[];
```

```
int donations[];
```

Because you can put the brackets after the information type instead of the variable name, the following statements also work:

```
String[] difficultWords;

Point[] hits;

int[] guesses;
```

You see both styles used in programs, and because there isn't a consensus on which style is more readable, the choice is largely a matter of personal preference.

Creating Array Objects

After you declare the array variable, the next step is to create an array object and assign it to that variable. The ways to do this step are as follows:

- Use the `new` operator.
- Initialize the contents of the array directly.

Because arrays are objects in Java, you can use the `new` operator to create a new instance of an array, as in the following statement:

```
String[] playerNames = new String[10];
```

This statement creates a new array of strings with 10 slots that can contain `String` objects. When you create an array object using `new`, you must indicate how many slots the array will hold. This statements does not put actual `String` objects in the slots—you must do that later.

Array objects can contain primitive types such as integers or Booleans, just as they can contain objects:

```
int[] temps = new int[99];
```

When you create an array object using `new`, all of its slots automatically are initialized (0 for numeric arrays, `false` for Boolean, `'\0'` for character arrays, and `null` for objects).

You also can create and initialize an array at the same time. Instead of using `new` to create the new array object, enclose the elements of the array inside braces, separated by commas:

```
String[] chiles = { "jalapeno", "anaheim", "serrano",
"habanero", "thai" };
```

Note

> The Java keyword `null` refers to a `null` object (and can be used for any object reference). It is not equivalent to zero or the `'\0'` character as the NULL constant is in C.

5

Each of the elements inside the braces must be the same type as the variable that holds the array. When you create an array with initial values in this manner, the array is the same size as the number of elements you have included within the braces. The preceding example creates an array of `String` objects named `chiles` that contains five elements.

Accessing Array Elements

Once you have an array with initial values, you can retrieve, change, and test the values in each slot of that array. The value in a slot is accessed with the array name followed by a subscript enclosed within square brackets. This name and subscript can be put into expressions, as in the following:

```
contestantScore[40] = 470;
```

The `contestantScore` part of this expression is a variable holding an array object, although it also can be an expression that results in an array. The subscript expression specifies the slot to access within the array. Array subscripts start with `0`, as they do in C and C++, so an array with 10 elements has array slots that are accessed by using subscripts `0` through `9`.

All array subscripts are checked to make sure that they are inside the array's boundaries, as specified when the array was created. In Java, it is impossible to access or assign a value to an array slot outside the array's boundaries, which avoids problems that result from overrunning the bounds of an array in C-like languages. Note the following two statements:

```
String[] beatleSpeak = new String[10];

beatleSpeak[10] = "I am the eggman.";
```

A program with the preceding two lines of code produces a compilation error when `beatleSpeak[10]` is used. The error occurs because the `beatleSpeak` array does not have a slot 10—it has 10 slots that begin at `0` and end at `9`. The Java compiler will catch this error.

The Java interpreter produces an error if the array subscript is calculated when the program is running (for example, as part of a loop), and the subscript ends up outside the array's boundaries. Actually, to be technically correct, it throws an exception. You learn more about exceptions on Day 16, "Exceptional Circumstances: Error Handling."

How can you keep from accidentally overrunning the end of an array in your programs? Test for the length of the array in your programs using the `length` instance variable—it's available for all array objects, regardless of type:

```
int len = beatleSpeak.length
```

To reiterate: The length of the array is 10, but its subscript can only go up to 9. Arrays start numbering from 0. Whenever you work with arrays, keep this in mind and subtract 1 from the length of the array to get its largest element.

Changing Array Elements

As you saw in the previous examples, you can assign a value to an array's specific slot by putting an assignment statement after the array name and subscript, as in the following:

```
myGrades[4] = 85;

sentence[0] = "The";

sentence[10] = sentence[0];
```

An important thing to note is that an array of objects in Java is an array of references to those objects. When you assign a value to a slot in that kind of array, you are creating a reference to that object. When you move values around inside arrays—as in the last of the preceding examples—you are reassigning the reference rather than copying a value from one slot to another. Arrays of a primitive data type such as int or float do copy the values from one slot to another.

Arrays are reasonably simple to create and modify, but they provide an enormous amount of functionality for Java. You'll find yourself running into arrays a lot the more you use the language.

To finish the discussion on arrays, Listing 5.1 shows a simple program that creates, initializes, modifies, and examines parts of an array.

5

TYPE **LISTING 5.1.** THE FULL TEXT OF ARRAYTEST.JAVA.

```
 1: class ArrayTest {
 2:
 3:     String[] firstNames = { "Dennis", "Grace", "Bjarne", "James" };
 4:     String[] lastNames = new String[firstNames.length];
 5:
 6:     void printNames() {
 7:         int i = 0;
 8:         System.out.println(firstNames[i]
 9:             + " " + lastNames[i]);
10:         i++;
11:         System.out.println(firstNames[i]
12:             + " " + lastNames[i]);
13:         i++;
```

continues

LISTING 5.1. CONTINUED

```
14:            System.out.println(firstNames[i]
15:                + " " + lastNames[i]);
16:            i++;
17:            System.out.println(firstNames[i]
18:                + " " + lastNames[i]);
19:        }
20:
21:        public static void main (String arguments[]) {
22:            ArrayTest a = new ArrayTest();
23:            a.printNames();
24:            System.out.println("-----");
25:            a.lastNames[0] = "Ritchie";
26:            a.lastNames[1] = "Hopper";
27:            a.lastNames[2] = "Stroustrup";
28:            a.lastNames[3] = "Gosling";
29:            a.printNames();
30:        }
31: }
```

The output of the program is as follows:

OUTPUT
```
Dennis null
Grace null
Bjarne null
James null
-----
Dennis Ritchie
Grace Hopper
Bjarne Stroustrup
James Gosling
```

This longer example shows how to create and use arrays. The class that is created here, ArrayTest, has two instance variables that hold arrays of String objects. The first, which is called firstNames, is declared and initialized on line 3 to contain four strings. The second instance variable, lastNames, is declared and created in line 4, but no initial values are placed in the slots. Note also that the lastNames array has exactly the same number of slots as the firstNames array, because the firstNames.length variable is used as the initial array index. When used on an array object, the length instance variable returns the number of slots in the array.

The ArrayTest class also has two methods: printNames() and main(). printNames(), defined in lines 6–19, is a utility method that goes through the firstNames and lastNames arrays sequentially, displaying the values of each slot. Note that the array index defined here (i) is set initially to 0 because Java array slots all start numbering from 0.

Finally, the `main()` method performs the following:

- Line 22 creates an initial instance of `ArrayTest` so its instance variables and methods can be used.
- Line 23 calls `printNames()` to show what the object looks like initially. The result is the first four lines of the output; note that the `firstNames` array was initialized, but the values in `lastNames` are all `null`. If an array is not initialized when it is declared, the values of the initial slots will be empty—`null` for object arrays, `0` for numbers, and `false` for Booleans.
- Lines 25–28 set the values of each of the slots in the `lastNames` array to actual strings.
- Line 29 calls `printNames()` once again to show that the `lastNames` array is now full of values, and each first and last name prints as you would expect. The results are shown in the last four lines of the output.

Note

If you don't recognize the names in this example, you might think the authors are working references to their friends into the book. These are all principal developers of computer programming languages: Dennis Ritchie (C), Bjarne Stroustrup (C++), Grace Hopper (COBOL), and James Gosling (Java).

One last note to make about Listing 5.1 is that it's a terrible example of programming style. Usually when dealing with arrays, you can use loops to cycle through an array's elements, rather than dealing with each individually. This makes the code a lot shorter, and easier to read in many cases. When you learn about loops later today, you see a rewrite of the current example.

5

Multidimensional Arrays

If you have used arrays in other languages, you might be wondering if Java can handle multidimensional arrays—arrays with more than one subscript, enabling more than one dimension to be represented.

Dimensions are useful when representing something such as an x,y grid of array elements.

Java does not support multidimensional arrays, but you can achieve the same functionality by declaring an array of arrays. Those arrays can also contain arrays, and so on, for as many dimensions as needed.

The following statements show how to declare and access these arrays of arrays:

```
int[][] coords = new int[12][12];

coords[0][0] = 1;

coords[0][1] = 2;
```

Block Statements

Statements in Java are grouped into blocks. The beginning and ending of a block are noted with brace characters—an opening brace ({) for the beginning and a closing brace (}) for the ending.

You already have used blocks throughout the programs during the first five days. You've used them for both of the following:

- To contain the variables and methods in a class definition
- To define the statements that belong in a method

Blocks also are called *block statements*, because an entire block can be used anywhere a single statement could be used. Each statement inside the block is then executed from top-to-bottom.

Blocks can be put inside other blocks, as you do when putting a method inside of a class definition.

An important thing to note about a block is that it creates a scope for the local variables that are created inside the block.

NEW TERM *Scope* is a programming term for the part of a program in which a variable exists and can be used. If the program leaves the scope of that variable, it doesn't exist and errors occur if you try to access the variable.

The scope of a variable is the block in which it was created. When you can declare and use local variables inside a block, those variables cease to exist after the block is finished executing. For example, the following `testBlock()` method contains a block:

```
void testBlock() {
    int x = 10;
    { // start of block
      int y = 40;
    y = y + x;
    } // end of block
}
```

There are two variables defined in this method: x and y. The scope of the y variable is the block it's in, and it can only be used within that block. An error would result if you tried to use it in another part of the testBlock() method. The x variable was created inside the method but outside of the inner block, so it can be used anywhere in the method. You can modify the value of x anywhere within the method and this value will be retained.

Block statements usually are not used alone in a method definition, as they are in the preceding example. You use them throughout class and method definitions, as well as in the logic and looping structures you learn about next.

if Conditionals

One of the key aspects of programming is a program's capability to decide what it will do. This is handled through a special type of statement called a conditional.

NEW TERM A *conditional* is a programming statement that only is executed if a specific condition is met.

The most basic conditional is the if keyword. The if conditional uses a Boolean expression to decide whether a statement should be executed. If the expression returns a true value, the statement is handled.

Here's a simple example that displays the message "You call that a haircut?" only on one condition: If the value of the age variable is greater than 39:

```
if (age > 39)
    System.out.println("You call that a haircut?");
```

If you want something else to happen in the case the if expression returns a false value, an optional else keyword can be used. The following example uses both if and else:

```
if (blindDateIsAttractive == true)
    restaurant = "Benihana's";
else
    restaurant = "Burrito Hut";
```

The if conditional executes different statements based on the result of a single Boolean test.

Note

The difference between if conditionals in Java and those in C or C++ is that Java requires the test to return a Boolean value (true or false). In C, the test can return an integer.

5

Using `if`, you only can include a single statement as the code to execute after the test. (The `restaurant` variable is assigned in the preceding example.) However, a block can appear anywhere in Java that a single statement can. If you want to do more than just one thing as a result of an `if` statement, you can enclose those statements inside a block. Note the following snippet of code, which is an extension of the `Jabberwock` object you created on Day 2, "A Taste of Object-Oriented Programming":

```
if (attitude == "angry" ) {
    System.out.println("The jabberwock is angry.");
    System.out.println ("Have you made out a will?");
} else {
    System.out.println ("The jabberwock is in a good mood.");
    if (hungry)
        System.out.println("It still is hungry, though.");
    else System.out.println("It wanders off.");
}
```

This example uses the test (`attitude == "angry"`) to determine whether to display that the jabberwock is angry or happy. If the jabberwock is happy, the test (`hungry`) is used to see whether the jabberwock also is hungry—assuming that a hungry jabberwock is a thing to avoid, even if it's a happy jabberwock. The conditional `if (hungry)` is another way of saying `if (hungry == true)`. For Boolean tests of this type, leaving off the last part of the expression is a common programming shortcut.

Listing 5.2 shows another simple example—this one in full application form. The `EvenSteven` class contains one utility method called `evenCheck()`, which tests a value to see if it's even. If it is, it displays `Steven!` onscreen.

TYPE   **LISTING 5.2.** THE FULL TEXT OF EVENSTEVEN.JAVA.

```
 1: class EvenSteven {
 2:
 3:     void evenCheck(int val) {
 4:         System.out.println("Value is "
 5:             + val + ". ");
 6:         if (val % 2 == 0)
 7:         System.out.println("Steven!");
 8:     }
 9:
10:     public static void main (String arguments[]) {
11:         EvenSteven e = new EvenSteven();
12:
13:         e.evenCheck(1);
14:         e.evenCheck(2);
15:         e.evenCheck(54);
16:         e.evenCheck(77);
```

```
17:          e.evenCheck(1346);
18:     }
19: }
```

The output of the program is as follows:

OUTPUT
```
Value is 1.
Value is 2.
Steven!
Value is 54.
Steven!
Value is 77.
Value is 1346.
Steven!
```

The heart of the EvenSteven class is the evenCheck() method (lines 3–8), where values are tested and an appropriate message is printed. Unlike the methods you've defined in previous examples, note that the definition of evenCheck() includes a single integer argument (see line 3). The evenCheck() method starts by printing out the value that was passed to it. That argument is then tested, using an if conditional, to see if it's an even number.

The modulus test from Day 3, "The ABCs of Java," returns the remainder of the division of its operands. If the remainder of a number divided by 2 is 0, it's an even number.

If the number is even, Steven! is displayed. (You learn more about defining methods with arguments tomorrow.)

The main() method in this application creates a new instance of EvenSteven and tests it, calling the evenCheck() method repeatedly with different values. In the output, only the values that are even get a Steven! message.

The Conditional Operator

An alternative to using the if and else keywords in a conditional statement is to use the conditional operator, sometimes called the *ternary operator*. The *conditional operator* is called a ternary operator because it has three terms.

The conditional operator is an expression, meaning that it returns a value—unlike the more general if, which only can result in a statement or block being executed. The conditional operator is most useful for short or simple conditionals and looks like the following line:

test ? trueresult : falseresult;

5

The *test* is an expression that returns `true` or `false`, just like the test in the `if` statement. If the test is `true`, the conditional operator returns the value of *trueresult*. If the test is `false`, the conditional operator returns the value of *falseresult*. For example, the following conditional tests the values of `myScore` and `yourScore`, returns the larger of the two as a value, and assigns that value to the variable `ourBestScore`:

```
int ourBestScore = myScore > yourScore ? myScore : yourScore;
```

This use of the conditional operator is equivalent to the following `if...else` code:

```
int ourBestScore;
if (myScore > yourScore)
    ourBestScore = myScore;
else
    ourBestScore = yourScore;
```

The conditional operator has a very low precedence—it usually is evaluated only after all its subexpressions are evaluated. The only operators lower in precedence are the assignment operators. For a refresher on operator precedence, see the precedence chart from Day 3.

`switch` Conditionals

A common programming practice in any language is to test a variable against some value, and to test it again against a different value if it doesn't match that value, and so on. This process can become unwieldy if you're using only `if` statements, depending on how many different values you have to test. For example, you might end up with a set of `if` statements something like the following:

```
if (oper == '+')
    addargs(arg1, arg2);
else if (oper == '-')
    subargs(arg1, arg2);
else if (oper == '*')
    multargs(arg1, arg2);
else if (oper == '/')
    divargs(arg1, arg2);
```

This use of `if` statements is called a nested `if` because each `else` statement contains another `if` until all possible tests have been made.

A shorthand mechanism for nested `if` statements that you can use in some programming languages is to group tests and actions together in a single statement. In Java, you can group actions together with the `switch` statement, which behaves as it does in C. The following is an example of `switch` usage:

```
switch (grade) {
    case 'A':
        System.out.println("Great job -- an A!");
        break;
    case 'B':
        System.out.println("Good job -- a B!");
        break;
    case 'C':
        System.out.println("Your grade was a C.");
        break;
    default: System.out.println("An F -- consider cheating!");
}
```

The `switch` statement is built on a test; in the preceding example, the test is on the value of the `grade` variable. The test variable, which can be any of the primitive types `byte`, `char`, `short`, or `int`, is compared in turn with each of the `case` values. If a match is found, the statement or statements after the test are executed. If no match is found, the `default` statement or statements are executed. The `default` is optional. If it is omitted and there is no match for any of the `case` statements, the `switch` statement completes without executing anything.

The Java implementation of `switch` is limited—tests and values can be only simple primitive types that are castable to `int`. You cannot use larger primitive types such as `long` or `float`, strings, or other objects within a `switch`, nor can you test for any relationship other than equality. These restrictions limit `switch` to the simplest cases. In contrast, nested `if` statements can work for any kind of test on any type.

The following is a revision of the nested `if` example shown previously. It has been rewritten as a `switch` statement:

5

```
switch (oper) {
    case '+':
        addargs(arg1, arg2);
        break;
    case '*':
        multargs(arg1, arg2);
        break;
    case '-':
        subargs(arg1, arg2);
        break;
    case '/':
        divargs(arg1, arg2);
        break;
}
```

There are two things to be aware of in this example: The first is that after each case, you can include a single result statement or more—you can include as many as you need.

Unlike with `if`, you don't need to surround multiple statements with braces for it to work. The second thing to note about this example are the `break` statements included with each `case` section. Without a `break` statement in a `case` section, once a match is made, the statements for that match and all the statements further down the `switch` are executed until a `break` or the end of the switch is found. In some cases, this might be exactly what you want to do. However, in most cases, you should include the `break` to ensure that only the right code is executed. Break, which you learn about in the section "Breaking Out of Loops," stops execution at the current point and jumps to the code outside of the next closing bracket (`}`)).

One handy use of falling through without a `break` occurs when multiple values should execute the same statements. To accomplish this task, you can use multiple `case` lines with no result; the `switch` will execute the first statements that it finds. For example, in the following `switch` statement, the string `x is an even number.` is printed if x has the values of 2, 4, 6, or 8. All other values of x cause the string `x is an odd number.` to be printed.

```
switch (x) {
    case 2:
    case 4:
    case 6:
    case 8:
        System.out.println("x is an even number.");
        break;
    default: System.out.println("x is an odd number.");
}
```

Listing 5.3 shows yet another example of a `switch`. This class, `NumberReader`, converts integer values to their actual English word equivalents using a method called `convertIt()`.

TYPE   **LISTING 5.3.** THE FULL TEXT OF NUMBERREADER.JAVA.

```
 1: class NumberReader {
 2:
 3:     String convertNum(int val) {
 4:         switch (val) {
 5:             case 0: return "zero ";
 6:             case 1: return "one ";
 7:             case 2: return "two ";
 8:             case 3: return "three ";
 9:             case 4: return "four ";
10:             case 5: return "five ";
11:             case 6: return "six ";
12:             case 7: return "seven ";
13:             case 8: return "eight ";
```

```
14:               case 9: return "nine ";
15:               default: return " ";
16:           }
17:      }
18:
19:      public static void main (String arguments[]) {
20:          NumberReader n = new NumberReader();
21:          String num = n.convertNum(4) + n.convertNum(1) +
                 n.convertNum(3);
22:          System.out.println("413 converts to " + num);
23:      }
24: }.
```

The output of the program is as follows: .

OUTPUT   413 converts to four one three

The heart of this example is, of course, the main switch statement in the middle of the convertNum() method in lines 4–16. This switch statement takes the integer argument that was passed into convertNum() and, when it finds a match, returns the appropriate string value. (Note that this method is defined to return a string as opposed to the other methods you've defined up to this point, which didn't return anything. You learn more about this tomorrow.)

There are no break statements needed in the NumberReader program because the return statement is used instead. return is similar to break except that it breaks out of the entire method definition and returns a single value. Again, you learn more about this tomorrow, when you learn all about how to define methods.

At this point you've probably seen enough main() methods to know what's going on, but run through this one quickly.

- Line 20 creates a new instance of the NumberReader class.
- Line 21 defines a string called num that will be the concatenation of the string values of three numbers. Each number is converted using a call to the convertNum() method.
- Line 22 displays the result.

for Loops

The for loop repeats a statement a specified number of times until a condition is met. Although for loops frequently are used for simple iteration in which a statement is repeated a certain number of times, for loops can be used for just about any kind of loop.

The `for` loop in Java looks roughly like the following:

```
for (initialization; test; increment) {
    statement;
}
```

The start of the `for` loop has three parts:

- *initialization* is an expression that initializes the start of the loop. If you have a loop index, this expression might declare and initialize it, such as `int i = 0`. Variables that you declare in this part of the `for` loop are local to the loop itself; they cease to exist after the loop is finished executing. You can initialize more than one variable in this section by separating each expression with a comma. The statement `int i = 0, int j = 10` in this section would declare the variables `i` and `j`, and both would be local to the loop.

- *test* is the test that occurs after each pass of the loop. The test must be a Boolean expression or a function that returns a `Boolean` value, such as `i < 10`. If the test is `true`, the loop executes. Once the test is `false`, the loop stops executing.

- *increment* is any expression or function call. Commonly, the increment is used to change the value of the loop index to bring the state of the loop closer to returning `false` and stopping the loop. Similar to the *initialization* section, you can put more than one expression in this section by separating each expression with a comma.

The *statement* part of the `for` loop is the statement that is executed each time the loop iterates. As with `if`, you can include either a single statement or a block statement; the previous example used a block because that is more common. The following example is a `for` loop that sets all slots of a `String` array to the value `Mr.`:

```
String[] salutation = new String[10];
int i; // the loop index variable

for (i = 0; i < salutation.length; i++)
    salutation[i] = "Mr.";
```

In this example, the variable `i` serves as a loop index—it counts the number of times the loop has been executed. Before each trip through the loop, the index value is compared to `salutation.length`, the number of elements in the `salutation` array. When the index is equal to or greater than `salutation.length`, the loop is exited.

The final element of the `for` statement is `i++`. This causes the loop index to increment by 1 each time the loop is executed. Without this statement, the loop would never stop.

The statement inside the loop sets an element of the `salutation` array equal to `"Mr."`. The loop index is used to determine which element is modified.

Any part of the for loop can be an empty statement—that is, you can include a semi-colon with no expression or statement and that part of the for loop will be ignored. Note that if you do use a null statement in your for loop, you may have to initialize or incre-ment any loop variables or loop indexes yourself elsewhere in the program.

You also can have an empty statement as the body of your for loop if everything you want to do is in the first line of that loop. For example, the following for loop finds the first prime number higher than 4,000. (It calls a method called notPrime(), which will theoretically have a way of figuring that out.)

```
for (i = 4001; notPrime(i); i += 2)
;
```

A common mistake in for loops is to accidentally put a semicolon at the end of the line that includes the for statement:

```
for (i = 0; i < 10; i++);
    x = x * i; // this line is not inside the loop!
```

In this example, the first semicolon ends the loop without executing x = x * i as part of the loop. The x = x * i line will be executed only once because it is outside the for loop entirely. Be careful not to make this mistake in your Java programs.

To finish up for loops, rewrite that example with the names from the array section. The original example is long and repetitive and only works with an array four elements long. This version, shown in Listing 5.4, is shorter and more flexible (but it returns the same output).

TYPE   **LISTING 5.4.** THE FULL TEXT OF NAMESLOOP.JAVA.

```
 1: class NamesLoop {
 2:
 3:     String[] firstNames = { "Dennis", "Grace", "Bjarne", "James" };
 4:     String[] lastNames = new String[firstNames.length];
 5:
 6:     void printNames() {
 7:         for (int i = 0; i < firstNames.length; i++)
 8:             System.out.println(firstNames[i] + " " + lastNames[i]);
 9:     }
10:
11:     public static void main (String arguments[]) {
12:         NamesLoop a = new NamesLoop();
13:         a.printNames();
14:         System.out.println("-----");
15:         a.lastNames[0] = "Ritchie";
16:         a.lastNames[1] = "Hopper";
```

continues

LISTING 5.4. CONTINUED

```
17:              a.lastNames[2] = "Stroustrup";
18:              a.lastNames[3] = "Gosling";
19:
20:              a.printNames();
21:      }
22: }.
```

The output of the program is as follows:

OUTPUT
```
Dennis null
Grace null
Bjarne null
James null
- - - - -
Dennis Ritchie
Grace Hopper
Bjarne Stroustrup
James Gosling
```

The only difference between this example and Listing 5.1 is in the `printNames()` method. Instead of going through the array slots one by one, this example uses a `for` loop to iterate through the array one slot at a time, stopping at the last element in the array. Using a more general-purpose loop to iterate over an array allows you to use `printNames()` for any array of any size and still have it print all the elements.

while and do Loops

The remaining types of loop are `while` and `do`. Like `for` loops, `while` and `do` loops enable a block of Java code to be executed repeatedly until a specific condition is met. Whether you use a `for`, `while`, or `do` loop is mostly a matter of your programming style. `while` and `do` loops are exactly the same as in C and C++, except that the test condition must be a Boolean in Java.

while Loops

The `while` loop is used to repeat a statement as long as a particular condition is `true`. The following is an example of a `while` loop:

```
while (i < 10) {
    x = x * i++; // the body of the loop
}
```

In the preceding example, the condition that accompanies the `while` keyword is a Boolean expression—`i < 10`. If the expression returns `true`, the `while` loop executes the body of the loop and then tests the condition again. This process repeats until the condition is `false`. Although the preceding loop uses opening and closing braces to form a block statement, the braces are not needed because the loop contains only one statement: `x = x * i++`. Using the braces does not create any problems, though, and the braces will be required if you add another statement inside the loop later on.

Listing 5.5 shows an example of a `while` loop that copies the elements of an array of integers (in `array1`) to an array of `floats` (in `array2`), casting each element to a `float` as it goes. The one catch is that if any of the elements in the first array is 1, the loop will immediately exit at that point.

TYPE   **LISTING 5.5.** THE FULL TEXT OF COPYARRAYWHILE.JAVA.

```
 1: class CopyArrayWhile {
 2:     public static void main (String arguments[]) {
 3:         int[] array1 = { 7, 4, 8, 1, 4, 1, 4 };
 4:         float[] array2 = new float[array1.length];
 5:
 6:         System.out.print("array1: [ ");
 7:         for (int i = 0; i < array1.length; i++) {
 8:             System.out.print(array1[i] + " ");
 9:         }
10:         System.out.println("]");
11:
12:         System.out.print("array2: [ ");
13:         int count = 0;
14:         while ( count < array1.length && array1[count] != 1) {
15:             array2[count] = (float) array1[count];
16:             System.out.print(array2[count++] + " ");
17:         }
18:         System.out.println("]");
19:     }
20: }
```

The output of the program is as follows:

OUTPUT
```
array1: [ 7 4 8 1 4 1 4 ]
array2: [ 7.0 4.0 8.0 ]
```

Here's what's going on in the `main()` method:

- Lines 3 and 4 declare the arrays; `array1` is an array of integers, which are initialized to some suitable numbers. `array2` is an array of floating-point numbers that is the same length as `array1` but doesn't have any initial values.

5

- Lines 6–10 are for output purposes; they simply iterate through array1 using a for loop to print out its values.

- Lines 13–17 are where the interesting stuff happens. This bunch of statements both assigns the values of array2 (converting the numbers to floating-point numbers along the array) and prints it out at the same time. You start with a count variable, which keeps track of the array index elements. The test in the while loop keeps track of the two conditions for exiting the loop, where those two conditions are running out of elements in array1 or encountering a 1 in array1. (Remember, that was part of the original description of what this program does.)

You can use the logical conditional && to keep track of the test; remember that && makes sure both conditions are true before the entire expression is true. If either one is false, the expression returns false and the loop exits. What goes on in this particular example? The output shows that the first four elements in array1 were copied to array2, but there was a 1 in the middle that stopped the loop from going any further. Without the 1, array2 should end up with all the same elements as array1. If the while loop's test initially is false the first time it is tested (for example, if the first element in that first array is 1), the body of the while loop will never be executed. If you need to execute the loop at least once, you can do one of two things:

- Duplicate the body of the loop outside the while loop.

- Use a do loop (which is described in the following section).

The do loop is considered the better solution of the two.

do...while Loops

The do loop is just like a while loop with one major difference: the place in the loop when the condition is tested. A while loop tests the condition before looping, so if the condition is false the first time it is tested, the body of the loop never will execute. A do loop executes the body of the loop at least once before testing the condition, so if the condition is false the first time it is tested, the body of the loop already will have executed once.

It's the difference between asking Dad to borrow the car and telling him later that you borrowed it. If Dad nixes the idea in the first case, you don't get to borrow it. If he nixes the idea in the second case, you already have borrowed it once.

do loops look like the following:

```
do {
    x = x * i++; // the body of the loop
} while (i < 10);
```

The body of the loop is executed once before the test condition, i < 10, is evaluated; then, if the test evaluates as true, the loop runs again. If it is false, the loop exits. Keep in mind that the body of the loop executes at least once with do loops.

Listing 5.6 shows a simple example of a do loop that prints a message each time the loop iterates (10 times, for this example):

TYPE **LISTING 5.6.** THE FULL TEXT OF DOTEST.JAVA.

```
 1: class DoTest {
 2:     public static void main (String arguments[]) {
 3:         int x = 1;
 4:
 5:         do {
 6:             System.out.println("Looping, round " + x);
 7:             x++;
 8:         } while (x <= 10);
 9:     }
10: }
```

The output of the program is as follows:

OUTPUT
```
Looping, round 1
Looping, round 2
Looping, round 3
Looping, round 4
Looping, round 5
Looping, round 6
Looping, round 7
Looping, round 8
Looping, round 9
Looping, round 10
```

5

Breaking Out of Loops

In all of the loops, the loop ends when a tested condition is met. There might be times when something occurs during execution of a loop and you want to exit the loop early. For that you can use the break and continue keywords.

You already have seen break as part of the switch statement; break stops execution of the switch statement, and the program continues. The break keyword, when used with a loop, does the same thing—it immediately halts execution of the current loop. If you have nested loops within loops, execution picks up with the next outer loop. Otherwise, the program merely continues executing the next statement after the loop.

For example, recall the `while` loop that copied elements from an integer array into an array of floating-point numbers until the end of the array or a 1 was reached. You can test for that latter case inside the body of the `while` loop, and then use `break` to exit the loop:

```
int count = 0;
while (count < userData1.length) {
    if (userData1[count] == 1)
        break;
    userData2[count] = (float) userData1[count++];
}
```

The `continue` keyword starts the loop over at the next iteration. For `do` and `while` loops, this means that the execution of the block statement starts over again; with `for` loops, the increment expression is evaluated and then the block statement is executed. The `continue` keyword is useful when you want to make a special case out of elements within a loop. With the previous example of copying one array to another, you could test for whether the current element is equal to 1, and use `continue` to restart the loop after every 1 so that the resulting array never will contain zero. Note that because you're skipping elements in the first array, you now have to keep track of two different array counters:

```
int count = 0;
int count2 = 0;
while (count++ <= userData1.length) {
    if (userData1[count] == 1)
        continue;

    userData2[count2++] = (float)userData1[count];
}
```

Labeled Loops

Both `break` and `continue` can have an optional label that tells Java where to resume execution of the program. Without a label, `break` jumps outside the nearest loop to an enclosing loop or to the next statement outside the loop. The `continue` keyword restarts the loop it is enclosed within. Using `break` and `continue` with a label enables you to use `break` to go to a point outside a nested loop or to use `continue` to go to a loop outside the current loop.

To use a labeled loop, add the label before the initial part of the loop, with a colon between the label and the loop. Then, when you use `break` or `continue`, add the name of the label after the keyword itself, as in the following:

```
out:
    for (int i = 0; i <10; i++) {
        while (x < 50) {
```

```
        if (i * x++ > 400)
            break out;
        // inner loop here
    }
    // outer loop here
}
```

In this snippet of code, the label out labels the outer loop. Then, inside both the for and while loops, when a particular condition is met, a break causes the execution to break out of both loops. Without the label out, the break statement would exit the inner loop and resume execution with the outer loop.

Here's another example: The program shown in Listing 5.7 contains a nested for loop. Inside the innermost loop, if the summed values of the two counters is greater than 4, both loops exit at once.

TYPE   **LISTING 5.7.** THE FULL TEXT OF LABELTEST.JAVA.

```
 1: class LabelTest {
 2:     public static void main (String arguments[]) {
 3:
 4:     thisLoop:
 5:         for (int i = 1; i <= 5; i++)
 6:         for (int j = 1; j <= 3; j++) {
 7:             System.out.println("i is " + i + ", j is " + j);
 8:             if (( i + j) > 4)
 9:             break thisLoop;
10:         }
11:         System.out.println("end of loops");
12:     }
13: }
```

The output of the program is as follows:

OUTPUT
```
i is 1, j is 1
i is 1, j is 2
i is 1, j is 3
i is 2, j is 1
i is 2, j is 2
i is 2, j is 3
end of loops
```

As you can see, the loop iterated until the sum of i and j was greater than 4, and then both loops exited to the outer block and the final message was displayed.

Summary

Now that you have been introduced to lists, loops, and logic, you can make a computer decide whether to repeatedly display the contents of an array.

You learned how to declare an array variable, assign an object to it, and access and change elements of the array. With the `if` and `switch` conditional statements, you can branch to different parts of a program based on a Boolean test. You learned about the `for`, `while`, and `do` loops, each enabling a portion of a program to be repeated until a given condition is met.

It bears repeating: You'll use all three of these features frequently in your Java programs.

You'll use all three of these features frequently in your Java programs.

Q&A

Q I declared a variable inside a block statement for an `if`. When the `if` was done, the definition of that variable vanished. Where did it go?

A In technical terms, block statements form a new *lexical scope*. What this means is that if you declare a variable inside a block, it's only visible and usable inside that block. When the block finishes executing, all the variables you declared go away.

It's a good idea to declare most of your variables in the outermost block in which they'll be needed—usually at the top of a block statement. The exception might be very simple variables, such as index counters in `for` loops, where declaring them in the first line of the `for` loop is an easy shortcut.

Q Why can't you use `switch` with strings?

A Strings are objects, and `switch` in Java works only for the primitive types `byte`, `char`, `short`, and `int`. To compare strings, you have to use nested `if`s, which enable more general expression tests, including string comparison.

DAY 6

Creating Classes

If you're coming to Java from another programming language, you might be going through a class struggle. The term "class" seems synonymous to the term "program," but you could be uncertain of the relationship between the two.

In Java, a program is made up of a main class and any other classes that are needed to support the main class. These support classes include any of those in Java's class library you might need (such as String, Math, and the like).

Today you go to the head of the class in terms of what you know on the subject. You create classes and read about each of the following:

- The parts of a class definition
- The creation and use of instance variables
- The creation and use of methods
- The main() method used in Java applications
- The use of arguments passed to a Java application

Defining Classes

Because you have created classes during each of the previous chapters, you should be familiar with the basics of class definition at this point. A class is defined via the class keyword and the name of the class, as in the following example:

```
class Ticker {
    // body of the class
}
```

By default, classes inherit from the Object class, which is the superclass of all classes in the Java class hierarchy.

If your class is a subclass, the extends keyword is used to indicate the new class' superclass. Look at the following subclass of Ticker:

```
class SportsTicker extends Ticker {
    // body of the class
}
```

Creating Instance and Class Variables

When you create a class that inherits from a superclass, you will have some kind of behavior that needs to be added to make the new class different than the class from which it inherits.

This behavior is defined by specifying the variables and methods of the new class. In this section you work with three kinds of variables: class variables, instance variables, and local variables. The next section details methods.

Defining Instance Variables

On Day 3, "The ABCs of Java," you learned how to declare and initialize local variables, which are variables inside method definitions. Instance variables are declared and defined in almost the same way local variables are. The main difference is their location in the class definition. Variables are considered instance variables if they are declared outside a method definition. Customarily, however, most instance variables are defined right after the first line of the class definition. Listing 6.1 contains a simple class definition for the class Jabberwock, which inherits from its superclass, Reptile.

TYPE   **LISTING 6.1.** THE FULL TEXT OF JABBERWOCK.JAVA.

```
1: class Jabberwock extends Reptile {
2:
3:     String color;
```

```
4:      String sex;
5:      boolean hungry;
6:      int age;
7: }
```

This class definition contains four variables. Because these variables are not defined inside a method, they are instance variables. The variables are as follows:

- color   The color of the jabberwock (for example, orange, lemon yellow, or burnt sienna)
- sex   A string that indicates the jabberwock's gender
- hungry   A Boolean variable that is true if the jabberwock is hungry and false otherwise
- age   The jabberwock's age in years

Constants

Variables are useful when you need to store information that can be changed as a program runs. If the value should never change during a program's runtime, you can use a special type of variable called a constant.

NEW TERM   A *constant*, which also is called a *constant variable*, is a variable with a value that never changes. This might seem like a misnomer, given the meaning of the word "variable."

Constants are useful in defining shared values for all methods of an object—in other words, for giving meaningful names to unchanging objectwide values. In Java, you can create constants for all kinds of variables: instance, class, and local.

Note

> Constant local variables were not possible in Java 1.0, but were added to the language as of Java 1.1. This becomes important if you're trying to create an applet that is fully compatible with Java 1.0. You learn more about this during Week 2, "Developing Web-Based and Graphical Programs."

6

To declare a constant, use the final keyword before the variable declaration and include an initial value for that variable, as in the following:

```
final float pi = 3.141592;
final boolean debug = false;
final int numberOfJenny = 8675309;
```

Constants can be useful for naming various states of an object and then testing for those states. Suppose you have a text label that can be aligned to the left, right, or center. You can define those values as constant integers:

```
final int LEFT = 0;
final int RIGHT = 1;
final int CENTER = 2;
```

As a place to store the value of the current alignment of the text, the variable `alignment` is declared as an `int`:

```
int alignment;
```

Later in the body of a method definition, you can set the alignment with the following:

```
this.alignment = CENTER;
```

You also can test for a given alignment:

```
switch (this.alignment) {
    case LEFT:
        // deal with left alignment
        break;
    case RIGHT:
        // deal with right alignment
        break;
    case CENTER:
        // deal with center alignment
        break;
}
```

Using constants often makes a program easier to understand. To illustrate this point, consider which of the following two statements is more informative of its function:

```
this.alignment = CENTER;
```

```
this.alignment = 2;
```

Class Variables

As you learned in previous lessons, class variables apply to a class as a whole, rather than being stored individually in objects of the class.

Class variables are good for communicating between different objects of the same class, or for keeping track of classwide information among a set of objects.

The `static` keyword is used in the class declaration to declare a class variable, as in the following:

```
static int sum;
static final int maxObjects = 10;
```

Creating Methods

As you learned on Day 4, "Object Lessons," methods define an object's behavior—anything that happens when the object is created and the various tasks the object can perform during its lifetime.

This section introduces method definition and how methods work. Tomorrow's lesson has more detail about advanced things you can do with methods.

Defining Methods

Method definitions have four basic parts:

- The name of the method
- The type of object or primitive type returned by the method
- A list of parameters
- The body of the method

The first three parts of the method definition form what's called the method's *signature*.

 Note

> To keep things simpler today, two optional parts of the method definition have been left out: a modifier, such as `public` or `private`, and the `throws` keyword, which indicates the exceptions a method can throw. You learn about these parts of a method definition during Week 3, "Using Swing and Other Advanced Features."

In other languages, the name of the method—which might be called a function, subroutine, or procedure—is enough to distinguish it from other methods in the program.

In Java, you can have several methods in the same class with the same name but differences in return type or argument list. This practice is called *method overloading*, and you learn more about it tomorrow.

Here's what a basic method definition looks like:

```
returnType methodName(type1 arg1, type2 arg2, type3 arg3 ...) {
    // body of the method
}
```

The `returnType` is the primitive type or class of the value returned by the method. It can be one of the primitive types, a class name, or `void` if the method does not return a value at all.

Note that if this method returns an array object, the array brackets can go either after `returnType` or after the parameter list. Because the former way is easier to read, it is used in this book's examples as in the following:

```
int[] makeRange(int lower, int upper) {
    // body of this method
}
```

The method's parameter list is a set of variable declarations, separated by commas, inside parentheses. These parameters become local variables in the body of the method, receiving their values when the method is called.

You can have statements, expressions, method calls to other objects, conditionals, loops, and so on inside the body of the method—everything you've learned about in the previous lessons.

Unless a method has been declared with `void` as its return type, the method returns some kind of value when it is completed. This value must be explicitly returned at some exit point inside the method, using the `return` keyword.

Listing 6.2 shows an example of a class that defines a `makeRange()` method. `makeRange()` takes two integers—a lower-bound and an upper-bound—and creates an array that contains all of the integers between those two boundaries. The boundaries themselves are included in the array of integers.

TYPE   **LISTING 6.2.** THE FULL TEXT OF RANGECLASS.JAVA.

```
 1: class RangeClass {
 2:     int[] makeRange(int lower, int upper) {
 3:         int arr[] = new int[ (upper - lower) + 1 ];
 4:
 5:         for (int i = 0; i < arr.length; i++) {
 6:             arr[i] = lower++;
 7:         }
 8:         return arr;
 9:     }
10:
11:     public static void main(String arguments[]) {
12:         int theArray[];
13:         RangeClass theRange = new RangeClass();
14:
15:         theArray = theRange.makeRange(1, 10);
16:         System.out.print("The array: [ ");
17:         for (int i = 0; i < theArray.length; i++) {
18:             System.out.print(theArray[i] + " ");
19:         }
20:         System.out.println("]");
```

```
21:     }
22:
23: }
```

The output of the program is the following:

OUTPUT   The array: [1 2 3 4 5 6 7 8 9 10]

The main() method in this class tests the makeRange() method by creating a range where the lower- and upper boundaries of the range are 1 and 10, respectively (see line 6), and then uses a for loop to print the new array's values.

The this Keyword

In the body of a method definition, you might want to refer to the current object—the object the method was called on. This can be done to use that object's instance variables or pass the current object as an argument to another method.

To refer to the current object in these cases, use the this keyword where you normally would refer to an object's name.

The this keyword refers to the current object, and you can use it anywhere the object might appear: in dot notation, as an argument to a method, as the return value for the current method, and so on. The following are some examples of using this:

```
t = this.x;            // the x instance variable for this object

this.resetData(this);  // call the resetData method, defined in
                       // this class, and pass it the current
                       // object

return this;           // return the current object
```

In many cases, you might not need to explicitly use the this keyword, because it will be assumed. For instance, you can refer to both instance variables and method calls defined in the current class simply by name, because the this is implicit in those references. Therefore, you could write the first two examples like the following:

```
t = x;              // the x instance variable for this object

resetData(this);    // call the resetData method, defined in this
                    // class
```

> **Note**
>
> The viability of omitting the this keyword for instance variables depends on whether variables of the same name are declared in the local scope. You see more on this subject in the next section.

6

Because this is a reference to the current instance of a class, you should use it only inside the body of an instance method definition. Class methods, methods declared with the static keyword, cannot use this.

Variable Scope and Method Definitions

One of the things you must know to use a variable is its scope.

NEW TERM *Scope* is the part of a program in which a variable or other information can be used. When the part defining the scope has completed execution, the variable ceases to exist.

When you declare a variable in Java, that variable always has a limited scope. A variable with local scope, for example, only can be used inside the block in which it was defined. Instance and class variables have a scope that extends to the entire class, so they can be used by any of the methods within their class.

When you refer to a variable within a method definition, Java checks for a definition of that variable first in the current scope (which might be a block), next in each outer scope, and finally, up to the current method definition. If the variable is not a local variable, Java then checks for a definition of that variable as an instance or class variable in the current class. If Java still does not find the variable definition, it searches each superclass in turn.

Because of the way Java checks for the scope of a given variable, it is possible for you to create a variable in a lower scope that hides (or replaces) the original value of that variable and introduce subtle and confusing bugs into your code.

For example, note the small Java program in Listing 6.3.

TYPE **LISTING 6.3.** THE FULL TEXT OF SCOPETEST.JAVA.

```
 1: class ScopeTest {
 2:     int test = 10;
 3:
 4:     void printTest () {
 5:         int test = 20;
 6:         System.out.println("test = " + test);
 7:     }
 8:
 9:     public static void main(String arguments[]) {
10:         ScopeTest st = new ScopeTest();
11:         st.printTest();
12:     }
13: }
```

The following is this program's output:

`test = 20`

In this class you have two variables with the same name and definition. The first, an instance variable, has the name `test` and is initialized with the value `10`. The second is a local variable with the same name, but with the value `20`. The local variable `test` within the `printTest()` method hides the instance variable `test`. The `printTest()` method inside `main()` displays that `test = 20`. You can get around this problem by using `this.test` to refer to the instance variable and using just `test` to refer to the local variable.

The conflict is avoided by referring explicitly to the instance variable via its object scope.

A more insidious example occurs when you redefine a variable in a subclass that already occurs in a superclass. This can create subtle bugs in your code; for example, you might call methods that are intended to change the value of an instance variable, but the wrong variable is changed. Another bug might occur when you cast an object from one class to another; the value of your instance variable might mysteriously change because it was getting that value from the superclass instead of your class.

The best way to avoid this behavior is to be aware of the variables defined in all your class' superclasses. This awareness prevents you from duplicating a variable that's in use higher up in the class hierarchy.

Passing Arguments to Methods

When you call a method with object parameters, the objects you pass into the body of the method are passed by reference. Whatever you do to the objects inside the method affects the original objects. Keep in mind that such objects include arrays and all objects that are contained in arrays. When you pass an array into a method and modify its contents, the original array is affected. Primitive types, on the other hand, are passed by value.

Listing 6.4 demonstrates how this works.

6

TYPE   **LISTING 6.4.** THE PASSBYREFERENCE CLASS.

```
1: class PassByReference {
2:     int onetoZero(int arg[]) {
3:         int count = 0;
```

continues

LISTING 6.4. CONTINUED

```
 4:
 5:            for (int i = 0; i < arg.length; i++) {
 6:                if (arg[i] == 1) {
 7:                    count++;
 8:                    arg[i] = 0;
 9:                }
10:            }
11:            return count;
12:        }
13:        public static void main(String arguments[]) {
14:            int arr[] = { 1, 3, 4, 5, 1, 1, 7 };
15:            PassByReference test = new PassByReference();
16:            int numOnes;
17:
18:            System.out.print("Values of the array: [ ");
19:            for (int i = 0; i < arr.length; i++) {
20:                System.out.print(arr[i] + " ");
21:            }
22:            System.out.println("]");
23:
24:            numOnes = test.onetoZero(arr);
25:            System.out.println("Number of Ones = " + numOnes);
26:            System.out.print("New values of the array: [ ");
27:            for (int i = 0; i < arr.length; i++) {
28:                System.out.print(arr[i] + " ");
29:            }
30:            System.out.println("]");
31:        }
32: }
```

The following is this program's output:

OUTPUT
```
Values of the array: [ 1 3 4 5 1 1 7 ]
Number of Ones = 3
New values of the array: [ 0 3 4 5 0 0 7 ]
```

Note the method definition for the onetoZero() method in lines 2 to 12, which takes a single array as an argument. The onetoZero() method does two things:

- It counts the number of 1s in the array and returns that value.
- For every 1 in the array, it substitutes a 0 in its place.

The main() method in the PassByReference class tests the use of the onetoZero() method. Go over the main() method line by line so you can see what is going on and why the output shows what it does.

Lines 14–16 set up the initial variables for this example. The first one is an array of integers; the second one is an instance of the class PassByReference, which is stored in the variable test. The third is a simple integer to hold the number of 1s in the array.

Lines 18–22 print out the initial values of the array; you can see the output of these lines in the first line of the output.

Line 24 is where the real work takes place; this is where you call the onetoZero() method defined in the object test and pass it the array stored in arr. This method returns the number of 1s in the array, which you then assign to the variable numOnes.

Got it so far? Line 25 prints out the number of 1s (the value you got back from the onetoZero() method). It returns 3, as you would expect.

The last section of lines prints out the array values. Because a reference to the array object is passed to the method, changing the array inside that method changes that array's original copy. Printing out the values in lines 27–30 proves this—that last line of output shows that all the 1s in the array have been changed to 0s.

Class Methods

The relationship between class and instance variables is directly comparable to how class and instance methods work.

Class methods are available to any instance of the class itself and can be made available to other classes. In addition, unlike an instance method, a class does not require an instance of the class in order for its methods to be called.

For example, the Java class libraries include a class called Math. The Math class defines a set of math operations that you can use in any program or any of the various number types, as in the following:

```
float root = Math.sqrt(453.0);

System.out.print("The larger of x and y is " + Math.max(x, y));
```

To define class methods, use the static keyword in front of the method definition, just as you would use static in front of a class variable. For example, the class method max() used in the preceding example might have the following signature:

```
static int max(int arg1, int arg2) {
    // body of the method
}
```

Java supplies wrapper classes for each of the base types; for example, Java supplies Integer, Float, and Boolean classes. By using class methods defined in those classes, you can convert objects to primitive types and convert primitive types to objects.

6

For example, the parseInt() class method in the Integer class can be used with a string. The string is sent to the method as an argument, and this is used to calculate a return value to send back as an int.

The following statement shows how the parseInt() method can be used:

```
int count = Integer.parseInt("42");
```

In the preceding statement, the String value "42" is returned by parseInt() as an integer with a value of 42, and this is stored in the count variable.

The lack of a static keyword in front of a method name makes it an instance method. Instance methods operate on a particular object, rather than a class of objects. On Day 2, "A Taste of Object-Oriented Programming," you created an instance method called feedJabberwock() that fed an individual jabberwock.

 Tip

> Most methods that operate on or affect a particular object should be defined as instance methods. Methods that provide some general capability, but do not directly affect an instance of the class, should be declared as class methods.

Creating Java Applications

Now that you know how to create classes, objects, class and instance variables, and class and instance methods, you can put it all together into a Java program.

Applications, to refresh your memory, are Java programs that run on their own. Applications are different from applets, which require a Java-enabled browser to view them. The projects you have been creating up to this point have been Java applications. You get a chance to dive into applets next week. Applets require a bit more background in order to get them to interact with the browser, as well as draw and update with the graphics system.

A Java application consists of one or more classes and can be as large or as small as you want it to be. Although all the Java applications you've created up to this point do nothing but output some characters to the screen or to a window, you also can create Java applications that use windows, graphics, and user-interface elements, just as applets do.

The only thing you need in order to make a Java application run, however, is one class that serves as the starting point for the rest of your Java program.

The starting-point class for your application needs only one thing: a `main()` method. When the application is run, the `main()` method is the first thing that gets called. None of this should be much of a surprise to you at this point; you've been creating Java applications with `main()` methods all along.

The signature for the `main()` method always looks like this:

```
public static void main(String arguments[]) {
    // body of method
}
```

Here's a rundown of the parts of the `main()` method:

- `public` means that this method is available to other classes and objects. The `main()` method must be declared `public`. You learn more about `public` and `private` methods during Week 3.
- `static` means that `main()` is a class method.
- `void` means that the `main()` method doesn't return a value.
- `main()` takes one parameter, which is an array of strings. This argument is used for program arguments, which you learn about in the next section.

The body of the `main()` method contains any code you need to start your application, such as the initialization of variables or the creation of class instances.

When Java executes the `main()` method, keep in mind that `main()` is a class method. An instance of the class that holds `main()` is not created automatically when your program runs. If you want to treat that class as an object, you have to create an instance of it in the `main()` method.

Helper Classes

Your Java application can have only one class, or in the case of most larger programs, it might be made up of several classes, where different instances of each class are created and used while the application is running. You can create as many classes as you want for your program.

6

> **Note**
>
> If you're using the JDK, the classes must be accessible from a folder that's listed in your CLASSPATH.

As long as Java can find the class, it will be used by your program when it runs. Note, however, that only the starting-point class needs a `main()` method. After it is called, the methods inside the various classes and objects used in your program take over. Although you can include `main()` methods in helper classes, they will be ignored when the program actually runs.

Java Applications and Command-Line Arguments

Because Java applications are standalone programs, it's useful to pass arguments or options to an application. You can use the arguments to determine how the application is going to run or enable a generic application to operate on different kinds of input. You can use program arguments for many different purposes, such as to turn on debugging input or to indicate a filename to load.

Passing Arguments to Java Applications

How you pass arguments to a Java application varies based on the platform you're running Java on. On Windows and UNIX, you can pass arguments to the Java program via the command line.

To pass arguments to a Java program on Windows or Solaris, the arguments should be appended to the command line when the program is run. The following shows an example:

```
java MyProgram argumentOne 2 three
```

In the preceding example, three arguments were passed to a program: `argumentOne`, the number 2, and `three`. Note that a space separates each of the arguments.

To group arguments that include spaces, the arguments should be surrounded with double quotation marks. For example, the argument `"No Shoes No Shirt No Service"` produces one argument for a program to deal with; the quotation marks prevent the spaces from being used to separate one argument from another. These quotation marks are not included in the argument when it is sent to the program and received using the `main()` method.

Handling Arguments in Your Java Application

When an application is run with arguments, Java stores the arguments as an array of strings and passes the array to the application's `main()` method. Take another look at the signature for `main()`:

```
public static void main(String arguments[]) {
    // body of method
}
```

Here, `arguments` is the name of the array of strings that contains the list of arguments. You can call this array anything you like.

Inside the `main()` method, you then can handle the arguments your program was given by iterating over the array of arguments and handling them in some manner. For example, Listing 6.5 is a simple class that prints out the arguments it gets, one per line.

TYPE   **LISTING 6.5.** THE FULL TEXT OF ECHOARGS.JAVA.

```
1: class EchoArgs {
2:     public static void main(String arguments[]) {
3:         for (int i = 0; i < arguments.length; i++) {
4:             System.out.println("Argument " + i + ": " + arguments[i]);
5:         }
6:     }
7: }
```

The following is an example of input to run this program:

INPUT   `java EchoArgs Wilhelm Niekro Hough 49`

If you run the `EchoArgs` application with the preceding command-line arguments, the following output is produced:

OUTPUT
```
Argument 0: Wilhelm
Argument 1: Niekro
Argument 2: Hough
Argument 3: 49
```

Here's another example of input to run this program:

`java EchoArgs "Hoyt Wilhelm" Charlie Hough`

Here's the output it produces:

OUTPUT
```
Argument 0: Hoyt Wilhelm
Argument 1: Charlie
Argument 2: Hough
```

Note how the arguments are grouped in the second input example; putting quotation marks around `Hoyt Wilhelm` causes that argument to be treated as one unit inside the argument array.

Note   The array of arguments in Java is not analogous to `argv` in C and UNIX. In particular, `arg[0]` or `arguments[0]`, the first element in the array of

6

arguments, is the first command-line argument after the name of the class—
not the name of the program as it would be in C. Be careful of this as you
write your Java programs.

An important thing to note: All arguments passed to a Java application are stored in an
array of strings. To treat them as something other than strings, you must convert them.

For example, suppose you have a simple Java program called SumAverage that takes any
number of numeric arguments and returns the sum and the average of those arguments.
Listing 6.6 shows a first pass at this program. Don't try compiling this one; just look at
the code and see if you can figure out what it does.

TYPE **LISTING 6.6.** A FIRST TRY AT SUMAVERAGE.JAVA.

```
 1: class SumAverage {
 2:     public static void main(String arguments[]) {
 3:         int sum = 0;
 4:
 5:         for (int i = 0; i < arguments.length; i++) {
 6:             sum += arguments[i];
 7:         }
 8:
 9:         System.out.println("Sum is: " + sum);
10:         System.out.println("Average is: " +
11:             (float)sum / arguments.length);
12:     }
13: }
```

At first glance, this program seems rather straightforward—a for loop iterates over the
array of arguments, summing them, and then the sum and the average are printed out as
the last step.

If you tried to compile this program, an error such as the following would be displayed
by the compiler:

OUTPUT SumAverage.java:6: Incompatible type for +=. Can't convert
java.lang.String to
int.
        sum += arguments[i];

This error occurs because the argument array is an array of strings. Even though you are
going to pass integers into the application, those integers will be converted to strings

before being stored in the array. You have to convert them from strings to integers using a class method for the `Integer` class called `parseInt`. Change line 6 to use that method, as follows:

```
sum += Integer.parseInt(arguments[i]);
```

The program compiles successfully. The following is an example of input to run this program:

INPUT   `Java SumAverage 123`

When you run the application with these arguments, you should see the following output:

OUTPUT
```
Sum is: 6
Average is: 2
```

Summary

After finishing today's chapter, you should have a pretty good idea why Java has class. Everything you create in Java involves the use of a main class that interacts with other classes as needed. It's a different programming mindset than you might be used to with other languages.

Today you put together everything you have learned about creating Java classes. Each of the following topics was covered:

- Instance and class variables, which hold the attributes of a class and objects created from it. You learned how to declare variables, how they differ from local variables, and how to declare constants.

- Instance and class methods, which define the behavior of a class. You learned how to define methods—including the parts of a method signature, how to return values from a method, how arguments are passed to methods, and how to use the `this` keyword to refer to the current object.

- Java applications. You learned how the `main()` method works and how to pass arguments to a Java application.

Tomorrow you finish off Week 1 by learning some advanced aspects of programming with methods.

Until then, class dismissed.

6

Q&A

Q You mentioned that constant local variables cannot be created in applets that are compatible with Java 1.02. Why would I want to create programs that don't use the current features of the language in Java 2?

A The most likely reason is that you're trying to create an applet that works on the largest number of browsers. Full support for versions of the language beyond 1.02 is lagging in browsers such as Netscape Navigator and Microsoft Internet Explorer, although Sun is working on ways to correct this. The situation is fully discussed during Day 8, "Putting Interactive Programs on the Web."

Q In my class, I have an instance variable called `origin`. I also have a local variable called `origin` in a method, which, because of variable scope, gets hidden by the local variable. Is there any way to get ahold of the instance variable's value?

A The easiest way is to avoid giving your local variables the same names your instance variables have. If you feel you must, you can use `this.origin` to refer to the instance variable and `origin` to refer to the local variable.

Q I wrote a program to take four arguments, but if I give it too few arguments, it crashes with a runtime error.

A Testing for the number and type of arguments your program expects is up to you in your Java program; Java won't do it for you. If your program requires four arguments, test that you have indeed been given four arguments, and return an error message if you haven't.

DAY 7

Using Methods to Accomplish Tasks

Methods are arguably the most important part of any object-oriented language, because they define every action an object takes.

Classes and objects provide a framework. Class and instance variables provide a way to describe what these classes and objects are. Only methods can define an object's behavior—the things it is capable of doing and the way it interacts with other classes and objects.

Yesterday, you learned some things about defining methods, and you could use this knowledge to create Java programs. You would, however, be missing some features that make methods powerful—features that make your objects and classes more efficient and easier to understand. Today you learn about the following features:

- *Overloading methods.* Creating methods with multiple signatures and definitions, but with the same name
- *Creating constructor methods.* Methods that enable you to initialize objects to set up their initial state when created

- *Overriding methods.* Creating a different definition for a method that has been defined in a superclass
- *Finalizer methods.* Methods that clean up after an object before it is removed from the system

Creating Methods with the Same Name, Different Arguments

When you work with Java's class library, you often encounter classes that have numerous methods with the same name. For example, the java.lang.String class has several different valueOf() methods.

Methods with the same name are differentiated from each other by two things:

- The number of arguments they take
- The data type or objects of each argument

These two things make up a method's signature, and using several methods with the same name and different signatures is called *overloading*.

In the example of String, the different overloaded valueOf() methods take different data types as a parameter.

Method overloading eliminates the need for entirely different methods that do essentially the same thing. Overloading also makes it possible for methods to behave differently based on the arguments they receive.

The overloaded valueOf() methods in String can be used to convert a variety of different data types and objects into String values. When you call a method in an object, Java matches the method name and arguments in order to choose which method definition to execute.

To create an overloaded method, you create different method definitions in a class, each with the same name but different argument lists. The difference can be the number, the type of arguments, or both. Java allows method overloading as long as each argument list is unique for the same method name.

Note that Java does not consider the return type when differentiating between overloaded methods. If you attempt to create two methods with the same signature and different return types, the class won't compile. In addition, variable names that you choose for each argument to the method are irrelevant—all that matters are the number and the type of arguments.

The next project is creating an overloaded method. Listing 7.1 shows a simple class definition for a class called MyRect, which defines a rectangular shape. The MyRect class defines a rectangular shape with four instance variables to define the upper-left and lower-right corners of the rectangle: x1, y1, x2, and y2.

TYPE   **LISTING 7.1.** THE BEGINNINGS OF MYRECT.JAVA.

```
1: class MyRect {
2:     int x1 = 0;
3:     int y1 = 0;
4:     int x2 = 0;
5:     int y2 = 0;
6: }
```

Note   Although you could successfully compile this program, it can't be run because there isn't a main() method. When you're finished building this class definition, the final version can be compiled and run.

When a new instance of the MyRect class is created, all of its instance variables are initialized to 0. You can add a buildRect() instance method to set the variables to their correct values as two corners of a rectangle. This method takes four integer arguments and returns the resulting rectangle object. Because the arguments have the same names as the instance variables, the keyword this is used inside the method when referring to the instance variables. The following is the code for buildRect():

```
MyRect buildRect(int x1, int y1, int x2, int y2) {
    this.x1 = x1;
    this.y1 = y1;
    this.x2 = x2;
    this.y2 = y2;
    return this;
}
```

This method can be used to create rectangles—but what if you wanted to define a rectangle's dimensions in a different way? An alternative would be to use Point objects rather than individual coordinates. To implement this alternative, you can overload buildRect() so that its argument list takes two Point objects. Look at the following:

```
MyRect buildRect(Point topLeft, Point bottomRight) {
    x1 = topLeft.x;
    y1 = topLeft.y;
    x2 = bottomRight.x;
```

7

```
        y2 = bottomRight.y;
        return this;
}
```

In order for the preceding method to work, the `Point` class must be imported at the top of the source file so that Java can find it.

Another possible way to define the rectangle is to use a top corner, a height and a width. The following is a definition for an overloaded method:

```
MyRect buildRect(Point topLeft, int w, int h) {
    x1 = topLeft.x;
    y1 = topLeft.y;
    x2 = (x1 + w);
    y2 = (y1 + h);
    return this;
}
```

To finish this example, a `printRect()` is created to display the rectangle's coordinates and a `main()` method tries everything out. Listing 7.2 shows the completed class definition with all its methods: three `buildRect()` methods, a `printRect()` method, and a `main()` method.

TYPE   **LISTING 7.2.** THE FULL TEXT OF MYRECT.JAVA.

```
 1: import java.awt.Point;
 2:
 3: class MyRect {
 4:     int x1 = 0;
 5:     int y1 = 0;
 6:     int x2 = 0;
 7:     int y2 = 0;
 8:
 9:     MyRect buildRect(int x1, int y1, int x2, int y2) {
10:         this.x1 = x1;
11:         this.y1 = y1;
12:         this.x2 = x2;
13:         this.y2 = y2;
14:         return this;
15:     }
16:
17:     MyRect buildRect(Point topLeft, Point bottomRight) {
18:         x1 = topLeft.x;
19:         y1 = topLeft.y;
20:         x2 = bottomRight.x;
21:         y2 = bottomRight.y;
22:         return this;
23:     }
24:
```

```
25:      MyRect buildRect(Point topLeft, int w, int h) {
26:          x1 = topLeft.x;
27:          y1 = topLeft.y;
28:          x2 = (x1 + w);
29:          y2 = (y1 + h);
30:          return this;
31:      }
32:
33:      void printRect(){
34:          System.out.print("MyRect: <" + x1 + ", " + y1);
35:          System.out.println(", " + x2 + ", " + y2 + ">");
36:      }
37:
38:      public static void main(String arguments[]) {
39:          MyRect rect = new MyRect();
40:
41:          System.out.println("Calling buildRect with coordinates 25,25,
             50,50:");
42:          rect.buildRect(25, 25, 50, 50);
43:          rect.printRect();
44:          System.out.println("***");
45:
46:          System.out.println("Calling buildRect with points (10,10),
             (20,20):");
47:          rect.buildRect(new Point(10,10), new Point(20,20));
48:          rect.printRect();
49:          System.out.println("***");
50:
51:          System.out.print("Calling buildRect with 1 point (10,10),");
52:          System.out.println(" width (50) and height (50):");
53:
54:          rect.buildRect(new Point(10,10), 50, 50);
55:          rect.printRect();
56:          System.out.println("***");
57:      }
58: }
```

The following is this program's output:

OUTPUT

```
Calling buildRect with coordinates 25,25, 50,50:
MyRect: <25, 25, 50, 50>
***
Calling buildRect with points (10,10), (20,20):
MyRect: <10, 10, 20, 20>
***
Calling buildRect with 1 point (10,10), width (50) and height (50):
MyRect: <10, 10, 60, 60>
***
```

7

As you can see from this example, all of the buildRect() methods work based on the arguments with which they are called. You can define as many versions of a method as you need to implement the behavior that is needed for that class.

When you have several methods that do similar things, using one method to call another is a shortcut technique to consider. For example, the buildRect() method in lines 17–23 can be replaced with the following, much shorter method:

```
MyRect buildRect(Point topLeft, Point bottomRight) {
    return buildRect(topLeft.x, topLeft.y,
        bottomRight.x, bottomRight.y);
}
```

The return statement in this method calls the buildRect() method in lines 9–15 with four integer arguments. It produces the same results in fewer statements.

Constructor Methods

In addition to regular methods, you also can define constructor methods in your class definition.

NEW TERM   A *constructor method* is method that is called on an object when it is created—in other words, when it is constructed.

Unlike other methods, a constructor cannot be called directly. Instead, Java calls constructor methods automatically.

Java does three things when new is used to create an instance of a class:

- Allocates memory for the object
- Initializes that object's instance variables, either to initial values or to a default (0 for numbers, null for objects, false for Booleans, or '\0' for characters)
- Calls the constructor method of the class, which might be one of several methods

If a class doesn't have any constructor methods defined, an object still is created when the new statement is used in conjunction with the class. However, you might have to set its instance variables or call other methods that the object needs to initialize itself. All examples you have created up to this point have behaved like this.

By defining constructor methods in your own classes, you can set initial values of instance variables, call methods based on those variables, call methods on other objects, and set the initial properties of an object. You also can overload constructor methods, as you can do with regular methods, to create an object that has specific properties based on the arguments you give to new.

Basic Constructors Methods

Constructors look a lot like regular methods, with two basic differences:

- Constructor methods always have the same name as the class.

- Constructor methods don't have a return type.

For example, Listing 7.3 shows a simple class called `Person`. The `Person` class uses a constructor method to initialize its instance variables based on arguments for `new`. The class also includes a method for the object to introduce itself.

TYPE **LISTING 7.3.** THE PERSON CLASS.

```
 1: class Person {
 2:     String name;
 3:     int age;
 4:
 5:     Person(String n, int a) {
 6:         name = n;
 7:         age = a;
 8:     }
 9:
10:     void printPerson() {
11:         System.out.print("Hi, my name is " + name);
12:         System.out.println(". I am " + age + " years old.");
13:     }
14:
15:     public static void main (String arguments[]) {
16:         Person p;
17:         p = new Person("Luke", 50);
18:         p.printPerson();
19:         System.out.println("----");
20:         p = new Person("Laura", 35);
21:         p.printPerson();
22:         System.out.println("----");
23:     }
24: }
```

The following is this program's output:

OUTPUT
```
Hi, my name is Luke. I am 50 years old.
----
Hi, my name is Laura. I am 35 years old.
----
```

7

The person class has three methods: The first is the constructor method, defined in lines 5–8, which initializes the class's two instance variables based on the arguments to the `Person()` constructor. The `Person` class also includes a method called `printPerson()` so that the object can "introduce" itself, and a `main()` method to test each of these things.

Calling Another Constructor Method

Earlier today you saw how one method could do the work of another—one `buildRect()` method called another `buildRect()` method.

You can do the same thing with any type of method, including constructors. If you have a constructor method that duplicates some of the behavior of an existing constructor method, you can call the first constructor from inside the body of the second constructor. Java provides a special syntax for doing this. Use the following to call a constructor method defined in the current class:

```
this(arg1, arg2, arg3);
```

The use of `this` with a constructor method is similar to how `this` can be used to access a current object's variables. In the preceding statement, the arguments with `this()` are the arguments for the constructor method. For example, consider a simple class that defines a circle using the (x,y) coordinate of its center and the length of its radius. The class, `MyCircle`, could have two constructors: one where the radius is defined, and one where the radius is set to a default value of 1. The following code could be used:

```
class MyCircle {
    int x, y, radius;

    MyCircle(int xPoint, int yPoint, int radiusLength) {
        this.x = xPoint;
        this.y = yPoint;
        this.radius = radiusLength;
    }

    MyCircle(int xPoint, int yPoint) {
        this(xPoint, yPoint, 1);
    }
}
```

The second constructor in `MyCircle` takes only the x and y coordinates of the circle's center. Because no radius is defined, the default value of 1 is used. The first constructor is called with `xPoint`, `yPoint`, and the integer literal 1, all as arguments.

Overloading Constructor Methods

Like regular methods, constructor methods also can take varying numbers and types of parameters. This capability enables you to create an object with exactly the properties you want it to have, or lets the object calculate properties from different kinds of input.

For example, the `buildRect()` methods that you defined in the `MyRect` class earlier today would make excellent constructor methods because they are being used to initialize an object's instance variables to the appropriate values. For example, instead of the original `buildRect()` method you had defined (which took four parameters for the coordinates of the corners), you could create a constructor.

Listing 7.4 shows a new class, `MyRect2`, that has the same functionality of the original `MyRect`, except that is uses overloaded constructor methods instead of overloaded `buildRect()` methods. The output shown at the end is the same although the code to produce it has changed.

TYPE   **LISTING 7.4.** THE FULL TEXT OF MYRECT2.JAVA.

```
 1: import java.awt.Point;
 2:
 3: class MyRect2 {
 4:     int x1 = 0;
 5:     int y1 = 0;
 6:     int x2 = 0;
 7:     int y2 = 0;
 8:
 9:     MyRect2(int x1, int y1, int x2, int y2) {
10:         this.x1 = x1;
11:         this.y1 = y1;
12:         this.x2 = x2;
13:         this.y2 = y2;
14:     }
15:
16:     MyRect2(Point topLeft, Point bottomRight) {
17:         x1 = topLeft.x;
18:         y1 = topLeft.y;
19:         x2 = bottomRight.x;
20:         y2 = bottomRight.y;
21:     }
22:
23:     MyRect2(Point topLeft, int w, int h) {
24:         x1 = topLeft.x;
25:         y1 = topLeft.y;
26:         x2 = (x1 + w);
27:         y2 = (y1 + h);
28:     }
29:
30:     void printRect() {
31:         System.out.print("MyRect: <" + x1 + ", " + y1);
32:         System.out.println(", " + x2 + ", " + y2 + ">");
33:     }
34:
35:     public static void main(String arguments[]) {
36:         MyRect2 rect;
```

7

continues

LISTING 7.4. CONTINUED

```
37:
38:            System.out.println("Calling MyRect2 with coordinates 25,25
               50,50:");
39:            rect = new MyRect2(25, 25, 50,50);
40:            rect.printRect();
41:            System.out.println("***");
42:
43:            System.out.println("Calling MyRect2 with points (10,10),
               (20,20):");
44:            rect= new MyRect2(new Point(10,10), new Point(20,20));
45:            rect.printRect();
46:            System.out.println("***");
47:
48:            System.out.print("Calling MyRect2 with 1 point (10,10)");
49:            System.out.println(" width (50) and height (50):");
50:            rect = new MyRect2(new Point(10,10), 50, 50);
51:            rect.printRect();
52:            System.out.println("***");
53:
54:    }
55: }.
```

The program produces the following output:

OUTPUT

```
Calling MyRect2 with coordinates 25,25 50,50:
MyRect: <25, 25, 50, 50>
***
Calling MyRect2 with points (10,10), (20,20):
MyRect: <10, 10, 20, 20>
***
Calling MyRect2 with 1 point (10,10) width (50) and height (50):
MyRect: <10, 10, 60, 60>
***
```

Overriding Methods

When you call an object's method, Java looks for that method definition in the object's class. If it doesn't find one, it passes the method call up the class hierarchy until a method definition is found. Method inheritance enables you to define and use methods repeatedly in subclasses without having to duplicate the code.

However, there might be times when you want an object to respond to the same methods but have different behavior when that method is called. In this case, you can override the method. To override a method, define a method in a subclass with the same signature as a method in a superclass. Then, when the method is called, the subclass method is found and executed instead of the one in the superclass.

Creating Methods That Override Existing Methods

To override a method, all you have to do is create a method in your subclass that has the same signature (name, return type, and argument list) as a method defined by your class' superclass. Because Java executes the first method definition it finds that matches the signature, the new signature hides the original method definition.

Here's a simple example; Listing 7.5 shows a simple class with a method called printMe(), which prints out the name of the class and the values of its instance variables.

TYPE   **LISTING 7.5.** THE FULL TEXT OF PRINTCLASS.JAVA.

```
 1: class PrintClass {
 2:     int x = 0;
 3:     int y = 1;
 4:
 5:     void printMe() {
 6:         System.out.println("x is " + x + ", y is " + y);
 7:         System.out.println("I am an instance of the class " +
 8:         this.getClass().getName());
 9:     }
10: }
```

Listing 7.6 shows a class called PrintSubClass, which is a subclass of PrintClass. The only difference between PrintClass and PrintSubClass is that the latter has a z instance variable.

TYPE   **LISTING 7.6.** THE FULL TEXT OF PRINTSUBCLASS.JAVA.

```
 1: class PrintSubClass extends PrintClass {
 2:     int z = 3;
 3:
 4:     public static void main(String arguments[]) {
 5:         PrintSubClass obj = new PrintSubClass();
 6:         obj.printMe();
 7:     }
 8: }
```

The output of the program is as follows:

OUTPUT
```
x is 0, y is 1
I am an instance of the class PrintSubClass
```

7

A PrintSubClass object was created and the printMe() method was called in the main() method of PrintSubClass. Because the PrintSubClass does not define this method, Java looks for it in the superclasses of PrintSubClass, starting with PrintClass. PrintClass has a printMe() method, so it is executed. Unfortunately, this method does not display the z instance variable, as you can see from the preceding output.

> **Note**
>
> There's an important feature of PrintClass to point out: It doesn't have a main() method. It doesn't need one; it isn't an application. PrintClass is simply a utility class for the PrintSubClass class, which is an application and therefore has a main() method. Only the class that you're actually executing the Java interpreter with needs a main() method.

Now create a third class. PrintSubClass2 is nearly identical to PrintSubClass, but the printMe() method is overridden to include the z variable. Listing 7.7 shows this class.

TYPE **LISTING 7.7.** THE PRINTSUBCLASS2 CLASS.

```
1: class PrintSubClass2 extends PrintClass {
2:     int z = 3;
3:
4:     void printMe() {
5:         System.out.println("x is " + x + ", y is " + y +
6:                 ", z is " + z);
7:         System.out.println("I am an instance of the class " +
8:                 this.getClass().getName());
9:     }
10:
11:     public static void main(String arguments[]) {
12:         PrintSubClass2 obj = new PrintSubClass2();
13:         obj.printMe();
14:     }
15: }
```

Now when a PrintSubClass object is instantiated and the printMe() method is called, the PrintSubClass version of printMe() is called instead of the one in the superclass PrintClass. The following would be the output:

OUTPUT
```
x is 0, y is 1, z is 3
I am an instance of the class PrintSubClass2
```

Calling the Original Method

Usually, there are two reasons why you want to override a method that a superclass already has implemented:

- To replace the definition of that original method completely
- To augment the original method with additional behavior

You already have learned about the first reason—overriding a method and giving the method a new definition hides the original method definition. There are times, however, when behavior should be added to the original definition instead of replacing it completely, particularly when behavior is duplicated in both the original method and the method that overrides it. By calling the original method in the body of the overriding method, you can add only what you need.

Use the `super` keyword to call the original method from inside a method definition. This keyword passes the method call up the hierarchy, as shown in the following:

```
void myMethod (String a, String b) {
    // do stuff here
    super.myMethod(a, b);
    // maybe do more stuff here
}
```

The `super` keyword, somewhat like the `this` keyword, is a placeholder for the class' superclass. You can use it anywhere that you use `this`, but `super` refers to the superclass rather than the current class.

For example, Listing 7.8 shows the two different `printMe()` methods used in the previous example.

TYPE   **LISTING 7.8.** THE `PRINTME()` METHODS.

```
1: // from PrintClass
2:     void printMe() {
3:         System.out.println("x is " + x + ", y is " + y);
4:         System.out.println("I am an instance of the class" +
5:                 this.getClass().getName());
6:     }
7:
8: //from PrintSubClass2
9:     void printMe() {
10:         System.out.println("x is " + x + ", y is " + y + ", z is " +
            z);
11:         System.out.println("I am an instance of the class " +
12:                 this.getClass().getName());
13:     }
```

7

Rather than duplicating most of the behavior of the superclass method in the subclass, you can rearrange the superclass method so that additional behavior can be added easily:

```
// from PrintClass
    void printMe() {
        System.out.println("I am an instance of the class" +
            this.getClass().getName());
        System.out.println("X is " + x);
        System.out.println("Y is " + y);
}
```

Then, when you override the `printMe()` method in the subclass, you can call the original method and just add the extra stuff:

```
// From PrintSubClass
    void printMe() {
        super.printMe();
        System.out.println("Z is " + z);
}
```

The following would be the result of calling `printMe()` on an instance of the subclass:

OUTPUT
```
I am an instance of the class PrintSubClass2
X is 0
Y is 1
Z is 3
```

Overriding Constructors

Technically, constructor methods cannot be overridden. Because they always have the same name as the current class, new constructor methods are created instead of being inherited. This system is fine much of the time; when your class' constructor method is called, the constructor method with the same signature for all your superclasses is also called. Therefore, initialization can happen for all parts of a class that you inherit.

However, when you are defining constructor methods for your own class, you might want to change how your object is initialized, not only by initializing new variables added by your class, but also by changing the contents of variables that already are there. To do this, explicitly call the constructor methods of the superclass and subsequently change whatever variables need to be changed.

To call a regular method in a superclass, you use super.*methodname*(*arguments*). Because constructor methods don't have a method name to call, the following form is used:

```
super(arg1, arg2, ...);
```

Note that Java has a specific rule for the use of super(): It must be the very first state-ment in your constructor definition. If you don't call super() explicitly in your construc-tor, Java does it for you—using super() with no arguments. Because a call to a super() method must be the first statement, you can't do something like the following in your overriding constructor:

```
if (condition == true)
    super(1,2,3); // call one superclass constructor
else
    super(1,2); // call a different constructor
```

Similar to using this(…) in a constructor method, super(…) calls the constructor method for the immediate superclass (which might, in turn, call the constructor of its superclass, and so on). Note that a constructor with that signature has to exist in the superclass in order for the call to super() to work. The Java compiler checks this when you try to compile the source file.

You don't have to call the constructor in your superclass that has the same signature as the constructor in your class; you only have to call the constructor for the values you need initialized. In fact, you can create a class that has constructors with entirely differ-ent signatures from any of the superclass's constructors.

Listing 7.9 shows a class called NamedPoint, which extends the class Point from the java.awt package. The Point class has only one constructor, which takes an x and a y argument and returns a Point object. NamedPoint has an additional instance variable (a string for the name) and defines a constructor to initialize x, y, and the name.

TYPE **LISTING 7.9.** THE NAMEDPOINT CLASS.

```
 1: import java.awt.Point;
 2:
 3: class NamedPoint extends Point {
 4:     String name;
 5:
 6:     NamedPoint(int x, int y, String name) {
 7:         super(x,y);
 8:         this.name = name;
 9:     }
10:
11:     public static void main (String[] arguments) {
12:         NamedPoint np = new NamedPoint(5, 5, "SmallPoint");
13:         System.out.println("x is " + np.x);
14:         System.out.println("y is " + np.y);
15:         System.out.println("Name is " + np.name);
16:     }
17: }.
```

7

The output of the program is as follows:

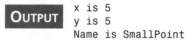

```
x is 5
y is 5
Name is SmallPoint
```

The constructor method defined here for `NamedPoint` calls `Point`'s constructor method to initialize the instance variables of `Point` (x and y). Although you can just as easily initialize x and y yourself, you might not know what other things `Point` is doing to initialize itself. Therefore, it is always is a good idea to pass constructor methods up the hierarchy to make sure everything is set up correctly.

Finalizer Methods

Finalizer methods are almost the opposite of constructor methods. A *constructor method* is used to initialize an object, and *finalizer methods* are called just before the object is collected for garbage and has its memory reclaimed.

The finalizer method is `finalize()`. The `Object` class defines a default finalizer method that does nothing. To create a finalizer method for your own classes, override the `finalize()` method using this signature:

```
protected void finalize() throws Throwable {
    super.finalize();
}
```

Note

The `throws Throwable` part of this method definition refers to the errors that might occur when this method is called. Errors in Java are called *exceptions*; you learn more about them on Day 16, "Exceptional Circumstances: Error Handling." For now, all you need to do is include these keywords in the method definition.

Include any cleaning up that you want to do for that object inside the body of that `finalize()` method. You also can call `super.finalize()` to enable your class' superclasses to finalize the object, if necessary.

You can call the `finalize()` method yourself at any time—it's a method just like any other. However, calling `finalize()` does not trigger an object to be collected in the garbage. Only removing all references to an object causes it to be marked for deletion.

Finalizer methods are used best for optimizing the removal of an object—for example, by removing references to other objects. In most cases, you don't need to use `finalize()` at all.

Summary

Today you learned all kinds of techniques for using, reusing, defining, and redefining methods. You learned about overloaded methods that reuse a method name by giving it different arguments, constructor methods that define the initial variables and other starting conditions of an object, and overriding method inheritance. You finished up with the methods that finish off an object: finalizers.

After being an understudy for a day in Java's style of method acting, you should be ready to step into a starring role with your own programs.

Next week you will be writing more sophisticated Java programs using the techniques of Java 1.0.2 for applets and Java 2 for applications. You will work with graphics, graphical user interfaces, mouse and keyboard events, and windowing. It's a chance to step into the big time.

Break a leg.

Q&A

Q I created two methods with the following signatures:

```
int total(int arg1, int arg2, int arg3) {...}
float total(int arg1, int arg2, int arg3) {...}
```

The Java compiler complains when I try to compile the class with these method definitions, but their signatures are different. What have I done wrong?

A Method overloading in Java works only if the parameter lists are different—either in number or type of arguments. Return type is not relevant for method overloading. Think about it—if you had two methods with exactly the same parameter list, how would Java know which one to call?

Q Can I overload overridden methods? (That is, can I create methods that have the same name as an inherited method, but a different parameter list?)

A Sure—as long as parameter lists vary, it doesn't matter whether you've defined a new method name or one that you've inherited from a superclass.

7

WEEK 2

Developing Web-Based and Graphical Programs

DAY **8**

Putting Interactive Programs on the Web

Java has been the rock star of computer languages since its introduction, receiving the kind of publicity normally reserved for presidential scandals, sugar substitutes, and professional athletes who turn to a life of crime.

The biggest reason for the hype has been applets: Java programs that run on the World Wide Web. The first exposure of most people to Java was when Netscape Navigator began running applets in late 1995.

Although Java can be used today for many things beyond the World Wide Web, a sizable number of programmers are still learning the language to write applets.

Last week you focused on learning about the Java language itself, and all but one of the programs you created were Java applications. This week you move on to applet development.

Today you start with the basics:

- The differences between applets and applications
- How to create a simple applet
- How to put an applet onto a Web page
- How to send information from a Web page to an applet
- How to store an applet in an archive for faster download off a Web page

How Applets and Applications Are Different

The difference between Java applets and applications lies in how they are run.

Applications are run by using a Java interpreter to load the application's main class file. This normally is done from a command-line prompt using the `java` tool from the JDK, as you have done since Day 1, "A Fistful of Java," of this book.

Applets, on the other hand, are run on any browser that supports Java. At the present time this includes current versions of Netscape Navigator, Microsoft Internet Explorer, and Sun's HotJava browser. They also can be tested using the `appletviewer` tool included with the Java Development Kit.

In order for an applet to run, it must be included on a Web page using HTML tags in the same way images and other elements are included. When a user with a Java-capable browser loads a Web page that includes an applet, the browser downloads the applet from a Web server and runs it on the Web user's own system. A separate Java interpreter is not needed—one is built into the browser. Like an application, a Java applet includes a class file and any other helper classes that are needed to run the applet. Java's standard class library is included automatically.

Because Java applets run inside a Java browser, some of the work of creating a user interface already is done for the applet programmer. There's an existing window for the applet to run in, a place to display graphics and receive information, and the browser's interface.

Note

> It is possible for a single Java program to function as both an applet and an application. Although different procedures are used to create these types of programs, they do not conflict with each other. The features specific to applets would be ignored when the program runs as an application, and vice versa.

Applet Security Restrictions

Because Java applets are run on a Web user's system, there are some serious restrictions to what an applet is capable of doing. If these were not in place, a malicious Java programmer could easily write an applet that deletes user files, collects private information from the system, and commits other security breaches.

As a general rule, Java applets run under a "better safe than sorry" security model. An applet cannot do any of the following:

- They cannot read or write files on the user's file system.
- They cannot communicate with an Internet site other than the one that served the Web page that included the applet.
- They cannot run any programs on the reader's system.
- They cannot load programs stored on the user's system, such as executable programs and shared libraries.

All these rules are true for Java applets running under Netscape Navigator or Microsoft Internet Explorer, the browsers favored by most Web users today. Other Java-capable browsers and Java development tools might enable you to configure the level of security you want, permitting some file access to specific folders or network connections to selected Internet sites.

As an example, the `appletviewer` tool enables an access control list to be set for the folders an applet can read or write files to. However, an applet developer can assume that most of the audience will be using a browser that implements the strictest security rules.

Java applications have none of the restrictions in place for applets. They can take full advantage of Java's capabilities.

Caution

Although Java's security model makes it extremely difficult for a malicious applet to do harm to a user's system, it will never be 100 percent secure. Search the Web for "hostile applets" and you'll find discussion of security issues in different versions of Java, and how they have been addressed. You might even find examples of applets that cause problems for people using Java browsers. Java is more secure than other Web programming solutions such as ActiveX, but all browser users should acquaint themselves fully with the issue.

Choosing a Java Version

A Java programmer who writes applets must address this issue: For which Java version should I write?

At the time of this writing, Java 1.02 is the only version of the language supported fully on both the Netscape Navigator and Microsoft Internet Explorer browsers, which comprise more than 90 percent of the applet-using world. Netscape has been slow to support 1.1 fully in version 4.0 of its browser, and Microsoft might never fully support it.

> **Note**
>
> Sun has developed a browser add-on called the Java Plug-in, which enables applet programmers to use Java 1.1 and 2.0 enhancements in their programs. The Java Plug-in is included with both the JDK 1.2, as well as the JRE 1.2. Both of which are available from:
>
> `http://java.sun.com/products`

Because of this split, the most widely used course of action among programmers seems to be the following:

- Applets are written using only Java 1.02 features, because they will run on all Java-capable browsers.
- Applications are written using Java 2, because they can run on any system with a Java 2 interpreter.

Java 2 has been designed so that a program using only Java 1.02 features can compile and run successfully on a Java 1.02 interpreter or 1.02-capable browser.

If an applet uses any feature that was introduced with Java 1.1 or Java 2, the program won't run successfully on a browser that doesn't support those versions of the language. The only test environment that fully supports these versions is the latest `appletviewer` from Sun.

This is a common source of errors for Java applet programmers. If you write a Java 2 applet and run it on a non-supporting browser such as Microsoft Internet Explorer 4.0, you get security errors, class-not-found errors, and other problems that prevent it from running.

In this book, most applet programming is taught using Java 1.02's techniques because that's still the standard for Web programming. Applets are normally smaller programs that do not require many of the enhancements to the language that were introduced in Java 1.1 or 2.

Application programming will use the latest and greatest features of Java 2. Once a way is found for browsers to catch up to the language developers, you will be able to use the Java 2 class libraries in your applets.

Version differences will be noted throughout this book. The Java compiler will occasionally note these differences when you use a Java 1.02 feature that has been replaced with a better solution as of Java 2, and you'll be warned about this as well.

Enhanced Control of Security

The security model described up to this point is the one introduced with Java 1.02. Java's current version includes a way for a Web user to trust an applet, so that applet can run without restriction on the user's system, just as an application can.

Java 2 enables very specific security controls to be put into place or removed from applets and applications. This is covered during Day 16, "Exceptional Circumstances: Error Handling."

Creating Applets

Most of the Java programs you've created up to this point have been Java applications—simple programs with a single `main()` method that is used to create objects, set instance variables, and call other methods.

Applets do not have a `main()` method that automatically is called to begin the program. Instead, there are several methods that are called at different points in the execution of an applet. You learn about these methods today.

All applets are subclasses of the `Applet` class in the `java.applet` package. The `Applet` class provides two kinds of behavior that all applets must have:

- Behavior to work as part of a browser and handle occurrences such as the browser page being reloaded
- Behavior to present a graphical user interface and take input from users

Although an applet can make use of as many other classes as needed, the `Applet` class is the main class that triggers the execution of the applet. The subclass of `Applet` that you create takes the following form:

```
public class YourApplet extends java.applet.Applet {
    // Applet code here
}
```

All applets must be declared `public` because the `Applet` class is a public class. This requirement is true only of your main `Applet` class, and any helper classes can be public or private. More information on this kind of access control is described on Day 15, "Class Roles: Packages, Interfaces, and Other Features."

When a browser's built-in Java interpreter encounters a Java applet on a Web page, that applet's class is loaded along with any other helper classes it uses. The browser automatically creates an instance of the applet's class and calls methods of the `Applet` class when specific events take place.

Different applets that use the same class use different instances, so you could place more than one copy of the same type of applet on a page, and each could behave differently.

Major Applet Activities

Instead of a `main()` method, applets have methods that are called when specific things occur as the applet runs.

An example of these methods is `paint()`, which is called whenever the applet's window needs to be displayed or redisplayed.

By default, these methods do nothing. For example, the `paint()` method that is inherited from `Applet` is an empty method. In order for anything to be displayed on the applet window, the `paint()` method must be overridden with behavior to display text, graphics, and other things.

You learn here about `Applet` class methods that should be overridden as the week progresses. The following sections describe five of the more important methods in an applet's execution: initialization, starting, stopping, destruction, and painting.

Initialization

Initialization occurs when the applet is loaded. *Initialization* might include creating the objects the applet needs, setting up an initial state, loading images or fonts, or setting parameters. To provide behavior for the initialization of an applet, you override the `init()` method as follows:

```
public void init() {
    // Code here
}
```

Starting

An applet is started after it is initialized. *Starting* also can occur if the applet were previously stopped. For example, an applet is stopped if the browser user follows a link to a different page, and it is started again when the user returns to the page containing the applet.

8

Starting can occur several times during an applet's life cycle, but initialization happens only once. To provide startup behavior for your applet, override the start() method as follows:

```
public void start() {
    // Code here
}
```

Functionality that you put in the start() method might include sending the appropriate messages to helper objects or in some way telling the applet to begin running. You learn more about starting applets on Day 10, "Adding Images, Animation, and Sound."

Stopping

Stopping and starting go hand-in-hand. *Stopping* occurs when the user leaves the page that contains a currently running applet, or when an applet stops itself by calling stop() directly. The following shows the form of a stop() method:

```
public void stop() {
    // Code here
}
```

Destruction

Destruction sounds more harsh than it is. The destroy() method enables the applet to clean up after itself just before it is freed from memory or the browser exits. You can use this method to kill any running threads or to release any other running objects. Generally, you won't want to override destroy() unless you have specific resources that need to be released, such as threads that the applet has created. To provide cleanup behavior for your applet, override the destroy() method as follows:

```
public void destroy() {
    // Code here
}
```

 Note

You might be wondering how destroy() is different from finalize(), which was described on Day 7, "Using Methods to Accomplish Tasks." The destroy() method applies only to applets; finalize() is a more general-purpose way for a single object of any type to clean up after itself.

Java has an automatic garbage collector that manages memory for you. The collector reclaims memory from resources after the program is done using them, so you don't normally have to use methods such as destroy().

Painting

Painting is how an applet displays something on-screen, be it text, a line, a colored background, or an image. Painting can occur many hundreds of times during an applet's life cycle: once after the applet is initialized, again if the browser window is brought out from behind another window onscreen, again if the browser window is moved to a different position onscreen, and so on. You must override the paint() method of your Applet subclass in order to display anything. The paint() method looks like the following:

```
public void paint(Graphics g) {
    // Code here
}
```

Note that unlike other methods described in this section, paint() takes an argument: an instance of the class Graphics. This object is created and passed to paint()by the browser, so you don't have to worry about it. However, you always must import the Graphics class (part of the java.awt package) into your applet code, usually through an import statement at the top of your Java source file, as in the following:

```
import java.awt.Graphics;
```

> **Tip**
>
> If you are importing several classes from the same package, such as the Abstract Windowing Toolkit classes, you can use a wildcard character to load all of them at the same time. For example, the statement import java.awt.*; makes every public class in the java.awt package available. The import statement does not include subclasses of the package, however, so the import java.awt.*; statement does not include the classes of the java.awt.image package.

A Simple Applet

On Day 2, "A Taste of Object-Oriented Programming," you created a simple applet called Palindrome that displayed the text "Go hang a salami, I'm a lasagna hog.". You created and used that applet as an example of creating a subclass.

That applet is reviewed here for a different reason: to look at it as an example of applet programming. Listing 8.1 shows the code for that applet.

TYPE **LISTING 8.1.** THE FULL TEXT OF PALINDROME.JAVA.

```
 1: import java.awt.Graphics;
 2: import java.awt.Font;
 3: import java.awt.Color;
 4:
 5: public class Palindrome extends java.applet.Applet {
 6:     Font f = new Font("TimesRoman", Font.BOLD, 36);
 7:
 8:     public void paint(Graphics screen) {
 9:         screen.setFont(f);
10:         screen.setColor(Color.red);
11:         screen.drawString("Go hang a salami, I'm a lasagna hog.", 5,
           40);
12:     }
13: }
```

This applet overrides the paint() method. Because the applet just displays a few words on the screen, there is nothing to initialize. Hence, the start(), stop(), and init() methods are not needed.

The paint() method is where this applet's real work occurs. The Graphics object passed into the paint() method holds the graphics state, which keeps track of the current attributes of the drawing surface. The state includes details on the current font and color to use for any drawing operation, for example.

Lines 9 and 10 set up the font and color for this graphics state. The Font object is held in the f instance variable and an object representing the color red is stored in the Color class variable red.

Line 11 uses the current font and color to draw the string "Go hang a salami, I'm a lasagna hog." at the position 5, 40. Note that the 0 point for x,y is at the top left of the applet's drawing surface, with positive y moving downward, so 40 is at the bottom of the applet. Figure 8.1 shows how the applet's bounding box and the string are drawn on the page.

FIGURE 8.1.

Drawing the applet.

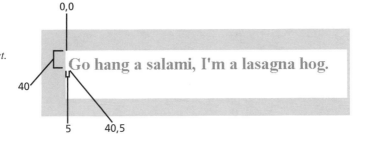

If you implement the right applet methods in your class (init(), start(), stop(), paint(), and so on), your applet just seamlessly works without needing an explicit jumping-off point.

Including an Applet on a Web Page

After you create the class or classes that compose your applet and compile them into class files, you must create a Web page to place the applet on.

Applets are placed on a page using the <APPLET> tag, an HTML programming command that works like other HTML elements. There also are numerous Web-page development tools such as Claris Home Page and Macromedia Dreamweaver that can be used to add applets to a page without using HTML.

The purpose of <APPLET> is to place an applet on a Web page and control how it looks in relation to other parts of the page.

Java-capable browsers use the information contained in the tag to find and execute the applet's compiled class files. In this section you learn how to put Java applets on a Web page and how to serve the executable Java files to the Web at large.

 Note

> The following section assumes that you have at least a passing understanding of writing HTML pages or know how to use a Web development tool to approximate HTML. If you need help in this area, Sams Publishing and this book's coauthors have several offerings, including *Sams Teach Yourself Web Publishing with HTML 4 in 21 Days* by Laura Lemay and *Sams Teach Yourself to Create a Home Page in 24 Hours* by Rogers Cadenhead.

The <APPLET> Tag

The <APPLET> tag is a special extension to HTML for including Java applets in Web pages; the tag is supported by all browsers that handle Java programs. Listing 8.2 shows a simple example of a Web page with an applet included.

TYPE   **LISTING 8.2.** THE FULL TEXT OF PALINDROMEPAGE.HTML.

```
1: <HTML>
2: <HEAD>
3: <TITLE>The Palindrome Page</TITLE>
4: </HEAD>
5: <BODY>
```

```
 6: <P>My favorite meat-related palindrome is:
 7: <BR>
 8: <APPLET CODE="Palindrome.class" WIDTH=600 HEIGHT=100>
 9: A secret if your browser does not support Java!
10: </APPLET>
11: </BODY>
12: </HTML>
```

8

In this example, the <APPLET> tag includes three attributes:

- CODE Specifies the name of the applet's main class file
- WIDTH Specifies the width of the applet window on the Web page
- HEIGHT Specifies the height of the applet window

The class file indicated by the CODE attribute must be in the same folder as the Web page containing the applet, unless you use a CODEBASE attribute to specify a different folder. You learn how to do that later today.

WIDTH and HEIGHT are required attributes, because the Web browser needs to know how much space to devote to the applet on the page. It's easy to draw to an area outside the applet window in a program, so you must be sure to provide a window large enough.

Text, images, and other Web page elements can be included between the <APPLET> and </APPLET> tags. These are only displayed on browsers that cannot handle Java programs, and including them is a good way to let people know they're missing out on a Java applet because their browser doesn't support them. If you don't specify anything between <APPLET> and </APPLET>, browsers that don't support Java display nothing in place of the applet.

In the current example, the text that displays above the applet reads My favorite meat-related palindrome is:. Users who have Java browsers see the Palindrome applet below this text. Users who don't have Java see the alternate text that has been provided—A secret if your browser does not support Java!

Testing the Result

Once you have a main applet class file and an HTML file that uses the applet, you can load the HTML file into a Java-capable browser from your local disk. Using Netscape Navigator, local files can be loaded with the File ¦ Open Page ¦ Choose File command. In Internet Explorer, choose File ¦ Open ¦ Browse to find the right file on your system. The browser loads your Web page and the applet contained on it.

If you don't have a Java-capable browser, there should be a way to load applets included with your development environment. The JDK includes the `appletviewer` tool for testing your applets. Unlike a browser, `appletviewer` only displays the applets that are included on a Web page. It does not display the Web page itself.

Figure 8.2 shows the `PalindromePage.html` page loaded in Netscape Navigator.

FIGURE 8.2.

The
`PalindromePage.html`
Web page in Navigator.

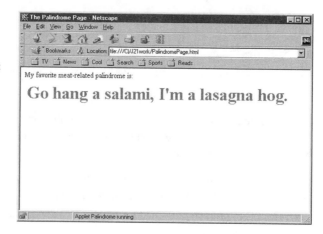

Putting Applets on the Web

After you have an applet that works successfully when you test it locally on your own system, you can make the applet available on the World Wide Web.

Java applets are presented by a Web server in the same way that HTML files, images, and other media are. You store the applet in a folder accessible to the Web server—often the same folder that contains the Web page that features the applet. The Web server should be configured to offer Java applets to browsers that support the language.

There are certain files you need to upload to a Web server:

- The HTML page containing the applet
- All `.class` files used by the applet that aren't part of Java's standard class library

If you know how to publish Web pages, image files, and other multimedia files, you don't have to learn any new skills to publish Java applets on your site.

More About the <APPLET> Tag

8

In its simplest form, the <APPLET> tag uses CODE, WIDTH, and HEIGHT attributes to create a space of the appropriate size, and then loads and runs the applet in that space. However, <APPLET> includes several other attributes that can help you better integrate an applet into a Web page's overall design.

 Note The attributes available for the <APPLET> tag are almost identical to those for the HTML <IMG> tag.

ALIGN

The ALIGN attribute defines how the applet will be aligned on a Web page in relation to other parts of the page. This attribute can have one of nine values:

- ALIGN=LEFT aligns the applet to the left of the text that follows the applet on the page.
- ALIGN=RIGHT aligns the applet to the right of the text that follows the applet on the page.
- ALIGN=TEXTTOP aligns the top of the applet with the top of the tallest text in the line.
- ALIGN=TOP aligns the applet with the topmost item in the line (which can be another applet, an image, or the top of the text).
- ALIGN=ABSMIDDLE aligns the middle of the applet with the middle of the largest item in the line.
- ALIGN=MIDDLE aligns the middle of the applet with the middle of the text's baseline.
- ALIGN=BASELINE aligns the bottom of the applet with the text's baseline. ALIGN=BASELINE is the same as ALIGN=BOTTOM, but ALIGN=BASELINE is a more descriptive name.
- ALIGN=ABSBOTTOM aligns the bottom of the applet with the lowest item in the line (which can be the text's baseline or another applet or image).

To end the formatting that is specified with the ALIGN attribute, you can use the HTML line break tag (<BR>) with the CLEAR attribute. This takes three values:

- <BR CLEAR=LEFT>   Continue displaying the rest of the Web page at the next clear left margin

- `<BR CLEAR=RIGHT>`   Continue displaying at the next clear right margin
- `<BR CLEAR=ALL>`   Continue displaying at the next clear left and right margin

Figure 8.3 shows the various alignment options, in which the smiley face is an applet.

FIGURE 8.3.

Applet alignment options.

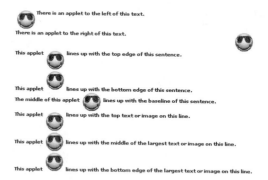

If you are using a Web development tool that enables you to place Java applets on a page, you should be able to set the ALIGN attribute by choosing LEFT, RIGHT, or one of the other values from within the program.

HSPACE and VSPACE

The HSPACE and VSPACE attributes are used to set the amount of space, in pixels, between an applet and its surrounding text. HSPACE controls the horizontal space to the left and right of the applet, and VSPACE controls the vertical space above and below the applet. For example, here's that sample snippet of HTML with vertical space of 50 and horizontal space of 10:

```
<APPLET CODE="ShowSmiley.class" WIDTH=45 HEIGHT=42
ALIGN=LEFT VSPACE=50 HSPACE=10>
Requires Java
</APPLET>
```

Figure 8.4 shows how this applet, which displays a smiley face on a white background, would be displayed with other elements of a Web page. The background of the page is a grid, and each grid is 10×10 pixels in size. You can use the grid to measure the amount of space between the applet and the text on the page.

CODE and CODEBASE

The CODE and CODEBASE attributes, unlike other parts of the <APPLET> tag, are used to indicate where the applet's main class file and other files can be found. They are used by a Java-capable browser when it attempts to run an applet after downloading it from a Web server.

FIGURE 8.4.

Vertical and horizontal space.

CODE indicates the filename of the applet's main class file. If CODE is used without an accompanying CODEBASE attribute, the class file will be loaded from the same place as the Web page containing the applet.

You must specify the .class file extension with the CODE attribute. The following is an example of an <APPLET> tag that loads an applet called Bix.class from the same folder as the Web page:

```
<APPLET CODE="Bix.class" HEIGHT=40 WIDTH=400>
</APPLET>
```

The CODEBASE attribute is used to cause the browser to look in a different folder for the applet and any other files it uses. CODEBASE indicates an alternate folder, or even an alternate World Wide Web site, to load the class and other files from. The following loads a class called Bix.class from a folder called Torshire:

```
<APPLET CODE="Bix.class" CODEBASE="Torshire" HEIGHT=40 WIDTH=400>
</APPLET>
```

Here's an example where the Java class files are loaded from an entirely different Web site than the one containing the page:

```
<APPLET CODE="Bix.class" CODEBASE="http://www.torshire.com/javaclasses"
HEIGHT=40 WIDTH=400>
</APPLET>
```

The <OBJECT> Tag

The <APPLET> tag is an HTML extension introduced specifically to present Java programs on Web pages. Today there are other types of programs that can run interactively on a page, including ActiveX controls, NetRexx applets, and Python programs. In order to deal with all of these program types without requiring a different tag for each, the <OBJECT> tag has been added to the HTML specification.

The <OBJECT> tag is used for all objects—interactive programs and other external elements—that can be presented as part of a Web page. It is supported by versions 4.0 and higher of Netscape Navigator and Microsoft Internet Explorer. Older browsers do not support this new tag, so you may still be using <APPLET> in many cases.

The <OBJECT> tag takes the following form:

```
<OBJECT CLASSID="java:Bix.class" CODEBASE="javaclasses" HEIGHT=40
WIDTH=400">
</OBJECT>
```

Switching from <APPLET> to <OBJECT> requires the following changes:

- The <OBJECT> tag should be used in place of <APPLET>.
- The CODE attribute should be replaced by CLASSID. In addition, the text "java:" should be placed before the name of the applet's class file. For example, if the applet is in GameApplet.class, the CLASSID attribute should be java:GameApplet.class.

Otherwise, attributes remain the same, including CODEBASE, HEIGHT, WIDTH, ALIGN. The <OBJECT> tag also can use optional <PARAM> tags, which are described later today.

Listing 8.3 contains a Web page that loads the Palindrome applet using the <OBJECT> tag. Everything else is the same as the previous example in Listing 8.2.

TYPE   **LISTING 8.3.** THE FULL TEXT OF PALINDROMEPAGE2.HTML.

```
 1:  <HTML>
 2:  <HEAD>
 3:  <TITLE>The Palindrome Page</TITLE>
 4:  </HEAD>
 5:  <BODY>
 6:  <P>My favorite meat-related palindrome is:
 7:  <BR>
 8:  <OBJECT CLASSID="java:Palindrome.class" WIDTH=600 HEIGHT=100>
 9:  A secret if your browser does not support Java!
10:  </OBJECT>
11:  </BODY>
12:  </HTML>
```

Java Archives

The standard way of placing a Java applet on a Web page is to use <APPLET> or <OBJECT> to indicate the primary class file of the applet. A Java-enabled browser then downloads and runs the applet. Any other classes and any other files needed by the applet are downloaded from the Web server.

The problem with running applets in this way is that every single file an applet needs—be it another helper class, image, audio file, text file, or anything else—requires a separate connection from a Web browser to the server containing the file. Because a fair amount of time is needed just to make the connection itself, this can increase the amount of time it takes to download an applet and everything it needs to run.

The solution to this problem is a Java archive, or JAR file. A *Java archive* is a collection of Java classes and other files packaged into a single file. By using a Java archive, the browser makes only one connection to the server rather than several. By reducing the number of files the browser has to load from the server, you can download and run your applet more quickly. Java archives also can be compressed, making the overall file size smaller and therefore faster to download—although it will take some time on the browser side for the files to be decompressed before they can run.

Versions 4.0 and higher of the Navigator and Internet Explorer browsers include support for JAR files. To create these archives, the JDK includes a tool called jar that can pack files into Java archives and unpack them. JAR files can be compressed using the Zip format or packed without using compression. The following command packs all of a folder's class and GIF image files into a single Java archive called Animate.jar:

```
jar cf Animate.jar *.class *.gif
```

The argument cf specifies two command-line options that can be used when running the jar program. The c option indicates that a Java archive file should be created, and f indicates that the name of the archive file will follow as one of the next arguments.

You also can add specific files to a Java archive with a command such as the following:

```
jar cf Smiley.jar ShowSmiley.class ShowSmiley.html spinhead.gif
```

This creates a Smiley.jar archive containing three files: ShowSmiley.class, ShowSmiley.html, and spinhead.gif.

Run jar without any arguments to see a list of options that can be used with the program.

After you create a Java archive, the ARCHIVE attribute is used with the <APPLET> tag to show where the archive can be found. You can use Java archives with an applet with tags such as the following:

```
<applet code="ShowSmiley.class" archive="Smiley.jar" width=45 height=42>
</applet>
```

This tag specifies that an archive called Smiley.jar contains files used by the applet. Browsers and browsing tools that support JAR files will look inside the archive for files that are needed as the applet runs.

Caution Although a Java archive can contain class files, the ARCHIVE attribute does not remove the need for the CODE attribute. A browser still needs to know the name of the applet's main class file in order to load it.

Other Archival Formats

Before Java's developers introduced the JAR file format, both Netscape and Microsoft offered their own archival solutions. They do not offer some of the advantages of Java archives, but they have the benefit of working with Java-enabled browsers that do not yet support versions of Java beyond 1.02.

Current versions of Netscape's Web browsers support the use of Zip archives with the ARCHIVE attribute, but they can be used only for class files, not images or other types of files that an applet might need. Within Netscape, you can use the ARCHIVE attribute to indicate the name of the archive, like this:

```
<APPLET CODE="MyApplet.class" ARCHIVE="appletstuff.zip" WIDTH=100
HEIGHT=100>
</APPLET>
```

The archive itself is an uncompressed Zip file. Standard Zip files, which use some form of compression to make the file smaller, are not recognized. Also, helper classes may be contained inside or outside the Zip file; Netscape browsers will look in both places. The ARCHIVE attribute is ignored by browsers or applet viewers that may run across this Web page.

Microsoft Internet Explorer recognizes a third type of archive format for the delivery of Java applets: the CAB file. CAB is short for cabinet, and it's a way to group files together and compress them for faster delivery over the Web.

Cabinet archives are created with a tool from Microsoft called CABarc. It currently is available for free download as part of the Cabinet Software Development kit from the following address:

```
http://www.microsoft.com/workshop/management/prog/cab/cabdl.asp
```

Using CABarc, you can compress all class files and other files needed by an applet into a single archive, which has the .cab file extension. To specify this archive, a parameter called cabbase is used with the <PARAM> tag in HTML, and the value of cabbase is set to the name of the .cab file. The following is an example:

```
<APPLET CODE="DanceFever.class" WIDTH=200 HEIGHT=450>
<PARAM NAME="cabbase" VALUE="DanceFever.cab">
</APPLET>
```

Like the ARCHIVE attribute, the cabbase parameter will be ignored by Web browsers that do not support its use.

Netscape and Microsoft's Java archival features work on the current editions of these companies' Web browsers and are not guaranteed to be supported on other browsers. If you use either solution, you ought to store both the archive and the individual files that comprise the archive on your Web server. This way, everyone with a Java-enabled browser will be able to use the applet.

Passing Parameters to Applets

With Java applications, you can pass parameters to the main() method by using arguments on the command line. You then can parse those arguments inside the body of your class, and the application acts accordingly based on the arguments it is given.

Applets, however, don't have a command line. Applets can get different input from the HTML file that contains the <APPLET> or <OBJECT> tag through the use of applet parameters. To set up and handle parameters in an applet, you need two things:

- A special parameter tag in the HTML file
- Code in your applet to parse those parameters

Applet parameters come in two parts: a name, which is simply a name you pick, and a value, which determines the value of that particular parameter. For example, you can indicate the color of text in an applet by using a parameter with the name color and the value red. You can determine an animation's speed using a parameter with the name speed and the value 5.

In the HTML file that contains the embedded applet, you indicate each parameter using the <PARAM> tag, which has two attributes for the name and the value called (surprisingly enough) NAME and VALUE. The <PARAM> tag goes inside the opening and closing <APPLET> tags, as in the following:

```
<APPLET CODE="QueenMab.class" WIDTH=100 HEIGHT=100>
<PARAM NAME=font VALUE="TimesRoman">
<PARAM NAME=size VALUE="24">
A Java applet appears here.
</APPLET>
```

This particular example defines two parameters to the QueenMab applet: one named font with a value of TimesRoman, and one named size with a value of 24.

The usage of the <PARAM> tag is the same for applets that use the <OBJECT> tag instead of <APPLET>.

Parameters are passed to your applet when it is loaded. In the `init()` method for your applet, you can retrieve these parameters by using the `getParameter()` method. The `getParameter()` method takes one argument, a string representing the name of the parameter you're looking for, and returns a string containing the corresponding value of that parameter. (Like arguments in Java applications, all parameter values are returned as strings.) To get the value of the `font` parameter from the HTML file, you might have a line such as the following in your `init()` method:

```
String theFontName = getParameter("font");
```

Note
The names of the parameters as specified in <PARAM> and the names of the parameters in getParameter() must match identically, including the same case. In other words, <PARAM NAME="eecummings"> is different from <PARAM NAME="EECummings">. If your parameters are not being properly passed to your applet, make sure the parameter cases match.

Note that if a parameter you expect has not been specified in the HTML file, `getParameter()` returns `null`. Most often, you will want to test for a `null` parameter and supply a reasonable default, as shown:

```
if (theFontName == null)
    theFontName = "Courier";
```

Keep in mind that `getParameter()` returns strings; if you want a parameter to be some other object or type, you have to convert it yourself. For example, consider the HTML file for the QueenMab applet. To parse the `size` parameter and assign it to an integer variable called `theSize`, you might use the following lines:

```
int theSize;
String s = getParameter("size");
if (s == null)
    theSize = 12;
else theSize = Integer.parseInt(s);
```

Create an example of an applet that uses this technique. You modify the Palindrome applet so that it displays a specific name, for example, `Dennis and Edna sinned` or `No, sir, prefer prison`. The name is passed into the applet through an HTML parameter. The project will be called NewPalindrome.

Start by copying the original `Palindrome` class, with a change to reflect the new class name, as shown in Listing 8.4.

TYPE **LISTING 8.4.** THE STARTING TEXT FOR NEWPALINDROME.JAVA.

```
 1: import java.awt.Graphics;
 2: import java.awt.Font;
 3: import java.awt.Color;
 4:
 5: public class NewPalindrome extends java.applet.Applet {
 6:     Font f = new Font("TimesRoman", Font.BOLD, 36);
 7:
 8:     public void paint(Graphics screen) {
 9:         screen.setFont(f);
10:         screen.setColor(Color.red);
11:         screen.drawString("Go hang a salami, I'm a lasagna hog.", 5,
            40);
12:     }
13: }
```

The first thing you need to add to this class is a place for the `palindrome` parameter to be stored in. Because you'll need that name throughout the applet, you add an instance variable for the name right after the variable for the font:

```
String palindrome;
```

To set a value for the name, you have to get the parameter. The best place to handle an applet's parameters is inside an `init()` method. The `init()` method is defined similarly to `paint()` (public, with no arguments, and a return type of `void`). Make sure when you test for a parameter that you test for a value of `null`. If a palindrome isn't indicated, the default, in this case, is to display `Dennis and Edna sinned`, as the following illustrates:

```
public void init() {
    palindrome = getParameter("palindrome");
        if (palindrome == null)
        palindrome = "Dennis and Edna sinned";
    }
```

Once this method has been added, all that's left is to modify the `paint()` method. The original `drawString()` method looked like this:

```
screen.drawString("Go hang a salami, I'm a lasagna hog.", 5, 50);
```

To draw the new string you have stored in the `name` instance variable, all you need to do is substitute that variable for the literal string:

```
screen.drawString(palindrome, 5, 50);
```

Listing 8.5 shows the final result of the `NewPalindrome` class. Compile it so that you have a class file ready.

TYPE **LISTING 8.5.** THE FULL TEXT OF NEWPALINDROME.JAVA.

```java
 1: import java.awt.Graphics;
 2: import java.awt.Font;
 3: import java.awt.Color;
 4:
 5: public class NewPalindrome extends java.applet.Applet {
 6:     Font f = new Font("TimesRoman", Font.BOLD, 36);
 7:     String palindrome;
 8:
 9:     public void paint(Graphics screen) {
10:         screen.setFont(f);
11:         screen.setColor(Color.red);
12:         screen.drawString(palindrome, 5, 50);
13:     }
14:
15:     public void init() {
16:         palindrome = getParameter("palindrome");
17:         if (palindrome == null)
18:             palindrome = "Dennis and Edna sinned";
19:     }
20: }
```

Now create the HTML file that contains this applet. Listing 8.6 shows a new Web page for the NewPalindrome applet.

TYPE **LISTING 8.6.** THE FULL TEXT OF NEWPALINDROME.HTML.

```html
 1: <HTML>
 2: <HEAD>
 3: <TITLE>The New Palindrome Page</TITLE>
 4: </HEAD>
 5: <BODY>
 6: <P>
 7: <APPLET CODE="NewPalindrome.class" WIDTH=600 HEIGHT=100>
 8: <PARAM NAME=palindrome VALUE="No, sir, prefer prison">
 9: Your browser does not support Java!
10: </APPLET>
11: </BODY>
12: </HTML>
```

Note the <APPLET> tag, which designates the class file for the applet and the appropriate width and height (600 and 100, respectively). Just below it (line 8) is the <PARAM> tag, which is used to pass the palindrome to the applet. In this example, the NAME parameter is palindrome, and the VALUE is the string No, sir, prefer prison.

Loading this HTML file in Netscape Navigator produces the result shown in Figure 8.5.

FIGURE 8.5.

The
NewPalindrome.html
page loaded with
Netscape Navigator.

If no palindrome is specified in the code for NewPalindrome, the default is Dennis and Edna sinned. Listing 8.7 creates an HTML file with no parameter tag for NAME.

TYPE **LISTING 8.7.** THE FULL TEXT OF NEWPALINDROME2.HTML.

```
 1: <HTML>
 2: <HEAD>
 3: <TITLE>The New Palindrome Page</TITLE>
 4: </HEAD>
 5: <BODY>
 6: <P>
 7: <APPLET CODE="NewPalindrome.class" WIDTH=600 HEIGHT=100>
 8: Your browser does not support Java!
 9: </APPLET>
10: </BODY>
```

Because no name was supplied here, the applet uses the default, and the result is what you might expect. Take a look at Figure 8.6.

FIGURE 8.6.

The
NewPalindrome2.html
page loaded with
Netscape Navigator.

Applet Effects

NEW TERM If you are an active Web surfer, you probably have seen Java applets that display messages along the *status line*—the part of a Web browser that indicates what a hyperlink is connected to, among other information. This section teaches you how to achieve this and how to provide information about the applet for the browser.

The showStatus() Method

The Applet class's showStatus() method enables you to display a string in the status bar of the browser running the applet. You can use this to display error messages, hyperlinks, help, and other status messages.

This method can be called with a statement such as the following:

```
getAppletContext().showStatus("Click applet window to begin");
```

The getAppletContext() method enables your applet to access features of the browser that contains it. showStatus() uses this mechanism to display status messages.

Applet Information

The Abstract Windowing Toolkit provides a mechanism for associating information with your applet such as the author, copyright date, and other relevant details. A Web browser may include a mechanism to display this information if the applet developer has provided it.

To provide information about your applet, override the getAppletInfo() method in the following method:

```
public String getAppletInfo() {
    return "GetRaven Copyright 1998 Laura Lemay";
}
```

Summary

It is arguable whether applets remain the focus of today's Java development, more than two years after the language was first released to the public.

However, applets remain the biggest public use of Java, because applets are featured on thousands of World Wide Web sites. According to the AltaVista search engine at http://www.altavista.digital.com, there are more than 1,200,000 Web pages containing applets.

Because they are executed and displayed within Web pages, applets can use the graphics, user interface, and event structure provided by the Web browser. This capability provides the applet programmer with a lot of functionality without a lot of extra toil.

Today you learned the basics of applet creation, including the following things:

- All applets are subclasses of the `java.applet.Applet` class, which provides the behavior the program needs to run within a Web browser.

- Applets have five main methods that cover activities an applet performs as it runs: `init()`, `start()`, `stop()`, `destroy()`, and `paint()`. These methods are overridden to provide functionality in an applet.

- Applets are placed on Web pages using the `<APPLET>` tag in HTML or a Web development tool that can handle applets. When a Java-capable browser loads a page containing an applet, it loads the class file described with the `<APPLET>` tag.

- To speed the time it takes to download an applet from a Web server, you can use Java archive files, Netscape's `ARCHIVE` attribute, and Microsoft's `cabbase` parameter.

- Applets can receive information from a Web page by using the `<PARAM>` tag in association with an applet. Inside the body of your applet, you can gain access to those parameters using the `getParameter()` method.

Q&A

Q **I have an applet that takes parameters and an HTML file that passes it those parameters, but when my applet runs, all I get are `null` values. What's going on here?**

A Do the names of your parameters (in the `NAME` attribute) match exactly with the names you're testing for in `getParameter()`? They must be exact, including case, for the match to be made. Make sure also that your `<PARAM>` tags are inside the opening and closing `<APPLET>` tags and that you haven't misspelled anything.

Q **Is any special configuration required so that my Web server software can present Java applets on Web pages?**

A Very little is required on the server side to offer Java applets along with HTML documents, image files, and other files. Many of the commercially available server packages offer out-of-the-box support for Java. If they don't, configuring the server to present Java applets requires that the `.class` file extension be associated with the MIME type `application/octet-stream`. Consult your server's documentation for more information regarding MIME types.

Q **Because applets don't have a command line or a standard output stream, how can I do simple debugging output like `System.out.println()` in an applet?**

A Depending on your browser or other Java-enabled environment, you may have a console window where debugging output (the result of `System.out.println()`) appears, or it may be saved to a log file. (Netscape has a Java Console under the Options menu; Internet Explorer uses a Java log file that you must enable by choosing Options I Advanced.)

You can continue to print messages using `System.out.println()` in your applets—just remember to remove them after you're done, so that they don't confuse your actual users.

WEEK 2

DAY 9

Making Programs Look Good with Graphics, Fonts, and Color

One of the best ways to impress a non-programming acquaintance is with a program that features graphics. Uncle Wade might not appreciate the nuances of a well-constructed `for` loop or an elegant class hierarchy, but show him your animated sequence of a toddler dancing the Funky Chicken, and he'll be impressed with your programming acumen.

Today you start learning how to win friends and influence people by writing applets that use graphics, fonts, and color.

To use graphical features in your programs, you utilize classes of the `java.awt` package, which delivers most of Java's visual pizzazz. With these classes you'll draw text and shapes like circles and polygons in an applet. You learn how to use different fonts and colors for the shapes you draw.

You also start using the improved drawing features in Java2D, a set of classes introduced with Java 1.2 that offers some eye-catching features:

- Anti-aliased objects
- Gradient fill patterns
- Drawing lines of different widths

The Graphics Class

One way to think of an applet is as a canvas for graphical operations. You already have used the drawString() method to draw text onto an applet. The text's font and color were chosen prior to drawing the characters, the same way an artist would choose a color and a brush before painting.

Text isn't the only thing you can draw onto an applet window. You can draw lines, ovals, circles, arcs, rectangles, and other polygons.

Most of the basic drawing operations are methods defined in the Graphics class. In an applet, you don't have to create a Graphics object in order to draw something—as you might recall, one of the paint() method's parameters is a Graphics object. This object represents the Applet window and its methods are used to draw onto the applet.

The Graphics class is part of the java.awt package, so all applets that draw something must use the import statement to make Graphics available in the program.

Listing 9.1 is a simple applet that uses the drawString() method to display text, as you have done previously with the Palindrome applet.

TYPE   **LISTING 9.1.** THE STARTING TEXT OF MAP.JAVA.

```
1: import java.awt.Graphics;
2:
3: public class Map extends java.applet.Applet {
4:     public void paint(Graphics screen) {
5:         screen.drawString("Florida", 185, 75);
6:     }
7: }
```

This applet uses the screen object's drawString() method to draw the string "Florida" at the coordinates 185,75. Listing 9.2 shows the HTML that displays this applet after it has been compiled into a class file.

TYPE   **LISTING 9.2.** THE FULL TEXT OF MAP.HTML.

```
1: <body bgcolor="#c4c4c4">
2: <div align="center">
3: <applet code="Map.class" height=350 width=350>
4: </applet>
5: </div>
6: </body>
```

Figure 9.1 shows the page and applet loaded on Netscape Navigator.

FIGURE 9.1.

Drawing text onto an Applet window.

All of the basic drawing commands you learn about today will be Graphics methods that are called within an applet's paint() method. This is an ideal place for all drawing operations because paint() automatically is called anytime the Applet window needs to be redisplayed. If another program's window overlaps the applet and it needs to be redrawn, putting all of the drawing operations in paint() makes sure that no part of the drawing is left out.

Continue to add to the Map applet with each of the drawing methods covered in this section.

The Graphics Coordinate System

Like `drawString()`, all of the drawing methods have arguments that indicate x,y coordinates. Some take more than one set of coordinates, such as a line, which has an x,y coordinate to identify its starting point and another x,y coordinate for its endpoint.

Java's coordinate system uses pixels as its unit of measure. The origin coordinate 0,0 is in the upper-left corner of the Applet window. The value of x coordinates increases to the right of 0,0, and y coordinates increase in a downward direction. This differs from other drawing systems in which the 0,0 origin is at the lower left and y values increase in an upward direction.

All pixel values are integers—you can't use decimal numbers to display something between integer values.

Figure 9.2 depicts Java's graphical coordinate system visually with the origin at 0,0. Two of the points of a rectangle are at 20,20 and 60,60.

FIGURE 9.2.

The Java graphics coordinate system.

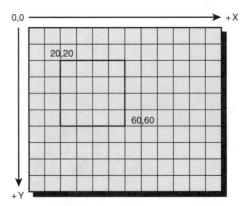

Drawing and Filling

There are two kinds of drawing methods available for many of the shapes you can draw onto an applet: draw methods, which draw an outline of the object, and fill methods, which fill in the object with the current color. In each type of method, the outline of the object also is drawn with the current color.

 Note

> You can also draw bitmap graphics files, such as GIF and JPG files, by using the `Image` class. You learn about this tomorrow.

Lines

The `drawLine()` method is used to draw a line between two points. The method takes four arguments: the x and y coordinates of the starting point and the x and y coordinates of the ending point, as follows:

```
drawLine(x1, y1, x2, y2);
```

This method draws a line from the point (x1, y1) to the point (x2, y2). The width of the line is fixed at 1 pixel.

Add the following statement to the Map applet's `paint()` method:

```
screen.drawLine(185,80,222,80);
```

This draws a line from 185,80 to 222,80—an underline under the text `Florida`, as you can see in Figure 9.3, a portion of the Applet window.

FIGURE 9.3.

Adding a line to the applet.

Florida

Note

To prevent whiplash that may result from repeatedly bouncing between this text and your Java source code editor, the final version of `Map.java` is listed in full at the end of this section. Until then, you can follow along with the text and enter the full Java code at one time.

Rectangles

There are `Graphics` methods for two kinds of rectangles: normal rectangles and those with rounded corners (like the edges of keys on most computer keyboards).

You can draw both types of rectangles in outline form or filled with the current color.

To draw a normal rectangle, use the `drawRect()` method for outlines and the `fillRect()` method for filled shapes.

Both of these methods take four arguments:

- The x and y coordinates of the rectangle's top-left corner
- The width of the rectangle
- The height of the rectangle

Add the following statement to the Map applet:

```
screen.drawRect(2, 2, 345, 345);
```

This adds a rectangle outline just inside the outer edges of the Applet window. If the `fillRect()` method had been used instead, a solid rectangle would have filled most of the applet area and overwritten the underlined text `Florida`.

Rectangles with rounded corners require the `drawRoundRect()` and `fillRoundRect()` methods. They take the same first four arguments that regular rectangles take, with two arguments added at the end.

These last two arguments define the width and height of the area where corners are rounded. The bigger the area, the more round the corners. You can even make a rectangle look like a circle or an oval by making these arguments large enough.

Figure 9.4 shows several examples of rectangles with rounded corners. One rectangle has a width of 30 and a height of 10 for each rounded corner. Another has a width of 20 and a height of 20, and it looks more like a circle than a rectangle.

FIGURE 9.4.

Rectangles with round-ed corners.

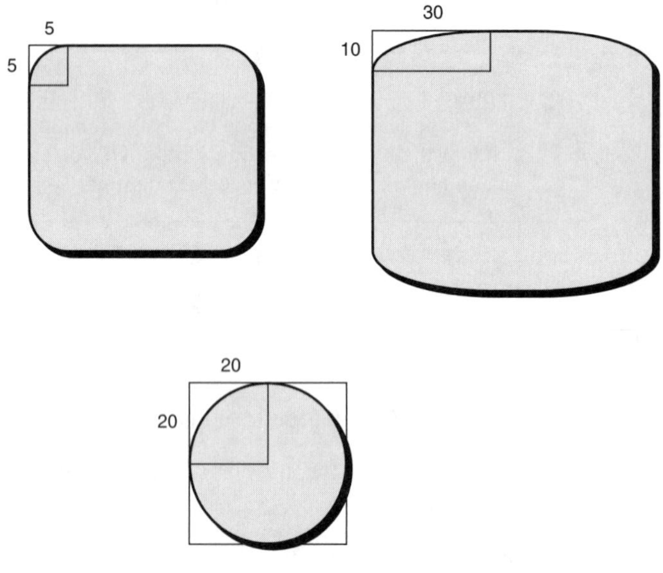

Add the following statement to the Map applet's `paint()` method:

```
screen.drawRoundRect(182,61,43,24,10,8);
```

This draws a rounded rectangle at the coordinates 182,61 with a width of 43 pixels and a height of 24. The rectangular area of each rounded corner is 10 pixels wide and 8 tall. The result is shown in Figure 9.5, a close-up of a portion of the applet.

9

FIGURE 9.5.

Adding a rounded rectangle to the applet.Polygons

Polygons can be drawn with the `drawPolygon()` and `fillPolygon()` methods.

To draw a polygon, you need x,y coordinates for each point on the polygon. Polygons can be thought of as a series of lines that are connected to each other—one line is drawn from starting point to end point, that end point is used to start a new line, and so on.

You can specify these coordinates two ways:

- As a pair of integer arrays, one holding all the x coordinates and one holding all the y coordinates
- As a `Polygon` object that is created using an integer array of x coordinates and an integer array of y coordinates

The second method is more flexible because it enables points to be added individually to a polygon before it is drawn.

In addition to the x and y coordinates, you must specify the number of points in the polygon. You cannot specify more x,y coordinates than you have points, or more points than you have x,y coordinates set up for. A compiler error will result in either case.

To create a `Polygon` object, the first step is to create an empty polygon with a new `Polygon()` statement such as the following:

```
Polygon poly = new Polygon();
```

As an alternative, you can create a polygon from a set of points using integer arrays. This requires a call to the `Polygon(int[], int[], int)` constructor, which specifies the array of x points, array of y points, and the number of points. The following example shows the use of this constructor:

```
int x[] = { 10, 20, 30, 40, 50 };
int y[] = { 15, 25, 35, 45, 55 };
int points = x.length;
Polygon poly = new Polygon(x, y, points);
```

After a `Polygon` object has been created, you can add points to it using the object's `addPoint()` method. This takes x,y coordinates as arguments and adds the point to the polygon. The following is an example:

```
poly.addPoint(60, 65);
```

When you have a `Polygon` object that has all the points it needs you can draw it with the `drawPolygon()` or `fillPolygon()` methods. These take only one argument—the `Polygon` object, as shown here:

```
screen.drawPolygon(poly);
```

If you use `drawPolygon()` under Java 1.02, you can close off the polygon by making its last x,y coordinate the same as its first. Otherwise, the polygon will be open on one side.

The `fillPolygon()` method automatically closes off the polygon without requiring matching points.

Caution

> The behavior of `drawPolygon()` changed after version 1.02 of Java. With versions 1.1 and 2.0, `drawPolygon()` automatically closes off a polygon the same way `fillPolygon()` does. If you want to create an open-edged polygon with those versions of the language, you can use the `drawPolyline()` method. It works just like `drawPolygon()` worked under Java 1.02.

Add the following statements to the `paint()` method of the Map applet to see polygons in action:

```
int x[] = { 10, 234, 253, 261, 344, 336, 295, 259, 205, 211,
    195, 191, 120, 94, 81, 12, 10 };
int y[] = { 12, 15, 25, 71, 209, 278, 310, 274, 188, 171, 174,
    118, 56, 68, 49, 37, 12 };
int pts = x.length;
Polygon poly = new Polygon(x, y, pts);
screen.drawPolygon(poly);
```

The `Polygon` class is part of the `java.awt` package, so you must make it available by adding the following statement at the top of the Map applet:

```
import java.awt.Polygon;
```

Figure 9.6 shows what the Map applet looks like with the polygon added to everything else already being drawn.

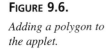

FIGURE 9.6.

Adding a polygon to the applet.

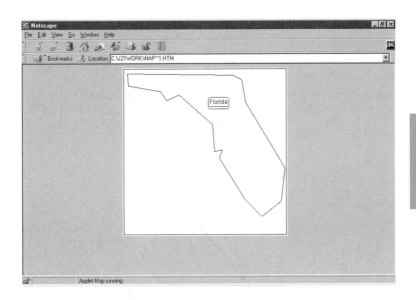

9

Ovals

The `drawOval()` and `fillOval()` methods are used to draw circles and ovals.

These methods take four arguments:

- the oval's x,y coordinates
- the oval's width and height, which are the same size on circles

Because an oval doesn't have any corners, you might be wondering what the x,y coordinate refers to. Ovals are handled in the same fashion as the corners of rounded rectangles. The x,y coordinate is at the upper-left corner of the area in which the oval is drawn, and will be to the left and above the actual oval itself.

Return to the Map applet and add the following statements:

```
screen.fillOval(235,140,15,15);
screen.fillOval(225,130,15,15);
screen.fillOval(245,130,15,15);
```

These are `fill` methods rather than `draw` methods, so they create three black circles connected together at a spot in central Florida, as shown in Figure 9.7.

FIGURE 9.7.

Adding a trio of circles to the applet.

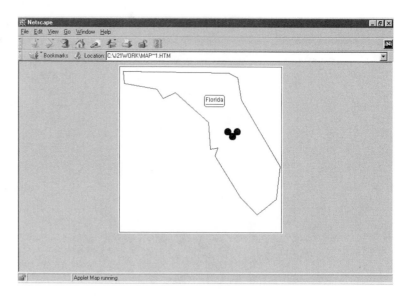

Arcs

Of all the drawing operations, arcs are the most complex to construct. An arc is part of an oval, and is implemented in Java as an oval that is partially drawn.

Arcs are drawn with the drawArc() and fillArc() methods, which take six arguments:

- the oval's x,y coordinates
- the oval's width and height
- the angle at which to start the arc
- the number of degrees traveled by the arc

The first four arguments are the same as those for an oval and function in the same manner.

The arc's starting angle ranges from 0 to 359 degrees in a counterclockwise direction. On a circular oval, 0 degrees is the same as 3 o'clock, 90 degrees is 12 o'clock, 180 degrees is 9 o'clock, and 270 degrees is 6 o'clock.

The number of degrees traveled by an arc ranges from 0 to 359 degrees in a counterclockwise direction, and 0 to –359 degrees in a clockwise direction.

Figure 9.8 shows how the last two arguments are calculated.

FIGURE 9.8.

Measuring an arc.

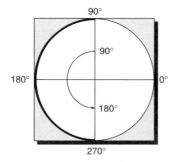

Filled arcs are drawn as if they were sections of a pie; instead of joining the two end-points, both endpoints are joined to the center of the arc's oval.

The following is an example of a `drawArc()` method call:

```
screen.drawArc(20,25,315,150,5,-190);
```

This statement draws an arc of an oval with the coordinates 20,25, a width of 315 pixels, and a height of 150 pixels. The arc begins at the 5-degree mark and travels 190 degrees in a clockwise direction. The arc is shown in Figure 9.9.

FIGURE 9.9.

An arc.

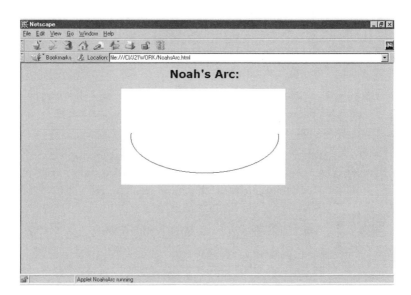

As a last wrinkle for the Map applet, a bunch of little arcs with four arguments that do not change will be drawn:

- Each arc's oval will have a width and height of 10 pixels, making the ovals circular.
- Each arc will begin at 0 degrees and head clockwise for 180 degrees, making them half circles.

The arc's x,y coordinates will change, and two for loops will cycle through a range of x and y values.

Add the following statements to the Map applet's paint() method:

```
for (int ax = 50; ax < 150; ax += 10)
    for (int ay = 120; ay < 320 ; ay += 10)
        screen.drawArc(ax, ay, 10, 10, 0, -180);
```

Putting one for loop inside another might appear confusing. Here are the first six x,y coordinates that are created by the loop:

50,120

50,130

50,140

50,150

50,160

50,170

As you can see, the x coordinate—specified by ax—does not change. It won't change until the entire ay loop has run its course. When that happens, ax increases by 10 and the ay loop runs again in full.

Compile the Map applet to see what effect these loops produce by drawing a bunch of small half circles. Listing 9.3 shows the full, final source code for Map.java, including all of the drawing statements that have been covered during this section.

TYPE   **LISTING 9.3.** THE FULL, FINAL TEXT OF MAP.JAVA.

```
1: import java.awt.Graphics;
2: import java.awt.Polygon;
3:
4: public class Map extends java.applet.Applet {
5:     public void paint(Graphics screen) {
6:         screen.drawString("Florida", 185, 75);
7:         screen.drawLine(185,80,222,80);
8:         screen.drawRect(2, 2, 345, 345);
```

```
 9:          screen.drawRoundRect(182,61,43,24,10,8);
10:          int x[] = { 10, 234, 253, 261, 344, 336, 295, 259, 205, 211,
11:              195, 191, 120, 94, 81, 12, 10 };
12:          int y[] = { 12, 15, 25, 71, 209, 278, 310, 274, 188, 171, 174,
13:              118, 56, 68, 49, 37, 12 };
14:          int pts = x.length;
15:          Polygon poly = new Polygon(x, y, pts);
16:          screen.drawPolygon(poly);
17:          screen.fillOval(235,140,15,15);
18:          screen.fillOval(225,130,15,15);
19:          screen.fillOval(245,130,15,15);
20:          for (int ax = 50; ax < 150; ax += 10)
21:              for (int ay = 120; ay < 320 ; ay += 10)
22:                  screen.drawArc(ax, ay, 10, 10, 0, -180);
23:      }
24: }
```

Figure 9.10 shows the Map applet that has been painted with Java's basic drawing methods.

FIGURE 9.10.

The Map applet.

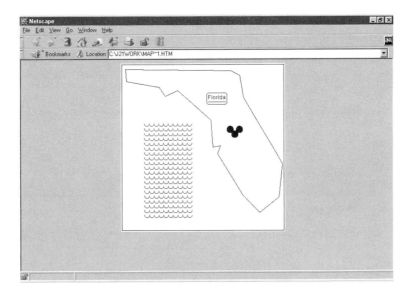

Although no cartographer would fear for his job security at this display of mapmaking, the applet combines a sampling of most drawing features that are available through the Graphics class. An applet like this could be expanded using Font and Color objects, and the drawing operations could be rearranged to improve the final product.

Copying and Clearing

The Graphics class also includes some cut-and-paste functionality involving the Applet window:

- The copyArea() method, which copies a rectangular region of the Applet window onto another region of the window
- The clearRect() method, which clears a rectangular region of the Applet window

The copyArea() method takes six arguments:

- The x,y coordinates of the rectangular region to copy
- The width and the height of that region
- The horizontal and vertical distance, in pixels, to move away from the region before displaying a copy of it

The following statement copies a 100×100 pixel region to an area 50 pixels to the right and 25 pixels down:

```
screen.copyArea(0,0,100,100,50,25);
```

The clearRect() method takes the same four arguments as the drawRect() and fillRect() methods, and it fills the rectangular region with the current background color of the applet. You learn how to set the background color later today.

You can determine the window's size via the size() method if you want to clear an entire Applet window. This returns a Dimension object, which has width and height variables; they represent the applet's dimensions.

To clear the entire applet, you can use the size() method, which returns a Dimension object representing the applet's width and height. You then can get to the actual values for width and height by using the width and height instance variables, as in the following statement:

```
screen.clearRect(0, 0, size().width, size().height);
```

Note

> The size() method was renamed after Java 1.02. It still works in Java 2, but the compiler will give a deprecation warning that means a replacement method is available. The getSize() method in Java 2 works exactly like size() does. The name change is part of Sun's effort for consistent method names throughout the class library.

Text and Fonts

`java.awt.Font` class objects are used in order to use the `drawString()` method with different fonts. Font objects represent the name, style, and point size of a font. Another class, `FontMetrics`, provides methods to determine the size of the characters being displayed with a specified font, which can be used for things like formatting and centering text.

Creating Font Objects

A `Font` object is created by sending three arguments to its constructor:

- The font's name
- The font's style
- The font's point size

The name of the font can be a specific font name such as Arial or Garamond Old Style, and it will be used if the font is present on the system on which the Java program is running.

There also are names that can be used to select Java's built-in fonts: TimesRoman, Helvetica, Courier, Dialog, and DialogInput.

 Caution

> For Java 1.1 and later, the font names TimesRoman, Helvetica, and Courier should be replaced with serif, sanserif, and monospaced, respectively. These generic names specify the style of the font without naming a specific font family used to represent it. This is a better choice because some font families may not be present on all implementations of Java, so the best choice for the selected font style (such as serif) can be used.

Three Font styles can be selected by using the constants `Font.PLAIN`, `Font.BOLD`, and `Font.ITALIC`. These constants are integers and you can add them to combine effects.

The last argument of the `Font()` constructor is the point size of the font.

The following statement creates a 24-point Dialog font that is bold and italicized.

```
Font f = new Font("Dialog", Font.BOLD + Font.ITALIC, 24);
```

Drawing Characters and Strings

To set the current font, the `Graphics class`' `setFont()` method is used with a `Font` object. The following statement uses a `Font` object named `ft`:

```
screen.setFont(ft);
```

Text can be displayed in an Applet window using the `drawString()` methods. This method uses the currently selected font; it uses the default if no font has been selected. A new current font can be set at any time using `setFont()`.

The following `paint()` method creates a new `Font` object, sets the current font to that object, and draws the string `"I'm very font of you."` at the coordinates 10,100.

```
public void paint(Graphics screen) {
    Font f = new Font("TimesRoman", Font.PLAIN, 72);
    screen.setFont(f);
    screen.drawString("I'm very font of you.", 10, 100);
}
```

The last two arguments to the `drawString()` method are x and y coordinates. The x value is the start of the leftmost edge of the text, and y is the baseline for the entire string.

Finding Information About a Font

The `FontMetrics` class can be used for detailed information about the current font, such as the width or height of characters it can display.

To use this class' methods, a `FontMetrics` object must be created using the `getFontMetrics()` method. The method takes a single argument: a `Font` object.

Table 9.1 shows some of the information you can find using font metrics. All these methods should be called on a `FontMetrics` object.

TABLE 9.1. FONT METRICS METHODS.

Method Name	Action
`stringWidth(String)`	Given a string, returns the full width of that string in pixels
`charWidth(char)`	Given a character, returns the width of that character
`getHeight()`	Returns the total height of the font

Listing 9.4 shows how the `Font` and `FontMetrics` classes can be used. The `SoLong` applet displays a string at the center of the Applet window, using `FontMetrics` to measure the string's width using the current font.

TYPE   **LISTING 9.4.** THE FULL TEXT OF SOLONG.JAVA.

```
1: import java.awt.Font;
2: import java.awt.Graphics;
3: import java.awt.FontMetrics;
```

```
4:
5: public class SoLong extends java.applet.Applet {
6:
7:     public void paint(Graphics screen) {
8:         Font f = new Font("Courier", Font.BOLD, 18);
9:         FontMetrics fm = getFontMetrics(f);
10:         screen.setFont(f);
11:         String s = "So long, and thanks for all the fish.";
12:         int x = (size().width - fm.stringWidth(s)) / 2;
13:         int y = size().height / 2;
14:         screen.drawString(s, x, y);
15:     }
16: }
```

Figure 9.11 shows two copies of the SoLong applet on a Web page, each with windows of different sizes.

FIGURE 9.11.

Two copies of the SoLong applet.

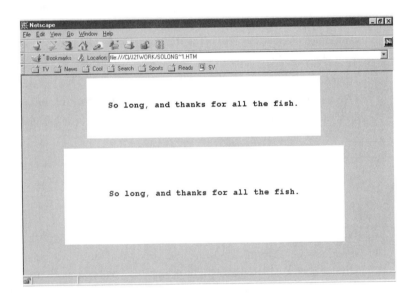

The size() method in lines 12 and 13 should be replaced with getSize() if you're writing a Java 1.1 or later applet. Determining the Applet window's size within the applet is preferable to defining the exact size in the applet, because it's more adaptable. You can change the applet's HTML code on the Web page without changing the program, and it still will work successfully.

Color

The `Color` and `ColorSpace` classes of the `java.awt` package can be used to make your applets and applications more colorful. With these classes you can set the current color for use in drawing operations, as well as the background color of an applet and other windows. You also can translate a color from one color-description system into another.

By default, Java uses colors according to a color-description system called sRGB. In this system a color is described by the amount of red, green, and blue it contains—that's where the R, G, and B come from. Each of the three components can be represented as an integer between `0` and `255`. Black is `0,0,0`—the complete absence of any red, green, or blue. White is `255,255,255`—the maximum amount of all three. You also can represent sRGB values using three floating-point numbers ranging from `0` to `1.0`. Java can represent millions of colors between the two extremes using sRGB.

A color-description system is called a *color space*, and sRGB is only one such space. There also is CMYK, a system used by printers that describes colors by the amount of cyan, magenta, yellow, and black they contain. Java 2 supports the use of any color space desired, as long as a `ColorSpace` object is used that defines the description system. You also can convert from any color space to sRGB, and vice versa.

Java's internal representation of colors using sRGB is just one color space that's being used in a program. An output device such as a monitor or printer also has its own color space.

When you display or print something of a designated color, the output device might not support the designated color. In this circumstance, a different color will be substituted or a *dithering* pattern will be used to approximate the unavailable color. This happens frequently on the World Wide Web, when an unavailable color is replaced by a dithering pattern of two or more colors that approximate the missing color.

The practical reality of color management is that the color you designated with sRGB will not be available on all output devices. If you need more precise control of the color, you can use `ColorSpace` and other classes in the `java.awt.color` package introduced in Java 2.

For most programs, the built-in use of sRGB to define colors will be sufficient.

Using `Color` Objects

To set the current drawing color, either a `Color` object must be created that represents the color or you must use one of the standard colors available from the `Color` class.

There are two ways to call the `Color` constructor method to create a color:

- Using three integers that represent the sRGB value of the desired color
- Using three floating-point numbers that represent the desired sRGB value

You can specify a color's sRGB value using either three `int` or `float` values. The following statements show examples of each:

```
Color c1 = new Color(0.807F,1F,0F);
```

```
Color c2 = new Color(255,204,102);
```

The c1 object describes a neon green color and c2 is butterscotch.

Note

> It's easy to confuse floating-point literals like `0F` and `1F` with hexadecimal numbers, which were discussed on Day 3, "The ABCs of Java." Colors often are expressed in hexadecimal, such as when a background color is set up for a Web page using the HTML `<BODY>` tag. None of the Java classes and methods you work with take hexadecimal arguments, so when you see a literal such as `1F` or `0F`, you're dealing with floating-point numbers.

Testing and Setting the Current Colors

The current color for drawing is designated by using the `Graphics` class's `setColor()` method. This method must be called on the `Graphics` object that represents the area you're drawing to. In an applet, this object is the one passed to the `paint()` method.

One way to set the color is to use one of the standard colors available as class variables in the `Color` class.

These colors use the following `Color` variables (with sRGB values indicated within parentheses):

black (0,0,0)	magenta (255,0,255)
blue (0,0,255)	orange (255,200,0)
cyan (0,255,255)	pink (255,175,175)
darkGray (64,64,64)	red (255,0,0)
gray (128,128,128)	white (255,255,255)
green (0,255,0)	yellow (255,255,0)
lightGray (192,192,192)	

The following statement sets the current color for the `screen` object using one of the standard class variables:

```
screen.setColor(Color.pink);
```

If you have created a `Color` object, it can be set in a similar fashion:

```
Color brush = new Color(255,204,102);
screen.setColor(brush);
```

After you set the current color, all drawing operations will occur in that color.

You can set the background color for an Applet window by using the applet's own `setBackground()` and `setForeground()` methods. These are inherited by the `Applet` class from one of its superclasses, so all applets you create will inherit them.

The `setBackground()` method sets the Applet window's background color. It takes a single argument, a `Color` object:

```
setBackground(Color.white);
```

There also is a `setForeground()` method that is called on user-interface components instead of `Graphics` objects. It works the same as `setColor()`, but changes the color of an interface component such as a button or a window.

Because an applet is a window, you can use `setForeground()` in the `init()` method to set the color for drawing operations. This color is used until another color is chosen with either `setForeground()` or `setColor()`.

If you want to find out what the current color is, you can use the `getColor()` method on a `Graphics` object, or the `getForeground()` or `getBackground()` methods of the `Applet` class.

The following statement sets the current color of `screen`—a `Graphics` object—to the same color as an applet's background:

```
screen.setColor(getBackground());
```

Advanced Graphics Operations Using Java2D

One of the enhancements offered with Java 2 is Java2D, a set of classes for offering high-quality 2D graphics, images, and text in your programs. The Java2D classes extend the capabilities of existing `java.awt` classes that handle graphics, such as those you have learned about today. They don't replace the existing classes—you can continue to use the other classes and programs that implement them.

Java2D features include the following:

- Special fill patterns such as gradients and patterns
- Strokes that define the width and style of a drawing stroke
- Anti-aliasing to smooth edges of drawn objects

User and Device Coordinate Spaces

One of the concepts introduced with Java2D is the difference between an output device's coordinate space and the coordinate space you refer to when drawing an object.

New Term *Coordinate space* is any 2D area that can be described using x,y coordinates.

For all drawing operations up to this point and all operations prior to Java 2, the only coordinate space used was the device coordinate space. You specified the x,y coordinates of an output surface such as an Applet window, and those coordinates were used to draw lines, text, and other elements.

Java2D requires a second coordinate space that you refer to when creating an object and actually drawing it. This is called the *user coordinate space*.

Before any 2D drawing has occurred in a program, the device space and user space have the 0,0 coordinate in the same place—the upper-left corner of the drawing area.

The user space's 0,0 coordinate can move as a result of the 2D drawing operations being conducted. The x and y axes even can shift because of a 2D rotation. You learn more about the two different coordinate systems as you work with Java2D.

Casting a `Graphics2D` Object

The drawing operations you have learned about thus far are called on a `Graphics` object that represents the area being drawn to—such as an Applet window. For Java2D, this object must be used to create a new `Graphics2D` object, as in the following `paint()` method:

```
public void paint(Graphics screen) {
    Graphics2D screen2D = (Graphics2D)screen;
}
```

The `screen2D` object in this example was produced via casting. It is the `screen` object converted from the `Graphics` class into the `Graphics2D` class.

All Java2D graphics operations must be called on a `Graphics2D` object. `Graphics2D` is part of the `java.awt` package.

Specifying the Rendering Attributes

The next step in 2D drawing is to specify how a drawn object will be rendered. Drawings that are not 2D only can select one attribute: color. 2D offers a wide range of attributes for designating color, line width, fill patterns, transparency, and many other features.

2D Colors

Colors are specified using the `setColor()` method, which works the same as the `Graphics` method of the same name. The following is an example:

```
screen2D.setColor(Color.black);
```

> **Caution**   Although some of the 2D methods work the same as their non-2D counter-parts, they must be called on a `Graphics2D` object in order to use Java2D's capabilities.

Fill Patterns

Fill patterns control how a drawn object will be filled in. With Java2D, you can use a solid color, gradient fill, texture, or a pattern of your own devising.

A fill pattern is defined by using the `setPaint()` method of `Graphics2D` with a `Paint` object as its only argument. The `Paint` interface is implemented by any class that can be a fill pattern, including `GradientPaint`, `TexturePaint`, and `Color`. The third might surprise you, but using a `Color` object with `setPaint()` is the same thing as filling with a solid color as the pattern.

 A *gradient fill* is a gradual shift from one color at one coordinate point to another color at a different coordinate point. The shift can occur once between the points, which is called an *acyclic gradient*, or it can happen repeatedly, which is a *cyclic gradient*.

Figure 9.12 shows examples of acyclic and cyclic gradients between white and a darker color. The arrows indicate the points that the colors shift between.

The coordinate points in a gradient do not refer directly to points on the `Graphics2D` object being drawn onto. Instead, they refer to user space and can even be outside the object being filled with a gradient.

Acyclic   Cyclic

FIGURE 9.12.

*Acyclic and cyclic gra-
dient shifts.*

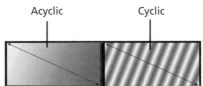

9

Figure 9.13 illustrates this. Both rectangles on the applet are filled using the same
`GradientPaint` object as a guide. One way to think of a gradient pattern is as a piece of
clothing fabric that has been spread out over a flat surface. The shapes being filled with a
gradient are the dress patterns cut from the fabric, and more than one pattern can be cut
out of the same piece of cloth.

FIGURE 9.13.

*Two rectangles using
the same
GradientPaint.*

A call to the `GradientPaint` constructor method takes the following format:

```
GradientPaint(x1,y1,color1,x2,y2,color2);
```

The point x1,y1 is where the color represented by `color1` begins, and x2,y2 is where the
shift ends at `color2`.

If you want to use a cyclic gradient shift, an extra argument is added at the end:

```
GradientPaint(x1,y1,color1,x2,y2,color2,true);
```

The last argument is a Boolean value that is `true` for a cyclic shift. A `false` argument
can be used for acyclic shifts, or you can leave this argument off entirely—acyclic shifts
is the default behavior.

After you have created a `GradientPaint` object, you set it as the current paint attribute
by using the `setPaint()` method. The following statements create and select a gradient:

```
GradientPaint pat = new GradientPaint(0f,0f,Color.white,
    100f,45f,Color.blue);
screen2D.setPaint(pat);
```

All subsequent drawing operations to the `screen2D` object will use this fill pattern until
another one is chosen.

Setting a Drawing Stroke

As you have learned, the lines drawn in all non-2D graphics operations are 1 pixel wide. Java2D adds the capability to vary the width of the drawing line by using the setStroke() method with a BasicStroke.

A simple BasicStroke constructor takes three arguments:

- A float value representing the line width, with 1.0 as the norm
- An int value determining the style of cap decoration drawn at the end of a line
- An int value determining the style of juncture between two line segments

NEW TERM The endcap- and juncture-style arguments use BasicStroke class variables. *Endcap* styles apply to the end of lines that do not connect to other lines. *Juncture* styles apply to the ends of lines that join other lines.

Possible endcap styles are CAP_BUTT for no endpoints, CAP_ROUND for circles around each endpoint, and CAP_SQUARE for squares. Figure 9.14 shows each endcap style. As you can see, the only visible difference between the CAP_BUTT and CAP_SQUARE styles is that CAP_SQUARE is longer because a square endcap is drawn.

FIGURE 9.14.

Endpoint cap styles.

CAP_BUTT   CAP_ROUND   CAP_SQUARE

Possible juncture styles are JOIN_MITER to join segments by extending their outer edges, JOIN_ROUND to round off a corner between two segments, and JOIN_BEVEL to join segments with a straight line. Figure 9.15 shows examples of each juncture style.

FIGURE 9.15.

Endpoint juncture styles.

JOIN_MITER   JOIN_ROUND   JOIN_BEVEL

The following statements create a BasicStroke object and make it the current stroke:

```
BasicStroke pen = BasicStroke(2.0f,
    BasicStroke.CAP_BUTT,
    BasicStroke.JOIN_ROUND);
screen2D.setStroke(pen);
```

The stroke has a width of 2 pixels, plain endpoints, and rounded segment corners.

Creating Objects to Draw

After you have created a Graphics2D object and specified the rendering attributes, the final two steps are to create the object and draw it.

Drawn objects in Java2D are created by defining them as geometric shapes using the java.awt.geom package classes. You can draw each of the things created earlier today, including lines, rectangles, ellipses, arcs, and polygons.

The Graphics2D class does not have different methods for each of the shapes you can draw. Instead, you define the shape and use it as an argument to draw() or fill() methods.

Lines

Lines are created using the Line2D.Float class. This class takes four arguments: the x,y coordinates of one endpoint followed by the x,y coordinates of the other. Here's an example:

```
Line2D.Float ln = new Line2D.Float(60F,5F,13F,28F);
```

This statement creates a line between 60,5 and 13,28. Note that an F is used with the literals sent as arguments—otherwise, the Java compiler would assume that they are integers.

Rectangles

Rectangles are created by using the Rectangle2D.Float or Rectangle2D.Double classes. The difference between the two is that one takes float arguments and the other takes double arguments.

Rectangle2D.Float takes four arguments: x coordinate, y coordinate, width, and height. The following is an example:

```
Rectangle2D.Float rc = new Rectangle2D.Float(10F,13F,40F,20F);
```

This creates a rectangle at 10,13 that is 40 pixels wide and 20 pixels tall.

Ellipses

NEW TERM Oval objects are called *ellipses* in Java2D, and they can be created with the Ellipse2D.Float class. It takes four arguments: x coordinate, y coordinate, width, and height.

The following statement creates an ellipse at 113,25 with a width of 22 pixels and a height of 40 pixels:

```
Ellipse2D.Float ee = new Ellipse2D.Float(113,25,22,40);
```

Arcs

Arcs are created with the `Arc2D.Float` class. They are created in a similar fashion to the non-2D counterpart, but there's an extra feature: You can define how the arc is closed.

`Arc2D.Float` takes seven arguments. The first four apply to the ellipse that the arc is a part of: x coordinate, y coordinate, width, and height. The last three arguments are the starting degree of the arc, the number of degrees it travels, and an integer describing how it is closed.

The number of degrees traveled by the arc is specified in a clockwise direction by using positive numbers. This is the opposite of the way a non-2D arc is handled.

The last argument uses one of three class variables: `Arc2D.OPEN` for an unclosed arc, `Arc2D.CHORD` to connect the arc's endpoints with a straight line, and `Arc2D.PIE` to connect the arc to the center of the ellipses like a pie slice. Figure 9.16 shows each of these styles.

FIGURE 9.16.

Arc closure styles.

Arc2D.OPEN   Arc2D.CHORD   Arc2D.PIE

 Note   The `Arc2D.OPEN` close style does not apply to filled arcs. A filled arc that has `Arc2D.OPEN` as its style will be closed using the same style as `Arc2D.CHORD`.

The following statement creates an `Arc2D.Float` object:

```
Arc2D.Float = new Arc2D.Float(27,22,42,30,33,90,Arc2D.PIE);
```

This creates an arc for an oval at 27,22 that is 42 pixels wide and 30 pixels tall. The arc begins at 33 degrees, extends 90 degrees in a clockwise direction, and will be closed like a pie slice.

Polygons

Polygons are created in Java2D by defining each movement from one point on the polygon to another. A polygon can be formed out of straight lines, quadratic curves, and bezier curves.

The movements to create a polygon are defined as a `GeneralPath` object, which also is part of the `java.awt.geom` package.

A `GeneralPath` object can be created without any arguments, as shown here:

```
GeneralPath polly = new GeneralPath();
```

The `moveTo()` method of `GeneralPath` is used to create the first point on the polygon. The following statement would be used if you wanted to start `polly` at the coordinates 5,0:

```
polly.moveTo(5f, 0f);
```

After creating the first point, the `lineTo()` method is used to create lines that end at a new point. This method takes two arguments: the x and y coordinates of the new point.

The following statements add three lines to the `polly` object:

```
polly.lineTo(205f, 0f);
polly.lineTo(205f, 90f);
polly.lineTo(5f, 90f);
```

The `lineTo()` and `moveTo()` methods require `float` arguments to specify coordinate points.

If you want to close a polygon, the `closePath()` method is used without any arguments, as shown here:

```
polly.closePath();
```

This method closes a polygon by connecting the current point with the point specified by the most recent `moveTo()` method. You can close a polygon without this method by using a `lineTo()` method that connects to the original point.

Once you have created an open or closed polygon, you can draw it like any other shape using the `draw()` and `fill()` methods. The `polly` object is a rectangle with points at 5,0, 205,0, 205,90, and 5,90.

Drawing Objects

After you have defined the rendering attributes, such as color and line width, and have created the object to be drawn, you're ready to draw something in all its 2D glory.

All drawn objects use the same `Graphics2D` class's methods: `draw()` for outlines and `fill()` for filled objects. These take an object as their only argument.

Strings in Java2D are drawn using the `drawString()` method. This takes three arguments: the `String` object to draw and its x,y coordinates. As with all coordinates in Java2D, floating-point numbers must be specified instead of integers.

A 2D Drawing Example

Earlier today you created a map of Florida using the drawing methods that are available through the Graphics class. The next applet you create is a revised version of that map, which uses 2D drawing techniques.

Because all of the Java2D classes are new with version 2 of Java, this applet only can be viewed with a Web browser that supports Java 2. At the time of this writing, the appletviewer tool included with JDK 1.2 is the only way to see it.

Listing 9.5 contains the Map2D applet. It's a longer program than many in this book, because 2D requires more statements to accomplish a drawing operation.

TYPE   **LISTING 9.5.** THE FULL TEXT OF MAP2D.JAVA.

```
1: import java.awt.*;
2: import java.awt.geom.*;
3:
4: public class Map2D extends java.applet.Applet {
5:     public void paint(Graphics screen) {
6:         Graphics2D screen2D = (Graphics2D)screen;
7:         setBackground(Color.blue);
8:         // Draw waves
9:         screen2D.setColor(Color.white);
10:        BasicStroke pen = new BasicStroke(2F,
11:            BasicStroke.CAP_BUTT, BasicStroke.JOIN_ROUND);
12:        screen2D.setStroke(pen);
13:        for (int ax = 10; ax < 340; ax += 10)
14:            for (int ay = 30; ay < 340 ; ay += 10) {
15:                Arc2D.Float wave = new Arc2D.Float(ax, ay,
16:                    10, 10, 0, 180, Arc2D.OPEN);
17:                screen2D.draw(wave);
18:            }
19:        // Draw Florida
20:        GradientPaint gp = new GradientPaint(0F,0F,Color.green,
21:            50F,50F,Color.orange,true);
22:        screen2D.setPaint(gp);
23:        GeneralPath fl = new GeneralPath();
24:        fl.moveTo(10F,12F);
25:        fl.lineTo(234F,15F);
26:        fl.lineTo(253F,25F);
27:        fl.lineTo(261F,71F);
28:        fl.lineTo(344F,209F);
29:        fl.lineTo(336F,278F);
30:        fl.lineTo(295F,310F);
31:        fl.lineTo(259F,274F);
32:        fl.lineTo(205F,188F);
33:        fl.lineTo(211F,171F);
34:        fl.lineTo(195F,174F);
```

```
35:            fl.lineTo(191F,118F);
36:            fl.lineTo(120F,56F);
37:            fl.lineTo(94F,68F);
38:            fl.lineTo(81F,49F);
39:            fl.lineTo(12F,37F);
40:            fl.closePath();
41:            screen2D.fill(fl);
42:            // Draw ovals
43:            screen2D.setColor(Color.black);
44:            BasicStroke pen2 = new BasicStroke();
45:            screen2D.setStroke(pen2);
46:            Ellipse2D.Float e1 = new Ellipse2D.Float(235,140,15,15);
47:            Ellipse2D.Float e2 = new Ellipse2D.Float(225,130,15,15);
48:            Ellipse2D.Float e3 = new Ellipse2D.Float(245,130,15,15);
49:            screen2D.fill(e1);
50:            screen2D.fill(e2);
51:            screen2D.fill(e3);
52:        }
53: }
```

In order to view the applet, you need to create a short HTML page that contains it, using Listing 9.6. Because it uses Java 2 classes and methods, the applet only can be viewed with a browser that supports this version of the language. At the time of this writing, the appletviewer tool included with the JDK is the only tool that runs Java 2 applets. appletviewer handles <APPLET> tags and ignores other HTML tags, so there's no reason to create a complicated page for something you only view with that tool.

TYPE   **LISTING 9.6.** THE FULL TEXT OF MAP2D.HTML.

```
1: <applet code="Map2D.class" height=370 width=350>
2: </applet>
```

Some observations about the Map2D applet:

- Line 2 imports the classes in the java.awt.geom package. This statement is required because import java.awt.*; in line 1 only handles classes, not packages available under java.awt.

- Line 6 creates the screen2D object that is used for all 2D drawing operations. It's a cast of the Graphics object that represents the Applet window.

- Lines 10–12 create a BasicStroke object that represents a line width of 2 pixels and then makes this the current stroke with the setStroke() method of Graphics2D.

- Lines 13–17 use two nested `for` loops to create waves out of individual arcs. This same technique was used for the Map applet, but there are more arcs covering the Applet window in Map2D.

- Lines 20 and 21 create a gradient fill pattern from the color green at 0,0 to orange at 50,50. The last argument to the constructor, `true`, causes the fill pattern to repeat itself as many times as needed to fill an object.

- Line 22 sets the current gradient fill pattern using the `setPaint()` method and the `gp` object that was just created.

- Lines 23–41 create the polygon shaped like the state of Florida and draw it. This polygon will be filled with green-to-orange strips because of the currently selected fill pattern.

- Line 43 sets the current color to black. This replaces the gradient fill pattern for the next drawing operation because colors are also fill patterns.

- Line 44 creates a new `BasicStroke()` object with no arguments, which defaults to a 1-pixel wide line width.

- Line 45 sets the current line width to the new `BasicStroke` object `pen2`.

- Lines 46–51 create three ellipses at 235,140, 225,130, and 245,130. Each is 15 pixels wide and 15 pixels tall, making them circles.

Figure 9.17 shows the output of the Map2D applet in `appletviewer`.

FIGURE 9.17.

The Map2D applet.

Summary

You now have some tools to improve the looks of an applet. You can draw with lines, rectangles, ellipses, polygons, fonts, colors, and patterns onto an Applet window, using non-2D and 2D classes.

Non-2D drawing operations require the use of methods in the Graphics class, with arguments that describe the object being drawn.

Java2D uses the same two methods for each drawing operation—draw() and fill(). Different objects are created using classes of the java.awt.geom package, and these are used as arguments for the drawing methods of Graphics2D.

Later in the book you learn how to draw to other components of a Java program the way you did to the Applet window. This enables you to use today's techniques in a Java application also.

You get more chances to impress Uncle Wade tomorrow, when the art lessons include animation and the display of image files.

Q&A

Q I want to draw a line of text with a boldface word in the middle. I understand that I need two Font objects—one for the regular font and one for the bold one—and that I'll need to reset the current font in between. The problem is that drawString() requires an x and a y position for the start of each string, and I can't find anything that refers to "current point." How can I figure out where to start the boldface word?

A Java's text display capabilities are fairly primitive. Java has no concept of the current point, so you have to figure out yourself where the end of one string was so that you can begin the next string. The stringWidth() methods can help you with this problem, both to find out the width of the string you just drew and to add the space after it.

DAY 10

Adding Images, Animation, and Sound

The first exposure to Java for many people was the sight of animated text or moving images on a Web page. These kinds of animation are simple, requiring only a few methods to implement in Java, but those methods are the basis for any applet that requires dynamic updates to the screen. Starting with simple animation is a good way to build up to more complicated applets.

Animation in Java is accomplished by using interrelated parts of the Abstract Windowing Toolkit (AWT). Today, you learn how the various parts of Java work together so that you can create moving figures and dynamically updated applets.

Creating animation is fun and easy to do in Java, but there's only so much you can do with the built-in Java methods for lines, fonts, and colors. For interesting animation, you have to provide your own images for each frame of the animation—and having sounds is nice as well.

Today you explore the following topics:

- How Java animations work—The `paint()` and `repaint()` methods, starting and stopping dynamic applets, and how to use and override these methods in your own applets
- Threads—What they are and how they can make your applets more well-behaved with other applets and with the system in general
- How to reduce animation flicker—A common problem with animation in Java
- Using bitmapped images such as GIF or JPEG files—Getting them from the server, loading them into Java, displaying them in your applet, and using them in animation
- Using sounds—Getting them and playing them at the appropriate times

Creating Animation in Java

Animation in Java is a relatively simple process that requires the following steps:

- Draw something using text, objects, or image files.
- Tell the windowing system to display what you have drawn.

These steps are repeated with different things being drawn to create an illusion of movement. You can vary the amount of time between different frames in the animated sequence or let Java draw as fast as it can.

Painting and Repainting

As you learned, the `paint()` method automatically is called when an applet's display area must be redrawn. This method is called when an applet begins because the window is blank and must be drawn for the first time. It also can be called when the Applet window is revealed after being obscured by another program's window.

You can ask Java's windowing system to repaint the window by using the `repaint()` method.

 Note

> The polite language is used here for a reason—`repaint()` really is a request rather than a command. The Java windowing system receives this request and processes it as soon as possible, but if `repaint()` requests stack up faster than Java can handle them, some might be skipped. In most cases, the delay between the call to `repaint()` and the actual window redisplay is negligible.

To change the appearance of what displays on an area such as an Applet window, you draw what you want displayed, call `repaint()`, draw something else, call `repaint()` again, and so on.

All these actions do not take place in the `paint()` method because it is responsible only for drawing a single frame of the animation—the most current frame. The real work occurs elsewhere in an applet.

In that other place, which might be its own method, you create objects, draw them, do any other necessary tasks, and finish by calling `repaint()`.

> **Caution**
>
> Although you can call the `paint()` method yourself, you should make all requests to draw the display area using calls to `repaint()`. The `repaint()` method is easier to use—it doesn't require a `Graphics` object as an argument—unlike `paint()`—and it takes care of all the behavior needed to update the display area. You'll see this later today when you call `repaint()` to create an animated sequence.

10

Starting and Stopping an Applet's Execution

As you recall from Day 8, "Putting Interactive Programs on the Web," the `start()` and `stop()` methods are called when an applet begins and ends execution.

These methods are empty when inherited from `java.applet.Applet`, so you have to override them to do anything at the start or the conclusion of your program. You didn't use `start()` or `stop()` yesterday because the applets only needed to use `paint()` once.

With animation and other Java applets that are processing and run over time, `start()` and `stop()` are needed to trigger the start of your applet's execution and to stop it from running when the page containing the applet is exited.

Controlling Animation Through Threads

Animation is an ideal use for threads, Java's means for handling more than one programming task at a time.

New Term   A *thread* is a part of a program that is set up to run on its own while the rest of the program does something else. This also is called *multitasking* because the program can handle more than one task simultaneously.

Threads are ideal for anything that takes up a lot of processing time and runs continuously, such as repeated drawing operations that create an animation.

By putting the workload of the animation into a thread, you free up the rest of the program to handle other things. You also make it easier for the applet's runtime environment to handle the program because all the intensive work is isolated into its own thread.

Writing Applets with Threads

To use a thread in an applet, you can make five modifications to its class file:

- Change the class declaration by adding the text `implements Runnable`.
- Create a `Thread` object to hold the thread.
- Override the applet's `start()` method to create a thread and start running it.
- Override the `stop()` method to set the running thread to `null`.
- Create a `run()` method that contains the statements that make the applet run continuously.

The `implements` keyword is similar to the `extends` keyword because it modifies the `class` that is declared on the same line. The following is an example of a class that uses both `extends` and `implements`:

```
public class DancingBaby extends java.applet.Applet
    implements Runnable {
    // ...
}
```

Although the class declaration has been split on two lines, everything from the keyword `public` to the left brace "{" defines the class.

`Runnable` is a special type of class called an interface. As you might recall from Day 2, "A Taste of Object-Oriented Programming," an *interface* is a way for a class to inherit methods not otherwise inherited from its superclasses.

These methods can be implemented by any class that needs the behavior. In this example, the `Runnable` interface is implemented by classes that will function as a thread. `Runnable` provides a definition for the `run()` method, which is called to start a thread.

The `Thread` class is part of the standard `java.lang` package, so it doesn't have to be made available through an `import` statement. Beginning the creation of a `Thread` object is as simple as giving one a name, as in the following statement:

```
Thread runner;
```

This object can be created in the applet's `start()` method. The variable `runner` will have the value `null` until the object actually has been created.

The ideal place to create it is in the applet's start() method. The following method checks to see if the thread has been created yet. If not, it creates it:

```
public void start() {
    if (runner == null) {
        runner = new Thread(this);
        runner.start();
    }
}
```

The this keyword used in the Thread() constructor is a way to refer to the object that the method is running in—the applet itself. By using this, the applet is identified as the class that provides the behavior to run the thread.

To run a thread, its start() method is called, as in this statement from the preceding example:

```
runner.start();
```

Calling a thread's start() method causes another method to be called—the run() method of the class that is handling the thread.

In this example, the applet implements the Runnable interface and has been linked to the runner object through the this keyword. A run() method must be added to the applet. The following is an example:

```
public void run() {
    // what your applet actually does
}
```

The run() method is the heart of the threaded applet. It should be used to drive the animated sequence by setting up anything needed for the drawings and to change things between each frame.

After the run() method has been filled with any behavior the thread needs, the last step in making an applet threaded is to use its stop() method to stop the thread.

The way to stop a thread is to set its object to null. This won't stop the thread, but you can design the run() method in such a way that it keeps running only while its Thread object is not equal to null.

Caution

There is a stop() method that could be called on Thread objects to stop them, but Sun has deprecated it as of Java 2. The use of a thread's stop() method creates instabilities in the runtime environment of the program and can introduce errors in its operation that are difficult to detect.

Programmers are strongly discouraged from using stop() to stop a thread any longer in Java, even in Java 1.02 and 1.1 programs. The alternative used today is recommended in release notes issued with Java 2 and should be suitable for all threaded programming.

By adding implements Runnable, creating a Thread object associated with the applet, and using the applet's start(), stop(), and run() methods, an applet becomes a threaded program.

Putting It Together

Threaded programming should become clearer when you actually see it in action. Listing 10.1 contains a simple animated applet that displays the date and time with constant updates. This creates a digital clock as shown in Figure 10.1.

FIGURE 10.1.

The DigitalClock applet on Netscape Navigator.

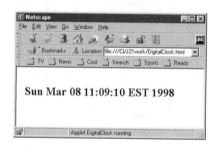

This applet uses the paint(), start(), and stop() methods. It also uses threads.

TYPE   **LISTING 10.1.** THE FULL TEXT OF DIGITALCLOCK.JAVA.

```
 1: import java.awt.Graphics;
 2: import java.awt.Font;
 3: import java.util.Date;
 4:
 5: public class DigitalClock extends java.applet.Applet
 6:     implements Runnable {
 7:
 8:     Font theFont = new Font("TimesRoman",Font.BOLD,24);
 9:     Date theDate;
10:     Thread runner;
11:
12:     public void start() {
13:         if (runner == null) {
14:             runner = new Thread(this);
```

```
15:                 runner.start();
16:         }
17:     }
18:
19:     public void stop() {
20:         if (runner != null) {
21:             runner = null;
22:         }
23:     }
24:
25:     public void run() {
26:         Thread thisThread = Thread.currentThread();
27:         while (runner == thisThread) {
28:             repaint();
29:             try {
30:                 Thread.sleep(1000);
31:             } catch (InterruptedException e) { }
32:         }
33:     }
34:
35:     public void paint(Graphics screen) {
36:         theDate = new Date();
37:         screen.setFont(theFont);
38:         screen.drawString("" + theDate.toString(), 10, 50);
39:     }
40: }
```

10

To test the applet, put it on a Web page in an Applet window with width=380 and
height=100.

> **Note**
>
> This applet uses the Date() class to get the current date and time, which
> makes it compatible with Java 1.02. For later versions of the language, the
> Calendar class should be used because it provides better support for interna-
> tional calendar systems. There is a Java 2-compliant version of the
> DigitalClock applet called DigitalClock12.java on the book's Web site at
> http://www.prefect.com/java21pre.

Animation is a good example of the kind of task that needs its own thread. Consider the
endless while() loop in the DigitalClock applet. If you didn't use threads, while()
would run in the default Java system thread, which also is responsible for painting the
screen, dealing with user input such as mouse clicks, and keeping everything internally
up-to-date. Unfortunately, if you run that while() loop in the main system thread, it

monopolizes Java's resources and prevents anything else—including painting—from happening. You'd never actually see anything onscreen because Java would be sitting and waiting for the while() loop to finish before it did anything else.

You look at this applet from the perspective of the actual animation parts in this section and deal with the parts that manage threads afterward.

Lines 8–9 define two basic instance variables: theFont and theDate, which hold objects representing the current font and the current date, respectively. You'll learn more about these later.

The start() and stop() methods here start and stop a thread; the bulk of the applet's work goes on in the run() method (lines 25–33).

Inside run() is where the animation actually takes place. Note the while loop inside this method (beginning with the statement on line 27); the expression runner == thisThread will return a value of true until the runner object is set to null (which occurs in the stop() method of the applet). A single animation frame is constructed inside that while loop.

The first thing that happens in the loop is that the repaint() statement is called in line 28 to repaint the applet. Lines 29–31, as complicated as they look, do nothing except pause for 1000 milliseconds (1 second) before the loop repeats.

The sleep()method of the Thread class is what causes the applet to pause. Without a specific sleep() method, the applet would run as fast as it possibly could. The sleep() method controls exactly how fast the animation takes place. The try and catch stuff around it enables Java to manage errors if they occur. These statements will be described on Day 16, "Exceptional Circumstances: Error Handling and Security."

In the paint()method in lines 35–39, a new instance of the Date class is created to hold the current date and time—note that it was specifically imported in line 3. This new Date object is assigned to the theDate instance variable.

In line 37 the current font is set using the value of the variable theFont and the date itself is displayed to the screen—note that you have to call the toString() method of Date to display the date and time as a string. Every time that paint() is called, a new theDate object is created that holds the current date and time.

Look at the lines of this applet that create and manage threads. First, look at the class definition itself in lines 5–6. Note that the class definition implements the Runnable interface. Any classes you create that use threads must include Runnable.

Line 10 defines a third instance variable for this class called runner of type Thread, which will hold the thread object for this applet.

Lines 12–23 define the boilerplate start() and stop() methods that do nothing except create and destroy threads. These method definitions will be similar from class to class because all they do is set up the infrastructure for the threads used by the program.

Finally, the bulk of your applet's work goes on inside the run() method in lines 25–33.

Reducing Animation Flickering

When the DigitalClock applet runs, you see an occasional flickering in the text as it displays. The extent of the flickering depends on the quality of the Java runtime environment the program runs on, as well as the processor speed. However, it is likely to be irritating even on a fast PC and well-implemented Java virtual machine.

Flickering is one of the side-effects of the way images are updated on a Java program, and it's one of the problems you will tackle as you create animation.

Flickering and How to Avoid It

Flickering is caused by the way Java repaints each frame of an applet. At the beginning of today's lesson, you learned that when the repaint() method is called, repaint() calls the paint() method.

There actually is a middleman involved. When repaint() is called, it calls the update() method, which clears the screen of any existing content by filling it with the background color of the Applet window. The update() method then calls paint().

The screen-clearing process in update() is the main culprit in the flickering problem. Because the screen is cleared between frames, the parts of the screen that do not change between frames alternate rapidly between being painted and being cleared—in other words, they flicker.

There are two major ways to avoid flickering in your Java applets:

- Override the update() method so that it either does not clear the screen or only clears the parts of the screen you changed.
- Override both the update() and paint() methods and use double-buffering.

The easiest way to reduce flickering is to override update() so that it does not clear the screen. The most successful way to take care of it is to use double-buffering.

How to Override `update()`

The default update () method of any applet takes the following form:

```
public void update(Graphics g) {
    g.setColor(getBackground());
    g.fillRect(0, 0, size().width, size().height);
    g.setColor(getForeground());
    paint(g);
}
```

The `update()` method clears the screen by filling the Applet window with the background color, sets the color back to normal, and then calls `paint()`. When you override `update()` with your own version of the method, you have to make sure that your version of `update()` does something similar. In the next two sections, you work through some examples of overriding `update()` to reduce flickering.

One Solution: Don't Clear the Screen

The first solution to reducing flickering is not to clear the screen at all. This solution works only for some applets, of course. For example, the ColorSwirl applet displays a single string (`Look to the cookie!`), but the string is presented in different colors that fade into each other dynamically. This applet flickers terribly when run. Listing 10.2 shows the initial source code for this applet and Figure 10.2 shows the result.

FIGURE 10.2.

Output of the ColorSwirl applet using Netscape Navigator.

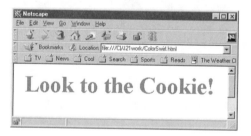

TYPE   **LISTING 10.2.** THE FULL TEXT OF COLORSWIRL.JAVA.

```
 1: import java.awt.Graphics;
 2: import java.awt.Color;
 3: import java.awt.Font;
 4:
 5: public class ColorSwirl extends java.applet.Applet
 6:     implements Runnable {
 7:
 8:     Font f = new Font("TimesRoman", Font.BOLD, 48);
 9:     Color colors[] = new Color[50];
10:     Thread runner;
```

```
11:
12:    public void start() {
13:        if (runner == null) {
14:            runner = new Thread(this);
15:            runner.start();
16:        }
17:    }
18:
19:    public void stop() {
20:        runner = null;
21:    }
22:
23:    public void run() {
24:        // initialize the color array
25:        float c = 0;
26:        for (int i = 0; i < colors.length; i++) {
27:            colors[i] =
28:            Color.getHSBColor(c, (float)1.0,(float)1.0);
29:            c += .02;
30:        }
31:
32:        // cycle through the colors
33:        int i = 0;
34:        Thread thisThread = Thread.currentThread();
35:        while (runner == thisThread) {
36:            setForeground(colors[i]);
37:            repaint();
38:
39:            i++;
40:            try {
41:                Thread.sleep(200);
42:            } catch (InterruptedException e) { }
43:            if (i == colors.length ) i = 0;
44:        }
45:    }
46:
47:    public void paint(Graphics screen) {
48:        screen.setFont(f);
49:        screen.drawString("Look to the Cookie!", 15, 50);
50:    }
51: }
```

To test this applet, put it on a Web page with an <APPLET> tag with height=150
width=450 attributes. Three things about this applet might look strange to you:

- Line 9 defines an instance variable colors, which is an array of 50 elements.
  When the applet starts, the first thing you do in the run() method (in lines 25–30)
  is to fill up that array with Color objects. By creating all the colors beforehand,

you can then just draw text in that color, one at a time; it's easier to precompute all the colors at once. (And, in fact, this `for` loop might make more sense in an `init()` method because it only needs to happen once.) The choice of 50 colors is arbitrary—the program just as easily can cycle through 20 or 250 colors.

- To create the different color objects, a method in the `Color` class called `getHSBColor()` is used, rather than just using `new` with various sRGB values. The `getHSBColor()` class method creates a `Color` object based on values for hue, saturation, and brightness, rather than the standard red, green, and blue. By incrementing the hue value while keeping saturation and brightness constant, you can create a range of colors without having to generate the sRGB value for each one. It's just a quick and easy way to create the color array.

- To create the animation, the applet cycles through the array of colors, setting the foreground color to each `Color` object in turn and calling `repaint()`. When it gets to the end of the array, it starts over again (line 45), so the process repeats again ad infinitum.

Now that you understand what the applet does, it's time to fix the flickering. The flickering is occurring because each time the applet is painted, there's a moment where the screen is cleared. Instead of the text cycling neatly from red to a nice pink to purple, the text is going from red to gray, to pink to gray, to purple to gray, and so on.

Because the screen clearing is all that's causing the problem, the solution is easy: override `update()` and remove the part where the screen is cleared. It doesn't need to get cleared anyhow because nothing is changing except for the color of the text. With the screen clearing behavior removed from `update()`, all `update()` needs to do is call `paint()`. Here's what the `update()` method should look like in the revised ColorSwirl applet:

```
public void update(Graphics screen) {
    paint(screen);
}
```

Adding these three lines stops the flickering.

Note You can find the first version of `ColorSwirl.java` under that name on the book's Web site at `http://www.prefect.com/java21pre` and the improved version in the same place as `BetterSwirl.java`.

You'll learn another method later today to reduce flickering—a technique called *double-buffering.*

Retrieving and Using Images

Basic image handling in Java is conducted through the Image class, which is part of the java.awt package. When you work with an applet, you can use methods of the Applet and Graphics classes to load and display images.

Getting Images

To display an image in your applet, you first must load that image over the World Wide Web into your Java program. Images are stored as separate files from Java class files, so you have to tell Java where to find them.

When you use the Image class, the image must be in .GIF or .JPG format.

A Web address is represented in Java as a URL object, an acronym that stands for Uniform Resource Locator. The URL class is part of the java.net package, so like Image, it requires an import statement to use in a Java program.

The URL object is created by sending a Web page address to the URL constructor method. Here's an example:

```
URL u = new URL("http://www.prefect.com/java21pre/images/book.gif");
```

When you have a URL object, you can use it to create an Image object that represents the graphics file.

The Applet class provides a method called getImage() to load an image into an Image object. There are two ways to use it:

- The getImage() method with a single argument (an object of type URL) retrieves the image at that URL.
- The getImage() method with two arguments: the base URL (also an URL object) and a string representing the relative path or filename of the actual image.

Although the first way might seem easier, the second is more flexible. If you use a specific Web address in your applet, you must change this address and recompile the program if your Web site is moved.

The Applet class has two methods that can be used to create a base URL without using a specific address into the program:

- The getDocumentBase() method returns an URL object that represents the folder containing the Web page presenting the applet. For example, if the page is located at http://www.prefect.com/java21pre/, getDocumentBase() returns a URL pointing to that path.

- The getCodeBase() method returns a URL object that represents the folder where the applet's main class file is located.

Relative File Paths

The relative path you use as the second argument to getImage() will change depending on what's used in the first argument.

For example, consider a Web page at http://www.prefect.com/java21pre/index.html that contains an image file called http://www.prefect.com/java21pre/book.gif. If you want to load this image into an applet, the following statement can be used:

```
Image img = getImage(getDocumentBase(), "book.gif");
```

As another example, if the book.gif file were moved to http://www.prefect.com/java21pre/images/book.gif, the following statement can be used:

```
Image img = getImage(getDocumentBase(), "images/book.gif");
```

Choosing between getDocumentBase() or getCodeBase() depends on whether your images are stored in subfolders of your Java applet or subfolders of the applet's Web page.

 Note   Using either getDocumentBase() or getCodeBase() also makes it possible for the image to load when you test it on your own computer. You don't have to store it onto a World Wide Web site before seeing if it works.

By using one of these methods, you make it possible to move your applet along with its Web page and make no changes to the program.

 Note   If you use a Java archive to present your applet, you can include image files and other data files in the archive. These files will be extracted from the archive automatically with any class files in the .JAR file.

Drawing Images

After you have loaded an image into an `Image` object, you can display it in an applet using the `drawImage()` method of the `Graphics` class.

To display an image at its actual size, you call the `drawImage()` method with four arguments:

- the `Image` object to display
- the x coordinate
- the y coordinate
- the keyword `this`

If a graphics file is stored in the `img` object, the following `paint()` method can be used to display it:

```
public void paint(Graphics screen) {
    screen.drawImage(img, 10, 10, this);
}
```

The x,y coordinates used with `drawImage()` are comparable to using x,y coordinates to display a rectangle. The point represents the upper-left corner of the image.

You can display an image at a different size by using six extra arguments:

- the `Image` object to display
- the x coordinate
- the y coordinate
- width
- height
- the keyword `this`

The width and height arguments describe the width and height, in pixels, that the image should occupy when displayed. If these aren't the actual size, the image will be scaled to fit in the modified width and height. This does not change the image, so you can use several `drawImage()` calls to display an `Image` object at several different sizes.

Two methods of the `Image` class are useful when displaying an image at anything other than actual size. The `getHeight()` method returns the height of the image as an integer, and the `getWidth()` method returns the width.

10

A Note About Image Observers

The last argument of the drawImage() method is the keyword this. As you might recall from previous days, this can be used inside an object to refer to itself.

The this keyword is used in drawImage() to identify that the applet can keep track of an image as it is loaded off of the World Wide Web. Image loading is tracked through the ImageObserver interface. Classes that implement this interface, such as Applet, can track the progress of an image. This would be useful to create a program that displays a message such as "Loading images …" while its graphics files are being loaded.

The existing support for ImageObserver should be sufficient for simple uses of images in applets, so the this keyword is used as an argument to drawImage().

Putting Images to Work

Before you dive into image animation, a simple applet will show an example of loading an image from a URL and displaying it at two different sizes. The Fillmore applet in Listing 10.3 displays an image of U.S. President Millard Fillmore, last of the Whigs.

TYPE   **LISTING 10.3.** THE FULL TEXT OF FILLMORE.JAVA.

```
 1: import java.awt.Graphics;
 2: import java.awt.Image;
 3:
 4: public class Fillmore extends java.applet.Applet {
 5:     Image whig;
 6:
 7:     public void init() {
 8:         whig = getImage(getCodeBase(),
 9:             "images/fillmore.jpg");
10:     }
11:
12:     public void paint(Graphics screen) {
13:         int iWidth = whig.getWidth(this);
14:         int iHeight = whig.getHeight(this);
15:         int xPos = 10;
16:         // 25%
17:         screen.drawImage(whig, xPos, 10,
18:             iWidth / 4, iHeight / 4, this);
19:         // 100%
20:         xPos += (iWidth / 4) + 10;
21:         screen.drawImage(whig, xPos, 10, this);
22:     }
23: }
```

To get ready to test the Fillmore applet, do the following:

- Create a new subfolder in the \J21work folder called images.
- Copy the file fillmore.jpg into this folder from the book's Web site at http://www.prefect.com/java21pre. As an alternative, you can use any .JPG file that's already on your system.
- Create a Web page that loads the applet, with height=400 width=420 attributes for the <APPLET> tag. If you use one of your own .JPG files, you might need to adjust the height and width attributes to make enough room in the Applet window for the image.

Figure 10.3 shows the output of the applet, which displays the fillmore.jpg graphics file at two sizes: 25 percent and 100 percent.

10

FIGURE 10.3.

The Fillmore applet.

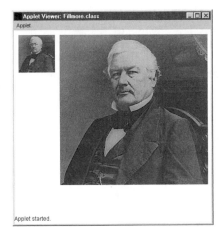

Line 5 of the applet associates the variable whig with the Image class. You don't have to use the new statement to create an object here because you receive an Image object from the getImage() method in lines 8–9.

Lines 13–14 use getWidth() and getHeight(), two methods of the Image class, and store their values in integer variables. These are needed to create a scaled-down version of the image in lines 17–18.

Line 15 creates the xPos variable, which stores the x coordinate to use for both versions of President Fillmore. In line 20, this variable is increased so that the large picture appears 10 pixels to the right of the smaller version.

Creating Animation Using Images

Creating animation with images is the same as animating fonts, colors, and other objects. You use the same methods and the same procedures for painting, repainting, and reducing flickering problems. The only difference is that you have a stack of images to flip through rather than a set of drawing operations.

The best way to show how to animate images is to work through an example. The next project is the longest you have undertaken, but it is covered in detail. The Neko applet is a good demonstration of threaded applet programming, image handling, and animation.

An Example: Neko

The images that you work with in the Neko applet will be familiar to many Macintosh users and some people on other platforms as well. Neko, whose name comes from the Japanese word for cat, is a Macintosh program written by Kenji Gotoh that features a small animated kitten. Neko chases the mouse pointer around the screen, sleeps, and engages in other Tamagotchi-like behavior.

For this example, you'll create animation based on the original Neko graphics. The Java-based Neko will run in from the left side of the Applet window, stop in the middle, yawn, scratch its ear, sleep a little, and then run off to the right.

Step 1: Collect Your Images

Before you begin writing Java code to construct an animation, you should have all the images that form the animation itself. For this version of Neko, there are nine of them (the original has 36), as shown in Figure 10.4.

FIGURE 10.4.

The images for the Neko applet.

To get ready for this project, copy the following nine image files from the book's Web site at http://www.prefect.com/java21pre into the \J21work\images folder you created earlier: Awake1.gif, Right1.gif, Right2.gif, Scratch1.gif, Scratch2.gif, Sleep1.gif, Sleep2.gif, Stop.gif, and Yawn.gif.

Step 2: Organize and Load the Images in Your Applet

The basic idea in the Neko applet is to take the series of images and display them one at a time to create the appearance of movement.

One way to manage this in Java is to store the images in an array of Image objects and use another Image object called currentImg to keep track of the current image to display.

For the Neko applet, the images will be stored in an array called nekoPics, and an Image object called currentImg will hold the current image. The following statements declare these objects:

```
Image nekoPics[] = new Image[9];
Image currentImg;
```

The image array has nine slots (0 through 8), which hold the images.

Because the Neko animation draws the cat images in different positions on the screen, the current x,y coordinates will be tracked as well in the x and y integer variables. Neko will move entirely from left to right, so the y integer variable will always have the same value: 50. The following statements create these variables:

```
int x;
int y = 50;
```

The applet's init() method will be used to load the images into the nekoPics array. You can do separate calls to getImage() for each of the nine filenames, but a less redundant way to do it is to create a String array that holds all nine of the filenames. This array will be used in a for loop to feed filenames to the getImage() method. Here's the result:

```
public void init() {
    String nekoSrc[] = { "right1.gif", "right2.gif",
        "stop.gif", "yawn.gif", "scratch1.gif",
        "scratch2.gif", "sleep1.gif", "sleep2.gif",
        "awake.gif" };

    for (int i=0; i < nekoPics.length; i++) {
        nekoPics[i] = getImage(getCodeBase(),
            "images/" + nekoSrc[i]);
    }
}
```

Because the images were stored in the images subfolder, it is part of the file reference sent to the getImage() method.

Step 3: Animate the Images

With the images loaded, the next step in the applet is to begin animating the elements of the applet. Because this is a threaded applet, the run() method will be used for this purpose.

Neko takes five successive actions in the program:

- Runs in from the left side of the screen
- Stops in the middle and yawns

- Scratches four times
- Sleeps
- Wakes up and runs off to the right side of the screen

Each of Neko's activities will be contained in its own method. This makes it possible to reuse some of the actions—such as Neko running across the applet—and to rearrange the order of things if desired.

The first method created is nekoRun(), which takes two integers as arguments: start and end. These determine the x coordinate where Neko begins and ends running. By using arguments, you make the method reusable. Here's the starting code for the method body:

```
void nekorun(int start, int end) {
  // to do
}
```

There are two images that represent Neko running: Right1.gif and Right2.gif. These are stored in elements 0 and 1 of the nekoPic array.

To make it appear that the virtual cat is scampering across the window, these images display in succession. At the same time, the x coordinate of the image increases, so the flip-flopping image is drawn a little further to the right each time. A for loop is used to cycle between the start and end values and increase the x coordinate.

To swap images, the currentImg object keeps track of the current image and switches from one value to the other each time through the for loop.

A call to repaint()causes the image tracked by currentImg to display.

The last thing to do in the nekoRun() method is to pause inside the for loop before the images are flopped and a new one appears.

Because each of the Neko-movement methods needs a pause, a pause() method is added to the applet that can be reused. This method uses the Thread.sleep() method, as shown here:

```
void pause(int time) {
    try {
        Thread.sleep(time);
    } catch (InterruptedException e) { }
}
```

After the call to pause() is added, the nekoRun() method consists of the following:

```
void nekoRun(int start, int end) {
    for (int i = start; i < end; i+=10) {
        x = i;
        // swap images
```

```
        if (currentImg == nekoPics[0])
            currentImg = nekoPics[1];
        else currentImg = nekoPics[0];
        repaint();
        pause(150);
    }
}
```

The last part of the for() statement increments the loop by 10 pixels each time, which kicks the images that distance to the right with each update. This choice, like the 150 millisecond pause in the pause() method call, was reached through trial and error to determine what looks best when the animation sequence runs.

You have seen that the nekoRun() method stores the current frame of the animation in the currentImg object before calling repaint(). The paint() method of the applet will do the actual work of displaying this image, as shown here:

```
public void paint(Graphics screen) {
    if (currentImg != null)
        screen.drawImage(currentImg, x, y, this);
}
```

Before calling drawImage(), the method tests to make sure that currentImg exists. If it didn't, the object would have a null value.

Now that there is a method to approximate some of Neko's movement, and the pause() and paint() methods have been set up, some statements can be added to the run() method, as follows:

```
// run from one side of the screen to the middle
nekoRun(0, size().width / 2);
```

> **Caution**
>
> The size() method of the Applet class has been deprecated after Java 1.02, so if you're writing this applet to be current with Java 2, it can be replaced with getSize(), which changes the nekoRun() call to the following:
>
> ```
> nekoRun(0, getSize().width / 2);
> ```

The second activity that Neko undertakes is to stop and yawn. Each of these is a single frame of the animation that isn't repeated, so they will be added to the run() method directly instead of being implemented as their own methods.

10

All that has to happen to display each of these images is the following:

- Change the value of currentImg to the Image object that should display
- Call repaint()
- Pause for a set amount of time

Here's the code:

```
// stop and pause
currentImg = nekoPics[2];
repaint();
pause(1000);
// yawn
currentImg = nekoPics[3];
repaint();
pause(1000);
```

The third part of the animation will be Neko scratching, which alternates between elements 4 and 5 of the nekoPics array. There's no horizontal movement during this part of the animation, so the only thing a nekoScratch() method needs to handle is the number of times to display Neko scratching itself.

The nekoScratch() method takes a single argument: the number of times to scratch. That argument is used in the for loop that displays both of the nekoPics images. The following statements comprise the method:

```
void nekoScratch(int numTimes) {
    for (int i = numTimes; i > 0; i--) {
        currentImg = nekoPics[4];
        repaint();
        pause(150);
        currentImg = nekoPics[5];
        repaint();
        pause(150);
    }
}
```

Inside the applet's run() method, the nekoScratch() method is called with an argument of 4:

```
// scratch four times
nekoScratch(4);
```

The next method, nekoSleep() will alternate two images to show Neko sleeping. These images occupy elements 6 and 7 of the array and will each appear followed by a 150 millisecond pause. This uses techniques you have already seen in other methods:

```
void nekoSleep(int numTimes) {
    for (int i = numTimes; i > 0; i--) {
```

```
            currentImg = nekoPics[6];
            repaint();
            pause(250);
            currentImg = nekoPics[7];
            repaint();
            pause(250);
        }
}
```

The `nekoSleep()` method is called in the applet's `run()` method with an argument of 5, as shown here:

```
// sleep for 5 "turns"
nekoSleep(5);
```

As the last of Neko's activities, the waking up image in `nekoPics[8]` will appear in the `run()` method, followed by another call to the `nekoRun()` method to make the cat exit stage right. These statements are used:

```
// wake up and run off
currentImg = nekoPics[8];
repaint();
pause(500);
nekoRun(x, size().width + 10);
```

Step 4: Finish Up

The images in the Neko animation all have white backgrounds. If your Applet window is any color other than white, each frame in the animation will have a white box around it.

To make each frame blend into the Applet window, add the following statement at the beginning of the `run()` method:

```
setBackground(Color.white);
```

There's a lot of code in this applet, which uses several different methods to accomplish a reasonably simple animation. Note that nothing is done to reduce the amount of flickering in this applet because the image size and drawing area are both small enough to minimize the problem. It generally is a good idea to write your animation the simplest way first and then add behavior to make it run cleaner.

To finish up this section, Listing 10.4 shows the complete code for the Neko applet.

TYPE   **LISTING 10.4.** THE FULL TEXT OF NEKO.JAVA.

```
1: import java.awt.Graphics;
2: import java.awt.Image;
```

continues

LISTING 10.4. CONTINUED

```
 3: import java.awt.Color;
 4:
 5: public class Neko extends java.applet.Applet
 6:     implements Runnable {
 7:
 8:     Image nekoPics[] = new Image[9];
 9:     Image currentImg;
10:     Thread runner;
11:     int x;
12:     int y = 50;
13:
14:     public void init() {
15:         String nekoSrc[] = { "right1.gif", "right2.gif",
16:             "stop.gif", "yawn.gif", "scratch1.gif",
17:             "scratch2.gif","sleep1.gif", "sleep2.gif",
18:             "awake.gif" };
19:
20:         for (int i=0; i < nekoPics.length; i++) {
21:             nekoPics[i] = getImage(getCodeBase(),
22:                 "images/" + nekoSrc[i]);
23:         }
24:     }
25:
26:     public void start() {
27:         if (runner == null) {
28:             runner = new Thread(this);
29:             runner.start();
30:         }
31:     }
32:
33:     public void stop() {
34:         runner = null;
35:     }
36:
37:     public void run() {
38:         setBackground(Color.white);
39:         // run from one side of the screen to the middle
40:         nekoRun(0, size().width / 2);
41:         // stop and pause
42:         currentImg = nekoPics[2];
43:         repaint();
44:         pause(1000);
45:         // yawn
46:         currentImg = nekoPics[3];
47:         repaint();
48:         pause(1000);
49:         // scratch four times
50:         nekoScratch(4);
51:         // sleep for 5 "turns"
```

```
52:         nekoSleep(5);
53:         // wake up and run off
54:         currentImg = nekoPics[8];
55:         repaint();
56:         pause(500);
57:         nekoRun(x, size().width + 10);
58:     }
59:
60:     void nekoRun(int start, int end) {
61:         for (int i = start; i < end; i += 10) {
62:             x = i;
63:             // swap images
64:             if (currentImg == nekoPics[0])
65:                 currentImg = nekoPics[1];
66:             else currentImg = nekoPics[0];
67:             repaint();
68:             pause(150);
69:         }
70:     }
71:
72:     void nekoScratch(int numTimes) {
73:         for (int i = numTimes; i > 0; i--) {
74:             currentImg = nekoPics[4];
75:             repaint();
76:             pause(150);
77:             currentImg = nekoPics[5];
78:             repaint();
79:             pause(150);
80:         }
81:     }
82:
83:     void nekoSleep(int numTimes) {
84:         for (int i = numTimes; i > 0; i--) {
85:             currentImg = nekoPics[6];
86:             repaint();
87:             pause(250);
88:             currentImg = nekoPics[7];
89:             repaint();
90:             pause(250);
91:         }
92:     }
93:
94:     void pause(int time) {
95:         try {
96:             Thread.sleep(time);
97:         } catch (InterruptedException e) { }
98:     }
99:
100:    public void paint(Graphics screen) {
```

10

continues

LISTING 10.4. CONTINUED

```
101:            if (currentImg != null)
102:                screen.drawImage(currentImg, x, y, this);
103:        }
104: }
```

When this applet is compiled using a Java 2 compiler, warning messages appear because of the use of the deprecated `size()` method. These can be disregarded and the applet will run successfully on Java 1.02- and 1.1-compliant browsers such as Netscape Navigator. A Java 2 version of this applet is available on the book's Web site at `http://www.prefect.com/java21pre`.

To test this applet, create a Web page where the Neko Applet window has a width of 300 pixels and a height of 200. Figure 10.5 shows the result.

FIGURE 10.5.

The Neko applet.

A Note on Disposing of `Graphics` Contexts

Although Java's garbage collector automatically gets rid of objects when they are no longer needed in a program, this can't be done for the `Graphics` objects that are created to handle offscreen buffers.

Because unused objects take up memory and can harm the performance of Java, you should use the `dispose()` method of the `Graphics` class to explicitly get rid of one of its objects when it is not needed. A good place to put this in an applet is the applet's `destroy()` method, which was described on Day 8, "Putting Interactive Programs on the Web." This method is called without any arguments, as shown in this example:

```
public void destroy() {
    offscreenGraphics.dispose();
}
```

Double-Buffering

The next example, the Checkers applet, uses a technique called double-buffering to improve the performance of the animation.

NEW TERM *Double-buffering* describes the process of drawing an entire frame of an animation to a nonvisible area before copying it into the visible window of a program. The offscreen area is called a *buffer*.

With double-buffering, you create a second surface (offscreen, so to speak), do all your painting to that offscreen surface, and then draw the whole surface at once onto the actual applet (and onto the screen) at the end—rather than drawing to the applet's actual graphics surface. Because all the work actually goes on behind the scenes, interim parts of the drawing process cannot appear accidentally and disrupt the smoothness of the animation.

Double-buffering isn't always the best solution. If your applet suffers from flickering, try overriding update() and drawing only portions of the screen first; that might solve your problem. Double-buffering is less efficient than regular buffering and also takes up more memory and space, so in some cases it might not be the optimal solution. To nearly eliminate animation flickering, however, double-buffering works exceptionally well.

To create an applet that uses double-buffering, you need two things: an offscreen image to draw on and a graphics context for that image. Those two together mimic the effect of the applet's drawing surface: the graphics context (an instance of Graphics) to provide the drawing methods, such as drawImage() (and drawString()), and the Image to hold the dots that get drawn.

There are four major steps to adding double-buffering to your applet. First, your offscreen image and graphics context need to be stored in instance variables so that you can pass them to the paint() method. Declare the following instance variables in your class definition:

```
Image offscreenImage;
Graphics offscreen;
```

Second, during the initialization of the applet, you'll create an Image and a Graphics object and assign them to these variables. (You have to wait until initialization so you know how big they're going to be.) The createImage() method gives you an instance of Image, which you can then send the getGraphics() method to get a new Graphics context for that image:

```
offscreenImage = createImage(size().width,
    size().height);
offscreen = offscreenImage.getGraphics();
```

Now, whenever you have to draw to the screen (usually in your `paint()` method), rather than drawing to paint's graphics, draw to the offscreen graphics. For example, to draw an image called `bug` at position 10,10, use this line:

```
offscreen.drawImage(bug, 10, 10, this);
```

Finally, at the end of your paint method, after all the drawing to the offscreen image is done, add the following line to place the offscreen buffer on the real screen:

```
screen.drawImage(offscreenImage, 0, 0, this);
```

Of course, you most likely will want to override `update()` so that it doesn't clear the screen between paintings:

```
public void update(Graphics g) {
    paint(g);
}
```

Now review those four steps:

1. Add instance variables to hold the image and graphics contexts for the offscreen buffer.

2. Create an image and a graphics context when your applet is initialized.

3. Do all your applet painting to the offscreen buffer, not the applet's drawing surface.

4. At the end of your `paint()` method, draw the offscreen buffer to the real screen.

The Checkers Applet

The Checkers applet draws a red piece from the game of checkers and moves it back and forth between a white and black square. If it were drawn using the same techniques as the Neko and ColorSwirl applets, there would be a terrible flicker as the piece passed over the different colored backgrounds. Overriding `update()` so that the window isn't cleared out would not remove the flickering problem in this instance.

The Checkers applet uses `fillRect()` and `fillOval()` methods to draw the checkerboard tiles and the checker. These are part of the applet's `paint()` method.

To move the checker from side to side, an integer variable called `xPos` keeps track of where it should appear at any given time. The value of this variable changes continuously in the `run()` method.

This is consistent with the animation applets you created up to this point. The way that the `paint()` method handles updates to the Applet window is new.

Instead of drawing each element of the animation directly to the Applet window, they will be drawn to an offscreen buffer first. When an entire frame of the animation is completed, this completed frame will then be drawn to the Applet window.

By using this "not until everything is done" method, no flickering will be displayed because of different objects appearing at slightly different times.

The first step in double-buffering is to create an `Image` object to hold the offscreen frame as it is being completed, and a `Graphics` object that enables you to draw to this offscreen image area. The following statements create these objects:

```
Image offscreenImg;
Graphics offscreen;
```

Objects will be assigned to these variables in the `init()` method of the applet:

```
public void init() {
    offscreenImg = createImage(size().width, size().height);
    offscreen = offscreenImg.getGraphics();
}
```

Next, the `paint()` method is modified to draw to the offscreen buffer instead of to the main `Graphics` object:

```
public void paint(Graphics screen) {
    // Draw background
    offscreen.setColor(Color.black);
    offscreen.fillRect(0, 0, 100, 100);
    offscreen.setColor(Color.white);
    offscreen.fillRect(100, 0, 100, 100);
    // Draw checker
    offscreen.setColor(Color.red);
    offscreen.fillOval(xPos, 5, 90, 90);
    screen.drawImage(offscreenImg, 0, 0, this);
}
```

Note the last statement of the method, which is the only one that displays anything on the Applet window. This statement displays the completed offscreen image at the coordinates (0,0). Because `offscreenImg` was created to be the same size as the onscreen area, it completely fills the Applet window.

To finish off, the `offscreen` object is disposed of in the applet's `destroy()` method, as indicated here:

```
public void destroy() {
    offscreen.dispose();
}
```

10

Listing 10.5 shows the full source code for the Checkers applet.

TYPE   **LISTING 10.5.** THE FULL TEXT OF CHECKERS.JAVA.

```
 1: import java.awt.*;
 2:
 3: public class Checkers extends java.applet.Applet implements Runnable {
 4:     Thread runner;
 5:     int xPos = 5;
 6:     int xMove = 4;
 7:     Image offscreenImg;
 8:     Graphics offscreen;
 9:
10:
11:     public void init() {
12:         offscreenImg = createImage(size().width, size().height);
13:         offscreen = offscreenImg.getGraphics();
14:     }
15:
16:     public void start() {
17:         if (runner == null) {
18:             runner = new Thread(this);
19:             runner.start();
20:         }
21:     }
22:
23:     public void stop() {
24:         runner = null;
25:     }
26:
27:     public void run() {
28:         Thread thisThread = Thread.currentThread();
29:         while (runner == thisThread) {
30:             xPos += xMove;
31:             if ((xPos > 105) ¦ (xPos < 5))
32:                 xMove *= -1;
33:             repaint();
34:             try {
35:                 Thread.sleep(100);
36:             } catch (InterruptedException e) { }
37:         }
38:     }
39:
40:     public void update(Graphics screen) {
41:         paint(screen);
42:     }
43:
44:     public void paint(Graphics screen) {
45:         // Draw background
46:         offscreen.setColor(Color.black);
```

```
47:        offscreen.fillRect(0,0,100,100);
48:        offscreen.setColor(Color.white);
49:        offscreen.fillRect(100,0,100,100);
50:        // Draw checker
51:        offscreen.setColor(Color.red);
52:        offscreen.fillOval(xPos,5,90,90);
53:        screen.drawImage(offscreenImg, 0, 0, this);
54:    }
55:
56:    public void destroy() {
57:        offscreen.dispose();
58:    }
59: }
```

You can test this applet on a Web page with an Applet window of `height=200` and `width=300`. Figure 10.6 shows the result.

FIGURE 10.6.

The Checkers applet.

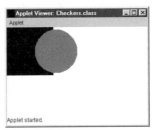

10

Retrieving and Using Sounds

Java supports the playback of sound files through the `Applet` class, and you can play a sound one time only or as a repeating sound loop.

Prior to Java 2, the language could handle only one audio format: 8KHz mono AU with mu-law encoding (named for the Greek letter "μ", or mu). If you wanted to use something that was in a format such as WAV, you had to translate it to mu-law AU, often at a loss of quality.

Java 2 adds much fuller support for audio. You can load and play digitized sound files in the following formats: AIFF, AU, and WAV. Three MIDI-based song file formats also are supported: Type 0 MIDI, Type 1 MIDI, and RMF. The greatly improved sound support can handle 8- or 16-bit audio data in mono or stereo, and the sample rates can range from 8KHz to 48KHz.

The simplest way to retrieve and play a sound is through the `play()` method of the `Applet` class. The `play()` method, like the `getImage()` method, takes one of two forms:

- `play()` with one argument—An `URL` object—loads and plays the audio clip stored at that URL.
- `play()` with two arguments—A base URL and a folder pathname—loads and plays that audio file. The first argument often will be a call to `getDocumentBase()` or `getCodeBase()`, as you have seen with `getImage()`.

The following statement retrieves and plays the sound `zap.au`, which is stored in the same place as the applet:

```
play(getCodeBase(), "zap.au");
```

The `play()` method retrieves and plays the given sound as soon as possible after it is called. If the sound file can't be found, the only indication you'll receive of a problem is the silence. No error message will be displayed.

To play a sound repeatedly, start and stop the sound, or play it repeatedly as a loop, you must load it into an `AudioClip` object by using the applet's `getAudioClip` method. `AudioClip` is part of the `java.applet` package, so it must be imported to be used in a program.

The `getAudioClip()` method takes one or two arguments in the same fashion as the `play()` method. The first (or only) argument is a `URL` argument identifying the sound file, and the second is a folder path reference.

The following statement loads a sound file into the `clip` object:

```
AudioClip clip = getAudioClip(getCodeBase(),
    "audio/marimba.wav");
```

In this example, the filename includes a folder reference, so the file `marimba.wav` will be loaded from the subfolder `audio`.

The `getAudioClip()` method can be called only within an applet. As of Java 2, applications can load sound files by using the `newAudioClip()` method of the `Applet` class. Here's the previous example rewritten for use in an application:

```
AudioClip clip = newAudioClip("audio/marimba.wav");
```

After you have created an `AudioClip` object, you can call the `play()`, `stop()`, and `loop()` methods on it. These do what you might expect—`play()` plays the sound, `stop()` halts playback, and `loop()` plays it repeatedly.

If the getAudioClip() or newAudioClip() methods can't find the sound file indicated by their arguments, the value of the AudioClip object will be null. Trying to play a null object results in an error, so test for this condition before using an AudioClip object.

More than one sound can play simultaneously—they will be mixed together during play-back.

An important thing to note when using a sound loop in an applet is that it won't stop automatically when the applet's running thread is stopped. If a Web user moves to another page, the sound continues playing, which isn't likely to win you any friends among the Web-surfing public.

You can fix this problem by using the stop() method on the looping sound at the same time the applet's thread is being stopped.

Listing 10.6 is an applet that plays two sounds: a looping sound named loop.au and a honking horn called beep.au that plays every five seconds.

TYPE   **LISTING 10.6.** THE FULL TEXT OF AUDIOLOOP.JAVA.

```
 1: import java.awt.Graphics;
 2: import java.applet.AudioClip;
 3:
 4: public class AudioLoop extends java.applet.Applet
 5:     implements Runnable {
 6:
 7:     AudioClip bgSound;
 8:     AudioClip beep;
 9:     Thread runner;
10:
11:     public void start() {
12:         if (runner == null) {
13:             runner = new Thread(this);
14:             runner.start();
15:         }
16:     }
17:
18:     public void stop() {
19:         if (runner != null) {
20:             if (bgSound != null)
21:                 bgSound.stop();
22:             runner = null;
23:         }
24:     }
25:
26:     public void init() {
```

continues

LISTING 10.6. CONTINUED

```
27:            bgSound = getAudioClip(getCodeBase(),"loop.au");
28:            beep = getAudioClip(getCodeBase(), "beep.au");
29:        }
30:
31:        public void run() {
32:            if (bgSound != null)
33:                bgSound.loop();
34:            Thread thisThread = Thread.currentThread();
35:            while (runner == thisThread) {
36:                try {
37:                    Thread.sleep(5000);
38:                } catch (InterruptedException e) { }
39:                if (beep != null)
40:                    beep.play();
41:            }
42:        }
43:
44:        public void paint(Graphics screen) {
45:            screen.drawString("Playing Sounds ...", 10, 10);
46:        }
47: }
```

To test `AudioLoop`, create a Web page with an Applet window that has a height of 100 and a width of 200. The audio files `loop.au` and `beep.au` should be copied from the book's Web site (`http://www.prefect.com/java21pre`) into the `\J21work` folder on your system. When you run the applet, the only visual output is a single string, but you should hear two sounds playing as the applet runs.

The `init()` method in lines 26–29 loads the `loop.au` and `beep.au` sound files. No attempt is made in this method to make sure the files actually loaded, which would result in `null` values for the `bgsound` and `beep` object. This will be tested elsewhere before the sound files are used, such as in lines 32 and 39, when the `loop()` and `play()` methods are used on the `AudioClip` objects.

Lines 20 and 21 turn off the looping sound if the thread also is stopped.

Summary

Today you learned about a plethora of methods to use and override—`start()`, `stop()`, `paint()`, `repaint()`, `run()`, and `update()`—and you got a basic foundation in creating and using threads. You also learned about using images in your applets—locating them, loading them, and using the `drawImage()` method to display and animate them.

An animation technique that you now can use is double-buffering, which virtually eliminates flickering in your animation at some expense of animation efficiency and speed. Using images and graphics contexts, you can create an offscreen buffer to draw to, the result of which is then displayed to the screen at the last possible moment.

You learned how to use sounds, which can be included in your applets any time you need them—at specific moments or as background sounds that can be repeated while the applet executes. You learned how to locate, load, and play sounds using both the `play()` and the `getAudioClip()` methods.

Q&A

Q In the Neko program, you put the image loading into the `init()` method. It seems to me that it might take Java a long time to load all those images, and because `init()` isn't in the main thread of the applet, there's going to be a distinct pause there. Why not put the image loading at the beginning of the `run()` method instead?

A Sneaky things happen behind the scenes. The `getImage()` method doesn't actually load the image; in fact, it returns an `Image` object almost instantaneously, so it isn't taking up a large amount of processing time during initialization. The image data that `getImage()` points to isn't actually loaded until the image is needed. This way, Java doesn't have to keep enormous images around in memory if the program is going to use only a small piece. Instead, it can just keep a reference to that data and retrieve what it needs later.

Q I compiled and ran the Neko applet. Something weird is going on; the animation starts in the middle and drops frames. It's as if only some of the images have loaded when the applet is run.

A That's precisely what's going on. Because image loading doesn't actually load the image right away, your applet might be merrily animating blank screens while the images are still being loaded. Depending on how long it takes those images to load, your applet might appear to start in the middle, to drop frames, or to not work at all.

There are three possible solutions to this problem. The first is to have the animation loop (that is, start over from the beginning when it stops). Eventually, the images will load and the animation will work correctly. The second solution, and not a very good one, is to sleep for a while before starting the animation, to pause while the images load. The third, and best solution, is to use image observers to make sure no part of the animation plays before its images have loaded. Check out the documentation for the `ImageObserver` interface for details.

10

DAY 11

Building Simple User Interfaces for Applets

With the popularity of Apple's Macintosh and Microsoft Windows operating systems, most of today's computer users expect their software to feature a graphical user interface and things they can control with a mouse. In the workplace, the right to point-and-click ranks up there with life, liberty, and the pursuit of a good 401(k) plan.

These software amenities are user-friendly but programmer-unfriendly in many languages. Writing windowing software can be one of the more challenging tasks for a novice developer.

Fortunately, Java has simplified the process with the Abstract Windowing Toolkit, a set of classes for the creation and usage of graphical user interfaces.

Today you'll use the toolkit to create a user interface for an applet. You'll use the techniques of Java 1.02, because that remains the standard version of the language among the applet-using audience.

Tomorrow you learn how to arrange all of the components on a user interface. On Day 13, "Responding to User Input in an Applet," you'll finish off a user interface by making it responsive to user control.

After you have learned how to create programs using the Abstract Windowing Toolkit, you'll be ready to use Java 2 techniques to create applications on Days 19 through 21.

The Abstract Windowing Toolkit

The Abstract Windowing Toolkit, also called the AWT, is a set of classes that enables you to create a graphical user interface and receive user input from the mouse and keyboard.

Because Java is a platform-independent language, the AWT offers a way to design an interface that will have the same general appearance and functionality on all systems it runs on.

 Caution

One thing you will learn as you create Java applets with the AWT is that some things are not entirely consistent across platforms. The different Java runtime environments created by Netscape, Microsoft, and other companies for their browsers don't always agree on how an AWT interface should function. It's important to test your windowing applets on as many platforms and browsers as possible.

Using the AWT, a user interface consists of three things:

- *Components*. Anything that can be put onto a user interface, including clickable buttons, scrolling lists, pop-up menus, check boxes, and text fields.
- *Containers*. A component that can contain other components. You have been working with one of these all along—the Applet window—and others include panels, dialog boxes, and standalone windows.
- *Layout managers*. An object that defines how the components in a container will be arranged. You don't see the layout manager in an interface, but you definitely see the results of its work.

The AWT's classes are all part of the java.awt package. To make all of its classes available in a program, the following statement can be used at the top of a source code file:

```
import java.awt.*;
```

This imports all of the components, containers, and layout managers that you will use to design an interface. You also can use individual import statements with the classes you are using in a program.

The AWT's classes, like all parts of the Java class library, are arranged into an inheritance hierarchy. When you learn how to use one AWT class, you learn some things about how to use other classes that inherit from the same superclass.

User-Interface Components

Components are placed onto a user interface by adding them to a container. A container is itself a component, so it can be added to other containers. You will be using this functionality when you start working with layout managers to arrange an interface.

The easiest way to demonstrate interface design is by using the container you've been working with all along—the Applet class.

Adding Components to a Container

A component is added to a container via the following two steps:

- Create the component.
- Call the container's add() method with the component.

Because all applets are containers, you can use the add() method inside an applet to add a component directly to the Applet window.

Each AWT user-interface component is a class, so you create a component by creating an object of that class.

The Button class represents clickable buttons on an interface. You can create a button by specifying the label of the button in its constructor method, as in the following statement:

```
Button panic = new Button("Panic!");
```

This creates a Button object that is labeled with the text "Panic!".

Once you have created a component, the simplest way to add it to a container is to call the container's add() method with the component as the only argument.

Because an applet is a container, the following statement could be used in an applet to add the panic object to the Applet window:

```
add(panic);
```

11

Adding a component does not immediately cause it to appear. Instead, it will appear when the paint() method of its container is called. This is something that Java handles behind the scenes, but you can force a call to paint() in an applet by using its repaint() method.

When you add a component to a container, you do not specify an x,y coordinate that indicates where the component should be placed. The arrangement of components is handled by the layout manager in effect for the container.

> **Note**
>
> You learn more about layout managers tomorrow. The default layout for a container is to place each component on one line from left to right until there is no more room, and then continue by placing components on the next line. This is called *flow layout*, and is handled by the FlowLayout class.

In an applet, the best place to create components and add them to containers is the init() method. This is demonstrated in a one-button applet shown in Listing 11.1. The Slacker applet creates a Button object and adds it to the Applet window. The button is displayed when the applet's paint() method—inherited from the Applet class—is called.

TYPE   **LISTING 11.1.** THE FULL TEXT OF SLACKER.JAVA.

```
 1: import java.awt.*;
 2:
 3: public class Slacker extends java.applet.Applet {
 4:     String note = "I am extremely tired and would prefer not " +
 5:         "to be clicked. Please interact somewhere else.";
 6:     Button tired = new Button(note);
 7:
 8:     public void init() {
 9:         add(tired);
10:     }
11: }
```

Test this applet on a page using the following <APPLET> tag:

```
<applet code="Slacker.class" width=550 height=75>
</applet>
```

Figure 11.1 shows the result using the appletviewer.

FIGURE 11.1.

The Slacker applet.

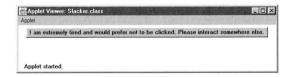

Labels

The simplest user-interface component is the label, created from the Label class. *Labels* often are used to identify the purpose of other components on an interface, and they cannot be edited directly by a user.

Using a label for text is preferable to using the drawString() method for the following reasons:

- Labels are drawn automatically after creation and don't have to be handled explicitly in the paint() method.
- Labels will be laid out according to the layout manager in use, rather than being specifically tied to an x,y address like a drawn string.

To create a label, use one of the following constructors:

- Label() creates an empty label with its text aligned to the left.
- Label(*String*) creates a label with the given text string, also aligned to the left.
- Label(*String*, *int*) creates a label with the given text string and the alignment indicated by the *int* argument. The following class variables are used to set the alignment: Label.RIGHT, Label.LEFT, and Label.CENTER.

You can change the label's font with the setFont() method you learned about during Day 9, "Making Programs Look Good with Graphics, Fonts, and Color." This method can be called on the label's container (such as an applet), which affects all components on the container, or on the label itself.

A label's setText(*String*) method can be used to change the label's text after it has been created. The new text indicated by *String* is displayed when the component is repainted. You also can use the getText() method to indicate what the label's current text is.

Listing 11.2 contains a simple applet that creates a few labels in Helvetica Bold.

11

```
 1: import java.awt.*;
 2:
 3: public class Labels extends java.applet.Applet {
 4:     Label lefty = new Label("Bleeding heart!");
 5:     Label center = new Label("Centrist!", Label.CENTER);
 6:     Label righty = new Label("Hardliner!", Label.RIGHT);
 7:     Font lf = new Font("Helvetica", Font.BOLD, 14);
 8:     GridLayout layout = new GridLayout(3,1);
 9:
10:     public void init() {
11:         setFont(lf);
12:         setLayout(layout);
13:         add(lefty);
14:         add(center);
15:         add(righty);
16:     }
17: }
```

Test this applet using the following <APPLET> tag:

```
<applet code="Labels.class" height=150 width=175>
</applet>
```

Figure 11.2 shows the output of this applet in appletviewer. This is a good tool to use for this program, because you can resize the window and see how it results in a realignment for the three labels. The "Hardliner!" label sticks to the right edge of the Applet window, and the "Centrist!" label remains centered.

FIGURE 11.2.

The Labels applet.

Lines 8 and 12 of this applet are used to create a GridLayout object and use that object to set the layout of the container. This is covered later—it has to be used here to illustrate alignment because labels are not aligned under the default behavior for containers, which is flow layout. Lines 8 and 12 are used to arrange components into a grid with one column and three rows.

Buttons

Clickable buttons can be created using the `Button` class, as you saw with the Slacker applet. Buttons are useful in an interface to trigger an action, such as a Quit button to exit a program.

To create a button, use one of the following constructors:

- `Button()` creates a button with no text label that indicates its function.
- `Button(String)` creates a button with the given string as a label.

After you create a `Button` object, you can set its label with the `setLabel(String)` method and get the label's text with the `getLabel()` method.

Listing 11.3 contains the VCR applet, which displays several familiar commands on buttons.

TYPE **LISTING 11.3.** THE FULL TEXT OF VCR.JAVA.

```
1: import java.awt.*;
2:
3: public class VCR extends java.applet.Applet {
4:     Button rewind = new Button("Rewind");
5:     Button play = new Button("Play");
6:     Button ff = new Button("Fast Forward");
7:     Button stop = new Button("Stop");
8:     Button eat = new Button("Eat Tape");
9:
10: public void init() {
11:     add(rewind);
12:     add(play);
13:     add(ff);
14:     add(stop);
15:     add(eat);
16:     }
17: }
```

Test the VCR applet using the following HTML:

```
<applet code="VCR.class" height=60 width=300>
</applet>
```

Figure 11.3 shows this applet loaded with `appletviewer`. Note that the Eat Tape button appears on a new line because there wasn't room for it on the preceding line. If you made the Applet window 500 pixels wide instead of 300, all five buttons would be aligned.

11

FIGURE 11.3.

The VCR applet.

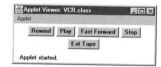

Check Boxes

Check boxes are labeled or unlabeled boxes that can be either "checked off" or empty. They are typically used to select or deselect some kind of option in a program, such as the Disable Sound and Password Protected check boxes from a Windows screen saver, which is shown in Figure 11.4.

FIGURE 11.4.

A dialog box that uses check boxes.

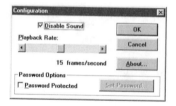

Check boxes normally are *nonexclusive*, meaning that if you have five check boxes in a container, all five can be checked or unchecked at the same time.

This component can be organized into check box groups, which are sometimes called *radio buttons*. They get their name from older car radios, where pushing one button pops out any other buttons that are pushed in.

Both kinds of check boxes are created using the Checkbox class. You can create a nonexclusive check box using one of the following constructors:

- Checkbox()creates an unlabeled check box that is not checked.
- Checkbox(*String*) creates an unchecked check box with the given string as a label.

After you create a Checkbox object, you can use the setState(*boolean*) method with a true value as the argument to check the box, and false to uncheck it. The getState() method will return a Boolean indicating the check box's current checked or unchecked status.

Five check boxes are created in Listing 11.4, which is an applet that enables you to select up to five Czechoslovakian-born celebrities. All five are Czech, but only one is checked—model/actress Paulina Porizkova.

TYPE **LISTING 11.4.** THE FULL TEXT OF CHECKACZECH.HTML.

```
1: import java.awt.*;
2:
3: public class CheckACzech extends java.applet.Applet {
4:     Checkbox c1 = new Checkbox("Milos Forman");
5:     Checkbox c2 = new Checkbox("Paulina Porizkova");
6:     Checkbox c3 = new Checkbox("Ivan Reitman");
7:     Checkbox c4 = new Checkbox("Tom Stoppard");
8:     Checkbox c5 = new Checkbox("Ivana Trump");
9:
10:     public void init() {
11:         add(c1);
12:         c2.setState(true);
13:         add(c2);
14:         add(c3);
15:         add(c4);
16:         add(c5);
17:     }
18: }
```

Figure 11.5 shows this applet's output, which can be tested with the following <APPLET> tag:

```
<applet code="CheckACzech.class" height=200 width=150>
</applet>
```

FIGURE 11.5.

The CheckACzech applet.

To organize several check boxes into a group so that only one can be selected at a time, a CheckboxGroup object is created with a statement such as the following:

```
CheckboxGroup radio = new CheckboxGroup();
```

The CheckboxGroup object keeps track of all check boxes in its group. You use this object as an extra argument to the Checkbox constructor.

Checkbox(*String*, *CheckboxGroup*, *boolean*) creates a check box labeled with the given string that belongs to the CheckboxGroup indicated by the second argument. The third argument equals true if the box is checked, false otherwise.

> **Caution**
>
> As of Java 1.2, the Checkbox(*String*, *CheckBoxGroup*, *boolean*) method has been deprecated, meaning that a better method is available. If you aren't writing a Java 1.02 applet, the Checkbox(*String*, *boolean*, *CheckboxGroup*) method should be used instead. The usage is the same, but the second and third arguments are reversed.

The following example creates a group and two check boxes that belong to it:

```
CheckboxGroup betterDarrin = new CheckboxGroup();
Checkbox r1 = new Checkbox("Dick York", betterDarrin, true);
Checkbox r2 = new Checkbox("Dick Sargent", betterDarrin, false);
```

The betterDarrin object is used to group together the r1 and r2 check boxes. The r1 object, which has the label "Dick York", is selected. Only one member of the group can be selected at a time, so it's impossible to use true as the third argument for both r1 and r2. (Besides, as all right-thinking fans of the '60s television sitcom *Bewitched* should attest, actor Dick York was the better Darrin Stevens than his successor, Dick Sargent.)

If you try to use true with more than one check box in a group, the last one will be the only one selected. A group can appear with none of the check boxes selected.

A check box group is demonstrated in Listing 11.5, an applet that provides check boxes for five Polish-born entertainers and selects one—Krzysztof Kieslowski, the late director of *Blue*, *White*, and *Red*.

TYPE **LISTING 11.5.** THE FULL TEXT OF PICKAPOLE.JAVA.

```
 1: import java.awt.*;
 2:
 3: public class PickAPole extends java.applet.Applet {
 4:     CheckboxGroup p = new CheckboxGroup();
 5:     Checkbox p1 = new Checkbox("Samuel Goldwyn", p, false);
 6:     Checkbox p2 = new Checkbox("Krzysztof Kieslowski", p, true);
 7:     Checkbox p3 = new Checkbox("Klaus Kinski", p, false);
 8:     Checkbox p4 = new Checkbox("Joanna Pacula", p, false);
 9:     Checkbox p5 = new Checkbox("Roman Polanski", p, false);
10:
11:     public void init() {
```

```
12:          add(p1);
13:          add(p2);
14:          add(p3);
15:          add(p4);
16:          add(p5);
17:    }
18: }
```

Use the following <APPLET> tag on a Web page to test this applet, which is shown in Figure 11.6:

```
<applet code="PickAPole.class" height=200 width=150>
</applet>
```

FIGURE 11.6.

The PickAPole applet.

The setCurrent(*Checkbox*) method can be used to make the set the currently selected check box in the group. There also is a getCurrent() method, which returns the currently selected check box.

Choice Lists

Choice lists, which are created from the Choice class, are components that enable a single item to be picked from a pull-down list. You encounter these lists often when filling out a form on a World Wide Web page. Figure 11.7 shows an example from the Macmillan Personal Bookshelf Web site.

Note

Personal Bookshelf is a Macmillan program that enables users to view up to five books, including those from Sams Publishing, in full text on the Web. For details, visit the following Web page:

http://www.mcp.com/personal/

FIGURE 11.7.

Example of a choice list.

The first step in creating a choice list is to create a `Choice` object to hold the list, as shown in the following statement:

```
Choice gender = new Choice();
```

Items are added to a choice list by using the `addItem(String)` method on the object. The following statements add two items to the gender choice list:

```
gender.addItem("Male");
gender.addItem("Female");
```

You can continue to use `addItem()` to add to the list after the choice list has been added to a container.

> **Caution**
>
> The `addItem(String)` method is deprecated after Java 1.02. Use the `add(String)` method instead when designing for later versions of the language.

After you build the choice list, it is added to a container like any other component—the container's `add()` method is used with the choice list as the argument.

Listing 11.6 shows an applet that continues the trend of using Java to recognize international entertainers. The SelectASpaniard applet builds a choice list of Spanish-born celebrities from which a single item can be selected.

TYPE   **LISTING 11.6.** THE FULL TEXT OF SELECTASPANIARD.JAVA.

```
 1: import java.awt.*;
 2:
 3: public class SelectASpaniard extends java.applet.Applet {
 4:     Choice span = new Choice();
 5:
 6:     public void init() {
 7:         span.addItem("Pedro Almodóvar");
 8:         span.addItem("Antonio Banderas");
 9:         span.addItem("Charo");
10:         span.addItem("Xavier Cugat");
```

```
11:          span.addItem("Julio Iglesias");
12:          add(span);
13:     }
14: }
```

Test this applet with the following HTML tag, and the result will resemble Figure 11.8.

```
<applet code="SelectASpaniard.class" height=200 width=150>
</applet>
```

FIGURE 11.8.

The SelectASpaniard applet.

The Choice class has several methods that can be used to control a choice list:

- The getItem(*int*) method returns the text of the list item at the index position specified by the integer argument. As with arrays, the first item of a choice list is at index position 0, the second at position 1, and so on.
- The countItems() method returns the number of items in the list. This is deprecated as of Java 1.2 and replaced with getItemCount(), which does the same thing.
- The getSelectedIndex() method returns the index position of the currently selected item in the list.
- The getSelectedItem() method returns the text of the currently selected item.
- The select(*int*) method selects the item at the indicated index position.
- The select(*String*) method selects the first item in the list with the given text.

Text Fields

Earlier, you used labels for text that cannot be modified by a user. Text fields are used to create a component for editable text. These are created from the TextField class.

To create a text field, use one of the following constructors:

- TextField() creates an empty text field with no specified width.

- TextField(*int*) creates an empty text field with enough width to display the specified number of characters. It has been deprecated as of Java 2 and should be replaced with TextField(*String*, *int*) for non-1.02 applets.
- TextField(*String*) creates a text field filled with the specified text and of no specified width.
- TextField(String, *int*) creates a text field with the specified text and specified width.

A text field's width attribute only has relevance under a layout manager that does not resize components, such as the FlowLayout manager. You get more experience with this when you work with layout managers tomorrow.

The following statement creates an empty text field that has enough space for 30 characters:

```
TextField name = new TextField(30);
```

The following statement could be used if you wanted to provide the starting text "Puddin N. Tane" in the name text field:

```
TextField name = new TextField("Puddin N. Tane", 30);
```

You also can create a text field that obscures the characters being typed in with a common character. This is used frequently in Enter Password fields to hide an entered password from prying eyes.

To set an obscuring character, the TextField class' setEchoCharacter (*char*) method is used in Java 1.02. (setEchoChar(*char*) should be used in subsequent versions of the language.) If a literal is used to specify the character, it should be surrounded by single quotation marks, as in '*'. Java interprets any literal in double quotation marks as a String object.

The following example creates a text field and sets a pound sign (#) as the character that will be shown as text is entered into the field:

```
TextField passkey = new TextField(16);
passkey.setEchoCharacter('#');
```

The applet in Listing 11.7 creates several text fields. Labels are used to identify the fields—you normally will use labels in this way, rather than providing text inside the text field explaining its use. One of the fields uses an obscuring character to hide the text being input.

TYPE   **LISTING 11.7.** THE FULL TEXT OF OUTOFSITE.JAVA.

```
 1: import java.awt.*;
 2:
 3: public class OutOfSite extends java.applet.Applet {
 4:     Label siteLabel = new Label("Site Name: ");
 5:     TextField site = new TextField(25);
 6:     Label addressLabel = new Label("Site Address: ");
 7:     TextField address = new TextField(25);
 8:     Label passwordLabel = new Label("Admin Password: ");
 9:     TextField password = new TextField(25);
10:
11:     public void init() {
12:         add(siteLabel);
13:         add(site);
14:         add(addressLabel);
15:         add(address);
16:         add(passwordLabel);
17:         password.setEchoCharacter('*');
18:         add(password);
19:     }
20: }
```

11

This applet can be tested using the following <APPLET> tag:

```
<applet code="OutOfSite.class" width=350 height=125>
</applet>
```

Because this applet uses the default layout manager, the only thing causing the six components to appear on three different lines is the width of the window. Depending on the platform you're using, you might need to adjust the width of the Applet window to produce output comparable to Figure 11.9. (You learn in the next section how to use layout managers to prevent this problem.)

FIGURE 11.9.

The OutOfSite applet.

The TextField class has several methods that can be used to control a text field:

- The getText() method returns the text contained in the field.
- The setText(*String*) method fills the field with the indicated text.

- The setEditable(*boolean*) method determines whether the field can be edited. A false argument prevents a field from being edited and true makes a field editable (which is the default).

- The isEditable() method returns a Boolean value indicating whether the field can be edited (true) or not (false).

Text Areas

Text areas, which are created with the TextArea class, are editable text fields that can handle more than one line of input. Text areas have horizontal and vertical scroll bars that enable users to scroll through the text contained in the component.

To create a text area, use one of the following constructors:

- TextArea() creates an empty text area of unspecified height and width.

- TextArea(*int*, *int*) creates an empty text area with the indicated number of lines (first argument) and the indicated width in characters (second argument).

- TextArea(*String*) creates a text area containing the indicated string of unspecified height and width.

- TextArea(*String*, *int*, *int*) creates a text area containing the indicated string, number of lines (first argument) and width in characters (second argument).

The applet shown in Listing 11.8 displays a text area that is filled with a string when the program begins running.

TYPE   **LISTING 11.8.** THE FULL TEXT OF VIRGINIA.JAVA.

```
 1: import java.awt.*;
 2:
 3: public class Virginia extends java.applet.Applet {
 4:     String letter = "Dear Editor:\n" +
 5:         "I am 8 years old.\n" +
 6:         "Some of my little friends say there is no Santa Claus." +
 7:             " Papa\n" +
 8:         "says, ''If you see it in The Sun it's so.'' Please tell" +
 9:             " me the truth,\n" +
10:         "is there a Santa Claus?\n\n" +
11:         "Virginia O'Hanlon\n" +
12:         "115 West 95th Street\n" +
13:         "New York";
14:     TextArea lt;
15:
16:     public void init() {
```

```
17:          lt = new TextArea(letter, 10, 50);
18:          add(lt);
19:          }
20: }
```

Test the `Virginia` applet with the following HTML tag:

```
<applet code="Virginia.class" height=250 width=450>
</applet>
```

The output of the applet loaded with `appletviewer` is shown in Figure 11.10.

FIGURE 11.10.

The Virginia applet.

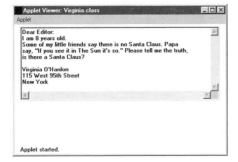

Both text areas and text fields inherit from the `TextComponent` class, so a lot of the behavior for text fields is usable on text areas as well. You can use the `setText()`, `getText()`, `setEditable()`, and `isEditable()` methods on text areas also, and text areas also can use the following methods:

- The `insertText(String, int)` method inserts the indicated string at the character index indicated by the integer. The index begins at 0 for the first character and counts upward. This method is deprecated after Java 1.02 and replaced with `insert(String, int)`.

- The `replaceText(String, int, int)` method replaces the text between the given integer positions with the indicated string. This method also is deprecated after Java 1.02 and replaced with `replace(String, int)`.

Scrolling Lists

Scrolling lists, which are created from the `List` class, are similar to choice lists with two significance differences:

- A scrolling list can be set up so that more than one item can be selected at a time.

- Scrolling lists do not pop up when selected. Instead, multiple items are displayed in a manner similar to a text area. If the list contains more items than can be displayed, a scrollbar is used to move through the entire list.

A scrolling list is developed by creating a `List` object and then adding individual items to the list. The `List` class has the following constructors:

- `List()` creates an empty scrolling list that enables only one item to be selected at a time.
- `List(int, boolean)` creates a scrolling list with the indicated number of items visible on the list, which might be lower than the total number of items. The `boolean` argument indicates whether multiple items can be selected (`true`) or not (`false`).

After a `List` object has been created, its `addItem(String)` method is used to add items to the list. (Deprecation note: The preferred method to use for Java 2 is `add(String)`).

The following example creates a list and adds two items to it:

```
List lackeys = new List();
lackeys.addItem("Rosencrantz");
lackeys.addItem("Guildenstern");
```

After creating the scrolling list and populating it with items, the list should be added to its container using the `add()` method. Listing 11.9 illustrates the creation of a scrolling list with seven items.

TYPE   **LISTING 11.9.** THE FULL TEXT OF HAMLET.JAVA.

```
 1: import java.awt.*;
 2:
 3: public class Hamlet extends java.applet.Applet {
 4:     List hm = new List(5, true);
 5:
 6:     public void init() {
 7:         hm.addItem("Hamlet");
 8:         hm.addItem("Claudius");
 9:         hm.addItem("Gertrude");
10:         hm.addItem("Polonius");
11:         hm.addItem("Horatio");
12:         hm.addItem("Laertes");
13:         hm.addItem("Ophelia");
14:         add(hm);
15:     }
16: }
```

The output for the applet is shown in Figure 11.11; the following applet tag is used:

```
<applet code="Hamlet.class" height=150 width=200>
</applet>
```

FIGURE 11.11.

The Hamlet applet with Claudius, Polonius, *and* Horatio *selected.*

Scrolling lists have several methods that work exactly the same as methods for choice lists: getItem(*int*), countItems(), getSelectedIndex(), getSelectedItem(), and select(*int*) all work the same. countItems() also has the same replacement for Java 2 programs: getItemCount().

Because more than one item can be selected for a scrolling list, the following methods also can be used:

- The getSelectedIndexes() method returns an array of integers containing the index position of each selected item.
- The getSelectedItems() method returns an array of strings containing the text of each selected item.

Scrollbars and Sliders

Scrollbars are components that enable a value to be selected by sliding a box between two arrows. Several components have built-in scrollbar functionality, including text areas and scrolling lists. The Scrollbar class is used for other scrollbars. A scrollbar can be horizontal or vertical.

Scrollbars are normally created by specifying the minimum and maximum values that can be set using the component.

To create a scrollbar, you can use the following constructors:

- Scrollbar() creates a vertical scroll bar with its initial maximum and minimum values equal to 0.
- Scrollbar(*int*) creates a scrollbar with minimum and maximum values of 0 and the indicated orientation. Class variables are used to set the orientation with the method's only argument: Scrollbar.HORIZONTAL or Scrollbar.VERTICAL.

11

You also can use a third constructor with five integer arguments: Scrollbar(*int*, *int*, *int*, *int*, *int*). The arguments for this method are in order here:

- Orientation is either Scrollbar.HORIZONTAL or Scrollbar.VERTICAL.
- The initial value of the scrollbar, which should equal or be between the minimum and maximum values of the bar.
- The overall width or height of the box used to change the scrollbar's value. This can be equal to 0 when using the default size.
- The minimum value of the scrollbar.
- The maximum value.

Listing 11.10 shows a simple applet that displays a scrollbar. The GridLayout object is used with the applet's setLayout() method to provide a layout in which a scrollbar fills its entire container. You learn about layout managers tomorrow.

TYPE   **LISTING 11.10.** THE FULL TEXT OF SLIDER.JAVA.

```
 1: import java.awt.*;
 2:
 3: public class Slider extends java.applet.Applet {
 4:     GridLayout gl = new GridLayout(1,1);
 5:     Scrollbar bar = new Scrollbar(Scrollbar.HORIZONTAL,
 6:     50,0,1,100);
 7:
 8:     public void init() {
 9:         setLayout(gl);
10:         add(bar);
11:     }
12: }
```

No matter what values are used for the height and width of the Applet window, the scrollbar will fill the entire area. Figure 11.12 was produced using the following tag:

```
<applet code="Slider.class" height=20 width=500>
</applet>
```

The Scrollbar class provides several methods for managing the values within scroll bars:

- The getValue() method returns the scroll bar's current value.
- The setValue(*int*) method sets the current value.

FIGURE 11.12.

The Slider applet.

Canvases

Canvases are components that are primarily used as a place on an interface to display images or animation. You can draw to other components, as you have done with the Applet window throughout this book, but Canvases are the simplest object for this kind of use.

In order to use a canvas, you must create a subclass of Canvas. That subclass can handle any drawing that needs to take place on the canvas in its paint() method.

Once you have created a canvas subclass, it can be used in a program by calling its constructor and adding the new Canvas object to a container.

This is demonstrated with the Crosshair applet, shown in Listing 11.11. This applet draws a target crosshair at the center of the Applet window and can immediately move the center if the window is resized.

11

TYPE   **LISTING 11.11.** THE FULL TEXT OF CROSSHAIR.JAVA.

```
 1: import java.awt.*;
 2:
 3: public class Crosshair extends java.applet.Applet {
 4:     GridLayout gl = new GridLayout(1,1);
 5:     MyCanvas can = new MyCanvas();
 6:
 7:     public void init() {
 8:         setLayout(gl);
 9:         add(can);
10:     }
11:
12: }
13:
14: class MyCanvas extends java.awt.Canvas {
15:     public void paint(Graphics g) {
16:         int x = size().width / 2;
17:         int y = size().height / 2;
18:         g.setColor(Color.black);
19:         g.drawLine(x-10,y,x-2,y);
20:         g.drawLine(x+10,y,x+2,y);
21:         g.drawLine(x,y-10,x,y-2);
22:         g.drawLine(x,y+10,x,y+2);
23:     }
24: }
```

The Crosshair program can be tested with a window of any size for the applet. The following <APPLET> tag was used to produce the output shown in Figure 11.13.

```
<applet code="Crosshair.class" height=100 width=100>
</applet>
```

FIGURE 11.13.

The Crosshair applet.

Listing 11.11 contains two class files. The first, `Crosshair`, is the applet itself. The second, listed on lines 14–24, is the `MyCanvas` class, which is a subclass of `Canvas`.

The following things are taking place in the `Crosshair` class:

- Line 4 creates a `GridLayout` object that will be set as the layout manager for the class in line 8.
- Line 5 creates a `MyCanvas` object called `can` using the subclass of `Canvas` that is created in lines 14–24.
- Line 9 adds `can` to the Applet window. Because a grid layout manager is in effect, the canvas expands to fill the entire window.

Most of the work in this project is done in `MyCanvas`, the helper class. The following things are taking place in the class:

- Lines 16 and 17 determine the point at the center of the Applet window. This is done dynamically each time the canvas is repainted. The `size().width` and `size().height` variables hold the width and height of the canvas, and they can be divided by 2 to determine the center point. If you're not writing a 1.02 applet, the `getSize().width` and `getSize().height` variables should be used instead to avoid deprecation warnings when you compile the program.
- Line 18 sets black as the currently active color for drawing operations. Note that this method is called on the `Graphics` object and not the canvas itself. The `Graphics` object sent to the `paint()` method handles all drawing operations that take place on the object.
- Lines 19–22 use the x,y center coordinates to draw four lines in a crosshair pattern around the center. Each line is 8 pixels long and ends 2 pixels from the center.

Summary

You now know how to paint a user interface onto a Java applet's window using the language's standard palette—the components of the Abstract Windowing Toolkit.

The toolkit includes classes for many of the buttons, bars, lists, and fields you would expect to see on a program. These components are used by creating an instance of their class and adding it to a container—such as an Applet window—by using the container's add() method.

Today you learned something about function by developing components and adding them to a program. During the next two days you learn more about two things that are needed to make a graphical interface usable:

Form: How to arrange components together to form a whole interface.

Feedback: How to receive input from a user through these components.

Q&A

Q With all the deprecated methods that are part of the Abstract Windowing Toolkit as of Java 2, why should I write applets in Java 1.02?

A Ideally, you shouldn't have to learn anything about past versions of Java when you're tackling Java 2. However, the leading browser developers have been extremely slow to introduce support for versions of the language beyond 1.02, and it appears at the time of this writing that Microsoft will never support Java 1.1 in full, much less Java 2. Because of this, Java 1.02 remains the standard when writing applets. Sun is working on a way for applet developers to specify their own runtime environment with an applet, which would make it possible to write Java 2 applets and be sure that the people using Java-enabled browsers could run the program.

Q My Java development tool has a way to design a program's interface visually—I can drag and drop buttons and other components and arrange them with a mouse. Do I need to learn the Abstract Windowing Toolkit?

A If you're happy with the results you're getting and confident in your ability to use the interface in a working program, the Abstract Windowing Toolkit is not a necessity. However, using the AWT to create a working graphical user interface is one of this book's major projects. It builds skills you will benefit from in other areas of Java.

11

DAY **12**

Arranging Components on a User Interface

If designing a graphical user interface is comparable to painting, you currently can produce only one kind of art: abstract expressionism. You can put components onto an interface but you don't have much control over where they go.

In order to impose some kind of form on a interface designed with the Abstract Windowing Toolkit, you must use a set of classes called *layout managers*.

Today you learn how to use five layout managers to arrange components into an interface. You'll take advantage of the flexibility of Java's windowing toolkit, which was designed to be presentable on the many different platforms that support the language.

When one arrangement doesn't quite suit what you have in mind for a program, you also learn how to put several different layout managers to work on the same interface.

The place to start is with the basic layout managers.

Basic Interface Layout

As you learned yesterday, a graphical user interface designed with the Abstract Windowing Toolkit is a very fluid thing. Resizing a window can wreak havoc on your interface, as components move to places on a container that might not have been what you had in mind.

This fluidity is by necessity. Java is implemented on many different platforms, and there are subtle differences in the way each platform displays things such as buttons, scroll-bars, and the like.

With programming languages such as Microsoft Visual Basic, a component's location on a window is precisely defined by its x,y coordinates. Some Java development tools allow similar control over an interface through the use of their own windowing classes.

When using the Abstract Windowing Toolkit, a programmer gains more control over the layout of an interface by using layout managers.

Laying Out an Interface

A layout manager determines how components will be arranged when they are added to a container.

The default layout manager is the `FlowLayout` class. This class lets components flow from left to right in the order they are added to a container. When there's no more room, a new row of components begins immediately below the first, and the left-to-right order continues.

The AWT includes five basic layout managers: `FlowLayout`, `GridLayout`, `BorderLayout`, `CardLayout`, and `GridBagLayout`. To create a layout manager for a container, an instance of the container is created using a statement such as the following:

```
FlowLayout flo = new FlowLayout();
```

After you create a layout manager, you make it the layout manager for a container by using the container's `setLayout()` method. The layout manager must be established before any components are added to the container. If no layout manager is specified, flow layout will be used.

The following statements represent the starting point for an applet that creates a layout manager and uses `setLayout()` so that it controls the arrangement of all components that will be added to the Applet window:

```
public class Starter extends java.applet.Applet {
    FlowLayout lm = new FlowLayout();
```

```
    public void init() {
        setLayout(lm);
    }
}
```

After the layout manager is set, you can start adding components to the container that it manages. For some of the layout managers such as FlowLayout, the order in which components are added is significant. You learn more in today's subsequent sections as you work with each of the managers.

Flow Layout

The FlowLayout class is the simplest of the layout managers. It lays out components in a manner similar to the way words are laid out on a page—from left to right until there's no more room, then on to the next row.

By default, the components on each row will be centered when you use the FlowLayout() constructor with no arguments. If you want the components to be aligned along the left or right edge of the container, the FlowLayout.LEFT or FlowLayout.RIGHT class variable should be the constructor's only argument, as in the following statement:

```
FlowLayout righty = new FlowLayout(FlowLayout.RIGHT);
```

The FlowLayout.CENTER class variable is used to specify centered components.

The applet in Listing 12.1 displays six buttons arranged by the flow layout manager. Because the FlowLayout.LEFT class variable was used in the FlowLayout() constructor, the components are lined up along the left side of the applet window.

12

TYPE **LISTING 12.1.** THE FULL TEXT OF ALPHABET.JAVA.

```
 1: import java.awt.*;
 2:
 3: public class Alphabet extends java.applet.Applet {
 4:     Button a = new Button("Alibi");
 5:     Button b = new Button("Burglar");
 6:     Button c = new Button("Corpse");
 7:     Button d = new Button("Deadbeat");
 8:     Button e = new Button("Evidence");
 9:     Button f = new Button("Fugitive");
10:     FlowLayout lm = new FlowLayout(FlowLayout.LEFT);
11:
12:     public void init() {
13:         setLayout(lm);
14:         add(a);
15:         add(b);
```

continues

LISTING 12.1. CONTINUED

```
16:          add(c);
17:          add(d);
18:          add(e);
19:          add(f);
20:      }
21: }
```

The following `<APPLET>` tag was used to produce the output shown in Figure 12.1 with the `appletviewer`:

```
<applet code="Alphabet.class" height=120 width=220>
</applet>
```

FIGURE 12.1.

Six buttons arranged in flow layout.

In the Alphabet applet, the flow layout manager puts a gap of three pixels between each component on a row and three pixels between each row. You also can change the horizontal and vertical gap between components with some extra arguments to the `FlowLayout()` constructor.

The `FlowLayout(int, int, int)` constructor takes the following three arguments, in order:

- The alignment, which must be `FlowLayout.CENTER`, `FlowLayout.LEFT`, or `FlowLayout.RIGHT`
- The horizontal gap between components, in pixels
- The vertical gap, in pixels

The following constructor creates a flow layout manager with centered components, a horizontal gap of 30 pixels and a vertical gap of 10:

```
FlowLayout flo = new FlowLayout(FlowLayout.CENTER, 30, 10);
```

Grid Layout

The grid layout manager arranges components into a grid of rows and columns. Components are added first to the top row of the grid, beginning with the leftmost grid cell and continuing to the right. When all of the cells in the top row are full, the next component is added to the leftmost cell in second row of the grid—if there is a second row—and so on.

Grid layouts are created with the GridLayout class. Two arguments are sent to the GridLayout constructor—the number of rows in the grid and the number of columns. The following statement creates a grid layout manager with 10 rows and 3 columns:

```
GridLayout gr = new GridLayout(10,3);
```

As with flow layout, you can specify a vertical and horizontal gap between components with two extra arguments. The following statement creates a grid layout with 10 rows, 3 columns, a horizontal gap of 5 pixels, and a vertical gap of 8 pixels:

```
GridLayout gr2 = new GridLayout(10,3,5,8);
```

The default gap between components under grid layout is 0 pixels in both vertical and horizontal directions.

Listing 12.2 contains an applet that creates a grid with 3 rows, 3 columns, and a 10-pixel gap between components in both the vertical and horizontal directions.

TYPE   **LISTING 12.2.** THE FULL TEXT OF BUNCH.JAVA.

```
 1: import java.awt.*;
 2:
 3: public class Bunch extends java.applet.Applet {
 4:     GridLayout family = new GridLayout(3,3,10,10);
 5:     Button marcia = new Button("Marcia");
 6:     Button carol = new Button("Carol");
 7:     Button greg = new Button("Greg");
 8:     Button jan = new Button("Jan");
 9:     Button alice = new Button("Alice");
10:     Button peter = new Button("Peter");
11:     Button cindy = new Button("Cindy");
12:     Button mike = new Button("Mike");
13:     Button bobby = new Button("Bobby");
14:
15:     public void init() {
16:         setLayout(family);
17:         add(marcia);
18:         add(carol);
19:         add(greg);
20:         add(jan);
21:         add(alice);
22:         add(peter);
23:         add(cindy);
```

12

continues

LISTING 12.2. CONTINUED

```
24:            add(mike);
25:            add(bobby);
26:        }
27: }
```

Figure 12.2 shows this applet on a page with the following <APPLET> tag:

```
<applet code="Bunch.class" height=160 width=160>
</applet>
```

FIGURE 12.2.

Nine buttons arranged in 3×3 grid layout.

One thing to note about the buttons in Figure 12.2 is that they expanded to fill the space available to them in each cell. This is an important difference between flow layout and some of the other layout managers. In grid layout, a component always will take up a cell's entire space. If you load the Bunch applet using the appletviewer tool, you can see that the buttons change size when you resize the Applet window.

Border Layout

Border layouts, which are created by using the BorderLayout class, divide a container into five sections: north, south, east, west, and center. The five areas of Figure 12.3 show how these sections are arranged.

FIGURE 12.3.

Component arrangement under border layout.

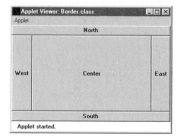

Under border layout, the components in the four compass points will take up as much space as they need—the center gets whatever space is left over. Ordinarily, this will result in an arrangement with a large central component and four thin components around it.

A border layout is created with either the BorderLayout() or BorderLayout(*int*, *int*) constructors. The first constructor creates a border layout with no gap between any of the components. The second constructor specifies the horizontal gap and vertical gap, respectively.

After you create a border layout and set it up as a container's layout manager, components are added using a different call to the add() method than you have seen previously:

add(String, component)

The second argument to this method is the component that should be added to the container.

The first argument is a string indicating which part of the border layout to assign the component to. There are five possible values: "North", "South", "East", "West", or "Center".

The following statement adds a button called quitButton to the north portion of a border layout:

add("North", quitButton);

Listing 12.3 contains the applet used to produce Figure 12.3.

LISTING 12.3. THE FULL TEXT OF BORDER.JAVA.

```
 1: import java.awt.*;
 2:
 3: public class Border extends java.applet.Applet {
 4:     BorderLayout b = new BorderLayout();
 5:     Button north = new Button("North");
 6:     Button south = new Button("South");
 7:     Button east = new Button("East");
 8:     Button west = new Button("West");
 9:     Button center = new Button("Center");
10:
11:     public void init() {
12:         setLayout(b);
13:         add("North", north);
14:         add("South", south);
15:         add("East", east);
16:         add("West", west);
17:         add("Center", center);
18:     }
19: }
```

12

The following <APPLET> tag was used:

```
<applet code="Border.class" height=120 width=120>
</applet>
```

Mixing Layout Managers

At this point, you might be wondering how the Abstract Windowing Toolkit's layout managers will work with the kind of graphical user interface you want to design. Choosing a layout manager is an experience akin to Goldilocks checking out the home of the three bears and finding it lacking: "This one is too square! This one is too disorganized! This one is too strange!"

To find the layout that is just right, you often have to combine more than one manager on the same interface.

This is done by adding containers to a main container like an Applet window, and giving each of these smaller containers their own layout managers.

The container to use for these smaller containers is the panel, which is created from the Panel class. *Panels* are containers that are used to group components together. There are two things to keep in mind when working with panels:

- The panel is filled with components before it is put into a larger container.
- The panel has its own layout manager.

Panels are created with a simple call to the constructor of the Panel class, as shown in the following example:

```
Panel pane = new Panel();
```

The layout method is set for a panel by calling the setLayout() method on that panel. This works identically to the setLayout() method you've been using for the applet window—both Applet and Panel are subclasses of the Container class, and they inherit the layout management behavior unchanged from that superclass.

The following statements create a layout manager and apply it to a Panel object called pane:

```
BorderLayout bo = new BorderLayout();
pane.setLayout(bo);
```

Components are added to a panel by calling the panel's add() method, which works the same for panels as it does for other containers like applets.

The following statement adds a text area called `dialogue` to a `Panel` object called `pane`:

```
pane.add(dialogue);
```

You'll see several examples of panel use in the rest of today's example programs.

Advanced Interface Layout

In addition to the three layout managers you have learned about—flow layout, grid layout, and border layout—the Abstract Windowing Toolkit includes two more sophisticated layout managers. The card layout and grid bag layout managers also can be mixed with the other managers by nesting one container inside another.

Card Layout

Card layouts differ from the other layouts because they hide some components from view. A *card layout* is a group of containers or components that are displayed one at a time, in the same way that a blackjack dealer reveals one card at a time from a deck. Each container in the group is called a *card*.

If you have used software such as HyperCard on the Macintosh or a tabbed dialog box such as the System Properties portion of the Windows 95 Control Panel, you have worked with a program that uses card layout.

The normal way to use a card layout is to use a panel for each card. Components are added to the panels first, and then the panels are added to the container that is set to use card layout.

A card layout is created from the `CardLayout` class with a simple constructor call:

```
CardLayout cc = new CardLayout();
```

The `setLayout()` method is used to make this the layout manager for the container, as in the following statement:

```
setLayout(cc);
```

After you set a container to use the card layout manager, you must use a slightly different `add()` method call to add cards to the layout.

The method to use is add(*String, container*). The second argument specifies the container or component that is the card. If it is a container, all components must have been added to it before the card is added.

12

The first argument to the add() method is a string that represents the name of the card. This can be anything you want to call the card. You might want to number the cards in some way and use the number in the name, as in "Card 1", "Card 2", "Card 3", and so on.

The following statement adds a panel called options to a container and gives this card the name "Options Card":

```
add("Options Card", options);
```

After you have added a card to the main container for a program, such as an Applet window, you can use the show() method of your card layout manager to display a card. The show() method takes two arguments:

- The container that all the cards have been added to. If the container is the applet, you can use the this keyword inside the applet for this argument.
- The name that was given to the card.

The following statement calls the show() method of a card layout manager called cc:

```
cc.show(this, "Fact Card");
```

The this keyword refers to the class that this statement is appearing in, and "Fact Card" is the name of the card to reveal. When a card is shown, the previously displayed card will be obscured. Only one card in a card layout can be viewed at a time.

In a program that uses the card layout manager, a card change will usually be triggered by a user's action. For example, in a program that displays mailing addresses on different cards, the user could select a card for display by selecting an item in a scrolling list. As an alternative, the applet in Listing 12.4 uses threaded animation to switch from one card's panel to the next.

TYPE   **LISTING 12.4.** THE FULL TEXT OF BURMASHAVE.JAVA.

```
 1: import java.awt.*;
 2:
 3: public class BurmaShave extends java.applet.Applet
 4:     implements Runnable {
 5:
 6:     CardLayout card = new CardLayout();
 7:     Label[] lab = new Label[6];
 8:     int current = 0;
 9:     Thread runner;
10:
11:     public void start() {
12:         if (runner == null) {
```

```
13:                runner = new Thread(this);
14:                runner.start();
15:          }
16:      }
17:
18:      public void stop() {
19:          runner = null;
20:      }
21:
22:      public void init() {
23:          lab[0] = new Label("Grandpa's beard");
24:          lab[1] = new Label("Was stiff and coarse.");
25:          lab[2] = new Label("And that's what caused");
26:          lab[3] = new Label("His fifth");
27:          lab[4] = new Label("Divorce.");
28:          lab[5] = new Label("Burma Shave.");
29:          setLayout(card);
30:          for (int i = 0; i < 6; i++)
31:              add("Card " + i, lab[i]);
32:      }
33:
34:      public void run() {
35:          Thread thisThread = Thread.currentThread();
36:          while (runner == thisThread) {
37:              card.show(this, "Card " + current);
38:              current++;
39:              if (current > 5)
40:                  current = 0;
41:              repaint();
42:              try {
43:                  Thread.sleep(5000);
44:              } catch (InterruptedException e) { }
45:          }
46:      }
47: }
```

12

The following <APPLET> tag was used to produce the output shown in Figure 12.4.

```
<applet code="BurmaShave.class" height=80 width=160>
</applet>
```

The BurmaShave applet features a card layout with six cards. Each card is a label component, and the animation is achieved by cycling through the six cards.

Some notes on the applet:

- Line 7—The lab array is created to hold the six labels.
- Line 8—The current variable is set up. This is used to keep track of the current card to display.

- Lines 23–28—The six Label objects are created and each is titled with a line from a Burma Shave roadside advertising slogan.
- Line 29—The layout manager for the applet is set to card layout.
- Lines 30 and 31—Using a for loop, all six labels in the lab array are added to the Applet window as cards. Each card is given a name beginning with the text "Card", followed by a space and a number from 0 to 5, such as "Card 0".
- Line 37—The show() method of the CardLayout class is used to show the current card. The name of the card is the text "Card", followed by a space and the value of the current variable.
- Line 38—The value of current is incremented by 1.
- Lines 39 and 40—The current variable is set back to 0 if it goes above 5.

FIGURE 12.4.

One card displayed in a multicard layout.

Grid Bag Layout

The last of the layout managers available through the AWT is grid bag layout, which is an extension of the grid layout manager. A grid bag layout differs from grid layout in the following ways:

- A component can take up more than one cell in the grid.
- The proportions between different rows and columns do not have to be equal.
- Components inside grid cells can be arranged in different ways.

To create a grid bag layout, you use the GridBagLayout class and a helper class called GridBagConstraints. GridBagLayout is the layout manager, and GridBagConstraints is used to define the properties of each component to be placed into the cell—its placement, dimensions, alignment, and so on. The relationship between the grid bag, the constraints, and each component defines the overall layout.

In its most general form, creating a grid bag layout involves the following steps:

1. Creating a GridBagLayout object and defining it as the current layout manager, as you would for any other layout manager
2. Creating a new instance of GridBagConstraints
3. Setting up the constraints for a component

4. Telling the layout manager about the component and its constraints

5. Adding the component to the container

The following example adds a single button to a container implementing grid bag layout. (Don't worry about the various values for the constraints; they are covered later in this section.)

```
// set up layout
GridBagLayout gridbag = new GridBagLayout();
GridBagConstraints constraints = new GridBagConstraints();
setLayout(gridbag);

// define constraints for the button
Button btn = new Button("Save");
constraints.gridx = 0;
constraints.gridy = 0;
constraints.gridwidth = 1;
constraints.gridheight = 1;
constraints.weightx = 30;
constraints.weighty = 30;
constraints.fill = GridBagConstraints.NONE;
constraints.anchor = GridBagConstraints.CENTER;

// attach constraints to layout, add button
gridbag.setConstraints(btn, constraints);
add(btn);
```

As you can see from this example, you have to set all of the constraints for every component you want to add to the panel. Given the numerous constraints, it helps to have a plan and to deal with each kind of constraint one at a time.

Step One: Design the Grid

The first place to start in the grid bag layout is on paper. Sketching out your user interface design beforehand—before you write even a single line of code—will help enormously in the long run with trying to figure out where everything goes. Put your editor aside for a second, pick up a piece of paper and a pencil, and build the grid.

Figure 12.5 shows the panel layout you'll be building in this example. Figure 12.6 shows the same layout with a grid imposed on top of it. Your layout will have a grid similar to this one, with rows and columns forming individual cells.

As you draw your grid, keep in mind that each component must have its own cell. You cannot put more than one component into the same cell. The reverse is not true, however; one component can span multiple cells in the x or y direction (as in the OK button in the bottom row, which spans two columns). In Figure 12.6, note that the labels and text fields have their own grids and that the button spans two column cells.

12

FIGURE 12.5.

A grid bag layout.

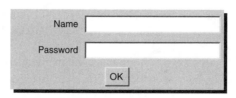

FIGURE 12.6.

The grid bag layout from Figure 12.5, with grid imposed.

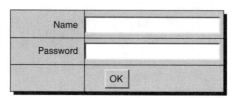

Label the cells with their x and y coordinates while you're still working on paper; this helps you later. They aren't pixel coordinates; rather, they're cell coordinates. The top-left cell is 0,0. The next cell to the right of it in the top row is 1,0. The cell to the right of that one is 2,0. Moving to the next row, the leftmost cell is 1,0, the next cell in the row is 1,1, and so on. Label your cells on the paper with these numbers; you'll need them later when you do the code for this example. Figure 12.7 shows the numbers for each of the cells in this example.

FIGURE 12.7.

The grid bag layout from Figure 12.5, with cell coordinates.

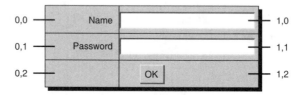

Step Two: Create the Grid

Now go back to Java and start implementing the layout you've just drawn on paper. Initially, you're going to focus exclusively on the layout—getting the grid and the proportions right. For that, it might be easier to use buttons as placeholders for the actual elements in the layout. They're easy to create and they clearly define the space that a component will take up in the layout manager—or managers—that are in use. Once everything is set up correctly, the buttons can be replaced with the right elements.

To cut down on the amount of typing you have to do to set up all those constraints, you can start by defining a helper method that takes several values and sets the constraints for those values. The `buildConstraints()` method takes seven arguments: a `GridBagConstraints` object and six integers representing the `GridBagConstraints` instance variables `gridx`, `gridy`, `gridwidth`, `gridheight`, `weightx`, and `weighty`. You'll learn later what these actually do; for now, here's the code to the helper method that you'll use later in this example:

```
void buildConstraints(GridBagConstraints gbc, int gx, int gy,
    int gw, int gh, int wx, int wy) {

    gbc.gridx = gx;
    gbc.gridy = gy;
    gbc.gridwidth = gw;
    gbc.gridheight = gh;
    gbc.weightx = wx;
    gbc.weighty = wy;
}
```

Now move on to the `init()` method, where all the layout actually occurs. Here's the basic method definition, where you'll define the `GridBagLayout` to be the initial layout manager and create a constraints object (an instance of `GridBagConstraints`):

```
public void init() {
    GridBagLayout gridbag = new GridBagLayout();
    GridBagConstraints constraints = new GridBagConstraints();
    setLayout(gridbag);

    constraints.fill = GridBagConstraints.BOTH;
}
```

One more small note of explanation: The last line, which sets the value of `constraints.fill`, will be removed (and explained) later. It's there so that the components will fill the entire cell in which they're contained, which helps you see what's going on. Add it for now; you'll get a clearer idea of what it's for later.

Now add the button placeholders to the layout. (Remember that you're focusing on basic grid organization at the moment, so you'll use buttons as placeholders for the actual user interface elements you'll add later.) Start with a single button so you can get a feel for setting its constraints. This code will go into the `init()` method just after the setLayout line:

```
// Name label
buildConstraints(constraints, 0, 0, 1, 1, 100, 100);
Button label1 = new Button("Name:");
gridbag.setConstraints(label1, constraints);
add(label1);
```

These four lines set up the constraints for an object, create a new button, attach the constraints to the button, and then add it to the panel. Note that constraints for a component are stored in the `GridBagConstraints` object, so the component doesn't even have to exist to set up its constraints.

Now you can get down to details: Just what are the values for the constraints that you've plugged into the helper method `buildConstraints()`?

The first two integer arguments are the `gridx` and `gridy` values of the constraints. They are the cell coordinates of the cell that contains this component. Remember how you wrote these components down on paper in step one? With the cells nearly numbered on paper, all you have to do is plug in the right values. Note that if you have a component that spans multiple cells, the cell coordinates are those of the cell in the top-left corner.

This button is in the top-left corner, so its `gridx` and `gridy` (the first two arguments to `buildConstraints()`) are 0 and 0, respectively.

The second two integer arguments are the `gridwidth` and `gridheight`. They are not the pixel widths and heights of the cells; rather, they are the number of cells this component spans: `gridwidth` for the columns and `gridheight` for the rows. Here this component spans only one cell, so the values for both are 1.

The last two integer arguments are for `weightx` and `weighty`. They are used to set up the proportions of the rows and columns—that is, how wide or deep they will be. Weights can become very confusing, so for now, set both values to 100. Weights are dealt with in step three.

After the constraints have been built, you can attach them to an object using the `setConstraints()` method. `setConstraints()`, which is a method defined in `GridBagLayout`, takes two arguments: the component (here a button) and the constraints for that button. Finally, you can add the button to the panel.

After you've set and assigned the constraints to one component, you can reuse that `GridBagConstraints` object to set up the constraints for the next object. You, therefore, duplicate these four lines for each component in the grid, with different values for the `buildConstraints()` method. To save space, the `buildConstraints()` methods will only be shown for the last four cells.

The second cell to add is the one that will hold the text box for the name. The cell coordinates for this one are 1,0 (second column, first row); it too spans only one cell, and the weights (for now) are both 100:

```
buildConstraints(constraints, 1, 0, 1, 1, 100, 100);
```

The next two components, which will be a label and a text field, are nearly exactly the same as the previous two; the only difference is in their cell coordinates. The password label is at 0,1 (first column, second row), and the password text field is at 1,1 (second column, second row):

```
buildConstraints(constraints, 0, 1, 1, 1, 100, 100);
buildConstraints(constraints, 1, 1, 1, 1, 100, 100);
```

Finally, you need the OK button, which is a component that spans two cells in the bottom row of the panel. Here the cell coordinates are the left and topmost cell, where the span starts (0,2). Here, unlike the previous components, you'll set `gridwidth` and `gridheight` to be something other than 1 because this cell spans multiple columns. The `gridwidth` is 2 (it spans two cells) and the `gridheight` is 1 (it spans only one row):

```
buildConstraints(constraints, 0, 2, 2, 1, 100, 100);
```

You've set the placement constraints for all the components that will be added to the grid layout. You also need to assign each component's constraints to the layout manager and then add each component to the panel. Figure 12.8 shows the result at this point. Note that you're not concerned about exact proportions here, or concerned about making sure everything lines up. What you should keep track of at this point is making sure the grid is working, that you have the right number of rows and columns, that the spans are correct, and that nothing strange is going on (cells in the wrong place, cells overlapping, that kind of thing).

FIGURE 12.8.

Grid bag layout, first pass.

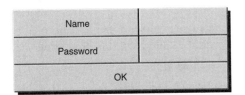

Step Three: Determine the Proportions

The next step is to determine the proportions of the rows and columns in relation to other rows and columns. For example, in this case you'll want the labels (name and password) to take up less space than the text boxes. You might want the OK button at the bottom to be only half the height of the two text boxes above it. You arrange the proportions of the cells within your layout using the `weightx` and `weighty` constraints.

The easiest way to think of `weightx` and `weighty` is that their values are either percentages of the total width and height of the panel, or 0 if the weight or height has been set by some other cell. The values of `weightx` and `weighty` for all your components, therefore, should sum to 100.

Note

Actually, the `weightx` and `weighty` values are not percentages; they're simply proportions—they can have any value whatsoever. When the proportions

12

> are calculated, all the values in a direction are summed so that each individual value is in proportion to that total. To make this process easier to understand: Look at the weights as percentages and make sure they sum up to 100 to make sure everything is coming out right.

Which cells get values and which cells get 0? Cells that span multiple rows or columns should always be 0 in the direction they span. Beyond that, deciding is simply a question of picking a cell to have a value, and then all the other cells in that row or columns should be 0.

Look at the five calls to `buildConstraints()` made in the preceding step:

```
buildConstraints(constraints, 0, 0, 1, 1, 100, 100); //name
buildConstraints(constraints, 1, 0, 1, 1, 100, 100); //name text
buildConstraints(constraints, 0, 1, 1, 1, 100, 100); //password
buildConstraints(constraints, 1, 1, 1, 1, 100, 100); //password text
buildConstraints(constraints, 0, 2, 2, 1, 100, 100); //OK button
```

You'll be changing those last two arguments in each call to `buildConstraints` to be either a value or 0. Start with the x direction (the proportions of the columns), which is the second-to-last argument in the preceding list.

If you look back to Figure 12.6 (the picture of the panel with the grid imposed), note that the second column is much larger than the first. If you were going to pick theoretical percentages for those columns, you might say that the first is 10 percent and the second is 90 percent. (This is a guess; that's all you need to do as well.) With these two guesses, you can assign them to cells. You don't want to assign any values to the cell with the OK button because that cell spans both columns, and percentages there wouldn't work. Add them to the first two cells, the name label and the name text field:

```
buildConstraints(constraints, 0, 0, 1, 1, 10, 100); //name
buildConstraints(constraints, 1, 0, 1, 1, 90, 100); //name text
```

What about the values of the remaining two cells, the password label and text field? Because the proportions of the columns have already been set up by the name label and field, you don't have to reset them here. Give both of these cells as well as the one for the OK box 0 values:

```
buildConstraints(constraints, 0, 1, 1, 1, 0, 100); //password
buildConstraints(constraints, 1, 1, 1, 1, 0, 100); //password text
buildConstraints(constraints, 0, 2, 2, 1, 0, 100); //OK button
```

Note here that a 0 value does not mean that the cell has 0 width. These values are proportions, not pixel values. A 0 simply means that the proportion has been set somewhere else; all 0 says is "stretch it to fit."

Now that the totals of all the `weightx` constraints are `100`, you can move on to the `weighty` arguments. Here you have three rows. Glancing over the grid you drew, it looks like the button has about 20 percent and the text fields have the rest (40 percent each). As with the x values, you have to set the value of only one cell per row (the two labels and the button), with all the other cells having a `weightx` of `0`.

Here are the final five calls to `buildConstraints()` with the weights in place:

```
buildConstraints(constraints, 0, 0, 1, 1, 10, 40); //name
buildConstraints(constraints, 1, 0, 1, 1, 90, 0); //name text
buildConstraints(constraints, 0, 1, 1, 1, 0, 40); //password
buildConstraints(constraints, 1, 1, 1, 1, 0, 0); //password text
buildConstraints(constraints, 0, 2, 2, 1, 0, 20); //OK button
```

Figure 12.9 shows the result with the correct proportions.

FIGURE 12.9.

Grid bag layout, second pass.

At this step, the goal is to try to come up with some basic proportions for how the rows and cells will be spaced on the screen. You can make some basic estimates based on how big you expect the various components to be, but chances are you're going to use a lot of trial and error in this part of the process.

Step Four: Add and Arrange the Components

With the layout and the proportions in place, you can now replace the button placeholders with actual labels and text fields. Because you set up everything already, it should all work perfectly, right? Well, almost. Figure 12.10 shows what you get if you use the same constraints as before and replace the buttons with actual components.

FIGURE 12.10.

Grid bag layout, almost there.

This layout is close, but it's weird. The text boxes are too tall, and the OK button stretches the width of the cell.

What's missing are the constraints that arrange the components inside the cell. There are two of them: `fill` and `anchor`.

The `fill` constraint determines—for components that can stretch in either direction—in which direction to stretch (such as text boxes and buttons). `fill` can have one of four values, defined as class variables in the `GridBagConstraints` class:

- `GridBagConstraints.BOTH`, which stretches the component to fill the cell in both directions
- `GridBagConstraints.NONE`, which causes the component to be displayed in its smallest size
- `GridBagConstraints.HORIZONTAL`, which stretches the component in the horizontal direction
- `GridBagConstraints.VERTICAL`, which stretches the component in the vertical direction

Note

Keep in mind that this layout is dynamic. You're not going to set up the actual pixel dimensions of any components; rather, you're telling these elements in which direction they can grow given a panel that can be of any size.

By default, the `fill` constraint for all components is `NONE`. Why are the text fields and labels filling the cells is this is the case? If you remember way back to the start of the code for this example, this line was added to the `init()` method:

```
constraints.fill = GridBagConstraints.BOTH;
```

Now you know what it does. For the final version of this applet, you'll want to remove that line and add `fill` values for each independent component.

The second constraint that affects how a component appears in the cell is `anchor`. This constraint applies only to components that aren't filling the whole cell, and it tells the AWT where inside the cell to place the component. The possible values for the anchor constraint are `GridBagConstraints.CENTER`, which aligns the component both vertically and horizontally inside the cell, or one of eight direction values:

`GridBagConstraints.NORTH`	`GridBagConstraints.SOUTH`
`GridBagConstraints.NORTHEAST,`	`GridBagConstraints.SOUTHWEST,`
`GridBagConstraints.EAST`	`GridBagConstraints.WEST`
`GridBagConstraints.SOUTHEAST,`	`GridBagConstraints.NORTHWEST`

The default value of anchor is `GridBagConstraints.CENTER`.

You set these constraints the same way you did all the other ones: by changing instance variables in the `GridBagConstraints` object. Here you can change the definition of `buildConstraints()` to take two more arguments (they're integers), or you could just set them in the body of the `init()` method. The latter is used on this project.

Be careful with defaults. Keep in mind that because you're reusing the same `GridBagConstraints` object for each component, you may have some values left over when you're done with one component. On the other hand, if a `fill` or `anchor` from one object is the same as the one before it, you don't have to reset that object.

For this example, three changes are going to be made to the `fill` and `anchor` values of the components:

- The labels will have no `fill` and will be aligned `EAST` (so they hug the right side of the cell).
- The text fields will be filled horizontally (so they start one line high, but stretch to the width of the cell).
- The button will have no `fill` and will be center-aligned.

This is reflected in the full code at the end of this section.

Step Five: Make Adjustments

As you working with your own programs and grid bag layouts, the resulting layout often requires some tinkering. You may need to play with various values of the constraints to get an interface to come out right. There's nothing wrong with that—the goal of following the preceding steps is to get things fairly close to the final positions, not to come out with a perfect layout every time.

Listing 12.5 shows the complete code for the layout you've been building up in this section. If you had trouble following the discussion up to this point, you might find it useful to go through this code line by line to make sure you understand the various parts.

TYPE   **LISTING 12.5.** THE FULL TEXT OF NAMEPASS.JAVA.

```
1: import java.awt.*;
2:
3: public class NamePass extends java.applet.Applet {
4:
5:    void buildConstraints(GridBagConstraints gbc, int gx, int gy,
6:        int gw, int gh, int wx, int wy) {
```

continues

LISTING 12.5. CONTINUED

```
 7:
 8:          gbc.gridx = gx;
 9:          gbc.gridy = gy;
10:          gbc.gridwidth = gw;
11:          gbc.gridheight = gh;
12:          gbc.weightx = wx;
13:          gbc.weighty = wy;
14:      }
15:
16:  public void init() {
17:      GridBagLayout gridbag = new GridBagLayout();
18:      GridBagConstraints constraints = new GridBagConstraints();
19:      setLayout(gridbag);
20:
21:      // Name label
22:      buildConstraints(constraints, 0, 0, 1, 1, 10, 40);
23:      constraints.fill = GridBagConstraints.NONE;
24:      constraints.anchor = GridBagConstraints.EAST;
25:      Label label1 = new Label("Name:", Label.LEFT);
26:      gridbag.setConstraints(label1, constraints);
27:      add(label1);
28:
29:      // Name text field
30:      buildConstraints(constraints, 1, 0, 1, 1, 90, 0);
31:      constraints.fill = GridBagConstraints.HORIZONTAL;
32:      TextField tfname = new TextField();
33:      gridbag.setConstraints(tfname, constraints);
34:      add(tfname);
35:
36:      // password label
37:      buildConstraints(constraints, 0, 1, 1, 1, 0, 40);
38:      constraints.fill = GridBagConstraints.NONE;
39:      constraints.anchor = GridBagConstraints.EAST;
40:      Label label2 = new Label("Password:", Label.LEFT);
41:      gridbag.setConstraints(label2, constraints);
42:      add(label2);
43:
44:      // password text field
45:      buildConstraints(constraints, 1, 1, 1, 1, 0, 0);
46:      constraints.fill = GridBagConstraints.HORIZONTAL;
47:      TextField tfpass = new TextField();
48:      tfpass.setEchoCharacter('*');
49:      gridbag.setConstraints(tfpass, constraints);
50:      add(tfpass);
51:
52:      // OK Button
53:      buildConstraints(constraints, 0, 2, 2, 1, 0, 20);
54:      constraints.fill = GridBagConstraints.NONE;
55:      constraints.anchor = GridBagConstraints.CENTER;
```

```
56:        Button okb = new Button("OK");
57:        gridbag.setConstraints(okb, constraints);
58:        add(okb);
59:   }
60: }
```

The following <APPLET> tag was used to test this applet:

```
<applet code="NamePass.class" height=180 width=240>
</applet>
```

When you compile the applet, the call to the setEchoCharacter() method in line 48 causes a deprecation warning, because this method was renamed after Java 1.02. It can be replaced with setEchoChar() if you're writing an applet for version 2 of the language.

Cell Padding

Before you finish up with grid bag layouts, two more constraints deserve mentioning: ipadx and ipady. These two constraints control the *padding* (the extra space around an individual component). By default, no components have extra space around them (which is easiest to see in components that fill their cells).

ipadx adds space to either side of the component, and ipady adds it above and below.

Insets

Horizontal and vertical gaps, created when you create a new layout manager (or using ipadx and ipady in grid bag layouts), are used to determine the amount of space between components in a panel. *Insets*, however, are used to determine the amount of space around the panel itself. The Insets class includes values for the top, bottom, left, and right insets, which are then used when the panel itself is drawn.

Insets determine the amount of space between the edges of a panel and that panel's components.

To include an inset for your layout, you override the insets() method for Java 1.02, or the getInsets() method for Java 2. These methods do the same thing.

Inside the insets() or getInsets() method, create a new Insets object, where the constructor to the Insets class takes four integer values representing the insets on the top, left, bottom, and right of the panel. The insets() method should then return that Insets object. Here's some code to add insets for a grid layout: 10 to the top and bottom and 30 to the left and right. Figure 12.11 shows the inset.

12

```
public Insets insets() {
    return new Insets(10, 30, 10, 30);
}
```

FIGURE 12.11.

A panel with insets of 10 pixels on the top and bottom and 30 pixels to the left and right.

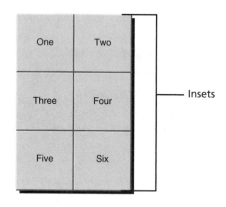

Insets

Summary

Abstract expressionism only goes so far, as you have seen during the day just completed. Layout managers require some adjustment for people who are used to more precise control over the place that components appear on an interface.

You now know how to use the five different layout managers and panels. As you work with the Abstract Windowing Toolkit, you'll find that it can approximate any kind of interface through the use of nested containers and different layout managers.

Once you master the development of a user interface in Java, your programs can offer something that most other visual programming languages can't: an interface that works on multiple platforms without modification.

To borrow an oft-repeated phrase: I don't know if it's art, but I like it.

Q&A

Q I really dislike working with layout managers; they're either too simplistic or too complicated (grid bag layout). Even with a whole lot of tinkering, I can never get my applets to look like I want them to. All I want to do is define the sizes of my components and put them at an x,y position on the screen. Can I do this?

A It's possible, but very problematic. The AWT was designed in such a way that a program's graphical user interface could run equally well on different platforms and with different screen resolutions, fonts, screen sizes, and the like. Relying on pixel coordinates can cause a program that looks good on one platform to be unusable on others, where components overlap each other, are cut off by the edge of a container, and other layout disasters. Layout managers, by dynamically placing elements on the screen, get around these problems. Although there might be some differences between the end result on different platforms, the differences are less likely to be catastrophic.

Still not convinced? Use a `null` layout manager and the `reshape()` method to make a component a specific size and place it at a particular position:

```
setLayout(null);
Button myButton = new Button("OK");
myButton.reshape(10, 10, 30, 15);
```

You can find out more about `reshape()` in the `Component` class.

Q **I was exploring the AWT classes and I saw this subpackage called `peer`. References to the peer classes also are sprinkled throughout the Java API documentation. What do peers do?**

A *Peers* are responsible for the platform-specific parts of the AWT. For example, when you create a Java AWT window, you have an instance of the `Window` class that provides generic window behavior, and then you have an instance of a class implementing `WindowPeer` that creates the very specific window for that platform—a motif window under X Window, a Macintosh-style window under the Macintosh, or a Windows 95 window under Windows 95. These peer classes also handle communication between the window system and the Java window itself. By separating the generic component behavior (the AWT classes) from the actual system implementation and appearance (the peer classes), you can focus on providing behavior in your Java application and let the Java implementation deal with the platform-specific details.

12

DAY **13**

Responding to User Input in an Applet

With the skills you have developed so far, you can design a graphical user interface with beauty but no brains. It might look like a working interface—receiving button clicks and other interactions like any other program—but nothing happens in response to those interactions.

To make an interface functional in Java, you must learn how to make a program respond to events. *Events* are method calls that Java's windowing system performs whenever any element of a user interface is manipulated. A wide variety of events cover mouse and keyboard use, including mouse-click events, mouse-movement events, and keypress events.

Today you learn how to make an applet handle events by using the techniques of Java 1.02 so that your programs can run on any Web browser that supports Java. On Day 20, "Handling User Events with Swing," you learn how to handle events using Java 2 techniques.

Event Handling

One of the things that you learned when creating applets for the first time is that forces are at work behind the scenes as the program is running. Java's windowing system calls methods such as paint(), init(), and start() automatically when they are needed, without any effort from you.

Like applet programming, event handling involves methods that are called automatically when a user action causes an event to take place.

Types of Events

An event is generated in response to just about anything that a user can do during the life cycle of a Java program. Every movement of the mouse, button click, or keypress generates an event.

In your programs, you don't have to deal with all events that might possibly occur. Instead, you handle the events you want the program to respond to, and the rest are ignored. For instance, if the user clicks the mouse somewhere inside the Applet window or presses a key on the keyboard, you might want the program to take action in response to that event.

The following events are some of those that can be handled in your own programs:

- *Mouse clicks.* Mouse down (button pressed), mouse up (button released), and mouse clicked (pressed and released in the same location)
- *Mouse movements.* The mouse cursor entering or exiting an interface component, or mouse drags (cursor motions that occur with the button pressed)
- *Keypresses.* Key pressed, key released, and key typed (pressed and released)
- *User-interface events.* Button clicked, scrollbar scrolled up and down, pop-up menus popped up, and so on

The handleEvent() Method

Event handling is the area in which Java has changed the most between Java 1.02 and its current incarnation, 2. Events are generated and flow through the system in roughly the same way, regardless of which version of the language you're using as you create a program. The difference lies in how events are received and processed.

In Java 1.02, all the events that occur during the life cycle of your Java program flow through that program and are handled by a method called handleEvent(). This method is defined in the Component class, which is inherited by java.applet.Applet, making it available to all your own applets.

When an event is sent to the handleEvent() method, this method then calls a more specific event-handling method depending on what kind of event it is. Some of these more specific methods are mouseDown(), mouseUp(), and keyDown().

To handle an event in your applets, you override one of these specific event-handling methods. Then, when that event occurs, your method is called. For example, you could override the mouseDown() method with behavior to display a message on the Applet window. When a mouse down event occurs, that message is displayed.

Handling Mouse Clicks

One of the most common events that you might be interested in is a mouse click. Mouse-click events occur when a user clicks the mouse anywhere on the program's interface.

You can intercept mouse clicks to do simple things—for example, to toggle the sound on and off in an applet, to move to the next slide in a presentation, or to clear the screen. You also can use mouse clicks in conjunction with mouse movements to perform more complex interaction with the user.

Mouse Down and Mouse Up Events

When a user clicks a mouse once, two events are generated: a mouse down event when the mouse button is pressed and a mouse up event when the button is released. This split enables different things to take place at different stages of the click.

Handling mouse events in your applet is easy; you override the right method definition in your applet, and it is called when that particular event occurs. Here's an example of the method signature for a mouse down event:

```
public boolean mouseDown(Event evt, int x, int y) {
    // ...
}
```

The mouseDown() method (and the mouseUp() method as well) takes three parameters: the event itself and the x and y coordinates where the mouse down or mouse up event occurred.

The evt argument is an instance of the class Event. All events generate an instance of the Event class, which contains information about where and when the event took place, the kind of event it is, and other information. Sometimes having a handle to that Event object is useful, as you'll discover later in this section.

13

The x and the y coordinates of the event, as passed in through the x and y arguments to the mouseDown() method, are particularly nice to know because you can use them to determine precisely where the mouse click took place. So, for example, if the mouse down event were over a graphical button, you could activate that button. Note that you can get to the x and y coordinates inside the Event object itself; in this method, they're passed in as separate variables to make them easier to deal with.

Here's a simple method that displays information about a mouse down event when it occurs:

```java
public boolean mouseDown(Event evt, int x, int y) {
    System.out.println("Mouse down at " + x + "," + y);
    return true;
}
```

If you include this method in your applet, every time a user clicks the mouse inside the applet, this message is displayed on the standard output device.

Note

> Using System.out.println() in an applet causes different behavior in different environments. The appletviewer displays the line in the same window where the appletviewer command was entered. Netscape Navigator displays the output on a separate window called the Java Console that is available as the Window | Java Console pull-down menu option. Microsoft Internet Explorer logs Java output to a separate file. Check with your environment to see where standard output from applets is sent.

Note that this method, unlike other methods from the Java class library you've studied thus far, returns a Boolean value instead of not returning anything (using the void keyword).

Having an event-handler method return true or false determines whether a given component can intercept an event or whether it needs to pass the event on to the enclosing component. The general rule is that if your method intercepts and does something with the event, it should return true. If, for any reason, the method doesn't do anything with that event, it should return false so that other components in the overall windowing system can have a chance to handle that event. In most of the examples in today's lesson, you'll be intercepting simple events, so most of the methods here will return true.

The second half of the mouse click is the mouseUp() method, which is called when the mouse button is released. To handle a mouse up event, add the mouseUp() method to your applet. This method looks just like mouseDown():

```
public boolean mouseUp(Event evt, int x, int y) {
    // ...
}
```

An Example: Spots

In this section, you'll create a sample applet that handles mouse down events. The Spots applet starts with a blank screen and then sits and waits. When you click the mouse on the Applet window, a blue dot is drawn. You can place up to 10 dots on the screen. Figure 13.1 shows the Spots applet.

FIGURE 13.1.

The Spots applet.

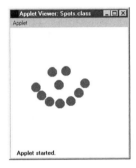

Start from the beginning and build this applet, starting from the initial class definition:

```
import java.awt.Graphics;
import java.awt.Color;
import java.awt.Event;

public class Spots extends java.applet.Applet {
    final int MAXSPOTS = 10;
    int xspots[] = new int[MAXSPOTS];
    int yspots[] = new int[MAXSPOTS];
    int currspots = 0;

}
```

This class uses three other Abstract Windowing Toolkit classes: Graphics, Color, and Event. The last class, Event, needs to be imported in any applets that handle events.

The Spots class has four instance variables: MAXSPOTS, a constant to determine the maximum number of spots that can be drawn, two arrays to store the x and y coordinates of the spots that already have been drawn, and an integer to keep track of the number of the current spot.

13

Note

> The `Event` class doesn't include the `implements` `Runnable` clause in its defini-tion. As you'll see later as you build this applet, it also doesn't have a `run()` method. Why not? Because it doesn't actually do anything on its own; it just waits for input and then does stuff when input happens. The applet doesn't need threads if it isn't actively doing something all the time.

Next, add the `init()` method, which does only one thing—set the background color to white:

```
public void init() {
    setBackground(Color.white);
}
```

You set the background here in `init()`, instead of in `paint()` as you have in past exam-ples, because you need to set the background only once. Because `paint()` is called repeatedly each time a new spot is added, setting the background in the `paint()` method unnecessarily slows down that method. Putting it here is a much better idea.

The main action of this applet occurs with the `mouseDown()` method, so you can add that one now:

```
public boolean mouseDown(Event evt, int x, int y) {
    if (currspots < MAXSPOTS) {
        addspot(x,y);
        return true;
    }
    else {
        System.out.println("Too many spots.");
        return false;
    }
}
```

When the mouse click occurs, the `mouseDown()` method tests to see whether you have fewer than 10 spots. If so, it calls the `addspot()` method (which you'll write soon) and returns `true` (the mouse down event was intercepted and handled). If not, it just prints an error message and returns `false`. What does `addspot()` do? It adds the coordinates of the spot to the arrays that store the coordinates, increments the `currspots` variable, and then calls `repaint()`:

```
void addspot(int x, int y) {
    xspots[currspots] = x;
    yspots[currspots] = y;
    currspots++;
    repaint();
}
```

You may be wondering why you have to keep track of all the past spots in addition to the current spot. You do so because of repaint(): Each time you paint the screen, you have to paint all the old spots in addition to the newest spot. Otherwise, each time you paint a new spot, the older spots are erased.

Now, on to the paint() method:

```
public void paint(Graphics g) {
    g.setColor(Color.blue);
    for (int i = 0; i < currspots; i++) {
    g.fillOval(xspots[i] -10, yspots[i] - 10, 20, 20);
    }
}
```

Inside paint(), you just loop through the spots you've stored in the xspots and yspots arrays, painting each one (actually, painting them a little to the right and upward so that the spot is painted around the mouse pointer rather than below and to the right).

That's all you need to create an applet that handles mouse clicks. Everything else is handled for you. You just have to add the appropriate behavior to mouseDown() or mouseUp() to intercept and handle that event.

Listing 13.1 shows the full text for the Spots applet.

TYPE   **LISTING 13.1.** THE FULL TEXT OF SPOTS.JAVA.

```
1: import java.awt.Graphics;
2: import java.awt.Color;
3: import java.awt.Event;
4:
5: public class Spots extends java.applet.Applet {
6:     final int MAXSPOTS = 10;
7:     int xspots[] = new int[MAXSPOTS];
8:     int yspots[] = new int[MAXSPOTS];
9:     int currspots = 0;
10:
11:     public void init() {
12:         setBackground(Color.white);
13:     }
14:
15:     public boolean mouseDown(Event evt, int x, int y) {
16:         if (currspots < MAXSPOTS) {
17:             addspot(x,y);
18:             return true;
19:         }
20:         else {
```

13

continues

LISTING 13.1. CONTINUED

```
21:                     System.out.println("Too many spots.");
22:                     return false;
23:             }
24:     }
25:
26:     void addspot(int x,int y) {
27:         xspots[currspots] = x;
28:         yspots[currspots] = y;
29:         currspots++;
30:         repaint();
31:     }
32:
33:     public void paint(Graphics g) {
34:         g.setColor(Color.blue);
35:         for (int i = 0; i < currspots; i++) {
36:             g.fillOval(xspots[i] - 10, yspots[i] - 10, 20, 20);
37:         }
38:     }
39: }
```

You can load this applet onto a page by using the following HTML:

```
<applet code="Spots.class" height=250 width=250>
</applet>
```

Double-Clicks

What if the mouse event you're interested in is more than a single mouse click? What if
you want to track double- or triple-clicks? The Java Event class provides a variable
called clickCount for tracking this information. clickCount is an integer representing
the number of consecutive mouse clicks that have occurred (where "consecutive" is usually determined by the operating system or the mouse hardware). If you're interested in
multiple mouse clicks in your applets, you can test this value in the body of your
mouseDown() method, like this:

```
public boolean mouseDown(Event evt, int x, int y) {
    switch (evt.clickCount) {
        case 1:  // single-click
        case 2:  // double-click
        case 3:  // triple-click
            // ...
    }
}
```

An important point to note when you're looking for double- and triple-clicks is that
mouseDown() is called once for each click of the button. Consider the following example:

```
public boolean mouseDown(Event evt, int x, int y) {
    system.out.println("Click count: " + evt.clickCount);
    return false;
}
```

If you put this method in an applet, the following is displayed on the standard output when the mouse is triple-clicked:

```
Click count: 1
Click count: 2
Click count: 3
```

As you'll learn later today, several components generate an action event when double-clicked. Therefore, it isn't always necessary to use `mouseDown()` to differentiate between single- and double-clicks generated by a component.

Handling Mouse Movements

Every time the mouse is moved, a mouse move event is generated. Moving the mouse from one side of the applet to the other can result in dozens of events. You'll discover two kinds of distinct mouse movement events in the AWT: mouse drags, in which the movement occurs with the mouse button pressed down, and plain mouse movements, in which the mouse button isn't pressed.

In addition, mouse enter and mouse exit events are generated each time the mouse enters or exits your applet or any component or container on the applet.

For each of these events, special methods intercept the events, just as the `mouseDown()` and `mouseUp()` methods intercept mouse clicks.

Mouse Drag and Mouse Move Events

To intercept and manage mouse movement events, use the `mouseDrag()` and `mouseMove()` methods.

The `mouseMove()` method, for handling plain mouse pointer movements without the mouse button pressed, looks much like the mouse click methods:

```
public boolean mouseMove(Event evt, int x, int y) {
    // ...
}
```

The `mouseDrag()` method handles mouse movements made with the mouse button pressed down (a complete dragging movement consists of a mouse down event, a series of mouse drag events for each pixel the mouse is moved, and a mouse up event when the button is released). The `mouseDrag()` method looks like this:

13

```
public boolean mouseDrag(Event evt, int x, int y) {
    // ...
}
```

Note that for both the `mouseMove()` and `mouseDrag()` methods, the arguments for the x and y coordinates are the new location of the mouse, not its starting location.

Mouse Enter and Mouse Exit Events

The `mouseEnter()` and `mouseExit()` methods are called when the mouse pointer enters or exits an applet or a portion of that applet. Both `mouseEnter()` and `mouseExit()` have signatures similar to the mouse click methods. They have three arguments: the event object and the x and y coordinates of the point where the mouse entered or exited the applet. The following examples show the signatures for `mouseEnter()` and `mouseExit()`:

```
public boolean mouseEnter(Event evt, int x, int y) {
    // ...
}

public boolean mouseExit(Event evt, int x, int y) {
    // ...
}
```

An Example: Drawing Lines

In this section, you'll create an applet that enables you to draw straight lines on the screen by dragging from the starting point to the end point. Figure 13.2 shows the applet at work.

FIGURE 13.2.

Drawing lines.

As you did with the Spots applet (on which this applet is based), start with the basic definition and work your way through it, adding the appropriate methods to build the applet. Here's a simple class definition for the Lines applet, with a number of initial instance variables and a simple `init()` method:

```
import java.awt.Graphics;
import java.awt.Color;
import java.awt.Event;
import java.awt.Point;

public class Lines extends java.applet.Applet {
    final int MAXLINES = 10;
    Point starts[] = new Point[MAXLINES]; // starting points
    Point ends[] = new Point[MAXLINES];   // ending points
    Point anchor;      // start of current line
    Point currentpoint; // current end of line
    int currline = 0; // number of lines

    public void init() {
        setBackground(Color.white);
    }
}
```

This applet uses a few more variables than the Spots applet. Unlike Spots, which keeps track of individual integer coordinates, the Lines applet keeps track of Point objects. Points represent an x and a y coordinate, encapsulated in a single object. To deal with points, you import the `Point` class (`java.awt.Point`) and set up a bunch of instance variables that hold points:

- The `starts` array holds points representing the starting points of lines already drawn.
- The `ends` array holds the end points of those same lines.
- `anchor` holds the starting point of the line currently being drawn.
- `currentpoint` holds the current end point of the line currently being drawn.
- `currline` holds the current number of lines (to make sure you don't go over `MAXLINES` and to keep track of which line in the array to access next).

Finally, the `init()` method, as in the Spots applet, sets the background of the applet to white.

The three main events this applet deals with are `mouseDown()`, to set the anchor point for the current line; `mouseDrag()`, to animate the current line as it's being drawn; and `mouseUp()`, to set the ending point for the new line. Given that you have instance variables to hold each of these values, you merely have to plug the right variables into the right methods. Here's `mouseDown()`, which sets the anchor point (but only if you haven't exceeded the maximum number of lines):

```
public boolean mouseDown(Event evt, int x, int y) {
    if (currline < MAXLINES) {
        anchor = new Point(x,y);
```

13

```
        return true;
    }
    else  {
        System.out.println("Too many lines.");
        return false;
    }
}
```

While the mouse is being dragged to draw the line, the applet animates the line being drawn. As you drag the mouse around, the new line moves with it from the anchor point to the tip of the mouse. The mouseDrag() event contains the current point each time the mouse moves, so use that method to keep track of the current point (and to repaint for each movement so the line "animates"). Note that if you've exceeded the maximum number of lines, you won't want to do any of this work. Here's the mouseDrag() method to do all those jobs:

```
public boolean mouseDrag(Event evt, int x, int y) {
    if (currline < MAXLINES) {
        currentpoint = new Point(x,y);
        repaint();
        return true;
    }
    else return false;
}
```

The new line doesn't get added to the arrays of old lines until the mouse button is released. Here's mouseUp(), which tests to make sure you haven't exceeded the maximum number of lines before calling the addline() method (described next):

```
public boolean mouseUp(Event evt, int x, int y) {
    if (currline < MAXLINES) {
    addline(x,y);
    return true;
    }
    else return false;
}
```

In the addline() method, the arrays of starting and ending points get updated, and the applet is repainted to take the new line into account:

```
void addline(int x,int y) {
    starts[currline] = anchor;
    ends[currline] = new Point(x,y);
    currline++;
    currentpoint = null;
    anchor = null;
    repaint();
}
```

Note that in this method you also set `currentpoint` and `anchor` to `null` because the current line you were drawing is over. By setting these variables to `null`, you can test for that value in the `paint()` method to see whether you need to draw a current line.

Painting the applet means drawing all the old lines stored in the `starts` and `ends` arrays, as well as drawing the current line in progress (whose end points are in `anchor` and `currentpoint`, respectively). To show the animation of the current line, draw it in blue. Here's the `paint ()` method for the Lines applet:

```java
public void paint(Graphics g) {
    // Draw existing lines
    for (int i = 0; i < currline; i++) {
        g.drawLine(starts[i].x, starts[i].y,
            ends[i].x, ends[i].y);
    }

    // Draw current line
    g.setColor(Color.blue);
    if (currentpoint != null)
        g.drawLine(anchor.x, anchor.y,
            currentpoint.x, currentpoint.y);
}
```

In `paint()`, when you're drawing the current line, you test first to see whether `currentpoint` is null. If it is, the applet isn't in the middle of drawing a line, so it doesn't have any reason to try drawing a line that doesn't exist. By testing for `currentpoint` (and by setting `currentpoint` to null in the `addline()` method), you can paint only what you need. That's it; just 68 lines of code and a few basic methods, and you have a basic drawing application in your Web browser. Listing 13.2 shows the full text of the Lines applet so that you can put the pieces together.

TYPE **LISTING 13.2.** THE FULL TEXT OF LINES.JAVA.

```java
1: import java.awt.Graphics;
2: import java.awt.Color;
3: import java.awt.Event;
4: import java.awt.Point;
5:
6: public class Lines extends java.applet.Applet {
7:     final int MAXLINES = 10;
8:     Point starts[] = new Point[MAXLINES]; // starting points
9:     Point ends[] = new Point[MAXLINES];    // endingpoints
10:    Point anchor;    // start of current line
11:    Point currentpoint; // current end of line
```

continues

13

LISTING 13.2. CONTINUED

```
12:     int currline = 0; // number of lines
13:
14:     public void init() {
15:         setBackground(Color.white);
16:     }
17:
18:     public boolean mouseDown(Event evt, int x, int y) {
19:         if (currline < MAXLINES) {
20:             anchor = new Point(x,y);
21:             return true;
22:         }
23:         else {
24:             System.out.println("Too many lines.");
25:             return false;
26:         }
27:     }
28:
29:     public boolean mouseUp(Event evt, int x, int y) {
30:         if (currline < MAXLINES) {
31:             addline(x,y);
32:             return true;
33:         }
34:         else return false;
35:     }
36:
37:     public boolean mouseDrag(Event evt, int x, int y) {
38:         if (currline < MAXLINES) {
39:             currentpoint = new Point(x,y);
40:             repaint();
41:             return true;
42:         }
43:         else return false;
44:     }
45:
46:     void addline(int x,int y) {
47:         starts[currline] = anchor;
48:         ends[currline] = new Point(x,y);
49:         currline++;
50:         currentpoint = null;
51:         anchor = null;
52:         repaint();
53:     }
54:
55:     public void paint(Graphics g) {
56:         // Draw existing lines
57:         for (int i = 0; i < currline; i++) {
```

```
58:                    g.drawLine(starts[i].x, starts[i].y,
59:                        ends[i].x, ends[i].y);
60:            }
61:
62:            // draw current line
63:            g.setColor(Color.blue);
64:            if (currentpoint != null)
65:                g.drawLine(anchor.x,anchor.y,
66:                    currentpoint.x,currentpoint.y);
67:        }
68: }
```

You can test this applet by using the following HTML:

```
<applet code="Lines.class" height=250 width=250>
</applet>
```

Handling Keyboard Events

A keyboard event is generated whenever a user presses a key on the keyboard. By using keyboard events, you can get hold of the values of the keys the user pressed to perform an action or merely to get character input from the users of your applet.

For a keyboard event to be received by a component, that component must have the focus; in other words, it must be the component on the interface that is currently selected to receive input. You'll learn more about focus later today when you work with focus events. Focus is easiest to understand when you're considering an interface that contains numerous text fields. The cursor blinks in the text field that has the focus, and a user can enter text into that field by using the keyboard. No other text fields can receive text until they receive the focus. All components, including containers, can be set up to have the focus.

To explicitly indicate that a component has the input focus, the component's requestFocus() method can be called with no arguments. The following statement gives the focus to a Button object called quit:

```
quit.requestFocus();
```

You can give an Applet window the focus by calling the applet's requestFocus() method.

13

Key Down and Key Up Events

To handle a keyboard event, use the `keyDown()` method:

```
public boolean keyDown(Event evt, int key) {
    // ...
}
```

The keys generated by key down events (and passed into `keyDown()` as the `key` argument) are integers representing Unicode character values, which include alphanumeric characters, function keys, tabs, returns, and so on. To use them as characters (for example, to print them), you need to cast them to characters, as follows:

```
currentchar = (char)key;
```

Here's a simple example of a `keyDown()` method that does nothing but print the key you just typed in both its Unicode and character representations (seeing which key characters produce which values can be fun):

```
public boolean keyDown(Event evt, int key) {
    System.out.println("ASCII value: " + key);
    System.out.println("Character: " + (char)key);
    return true;
}
```

As with mouse clicks, each key down event also has a corresponding key up event. To intercept key up events, use the `keyUp()` method:

```
public boolean keyUp(Event evt, int key)  {
    // ...
}
```

Default Keys

The `Event` class provides a set of class variables that refer to several standard non-alphanumeric keys, such as the arrow and function keys. If your applet's interface uses these keys, you can provide more readable code by testing for these names in your `keyDown()` method rather than testing for their numeric values (and your code is also more likely to work across different platforms if you use these variables). For example, to test whether the up arrow was pressed, you might use the following snippet of code:

```
if (key == Event.UP) {
    // ...
}
```

Because the values these class variables hold are integers, you also can use the `switch` statement to test for them.

Table 13.1 shows the standard Event class variables for various keys and the actual keys they represent.

TABLE 13.1. STANDARD KEYS DEFINED BY THE EVENT CLASS.

Class Variable	Represented Key
Event.HOME	Home key
Event.END	End key
Event.PGUP	Page Up key
Event.PGDN	Page Down key
Event.UP	Up arrow
Event.DOWN	Down arrow
Event.LEFT	Left arrow
Event.RIGHT	Right arrow
Event.F1	F1 key
Event.F2	F2 key
Event.F3	F3 key
Event.F4	F4 key
Event.F5	F5 key
Event.F6	F6 key
Event.F7	F7 key
Event.F8	F8 key
Event.F9	F9 key
Event.F10	F10 key
Event.F11	F11 key
Event.F12	F12 key

13

An Example: Entering, Displaying, and Moving Characters

Take a moment now to look at an applet that demonstrates keyboard events. With this applet, you type a character, and that character is displayed in the center of the Applet window. You then can move that character around on the screen by using the arrow keys. Typing another character at any time changes the character as it's currently displayed. Figure 13.3 shows an example.

Figure 13.3.

The Keys applet.

This applet is actually less complicated than the previous applets you've used. This one has only three methods: `init()`, `keyDown()`, and `paint()`. The instance variables are also simpler because the only things you need to keep track of are the x and y positions of the current character and the values of that character itself. Here's the initial class definition:

```
import java.awt.Graphics;
import java.awt.Event;
import java.awt.Font;
import java.awt.Color;

public class Keys extends java.applet.Applet {

    char currkey;
    int currx;
    int curry;
}
```

Start by adding an `init()` method. Here, `init()` is responsible for three tasks: setting the background color, setting the applet's font (here, 36-point Helvetica bold), and setting the beginning position for the character (the middle of the screen, minus a few points to nudge it up and to the right).

```
public void init() {
    currx = (size().width / 2) - 8;
    curry = (size().height / 2) - 16;
    setBackground(Color.white);
    setFont(new Font("Helvetica", Font.BOLD, 36));
    requestFocus();
}
```

The last statement in the `init()` method gives the Applet window the input focus. This statement is needed to ensure that the keyboard input is received by the component that is handling it—the Applet window itself.

Note

In previous versions of Java, calling `requestFocus()` was not required for the Applet window to receive keyboard input, and you could give the window the focus by clicking it. This is still true of the latest versions of

> Netscape Navigator and Microsoft Internet Explorer. However, the Java 2 `appletviewer` requires that `requestFocus()` be used; otherwise, the Applet window will never receive the focus for keyboard input. Keep this difference in mind when you're testing applets that use keyboard events. Using `requestFocus()` to explicitly request the focus for an Applet window is probably best.

Because this applet's behavior is based on keyboard input, most of the work of the applet takes place in the keyDown() method:

```
public boolean keyDown(Event evt, int key) {
    switch (key) {
        case Event.DOWN:
            curry += 5;
            break;
        case Event.UP:
            curry -= 5;
            break;
        case Event.LEFT:
            currx -= 5;
            break;
        case Event.RIGHT:
            currx += 5;
            break;
        default:
            currkey = (char)key;
    }
    repaint();
    return true;
}
```

In the center of the keyDown() applet is a switch statement that tests for different key events. If the event is an arrow key, the appropriate change is made to the character's position. If the event is any other key, the character itself is changed (that's the default part of the switch). The method finishes up with a repaint() and returns true.

The paint() method here is almost trivial; just display the current character at the current position. However, note that when the applet starts, it has no initial character and nothing to draw, so you have to take that point into account. The currkey variable is initialized to 0, so you paint the applet only if currkey has an actual value:

```
public void paint(Graphics g) {
    if (currkey != 0) {
        g.drawString(String.valueOf(currkey), currx,curry);
    }
}
```

13

Listing 13.3 shows the complete source code for the Keys applet.

TYPE   **LISTING 13.3.** THE FULL TEXT OF KEYS.JAVA.

```
 1: import java.awt.Graphics;
 2: import java.awt.Event;
 3: import java.awt.Font;
 4: import java.awt.Color;
 5:
 6: public class Keys extends java.applet.Applet {
 7:
 8:     char currkey;
 9:     int currx;
10:     int curry;
11:
12:     public void init() {
13:         currx = (size().width / 2) -8;   // default
14:         curry = (size().height / 2) -16;
15:
16:         setBackground(Color.white);
17:         setFont(new Font("Helvetica",Font.BOLD,36));
18:         requestFocus();
19:     }
20:
21:     public boolean keyDown(Event evt, int key) {
22:         switch (key) {
23:         case Event.DOWN:
24:             curry += 5;
25:             break;
26:         case Event.UP:
27:             curry -= 5;
28:             break;
29:         case Event.LEFT:
30:             currx -= 5;
31:             break;
32:         case Event.RIGHT:
33:             currx += 5;
34:             break;
35:         default:
36:             currkey = (char)key;
37:         }
38:
39:         repaint();
40:         return true;
41:     }
42:
43:     public void paint(Graphics g) {
44:         if (currkey != 0) {
```

```
45:                    g.drawString(String.valueOf(currkey), currx,curry);
46:            }
47:      }
48: }
```

You can test the applet by using the following HTML:

```
<applet code="Keys.class" height=100 width=100>
</applet>
```

Testing for Modifier Keys and Multiple Mouse Buttons

Shift, Control (Ctrl), and Meta are modifier keys. They don't generate key events them-selves, but when you get an ordinary mouse or keyboard event, you can test to see whether these modifier keys were held down when the event occurred. Sometimes this fact may be obvious; shifted alphanumeric keys produce different key events than unshifted ones, for example. For other events, however—mouse events in particular—you may want to handle an event with a modifier key held down differently from a regu-lar version of that event.

Note

> The Meta key is commonly used on UNIX systems; it's usually mapped to Alt on PC keyboards and Command (apple) on Macintosh keyboards.

The Event class provides three methods for testing whether a modifier key is held down: shiftDown(), metaDown(), and controlDown(). All return Boolean values based on whether that modifier key is indeed held down. You can use these three methods in any of the event-handling methods (mouse or keyboard) by calling them on the event object passed into that method:

```
public boolean mouseDown(Event evt, int x, int y) {
    if (evt.shiftDown())
        // handle shift-click
    else if controlDown()
        // handle control-click
    else // handle regular click
}
```

One other significant use of these modifier key methods is to test for which mouse but-ton generated a particular mouse event on systems with two or three mouse buttons. By default, mouse events (such as mouse down and mouse drag) are generated regardless of which mouse button is used. However, Java events internally map right and middle

13

mouse actions to Meta and Control (Ctrl) modifier keys, respectively, so testing for the key tests for the mouse button's action. By testing for modifier keys, you can find out which mouse button was used and execute different behavior for those buttons than you would use for the left button. Use an if statement to test each case, like this:

```
public boolean mouseDown(Event evt, int x, int y) {
    if (evt.metaDown())
        // handle a right-click
    else if (evt.controlDown())
        // handle a middle-click
    else // handle a regular click
}
```

Note that because this mapping from multiple mouse buttons to keyboard modifiers happens automatically, you don't have to do a lot of work to make sure your applets or applications work on different systems with different kinds of mouse devices. Because left-button or right-button mouse clicks map to modifier key events, you can use the actual modifier keys on systems with fewer mouse buttons to generate exactly the same results. So, for example, the act of holding down the Ctrl key and clicking the mouse on Windows or holding the Control key on the Macintosh is the same as clicking the middle button on a three-button mouse; the act of holding down the Command (apple) key and clicking the mouse on the Mac is the same as clicking the right button on a two- or three-button mouse.

Consider, however, that the use of different mouse buttons or modifier keys may not be immediately obvious if your applet or application runs on a system with fewer buttons than you're used to working with. Consider restricting your interface to a single mouse button or to providing help or documentation to explain the use of your program in this case.

The Generic Event Handler

The default methods you've learned about today for handling basic events in applets are called by a generic event-handler method called handleEvent(). When you use the handleEvent() method, the Abstract Windowing Toolkit generically deals with events that occur between application components and events based on user input.

In the default handleEvent() method, basic events are processed and the methods you learned about today are called. To handle events other than those mentioned here (such as events for scrollbars or for other user interface elements), to change the default event handling behavior, or to create and pass around your own events, you need to override handleEvent() in your own programs.

The `handleEvent()` method looks like this:

```
public boolean handleEvent(Event evt) {
    // ...
}
```

To test for specific events, examine the `id` instance variable of the `Event` object that gets passed in to `handleEvent()`. The event ID is an integer, but fortunately the `Event` class defines a whole set of event IDs as class variables whose names you can test for in the body of `handleEvent()`. Because these class variables are integer constants, a `switch` statement works particularly well. For example, here's a simple `handleEvent()` method to print out debugging information about mouse events:

```
public boolean handleEvent(Event evt) {
    switch (evt.id) {
        case Event.MOUSE_DOWN:
            System.out.println("MouseDown: " +
                evt.x + "," + evt.y);
            return true;
        case Event.MOUSE_UP:
            System.out.println("MouseUp: " +
                evt.x + "," + evt.y);
            return true;
        case Event.MOUSE_MOVE:
            System.out.println("MouseMove: " +
                evt.x + "," + evt.y);
            return true;
        case Event.MOUSE_DRAG:
            System.out.println("MouseDrag: " +
                evt.x + "," + evt.y);
            return true;
        default:
            return false;
    }
}
```

You can test for the following keyboard events:

- `Event.KEY_PRESS` is generated when a key is pressed (the same as the `keyDown()` method).
- `Event.KEY_RELEASE` is generated when a key is released.
- `Event.KEY_ACTION` and `Event.KEY_ACTION_RELEASE` are generated when an "action" key (a function key, an arrow key, Page Up, Page Down, or Home) is pressed or released.

You can test for these mouse events:

- `Event.MOUSE_DOWN` is generated when the mouse button is pressed (the same as the `mouseDown()` method).

13

- `Event.MOUSE_UP` is generated when the mouse button is released (the same as the `mouseUp()` method).

- `Event.MOUSE_MOVE` is generated when the mouse is moved (the same as the `mouseMove()` method).

- `Event.MOUSE_DRAG` is generated when the mouse is moved with the button pressed (the same as the `mouseDrag()` method).

- `Event.MOUSE_ENTER` is generated when the mouse enters the applet (or a component of that applet). You can also use the `mouseEnter()` method.

- `Event.MOUSE_EXIT` is generated when the mouse exits the applet. You can also use the `mouseExit()` method.

Note that if you override `handleEvent()` in your class, none of the default event-handling methods you learned about today are called unless you explicitly call them in the body of `handleEvent()`. So be careful if you decide to override this event. The best way to get around this problem is to test for the event you're interested in, and if that event isn't it, call `super.handleEvent()` so that the superclass that defines `handleEvent()` can process things. Here's an example:

```
public boolean handleEvent(Event evt) {
    if (evt.id == Event.MOUSE_DOWN) {
        // process the mouse down
        return true;
    } else
        return super.handleEvent(evt);
}
```

Also, note that like the individual methods for individual events, `handleEvent()` also returns a Boolean value. The value returned here is particularly important; if you pass handling of the event to another method, you must return `false` (the method you call returns `true` or `false` itself). If you handle the event in the body of this method, return `true`. If you pass the event up to a superclass, that method returns `true` or `false`; you don't have to return it yourself.

Handling Component Events

The event-handling techniques you have learned about up to this point have focused on the user's interaction—clicking a mouse, pressing keys on a keyboard, and the like. There also are events to handle specific events that take place on components such as buttons, text areas, and other interface elements. For example, buttons use action events that are triggered when the button is pressed. You don't have to worry about mouse down or mouse up or determining where the mouse interaction took place; the component handles all of that for you.

The following events can be generated from interaction with interface components:

- *Action events.* The primary events for most interface components to indicate that component has been "activated." Action events are generated when a button is pressed, when a check box or radio button is selected or deselected, when a choice menu item is picked, or when the user presses Return or Enter inside a text field.

- *List select and deselect events.* These events are generated when a check box or choice menu item is selected (which also generates an action event).

- *Got focus or lost focus events.* These events can be generated by any component either in response to a mouse click or as part of focus traversal using the Tab key. "Got focus" means just that; the component has the input focus and can now be selected, typed into, or activated. "Lost focus" means that the input focus has moved to some other component.

Handling Action Events

An action event is by far the most commonly used interface event, and for that reason a special method is used to handle it, just like basic mouse and keyboard event methods.

To intercept an action event generated by any component, define an `action()` method in your applet or class with the following signature:

```
public boolean action(Event evt, Object arg) {
    // ...
}
```

This `action()` method should look similar to the basic mouse and keyboard event methods. Like those methods, this one gets passed the event object that represents this event. It's also passed an extra object (in this code, the parameter `arg`), which can be of any class type.

What kind of object that second argument to the action method is depends on the interface component generating the action. The basic definition is that it's "any arbitrary argument," determined by the component itself, to pass along any extra information that might be useful for you to use in processing that action. Table 13.2 shows the extra arguments for each interface component.

TABLE 13.2. ACTION ARGUMENTS FOR EACH COMPONENT.

Component	Argument Type	Contains
Buttons	String	The label of the button
Check boxes	Boolean	Always `true`

continues

TABLE 13.2. CONTINUED

Radio buttons	Boolean	Always true
Choice menus	String	The label of the item selected
Text fields	String	The text inside the field

Inside the action() method, the first thing to do is to test to see which component generated the action (unlike with mouse or keyboard events, in which it doesn't really matter because different components can all generate actions). Fortunately, the Event object you get when action() is called contains an instance variable called target that contains a reference to the object that received the event. You can use the instanceof operator to find out which component generated the event, like this:

```
public boolean action(Event evt, Object arg) {
    if (evt.target instanceof TextField)
        return handleText(evt.target);
    else if (evt.target instanceof Choice)
        return handleChoice(arg);
        // ...
    return false;
}
```

In this example, action() could have been generated by either a TextField or a choice menu; the if statements determine which one actually generated the event and call some other method (handleText() or handleChoice() here) to actually deal with it. (Neither handleText() nor handleChoice() is an AWT method; they're just examples of names that could be used for helper methods. A common practice is to create helper methods so that action() doesn't get cluttered with a lot of code.)

As with the other event methods, action() returns a Boolean value. As with all the event methods, you should return true if action() itself deals with the method or false if it passes the method on somewhere else (or ignores it). In this example, you passed control to the handleText() or handleChoice() methods, and they must return true or false, so you can return false (remember, you return true only if that method processed the event).

Extra complications occur when you have lots of components that all have the same class—for example, a whole bunch of buttons. All of them generate actions, and all of them are instances of Button. That extra argument comes in here: You can use the labels, items, or contents of the component to determine which one generated the event and use simple string comparisons to choose among them. (Don't forget to cast the argument to the right object.)

```
public boolean action(Event evt, Object arg) {
    if (evt.target instanceof Button) {
        String labl = (String)arg;
        if (labl.equals("OK"))
            // handle OK button
        else if (labl.equals("Cancel"))
            // handle Cancel button
        else if (labl.equals("Browse"))
            // handle Browse button
        // ...
    }
}
```

Note

> What about check boxes and radio buttons? Their extra argument is always true, which isn't really useful for testing against. Generally, you shouldn't react to a check box or radio button when it's actually checked. Usually, check boxes and radio buttons can be selected or deselected by the user at will, and then their values are checked at some other point (for example, when a button is pressed).
>
> If you really want your program to react to a check box or radio button as it's checked, you can use the getLabel() method to extract the label for the check box from inside action() instead of using the extra argument. (Actually, all components have some sort of method of this type; it's just easier to use when it's passed in as the extra argument.)

Handling Focus Events

As mentioned earlier, action events are by far the most common interface events that you'll deal with for the components you've learned about in this lesson. However, you can use four other events in your own programs: list select, list deselect, got focus, and lost focus.

For the got focus and lost focus events, you can use the gotFocus() and lostFocus() methods, which are used the same as action(). Here are their signatures:

```
public boolean gotFocus(Event evt, Object arg) {
    // ...
}
```

```
public boolean lostFocus(Event evt, Object arg) {
    // ...
}
```

13

For list select and list deselect events, no easily overrideable methods are available for use. You have to use `handleEvent()` for those events, like this:

```
public boolean handleEvent(Event evt) {
    if (evt.id == Event.LIST_SELECT)
        handleSelect(Event);
    else if (evt.id == Event.LIST_DESELECT)
        handleDeselect(Event);
    else return super.handleEvent(evt);
}
```

In this snippet of code, `Event.LIST_SELECT` and `Event.LIST_DESELECT` are the official event IDs for the list select and deselect events, and here control has been passed to two helper methods (`handleSelect()` and `handleDeselect()`), which are theoretically defined elsewhere. Note also the call to `super.handleEvent()` at the bottom; this call lets other events pass gracefully back up to the original `handleEvent()` method.

Text Area Events

Text areas have the same events as text fields. You can use the `gotFocus()` and `lostFocus()` methods to trap focus events:

```
public boolean gotFocus(Event evt, Object arg) {
    // ...
}

public boolean lostFocus(Event evt, Object arg) {
    // ...
}
```

Scrolling List Events

Scrolling lists generate three different kinds of events: selecting or deselecting an individual list item results in a list select or list deselect event, and double-clicking a list item results in an action event.

You can override the `action()` event to handle a list item being double-clicked. For list select and list deselect, you have to override `handleEvent()` and test for the event IDs `LIST_SELECT` and `LIST_DESELECT`.

Scrollbar Events

If you like messing with events, you're going to love scrollbars. A whole set of events is generated and handled by different scrollbar movements only. You have to use `handleEvent()` for all these events. Table 13.3 shows the event IDs to look for and the motions that trigger them.

TABLE 13.3. SCROLLBAR EVENTS.

Event ID	What It Represents
SCROLL_ABSOLUTE	Generated when a scrollbar's box is moved
SCROLL_LINE_DOWN	Generated when a scrollbar's bottom or left end point (button) is selected
SCROLL_LINE_UP	Generated when a scrollbar's top or right end point (button) is selected
SCROLL_PAGE_DOWN	Generated when the scrollbar's field below (or to the left of) the box is selected
SCROLL_PAGE_UP	Generated when the scrollbar's field above (or to the right of) the box is selected

An Example: Background Color Switcher

If you have only snippets of code to work from, getting an idea of how all the parts fit together is hard. To fix that problem now, you can create a simple AWT applet.

The applet you'll build in this section, shown in Figure 13.4, uses five buttons, arranged neatly across the top of the screen, each one labeled with a color. Each button changes the background color of the applet to the label on the button.

FIGURE 13.4.

The SetBack applet.

13

For the first step of this section, you'll create the user interface code for the applet. That's usually the best way to approach any AWT-based applet: create the components and the layout, and make sure everything looks right before hooking up the events to actually make the applet work.

For this applet, the components and layout couldn't be any simpler. The applet contains five simple buttons, arranged at the top of the screen in a row. A flow layout works best for this arrangement and requires little work.

Here's the code for the class structure and `init()` method created for this applet. The `FlowLayout` is centered, and each button will have 10 points between it. After that, you just need to create and add each of the buttons.

```java
import java.awt.*;

public class SetBack extends java.applet.Applet {

    Button redButton,blueButton,greenButton,
        whiteButton,blackButton;

    public void init() {
        setBackground(Color.white);
        setLayout(new FlowLayout(FlowLayout.CENTER, 10, 10));

        redButton = new Button("Red");
        add(redButton);
        blueButton = new Button("Blue");
        add(blueButton);
        greenButton = new Button("Green");
        add(greenButton);
        whiteButton = new Button("White");
        add(whiteButton);
        blackButton = new Button("Black");
        add(blackButton);
        }
```

Adding the Event Code

Buttons, when they're pressed, result in action events. And, as you learned earlier, to handle an action event, you use the `action()` method. The `action()` method here does the following:

- It tests to make sure the target of the event is indeed a button.
- It further tests to find out exactly which button was pressed.
- It changes the background to the color named by the button.
- It calls `repaint()` (the action of changing the background isn't enough).

Before actually writing `action()`, let me help you make one more design decision. The last three steps are essentially identical for each button, with minor differences, so it actually makes sense to put them into their own method, which you can call `changeColor()`. Doing so simplifies the logic in `action()` itself.

With that decision made, creating the `action()` method itself is easy:

```java
public boolean action(Event evt, Object arg) {
    if (evt.target instanceof Button) {
```

```
        changeColor((Button)evt.target);
        return true;
    } else return false;
}
```

Not much is different about this `action()` from the simple ones created in the section on actions. The first step is to use `evt.target` to make sure the component is a button, at which time you pass control to the yet-to-be-written `changeColor()` method and return `true`. If the event isn't a button, you return `false`.

Note the one argument to `changeColor()`. With this argument, you pass the actual button object that received the event to the `changeColor()` method. (The object in `evt.target` is an instance of the class `Object`, so it has to be cast into a `Button` so that you can use it as a button.) The `changeColor()` method will deal with it from here.

Go ahead and define the `changeColor()` method now. The main focus of `changeColor()` is to decide which button was clicked. Remember that the extra argument to `action()` was the label of the button. Although you can use a string comparison in `changeColor()` to figure out which button was pressed, that solution is not the most elegant, and it ties your event code too tightly to the user interface. If you decide to change a button label, you'll have to go back and work through your event code as well. So, in this applet, you can ignore the extra argument altogether.

So how do you tell which button was pressed? At this point, the button instance variables come into play. The object contained in the event's target instance variable—the one you passed to `changeColor()`—is an instance of `Button`, and one of those instance variables contains a reference to that very same object. In `changeColor()`, you just have to compare the two to see whether they're the same object, set the background, and repaint, like this:

```
void changeColor(Button b) {
    if (b == redButton) setBackground(Color.red);
    else if (b == blueButton) setBackground(Color.blue);
    else if (b == greenButton) setBackground(Color.green);
    else if (b == whiteButton) setBackground(Color.white);
    else setBackground(Color.black);
    repaint();
}
```

13

From the user interface, a button press calls `action()`, `action()` calls `changeColor()`, and `changeColor()` sets the appropriate background. Easy! Listing 13.4 shows the final applet.

TYPE **LISTING 13.4.** THE FULL TEXT OF SETBACK.JAVA.

```
1: import java.awt.*;
2:
3: public class SetBack extends java.applet.Applet {
4:
5:     Button redButton,blueButton,greenButton,whiteButton,blackButton;
6:
7:     public void init() {
8:         setBackground(Color.white);
9:         setLayout(new FlowLayout(FlowLayout.CENTER, 10, 10));
10:
11:         redButton = new Button("Red");
12:         add(redButton);
13:         blueButton = new Button("Blue");
14:         add(blueButton);
15:         greenButton = new Button("Green");
16:         add(greenButton);
17:         whiteButton = new Button("White");
18:         add(whiteButton);
19:         blackButton = new Button("Black");
20:         add(blackButton);
21:     }
22:
23:     public boolean action(Event evt, Object arg) {
24:         if (evt.target instanceof Button) {
25:             changeColor((Button)evt.target);
26:             return true;
27:         } else return false;
28:     }
29:
30:     void changeColor(Button b) {
31:         if (b == redButton) setBackground(Color.red);
32:         else if (b == blueButton) setBackground(Color.blue);
33:         else if (b == greenButton) setBackground(Color.green);
34:         else if (b == whiteButton) setBackground(Color.white);
35:         else setBackground(Color.black);
36:
37:         repaint();
38:     }
39: }
```

You can test the applet by using the following HTML:

```
<applet code="SetBack.class" width=200 height=200>
</applet>
```

Summary

The completion of this day's work is a big event in your Java programming career. The ability to handle events makes it possible for you to write full-fledged Java applets, with graphical user interfaces that can be used for user interaction.

Tomorrow, you'll round out your knowledge of the Abstract Windowing Toolkit with a more sophisticated project and coverage of features such as standalone windows.

During Week 3 you get a chance to create a working application that uses Swing, the new windowing package introduced with Java 2.

Q&A

Q I have a new button class defined to look different from the standard AWT button objects in 1.02. I'd like to implement callbacks on this button (that is, to execute an arbitrary function when the button is pressed), but I can't figure out how to get Java to execute an arbitrary method. In C++, I'd just have a pointer to a function. In Smalltalk, I'd use `perform:`. How can I do this in Java?

A You can't do this using Java 1.02; button actions are executed from an `action()` event, which must be contained in the same class as the button. You need to subclass your button class each time you want to create different behavior for that button. This aspect of the language is one of the reasons the event-handling model was changed after Java 1.02. Creating your own components is much easier and more efficient when the event code isn't tied too closely to the user interface code.

13

DAY 14

Developing Advanced User Interfaces with the AWT

This is the last day you learn about the Abstract Windowing Toolkit. Whether you regard that as good or bad news probably depends on how comfortable you have become working with its classes.

If you believe it's good news, you should feel better about the AWT after you learn about some of its advanced features today.

You will build on everything you learned in previous days about components, layout managers, and user-interface events, and are introduced to several new concepts:

- How components work and the various things you can do to them
- Windows, frames, and dialog boxes
- Menus
- Creating standalone AWT applications

Windows, Frames, and Dialog Boxes

In addition to what has been covered thus far, the AWT provides features for creating user-interface elements outside of the applet and browser framework including windows, frames, and dialog boxes. These features enable you to create fully featured applications either as part of your applet or independently, for standalone Java applications.

The Window Classes

The AWT classes to produce windows and dialog boxes inherit from a single class: Window. The Window class inherits from Container as panels and applets do, and it provides generic behavior for all window-like elements.

You don't generally use instances of Window. Instead, you use two of its subclasses: Frame and Dialog.

The Frame class provides a window with a title bar, close boxes, and other platform-specific window features. Frames also let you add menu bars. Dialog is a more limited form of Frame that typically doesn't have a title. FileDialog, a subclass of Dialog, provides a standard file-picker dialog box (usually only usable from inside Java applications because of security restrictions on applets).

When you want to add a new window or dialog box to your applet or application, you create subclasses of the Frame and Dialog classes.

Frames

NEW TERM *Frames* are windows that are independent of an applet and of the browser that contains the applet; they are separate windows with their own titles, resize handles, close boxes, and menu bars. You can create frames for your own applets to produce windows, or you can use frames in Java applications to hold the contents of that application.

A frame is a platform-specific window with a title, a menu bar, close boxes, resize handles, and other window features.

Use one of the following constructors to create a frame:

- new Frame() creates a basic frame without a title.
- new Frame(*String*) creates a basic frame with the given title.

Because frames inherit from Window, which inherits from Container, which inherits from Component, frames are created and used much in the same way other AWT components are created and used. Frames are containers, just like panels are, so you can add other components to them just as you would regular panels, using the add() method. The default layout for frames is BorderLayout. Here's a single example that creates a frame, sets its layout, and adds two buttons:

```
win = new Frame("My Cool Window");
win.setLayout(new BorderLayout(10, 20));
win.add("North", new Button("Start"));
win.add("Center", new Button("Move"));
```

To set a size for the new frame, use the resize() method with the width and height of the new frame. For example, this line of code resizes the window at 100 pixels wide and 200 pixels high:

```
win.resize(100, 200);
```

Because different systems have different ideas of what a pixel is and different resolutions for these pixels, creating a window that is the "right" size for every platform is difficult. Windows that work fine for one may be way too large or too small for another.

One way around this problem is to use the pack() method instead of resize(). The pack() method, which has no arguments, creates a window of the smallest possible size given the current sizes of all the components inside the window and the layout manager and insets in use. The following example creates two buttons and adds them to a window. The window is then resized to the smallest possible window that can still hold these buttons.

```
FlowLayout flo = new FlowLayout();
Button ok = new Button("OK");
Button cancel = new Button("Cancel");
win = new Frame("My Other Cool Window");
win.setLayout(flo);
win.add(ok);
win.add(cancel);
win.pack();
```

When you create a window, it's invisible. You need to use the show() method to make the window appear onscreen. You can use hide() to hide it again:

```
win.show();
```

Note that when you pop up windows from inside applets, the browser may indicate in some way that the window is not a regular browser window—usually with a warning in the window itself.

In Netscape, a message at the bottom of every window states Unsigned Java Applet Window. This warning is intended to let users know that the window comes from the applet, not from the browser itself. (Remember that the Frame class produces windows

14

that look just like normal system windows.) The warning is to prevent a malicious programmer from creating an applet that mimics other programs to acquire user passwords and other information. It appears unless your applet takes steps to request—and receive—certification from the user that it's a trusted program. This is described during Day 16, "Exceptional Circumstances: Error Handling."

Listings 14.1 and 14.2 show the classes that make up a simple applet with a pop-up window frame. Both the applet and the window are shown in Figure 14.1. The applet has two buttons: one to show the window and one to hide the window. The window frame itself, created from a subclass called BaseFrame1, contains a single label: This is a Window. This basic window and applet are referred to throughout this section, so the more you understand what's going on here, the easier it will be later.

FIGURE 14.1.

Windows.

TYPE   **LISTING 14.1.** THE FULL TEXT OF POPUPWINDOW.JAVA.

```
 1: import java.awt.*;
 2:
 3: public class PopUpWindow extends java.applet.Applet {
 4:     Frame window;
 5:     Button open, close;
 6:
 7:     public void init() {
 8:         open = new Button("Open Window");
 9:         add(open);
10:         close = new Button("Close Window");
11:         add(close);
12:
13:         window = new BaseFrame1("A Pop Up Window");
14:         window.resize(150,150);
15:     }
16:
17:     public boolean action(Event evt, Object arg) {
18:         if (evt.target instanceof Button) {
19:             String label = (String)arg;
20:             if (label.equals("Open Window")) {
```

```
21:                    if (!window.isShowing())
22:                        window.show();
23:                } else {
24:                    if (window.isShowing())
25:                        window.hide();
26:                }
27:                return true;
28:            } else
29:                return false;
30:        }
31: }
```

TYPE **LISTING 14.2.** THE FULL TEXT OF BASEFRAME1.JAVA.

```
1: import java.awt.*;
2:
3: class BaseFrame1 extends Frame {
4:     String message = "This is a Window";
5:     Label l;
6:
7:     BaseFrame1(String title) {
8:         super(title);
9:         setLayout(new BorderLayout());
10:
11:         l = new Label(message, Label.CENTER);
12:         l.setFont(new Font("Helvetica", Font.PLAIN, 12));
13:         add("Center", l);
14:     }
15:
16:     public Insets getInsets() {
17:         return new Insets(20,0,25,0);
18:     }
19: }
```

After both of these classes have been compiled, the applet can be tested with the following HTML:

```
<applet code="PopUpWindow.class" height=200 width=200>
</applet>
```

Two classes make up this example: The first, PopUpWindow, is the applet class that creates and controls the pop-up window. In this class's init() method, and in particular in lines 7–15 of Listing 14.1, you add two control buttons to the applet to control the window; you then create, resize, and show the window itself.

14

The control in this applet occurs when one of the buttons is pressed. The `action()` method in lines 17–30 of Listing 14.1 handles these button clicks, which generate action events. In this method, the Open Window button simply shows the window if it's hidden (lines 20–22 of Listing 14.1), and hides it if it's showing (lines 23–25).

The pop-up window itself is a special kind of frame called `BaseFrame1`. In this example the frame is fairly simple; it uses a `BorderLayout` and displays a label in the center of the frame. Note that the initialization of the frame takes place in a constructor, not in an `init()` method. Because frames are regular objects and not applets, you have to initialize them in a more conventional way.

In `BaseFrame1`'s constructor, note that the first line (line 8) is a call to the constructor of `BaseFrame1`'s superclass. As you learned way back on Day 6, "Creating Classes," the first step to initializing a new class is to make this call. Don't forget this step in your own classes; you never know what important things your superclass may be doing in that constructor.

Dialog Boxes

Dialog boxes are functionally similar to frames in that they pop up new windows on the screen. However, dialog boxes are intended to be used for transient windows—windows that let you know about warnings, windows that ask you for specific information, and so on.

NEW TERM Dialog boxes don't usually have title bars or many of the more general features that windows have (although you can create a dialog box with a title bar). They can be made nonresizable or *modal*. (Modal dialogs prevent input to any other windows on the screen until they are dismissed.)

Dialogs are transient windows intended to alert the user to some event or to get input from the user. Unlike frames, dialogs do not generally have title bars or close boxes.

A modal dialog prevents input to any of the other windows on the screen until that dialog box is dismissed. You won't be able to bring other windows to the front or iconify a modal dialog box window; you must actually dismiss the modal dialog box before being able to do anything else on the system. Warnings and alerts are typically modal dialog boxes.

The AWT provides two kinds of dialog boxes: the `Dialog` class, which provides a generic dialog box, and `FileDialog`, which produces the platform-specific file browser dialog box.

Dialog Objects

Dialog boxes are created and used in much the same way as windows. Use one of these constructors to create a generic dialog box:

- `Dialog(Frame, boolean)` creates an invisible dialog box attached to the current frame, which is either modal (`true`) or not (`false`).

- `Dialog(Frame, String, boolean)` creates an invisible dialog box with the given title, which is either modal (`true`) or not (`false`).

NEW TERM The *dialog window*, like the frame window, is a panel on which you can lay out and draw user-interface components and perform graphics operations, just as you would any other panel. Like other windows, the dialog is initially invisible, but you can show it with `show()` and hide it with `hide()`.

Add a dialog to the example with the pop-up window. Of the three classes in this applet, `BaseFrame2` is the only one that needs changing. Here you modify the class to include a Set Text button and add a new class, `TextDialog`, which produces a text entry dialog similar to the one shown in Figure 14.2.

FIGURE 14.2.

The Enter Text dialog.

Note

> This project is an expansion of the previous one. To avoid overwriting the last project's source files, make a copy of `BaseFrame1.java` called `BaseFrame2.java`, and a copy of `PopUpWindow.java` called `PopUpWindowDialog.java`. Use these copies in the upcoming project.

14

The changes are minor when adding the dialog to the `BaseFrame2` class. First, the name of the class should be changed from `BaseFrame1` to `BaseFrame2`, and the constructor should be renamed `BaseFrame2(String title)`. Next, you need an instance variable to hold the dialog because you refer to it throughout this class:

```
TextDialog dl;
```

In `BaseFrame2`'s constructor method, you can create the dialog (an instance of the new class `TextDialog` you'll create in a bit), assign it to the `dl` instance variable, and resize it; the resizing is shown in the next two lines of code. You don't want to show it yet because it should only appear when the Set Text button is clicked.

```
dl = new TextDialog(this, "Enter Text", true);
dl.resize(150,150);
```

Now create the Set Text button to function similarly to how other buttons work, and add it to the `BorderLayout` in the `"South"` position (which puts it directly below the label).

```
Button b = new Button("Set Text");
add("South", b);
```

After you have added the `TextDialog` and a Set Text button to the `BaseFrame2` class, you need to add the following event-handling method:

```
public boolean action(Event evt, Object arg) {
    if (evt.target instanceof Button) {
        dl.show();
        return true;
    } else
        return false;
}
```

This displays the `TextDialog` object `dl` when any button on the frame is clicked. In this example, there's only one button—Set Text.

That's the end of the behavior you have to add to the pop-up window to create a dialog. Only two changes are needed in `PopUpWindowDialog`. First, the class name must be changed from `PopUpWindow` to `PopUpWindowDialog`. Next, the `BaseFrame2` class should be referenced instead of `BaseFrame1`, as illustrated in the following statement:

```
window = new BaseFrame2("A Pop Up Window");
```

The rest of the new behavior goes into the `TextDialog` class, the code for which is shown in Listing 14.3.

TYPE   **LISTING 14.3.** THE FULL TEXT OF TEXTDIALOG.JAVA.

```
1: import java.awt.*;
2:
3: class TextDialog extends Dialog {
4:     TextField tf;
```

```
 5:        BaseFrame2 theFrame;
 6:
 7:        TextDialog(Frame parent, String title, boolean modal) {
 8:            super(parent, title, modal);
 9:
10:            theFrame = (BaseFrame2)parent;
11:            setLayout(new BorderLayout(10,10));
12:            setBackground(Color.white);
13:            tf = new TextField(theFrame.message,20);
14:            add("Center", tf);
15:
16:            Button b = new Button("OK");
17:            add("South", b);
18:        }
19:
20:        public Insets insets() {
21:            return new Insets(30,10,10,10);
22:        }
23:
24:        public boolean action(Event evt, Object arg) {
25:            if (evt.target instanceof Button) {
26:                String label = (String)arg;
27:                if (label == "OK") {
28:                    hide();
29:                    theFrame.l.setText(tf.getText());
30:                }
31:                return true;
32:            } else
33:                return false;
34:        }
35: }
```

You should note a few points about this code. First, unlike the other two windows in this applet, the event handling is inside the class so that the dialog serves as its own handler.

Despite this fact, this dialog has a lot of the same elements as the BaseFrame2 class. Note that the constructor for TextDialog is identical to one of the constructors for its super-class Dialog because despite the fact that TextDialog is attached to an object whose class is BaseFrame2, dialogs must be attached to an actual Frame object. You can more easily make the constructor more generic and then specialize it after the superclass's constructor has been called—which is precisely what you do in lines 8 and 10 of Listing 14.3. Line 8 is the call to the superclass's constructor to hook up the dialog with the frame, and line 10 actually sets the instance variable to the specific instance of the Frame class defined in the BaseFrame2 class.

14

The remainder of the `TextDialog` constructor simply sets up the rest of the layout: a text field and a button in a border layout. The `getInsets()` method adds a few insets and the `action()` method, which handles the action of the dialog's OK button. The `action()` method does two things: In line 28 it hides the dialog to dismiss it, and in line 29 it changes the value of the label in the parent frame to be the new value of the text.

All these classes just for a simple applet! The different windows and associated event classes make the applet complicated. At this point, though, you should feel comfortable with how each part of an applet has its own components and actions and how all the parts of the applet fit together.

Attaching Dialogs to Applets

Dialogs can be attached to frames only. To create a dialog, you have to pass an instance of the `Frame` class to one of the dialog's constructor methods. This implies that you cannot create dialog boxes that are attached to applets. Because applets don't have explicit frames, you cannot give the `Dialog` class a frame argument. Through a bit of sneaky code, however, you can get ahold of the frame object that contains that applet (often the browser or applet viewer window itself) and then use that object as the dialog's frame.

This sneaky code makes use of the `getParent()` method, defined for all AWT components. The `getParent()` method returns the object that contains this object. The parent of all AWT applications, then, must be a frame. Applets behave this same way. By calling `getParent()` repeatedly, eventually you should be able to get ahold of an instance of `Frame`. Here's the sneaky code you can put inside your applet:

```
Object anchorpoint = getParent()
while (! (anchorpoint instanceof Frame))
    anchorpoint = ( (Component) anchorpoint ).getParent();
```

In the first line of this code you create a local variable, called `anchorpoint`, to hold the eventual frame for this applet. The object assigned to `anchorpoint` may be one of many classes, so declare its type as `Object`.

The second two lines of this code are a `while` loop that calls `getParent()` on each different object up the chain until it gets to an actual `Frame` object. Note here that because the `getParent()` method is defined only on objects that inherit from `Component`, you have to cast the value of `anchorpoint` to `Component` each time for the `getParent()` method to work.

After the loop exits, the object contained in the `anchorpoint` variable will be an instance of the `Frame` class (or one of its subclasses). You can then create a `Dialog` object attached to that frame, casting `anchorpoint` one more time to make sure you have a `Frame` object:

```
TextDialog dl = new TextDialog((Frame)anchorpoint,
    "Enter Text", true);
```

File Dialog Objects

The `FileDialog` class provides a basic File Open/Save dialog box that enables you to access the local file system. The `FileDialog` class is system independent, but depending on the platform, the standard Open File or Save File dialog is brought up.

 Note

> Whether you can even use instances of `FileDialog` for applets is dependent on the browser. Because of the default security restrictions in place for applets, most browsers produce a security exception when you try. `FileDialog` is much more useful in standalone applications.

Use the following constructors to create a file dialog:

- `FileDialog(Frame, String)` creates a file dialog, attached to the given frame, with the given title. This form creates a dialog to load a file.

- `FileDialog(Frame, String, int)` also creates a file dialog, but the integer argument is used to determine whether the dialog is for loading a file or saving a file. (The only difference is the labels on the buttons; the file dialog does not actually open or save anything.) The options for the mode argument are `FileDialog.LOAD` and `FileDialog.SAVE`.

After you create a `FileDialog` instance, use `show()` to display it:

```
FileDialog fd = new FileDialog(this, "FileDialog");
fd.show();
```

When the reader chooses a file in the File dialog and dismisses it, you can then access the filename the reader chose by using the `getDirectory()` and `getFile()` methods. Both of these methods return strings indicating the values the reader chose. You can then open the file by using the stream- and file-handling methods (which you learn about next week) and then read from or write to that file.

Window Events

You're down to the last set of events you can handle in the AWT: the events for windows and dialogs. (In terms of events, a dialog is considered just another kind of window.) Window events result when the state of a window changes in any way: when the window is moved, resized, iconified, deiconified, moved to the front, or closed. In a well-behaved application, you'll want to handle at least some of these events—for example, to stop running threads when a window is iconified, or to clean up when the window is closed.

14

You can use `handleEvent()` to test for each of the events shown in Table 14.1, using the standard `switch` statement with the `id` instance variable.

TABLE 14.1. WINDOW EVENTS.

Event Name	When It Occurs
WINDOW_DESTROY	Generated when a window is destroyed using the Close box or the Close menu item
WINDOW_EXPOSE	Generated when the window is brought forward from behind other windows
WINDOW_ICONIFY	Generated when the window is iconified
WINDOW_DEICONIFY	Generated when the window is restored from an icon
WINDOW_MOVED	Generated when the window is moved

Menus

Only one user interface element in the AWT is left to talk about: menus.

A menu bar is a collection of menus. A menu, in turn, contains a collection of menu items, which can have names and sometimes optional shortcuts. The AWT provides classes for all of these menu elements, including `MenuBar`, `Menu`, and `MenuItem`.

Menus and Menu Bars

NEW TERM A *menu bar* is a set of menus that appears across the top of a window. Because they are rooted to windows, you cannot create menu bars in applets (but if that applet pops up an independent window, the window can have a menu bar).

To create a menu bar for a given window, you create a new instance of the class `MenuBar`:

```
MenuBar mbar = new MenuBar();
```

You use the `setMenuBar()` method (defined in the `Frame` class) to set this menu bar as the default menu for the window:

```
window.setMenuBar(mbar);
```

You can add individual menus (File, Edit, and so on) to the menu bar by creating them and then adding them to the menu bar using `add()`. The argument to the `Menu` constructor is the name of the Menu as it will appear in the menu bar.

```
Menu myMenu = new Menu("File");
mbar.add(myMenu);
```

Some systems provide a special Help menu, which is drawn on the right side of the menu bar as opposed to the left side. You can indicate that a specific menu is the Help menu by using the `setHelpMenu()` method. The given menu should already be added to the menu itself before being made a Help menu.

```
Menu helpmenu = new Menu("Help");
mbar.add(helpmenu);
mbar.setHelpMenu(helpmenu);
```

If for any reason you want to prevent a user from selecting a menu, you can use the `disable()` command on that menu (and the `enable()`command to make it available again):

```
myMenu.disable();
```

Menu Items

You can add four kinds of items to individual menus:

- Instances of the class `MenuItem`, for regular menu items
- Instances of the class `CheckBoxMenuItem`, for toggled menu items
- Other menus, with their own menu items
- Separators, for lines that separate groups of items on menus

Creating Menu Items

Regular menu items are created and added to a menu using the `MenuItem` class. First create a new instance of `MenuItem`, and then add it to the `Menu` component using the `add()` method:

```
Menu myMenu = new Menu("Tools");
myMenu.add(new MenuItem("Info"));
myMenu.add(new MenuItem("Colors"));
```

Submenus can be added simply by creating a new instance of `Menu` and adding it to the first menu. You can then add items to that menu:

```
Menu submenu = new Menu("Sizes");
myMenu.add(submenu);
submenu.add(new MenuItem("Small"));
submenu.add(new MenuItem("Medium"));
submenu.add(new MenuItem("Large"));
```

The `CheckBoxMenuItem` class creates a menu item with a check box on it, enabling the menu state to be toggled on and off. (Selecting it once makes the check box appear selected; selecting it again deselects the check box.) Create and add a check box menu item the same way you create and add regular menu items:

14

```
CheckboxMenuItem coords =
new CheckboxMenuItem("Show Coordinates");
myMenu.add(coords);
```

Finally, to add a separator to a menu (a line used to separate groups of items in a menu), create and add a menu item with a single dash (-) as the label. That special menu item will be drawn with a separator line. These next two lines of Java code create a separator menu item and add it to the menu myMenu:

```
MenuItem msep = new MenuItem("-");
myMenu.add(msep);
```

Any menu item can be disabled by using the disable() method and enabled again using enable(). Disabled menu items cannot be selected.

```
MenuItem item = new MenuItem("Fill");
myMenu.addItem(item);
item.disable();
```

Menu Events

The act of selecting a menu item with the mouse or choosing the menu item's keyboard shortcut causes an action event to be generated. You can handle that event using the action() method, just as you have over the last two days.

In addition to action events, CheckBoxMenuItems generate list-select and list-deselect events, which can be handled via handleEvent().

As you process events generated by menu items and check box menu items, keep in mind that because CheckboxMenuItem is a subclass of MenuItem, you don't have to treat this menu item as a special case. You can handle this action the same way you handle other action methods.

Creating Standalone AWT Applications

Although you learn how to create graphical user interfaces for applications next week using the new Swing classes, you already have most of the skills you need to create a Java 1.02 application.

There actually isn't a lot of difference between a Java applet and a graphical Java application. Everything you've learned up to this point about the AWT, including the graphics methods, animation techniques, events, user-interface components, windows, and dialogs, can be used the same way in Java applications as they can in applets.

How do you go about creating a graphical Java application? The code to create it is almost trivial. Your main application class should inherit from Frame. If it uses threads (for animation or other processing), it should also implement Runnable:

```
class MyAWTApplication extends Frame implements Runnable {
    // ...
}
```

You create a new instance of your class inside the main() method for your application—because your class extends Frame, that'll give you a new AWT window that you can then resize and show as you would any AWT window.

Set up the usual AWT features for a window that you might usually do in an init() method for an applet inside the constructor method for your class: Set the title, add a layout manager, create and add components such as a menu bar or other user interface elements, start up a thread, and so on.

Here's an example of a very simple application:

```
import java.awt.*;

class MyAWTApplication extends Frame {

    MyAWTApplication(String title) {
        super(title);
        setLayout(new FlowLayout());
        add(new Button("OK"));
        add(new Button("Reset"));
        add(new Button("Cancel"));
    }

    public static void main(String args[]) {
        MyAWTApplication app = new MyAWTApplication("Hi! I'm an
application");
        app.resize(300,300);
        app.show();
    }
}
```

For the most part you can use any of the methods you've learned about this week to control and manage your application. The only methods you cannot use are those specific to applets (that is, those defined in java.applet.Applet, which includes methods for retrieving URL information and playing audio clips).

You should know one other difference between applications and applets: When you handle a window-closing event, in addition to hiding or destroying the window, you should also call System.exit(0) to indicate to the system that your application has exited.

14

```
public void windowClosing(WindowEvent e) {
    win.hide();
    win.destroy();
    System.exit(0);
}
```

A Complete Example: RGB-to-HSB Converter

As an opportunity to put the past several days' material to more use, the following sample applet demonstrates layout creation, nested panels, interface creation, and event handling.

Figure 14.3 shows the applet you create in this example. The ColorTest applet enables you to pick colors based on the sRGB and HSB color spaces—which describe colors based on their red, green, and blue content or hue, saturation, and brightness values, respectively.

FIGURE 14.3.

The ColorTest applet.

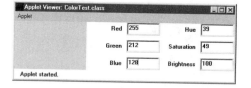

The ColorTest applet has three main parts: a colored box on the left side and two groups of text fields on the right. The first group indicates RGB values; the second group, HSB. If you change any of the values in any of the text boxes, the colored box is updated to the new color, as are the values in the other group of text boxes.

This applet uses two classes:

- ColorTest, which inherits from Applet. It is the controlling class for the applet itself.

- ColorControls, which inherits from Panel. You create this class to represent a group of three text fields and to handle actions from them. Two instances of this class, one for the sRGB values and one for the HSB ones, are created and added to the applet.

Because it's very complicated and can get confusing, work through this example step by step. All the code for this applet is shown at the end of this section.

Designing and Creating the Applet Layout

The best way to start creating an applet that uses AWT components is to first worry about the layout and then worry about the functionality. When dealing with the layout, you should start with the outermost panel first and work inward.

Making a sketch of your user-interface design can help you figure out how to organize the panels inside your applet or window to best take advantage of layout and space. Paper designs are helpful even when you're not using grid bag layouts, but doubly so when you are. (You'll be using a simple grid layout for this applet.)

Figure 14.4 shows the ColorTest applet with a grid drawn over it so that you can get an idea of how the panels and embedded panels work.

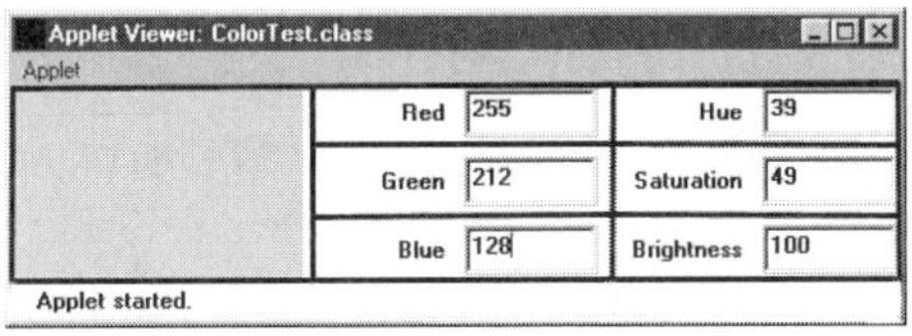

FIGURE 14.4.

The ColorTest applet panels and components.

Start with the outermost panel—the applet itself. This panel has three parts: the color box on the left, the RGB text fields in the middle, and the HSB fields on the right.

Because the outermost panel is the applet itself, the `ColorTest` class will be the applet class and will inherit from `Applet`. You also import the AWT classes here. (Note that because you use so many of them in this program, importing the entire package is easiest.)

```
import java.awt.*;

public class ColorTest extends java.applet.Applet {
    // ...
}
```

This applet has three main elements to keep track of: the color box and the two subpanels. Each of the two subpanels refers to different things, but they're essentially the same panel and behave in the same ways. Rather than duplicate a lot of code in this class, you can take this opportunity to create another class strictly for the subpanels, use instances of that class in the applet, and communicate between everything using methods. The new class called `ColorControls` will be defined in a bit.

For now, however, you know you need to keep a handle to all three parts of the applet, so you can update them when they change. Create three instance variables: one of type `Canvas` for the color box and the other two of type `ColorControls` for the control panels:

14

```
ColorControls RGBcontrols, HSBcontrols;
Canvas swatch;
```

Now you can move onto the `init()` method, where all the basic initialization and layout of the applet take place. Follow these three steps to initialize the applet:

1. Create the layout for the big parts of the panel. Although a flow layout would work, creating a grid layout with one row and three columns is a much better idea.

2. Create and initialize the three components of this applet: a canvas for the color box and two subpanels for the text fields.

3. Add these components to the applet.

Step 1 is the layout. Use a grid layout and a gap of 10 points to separate each of the components:

```
setLayout(new GridLayout(1, 3, 5, 15));
```

Step 2 is creating the components—the canvas first. You have an instance variable to hold that one. Here you create the canvas and initialize its background to black:

```
swatch = new Canvas();
swatch.setBackground(Color.black);
```

You need also to create two instances of the currently nonexistent `ColorControls` panels here. Because you haven't created the class yet, you don't know what the constructors to that class will look like. In that case, put in some placeholder constructors here; you can fill in the details later.

```
RGBcontrols = new ColorControls(...);
HSBcontrols = new ColorControls(...);
```

Step 3 is adding all three components to the applet panel, like this:

```
add(swatch);
add(RGBcontrols);
add(HSBcontrols);
```

Add insets for the applet while you're working on layout (10 points along all the edges):

```
public Insets getInsets() {
    return new Insets(10, 10, 10, 10);
}
```

Got it so far? At this point you should have three instance variables, an `init()` method with two incomplete constructors, and a `getInsets()` method in your `ColorTest` class. Move on now to creating the subpanel layout in the `ColorControls` class, so you can fill in these constructors and finish up the layout.

Defining the Subpanels

The `ColorControls` class will have behavior for laying out and handling the subpanels that represent the RGB and HSB values for the color. `ColorControls` doesn't need to be a subclass of `Applet` because it isn't actually an applet; it's just a panel. Define it to inherit from `Panel`:

```
import java.awt.*;

class ColorControls extends Panel {
    // ...
}
```

The `ColorControls` class needs a number of instance variables so that information from the panel can get back to the applet. The first of these instance variables is a hook back up to the applet class that contains this panel. Because the outer applet class controls the updating of each panel, this panel needs a way to tell the applet that something has changed. To call a method in that applet, you need a reference to the object; instance variable number one is a reference to an instance of the class `ColorTest`:

```
ColorTest applet;
```

If you figure that the `applet` class is updating everything, that class will be interested in the individual text fields in this subpanel. You create instance variables for these text fields:

```
TextField tfield1, tfield2, tfield3;
```

Now you can move on to the constructor for this class. Because this class isn't an applet, you won't use `init()` to initialize it; instead, you'll use a constructor method. Inside the constructor you do much of what you did inside `init()`: create the layout for the subpanel, create the text fields, and add them to the panel.

The goal here is to make the `ColorControls` class generic enough so that you can use it for both the RGB fields and the HSB fields. These two panels differ in only one respect: the labels for the text—that's three values to get before you can create the object. You can pass these three values in through the constructors in `ColorTest`. You also need one more: the reference to the enclosing applet, which you can get from the constructor as well.

You now have four arguments to the basic constructor for the `ColorControls` class. Here's the signature for the constructor:

```
ColorControls(ColorTest parent,
    String l1, String l2, String l3) {
}
```

14

Start this constructor by first setting the value of `parent` to the `applet` instance variable:

```
applet = parent;
```

Next, create the layout for this panel. You can also use a grid layout for these subpanels, as you did for the applet panel, but this time the grid will have three rows (one for each of the text field and label pairs) and two columns (one for the labels and one for the fields). Also define a 10-point gap between the components in the grid:

```
setLayout(new GridLayout(3,2,10,10));
```

Now you can create and add the components to the panel. First create the text field objects (initialized to the string `"0"`) and assign them to the appropriate instance variables:

```
tfield1 = new TextField("0");
tfield2 = new TextField("0");
tfield3 = new TextField("0");
```

Now add these fields and the appropriate labels to the panel using the remaining three parameters to the constructor as the text for the labels:

```
add(new Label(l1, Label.RIGHT));
add(tfield1);
add(new Label(l2, Label.RIGHT));
add(tfield2);
add(new Label(l3, Label.RIGHT));
add(tfield3);
```

You've finished the constructor for the subpanel class `ColorControls`. Are you done with the layout? Not quite. You also add an inset around the subpanel—only on the top and bottom edges—to tinker the layout. Add the inset here as you did in the `ColorTest` class using the `getInsets()` method:

```
public Insets getInsets() {
    return new Insets(10, 10, 0, 0);
}
```

You're almost there. You have 98 percent of the basic structure in place and ready to go, but you have one step left: going back to `ColorTest` and fixing the placeholder constructors for the subpanel so that they match the actual constructors for `ColorControls`.

The constructor for `ColorControls` that you just created now has four arguments: the `ColorTest` object and three labels (strings). Remember when you created the `init()` method for `ColorTest`. You added two placeholders for creating new `ColorControls` objects. Replace these placeholders with the correct versions now. Make sure you add the four arguments the constructor needs to work: the `ColorTest` object and three strings. You can use the `this` keyword to pass the `ColorTest` object to these constructors:

```
RGBcontrols = new ColorControls(this, "Red",
    "Green", "Blue");
HSBcontrols = new ColorControls(this, "Hue",
    "Saturation", "Brightness");
```

 Note

The number 0 (actually, the string "0") is used for the initial values of all the text fields in this example. For the color black, both the RGB and the HSB values are 0, which is why this assumption can be made. If you want to initialize the applet to some other color, you might want to rewrite the `ColorControls` class to use initializer values as well as to initialize labels. The way it was done made for a shorter example.

Handling the Events

After creating the layout, you set up actions with the user-interface components so that the applet can respond when the user interacts with it.

This applet's action occurs when the user changes a value in any of the text fields. By causing an action in a text field, the color changes, the color box updates to the new color, and the value of the fields in the opposite subpanel change to reflect the new color.

The `ColorTest` class is responsible for actually doing the updating because it keeps track of all the subpanels. You should be tracking and intercepting events in the subpanel in which they occur, however. Because the applet's action is an actual text action, you can use an `action()` method to intercept it in the `ColorControls` class:

```
public boolean action(Event evt, Object arg) {
    if (evt.target instanceof TextField) {
        applet.update(this);
        return true;
    }
    else return false;
}
```

In the `action()` method, you test to make sure the action was indeed generated by a text field (because there are only text fields available, that's the only action you'll get; it is a good idea to test for it anyway). If so, call the `update()` method defined in `ColorTest` to update the applet to reflect the new values. Because the outer applet is responsible for doing all the updating, this is precisely why you need that hook back to the applet—so you can call the right method at the right time.

14

Updating the Result

Now comes the hard part: actually doing the updating based on the new values of whatever text field was changed. For this step you define the update() method in the ColorTest class. This update() method takes a single argument: the ColorControls instance that contains the changed value. (You get the argument from the event methods in the ColorControls object.)

> **Note**
>
> Won't this update() method interfere with the system's update() method? No. Remember, methods can have the same name, but different signatures and definitions. Because this update() has a single argument of type ColorControls, it doesn't interfere with the other version of update(). Normally, all methods called update() should mean basically the same thing. That's not the case here, but this is only an example.

The update() method is responsible for updating all the panels in the applet. To know which panel to update, you need to know which panel changed. You can find out by testing to see whether the argument you got passed from the panel is the same as the subpanels you have stored in the RGBcontrols and HSBcontrols instance variables:

```
void update(ColorControls controlPanel) {

    if (controlPanel == RGBcontrols) {  // RGB has changed, update HSB
        // ...
    } else {  // HSB has changed, update RGB
        // ...
    }
}
```

This test is the heart of the update() method. Start with the first case—a number has been changed in the RGB text fields. Now, based on these new RGB values, you have to generate a new Color object and update the values on the HSB panel. You can create a few local variables to hold some basic values in order to reduce some typing. In particular, the values of the text fields are strings whose values you can get to using the getText() method defined in the TextField objects of the ColorControls object. Because most of the time in this method you'll want to deal with these values as integers, you can get these string values, convert them to integers, and store them in local variables (value1, value2, value3). Here's the code to take care of this job (it looks more complicated than it actually is):

```
int value1 = Integer.parseInt(controlPanel.tfield1.getText());
int value2 = Integer.parseInt(controlPanel.tfield2.getText());
int value3 = Integer.parseInt(controlPanel.tfield3.getText());
```

While you're defining local variables, you also need one for the new `Color` object:

```
Color c;
```

Now assume one of the text fields in the RGB side of the applet has changed and add the code to the `if` part of the `update()` method. You need to create a new `Color` object and update the HSB side of the panel. That first part is easy. Given the three RGB values, you can create a new `Color` object using these values as arguments to the constructor:

```
c = new Color(value1, value2, value3);
```

Note

> This part of the example isn't very robust. It assumes that the user has indeed entered integers from 0 to 255 into the text fields. A better version would test to make sure that no data-entry errors had occurred, but this example was kept small.

Now you convert the RGB values to HSB. Standard algorithms can convert an RGB-based color to an HSB color, but you don't have to look them up. The `Color` class has a class method called `RGBtoHSB()` you can use. This method does the work for you—most of it, at least. The `RGBtoHSB()` method poses two problems, however:

- The `RGBtoHSB()` method returns an array of the three HSB values, so you have to extract these values from the array.
- The HSB values are measured in floating-point values from `0.0` to `1.0`. I prefer to think of HSB values as integers, where the hue is a degree value around a color wheel (`0` through `360`), and saturation and brightness are percentages from `0` to `100`.

Neither of these problems is insurmountable; you just have to add some extra lines of code. Start by calling `RGBtoHSB()` with the new RGB values you have. The return type of that method is an array of `float`s, so you create a local variable (`HSB`) to store the results of the `RBGtoHSB()` method. (Note that you also need to create and pass in an empty array of `float`s as the fourth argument to `RGBtoHSB()`.)

```
float[] HSB = Color.RGBtoHSB(value1, value2,
    value3, (new float[3]));
```

Now convert these floating-point values that range from `0.0` to `1.0` to values that range from `0` and `100` (for the saturation and brightness) and `0` to `360` for the hue by multiplying the appropriate numbers and reassigning the value back to the array:

```
HSB[0] *= 360;
HSB[1] *= 100;
HSB[2] *= 100;
```

Now you have the numbers you want. The last part of the update puts these values back into the text fields. Of course, these values are still floating-point numbers, so you have to cast them to ints before turning them into strings and storing them:

```
HSBcontrols.tfield1.setText(String.valueOf((int)HSB[0]));
HSBcontrols.tfield2.setText(String.valueOf((int)HSB[1]));
HSBcontrols.tfield3.setText(String.valueOf((int)HSB[2]));
```

You're halfway there. The next part of the applet is the part that updates the RGB values when a text field on the HSB side has changed. This is the else in the big if...else that defines this method and determines what to update, given a change.

Generating RGB values from HSB values is actually easier than doing the process the other way around. A class method in the Color class, getHSBColor(), creates a new Color object from three HSB values. After you have a Color object, you can easily pull the RGB values out of there. The catch, of course, is that getHSBColor takes three floating-point arguments, and the values you have are the integer values that I prefer to use. In the call to getHSBColor, you'll have to cast the integer values from the text fields to floats and divide them by the proper conversion factor. The result of getHSBColor is a Color object. You therefore can simply assign the object to the c local variable so that you can use it again later:

```
c = Color.getHSBColor((float)value1 / 360,
    (float)value2 / 100, (float)value3 / 100);
```

With the Color object all set, updating the RGB values involves extracting these values from that Color object. The getRed(), getGreen(), and getBlue() methods, defined in the Color class, will do just that job:

```
RGBcontrols.tfield1.setText(String.valueOf(c.getRed()));
RGBcontrols.tfield2.setText(String.valueOf(c.getGreen()));
RGBcontrols.tfield3.setText(String.valueOf(c.getBlue()));
```

Finally, regardless of whether the RGB or HSB value has changed, you need to update the color box on the left to reflect the new color. Because you have a new Color object stored in the variable c, you can use the setBackground method to change the color. Also note that setBackground doesn't automatically repaint the screen, so fire off a repaint() as well:

```
swatch.setBackground(c);
swatch.repaint();
```

That's it! You're done. Now compile both the ColorTest and ColorControls classes, create an HTML file to load the ColorTest applet, and check it out.

The Complete Source Code

Listing 14.4 shows the complete source code for the applet class ColorTest, and Listing 14.5 shows the source for the helper class ColorControls. Figuring out what's going on in an applet is often easier when the code is all in one place, and you can follow the method calls and how values are passed back and forth. Start with the init() method in the ColorTest applet and go from there.

TYPE **LISTING 14.4.** THE FULL TEXT OF COLORTEST.JAVA.

```
 1: import java.awt.*;
 2:
 3: public class ColorTest extends java.applet.Applet {
 4:     ColorControls RGBcontrols, HSBcontrols;
 5:     Canvas swatch;
 6:
 7:     public void init() {
 8:         setLayout(new GridLayout(1, 3, 5, 15));
 9:         swatch = new Canvas();
10:         swatch.setBackground(Color.black);
11:         RGBcontrols = new ColorControls(this, "Red",
12:             "Green", "Blue");
13:         HSBcontrols = new ColorControls(this, "Hue",
14:             "Saturation", "Brightness");
15:         add(swatch);
16:         add(RGBcontrols);
17:         add(HSBcontrols);
18:     }
19:
20:     public Insets getInsets() {
21:         return new Insets(10, 10, 10, 10);
22:     }
23:
24:     void update(ColorControls controlPanel) {
25:         int value1 = Integer.parseInt(controlPanel.tfield1.getText());
26:         int value2 = Integer.parseInt(controlPanel.tfield2.getText());
27:         int value3 = Integer.parseInt(controlPanel.tfield3.getText());
28:         Color c;
29:         if (controlPanel == RGBcontrols) {   // RGB has changed, update HSB
30:             c = new Color(value1, value2, value3);
31:             float[] HSB = Color.RGBtoHSB(value1, value2,
32:                 value3, (new float[3]));
33:             HSB[0] *= 360;
34:             HSB[1] *= 100;
35:             HSB[2] *= 100;
```

continues

14

LISTING **14.4.** CONTINUED

```
36:            HSBcontrols.tfield1.setText(String.valueOf((int)HSB[0]));
37:            HSBcontrols.tfield2.setText(String.valueOf((int)HSB[1]));
38:            HSBcontrols.tfield3.setText(String.valueOf((int)HSB[2]));
39:        } else {  // HSB has changed, update RGB
40:            c = Color.getHSBColor((float)value1 / 360,
41:                (float)value2 / 100, (float)value3 / 100);
42:            RGBcontrols.tfield1.setText(String.valueOf(c.getRed()));
43:            RGBcontrols.tfield2.setText(String.valueOf(c.getGreen()));
44:            RGBcontrols.tfield3.setText(String.valueOf(c.getBlue()));
45:        }
46:        swatch.setBackground(c);
47:        swatch.repaint();
48:    }
49: }
```

TYPE   LISTING **14.5.** THE FULL TEXT OF COLORCONTROLS.JAVA.

```
1: import java.awt.*;
2:
3: class ColorControls extends Panel {
4:     ColorTest applet;
5:     TextField tfield1, tfield2, tfield3;
6:
7:     ColorControls(ColorTest parent,
8:         String l1, String l2, String l3) {
9:
10:         applet = parent;
11:         setLayout(new GridLayout(3,2,10,10));
12:         tfield1 = new TextField("0");
13:         tfield2 = new TextField("0");
14:         tfield3 = new TextField("0");
15:         add(new Label(l1, Label.RIGHT));
16:         add(tfield1);
17:         add(new Label(l2, Label.RIGHT));
18:         add(tfield2);
19:         add(new Label(l3, Label.RIGHT));
20:         add(tfield3);
21:
22:     }
23:
24:     public Insets getInsets() {
25:         return new Insets(10, 10, 0, 0);
26:     }
27:
28:     public boolean action(Event evt, Object arg) {
29:         if (evt.target instanceof TextField) {
30:             applet.update(this);
```

```
31:                return true;
32:            }
33:            else return false;
34:        }
35: }
```

After both of these class files have been compiled, the ColorTest applet can be loaded on a page with the following HTML:

```
<applet code="ColorTest.class" width=475 height=100>
</applet>
```

Summary

Four days is a long time to focus on a specific element of the Java language, but the Abstract Windowing Toolkit is an essential part of any Java programmer's skill set.

You now can create a graphical user interface for an applet, or even create an application using the AWT and Java 1.02 techniques. During this book's third week you learn how to accomplish some of the same tasks using the Swing windowing classes.

Whether your response is a tearful goodbye or a joyful good riddance, you'll be moving from the AWT to new subjects beginning tomorrow.

This response to you is well deserved: Good job!

Q&A

Q In your discussion on standalone applications, I got the impression that there's absolutely no difference between an applet and an application. Why is that?

A Both applets and applications use the same procedures inside the AWT to build components, display them, and handle events. Aside from security restrictions, the only differences are that applications initialize from main() and display in their own windows, and applets initialize and start from init() and start(), respectively. Given the vast number of similarities between applets and applications, 99 percent of what you learn regarding applets can be used with applications. In fact, because applets ignore the main() method if it happens to exist in a class, there's no reason you can't create a single program that runs equally well as an applet and as an application.

14

Q I created a standalone application, but nothing happens when I click on the Close box. What do I need to do to get my application to actually close?

A Trap the window-close event with `WINDOW_CLOSE` in the 1.02 event model. In response to that event, either call `hide()` if it may come back later, or call `destroy()` to get rid of it for good. If the window-close event results in your entire program exiting, also call `System.exit()`.

WEEK 3

Using Swing and Other Advanced Features

DAY 15

Class Roles: Packages, Interfaces, and Other Features

The third week of this course extends what you already know. You could quit at this point and develop functional programs, but you would be missing some of the advanced features that express the real strengths of the language.

Today, you'll extend your knowledge of classes and how they interact with other classes in a Java program. The following subjects will be covered:

- Controlling access to methods and variables from outside a class
- Finalizing classes, methods, and variables so their values or definitions cannot be subclasses or cannot be overridden
- Creating abstract classes and methods for factoring common behavior into superclasses
- Grouping classes into packages
- Using interfaces to bridge gaps in a class hierarchy

Modifiers

The techniques for programming you'll learn today involve different strategies and ways of thinking about how a class is organized. But the one thing all these techniques have in common is that they all use special modifier keywords in the Java language.

In Week 1, "Getting Started with Java Programming," you learned how to define classes, methods, and variables in Java. Modifiers are keywords you add to those definitions to change their meaning.

The Java language has a wide variety of modifiers, including

- Modifiers for controlling access to a class, method, or variable: `public`, `protected`, and `private`
- The `static` modifier, for creating class methods and variables
- The `final` modifier, for finalizing the implementations of classes, methods, and variables
- The `abstract` modifier, for creating abstract classes and methods
- The `synchronized` and `volatile` modifiers, which are used for threads

To use a modifier, you include its keyword in the definition of the class, method, or variable that is being modified. The modifier precedes the rest of the statement, as in the following examples:

```
public class MyApplet extends java.applet.Applet { ... }

private boolean killJabberwock;

static final double weeks = 9.5;

protected static final int MEANINGOFLIFE = 42;

public static void main(String arguments[]) { ...}
```

If you're using more than one modifier in a statement, you can place them in any order, as long as all modifiers precede the element they are modifying. Make sure to avoid treating a method's return type—such as `void`—as if it were one of the modifiers.

Modifiers are optional—which you should realize, after using very few of them in the preceding two weeks. You can come up with many good reasons to use them, though, as you'll see.

Access Control for Methods and Variables

The modifiers that you will use the most often in your programs are the ones that control access to methods and variables: `public`, `private`, and `protected`. These modifiers determine which variables and methods of a class are visible to other classes.

15

By using access control, you control how your class will be used by other classes. Some variables and methods in a class will be of use only within the class itself, and they should be hidden from other classes that might interact with the class. This process is called encapsulation: An object controls what the outside world can know about it and how the outside world can interact with it.

NEW TERM *Encapsulation* is the process of preventing the variables of a class from being read or modified by other classes. The only way to use these variables is by calling methods of the class, if they are available.

The Java language provides four levels of access control: `public`, `private`, `protected`, and a default level that is specified by using no modifier.

Default Access

For most of the examples in this book, you have not specified any kind of access control. Variables and methods were declared with statements such as the following:

```
String singer = "Phil Harris";
boolean digThatCrazyBeat() {
    return true;
}
```

A variable or method declared without any access control modifier is available to any other class in the same package. Previously, you saw how classes in the Java class library are organized into packages. The `java.awt` package is one of them—a set of related classes for behavior related to Java's Abstract Windowing Toolkit.

Any variable declared without a modifier can be read or changed by any other class in the same package. Any method declared the same way can be called by any other class in the same package. No other classes can access these elements in any way.

This level of access control doesn't control much access. When you start thinking more about how your class will be used by other classes, you'll be using one of the three modifiers more often than accepting the default control.

Note

The preceding discussion raises the question about what package your own classes have been in up to this point. As you'll see later today, you can make your class a member of a package by using the `package` statement. If you don't use this approach, the class is put into a package with all other classes that don't belong to any other packages.

Private Access

To completely hide a method or variable from being used by any other classes, you use the private modifier. The only place these methods or variables can be seen is from within their own class.

A private instance variable, for example, can be used by methods in its own class but not by objects of any other class. In the same vein, private methods can be called by other methods in their own class but by no others. This restriction also affects inheritance: Neither private variables nor private methods are inherited by subclasses.

Private variables are extremely useful in two circumstances:

- When other classes have no reason to use that variable
- When another class could wreak havoc by changing the variable in an inappropriate way

For example, consider a Java class called BingoBrain that generates bingo numbers for an Internet gambling site. A variable in that class called winRatio could control the number of winners and losers that are generated. As you can imagine, this variable has a big impact on the bottom line at the site. If the variable was changed by other classes, the performance of BingoBrain would change greatly. To guard against this scenario, you can declare the winRatio variable as private.

The following class uses private access control:

```
class  Writer {
    private boolean writersBlock = true;
    private String mood;
    private int income = 0;

    private void getIdea(Inspiration in) {
        // ...
    }

    Manuscript createManuscript(int numDays, long numPages) {
        // ...
    }
}
```

In this code example, the internal data to the class Writer (the variables writersBlock, mood, and income and the method getIdea()) is all private. The only method accessible from outside the Writer class is the createManuscript() method. createManuscript() is the only task other objects can ask the Writer object to perform. Editor and Publisher objects might prefer a more direct means of extracting a Manuscript object from the Writer, but they don't have the access to do so.

Using the `private` modifier is the main way that an object encapsulates itself. You can't limit the ways in which a class is used without using `private` in many places to hide variables and methods. Another class is free to change the variables inside a class and call its methods in any way desired if you don't control access.

Public Access

In some cases, you may want a method or variable in a class to be completely available to any other class that wants to use it. Think of the class variable `black` from the `Color` class. This variable is used when a class wants to use the color black, so `black` should have no access control at all.

Class variables often are declared to be `public`. An example would be a set of variables in a `Football` class that represent the number of points used in scoring. The `TOUCHDOWN` variable could equal 7, the `FIELDGOAL` variable could equal 3, and so on. These variables would need to be public so that other classes could use them in statements such as the following:

```
if (position < 0) {
    System.out.println("Touchdown!");
    score = score + Football.TOUCHDOWN;
}
```

The `public` modifier makes a method or variable completely available to all classes. You have used it in every application you have written so far, with a statement such as the following:

```
public static void main(String[] arguments) {
    // ...
}
```

The `main()` method of an application has to be public. Otherwise, it could not be called by the `java` interpreter to run the class.

Because of class inheritance, all public methods and variables of a class are inherited by its subclasses.

Protected Access

The third level of access control is to limit a method and variable to use by the following two groups:

- Subclasses of a class
- Other classes in the same package

You do so by using the `protected` modifier, as in the following statement:

```
protected boolean weNeedMoreCalgon = true;
```

Note

> You might be wondering how these two groups are different. After all, aren't subclasses part of the same package as their superclass? Not always. An example is the `Applet` class. It is a subclass of `java.awt.Panel` but is actually in its own package, `java.applet`. Protected access differs from default access this way; protected variables are available to subclasses, even if they aren't in the same package.

This level of access control is useful if you want to make it easier for a subclass to implement itself. Your class might use a method or variable to help the class do its job. Because a subclass inherits much of the same behavior and attributes, it might have the same job to do. Protected access gives the subclass a chance to use the helper method or variable, while preventing a nonrelated class from trying to use it.

Consider the example of a class called `AudioPlayer` that plays a digital audio file. `AudioPlayer` has a method called `openSpeaker()`, which is an internal method that interacts with the hardware to prepare the speaker for playing. `openSpeaker()` isn't important to anyone outside the `AudioPlayer` class, so at first glance you might want to make it `private`. A snippet of `AudioPlayer` might look something like this:

```
class AudioPlayer {

    private boolean openSpeaker(Speaker sp_ {
        // implementation details
    }
}
```

This code works fine if `AudioPlayer` isn't going to be subclassed. But what if you were going to create a class called `StreamingAudioPlayer` that is a subclass of `AudioPlayer`? This class would want access to the `openSpeaker()` method so that it can override it and provide streaming audio-specific speaker initialization. You still don't want the method generally available to random objects (and so it shouldn't be `public`), but you want the subclass to have access to it.

Comparing Levels of Access Control

The differences between the various protection types can become very confusing, particularly in the case of `protected` methods and variables. Table 15.1, which summarizes exactly what is allowed where, helps clarify the differences from the least restrictive (`public`) to the most restrictive (`private`) forms of protection.

TABLE 15.1. THE DIFFERENT LEVELS OF ACCESS CONTROL.

Visibility	public	protected	default	private
From the same class	yes	yes	yes	yes
From any class in the same package	yes	yes	yes	no
From any class outside the package	yes	no	no	no
From a subclass in the same package	yes	yes	yes	no
From a subclass outside the same package	yes	yes	no	no

15

Access Control and Inheritance

One last issue regarding access control for methods involves subclasses. When you create a subclass and override a method, you must consider the access control in place on the original method.

You might recall that Applet methods such as init() and paint() must be public in your own applets.

As a general rule, you cannot override a method in Java and make the new method more controlled than the original. You can, however, make it more public. The following rules for inherited methods are enforced:

- Methods declared public in a superclass must also be public in all subclasses (for this reason, most of the applet methods are public).
- Methods declared protected in a superclass must either be protected or public in subclasses; they cannot be private.
- Methods declared without access control (no modifier was used) can be declared more private in subclasses.

Methods declared private are not inherited at all, so the rules don't apply.

Accessor Methods

In many cases, you may have an instance variable in a class that has strict rules for the values it can contain. An example would be a zipCode variable. A zip code in the United States must be a number that is five digits long: 10000 to 99999 are valid values, but other integers outside that range cannot be zip codes.

To prevent an external class from setting the zipCode variable incorrectly, you can declare it private with a statement such as the following:

```
private int zipCode;
```

However, what if other classes must be able to set the zipCode variable for the class to be useful? In this circumstance, you can give other classes access to a private variable by using an accessor method inside the same class as zipCode.

Accessor methods get their name because they provide access to something that otherwise would be off limits. By using a method to provide access to a private variable, you can control how that variable is used. In the zip code example, the class could prevent anyone else from setting zipCode to an incorrect value.

Often, separate accessor methods to read and write a variable are available. Reading methods have a name beginning with get, and writing methods have a name beginning with set, as in setZipCode(*int*) and getZipCode(*int*).

 Note

This convention is becoming more standard with each version of Java. You might recall how the size() method of the Dimension class has been changed to getSize() as of Java 2. You might want to use the same naming convention for your own accessor methods, as a means of making the class more understandable.

Using methods to access instance variables is a frequently used technique in object-oriented programming. This approach makes classes more reusable because it guards against a class being used improperly.

Static Variables and Methods

A modifier you already have used in programs is static, which was introduced during Day 6, "Creating Classes." The static modifier is used to create class methods and variables, as in the following example:

```
public class Circle {
    public static float pi = 3.14159265F;

    public float  area(float r) {
        return  pi * r * r;
    }
}
```

Class variables and methods can be accessed using the class name followed by a dot and the name of the variable or method, as in Color.black or Circle.pi. You also can use the name of an object of the class, but for class variables and methods, using the class name is better. This approach makes more clear what kind of variable or method you're working with; instance variables and methods can never be referred to by class name.

The following statements use class variables and methods:

```
float circumference = 2 * Circle.pi * getRadius();
float randomNumer = Math.random();
```

Tip

For the same reason that holds true for instance variables, class variables can benefit from being private and limiting their use to accessor methods only.

Listing 15.1 shows a class called CountInstances that uses class and instance variables to keep track of how many instances of that class have been created.

TYPE   **LISTING 15.1.** THE FULL TEXT OF COUNTINSTANCES.JAVA.

```
 1: public class CountInstances {
 2:     private static int numInstances = 0;
 3:
 4:     protected static int getNumInstances() {
 5:         return numInstances;
 6:     }
 7:
 8:     private static void addInstance() {
 9:         numInstances++;
10:     }
11:
12:     CountInstances() {
13:         CountInstances.addInstance();
14:     }
15:
16:     public static void main(String arguments[]) {
17:         System.out.println("Starting with " +
18:             CountInstances.getNumInstances() + " instances");
19:         for (int  i = 0; i < 10; ++i)
20:             new CountInstances();
21:         System.out.println("Created " +
22:             CountInstances.getNumInstances() + " instances");
23:     }
24: }
```

The output of this program is as follows:

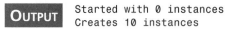

```
Started with 0 instances
Creates 10 instances
```

This example has a number of features, so take the time to go through it line by line. In line 2, you declare a `private` class variable to hold the number of instances (called `numInstances`). It is a class variable (declared `static`) because the number of instances is relevant to the class as a whole, not to any one instance. And it's private so that it follows the same rules as instance variables' accessor methods.

Note the initialization of `numInstances` to `0` in that same line. Just as an instance variable is initialized when its instance is created, a class variable is initialized when its class is created. This class initialization happens essentially before anything else can happen to that class, or its instances, so the class in the example will work as planned.

In lines 4–6, you create a `get` method for that private instance variable to get its value (`getNumInstances()`). This method is also declared as a class method, as it applies directly to the class variable. The `getNumInstances()` method is declared `protected`, as opposed to `public`, because only this class and perhaps subclasses will be interested in that value; other random classes are therefore restricted from seeing it.

Note that you don't have an accessor method to set the value. The reason is that the value of the variable should be incremented only when a new instance is created; it should not be set to any random value. Instead of creating an accessor method, therefore, you create a special private method called `addInstance()` in lines 8–10 that increments the value of `numInstances` by 1.

Lines 12–14 create the constructor method for this class. Remember, constructors are called when a new object is created, which makes this the most logical place to call `addInstance()` and to increment the variable.

Finally, the `main()` method indicates that you can run this as a Java application and test all the other methods. In the `main()` method, you create 10 instances of the `CountInstances` class, reporting after you're done the value of the `numInstances` class variable (which, predictably, prints `10`).

Final Classes, Methods, and Variables

The `final` modifier is used with classes, methods, and variables to indicate that they will not be changed. It has different meanings for each thing that can be finalized, as follows:

- A `final` class cannot be subclassed.
- A `final` method cannot be overridden by any subclasses.
- A `final` variable cannot change in value.

15

Variables

You got a chance to work with final variables during Day 6. They are often called constant variables (or just constants) because they do not change in value at any time.

With variables, the `final` modifier often is used with `static` to make the constant a class variable. If the value never changes, you don't have much reason to give each object in the same class its own copy of the value. They all can use the class variable with the same functionality.

The following statements are examples of declaring constants:

```
public static final int touchdown = 7;
static final title = "Captain";
```

As of Java 2, any kind of variable can be a final variable: class, instance, or local variables. A local variable could not be final in Java 1.02, but that was changed as part of the addition of inner classes to the language.

Methods

Final methods are those that can never be overridden by a subclass. You declare them using the `final` modifier in the class declaration, as in the following example:

```
public final void getMaxwellSmart() {
    // ...
}
```

The only reason to declare a method `final` is to make the class run more efficiently. Normally, when a Java runtime environment such as the `java` interpreter runs a method, it checks the current class to find the method first, checks its superclass second, and onward up the class hierarchy until the method is found. This process sacrifices some speed in the name of flexibility and ease of development.

If a method is `final`, the Java compiler can put the executable bytecode of the method directly into any program that calls the method. After all, the method won't ever change because of a subclass that overrides it.

When you are first developing a class, you won't have much reason to use `final`. However, if you need to make the class execute more quickly, you can change a few methods into `final` methods to speed up the process. Doing so removes the possibility of the method being subclassed later on, so consider this change carefully before continuing.

The Java class library declares many of the commonly used methods `final` so that they can be executed more quickly when utilized in programs that call them.

Note Private methods are final without being declared that way because they can't be subclassed under any circumstance.

Classes

You finalize classes by using the `final` modifier in the declaration for the class, as in the following:

```
public final class AnotherFineMess {
    // ....
}
```

A final class cannot be subclassed by another class. As with final methods, this process introduces some speed benefits to the Java language at the expense of flexibility.

If you're wondering what you're losing by using `final` classes, you must not have tried to subclass something in the Java class library yet. Many of the popular classes are final, such as `java.lang.String`, `java.lang.Math`, and `java.net.InetAddress`. If you want to create a class that behaves like strings but with some new changes, you can't subclass `String` and define only the behavior that is different. You have to start from scratch.

All methods in a `final` class automatically are final themselves, so you don't have to use a modifier in their declarations.

You won't have many reasons to make your own classes final because classes that can bequeath their behavior and attributes to subclasses are much more useful.

Abstract Classes and Methods

In a class hierarchy, the higher the class, the more abstract its definition. A class at the top of a hierarchy of other classes only can define the behavior and attributes that are common to all the classes. More specific behavior and attributes are going to fall somewhere lower down the hierarchy.

When you are factoring out common behavior and attributes during the process of defining a hierarchy of classes, you may sometimes find yourself with a class that doesn't ever need to be instantiated directly. Instead, these classes serve as a place to hold common behavior and attributes shared by their subclasses.

These classes are called abstract classes, and they are created using the `abstract` modifier. The following is an example:

```
public abstract class BroadwayBoogieWoogie {
    // ...
}
```

15

An example of an abstract class is `java.awt.Component`, the superclass of all Abstract Windowing Toolkit components. All components inherit from this class, so it contains methods and variables useful to each of them. However, there's no such thing as a generic component that can be added to an interface, so you would never need to create a `Component` object in a program.

Abstract classes can contain anything a normal class can, including constructor methods, because their subclasses may need to inherit the methods. Abstract classes also can contain abstract methods, which are method signatures with no implementation. These methods are implemented in subclasses of the abstract class. Abstract methods are declared with the `abstract` modifier. You cannot declare an abstract method in a nonabstract class.If an abstract class has nothing but abstract methods, you're better off using an interface, as you'll see later today.

Packages

Using packages, as mentioned previously, is a way of organizing groups of classes. A package contains any number of classes that are related in purpose, in scope, or by inheritance.

If your programs are small and use a limited number of classes, you may find that you don't need to explore packages at all. But the more Java programming you create, the more classes you'll find you have. And although those classes may be individually well designed, reusable, encapsulated, and with specific interfaces to other classes, you may find the need for a bigger organizational entity that allows you to group your packages.

Packages are useful for several broad reasons:

- They allow you to organize your classes into units. Just as you have folders or directories on your hard disk to organize your files and applications, packages allow you to organize your classes into groups so that you use only what you need for each program.

- They reduce problems with conflicts in names. As the number of Java classes grows, so does the likelihood that you'll use the same class name as someone else, opening up the possibility of naming clashes and errors if you try to integrate groups of classes into a single program. Packages allow you to "hide" classes so that conflicts can be avoided.

- They allow you to protect classes, variables, and methods in larger ways than on a class-by-class basis, as you learned today. You'll learn more about protections with packages later.

- They can be used to identify your classes. For example, if you implement a set of classes to perform some task, you could name a package of those classes with a unique identifier that identifies you or your organization.

Although a package is most typically a collection of classes, packages can also contain other packages, forming yet another level of organization somewhat analogous to the inheritance hierarchy. Each "level" usually represents a smaller, more specific grouping of classes. The Java class library itself is organized along these lines. The top level is called java; the next level includes names such as io, net, util, and awt. The last of them has an even lower level, which includes the package image.

Note

By convention, the first level of the hierarchy specifies the globally unique name to identify the author or owner of those packages. For example, Sun Microsystems' classes, which are not part of the standard Java environment, all begin with the prefix sun. Classes that Netscape includes with its implementation are contained in the netscape package. The standard package, java, is an exception to this rule because it is so fundamental and because it might someday be implemented by multiple companies.

Using Packages

You've been using packages all along in this book. Every time you use the import command, and every time you refer to a class by its full package name (java.awt.Color, for example), you use packages.

To use a class contained in a package, you can use one of three mechanisms:

- If the class you want to use is in the package java.lang (for example, System or Date), you can simply use the class name to refer to that class. The java.lang classes are automatically available to you in all your programs.
- If the class you want to use is in some other package, you can refer to that class by its full name, including any package names (for example, java.awt.Font).
- For classes that you use frequently from other packages, you can import individual classes or a whole package of classes. After a class or a package has been imported, you can refer to that class by its class name.

If you don't declare that your class belongs to a package, they're put into an unnamed default package. You can refer to those classes simply by class name from anywhere in your code.

Full Package and Class Names

To refer to a class in some other package, you can use its full name: the class name preceded by any package names. You do not have to import the class or the package to use it this way:

```
java.awt.Font f = new java.awt.Font()
```

For classes that you use only once or twice in your program, using the full name makes the most sense. If, however, you use that class multiple times, or if the package name is really long with lots of subpackages, you should import that class instead to save yourself some typing.

The `import` Command

To import classes from a package, use the `import` command, as you've used throughout the examples in this book. You can either import an individual class, like this:

```
import java.util.Vector;
```

Or you can import an entire package of classes, using an asterisk (*) to replace the individual class names, like this:

```
import java.awt.*
```

Note

Actually, let me be technically correct by saying that this command doesn't import all the classes in a package; it imports only the classes that have been declared `public`, and even then imports only those classes that the code itself refers to. You'll learn more about this topic in the section titled "Packages and Class Access Control."

Note that the asterisk (*) in this example is not like the one you might use at a command prompt to specify the contents of a folder or to indicate multiple files. For example, if you ask to list the contents of the directory `classes/java/awt/*`, that list includes all the `.class` files and subdirectories, such as `image` and `peer`. Writing `import java.awt.*` imports all the public classes in that package but does not import subpackages such as `image` and `peer`. To import all the classes in a complex package hierarchy, you must explicitly import each level of the hierarchy by hand. Also, you cannot indicate partial class names (for example, `L*` to import all the classes that begin with L). The only options when using an `import` statement are to load all of the classes in a package or just a single class.

The `import` statements in your class definition go at the top of the file, before any class definitions (but after the package definition, as you'll see in the next section).

So should you take the time to import classes individually or just import them as a group? The answer depends on how specific you want to be. Importing a group of classes does not slow down your program or make it any larger; only the classes you actually use in your code are loaded as they are needed. But importing a package does make it a little more confusing for readers of your code to figure out where your classes are coming from. Using individual `import` statements or importing packages is mostly a question of your own coding style.

> **Note**
>
> If you're coming to Java from C or C++, you might expect the `import` statement to work like `#include`, which results in a very large program by including source code from another file. This isn't the case; `import` indicates only where a class can be found. It doesn't do anything to expand the size of a class.

Name Conflicts

After you have imported a class or a package of classes, you can usually refer to a class name simply by its name, without the package identifier. In one case you may have to be more explicit: when you have multiple classes with the same name from different packages.

Here's an example. Say you import the classes from two packages from two different programmers (Jonathan and Bourne):

```
import jonathanclasses.*;
import bourneclasses.*;
```

Inside Jonathan's package is a class called `Defenestrate`. Unfortunately, inside Bourne's package, you also find a class called `Defenestrate` that has an entirely different meaning and implementation. You might wonder whose version of `Defenestrate` is used if you refer to the `Defenestrate` class in your own program like this:

```
Defenestrate outWindow = new Defenestrate("Phil");
```

The answer is neither; the Java compiler complains about a naming conflict and refuses to compile your program. In this case, despite the fact that you imported both classes, you still have to refer to the appropriate `Defenestrate` class by full package name, as follows:

```
jonathanclasses.Defenestrate outWindow = new
    jonathanclasses.Defenestrate("Phil");
```

15

A Note About CLASSPATH and Where Classes Are Located

For Java to be able to use a class, it has to be able to find that class on the file system. Otherwise, you get an error that the class does not exist. Java uses two elements to find classes: the package name itself and the directories listed in your CLASSPATH variable (if you're on a Windows or Solaris system).

First, the package names. Package names map to directory names on the file system, so the class java.applet.Applet is actually found in the applet directory, which in turn is inside the java directory (java\applet\Applet.class, in other words).

Java looks for those directories, in turn, inside the directories listed in your CLASSPATH variable, if one is provided in your configuration. If you remember back to Day 1, "A Fistful of Java," when you installed the JDK, you might have needed a CLASSPATH variable to point to the various places where your Java classes live. If no CLASSPATH is provided, the JDK looks for the default—java\lib directory in your JDK release and the current folder. When Java looks for a class you've referenced in your source, it looks for the package and class name in each of those directories and returns an error if it can't find the class file. Most class not found errors result because of misconfigured CLASSPATH variables.

Creating Your Own Packages

Creating a package for some of your classes in Java is not much more complicated than creating a class. You must follow three basic steps, as outlined next.

Picking a Package Name

The first step is to decide on a name. The name you choose for your package depends on how you are going to be using those classes. Perhaps you will name your package after you or perhaps after the part of the Java system you're working on (such as graphics or hardware_interfaces). If you intend to distribute your package to the Net at large or as part of a commercial product, you should use a package name that uniquely identifies the author.

A convention for naming packages recommended by Sun is to use your Internet domain name with the elements reversed. For example, if Sun followed this recommendation, its packages would be referred to under the name com.sun.java rather than just java. If your Internet domain name is prefect.com, your package name might be com.prefect You might want to lengthen the name with something that describes the classes in the package, such as com.prefect.canasta.

The idea is to make sure your package name is unique. Although packages can hide conflicting class names, the protection stops there. You cannot make sure your package won't conflict with someone else's package if you both use the same package name.

By convention, package names tend to begin with a lowercase letter to distinguish them from class names. Thus, for example, in the full name of the built-in String class, java.lang.String, you can more easily separate the package name from the class name visually. This convention helps reduce name conflicts.

Creating the Folder Structure

Step two in creating packages is to create a folder structure on your hard drive that matches the package name. If your package has just one name (mypackage), you must create a folder for that one name only. If the package name has several parts, you have to create folders within folders. For the package name com.prefect.canasta, for example, you need to create a com folder, a prefect folder inside com, and a canasta folder inside prefect. Your classes and source files can then go inside the prefect directory.

Adding a Class to a Package

The final step to putting your class inside packages is to add a statement to the class file above any import statements that are being used. The package statement is used along with the name of the package, as in the following:

```
package com.prefect.canasta;
```

The single package command, if any, must be the first line of code in your source file, after any comments or blank lines and before any import commands.

After you start using packages, you should make sure all your classes belong to some package to reduce the chance of confusion about where your classes belong.

Packages and Class Access Control

Previously, you learned about access control modifiers for methods and variables. You also can control access to classes, as you may have noticed when the public modifier was used in some class declarations on past projects.

Classes have the default access control if no modifier is specified, which means that the class is available to all other classes in the same package but is not visible or available outside that package—not even to subpackages. It cannot be imported or referred to by name; classes with package protection are hidden inside the package in which they are contained.

Package protection comes about when you define a class as you have throughout this book, like this:

```
class TheHiddenClass extends AnotherHiddenClass {
    // ...
}
```

To allow a class to be visible and importable outside your package, you can give it public protection by adding the `public` modifier to its definition:

```
public class TheVisibleClass {
    // ...
}
```

Classes declared as `public` can be imported by other classes outside the package.

Note that when you use an `import` statement with an asterisk, you import only the public classes inside that package. Hidden classes remain hidden and can be used only by the other classes in that package.

Why would you want to hide a class inside a package? For the same reason you want to hide variables and methods inside a class: so you can have utility classes and behavior that are useful only to your implementation, or so you can limit the interface of your program to minimize the effect of larger changes. As you design your classes, you should take the whole package into consideration and decide which classes you want to declare public and which you want to be hidden.

Listing 15.2 shows two classes that illustrate this point. The first is a public class that implements a linked list; the second is a private node of that list.

TYPE   **LISTING 15.2.** THE FULL TEXT OF LINKEDLIST.JAVA.

```
1: package  collections;
2:
3: public class  LinkedList {
4:     private Node  root;
5:
6:     public  void  add(Object o) {
7:         root = new Node(o, root);
8:     }
9:     // ...
```

continues

LISTING 15.2. CONTINUED

```
10: }
11:
12: class  Node {    // not public
13:     private Object  contents;
14:     private Node    next;
15:
16:     Node(Object o, Node n) {
17:         contents = o;
18:         next     = n;
19:     }
20:     // ...
21: }
```

Note

You can include as many class definitions per file as you want, but only one of them can be declared public, and that filename must have the same name as the one public class. When Java compiles the file, it will create separate .class files for each class definition inside the file.

The public LinkedList class provides a set of useful public methods (such as add()) to any other classes that might want to use them. These other classes don't need to know about any support classes LinkedList needs to get its job done. Node, which is one of those support classes, is therefore declared without a public modifier and will not appear as part of the public interface to the collections package.

Just because Node isn't public doesn't mean LinkedList won't have access to it after it's been imported into some other class. Think of protections not as hiding classes entirely, but more as checking the permissions of a given class to use other classes, variables, and methods. When you import and use LinkedList, the Node class will also be loaded into the system, but only instances of LinkedList will have permission to use it.

Creating a good package consists of defining a small, clean set of public classes and methods for other classes to use, and then implementing them by using any number of hidden support classes. You'll see another use for hidden classes later today.

Interfaces

Interfaces, like abstract classes and methods, provide templates of behavior that other classes are expected to implement. Interfaces, however, provide far more functionality to Java and to class and object design than do simple abstract classes and methods.

The Problem of Single Inheritance

After some deeper thought or more complex design experience, however, you may discover that the pure simplicity of the class hierarchy is restrictive, particularly when you have some behavior that needs to be used by classes in different branches of the same tree.

Look at an example that will make the problems clearer. Say you have a biological hierarchy with `Animal` at the top, and the classes `Mammal` and `Bird` underneath. Things that define a mammal include bearing live young and having fur. Behavior or features of birds include having a beak and laying eggs. So far, so good, right? So how do you go about creating a class for the platypus, which has fur and a beak and lays eggs? You would need to combine behavior from two classes to form the `Platypus` class. And, because classes can have only one immediate superclass in Java, this sort of problem simply cannot be solved elegantly.

Other OOP languages include the concept of multiple inheritance, which solves this problem. With multiple inheritance, a class can inherit from more than one superclass and get behavior and attributes from all its superclasses at once. A problem with multiple inheritance is that it makes a programming language far more complex to learn, to use, and to implement. Questions of method invocation and how the class hierarchy is organized become far more complicated with multiple inheritance, and more open to confusion and ambiguity. And because one of the goals for Java was that it be simple, multiple inheritance was rejected in favor of the simpler single inheritance.

So how do you solve the problem of needing common behavior that doesn't fit into the strict class hierarchy? Java has another hierarchy altogether separate from the main class hierarchy, a hierarchy of mixable behavior classes. Then, when you create a new class, that class has only one primary superclass, but it can pick and choose different common behaviors from the other hierarchy. This other hierarchy is the interface hierarchy. A Java interface is a collection of abstract behavior that can be mixed into any class to add to that class behavior that is not supplied by its superclasses. Specifically, a Java interface contains nothing but abstract method definitions and constants—no instance variables and no method implementations.

Interfaces are implemented and used throughout the Java class library whenever a behavior is expected to be implemented by a number of disparate classes. The Java class hierarchy, for example, defines and uses the interfaces `java.lang.Runnable`, `java.util.Enumeration`, `java.util.Observable`, `java.awt.image.ImageConsumer`, and `java.awt.image.ImageProducer`. Some of these interfaces you've seen before; others you'll see later in this book.

15

Interfaces and Classes

Classes and interfaces, despite their different definitions, have a great deal in common. Interfaces, like classes, are declared in source files, one interface to a file. Like classes, they also are compiled into .class files using the Java compiler. And, in most cases, anywhere you can use a class (as a data type for a variable, as the result of a cast, and so on), you can also use an interface.

Almost everywhere that this book has a class name in any of its examples or discussions, you can substitute an interface name. Java programmers often say "class" when they actually mean "class or interface." Interfaces complement and extend the power of classes, and the two can be treated almost the same. One of the few differences between them is that an interface cannot be instantiated: new can only create an instance of a class.

Implementing and Using Interfaces

You can do two things with interfaces: use them in your own classes and define your own. For now, start with the former.

To use an interface, you include the implements keyword as part of your class definition. You did this back on Day 10, "Adding Images, Animation, and Sound," when you learned about threads and included the Runnable interface in your applet definition:

```
public class Neko extends java.applet.Applet
    implements Runnable {

    //...
}
```

In this example, java.applet.Applet is the superclass, but the Runnable interface extends the behavior that it implements.

Because interfaces provide nothing but abstract method definitions, you then have to implement those methods in your own classes, using the same method signatures from the interface. Note that once you include an interface, you have to implement all the methods in that interface; you can't pick and choose the methods you need. By implementing an interface, you're telling users of your class that you support all of that interface. (Note that this is another difference between interfaces and abstract classes; subclasses of the latter can pick which methods to implement or override and can ignore others.)

After your class implements an interface, subclasses of your class inherit those new methods (and can override or overload them) just as if your superclass had actually defined them. If your class inherits from a superclass that implements a given interface, you don't have to include the implements keyword in your own class definition.

Examine one simple example now—creating the new class Orange. Suppose you already have a good implementation of the class Fruit and an interface, Fruitlike, that represents what a Fruit is expected to be able to do. You want an orange to be a fruit, but you also want it to be a spherical object that can be tossed, rotated, and so on. Here's how to express it all (don't worry about the definitions of these interfaces for now; you'll learn more about them later today):

```
interface  Fruitlike {
    void  decay();
    void  squish();
    // ...
}

class  Fruit implements Fruitlike {
    private Color myColor;
    private int daysTilIRot;
    // ...
}

interface  Spherelike {
    void  toss();
    void  rotate();
    // ...
}

class  Orange extends Fruit implements Spherelike {
    // toss()ing may squish() me (unique to me)
}
```

Note that the class Orange doesn't have to say implements Fruitlike because, by extending Fruit, it already has! One of the nice things about this structure is that you can change your mind about what class Orange extends (if a really great Sphere class is suddenly implemented, for example), yet class Orange still understands the same two interfaces:

```
class  Sphere implements Spherelike {   // extends Object
    private float  radius;
    // ...
}

class  Orange extends Sphere implements Fruitlike {
    // ... users of Orange never need know about the change!
}
```

Implementing Multiple Interfaces

In contrast to the singly inherited class hierarchy, you can include as many interfaces as you need in your own classes, and your class will implement the combined behavior of all the included interfaces. To include multiple interfaces in a class, just separate their names with commas:

```
public class Neko extends java.applet.Applet
    implements Runnable, Eatable, Sortable, Observable {

    // ...
}
```

Note that complications may arise from implementing multiple interfaces. What happens if two different interfaces both define the same method? You can solve this problem in three ways:

- If the methods in each of the interfaces have identical signatures, you implement one method in your class and that definition satisfies both interfaces.
- If the methods have different parameter lists, it is a simple case of method overloading; you implement both method signatures, and each definition satisfies its respective interface definition.
- If the methods have the same parameter lists but differ in return type, you cannot create a method that satisfies both (remember, method overloading is triggered by parameter lists, not by return type). In this case, trying to compile a class that implements both interfaces produces a compiler error. Running across this problem suggests that your interfaces have some design flaws that you might need to reexamine.

Other Uses of Interfaces

Remember that almost everywhere that you can use a class, you can use an interface instead. So, for example, you can declare a variable to be of an interface type:

```
Runnable aRunnableObject = new MyAnimationClass()
```

When a variable is declared to be of an interface type, it simply means that any object the variable refers to is expected to have implemented that interface; that is, it is expected to understand all the methods that interface specifies. It assumes that a promise made between the designer of the interface and its eventual implementors has been kept. In this case, because aRunnableObject contains an object of the type Runnable, the assumption is that you can call aRunnableObject.run().

The important point to realize here is that although aRunnableObject is expected to be able to have the run() method, you could write this code long before any classes that qualify are actually implemented (or even created!). In traditional object-oriented programming, you are forced to create a class with "stub" implementations (empty methods, or methods that print silly messages) to get the same effect. You can also cast objects to an interface, just as you can cast objects to other classes. So, for example, go back to that definition of the Orange class, which implemented both the Fruitlike interface (through its superclass, Fruit) and the Spherelike interface. Here you can cast instances of Orange to both classes and interfaces:

```
Orange anOrange = new Orange();
Fruit aFruit = (Fruit)anOrange;
Fruitlike aFruitlike = (Fruitlike)anOrange;
Spherelike aSpherelike = (Spherelike)anOrange;


aFruit.decay(); // fruits decay
aFruitlike.squish(); //  and squish

aFruitlike.toss(); // things that are fruitlike do not toss
aSpherelike.toss(); // but things that are spherelike do

anOrange.decay(); // oranges can do it all
anOrange.squish();
anOrange.toss();
anOrange.rotate();
```

Declarations and casts are used in this example to restrict an orange's behavior to acting more like a mere fruit or sphere.

Finally, note that although interfaces are usually used to mix in behavior to other classes (method signatures), interfaces can also be used to mix in generally useful constants. So, for example, if an interface defines a set of constants, and then multiple classes use those constants, the values of those constants could be globally changed without having to modify multiple classes. This is yet another example of a case in which the use of interfaces to separate design from implementation can make your code more general and more easily maintainable.

Creating and Extending Interfaces

After you use interfaces for a while, the next step is to define your own interfaces. Interfaces look a lot like classes; they are declared in much the same way and can be arranged into a hierarchy. However, you must follow certain rules for declaring interfaces.

New Interfaces

To create a new interface, you declare it like this:

```
public interface Growable {
    // ...
}
```

This declaration is, effectively, the same as a class definition, with the word interface replacing the word class. Inside the interface definition, you have methods and constants. The method definitions inside the interface are public and abstract methods; you can either declare them explicitly as such, or they are turned into public and abstract methods if you do not include those modifiers. You cannot declare a method inside an interface to be either private or protected. So, for example, here's a Growable interface with one method explicitly declared public and abstract (growIt()) and one implicitly declared as such (growItBigger()):

```
public interface Growable {
    public abstract void growIt(); // explicitly public and abstract
    void growItBigger(); // effectively public and abstract
}
```

Note that, as with abstract methods in classes, methods inside interfaces do not have bodies. Remember, an interface is pure design; no implementation is involved.

In addition to methods, interfaces can also have variables, but those variables must be declared public, static, and final (making them constant). As with methods, you can explicitly define a variable to be public, static, and final, or it is implicitly defined as such if you don't use those modifiers. Here's that same Growable definition with two new variables:

```
public interface Growable {
    public static final int increment = 10;
    long maxnum = 1000000; // becomes public static and final

    public abstract void growIt(); //explicitly public and abstract
    void growItBigger(); // effectively public and abstract
}
```

Interfaces must have either public or package protection, just like classes. Note, however, that interfaces without the public modifier do not automatically convert their methods to public and abstract nor their constants to public. A non-public interface also has non-public methods and constants that can be used only by classes and other interfaces in the same package.

Interfaces, like classes, can belong to a package if you add a package statement to the first line of the class file. Interfaces can also import other interfaces and classes from other packages, just as classes can.

Methods Inside Interfaces

Here's one trick to note about methods inside interfaces: Those methods are supposed to be abstract and apply to any kind of class, but how can you define parameters to those methods? You don't know what class will be using them! The answer lies in the fact that you use an interface name anywhere a class name can be used, as you learned earlier. By defining your method parameters to be interface types, you can create generic parameters that apply to any class that might use this interface.

So, for example, consider the interface Fruitlike, which defines methods (with no arguments) for decay() and squish(). You might also have a method for germinateSeeds(), which has one argument: the fruit itself. Of what type is that argument going to be? It can't be simply Fruit because you may have a class that's Fruitlike (that is, one that implements the Fruitlike interface) without actually being a fruit. The solution is to declare the argument as simply Fruitlike in the interface:

```
public interface Fruitlike {
    public abstract germinate(Fruitlike self) {
        // ...
    }
}
```

Then, in an actual implementation for this method in a class, you can take the generic Fruitlike argument and cast it to the appropriate object:

```
public class Orange extends Fruit {

public germinate(Fruitlike self) {
    Orange theOrange = (Orange)self;
    // ...
    }
}
```

Extending Interfaces

As you can do with classes, you can organize interfaces into a hierarchy. When one interface inherits from another interface, that "subinterface" acquires all the method definitions and constants that its "superinterface" defined. To extend an interface, you use the extends keyword just as you do in a class definition:

```
public interface Fruitlike extends Foodlike {
    ...
}
```

Note that, unlike classes, the interface hierarchy has no equivalent of the Object class; this hierarchy is not rooted at any one point. Interfaces can either exist entirely on their own or inherit from another interface.

Note also that, unlike the class hierarchy, the inheritance hierarchy is multiply inherited. So, for example, a single interface can extend as many classes as it needs to (separated by commas in the extends part of the definition), and the new interface will contain a combination of all its parent's methods and constants. Here's an interface definition for an interface called BusyInterface that inherits from a whole lot of other interfaces:

```
public interface BusyInterface extends Runnable, Growable, Fruitlike,
    Observable {

    // ...
}
```

In multiply inherited interfaces, the rules for managing method name conflicts are the same as for classes that use multiple interfaces; methods that differ only in return type result in a compiler error.

An Example: Enumerating Linked Lists

To finish up this lesson, look at the following example, which uses packages, package protection, and defines a class that implements the Enumeration interface (part of the java.util package). Listing 15.3 shows the code.

TYPE   **LISTING 15.3.** THE FULL TEXT OF LINKEDLIST.JAVA.

```
 1: package collections;
 2:
 3: public class LinkedList {
 4:     private Node  root;
 5:
 6:     // ...
 7:     public Enumeration enumerate() {
 8:         return new LinkedListEnumerator(root);
 9:     }
10: }
11:
12: class Node {
13:     private Object contents;
14:     private Node next;
15:
16:     // ...
17:     public Object contents() {
18:         return contents;
19:     }
20:
21:     public Node next() {
22:         return next;
23:     }
24: }
25:
26: class LinkedListEnumerator implements Enumeration {
27:     private Node currentNode;
28:
29:     LinkedListEnumerator(Node root) {
30:         currentNode = root;
```

15

```
31:     }
32:
33:     public boolean hasMoreElements() {
34:         return currentNode != null;
35:     }
36:
37:     public Object nextElement() {
38:         Object anObject = currentNode.contents();
39:
40:         currentNode = currentNode.next();
41:         return  anObject;
42:     }
43: }
```

Here is a typical use of the enumerator:

```
collections.LinkedList aLinkedList = createLinkedList();
java.util.Enumeration e = aLinkedList.enumerate();

while (e.hasMoreElements()) {
    Object  anObject = e.nextElement();
    // do something useful with anObject
}
```

Notice that although you are using the Enumeration e as though you know what it is, you actually do not. In fact, it is an instance of a hidden class (LinkedListEnumerator) that you cannot see or use directly. By using a combination of packages and interfaces, the LinkedList class has managed to provide a transparent public interface to some of its most important behavior (via the already defined interface java.util.Enumeration) while still encapsulating (hiding) its two implementation (support) classes.

Handing out an object like this is sometimes called vending. Often the "vendor" gives out an object that a receiver can't create itself but that it knows how to use. By giving the object back to the vendor, the receiver can prove it has a certain capability, authenticate itself, or do any number of useful tasks—all without knowing much about the vended object. This powerful metaphor can be applied in a broad range of situations. You'll learn more about enumeration and linked lists during Day 26, "Data Structures."

Inner Classes

The classes you have worked with thus far are all members of a package, either because you specified a package name with the package statement or because the default package was used. Classes that belong to a package are known as top-level classes. When Java was introduced, they were the only classes supported by the language.

Beginning with Java 1.1, you could define a class inside a class, as if it were a method or a variable. These types of classes are called inner classes. Listing 15.4 contains the Inner applet, which uses an inner class called BlueButton to represent clickable buttons that have a default background color of blue.

TYPE   **LISTING 15.4.** THE FULL TEXT OF INNER.JAVA.

```
 1: import java.awt.Button;
 2: import java.awt.Color;
 3:
 4: public class Inner extends java.applet.Applet {
 5:     Button b1 = new Button("One");
 6:     BlueButton b2 = new BlueButton("Two");
 7:
 8:     public void init() {
 9:         add(b1);
10:         add(b2);
11:     }
12:     class BlueButton extends Button {
13:         BlueButton(String label) {
14:             super(label);
15:             this.setBackground(Color.blue);
16:         }
17:     }
18: }
```

Figure 15.1 was produced on appletviewer using the following HTML tag:

```
<applet code="Inner.class" width=100 height=100>
</applet>
```

FIGURE 15.1.

The Inner applet.

In this example, the BlueButton class isn't any different from a helper class that is included in the same source file as a program's main class file. The only difference is that the helper is defined inside the class file, which has several advantages:

- Inner classes are invisible to all other classes, which means you don't have to worry about name conflicts between it and other classes.

- Inner classes can have access to variables and methods within the scope of a top-level class that they would not have as a separate class.

In many cases, an inner class is a short class file that exists only for a limited purpose. In the Inner applet, because `BlueButton` doesn't contain a lot of complex behavior and attributes, it is well suited for implementation as an inner class.

The name of an inner class is associated with the name of the class in which it is contained, and it is assigned automatically when the program is compiled. In the example of the `BlueButton` class, it is given the name `Inner$BlueButton.class` by the JDK.

> **Caution**
>
> When you're using inner classes, you must be more careful to include all `.class` files when making a program available. Each inner class has its own class file, and these class files must be included along with any top-level classes. If you publish the Inner applet on the World Wide Web, for example, you must publish both the `Inner.class` and `Inner$BlueButton.class` files together.

Inner classes, although seemingly a minor enhancement to the Java language, actually represent a significant modification to the language.

Rules governing the scope of an inner class closely match those governing variables. An inner class's name is not visible outside its scope, except in a fully qualified name, which helps in structuring classes within a package. The code for an inner class can use simple names from enclosing scopes, including class and member variables of enclosing classes, as well as local variables of enclosing blocks.

In addition, you can define a top-level class as a static member of another top-level class. Unlike an inner class, a top-level class cannot directly use the instance variables of any other class. The ability to nest classes in this way allows any top-level class to provide a package-style organization for a logically related group of secondary top-level classes.

Summary

Today, you learned how to encapsulate an object by using access control modifiers for its variables and methods. You also learned how to use other modifiers such as `static`, `final`, and `abstract` in the development of Java classes and class hierarchies.

To further the effort of developing a set of classes and using them, you learned how classes can be grouped into packages. These groupings better organize your programs and enable the sharing of classes with the many other Java programmers who are making their code publicly available.

Finally, you learned how to implement interfaces and inner classes, two structures that are helpful when designing a class hierarchy.

Q&A

Q Won't using accessor methods everywhere slow down my Java code?

A Not always. As Java compilers improve and can create more optimizations, they will be able to make accessor methods fast automatically, but if you're concerned about speed, you can always declare accessor methods to be `final`, and they'll be just as fast as direct instance variable accesses.

Q Are class (`static`) methods inherited just like instance methods?

A No. `static` (class) methods are now `final` by default. How, then, can you ever declare a non-`final` class method? The answer is that you can't. Inheritance of class methods is not allowed, breaking the symmetry with instance methods.

Q Based on what I've learned, `private abstract` methods and `final abstract` methods or classes don't seem to make sense. Are they legal?

A Nope, they're compile-time errors, as you have guessed. To be useful, `abstract` methods must be overridden, and `abstract` classes must be subclassed, but neither of those two operations would be legal if it were also `private` or `final`.

DAY 16

Exceptional Circumstances: Error Handling

Programmers in any language endeavor to write bug-free programs, programs that never crash, programs that can handle any situation with grace and that can recover from unusual situations without causing the user any undue stress. Good intentions aside, programs like this don't exist.

In real programs, errors occur either because the programmer didn't anticipate every situation your code would get into (or didn't have the time to test the program enough), or because of situations out of the programmer's control—bad data from users, corrupt files that don't have the right data in them, network connections that don't connect, hardware devices that don't respond, sun spots, gremlins, whatever.

In Java, these sorts of strange events that may cause a program to fail are called *exceptions*. Java defines a number of language features that deal with exceptions, including the following:

- How to handle them in your code and recover gracefully from potential problems
- How to tell Java and your methods' users that you're expecting a potential exception
- How to create an exception if you detect one
- How your code is limited, yet made more robust by exceptions

Exceptions, the Old and Confusing Way

Handling error conditions with most programming languages requires much more work than handling a program that is running properly. It can create a very confusing structure of statements similar in functionality to Java's if...else and switch blocks to deal with errors that might occur.

As an example, consider the following statements, which show the structure of how a file might be loaded from disk. Loading a file is something that can be problematic, due to a number of different circumstances—disk errors, file-not-found errors, and the like. If the program must have the data from the file in order to operate properly, it must deal with any of these circumstances before continuing.

Here's the structure of one possible solution:

```
int status = loadTextfile();
if (status != 1) {
    // something unusual happened, describe it
    switch (status) {
        case 2:
            // file not found
        case 3:
            // disk error
        case 4:
            // file corrupted
        default:
            // other error
    }
} else {
    // file loaded OK, continue with program
}
```

This code tries to load a file with a method call to `loadTextfile()`, which has been defined elsewhere in the program. This method returns an integer that indicates whether the file loaded properly (`status == 1`) or an error occurred (`status` equals anything other than 1).

Depending on the error that occurs, the program uses a `switch` statement to try to work around it. The end result is an elaborate block of code in which the most common circumstance—a successful file load—can be lost amid the error-handling code. This is just to handle one possible error. If you have other errors that might take place later in the program, you may end up with more nested `if...else` and `switch/case` blocks.

Error management can become a major problem once you start creating larger systems. Different programmers may use different special values for handling errors, and may not document them well, if at all. You may inconsistently use errors in your own programs. Code to manage these kinds of errors can often obscure the program's original intent, making that code difficult to read and to maintain. Finally, if you try dealing with errors in this kludgey way, there's no easy way for the compiler to check for consistency the way it can check to make sure you called a method with the right arguments.

Although the previous example uses Java syntax, you don't have to deal with errors that way in your programs. The language introduces a better way to deal with exceptional circumstances in a program: through the use of a group of classes called exceptions.

Exceptions include errors that could be fatal to your program, but also include other unusual situations. By managing exceptions you can manage errors and possibly work around them.

Through a combination of special language features, consistency checking at compile time, and a set of extensible exception classes, errors and other unusual conditions in Java programs can be much more easily managed.

Given these features, you can now add a whole new dimension to the behavior and design of your classes, of your class hierarchy, and of your overall system. Your class and interface definitions describe how your program is supposed to behave given the best circumstances. By integrating exception handling into your program design, you can consistently describe how the program will behave when circumstances are not quite good and allow people who use your classes to know what to expect in those cases.

Java Exceptions

At this point in the book, chances are you've run into at least one Java exception—perhaps you mistyped a method name or made a mistake in your code that caused a problem. Maybe you tried to run a Java applet written using version 2.0 of the language in a browser that doesn't support it yet, and saw a `Security Exception` message on the browser's status line.

Chances are, a program quit and spewed a bunch of mysterious errors to the screen. Those mysterious errors are exceptions. When your program quits, it's because an exception was *thrown*. Exceptions can be thrown by the system or explicitly thrown by the programs you write.

The term "thrown" is fitting because exceptions also can be caught. Catching an exception involves dealing with the exceptional circumstance so that your program doesn't crash—you learn more about this later. *An exception was thrown* is the proper Java terminology for "an error happened."

The heart of the Java exception system is the exception itself. Exceptions in Java are actual objects, instances of classes that inherit from the class `Throwable`. An instance of a `Throwable` class is created when an exception is thrown. Figure 16.1 shows a partial class hierarchy for exceptions.

FIGURE 16.1.

The exception class hierarchy.

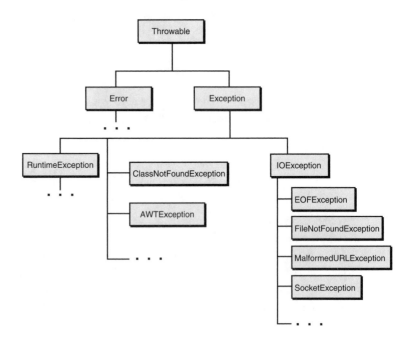

`Throwable` has two subclasses: `Error` and `Exception`. Instances of `Error` are internal errors in the Java runtime environment (the virtual machine). These errors are rare and usually fatal; there's not much you can do about them (either to catch them or to throw them yourself), but they exist so that Java can use them if it needs to.

The class Exception is more interesting. Subclasses of Exception fall into two general groups:

- Runtime exceptions (subclasses of the class RuntimeException) such as ArrayIndexOutofBounds, SecurityException, or NullPointerException
- Other exceptions such as EOFException and MalformedURLException

Runtime exceptions usually occur because of code that isn't very robust. An ArrayIndexOutofBounds exception, for example, should never be thrown if you're properly checking to make sure your code stays within the bounds of an array. NullPointerException exceptions won't happen unless you try to use a variable before it has been set up to hold an object.

16

> **Caution**
>
> If your program is causing runtime exceptions under any circumstances whatsoever, you should fix those problems before you even begin dealing with exception management.

The final group of exceptions is the most interesting because these are the exceptions that indicate something very strange and out of control is happening. EOFExceptions, for example, happen when you're reading from a file and the file ends before you expect it to. MalformedURLExceptions happen when an URL isn't in the right format (perhaps your user typed it wrong). This group includes exceptions that you create to signal unusual cases that may occur in your own programs.

Exceptions are arranged in a hierarchy like other classes, where the Exception superclasses are more general errors and subclasses are more specific errors. This organization becomes more important to you as you deal with exceptions in your own code.

Most of the exception classes are part of the java.lang package (including Throwable, Exception, and RuntimeException). Many of the other packages define other exceptions, and those exceptions are used throughout the class library. For example, the java.io package defines a general exception class called IOException, which is subclassed not only in the java.io package for input and output exceptions (EOFException, FileNotFoundException), but also in the java.net classes for networking exceptions such as MalFormedURLException.

Managing Exceptions

Now that you know what an exception is, how do you deal with them in your own code? In many cases the Java compiler enforces exception management when you try to use methods that use exceptions; you need to deal with those exceptions in your own code or it simply won't compile. In this section you learn about that consistency checking and how to use the `try`, `catch`, and `finally` language keywords to deal with exceptions that may occur.

Exception Consistency Checking

The more you work with the Java class libraries, the more likely it is that you'll run into a compiler error (an exception!) similar to this one:

```
BoogieDown.java:32: Exception java.lang.InterruptedException
must be caught or it must be declared in the throws clause
of this method.
```

What on earth does that mean? In Java a method can indicate the kinds of errors it might possibly throw. For example, methods that read from files might potentially throw `IOException` errors, so those methods are declared with a special modifier that indicates potential errors. When you use those methods in your own Java programs, you have to protect your code against those exceptions. This rule is enforced by the compiler itself, the same way the compiler checks to make sure you're using methods with the right number of arguments and that all your variable types match the thing you're assigning to them.

Why is this check in place? It makes your programs less likely to crash with fatal errors because you know, up front, the kind of exceptions that can be thrown by the methods a program uses. You no longer have to carefully read the documentation or the code of an object you're going to use to ensure you've dealt with all the potential problems—Java does the checking for you. On the other side, if you define your methods so that they indicate the exceptions they can throw, Java can tell your objects' users to handle those errors.

Protecting Code and Catching Exceptions

Assume that you've been happily coding and you ran into that exception message during a test compile. According to the message you have to either catch the error or declare that your method throws it. Deal with the first case: catching potential exceptions.

You do two things to catch an exception:

- You protect the code that contains the method that might throw an exception inside a `try` block.
- You test for and deal with an exception inside a `catch` block.

What `try` and `catch` effectively mean is "try this bit of code that might cause an exception. If it executes okay, go on with the program. If it doesn't, catch the exception and deal with it."

You've seen `try` and `catch` once before, when you first dealt with threads. On Day 10, "Adding Images, Animation, and Sound," you learned about an applet that created a digital clock; the animation paused once a second using this bit of code:

```
try {
    Thread.sleep(1000);
} catch (InterruptedException e) { }
```

While this example uses `try` and `catch`, it's not a very good use of it. Here's what's happening in these statements: The `Thread.sleep()` class method could potentially throw an exception of type `InterruptedException`, which signifies that the thread has been interrupted for some reason.

To handle this exception, the call to `sleep()` is placed inside a `try` block and an associated `catch` block has been set up. This `catch` block receives any `InterruptedException` objects that are thrown within the `try` block.

The reason this isn't a good example of exception handling is that there isn't anything inside the `catch` clause—in other words, you'll catch the exception if it happens, but then you'll do nothing to respond to its occurrence. In all but the simplest cases (such as this one, where the exception really doesn't matter), you're going to need something inside the `catch` block that does something to clean up after the exception happens.

The part of the `catch` clause inside the parentheses is similar to a method definition's argument list. It contains the class of exception to be caught and a variable name (e is commonly used). You can refer to that exception object inside the `catch` block.

One common use for this object is to call its `getMessage()` method. This method is present in all exceptions, and it displays a detailed error message describing what happened.

The following example is a revised version of the `try...catch` statement used on Day 10's DigitalClock applet:

```
try {
    Thread.sleep(1000);
} catch (InterruptedException e) {
    System.out.println("Error: " + e.getMessage());
}
```

For another example, revisit the subject of file handling in Java. If you have a program that reads from a file, it's likely to use one of the input/output stream classes you learn about on Day 17, "Handling Data Through Java Streams." The basic idea is that you open a connection to a file and use the `read()` method to get data from it. This can cause several exceptions, such as a disk error or an attempt to read more data than the file contains. In either of these cases, the `read()` method throws an `IOException`, which would either cause the program to stop executing if you didn't catch it or cause the program to crash.

By putting your `read()` method inside a `try` block, you then can deal gracefully with that error inside a `catch` block. You could clean up after the error and return to some safe state, patch things up enough for the program to proceed, or if all else fails, save as much of the current program's state as possible and exit.

The following example tries to read from the file and catches exceptions if they happen:

```
try {
    while (numBytes <= mybuffer.length) {
        myInputStream.read(myBuffer);
        numBytes++;
    }
} catch (IOException e) {
    System.out.println("Oops! IO Exception -- only read " + numBytes);
    // other cleanup code
}
```

Here, the "other cleanup code" can be anything you want it to be; you can go on with the program using the partial information you got from the file, or perhaps you want to display a dialog box enabling the user to select a different file.

The examples you have seen thus far catch a specific type of exception. Because exception classes are organized into a hierarchy and you can use a subclass anywhere a superclass is expected, you can catch groups of exceptions within the same `catch` statement.

As an example, there are several different types of `IOException` exceptions, such as `EOFException` and `FileNotFoundException`. By catching `IOException`, you also catch instances of any `IOException` subclass.

What if you do want to catch very different kinds of exceptions that aren't related by inheritance? You can use multiple `catch` blocks for a single `try`, like this:

```
try {
    // code that might generate exceptions
} catch (IOException e) {
    // handle IO exceptions
} catch (ClassNotFoundException e2) {
    // handle class not found exceptions
} catch (InterruptedException e3) {
    // handle interrupted exceptions
}
```

Because the scope of local variables in a `catch` statement is the same as the scope of the outer block the `try...catch` block is in, you have to use different local variables for each individual `catch` statement.

In a multiple `catch` block, the first `catch` block that matches will be executed and the rest ignored.

The `finally` Clause

Suppose there is some action in your code that you absolutely must do, no matter what happens, whether an exception is thrown or not. This is usually to free some external resource after acquiring it, to close a file after opening it, or something similar. While you could put that action both inside a `catch` block and outside it, that would be duplicating the same code in two different places. Instead, put one copy of that code inside a special optional part of the `try...catch` block called `finally`. The following example shows how a `try...catch...finally` block is structured:

```
try {
    readTextfile();
} catch (IOException e) {
    // deal with IO errors
} finally {
    closeTextfile();
}
```

The `finally` statement is actually useful outside exceptions; you can also use it to execute cleanup code after a `return`, a `break`, or a `continue` inside loop. For the latter case, you can use a `try` statement with a `finally` but without a `catch` statement.

The next project shows how a `finally` statement can be used inside a method.

TYPE   **LISTING 16.1.** THE FULL TEXT OF FINAL.JAVA.

```
 1: class Final {
 2:     int[] num1 = { 12, 15, 10, 8, -1, 7 };
 3:     int[] num2 = { 1, 5, 20, 8, 1, 13 };
 4:
 5:     public static void main(String[] arguments) {
 6:         Final fin = new Final();
 7:         System.out.println("First array: ");
 8:         fin.readNumbers(fin.num1);
 9:         System.out.println("Second array: ");
10:         fin.readNumbers(fin.num2);
11:     }
12:
```

continues

LISTING 16.1. CONTINUED

```
13:        void readNumbers(int[] numArray) {
14:            int count = 0;
15:            int lastNum = 0;
16:            try {
17:                while (count < numArray.length) {
18:                    lastNum = numArray[count++];
19:                    if (lastNum == -1)
20:                        return;
21:                }
22:            } finally {
23:                System.out.println("Last number read: " + lastNum);
24:            }
25:            return;
26:        }
27: }
```

The output of this program is as follows:

```
First array:
Last number read: -1
Second array:
Last number read: 13
```

The try...finally block in lines 16–24 causes an unusual thing to happen when the return statement is encountered at line 20. You would expect return to cause the method to be exited immediately.

Because it is within a try...finally block, the statements within the finally block are executed no matter how the try block is exited. The "Last number read" text always is displayed.

Declaring Methods That Might Throw Exceptions

In previous examples you learned how to deal with methods (by protecting code and catching any exceptions that occur) that might throw exceptions. The Java compiler checks to make sure you've somehow dealt with a method's exceptions—but how did it know which exceptions to tell you about in the first place?

The answer is that the original method indicated in its signature contains the exceptions that it might possibly throw. You can use this mechanism in your own methods—in fact, it's good style to do so to make sure your classes' other users are alerted to the errors your methods may come across.

To indicate that a method may possibly throw an exception, you use a special clause in the method definition called `throws`.

The `throws` Clause

To indicate that some code in your method's body may throw an exception, simply add the `throws` keyword after the signature for the method (before the opening brace) with the name or names of the exception that your method throws:

```
public boolean myMethod (int x, int y) throws AnException {
    // ...
}
```

16

If your method may throw multiple kinds of exceptions, you can put all of them in the `throws` clause, separated by commas:

```
public boolean myOtherMethod (int x, int y)
    throws AnException, AnotherException, AThirdException {
        // ...
}
```

Note that as with `catch`, you can use a superclass of an exceptions group to indicate that your method may throw any subclass of that exception:

```
public void YetAnotherMethod() throws IOException {
    // ...
}
```

Keep in mind that adding a `throws` method to your method definition simply means that the method might throw an exception if something goes wrong, not that it actually will. The `throws` clause simply provides extra information to your method definition about potential exceptions and allows Java to make sure that your method is being used correctly by other people.

Think of a method's overall description as a contract between the designer of that method (or class) and the caller of the method (you can be on either side of that contract, of course). Usually the description indicates the types of a method's arguments, what it returns, and the general semantics of what it normally does. By using `throws` you add information about the abnormal things it can do as well. This new part of the contract helps separate and make explicit all the places where exceptional conditions should be handled in your program, and that makes large-scale design easier.

Which Exceptions Should You Throw?

Once you decide to declare that your method might throw an exception, you have to decide which exceptions it might throw (and actually throw them or call a method that will throw them—you'll learn about throwing your own exceptions in the next section). In many instances this is apparent from the operation of the method itself. Perhaps you're creating and throwing your own exceptions, in which case you'll know exactly which exceptions to throw.

You don't really have to list all the possible exceptions that your method could throw; some exceptions are handled by the runtime itself and are so common (not common per se, but ubiquitous) that you don't have to deal with them. In particular, exceptions of either class `Error` or `RuntimeException` (or any of their subclasses) do not have to be listed in your `throws` clause. They get special treatment because they can occur anywhere within a Java program and are usually conditions that you, as the programmer, did not directly cause. One good example is `OutOfMemoryError`, which can happen anywhere, at any time, and for any number of reasons. These two kinds of exceptions are called *implicit exceptions*, and you don't have to worry about them.

Implicit exceptions are exceptions that are `RuntimeException` and `Error` subclasses. Implicit exceptions are usually thrown by the Java runtime itself. You do not have to declare that your method throws them.

 Note

> You can, of course, choose to list these errors and runtime exceptions in your `throws` clause if you like, but your methods' callers will not be forced to handle them; only non-runtime exceptions must be handled.

All other exceptions are called *explicit exceptions* and are potential candidates of a `throws` clause in your method.

Passing On Exceptions

In addition to declaring methods that throw exceptions, there's one other instance in which your method definition may include a `throws` clause. In this case you want to use a method that throws an exception, but you don't want to catch or deal with that exception. In many cases it might make more sense for the method that calls your method to deal with that exception rather than for you to deal with it. There's nothing wrong with this; it's a fairly common occurrence that you won't actually deal with an exception, but will pass it back to the method that calls yours. At any rate, it's a better idea to pass on exceptions to calling methods than to catch them and ignore them.

Rather than using the `try` and `catch` clauses in your method's body, you can declare your method with a `throws` clause such that it, too, might possibly throw the appropriate exception. It's then the responsibility of the method that calls your method to deal with that exception. This is the other case that satisfies the Java compiler that you have done something with a given method. Here's another way of implementing an example that reads characters from a stream:

```
public void readFile(String filename) throws IOException {
    // open the file, initialize the stream here
    while (numBytes <= myBuffer.length) {
        myInputStream.read(myBuffer);
        numBytes;++
}
```

This example is similar to an example used previously today; remember that the read() method was declared to throw an IOException, so you had to use try and catch to use it. Once you declare your method to throw an exception, however, you can use other methods that also throw those exceptions inside the body of this method, without needing to protect the code or catch the exception.

Note You can, of course, deal with other exceptions using try and catch in the body of your method in addition to passing on the exceptions you listed in the throws clause. You also can both deal with the exception in some way and then rethrow it so that your method's calling method has to deal with it anyhow. You learn how to throw methods in the next section.

throws and Inheritance

If your method definition overrides a method in a superclass that includes a throws clause, there are special rules for how your overridden method deals with throws. Unlike other parts of the method signature that must mimic those of the method it is overriding, your new method does not require the same set of exceptions listed in the throws clause.

Because there's a possibility that your new method may deal better with exceptions rather than just throwing them, your method can potentially throw fewer types of exceptions. It could even throw no exceptions at all. That means that you can have the following two class definitions and things will work just fine:

```
public class RadioPlay {
    public void startPlaying() throws SoundException {
        // ...
    }
}
public class StereoPlay extends RadioPlay {
    public void startPlaying() {
        // ...
    }
}
```

The converse of this rule is not true: A subclass method cannot throw more exceptions (either exceptions of different types or more general exception classes) than its super-class method.

Creating and Throwing Your Own Exceptions

There are two sides to every exception: the side that throws the exception and the side that catches it. An exception can be tossed around a number of times to a number of methods before it's caught, but eventually it will be caught and dealt with.

Who does the actual throwing? Where do exceptions come from? Many exceptions are thrown by the Java runtime or by methods inside the Java classes themselves. You can also throw any of the standard exceptions that the Java class libraries define, or you can create and throw your own exceptions. This section describes all these things.

Throwing Exceptions

Declaring that your method throws an exception is useful only to your method's users and to the Java compiler, which checks to make sure all your exceptions are being dealt with—but the declaration itself doesn't do anything to actually throw that exception should it occur; you have to do that yourself in the body of the method.

Remember that exceptions are all instances of some exception class, of which there are many defined in the standard Java class library. You need to create a new instance of an exception class in order to throw an exception. Once you have that instance, use the throw statement to throw it. The simplest way to throw an exception is like this:

```
NotInServiceException() nis = new NotInServiceException();
throw nis;
```

 Note

> You only can throw objects that are subclasses of Throwable. This is different from C++'s exceptions, which allow you to throw objects of any type.

Depending on the exception class you're using, the exception also may have arguments to its constructor that you can use. The most common of these is a string argument, which lets you describe the actual problem in greater detail (which can be very useful for debugging purposes). Here's an example:

```
NotInServiceException() nis = new
    NotInServiceException("Exception: Database Not in Service");
throw nis;
```

Once an exception is thrown, the method exits immediately, without executing any other code (other than the code inside `finally`, if that block exists) and without returning a value. If the calling method does not have a `try` or `catch` surrounding the call to your method, the program may very well exit based on the exception you threw.

Creating Your Own Exceptions

Although there are a fair number of exceptions in the Java class library that you can use in your own methods, you might need to create your own exceptions to handle different kinds of errors your programs run into. Fortunately, creating new exceptions is easy.

Your new exception should inherit from some other exception in the Java hierarchy. All user-created exceptions should be part of the `Exception` hierarchy rather than the `Error` hierarchy, which is reserved for errors involving the Java virtual machine. Look for an exception that's close to the one you're creating; for example, an exception for a bad file format would logically be an `IOException`. If you can't find a closely related exception for your new exception, consider inheriting from `Exception`, which forms the "top" of the exception hierarchy for explicit exceptions. (Remember that implicit exceptions, which include subclasses of `Error` and `RuntimeException`, inherit from `Throwable`.)

Exception classes typically have two constructors: The first takes no arguments and the second takes a single string as an argument. In the latter case you should call `super()` in that constructor to make sure the string is applied to the right place in the exception.

Beyond those three rules, exception classes look just like other classes. You can put them in their own source files and compile them just as you would other classes:

```
public class SunSpotException extends Exception {
    public SunSpotException() {}
    public SunSpotException(String msg) {
        super(msg);
    }
}
```

Combining `throws`, `try`, and `throw`

What if you want to combine all the approaches shown so far? You'd like to handle incoming exceptions yourself in your method, but also you'd like to pass the exception up to your caller. Simply using `try` and `catch` doesn't pass on the exception, and simply adding a `throws` clause doesn't give you a chance to deal with the exception. If you want to both manage the exception and pass it on to the caller, use all three mechanisms: the `throws` clause, the `try` statement, and a `throw` statement explicitly rethrowing the exception.

```
public void responsibleExceptionalMethod() throws IOException {
    MessageReader mr = new MessageReader();

    try {
        mr.loadHeader();
    } catch (IOException e) {
        // do something to handle the
        // IO exception
        throw e; // rethrow the exception
    }
}
```

This works because exception handlers can be nested. You handle the exception by doing something responsible with it, but decide that it is too important to not give an exception handler that might be in your caller a chance to handle it as well. Exceptions float all the way up the chain of method callers this way (usually not being handled by most of them) until at last the system itself handles any uncaught ones by aborting your program and printing an error message. This is not such a bad idea in a standalone program, but it can cause the browser to crash in an applet. Most browsers protect themselves from this disaster by catching all exceptions themselves whenever they run an applet, but you can never tell. If it's possible for you to catch an exception and do something intelligent with it, you should.

When and When Not to Use Exceptions

Because throwing, catching, and declaring exceptions are related concepts and can be very confusing, here's a quick summary of when to do what.

When to Use Exceptions

You can do one of three things if your method calls another method that has a `throws` clause:

- Deal with the exception using `try` and `catch` statements.
- Pass the exception up the calling chain by adding your own `throws` clause to your method definition.
- Perform both of the preceding methods by catching the exception using `catch` and then explicitly rethrowing it using `throw`.

In cases where a method throws more than one exception, you can handle each of those exceptions differently. For example, you might catch some of those exceptions while allowing others to pass up the calling chain.

If your method throws its own exceptions, you should declare that it throws those methods using the `throws` statement. If your method overrides a superclass method that has a `throws` statement, you can throw the same types of exceptions or subclasses of those exceptions; you cannot throw any different types of exceptions.

Lastly, if your method has been declared with a `throws` clause, don't forget to actually throw the exception in the body of your method using the `throw` statement.

When Not to Use Exceptions

There are several cases in which you should not use exceptions, even though they may seem appropriate at the time.

First, you should not use exceptions if the exception is something that you expect and could avoid easily with a simple expression. For example, although you can rely on an `ArrayIndexOutofBounds` exception to indicate when you've gone past the end of the array, it's easy to use the array's `length` variable to prevent you from going out of bounds.

In addition, if your users are going to enter data that must be an integer, testing to make sure it is an integer is a much better idea than throwing an exception and dealing with it somewhere else.

Exceptions take up a lot of processing time for your Java program. A simple test or series of tests will run much faster than exception handling and make your program more efficient. Exceptions should only be used for truly exceptional cases that are out of your control.

It's also easy to get carried away with exceptions and to try to make sure that all your methods have been declared to throw all the possible exceptions that they can possibly throw. This makes your code more complex in general; in addition, if other people will be using your code, they'll have to deal with handling all the exceptions that your methods might throw. You're making more work for everyone involved when you get carried away with exceptions. Declaring a method to throw either few or lots of exceptions is a trade-off; the more exceptions your method can throw, the more complex that method is to use. Declare only the exceptions that have a reasonably fair chance of happening and that make sense for the overall design of your classes.

Bad Style Using Exceptions

When you first start using exceptions, it might be appealing to work around the compiler errors that result when you use a method that declared a `throws` statements. Although it is legal to add an empty `catch` clause or to add a `throws` statement to your own method (and there are appropriate reasons for doing both of these things), intentionally dropping exceptions without dealing with them subverts the checks the Java compiler does for you.

The Java exception system was designed so that if an error can occur, you're warned about it. Ignoring those warnings and working around them makes it possible for fatal errors to occur in your program—errors that you could have avoided with a few lines of code. Even worse, adding throws statements to your methods to avoid exceptions means that the users of your methods (objects further up in the calling chain) will have to deal with them. You've just made your methods more difficult to use.

Compiler errors regarding exceptions are there to remind you to reflect on these issues. Take the time to deal with the exceptions that may affect your code. This extra care will richly reward you as you reuse your classes in later projects and in larger and larger programs. Of course, the Java class library has been written with exactly this degree of care, and that's one of the reasons it's robust enough to be used in constructing all your Java projects.

Summary

Today you learned about how exceptions aid your program's design and robustness. Exceptions give you a way of managing potential errors in your programs and of alerting your programs' users that potential errors can occur. By using try, catch, and finally, you can protect code that may result in exceptions, catch and handle those exceptions if they occur, and execute code whether an exception was generated or not.

Handling exceptions is only half of the equation; the other half is generating and throwing exceptions yourself. Today you learned about the throws clause, which tells your methods' users that the method might throw an exception. throws can also be used to pass on an exception from a method call in the body of your method.

In addition to the information given by the throws clause, you learned how to actually create and throw your own methods by defining new exception classes and by throwing instances of any exception classes using throw.

Q&A

Q I'm still not sure I understand the differences between exceptions, errors, and runtime exceptions. Is there another way of looking at them?

A Errors are caused by dynamic linking or virtual machine problems, and are thus too low-level for most programs to care about—or be able to handle even if they did care about them. Runtime exceptions are generated by the normal execution of

Java code, and although they occasionally reflect a condition you will want to handle explicitly, more often they reflect a coding mistake made by the programmer, and thus simply need to print an error to help flag that mistake. Exceptions that are non-runtime exceptions (IOException exceptions, for example) are conditions that, because of their nature, should be explicitly handled by any robust and well thought out code. The Java class library has been written using only a few of these, but those few are extremely important to using the system safely and correctly. The compiler helps you handle these exceptions properly via its throws clause checks and restrictions.

16

Q Is there any way to get around the strict restrictions placed on methods by the throws clause?

A Yes. Suppose you have thought long and hard and have decided that you need to circumvent this restriction. This is almost never the case because the right solution is to go back and redesign your methods to reflect the exceptions that you need to throw. Imagine, however, that for some reason a system class has you in a straitjacket. Your first solution is to subclass RuntimeException to make up a new, exempt exception of your own. Now you can throw it to your heart's content, because the throws clause that was annoying you does not need to include this new exception. If you need a lot of such exceptions, an elegant approach is to mix in some novel exception interfaces to your new Runtime classes. You're free to choose whatever subset of these new interfaces you want to catch (none of the normal Runtime exceptions need be caught), while any leftover Runtime exceptions are allowed to go through that otherwise annoying standard method in the library.

WEEK 3

DAY 17

Handling Data Through Java Streams

Many of the programs you create with Java will need to interact with some kind of data source. There are countless ways in which information can be stored on a computer, including files on a hard drive or CD-ROM, pages on a Web site, and even the computer's memory itself.

You might expect there to be different techniques to handle each of the different storage devices. Fortunately, this isn't the case.

In Java, information can be stored and retrieved using a communications system called streams, which are implemented in the `java.io` package.

Today you learn how to create input streams to read information and output streams to store information. You'll work with each of the following:

- Byte streams, which are used to handle bytes, integers, and other simple data types
- Character streams, which handle text files and other text sources

You can deal with all data the same way once you know how to work with an input stream, whether it's coming from a disk, the Internet, or even another program. The converse is true for output streams.

Streams are a powerful mechanism for handling data, but you don't pay for that power with classes that are difficult to implement.

Introduction to Streams

All data in Java is written and read using streams. Streams, like the bodies of water that share the same name, carry something from one place to another.

NEW TERM   A *stream* is a path traveled by data in a program. An *input stream* sends data from a source into a program, and an *output stream* sends data out of a program to a destination.

You deal with two different types of streams today: byte streams and character streams. *Bytes* carry integers with values that range from 0 to 255. A diverse assortment of data can be expressed in byte format, including numerical data, executable programs, Internet communications, and bytecode—the class files that are run by a Java virtual machine.

In fact, every kind of data imaginable can be expressed using either individual bytes or a series of bytes combined with each other.

NEW TERM   *Character streams* are a specialized type of byte stream that only handles textual data. They're distinguished from byte streams because Java's character set supports Unicode, a standard that includes many more characters than could be expressed easily using bytes.

Any kind of data that involves text should use character streams, including text files, Web pages, and other common types of text.

Using a Stream

Whether you're using a byte stream or a character stream, the procedure for using either in Java is largely the same. Before you start working with the specifics of the `java.io` classes, it's useful to walk through the process of creating and using streams.

For an input stream, the first step is to create an object that is associated with the data source. For example, if the source is a file on your hard drive, a `FileInputStream` object could be associated with this file.

Once you have a stream object, you can read information from that stream by using one of the object's methods. `FileInputStream` includes a `read()` method that returns a byte read from the file.

When you're done reading information from the stream, you call the `close()` method to indicate that you're done using the stream.

For an output stream, you begin by creating an object that's associated with the data's destination. One such object can be created from the `BufferedReader` class, which represents an efficient way to create text files.

The `write()` method is the simplest way to send information to the output stream's destination. For instance, a `BufferedReader write()` method can send individual characters to an output stream.

As you do with input streams, the `close()` is called on an output stream when you have no more information to send.

Filtering a Stream

The simplest way to use a stream is to create it and then call its methods to send or receive data, depending on whether it's an output stream or an input stream.

Many of the classes you work with today achieve more sophisticated results by associating a filter with a stream before reading or writing any data.

NEW TERM   A *filter* is a type of stream that modifies the way an existing stream is handled. Think of a beaver dam on a mountain stream. The dam regulates the flow of water from the points upstream to the points downstream. The dam is a type of filter—remove it, and the water would flow in a fashion much less controlled.

The procedure for using a filter on a stream is basically as follows:

- Create a stream associated with a data source or a data destination.
- Associate a filter with that stream.
- Read or write data from the filter rather than the original stream.

The methods you call on a filter are the same as the methods you would call on a stream: There are `read()` or `write()` methods, just as there would be on an unfiltered stream.

You can even associate a filter with another filter, so the following path for information is possible: an input stream associated with a text file, which is filtered through a Spanish-to-English translation filter, which is then filtered through a no-profanity filter, and is finally sent to its destination—a human being who wants to read it.

If this is still confusing in the abstract, you get plenty of opportunity to see it in practice in the following sections.

17

Byte Streams

All byte streams are either a subclass of InputStream or OutputStream. These classes are abstract, so you cannot create a stream by creating objects of these classes directly. Instead, you create streams through one of their subclasses, such as the following:

- FileInputStream and FileOutputStream   Byte streams stored in files on disk, CD-ROM, or other storage devices.
- DataInputStream and DataOutputStream   A filtered byte stream from which data such as integers and floating-point numbers can be read.

InputStream is the superclass of all input streams.

File Streams

The byte streams you work with most are likely to be file streams, which are used to exchange data with files on your disk drives, CD-ROMs, or other storage devices you can refer to by using a folder path and filename.

You can send bytes to a file output stream and receive bytes from a file input stream.

File Input Streams

A file input stream can be created with the FileInputStream(*string*) constructor. The string argument should be the name of the file. You can include a path reference with the filename, which enables the file to be in a different folder than the class loading it. The following statement creates a file input stream from the file scores.dat:

```
FileInputStream fis = new FileInputStream("scores.dat");
```

After you create a file input stream, you can read bytes from the stream by calling its read() method. This method returns an integer containing the next byte in the stream. If the method returns a -1, which is not a possible byte value, this signifies that the end of the file stream has been reached.

To read more than one byte of data from the stream, call its read(*byte[ ]*, *int*, *int*) method. The arguments to this method are as follows:

- A byte array where the data will be stored
- The element inside the array where the data's first byte should be stored
- The number of bytes to read

Unlike the other read() method, this does not return data from the stream. Instead, it returns an integer that represents the number of bytes read or -1 if no bytes were read before the end of the stream was reached.

The following statements use a `while` loop to read the data in a `FileInputStream` object called `df`:

```
int newByte = 0;
while (newByte != -1) {
    newByte = df.read();
    System.out.print(newByte + " ");
}
```

This loop reads the entire file referenced by `df` one byte at a time and displays each byte followed by a space character. It also will display a -1 when the end of the file has been reached—you could guard against this easily with an `if` statement.

The `ReadBytes` application in Listing 17.1 uses a similar technique to read a file input stream. The input stream's `close()` method is used to close the stream after the last byte in the file is read. This must be done to free system resources associated with the open file.

17

TYPE   **LISTING 17.1.** THE FULL TEXT OF READBYTES.JAVA.

```
 1: import java.io.*;
 2:
 3: public class ReadBytes {
 4:     public static void main(String[] arguments) {
 5:         try {
 6:             FileInputStream file = new
 7:                 FileInputStream("class.dat");
 8:             boolean eof = false;
 9:             int count = 0;
10:             while (!eof) {
11:                 int input = file.read();
12:                 System.out.print(input + " ");
13:                 if (input == -1)
14:                     eof = true;
15:                 else
16:                     count++;
17:             }
18:             file.close();
19:             System.out.println("\nBytes read: " + count);
20:         } catch (IOException e) {
21:             System.out.println("Error -- " + e.toString());
22:         }
23:     }
24: }
```

If you run this program, you'll get the following error message:

OUTPUT   `Error -- java.io.FileNotFoundException: class.dat`

This error message looks like the kind of exceptions generated by the compiler, but it's actually coming from the `catch` block in lines 21–23 of the `ReadBytes` application. The exception is being thrown by lines 6 and 7 because the `class.dat` file cannot be found.

You need a file of bytes in which to read. This can be any file—a suitable choice is the program's class file, which contains the bytecode instructions executed by the Java virtual machine. Create this file by making a copy of `ReadBytes.class` and renaming the copy `class.dat`. Don't rename `ReadBytes.class` itself, or you won't be able to run the program.

 Tip

> Windows 95 and Windows NT users can use the MS-DOS prompt to create `class.dat`. Go to the folder that contains `ReadBytes.class` and use the following DOS command:
>
> `copy ReadBytes.class class.dat`
>
> UNIX users can type the following at a command line:
>
> `cp ReadBytes.class class.dat`

When you run the program, each byte in `class.dat` will be displayed, followed by a count of the total number of bytes. If you used `ReadBytes.class` to create `class.dat`, the last several lines of output should resemble the following:

OUTPUT
```
49 43 182 0 23 54 4 178 0 20 187 0 11 89 21 4 184 0 26 183 0 16 18
 2 182 0 18 182 0 24 182 0 21 21 4 2 160 0 8 4 61 167 0 6 132 3 1
28 153 255 209 43 182 0 19 178 0 20 187 0 11 89 18 1 183 0 16 29 1
82 0 17 182 0 24 182 0 22 167 0 29 76 178 0 20 187 0 11 89 18 3 18
3 0 16 43 182 0 25 182 0 18 182 0 24 182 0 22 177 0 1 0 0 0 93 0 9
6 0 7 0 1 0 53 0 0 0 90 0 22 0 0 0 5 0 0 0 6 0 4 0 7 0 6 0 6 0 10
0 8 0 12 0 9 0 14 0 10 0 17 0 11 0 23 0 12 0 49 0 13 0 55 0 14 0 5
7 0 13 0 60 0 16 0 63 0 10 0 67 0 18 0 71 0 19 0 83 0 20 0 90 0 19
 0 93 0 5 0 96 0 21 0 97 0 22 0 122 0 4 0 1 0 58 0 0 0 2 0 57 -1
Bytes read: 1121
```

The number of bytes displayed on each line of output depends on the column width that text can occupy on your system. The bytes shown depend on the file used to create `class.dat`.

File Output Streams

A file output stream can be created with the FileOutputStream(*String*) constructor. The usage is the same as the FileInputStream(*String*) constructor, so you can specify a path along with a filename.

You have to be careful when specifying the file to which to write an output stream. If it's the same as an existing file, the original will be wiped out when you start writing data to the stream.

You can create a file output stream that appends data after the end of an existing file with the FileOutputStream(*String*, *boolean*) constructor. The string specifies the file and the Boolean argument should equal true to append data instead of overwriting any existing data.

The file output stream's write(*int*) method is used to write bytes to the stream. After the last byte has been written to the file, the stream's close() method closes the stream.

To write more than one byte, the write(*byte[]*, *int*, *int*) method can be used. This works in a manner similar to the read(*byte[]*, *int*, *int*) method described previously. The arguments to this method are the byte array containing the bytes to output, the starting point in the array, and the number of bytes to write.

The WriteBytes application in Listing 17.2 writes an integer array to a file output stream.

TYPE **LISTING 17.2.** THE FULL TEXT OF WRITEBYTES.JAVA.

```
1: import java.io.*;
2:
3: public class WriteBytes {
4:     public static void main(String[] arguments) {
5:         int[] data = { 71, 73, 70, 56, 57, 97, 15, 0, 15, 0,
6:             128, 0, 0, 255, 255, 255, 0, 0, 0, 44, 0, 0, 0,
7:             0, 15, 0, 15, 0, 0, 2, 33, 132, 127, 161, 200,
8:             185, 205, 84, 128, 241, 81, 35, 175, 155, 26,
9:             228, 254, 105, 33, 102, 121, 165, 201, 145, 169,
10:             154, 142, 172, 116, 162, 240, 90, 197, 5, 0, 59 };
11:         try {
12:             FileOutputStream file = new
13:                 FileOutputStream("pic.gif");
14:             for (int i = 0; i < data.length; i++)
15:                 file.write(data[i]);
16:             file.close();
17:         } catch (IOException e) {
18:             System.out.println("Error — " + e.toString());
19:         }
20:     }
21: }
```

The following things are taking place in this program:

- Lines 5–10   An integer array called data is created with 66 elements.
- Lines 12 and 13   A file output stream is created with the filename pic.gif in the same folder as the WriteBytes.class file.
- Lines 14 and 15   A for loop is used to cycle through the data array and write each element to the file stream.
- Line 16   The file output stream is closed.

After you run this program, you can display the pic.gif file in any Web browser or graphics editing tool. It's a small image file in the GIF format, as shown in Figure 17.1.

FIGURE 17.1.

The pic.gif file (enlarged).

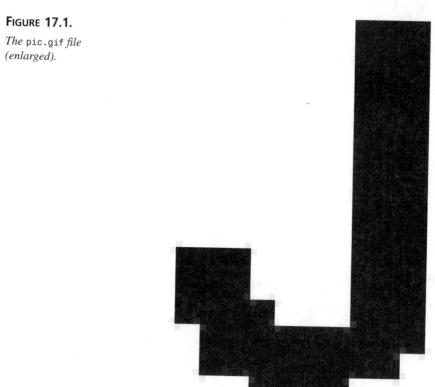

Filtering a Stream

NEW TERM   *Filtered streams* are streams that modify the information sent through an existing stream. They are created using the subclasses FilterInputStream or FilterOutputStream.

These classes do not handle any filtering operations themselves. Instead, they have sub-classes such as `BufferInputStream` and `DataOutputStream` that handle specific types of filtering.

Byte Filters

Information is delivered more quickly if it can be sent in large chunks, even if those chunks are received faster than they can be handled.

As an example of this, consider which of the following book-reading techniques is faster:

- A friend loans you a book in its entirety and you read it.
- A friend loans you a book one page at a time, and doesn't give you a new page until you finish the previous one.

Obviously, the first technique is going to be faster and more efficient. The same benefits are true of buffered streams in Java.

NEW TERM   A *buffer* is a storage place where data can be kept before it is needed by a program that reads or writes that data. By using a buffer, you can get data without always going back to the original source of the data.

Buffered Streams

A buffered input stream fills a buffer with data that hasn't been handled yet, and when a program needs this data, it looks to the buffer first before going to the original stream source. This is much more efficient—using a stream without a buffer is analogous to being given a book one page at a time. Any slowdowns from that stream are going to slow down efforts to use it.

Buffered byte streams use the `BufferedInputStream` and `BufferedOutputStream` classes.

A buffered input stream is created using one of the following two constructors:

- `BufferedInputStream(InputStream)` Creates a buffered input stream for the specified *InputStream* object.
- `BufferedInputStream(InputStream, int)` Creates the specified *InputStream* buffered stream with a buffer of *int* size.

The simplest way to read data from a buffered input stream is to call its `read()` method with no arguments, which normally returns an integer from 0 to 255 representing the next byte in the stream. If the end of the stream has been reached and no byte is available, -1 is returned.

You also can use the read(*byte[]*, *int*, *int*) method available for other input streams, which loads stream data into a byte array.

A buffered output stream is created using one of these two constructors:

- BufferedOutputStream(*OutputStream*)   Creates a buffered output stream for the specified *OutputStream* object.

- BufferedOutputStream(*OutputStream*, *int*)   Creates the specified *OutputStream* buffered stream with a buffer of *int* size.

The output stream's write(*int*) method can be used to send a single byte to the stream, and the write(*byte[]*, *int*, *int*) method writes multiple bytes from the specified byte array. The arguments to this method are the byte array, array starting point, and number of bytes to write.

> **Note**
>
> Although the write() method takes an integer as input, the value should be from 0 to 255. If you specify a number higher than 255, it will be stored as the remainder of the number divided by 256. You can test this when running the project created later in this section.

When data is directed to a buffered stream, it will not be output to its destination until the stream fills up or the buffered stream's flush() method is called.

The next project, the BufferDemo application, writes a series of bytes to a buffered output stream associated with a text file. The first and last integer in the series are specified as two command-line arguments, as in the following statement:

```
java BufferDemo 7 64
```

After writing to the textfile, BufferDemo creates a buffered input stream from the file and reads the bytes back in. Listing 17.3 contains the source code.

TYPE   **LISTING 17.3.** THE FULL TEXT OF BUFFERDEMO.JAVA.

```
1: import java.io.*;
2:
3: public class BufferDemo {
4:     public static void main(String[] arguments) {
5:         int start = 0;
6:         int finish = 255;
7:         if (arguments.length > 1) {
8:             start = Integer.parseInt(arguments[0]);
9:             finish = Integer.parseInt(arguments[1]);
```

```
10:            } else if (arguments.length > 0)
11:                start = Integer.parseInt(arguments[0]);
12:            ArgStream as = new ArgStream(start, finish);
13:            System.out.println("\nWriting: ");
14:            boolean success = as.writeStream();
15:            System.out.println("\nReading: ");
16:            boolean readSuccess = as.readStream();
17:        }
18: }
19:
20: class ArgStream {
21:        int start = 0;
22:        int finish = 255;
23:
24:        ArgStream(int st, int fin) {
25:            start = st;
26:            finish = fin;
27:        }
28:
29:        boolean writeStream() {
30:            try {
31:                FileOutputStream file = new
32:                    FileOutputStream("numbers.dat");
33:                BufferedOutputStream buff = new
34:                    BufferedOutputStream(file);
35:                for (int out = start; out <= finish; out++) {
36:                    buff.write(out);
37:                    System.out.print(" " + out);
38:                }
39:                buff.close();
40:                return true;
41:            } catch (IOException e) {
42:                System.out.println("Exception: " + e.getMessage());
43:                return false;
44:            }
45:        }
46:
47:        boolean readStream() {
48:            try {
49:                FileInputStream file = new
50:                    FileInputStream("numbers.dat");
51:                BufferedInputStream buff = new
52:                    BufferedInputStream(file);
53:                int in = 0;
54:                do {
55:                    in = buff.read();
56:                    if (in != -1)
57:                        System.out.print(" " + in);
58:                } while (in != -1);
```

continues

LISTING 17.3. CONTINUED

```
59:                buff.close();
60:                return true;
61:           } catch (IOException e) {
62:                System.out.println("Exception: " + e.getMessage());
63:                return false;
64:           }
65:      }
66: }
```

This program's output depends on the two arguments specified at the command line. If you use `java BufferDemo 4 13`, the following output is shown:

OUTPUT
```
Writing:
  4 5 6 7 8 9 10 11 12 13
Reading:
  4 5 6 7 8 9 10 11 12 13
```

This application consists of two classes: `BufferDemo` and a helper class called `ArgStream`. `BufferDemo` gets the two arguments' values, if they are provided, and uses them in the `ArgStream()` constructor.

The `writeStream()` method of `ArgStream` is called in line 14 to write the series of bytes to a buffered output stream, and the `readStream()` method is called in line 16 to read those bytes back.

Even though they are moving data in two different directions, the `writeStream()` and `readStream()` methods are substantially the same. They take the following format:

- The filename, `numbers.dat`, is used to create a file input or output stream.
- The file stream is used to create a buffered input or output stream.
- The buffered stream's `write()` method is used to send data, or the `read()` method is used to receive data.
- The buffered stream is closed.

Because file- and buffered streams throw `IOException` objects if an error occurs, all operations involving the streams are enclosed in a `try...catch` block for this exception.

Tip

The Boolean return values in `writeStream()` and `readStream()` indicate whether the stream operation was completed successfully. They aren't used in this program, but it's good practice to let callers of these methods know if something goes wrong.

Data Streams

If you need to work with data that isn't represented as bytes or characters, you can use data input and data output streams. These streams filter an existing byte stream so that each of the following primitive types can be read or written directly from the stream: boolean, byte, double, float, int, long, and short.

A data input stream is created with the DataInputStream(*InputStream*) constructor. The argument should be an existing input stream such as a buffered input stream or a file input stream.

Conversely, a data output stream requires the DataOutputStream(*OutputStream*) constructor, which indicates the associated output stream.

The following list indicates the read and write methods that apply to data input and output streams, respectively:

- readBoolean(), writeBoolean(*boolean*)
- readByte(), writeByte(*integer*)
- readDouble(), writeDouble(*double*)
- readFloat(), writeFloat(*float)*
- readInt(), writeInt(*int*)
- readLong(), writeLong(*long*)
- readShort(), writeShort(*int*)

Each of the input methods returns the primitive data type indicated by the name of the method. For example, the readFloat() method returns a float value.

There also are readUnsignedByte() and readUnsignedShort() methods that read in unsigned byte and short values. These are not data types supported by Java, so they are returned as int values.

Note

> Unsigned bytes have values ranging from 0 to 255. This differs from Java's byte variable type, which ranges from -128 to 127. Along the same lines, an unsigned short value ranges from 0 to 65,535, instead of the -32,768 to 32,767 range supported by Java's short type.

A data input stream's different read methods do not all return a value that can be used as an indicator that the end of the stream has been reached.

As an alternative, you can wait for an EOFException (end-of-file exception) to be thrown when a read method reaches the end of a stream. The loop that reads the data can be enclosed in a try block, and the associated catch statement should only handle EOFException objects. You can call close() on the stream and take care of other cleanup tasks inside the catch block.

This is demonstrated in the next project. Listings 17.4 and 17.5 contain two programs that use data streams. The WritePrimes application writes the first 400 prime numbers as integers to a file called 400primes.dat. The ReadPrimes application reads the integers from this file and displays them.

TYPE   **LISTING 17.4.** THE FULL TEXT OF WRITEPRIMES.JAVA.

```
 1: import java.io.*;
 2:
 3: class WritePrimes {
 4:     public static void main(String arguments[]) {
 5:         int[] primes = new int[400];
 6:         int numPrimes = 0;
 7:         // candidate: the number that might be prime
 8:         int candidate = 2;
 9:         while (numPrimes < 400) {
10:             if (isPrime(candidate)) {
11:                 primes[numPrimes] = candidate;
12:                 numPrimes++;
13:             }
14:             candidate++;
15:         }
16:
17:         try {
18:             // Write output to disk
19:             FileOutputStream file = new
20:                 FileOutputStream("400primes.dat");
21:             BufferedOutputStream buff = new
22:                 BufferedOutputStream(file);
23:             DataOutputStream data = new
24:                 DataOutputStream(buff);
25:
26:             for (int i = 0; i < 400; i++)
27:                 data.writeInt(primes[i]);
28:             data.close();
29:         } catch (IOException e) {
30:             System.out.println("Error -- " + e.toString());
31:         }
32:     }
33:
34:     public static boolean isPrime(int checkNumber) {
```

```
35:            double root = Math.sqrt(checkNumber);
36:            for (int i = 2; i <= root; i++) {
37:                if (checkNumber % i == 0)
38:                    return false;
39:            }
40:            return true;
41:        }
42: }
```

TYPE   **LISTING 17.5.** THE FULL TEXT OF READPRIMES.JAVA.

```
 1: import java.io.*;
 2:
 3: class ReadPrimes {
 4:     public static void main(String arguments[]) {
 5:         try {
 6:             FileInputStream file = new
 7:                 FileInputStream("400primes.dat");
 8:             BufferedInputStream buff = new
 9:                 BufferedInputStream(file);
10:             DataInputStream data = new
11:                 DataInputStream(buff);
12:
13:             try {
14:                 while (true) {
15:                     int in = data.readInt();
16:                     System.out.print(in + " ");
17:                 }
18:             } catch (EOFException eof) {
19:                 buff.close();
20:             }
21:         } catch (IOException e) {
22:             System.out.println("Error -- " + e.toString());
23:         }
24:     }
25: }
```

17

Most of the WritePrimes application is taken up with logic to find the first 400 prime numbers. Once you have an integer array containing the first 400 primes, it is written to a data output stream in lines 17–31.

This application is an example of using more than one filter on a stream. The stream is developed in a three-step process:

- A file output stream that is associated with a file called 400primes.dat is created.
- A new buffered output stream is associated with the file stream.
- A new data output stream is associated with the buffered stream.

The writeInt() method of the data stream is used to write the primes to the file.

The ReadPrimes application is simpler because it doesn't need to do anything regarding prime numbers—it just reads integers out of a file using a data input stream.

Lines 6–11 of ReadPrimes are nearly identical to statements in the WritePrimes application, except that input classes are used instead of output classes.

The try...catch block that handles EOFException objects is in lines 13–20. The work of loading the data takes place inside the try block.

The while(true) statement creates an endless loop. This isn't a problem—an EOFException will automatically occur when the end of the stream is encountered at some point as the data stream is being read. The readInt() method in line 15 reads integers from the stream.

The last several output lines of the ReadPrimes application should resemble the following:

 2137 2141 2143 2153 2161 2179 2203 2207 2213 2221 2237 2239 2243 22
51 2267 2269 2273 2281 2287 2293 2297 2309 2311 2333 2339 2341 2347
2351 2357 2371 2377 2381 2383 2389 2393 2399 2411 2417 2423 2437 2
441 2447 2459 2467 2473 2477 2503 2521 2531 2539 2543 2549 2551 255
7 2579 2591 2593 2609 2617 2621 2633 2647 2657 2659 2663 2671 2677
2683 2687 2689 2693 2699 2707 2711 2713 2719 2729 2731 2741

Character Streams

Once you know how to handle byte streams, you have most of the skills needed to handle character streams as well. These streams are used to work with any text that is represented by the ASCII character set or Unicode, an international character set that includes ASCII.

Examples of files you can work with through a character stream are plain text files, HTML documents, and Java source files.

The classes used to read and write these streams are all subclasses of Reader and Writer. These should be used for all text input instead of dealing directly with byte streams.

 Note   The techniques for handling character streams were greatly improved after Java 1.02 with the introduction of the Reader and Writer classes and their subclasses; they enable Unicode character support and better handling of text. A Java applet that's 1.02-ready can read characters by using the byte stream classes described previously.

Reading Text Files

`FileReader` is the main class used when reading character streams from a file. This class inherits from `InputStreamReader`, which reads a byte stream and converts the bytes into integer values that represent Unicode characters.

A character input stream is associated with a file using the `FileReader(String)` constructor. The string indicates the file, and it can contain path folder references in addition to a filename.

The following statement creates a new `FileReader` called `look` and associates it with a text file called `index.html`:

```
FileReader look = new FileReader("index.html");
```

Once you have a file reader, you can call the following methods on it to read characters from the file:

- `read()` returns the next character on the stream as an integer.
- `read(char[], int, int)` reads characters into the specified character array with the indicated starting point and number of characters read.

The second method works like methods similar for the byte input stream classes. Instead of returning the next character, it either returns the number of characters that were read or returns –1 if no characters were read before the end of the stream was reached.

The following method loads a text file using the `FileReader` object `text` and displays its characters:

```
FileReader text = new
    FileReader("readme.txt");
int inByte;
do {
    inByte = text.read();
    if (inByte != -1)
        System.out.print( (char)inByte );
} while (inByte != -1);
System.out.println("");
text.close();
```

Because a character stream's `read()` method returns an integer, you must cast this to a character before displaying it or storing it in an array or using it to form a string. Every character has a numeric code that represents its position in the Unicode character set. The integer read off the stream is this numeric code.

If you want to read a line of text at a time instead of reading a file character by character, you can use the `BufferedReader` class in conjunction with a `FileReader`.

17

The BufferedReader class reads a character input stream and buffers it for better efficiency. You must have an existing Reader object of some kind in order to created a buffered version. The following constructors can be used to create a BufferedReader:

- BufferedReader(*Reader*)   Creates a buffered character stream associated with the specified Reader object, such as FileReader.

- BufferedReader(*Reader, int*)   Creates a buffered character stream associated with the specified Reader and with a buffer of *int* size.

A buffered character stream can be read using the read() and read(*char[], int, int*) methods described for FileReader. You can read a line of text using the readLine() method.

The readLine() method returns a String object containing the next line of text on the stream, not including the character or characters that represent the end of a line. If the end of the stream is reached, the value of the string returned will be equal to null.

An end-of-line is indicated by any of the following:

- A newline character ('\n')

- A carriage return character ('\r')

- A carriage return followed by a newline

The project contained in Listing 17.6 is a Java application that reads its own source file through a buffered character stream.

TYPE **LISTING 17.6.** THE FULL TEXT OF READSOURCE.JAVA.

```
 1: import java.io.*;
 2:
 3: public class ReadSource {
 4:     public static void main(String[] arguments) {
 5:         try {
 6:             FileReader file = new
 7:                 FileReader("ReadSource.java");
 8:             BufferedReader buff = new
 9:                 BufferedReader(file);
10:             boolean eof = false;
11:             while (!eof) {
12:                 String line = buff.readLine();
13:                 if (line == null)
14:                     eof = true;
15:                 else
16:                     System.out.println(line);
17:             }
18:             buff.close();
```

```
19:          } catch (IOException e) {
20:              System.out.println("Error -- " + e.toString());
21:          }
22:     }
23: }
```

Much of this program is comparable to projects created earlier today, as illustrated:

- Lines 6 and 7   An input source is created—the `FileReader` object associated with the file `ReadSource.java`.
- Lines 8 and 9   A buffering filter is associated with that input source—the `BufferedReader` object `buff`.
- Lines 11–17   A `readLine()` method is used inside a `while` loop to read the text file one line at a time. The loop ends when the method returns the value `null`.

The `ReadSource` application's output is the text file `ReadSource.java`.

Writing Text Files

The `FileWriter` class is used to write a character stream to a file. It's a subclass of `OutputStreamWriter`, which has behavior to convert Unicode character codes to bytes.

There are two `FileWriter` constructors: `FileWriter(String)` and `FileWriter(String, boolean)`. The string indicates the name of the file that the character stream will be directed into, which can include a folder path. The optional Boolean argument should equal `true` if the file is to be appended to an existing text file. As with other stream-writing classes, you must take care not to accidentally overwrite an existing file when you're not appending data.

There are three methods of `FileWriter` that can be used to write data to a stream:

- `write(int)`   Write a character.
- `write(char[], int, int)`   Write characters from the specified character array with the indicated starting point and number of characters written.
- `write(String, int, int)`   Write characters from the specified string with the indicated starting point and number of characters written.

The following example writes a character stream to a file using the `FileWriter` class and the `write(int)` method:

```
FileWriter letters = new FileWriter("alphabet.txt");
for (int i = 65; i < 91; i++)
    letters.write( (char)i );
letters.close();
```

The `close()` method is used to close the stream after all characters have been sent to the destination file. The following is the `alphabet.txt` file produced by this code:

ABCDEFGHIJKLMNOPQRSTUVWXYZ

The `BufferedWriter` class can be used to write a buffered character stream. This class' objects are created with the `BufferedWriter(Writer)` or `BufferedWriter(Writer, int)` constructors. The `Writer` argument can be any of the character output stream classes, such as `FileWriter`. The optional second argument is an integer indicating the size of the buffer to use.

`BufferedWriter` has the same three output methods as `FileWriter`: `write(int)`, `write(char[], int, int)`, and `write(String, int, int)`.

Another useful output method is `newLine()`, which sends the preferred end-of-line character (or characters) for the platform being used to run the program.

Tip	The different end-of-line markers can create conversion hassles when transferring files from one operating system to another, such as when a Windows 95 user uploads a file to a Web server that's running the Linux operating system. Using `newLine()` instead of a literal (such as `'\n'`) makes your program more user-friendly across different platforms.

The `close()` method is called to close the buffered character stream and make sure that all buffered data is sent to the stream's destination.

Files and Filename Filters

In all of the examples thus far, a string has been used to refer to the file that's involved in a stream operation. This often is sufficient for a program that uses files and streams, but if you want to copy files, rename files, or handle other tasks, a `File` object can be used.

`File`, which also is part of the `java.io` package, represents a file or folder reference. The following `File` constructors can be used:

- `File(String)` Creates a `File` object with the specified folder—no filename is indicated, so this refers only to a file folder.
- `File(String, String)` Creates a `File` object with the specified folder path and the specified name.
- `File(File, String)` Creates a `File` object with its path represented by the specified `File` and its name indicated by the specified `String`.

You can call several useful methods on a `File` object.

The `exists()` method returns a Boolean value indicating whether the file exists under the name and folder path established when the `File` object was created. If the file exists, you can use the `length()` method to return a `long` integer indicating the size of the file in bytes.

The `renameTo(File)` method renames the file to the name specified by the `File` argument. A Boolean value is returned, indicating whether the operation was successful.

The `delete()` or `deleteOnExit()` method should be called to delete a file or a folder. The `delete()` method attempts an immediate deletion (returning a Boolean value indicating whether it worked). The `deleteOnExit()` method waits to attempt deletion until the rest of the program has finished running. This method does not return a value—you couldn't do anything with the information—and the program must finish at some point for it to work.

The `mkdir()` method can be used to create the folder specified by the `File` object it is called on. It returns a Boolean value indicating success or failure. There is no comparable method to remove folders, since `delete()` can be used on folders as well as files.

As with any file-handling operations, these methods must be handled with care to avoid deleting the wrong files and folders or wiping out data. There's no method available to undelete a file or folder.

Each of the methods will throw a `SecurityException` if the program does not have the security to perform the file operation in question, so these need to be dealt with through a `try...catch` block or a `throws` clause in a method declaration.

The program in Listing 17.7 converts all of the text in a file to uppercase characters. The file is pulled in using a buffered input stream, and one character is read at a time. After the character is converted to uppercase, it is sent to a temporary file using a buffered output stream. `File` objects are used instead of strings to indicate the files involved, which makes it possible to rename and delete files as needed.

TYPE **LISTING 17.7.** THE FULL TEXT OF ALLCAPSDEMO.JAVA.

```
1: import java.io.*;
2:
3: public class AllCapsDemo {
4:     public static void main(String[] arguments) {
5:         AllCaps cap = new AllCaps(arguments[0]);
```

continues

LISTING **17.7.** CONTINUED

```
 6:            cap.convert();
 7:        }
 8: }
 9:
10: class AllCaps {
11:     String sourceName;
12:
13:     AllCaps(String sourceArg) {
14:         sourceName = sourceArg;
15:     }
16:
17:     void convert() {
18:         try {
19:             // Create file objects
20:             File source = new File(sourceName);
21:             File temp = new File("cap" + sourceName + ".tmp");
22:
23:             // Create input stream
24:             FileReader fr = new
25:                 FileReader(source);
26:             BufferedReader in = new
27:                 BufferedReader(fr);
28:
29:             // Create output stream
30:             FileWriter fw = new
31:                 FileWriter(temp);
32:             BufferedWriter out = new
33:                 BufferedWriter(fw);
34:
35:             boolean eof = false;
36:             int inChar = 0;
37:             do {
38:                 inChar = in.read();
39:                 if (inChar != -1) {
40:                   char outChar = Character.toUpperCase( (char)inChar );
41:                   out.write(outChar);
42:                 } else
43:                     eof = true;
44:             } while (!eof);
45:             in.close();
46:             out.close();
47:
48:             boolean deleted = source.delete();
49:             if (deleted)
50:                 temp.renameTo(source);
51:         } catch (IOException e) {
52:             System.out.println("Error -- " + e.toString());
53:         } catch (SecurityException se) {
54:             System.out.println("Error -- " + se.toString());
```

```
55:            }
56:        }
57: }
```

After you compile the program, you need a text file that can be converted to all-capital letters. One option is to make a copy of AllCapsDemo.java and give it a name like TempFile.java.

The name of the file to convert is specified at the command line when running AllCapsDemo, as in the following example:

```
java AllCapsDemo TempFile.java
```

This program does not produce any output. Load the converted file into a text editor to see the result of the application.

Summary

You learned how to work with streams today in two different directions: pulling data into a program over an input stream and sending data out of a program using an output stream.

You used byte streams for many types of non-textual data and character streams to handle text. Filters were associated with streams to alter the way information was delivered through a stream, or to alter the information itself.

Today's lesson covers most java.io package classes, but there are other types of streams you might want to explore. Piped streams are useful when communicating data between different threads, and byte array streams can connect programs to a computer's memory.

Because the stream classes in Java are so closely coordinated, you already possess most of the knowledge you need to use these other types of streams. The constructors, read methods, and write methods are largely identical.

Streams are a powerful way to extend the functionality of your Java programs because they offer a connection to any kind of data you might want to work with.

Tomorrow you see how streams reach the largest data source imaginable: the Internet.

17

Q&A

Q A C program that I use creates a file of integers and other data. Can I read this using a Java program?

A You can, but one thing you have to consider is whether your C program represents integers in the same manner a Java program represents them. As you may recall, all data can be represented as an individual byte or a series of bytes. An integer is represented in Java using four bytes that are arranged in what is called big-endian order. You can determine the integer value by combining the bytes from left-to-right. A C program implemented on an Intel PC is likely to represent integers in little-endian order, which means the bytes must be arranged from right-to-left to determine the result. You may have to learn about advanced techniques such as bit shifting in order to use a data file created with a programming language other than Java.

WEEK 3

DAY 18

Communicating Across the Internet

One of the more remarkable things about Java since its introduction is how Internet-aware the language is. As you might recall from Day 1, "A Fistful of Java," Java was developed initially as a language that would control a network of interactive devices called the Star7. Duke—the animated mascot of Sun who looks a bit like a dancing bicuspid—was the star of these devices.

Java's class library includes the `java.net` package, which makes it possible to communicate over a network with your Java programs. The package provides cross-platform abstractions for simple networking operations, including connecting and retrieving files by using common Web protocols and creating basic UNIX-like sockets.

Used in conjunction with input and output streams, reading and writing files over the network becomes as easy as reading or writing to files on the local disk.

Today you write some Java applications that are Net-aware and learn why it's harder to do the same thing with an applet. You create a program that can load a document over the World Wide Web and investigate how client-server programs are created.

Networking in Java

NEW TERM *Networking* is the capability of making connections from your applet or application to a system over the network. Networking in Java involves classes in the java.net package, which provide cross-platform abstractions for simple networking operations, including connecting and retrieving files by using common Web protocols and creating basic UNIX-like sockets. Used in conjunction with input and output streams, reading and writing files over the network becomes as easy as reading or writing to files on the local disk.

There are restrictions, of course. Java applets usually cannot read or write from the disk on the machine where the browser is running. Java applets cannot connect to systems other than the one on which they were originally stored. Even given these restrictions, you can accomplish a great deal and take advantage of the Web to read and process information over the Net.

This section describes two simple ways you can communicate with systems on the Net:

- getInputStream(), a method that opens a connection to an URL and enables you to extract data from that connection

- The socket classes, Socket and ServerSocket, which enable you to open standard socket connections to hosts and read to and write from those connections

Opening Web Connections

Rather than asking the browser to just load the contents of a file, sometimes you might want to get ahold of that file's contents so that your applet can use them. If the file you want to grab is stored on the Web and can be accessed using the more common URL forms (http, FTP, and so on), your Java program can use the URL class to get it.

For security reasons, applets by default can connect only to the same host from which they originally loaded. This means that if you have your applets stored on a system called www.prefect.com, the only machine your applet can open a connection to will be that same host—and that same hostname, so be careful with host aliases. If the file the applet wants to retrieve is on that same system, using URL connections is the easiest way to get it.

This security restriction will change how you write and test applets that load files through their URLs. Because you haven't been dealing with network connections, you've been able to do all your testing on the local disk simply by opening the HTML files in a browser or with the `appletviewer` tool. You cannot do this with applets that open network connections. In order for those applets to work correctly, you must do one of two things:

- Run your browser on the same machine on which your Web server is running. If you don't have access to your Web server, you can often install and run a Web server on your local machine.
- Upload your class and HTML files to your Web server each time you want to test them. You then run the applet off the uploaded Web page instead of running it locally.

You'll know when you're not doing things right in regard to making sure your applet and the connection it's opening are on the same server. If you try to load an applet or a file from different servers, you get a security exception, along with a lot of other scary error messages printed to your screen or to the Java console.

Because of this, you might want to work with applications when you're connecting to the Internet and using its resources.

Move on to the methods and classes for retrieving files from the Web.

Opening a Stream Over the Net

As you learned during Day 17, "Handling Data Through Java Streams," there are several ways you can pull information through a stream into your Java programs. The classes and methods you choose depend on what form the information is in and what you want to do with it.

One of the resources you can reach from your Java programs is a text document on the World Wide Web, whether it's an HTML file or some other kind of plain text document.

You can use a four-step process to load a text document off the Web and read it line by line:

- Create an `URL` object that represents the resource's World Wide Web address.
- Create an `URLConnection` object that can load that URL and make a connection to the site hosting it.
- Using the `getInputStream()` method of that `URLConnection` object, create an `InputStreamReader` that can read a stream of data from the URL.

18

- Using that input stream reader, create a `BufferedReader` object that can efficiently read characters from an input stream.

There's a lot of interaction going on between Point A—the Web document—and Point B—your Java program. The URL is used to set up an URL connection, which is used to set up an input stream reader, which is used to set up a buffered input stream reader. The need to catch any exceptions that occur along the way adds more complexity to the process.

This is a confusing process, so it's useful to step through a program that implements it. Here's an example of an application that uses the four-step technique to open a connection to a Web site and read an HTML document from it. When the document is fully loaded, it is displayed in a text area.

Listing 18.1 shows the code; Figure 18.1 shows the result after the file has been read.

FIGURE 18.1.

The GetFile *application.*

LISTING 18.1. THE FULL TEXT OF GETFILE.JAVA.

```
 1: import java.awt.*;
 2: import java.awt.event.*;
 3: import java.net.*;
 4: import java.io.*;
 5:
 6: public class GetFile extends Frame implements Runnable {
 7:     Thread runner;
 8:     URL page;
 9:     TextArea box = new TextArea("Getting text ...");
10:
11:     public GetFile() {
12:         super("Get File");
13:         add(box);
14:         try {
15:             page = new
                 URL("http://www.prefect.com/java21pre/index.html");
16:         }
17:         catch (MalformedURLException e) {
18:             System.out.println("Bad URL: " + page);
19:         }
20:     }
```

```
21:
22:     public static void main(String[] arguments) {
23:         GetFile frame = new GetFile();
24:
25:         WindowListener l = new WindowAdapter() {
26:             public void windowClosing(WindowEvent e) {
27:                 System.exit(0);
28:             }
29:         };
30:         frame.addWindowListener(l);
31:
32:         frame.pack();
33:         frame.setVisible(true);
34:         if (frame.runner == null) {
35:             frame.runner = new Thread(frame);
36:             frame.runner.start();
37:         }
38:     }
39:
40:     public void run() {
41:         URLConnection conn = null;
42:         InputStreamReader in;
43:         BufferedReader data;
44:         String line;
45:         StringBuffer buf = new StringBuffer();
46:         try {
47:             conn = this.page.openConnection();
48:             conn.connect();
49:             box.setText("Connection opened ...");
50:             in = new InputStreamReader(conn.getInputStream());
51:             data = new BufferedReader(in);
52:             box.setText("Reading data ...");
53:             while ((line = data.readLine()) != null) {
54:                 buf.append(line + "\n");
55:             }
56:             box.setText(buf.toString());
57:         }
58:         catch (IOException e) {
59:             System.out.println("IO Error:" + e.getMessage());
60:         }
61:     }
62: }
```

This application is a subclass of the Frame class, and it contains only one component: a text area. The program is threaded so that the work of loading the HTML document occurs in its own thread. This becomes necessary because network connections and stream input can be processor-intensive and time-intensive undertakings. Putting this work into its own thread leaves the rest of the Java windowing system free to handle its normal tasks like updating the display area and receiving user input.

The constructor method `GetFile()` in lines 11–20 sets up the `URL` object and the text area in which that document will be displayed. The URL in this example is `http://www.prefect.com/java21pre/index.html`, which is the main page of this book's Web site. It could easily be any other Web page you know about—experiment with others if you like.

The work takes place inside the `run()` method (lines 40–61). First, the three objects you need to get to the document's data are initialized—`URLConnection`, `InputStreamReader`, and `BufferedReader`. In addition, two objects are created to actually hold the data when it arrives—a `String` and a `StringBuffer`.

Lines 47 and 48 open an URL connection, which is necessary to getting an input stream from that connection.

Line 50 uses the URL connection's `getInputStream()` method to create a new input stream reader.

Line 51 uses that input stream reader to create a new buffered input stream reader—a `BufferedReader` object called `data`.

Once you have this buffered reader, you can use its `readLine()` method to read a line of text from the input stream. The buffered reader puts characters in a buffer as they arrive, and pulls them out of the buffer when requested.

The `while` loop in lines 53–55 reads the Web document line by line, appending each line to the `StringBuffer` object that was created to hold the page's text. A string buffer is used instead of a string because you can't modify a string at runtime in this manner.

Once all the data has been read, line 56 converts the string buffer into a string with the `toString()` method and then puts that result in the program's text area.

One thing to note about this example is that the part of the code that opened a network connection, read from the file, and created a string is surrounded by a `try` and `catch` statement. If any errors occur while you're trying to read or process the file, these statements enable you to recover from them without the entire program crashing. (In this case the program exits with an error because there's little else to be done if the application can't read the file.) The `try` and `catch` give you the ability to handle and recover from errors.

 Note

> One thing that isn't discussed here is the event-handling code in lines 25–30. This is required for the application to close successfully when its window is closed—you'll learn about event handlers for applications during Day 20, "Handling User Events with Swing."

Sockets

For networking applications beyond what the URL and URLconnection classes offer (for example, for other protocols or for more general networking applications), Java provides the Socket and ServerSocket classes as an abstraction of standard TCP socket programming techniques.

> **Note**
>
> Java also provides facilities for using datagram (UDP) sockets, which are not covered here. See the Java documentation for the java.net package if you're interested in working with datagrams.

The Socket class provides a client-side socket interface similar to standard UNIX sockets. Create a new instance of Socket to open a connection (where *hostName* is the host to connect to and *portNum* is the port number):

```
Socket connection = new Socket(hostName, portNum);
```

> **Note**
>
> When using sockets in an applet, you are still subject to the default applet security restrictions that prevent you from connecting to any system other than the same one the applet came from.

18

Once the socket is open, you can use input and output streams to read and write from that socket:

```
BufferedInputStream bis = new
    BufferedInputStream(connection.getInputStream());
DataInputStream in = new DataInputStream(bis);
BufferedOutputStream bos = new
    BufferedOutputStream(connection.getOutputStream());
DataOutputStream out= new DataOutputStream(bos);
```

Once you're done with the socket, don't forget to close it. (This also closes all the input and output streams you may have set up for that socket.)

```
connection.close();
```

Server-side sockets work similarly, with the exception of the accept() method. A server socket listens on a TCP port for a connection from a client; when a client connects to that port, the accept() method accepts a connection from that client. By using both client and server sockets, you can create applications that communicate with each other over the network.

Create a new instance of `ServerSocket` with the port number in order to create a server socket and bind it to a port:

```
ServerSocket sConnection = new ServerSocket(8888);
```

Use the `accept()` method to listen on that port (and to accept a connection from any clients if one is made):

```
sConnection.accept();
```

Once the socket connection is made you can use input and output streams to read from and write to the client.

In the next section, "Trivia: A Simple Socket Client and Server," you work through some code to implement a simple socket-based application.

To extend the behavior of the socket classes—for example, to allow network connections to work across a firewall or a proxy—you can use the abstract class `SocketImpl` and the interface `SocketImplFactory` to create a new transport-layer socket implementation. This design fits with the original goal of Java's socket classes: to allow those classes to be portable to other systems with different transport mechanisms. The problem with this mechanism is that while it works for simple cases, it prevents you from adding other protocols on top of TCP (for example, to implement an encryption mechanism such as SSL) or for having multiple socket implementations per Java runtime.

For these reasons, sockets were extended after Java 1.02 so that the `Socket` and `ServerSocket` classes are not final and extendable. You can create subclasses of these classes that use either the default socket implementation or one of your own making. This allows much more flexible network capabilities.

Several other new features to the `java.net` package have been added:

- New options for sockets, based on BSD's socket options (for example, `TCP_NODELAY`, `IP_MULTICAST_LOOP`, `SO_BINDADDR`)
- Many new subclasses of the `SocketException` class, to represent network errors on a finer level of granularity than in Java 1.02 (for example, `NoRouteToHostException` or `ConnectException`)

Trivia: A Simple Socket Client and Server

To finish up the discussion on networking in Java, here's an example of a Java program that uses the Socket classes to implement a simple network-based application called `Trivia`.

The Trivia example works like this: The server program waits patiently for a client to connect. When a client connects, the server sends a question and waits for a response. On the other end, the client receives the question and prompts the user for an answer. The user types in an answer, which is sent back to the server. The server then checks to see whether the answer is correct and notifies the user. The server follows this up by asking the client whether it wants another question. If so, the process repeats.

Designing Trivia

It's usually a good idea to perform a brief preliminary design before you start churning out code. With that in mind, take a look at what is required of the Trivia server and client. On the server side you need a program that monitors a particular port on the host machine for client connections. When a client is detected, the server picks a random question and sends it to the client over the specified port. The server then enters a wait state until it hears back from the client. When it gets an answer from the client, the server checks it and notifies the client whether it is correct or incorrect. The server then asks the client whether it wants another question, upon which it enters another wait state until the client answers. Finally, the server either repeats the process by asking another question or it terminates the connection with the client. In summary, the server performs the following tasks:

1. Waits for a client to connect
2. Accepts the client connection
3. Sends a random question to the client
4. Waits for an answer from the client
5. Checks the answer and notifies the client
6. Asks the client whether it wants another question
7. Waits for an answer from the client
8. Goes back to step 3 if necessary

The client side of this Trivia example is an application that runs from a command line (it's easier to demonstrate that way). The client is responsible for connecting to the server and waiting for a question. When it receives a question from the server, the client displays it to the user and allows the user to type in an answer. This answer is sent back to the server and the client again waits for the server's response. The client displays the server's response to the user and allows the user to confirm whether he or she wants another question. The client then sends the user's response to the server and exits if the user declined any more questions. The client's primary tasks are as follows:

18

1. Connect to the server

2. Wait for a question to be sent

3. Display the question and input the user's answer

4. Send the answer to the server

5. Wait for a reply from the server

6. Display the server's reply and prompt the user to confirm another question

7. Send the user's reply to the server

8. Go back to step 2 if necessary

Implementing the Trivia Server

The heart of the Trivia example lies in the server. The Trivia server program is called TriviaServer. The instance variables defined in the TriviaServer class follow:

```
private static final int PORTNUM = 1234;
private static final int WAITFORCLIENT = 0;
private static final int WAITFORANSWER = 1;
private static final int WAITFORCONFIRM = 2;
private String[] questions;
private String[] answers;
private ServerSocket serverSocket;
private int numQuestions;
private int num = 0;
private int state = WAITFORCLIENT;
private Random rand = new Random();
```

The WAITFORCLIENT, WAITFORANSWER, and WAITFORCONFIRM variables are all state constants that define different states the server can be in; you see these constants in action in a moment. The questions and answers variables are string arrays used to store the questions and corresponding answers. The serverSocket instance variable keeps up with the server-socket connection. numQuestions is used to store the total number of questions, while num is the number of the current question being asked. The state variable holds the current state of the server as defined by the three state constants (WAITFORCLIENT, WAITFORANSWER, and WAITFORCONFIRM). Finally, the rand variable is used to pick questions at random.

The TriviaServer constructor doesn't do much except create a ServerSocket rather than a DatagramSocket. Check it out:

```
public TriviaServer() {
    super("TriviaServer");
    try {
        serverSocket = new ServerSocket(PORTNUM);
        System.out.println("TriviaServer up and running ...");
```

```
        }
    catch (IOException e) {
        System.err.println("Exception: couldn't create socket");
        System.exit(1);
    }
}
```

It's the `run()` method in the `TriviaServer` class where most of the action is. The source code for the `run()` method is as follows:

```
public void run() {
    Socket clientSocket = null;

    // Initialize the arrays of questions and answers
    if (!initQnA()) {
        System.err.println("Error: couldn't initialize questions and
answers");
        return;
    }

    // Look for clients and ask trivia questions
    while (true) {
        // Wait for a client
        if (serverSocket == null)
            return;
        try {
            clientSocket = serverSocket.accept();
        }
        catch (IOException e) {
            System.err.println("Exception: couldn't connect to client
socket");
            System.exit(1);
        }

        // Perform the question/answer processing
        try {
            InputStreamReader isr = new
InputStreamReader(clientSocket.getInputStream());
            BufferedReader is = new BufferedReader(isr);
            PrintWriter os = new PrintWriter(new
                BufferedOutputStream(clientSocket.getOutputStream()),
false);
            String outLine;

            // Output server request
            outLine = processInput(null);
            os.println(outLine);
            os.flush();

            // Process and output user input
            while (true) {
```

18

```
            String inLine = is.readLine();
            if (inLine.length() > 0) {
                outLine = processInput(inLine);
                os.println(outLine);
                os.flush();
                if (outLine.equals("Bye."))
                    break;
            }
        }

        // Cleanup
        os.close();
        is.close();
        clientSocket.close();
    }
    catch (Exception e) {
        System.err.println("Exception: " + e);
        e.printStackTrace();
    }
  }
}
```

The run() method first initializes the questions and answers by calling initQnA(). You learn about the initQnA() method in a moment. An infinite while loop that waits for a client connection is then entered. When a client connects, the appropriate I/O streams are created and the communication is handled via the processInput() method. You learn about processInput() next. processInput() continually processes client responses and handles asking new questions until the client decides not to receive any more questions. This is evidenced by the server sending the string "Bye.". The run() method then cleans up the streams and client socket.

The processInput()method keeps up with the server state and manages the logic of the whole question/answer process. The source code for processInput is as follows:

```
String processInput(String inStr) {
    String outStr = null;

    switch (state) {
        case WAITFORCLIENT:
            // Ask a question
            outStr = questions[num];
            state = WAITFORANSWER;
            break;

        case WAITFORANSWER:
            // Check the answer
            if (inStr.equalsIgnoreCase(answers[num]))
                outStr = "That's correct! Want another? (y/n)";
            else
```

```
                    outStr = "Wrong, the correct answer is " + answers[num] +
                        ". Want another? (y/n)";
                state = WAITFORCONFIRM;
                break;

            case WAITFORCONFIRM:
                // See if they want another question
                if (inStr.equalsIgnoreCase("Y")) {
                    num = Math.abs(rand.nextInt()) % questions.length;
                    outStr = questions[num];
                    state = WAITFORANSWER;
                }
                else {
                    outStr = "Bye.";
                    state = WAITFORCLIENT;
                }
                break;
        }
        return outStr;
    }
}
```

The first thing to note about the processInput() method is the outStr local variable. This string's value is sent back to the client in the run method when processInput returns, so keep an eye on how processInput uses outStr to convey information to the client.

In TriviaServer, the state WAITFORCLIENT represents the server when it is idle and waiting for a client connection. Understand that each case statement in processInput() represents the server leaving the given state. For example, the WAITFORCLIENT case statement is entered when the server has just left the WAITFORCLIENT state—a client has just connected to the server. When this occurs, the server sets the output string to the current question and sets the state to WAITFORANSWER.

If the server is leaving the WAITFORANSWER state, the client has responded with an answer. processInput() checks the client's answer against the correct answer and sets the output string accordingly. It then sets the state to WAITFORCONFIRM.

The WAITFORCONFIRM state represents the server waiting for a confirmation answer from the client. In processInput(), the WAITFORCONFIRM case statement indicates that the server is leaving the state because the client has returned a confirmation (yes or no). If the client answered yes with a y, processInput picks a new question and sets the state back to WAITFORANSWER. Otherwise, the server tells the client "Bye." and returns the state to WAITFORCLIENT to await a new client connection.

The questions and answers in Trivia are stored in a text file called QnA.txt, which is organized with questions and answers on alternating lines. Each question is followed by

18

its answer on the following line, which is in turn followed by the next question. A listing
of the QnA.txt file follows:

```
What caused the craters on the moon?
meteorites
How far away is the moon (in miles)?
239000
How far away is the sun (in millions of miles)?
93
Is the Earth a perfect sphere?
no
What is the internal temperature of the Earth (in degrees F)?
9000
```

The initQnA()method handles the work of reading the questions and answers from the
text file and storing them in separate string arrays, as shown here:

```
private boolean initQnA() {
    try {
        File inFile = new File("QnA.txt");
        FileInputStream inStream = new FileInputStream(inFile);
        byte[] data = new byte[(int)inFile.length()];

        // Read the questions and answers into a byte array
        if (inStream.read(data) <= 0) {
            System.err.println("Error: couldn't read questions and
answers");
            return false;
        }
        // See how many question/answer pairs there are
        for (int i = 0; i < data.length; i++)
            if (data[i] == (byte)'\n')
                numQuestions++;
        numQuestions /= 2;
        questions = new String[numQuestions];
        answers = new String[numQuestions];

        // Parse the questions and answers into arrays of strings
        int start = 0, index = 0;
        boolean isQ = true;
        for (int i = 0; i < data.length; i++)
            if (data[i] == (byte)'\n') {
                if (isQ) {
                    questions[index] = new String(data, start, i - start - 1);
                    isQ = false;
                }
                else {
                    answers[index] = new String(data, start, i - start - 1);
                    isQ = true;
```

```
                        index++;
                  }
            start = i + 1;
            }
      }
      catch (FileNotFoundException e) {
            System.err.println("Exception: couldn't find the question file");
            return false;
      }
      catch (IOException e) {
            System.err.println("Exception: I/O error trying to read
questions");
            return false;
      }

      return true;
}
```

The `initQnA()` method uses two arrays and fills them with alternating strings from the `QnA.txt` file: first a question, then an answer, alternating until the end of the file is reached.

The only remaining method in `TriviaServer` is `main()`; `main` simply creates the server object and gets it started with a call to the `start` method:

```
public static void main(String[] arguments) {
    TriviaServer server = new TriviaServer();
    server.start();
}
```

Listing 18.2 contains the full source code for the server application.

TYPE   **LISTING 18.2.** THE FULL TEXT OF TRIVIASERVER.JAVA.

```
 1: import java.io.*;
 2: import java.net.*;
 3: import java.util.Random;
 4:
 5: public class TriviaServer extends Thread {
 6:     private static final int PORTNUM = 1234;
 7:     private static final int WAITFORCLIENT = 0;
 8:     private static final int WAITFORANSWER = 1;
 9:     private static final int WAITFORCONFIRM = 2;
10:     private String[] questions;
11:     private String[] answers;
12:     private ServerSocket serverSocket;
13:     private int numQuestions;
14:     private int num = 0;
```

continues

LISTING 18.2. CONTINUED

```
15:     private int state = WAITFORCLIENT;
16:     private Random rand = new Random();
17:
18:     public TriviaServer() {
19:         super("TriviaServer");
20:         try {
21:             serverSocket = new ServerSocket(PORTNUM);
22:             System.out.println("TriviaServer up and running ...");
23:         }
24:         catch (IOException e) {
25:             System.err.println("Exception: couldn't create socket");
26:             System.exit(1);
27:         }
28:     }
29:
30:     public static void main(String[] arguments) {
31:         TriviaServer server = new TriviaServer();
32:         server.start();
33:     }
34:
35:     public void run() {
36:         Socket clientSocket = null;
37:
38:         // Initialize the arrays of questions and answers
39:         if (!initQnA()) {
40:             System.err.println("Error: couldn't initialize questions
                and answers");
41:             return;
42:         }
43:
44:         // Look for clients and ask trivia questions
45:         while (true) {
46:             // Wait for a client
47:             if (serverSocket == null)
48:                 return;
49:             try {
50:                 clientSocket = serverSocket.accept();
51:             }
52:             catch (IOException e) {
53:                 System.err.println("Exception: couldn't connect to
                    client socket");
54:                 System.exit(1);
55:             }
56:
57:             // Perform the question/answer processing
58:             try {
59:                 InputStreamReader isr = new
                    InputStreamReader(clientSocket.getInputStream());
```

```
60:                    BufferedReader is = new BufferedReader(isr);
61:                    PrintWriter os = new PrintWriter(new
62:                    BufferedOutputStream(clientSocket.getOutputStream()),
                       false);
63:                    String outLine;
64:
65:                    // Output server request
66:                    outLine = processInput(null);
67:                    os.println(outLine);
68:                    os.flush();
69:
70:                    // Process and output user input
71:                    while (true) {
72:                        String inLine = is.readLine();
73:                        if (inLine.length() > 0) {
74:                            outLine = processInput(inLine);
75:                            os.println(outLine);
76:                            os.flush();
77:                            if (outLine.equals("Bye."))
78:                                break;
79:                        }
80:                    }
81:
82:                    // Cleanup
83:                    os.close();
84:                    is.close();
85:                    clientSocket.close();
86:                }
87:            catch (Exception e) {
88:                System.err.println("Exception: " + e);
89:                e.printStackTrace();
90:            }
91:        }
92:    }
93:
94:    private boolean initQnA() {
95:        try {
96:            File inFile = new File("QnA.txt");
97:            FileInputStream inStream = new FileInputStream(inFile);
98:            byte[] data = new byte[(int)inFile.length()];
99:
100:            // Read the questions and answers into a byte array
101:            if (inStream.read(data) <= 0) {
102:                System.err.println("Error: couldn't read questions
                    and answers");
103:                return false;
104:            }
105:
```

continues

18

LISTING 18.2. CONTINUED

```
106:                    // See how many question/answer pairs there are
107:                    for (int i = 0; i < data.length; i++)
108:                        if (data[i] == (byte)'\n')
109:                            numQuestions++;
110:                    numQuestions /= 2;
111:                    questions = new String[numQuestions];
112:                    answers = new String[numQuestions];
113:
114:                    // Parse the questions and answers into arrays of strings
115:                    int start = 0, index = 0;
116:                    boolean isQ = true;
117:                    for (int i = 0; i < data.length; i++)
118:                        if (data[i] == (byte)'\n') {
119:                            if (isQ) {
120:                                questions[index] = new String(data, start,
                                    i - start - 1);
121:                                isQ = false;
122:                            }
123:                            else {
124:                                answers[index] = new String(data, start,
                                    i - start - 1);
125:                                isQ = true;
126:                                index++;
127:                            }
128:                            start = i + 1;
129:                        }
130:                }
131:            catch (FileNotFoundException e) {
132:                System.err.println("Exception: couldn't find the question
                    file");
133:                return false;
134:            }
135:            catch (IOException e) {
136:                System.err.println("Exception: I/O error trying to read
                    questions");
137:                return false;
138:            }
139:
140:            return true;
141:        }
142:
143:        String processInput(String inStr) {
144:            String outStr = null;
145:
146:            switch (state) {
147:                case WAITFORCLIENT:
148:                    // Ask a question
```

```
149:                    outStr = questions[num];
150:                    state = WAITFORANSWER;
151:                    break;
152:
153:                case WAITFORANSWER:
154:                    // Check the answer
155:                    if (inStr.equalsIgnoreCase(answers[num]))
156:                        outStr = "That's correct! Want another? (y/n)";
157:                    else
158:                        outStr = "Wrong, the correct answer is " +
                             answers[num] +
159:                            ". Want another? (y/n)";
160:                    state = WAITFORCONFIRM;
161:                    break;
162:
163:                case WAITFORCONFIRM:
164:                    // See if they want another question
165:                    if (inStr.equalsIgnoreCase("Y")) {
166:                        num = Math.abs(rand.nextInt()) %
                             questions.length;
167:                        outStr = questions[num];
168:                        state = WAITFORANSWER;
169:                    }
170:                    else {
171:                        outStr = "Bye.";
172:                        state = WAITFORCLIENT;
173:                    }
174:                    break;
175:            }
176:            return outStr;
177:    }
178: }
```

Implementing the Trivia Client

Because the client side of the Trivia example requires the user to type in answers and receive responses from the server, it is more straightforward to implement as a command-line application. This might not be as cute as a graphical applet, but it makes it very easy to see the communication events as they unfold. The client application is called Trivia.java.

The only instance variable defined in the Trivia class is PORTNUM, which defines the port number used by both the client and server. There is also only one method defined in the Trivia class: main(). The source code for the main() method is included in Listing 18.3.

TYPE   **LISTING 18.3.** THE FULL TEXT OF TRIVIA.JAVA.

```
 1: import java.io.*;
 2: import java.net.*;
 3:
 4: public class Trivia {
 5:     private static final int PORTNUM = 1234;
 6:
 7:     public static void main(String[] arguments) {
 8:         Socket socket = null;
 9:         InputStreamReader isr = null;
10:         BufferedReader in = null;
11:         PrintWriter out = null;
12:         String address;
13:
14:         // Check the command-line args for the host address
15:         if (arguments.length != 1) {
16:             System.out.println("Usage: java Trivia <address>");
17:             return;
18:         }
19:         else
20:             address = arguments[0];
21:
22:         // Initialize the socket and streams
23:         try {
24:             socket = new Socket(address, PORTNUM);
25:             isr = new InputStreamReader(socket.getInputStream());
26:             in = new BufferedReader(isr);
27:             out = new PrintWriter(socket.getOutputStream(),true);
28:         }
29:         catch (IOException e) {
30:             System.err.println("Exception: couldn't create stream
                socket "
31:                 + e.getMessage());
32:             System.exit(1);
33:         }
34:
35:         // Process user input and server responses
36:         try {
37:             StringBuffer str = new StringBuffer(128);
38:             String inStr;
39:             int c;
40:
41:             while ((inStr = in.readLine()) != null) {
42:                 System.out.println("Server: " + inStr);
43:                 if (inStr.equals("Bye."))
44:                     break;
45:                 while ((c = System.in.read()) != '\n')
46:                     str.append((char)c);
47:                 System.out.println("Client: " + str);
```

```
48:                        out.println(str.toString());
49:                        out.flush();
50:                        str.setLength(0);
51:                    }
52:                    // Cleanup
53:                    out.close();
54:                    in.close();
55:                    socket.close();
56:                }
57:                catch (IOException e) {
58:                    System.err.println("I/O error: "+ e.toString());
59:                }
60:        }
61: }
```

The first interesting thing you might notice about the `main()` method is that it looks for a command-line argument. The server address, such as `prefect.com`, is the command-line argument required of the `Trivia` client. Because this is a Java application and not an applet, it's not enough to connect back to the server where the applet came from—there is no default server, so you can connect to any server you want to. In the client application you either have to hard-code the server address or ask for it as a command-line argument. If you hard-code this, you must recompile any time you want to change something. Hence the command-line argument!

Note

> Most readers probably won't have access to a Web server that runs server-side Java programs like the `TriviaServer` application. On some operating systems, you can test server programs by running the `Trivia` server in one window and the `Trivia` client in another window, using the domain name `"localhost"`. The following is an example:
>
> `java Trivia "localhost"`
>
> This causes Java to look at the local host—in other words, the system running the application—for a server to make contact with. Depending on how Internet connections have been configured on your system, you might need to log on to the Internet before a successful socket connection can be made between the `Trivia` client and its server.

If the server address command-line argument is valid (not `null`), the `main()` method creates the necessary socket and I/O streams. It then enters a `while` loop, where it processes information from the server and transmits user requests back to the server. When the server quits sending information, the `while` loop falls through and the `main()` method cleans up the socket and streams—and that's all there is to the `Trivia` client!

18

Running Trivia

Like Fortune, the Trivia server must be running in order for the client to work. To get things started you must first run the server by using the Java interpreter. This is done from a command line, like this:

```
java TriviaServer
```

The Trivia client is also run from a command line, but you must specify a server address as the only argument. An example of running the Trivia client and connecting to the server localhost follows:

```
java Trivia "localhost"
```

You also can try to run it using the IP address representing the "localhost" port. This command is as follows:

```
java Trivia "127.0.0.1"
```

After running the Trivia client and answering a few questions, you should see output similar to this:

```
Server: What is the internal temperature of the Earth (in degrees
F)?
Client: meteorites
Server: Wrong, the correct answer is 9000. Want another? (y/n)
Client: y
Server: Is the Earth a perfect sphere?
Client: 93
Server: Wrong, the correct answer is no. Want another? (y/n)
Client: y
Server: What is the internal temperature of the Earth (in degrees
F)?
Client: 9000
Server: That's correct! Want another? (y/n)
Client: n
Server: Bye.
```

Applets and URL Objects

Because applets run inside Web browsers, it's nice to be able to use the capability of a browser to load new Web pages. Java provides a mechanism to tell the browser to load a new page. One use for this mechanism would be to create animated image maps that load a new page when clicked.

Creating Links Inside Applets

As you have learned, addresses on the World Wide Web are represented in Java by URL objects. A URL represents anything you can link to on the Web, including pages, graphics, sound files, and other types of information. You create a new instance of the class URL to link to a new page.

To create a new URL object, use one of four different constructors:

- URL*(String)* creates an URL object from a full Web address such as
  `http://www.prefect.com/java21pre` or `ftp://ftp.netscape.com`.

- URL*(URL, String)* creates an URL object with a base address provided by the specified *URL* and a relative path provided by the *String*. You can use getDocumentBase() for the URL of the page containing your applet, or getCodeBase() for the URL of the applet's class file. The relative path will be tacked onto the base address.

- URL*(String, String, int, String)* creates a new URL object, given a protocol (such as HTTP, or FTP), host name (such as `www.prefect.com` or `ftp.netcom.com`), port number (80 for HTTP), and a filename or path name.

- URL*(String, String, String)* is the same as the previous constructor minus the port number.

When you use the URL*(String)* constructor, you must deal with MalformedURLException objects. You could use a try...catch block, as shown in the following code:

```
try {
    theURL = new URL("http://www.mcp.com");
} catch (MalformedURLException e) {
    System.out.println("Bad URL: " + theURL);
}
```

Once you have an URL object, all you have to do is pass it to the browser. This causes the browser to load the address:

```
getAppletContext().showDocument(theURL);
```

The browser that contains the Java applet with this code will then load and display the document at that URL.

Listing 18.4 contains two classes: ButtonLink and a helper class called Bookmark. The ButtonLink applet displays three buttons that represent important Web locations; the buttons are shown in Figure 18.2. Clicking the buttons causes the document to be loaded from the locations to which those buttons refer.

FIGURE **18.2.**

The ButtonLink applet.

This applet must be run from inside a browser for the links to work, and is written using 1.02 event-handling techniques so that it can run on the widest range of browsers. You get a deprecated warning when compiling it with the Java 2 javac tool.

TYPE **LISTING 18.4.** THE FULL TEXT OF BUTTONLINK.JAVA.

```
1: import java.awt.*;
2: import java.net.*;
3:
4: public class ButtonLink extends java.applet.Applet {
5:     Bookmark bmList[] = new Bookmark[3];
6:
7:     public void init() {
8:         bmList[0] = new Bookmark("Sams Teach Yourself Java 1.2 in 21
            Days",
9:             "http://www.prefect.com/java21pre");
10:        bmList[1] = new Bookmark("Macmillan Computer Publishing",
11:            "http://www.mcp.com");
12:        bmList[2]= new Bookmark("Sun's Java Site",
13:            "http://java.sun.com");
14:
15:        GridLayout gl = new GridLayout(bmList.length, 1, 10, 10);
16:        setLayout(gl);
17:        for (int i = 0; i < bmList.length; i++) {
18:            add(new Button(bmList[i].name));
19:        }
20:    }
21:
22:    public boolean action(Event evt, Object arg) {
23:        if (evt.target instanceof Button) {
24:            linkTo( (String)arg );
25:            return true;
```

```
26:            }
27:            else return false;
28:     }
29:
30:     void linkTo(String name) {
31:            URL theURL = null;
32:            for (int i = 0; i < bmList.length; i++) {
33:                if (name.equals(bmList[i].name))
34:                    theURL = bmList[i].url;
35:            }
36:            if (theURL != null)
37:                getAppletContext().showDocument(theURL);
38:     }
39: }
40:
41: class Bookmark {
42:     String name;
43:     URL url;
44:
45:     Bookmark(String name, String theURL) {
46:            this.name = name;
47:            try {
48:                this.url = new URL(theURL);
49:            } catch (MalformedURLException e) {
50:                System.out.println("Bad URL: " + theURL);
51:            }
52:     }
53: }
```

This applet can be tested using the following HTML:

```
<APPLET CODE="ButtonLink.class" HEIGHT=120 WIDTH=240>
</APPLET>
```

Two classes make up this applet. The first, ButtonLink, implements the actual applet itself; the second, Bookmark, is a class representing a bookmark. Bookmarks have two parts: a name and an URL.

This particular applet creates three bookmark instances (lines 8-13) and stores them in an array of bookmarks. This applet easily could be modified to accept bookmarks as parameters from an HTML file. For each bookmark, a button is created whose label is the value of the bookmark's name.

The linkTo() method is called when the buttons are pressed. linkTo(), defined in lines 30-38, extracts the name of the button from the event, uses it to look up the actual URL from the Bookmark object, and then tells the browser to load the URL referenced by that bookmark.

Communicating Between Applets

Sometimes you want to have an HTML page that has several different applets on it. To do this, all you have to do is include several different iterations of the <APPLET> tag. The browser will create different instances of your applet for each one that appears on the HTML page.

What if you want to communicate between those applets? What if you want a change in one applet to affect the other applets in some way? The best way to do this is to use the applet context to get to different applets on the same page.

> **Note**
>
> Before you do extensive work with interapplet communication, be fore-warned that the mechanism described in this section is implemented differently (and often unreliably) in different browsers and different Java environments. If you need to rely on communicating between applets for your Web pages, make sure you test those applets extensively in different browsers on different platforms.

 As you have learned when dealing with graphics, a *context* is a means of describing the environment of which something is a part. An *applet context*, which is defined in the AppletContext class, is used for interapplet communication.

To get an instance of this class for your applet, you use the getAppletContext()method rather than calling a constructor of some kind. You've already seen the getAppletContext() method used for other things; you also can use it to work with the other applets on the page.

For example, to call a method named sendMessage() on all applets on a page, including the current one, use the getApplets() method and a for loop that looks something like this:

```
for (Enumeration e = getAppletContext().getApplets();
    e.hasMoreElements();) {
    Applet current = (MyAppletSubclass)(e.nextElement());
    current.sendMessage();
}
```

The getApplets() method returns an Enumeration object with a list of the applets on the page. Iterating over the Enumeration object in this way enables you to access each element in the Enumeration in turn. Note that each element in the Enumeration object is an instance of the Object class; to get that applet to behave the way you want it to (and accept messages from other applets), you have to cast it to be an instance of your applet subclass (here, the class MyAppletSubclass).

It's slightly more complicated to call a method in a specific applet. To do this, you give your applets names and then refer to each one by name inside the body of code for it.

To give an applet a name, use the NAME attribute to <APPLET> in your HTML file:

```
<P>This applet sends information:
<APPLET CODE="MyApplet.class" WIDTH=100 HEIGHT=150
NAME="sender">
</APPLET>
<P>This applet receives information from the sender:
<APPLET CODE="MyApplet.class" WIDTH=100 HEIGHT=150
NAME="receiver">
</APPLET>
```

To get a reference to another applet on the same page, use the getApplet() method from the applet context with the name of that applet. This gives you a reference to the applet with that name. You can then refer to that applet as if it were just another object: calling methods, setting its instance variables, and so on. Here's some code that does just that:

```
// get ahold of the receiver applet
Applet receiver = (MyAppletSubclass)
getAppletContext().getApplet("receiver");
// tell it to update itself.
receiver.update(text, value);
```

18

In this example, you use the getApplet() method to get a reference to the applet with the name receiver. Note that the object returned by getApplet() is an instance of the generic Applet class; you'll most likely want to cast that object to an instance of your subclass. Given the reference to the named applet, you can then call methods in that applet as if it were just another object in your own environment. For example, if both applets have an update() method, you can tell the receiver to update itself by using the information the current applet has.

Naming your applets and then referring to them by using the methods described in this section enables them to communicate and stay in sync with each other, providing uniform behavior for all the applets on your page.

Summary

Networking has many applications of which your applications can make use. You may not have realized it, but the GetFile project was a rudimentary Web browser. It brought a Web page's text into a Java program and displayed it. Of course, the HTML parsing is what turns a bunch of markup tags into a real Web page. Sun wrote an entire Web browser in Java—HotJava.

Today you learned how to use URLs, URL connections, and input streams in conjunction to pull data from the World Wide Web into your program.

You also learned how client and server programs are written in Java and how a server program sits on an Internet port waiting for a client program to contact it.

A simple but useful aspect of network programming also was introduced today: the ability of an applet to tell a Web browser to load a new page.

Q&A

Q How can I mimic an HTML form submission in a Java applet?

A Currently, applets make it difficult to do this. The best (and easiest way) is to use GET notation to get the browser to submit the form contents for you.

HTML forms can be submitted two ways: either by using the GET request or by using POST. If you use GET, your form information is encoded in the URL itself, something like this:

```
http://www.blah.com/cgi-bin/myscript?foo=1&bar=2&name=Laura
```

Because the form input is encoded in the URL, you can write a Java applet to mimic a form, get input from the user, and then construct a new URL object with the form data included on the end; then just pass that URL to the browser by using getAppletContext(), showDocument() and the browser will submit the form results itself. For simple forms, this is all you need.

Q How can I do POST form submissions?

A You have to mimic what a browser does to send forms using POST. Open a socket to the server and send the data, which looks something like the following. (The exact format is determined by the HTTP protocol; this is only a subset of it.)

```
POST /cgi-bin/mailto.cgi HTTP/1.0
Content-type: application/x-www-form-urlencoded
Content-length: 36

{your encoded form data here}
```

If you've done it right, you get the CGI form output back from the server. It's then up to your applet to handle that output properly. Note that if the output is in HTML, there really isn't a way to pass that output to the browser that is running your applet yet. This capability may end up in future Java releases. If you get an URL in return, however, you can redirect the browser to that URL.

DAY **19**

Designing a User Interface with Swing

During the last three days of this book, you'll work with a set of classes called Swing that can implement a user-interface style called Metal. (Sounds like somebody at Sun is either a music buff or a frustrated musician. The next technology that borrows the name of a musical genre should be called Ska, Hip-Hop, or Beer Barrel Polka.)

Swing, which is part of the Java Foundation Classes (JFC) library, is an extension of the Abstract Windowing Toolkit (AWT) that has been integrated into Java 2. It offers much improved functionality over its predecessor—new components, expanded component features, better event handling, and a selectable look and feel.

Today you'll use Swing to create Java interfaces, and tomorrow you'll learn how to turn those interfaces into full programs.

Note

Swing is also available as a separate add-on to Java 1.1. If you're writing an applet or application using Java 1.1 instead of 2, you can use Swing classes by downloading the 1.1-compatible version of JFC from Sun:

`http://java.sun.com/products/jfc/`

Because Swing has been fully incorporated into Java 2, you don't need to download Swing separately if you're using that version of Java.

The Benefits of Swing

"Look and feel" is an expression that's used often when describing interface programming. It's pretty self-explanatory—it describes how a graphical user interface looks and feels to a user. Look and feel is something that becomes relevant in Java with the introduction of Swing, the set of windowing classes included with Java 2. You'll work with Swing throughout the last two days of this book.

Swing enables a Java program to use a different look and feel at the control of the program or even the user of a program.

This feature offers the most visually dramatic change from the AWT. Swing enables you to create a Java program with an interface that uses the style of the native operating system, such as Windows or Solaris, or a new style unique to Java that has been dubbed Metal.

Swing components, unlike their predecessors in previous versions of Java, are implemented entirely in Java. This makes them more compatible across different platforms than programs you might have created using the AWT.

All elements of Swing are part of the `javax.swing` package. To use a Swing class, you must either use an `import` statement with that class or a catchall statement such as the following:

```
import javax.swing.*;
```

 Note

There's been some confusion about the name of the Swing package because it has been renamed several times during the development of Java 1.2/2. In versions prior to JDK 1.2 Beta 4, the name was `java.awt.swing`. In JDK 1.2 Beta 4, it was `com.sun.java.swing`. After soliciting feedback from programmers, Sun decided that the final name for the package should be `javax.swing`. If you come across these other package names in Java 2 source code on the Net and other places, a name change should be all that's required to update the code for the current JDK.

Using a Swing component is no different than using AWT components. You create the component by calling its constructor method, calling methods of the component if they're needed for proper setup, and adding the component to a container.

> **Caution**
>
> Swing uses the same infrastructure of classes that the AWT uses, which makes it possible to use Swing and AWT components in the same interface. However, in some cases the two types of components will not be rendered correctly in a container. To avoid these problems, it's best to use one windowing system exclusively.

Swing components all are subclasses of the JComponent class.

An Application Framework

The first step in creating a simple Swing application is to create a class that is a subclass of JFrame. The JFrame class is an extension of Frame, and it can be used in a similar manner.

The code in Listing 19.1 can be a framework—pun intended—for any applications you create that use a main window.

TYPE   **LISTING 19.1.** THE FULL TEXT OF FRAMEWORK.JAVA.

19

```
 1: import java.awt.GridLayout;
 2: import java.awt.event.*;
 3: import javax.swing.*;
 4:
 5: public class Framework extends JFrame {
 6:
 7:     public Framework() {
 8:         super("Application Title");
 9:
10:         // Add components here
11:     }
12:
13:     public static void main(String[] args) {
14:         JFrame frame = new Framework();
15:
16:         WindowListener l = new WindowAdapter() {
17:             public void windowClosing(WindowEvent e) {
18:                 System.exit(0);
19:             }
20:         };
21:         frame.addWindowListener(l);
```

continues

LISTING 19.1. CONTINUED

```
22:
23:            frame.pack();
24:            frame.setVisible(true);
25:      }
26: }
```

This application is a subclass of JFrame, and all the work involved in creating the frame's user interface is done in the Framework() constructor method.

Line 8 of the constructor provides text for the title bar of the frame by using the super(String) method. The user interface should be constructed within this constructor—components can be added to containers here, and containers added to the frame.

The following takes place in the application's main() method:

- Line 14—The Framework() constructor creates a new instance of the JFrame class. This instance is the application's main window.
- Lines 16–21—This standard event-handling code closes the application when the frame is closed. You'll learn about event handlers like WindowListener tomorrow.
- Line 23—Calls the frame's pack() method to shrink the frame to the smallest possible size to contain all of its components. By using pack(), you can add components to the frame and know that there will be room for them.
- Line 24—Makes the frame visible using its setVisible(boolean) method. If the argument were false instead of true, the frame would become invisible.

Although you can compile this framework successfully, it doesn't produce anything useful—the frame window will open to a minimum size and you won't even be able to see the full title bar on the frame. Components must be added before it begins to look like a real application.

Adding Components to a Swing Frame

NEW TERM Working with a JFrame object is more complicated than working with its AWT counterpart. Instead of adding containers and components directly to the frame, you must add them to an intermediate container called the *content pane*.

A JFrame is subdivided into several different panes. The main pane you work with is the content pane, which represents the full area of a frame in which components can be added.

Do the following to add a component to a content pane:

- Create a JPanel object (the Swing version of a panel).
- Add all components (which can be containers) to the JPanel by using its add(*Component*) method.
- Make this JPanel the content pane by using the setContentPane(*Container*) method. The JPanel object should be the only argument.

The program in Listing 19.2 uses the application framework and adds a button to the frame's content pane. The button is created from the JButton class, the Swing version of a clickable button. This program is similar to the Slacker project from Day 11, "Building Simple User Interfaces for Applets."

TYPE **LISTING 19.2.** THE FULL TEXT OF SWINGER.JAVA.

```
 1: import java.awt.GridLayout;
 2: import java.awt.event.*;
 3: import javax.swing.*;
 4:
 5: public class Swinger extends JFrame {
 6:
 7:     public Swinger() {
 8:         super("Swinger");
 9:
10:         String note = "I receive a disproportionate amount of " +
11:             "joy from being clicked. Please interact with me.";
12:         JButton hotButton = new JButton(note);
13:
14:         JPanel pane = new JPanel();
15:         pane.add(hotButton);
16:
17:         setContentPane(pane);
18:     }
19:
20:     public static void main(String[] args) {
21:         JFrame frame = new Swinger();
22:
23:         WindowListener l = new WindowAdapter() {
24:             public void windowClosing(WindowEvent e) {
25:                 System.exit(0);
26:             }
27:         };
28:         frame.addWindowListener(l);
29:
30:         frame.pack();
31:         frame.setVisible(true);
32:     }
33: }
```

19

Figure 19.1 shows the output from this application after you run it with the Java interpreter.

FIGURE **19.1.**

The Swinger
application.

The only new material in Listing 19.2 is lines 10–17, in which the following takes place:

- Lines 12 and 13—A JButton object is created using a string as its label. This use
  is identical to one of the constructors for the Button class.
- Lines 14 and 15—A JPanel object is created and the button is added to this panel.
- Line 17—The setContentPane(*Container*) method makes the panel the frame's
  content pane.

Once you have set the content pane for a frame, you use methods such as
setLayout(*LayoutManager*) and add(*Component*) on that pane. You don't call these
methods on the frame itself.

Note

> This holds true for applets as well, which are implemented in Swing through
> the JApplet class. You must create a JPanel object, add components to it,
> and make that panel the content pane for the applet. Note that any applets
> you create with Swing and Java 2 will not work in Web browsers that only
> support Java 1.02. You also have to find a way to make the Swing classes
> available to the applet; they will take a long time to download on the Web
> page with the files that make up the applet.

Working with Swing

There are Swing components for each of the AWT components you have learned about
thus far. In most cases there is a constructor for the Swing component that matches its
AWT counterpart, so you don't have to learn something new to work with the components in Swing.

NEW TERM   There are also new constructors for many components that take an Icon object as
an argument. An *icon* is a small graphic, usually in GIF format, that can be
placed on a button, label, or other interface element to identify it. You see icons all the
time in file folders on graphical operating systems like Windows 95, Windows 98, and
MacOS.

An Icon object is created in a manner similar to that of an Image object. The constructor takes a graphic's filename or URL as the only argument. The following example loads an icon from the file unabom.gif and creates a JButton with the icon as its label:

```
ImageIcon una = new ImageIcon("unabom.gif");
JButton button = new JButton(una);

JPanel pane = new JPanel();
pane.add(button);

setContentPane(pane);
```

Figure 19.2 shows the result.

FIGURE 19.2.

An icon on a JButton.

Note

The Unabomber icon comes from Jeffrey Zeldman's Pardon My Icons! collection, which includes hundreds of icons you can use in your own projects. If you're looking for icons to play with in Swing applications, you can find Pardon My Icons at the following address:

http://www.zeldman.com/icon.html

This example's source code is available on this book's CD-ROM and on its official Web site at http://www.prefect.com/java21pre under the filename UnaButton.java, and the icon graphic is in the file unabom.gif.

Labels

Labels are implemented in Swing with the JLabel class. The functionality is comparable to AWT labels, but now you can include icons. In addition, the alignment of a label can be specified with one of three class variables from the SwingConstants class: LEFT, CENTER, or RIGHT.

Some constructor methods you can use include the following:

- JLabel(*String, int*)—A label with the specified text and alignment.
- JLabel(*String, Icon, int*)—A label with the specified text, icon, and alignment.

19

Buttons

As you have learned, Swing buttons are embodied by the JButton class. A Swing button can feature a text label (just like AWT buttons), an icon label, or a combination of both.

Some constructor methods you can use include the following:

- JButton(*String*)—A button with the specified text.
- JButton(*Icon*)—A button with the specified icon.
- JButton(*String*, *Icon*)—A button with the specified text and icon.

Text Fields

Text fields are implemented in Swing by the JTextField class. A difference between these text fields and their AWT counterparts is that the setEchoChar(*char*) method is not supported in JTextField for obscuring text input.

Constructor methods you can use include the following:

- JTextField(*int*)—A text field with the specified width.
- JTextField(*String*, *int*)—A text field with the specified text and width.

The JPasswordField class creates a text field that can use a character to obscure input. This class has the same constructor methods as JTextField: JPasswordField(*int*) and JPasswordField(*String*, *int*).

Once you have created a password text field, you can use the setEchoChar(*char*) method on it to obscure input with the specified character.

Text Areas

Text areas are implemented in Swing with the JTextArea class. It takes the following constructor methods:

- JTextArea(*int*, *int*)—A text area with the specified number of rows and columns.
- JTextArea(*String*, *int*, *int*)—A text area with the specified text, rows, and columns.

Check Boxes and Radio Buttons

The JCheckBox class is the implementation of check boxes in Swing. The functionality is the same as the AWT, with the addition of icon labels.

Constructor methods you can use include the following:

- JCheckBox(*String*)—A check box with the specified text label.
- JCheckBox(*String*, *boolean*)—A check box with the specified text label that is selected if the second argument is `true`.
- JCheckBox(*Icon*)—A check box with the specified icon label.
- JCheckBox(*Icon*, *boolean*)—A check box with the specified icon label that is selected if the second argument is `true`.
- JCheckBox(*String*, *Icon*)—A check box with the specified text label and icon label.
- JCheckBox(*String*, *Icon*, *boolean*)—A check box with the specified text label and icon label that is selected if the second argument is `true`.

Check box groups are implemented in Swing with the ButtonGroup class. As you have seen, only one component in a check box group can be selected at one time. You create a ButtonGroup object and add check boxes to it using the add(*Component*) method to add a component to the group.

Radio buttons are implemented in Swing through the JRadioButton class. The constructor methods are the same as those for the JCheckBox class.

The name change from CheckboxGroup to ButtonGroup reflects expanded functionality—buttons and radio buttons also can be grouped together.

Choice Lists

Choice lists, which were created in the AWT using the Choice class, are one of the implementations possible with the JComboBox class.

The following steps show how a choice list is created:

1. The JComboBox() constructor is used with no arguments.
2. The combo box's addItem(*Object*) method adds items to the list.
3. The combo box's setEditable(*boolean*) method is used with `false` as the argument.

This last method makes the combo box into a choice list—the only choices a user can make are those items added to the list.

If the combo box is editable, the user can enter text into the field instead of using the choice list to pick an item. This is the combination that gives combo boxes their name.

Scrollbars

Scrollbars are implemented in Swing with the JScrollBar class. The functionality is identical to AWT scrollbars, and you can use the following constructor methods:

19

- JScrollBar(*int*)—A scrollbar with the specified orientation.
- JScrollBar(*int, int, int, int, int*)—A scrollbar with the specified orientation, starting value, scroll box size, minimum value, and maximum value.

The orientation is indicated by the SwingConstants class variables HORIZONTAL and VERTICAL.

An Example: The SwingColorTest Application

One of the projects in Day 14, "Developing Advanced User Interfaces with the AWT," was the ColorTest applet, which enabled a color to be selected using its RGB or HSB values. The next project creates the graphical user interface for this project using Swing and makes it an application instead of an applet. You'll create the event handling methods for it tomorrow.

TYPE   **LISTING 19.3.** THE FULL TEXT OF SWINGCOLORTEST.JAVA.

```
 1: import java.awt.*;
 2: import java.awt.event.*;
 3: import javax.swing.*;
 4:
 5: public class SwingColorTest extends JFrame {
 6:     SwingColorControls RGBcontrols, HSBcontrols;
 7:     JPanel swatch;
 8:
 9:     public SwingColorTest() {
10:         super("Color Test");
11:
12:         JPanel pane = new JPanel();
13:         pane.setLayout(new GridLayout(1, 3, 5, 15));
14:         swatch = new JPanel();
15:         swatch.setBackground(Color.black);
16:         RGBcontrols = new SwingColorControls(this, "Red",
17:             "Green", "Blue");
18:         HSBcontrols = new SwingColorControls(this, "Hue",
19:             "Saturation", "Brightness");
20:         pane.add(swatch);
21:         pane.add(RGBcontrols);
22:         pane.add(HSBcontrols);
23:
24:         setContentPane(pane);
25:     }
26:
27:     public static void main(String[] args) {
28:         JFrame frame = new SwingColorTest();
29:
30:         WindowListener l = new WindowAdapter() {
```

```
31:            public void windowClosing(WindowEvent e) {
32:                System.exit(0);
33:            }
34:        };
35:        frame.addWindowListener(1);
36:
37:        frame.pack();
38:        frame.setVisible(true);
39:    }
40:
41:    public Insets getInsets() {
42:        return new Insets(10, 10, 10, 10);
43:    }
44: }
45:
46: class SwingColorControls extends JPanel {
47:    SwingColorTest frame;
48:    JTextField tfield1, tfield2, tfield3;
49:
50:    SwingColorControls(SwingColorTest parent,
51:        String l1, String l2, String l3) {
52:
53:        frame = parent;
54:        setLayout(new GridLayout(3,2,10,10));
55:        tfield1 = new JTextField("0");
56:        tfield2 = new JTextField("0");
57:        tfield3 = new JTextField("0");
58:        add(new JLabel(l1, JLabel.RIGHT));
59:        add(tfield1);
60:        add(new JLabel(l2, JLabel.RIGHT));
61:        add(tfield2);
62:        add(new JLabel(l3, JLabel.RIGHT));
63:        add(tfield3);
64:    }
65:
66:    public Insets getInsets() {
67:        return new Insets(10, 10, 0, 0);
68:    }
69: }
```

19

Figure 19.3 shows the interface that's developed for this application after you run it with the Java interpreter. Although the buttons and other components exhibit a different look and feel than the ColorTest applet, which you'll learn about in today's "Setting the Look and Feel" section, the interface performs the same functions as its non-Swing counterpart.

FIGURE 19.3.

The SwingColorTest
application.

The SwingColorTest program uses the application framework introduced earlier, so many parts of it have been introduced previously. This program is composed of three classes: the main class SwingColorTest, the private helper class SwingColorControls, and the inner class that's defined in lines 30–34.

Both the SwingColorTest and SwingColorControls classes override the getInsets() method, which enables these components to be inset from their container edges by a designated number of pixels. Like many aspects of Swing, this is supported in the same manner as with AWT components.

The SwingColorControls class is a subclass of JPanel and was updated for Swing by changing the text fields and labels from AWT components into Swing components. No other changes were necessary.

In the SwingColorTest class, the following changes updated the windowing code to work with Swing instead of the AWT:

- The program is a subclass of JFrame.
- The swatch object, which displays the currently selected color, became a JPanel object instead of a Canvas. There is no Canvas object in Swing, so panels should be used instead.
- A JPanel object was created to be the frame's main content pane.
- The components swatch, RGBcontrols, and HSBcontrols were added to the content pane instead of the program's main window.

In many cases, an interface created for the AWT can be implemented by using Swing with few major changes. If you are converting an applet written for Java 1.02 into a Swing program written for Java 2, you'll run into more significant changes in the event-handling methods, which are discussed tomorrow.

New Features of Swing

In addition to components and containers that extend the functionality of the AWT, Swing offers numerous features that are completely new, including a definable look and feel, keyboard mnemonics, ToolTips, and standard dialog boxes.

Setting the Look and Feel

You're already familiar with layout managers, classes that control the arrangement of components in a user interface. Swing has a user-interface manager that controls the look and feel of components—the way that the buttons, labels, and other elements are rendered onscreen.

Management of look and feel is handled by the UIManager class in the com.sun.java.swing.* package. The choices for look and feel vary depending on the Java development environment you're using. The following are available with Java 2:

- A Windows 95, 98, or NT look and feel
- A Motif X-Window system look and feel
- Metal, Swing's new cross-platform look and feel

The UIManager class has a setLookAndFeel(LookAndFeel) method that is used to choose a program's look and feel. To get a LookAndFeel object that you can use with setLookAndFeel(), use one of the following UIManager methods:

- getCrossPlatformLookAndFeelClassName()—This method returns a LookAndFeel object representing Java's cross-platform Metal look and feel.
- getSystemLookAndFeelClassName()—This method returns a LookAndFeel object representing your system's look and feel.

The setLookAndFeel() method throws an UnsupportedLookAndFeelException if it can't set the look and feel.

The following statements can be used in any program to designate Metal as the look and feel:

```
try {
    UIManager.setLookAndFeel(
        UIManager.getCrossPlatformLookAndFeelClassName());
    } catch (Exception e) {
        System.err.println("Can't set look and feel: " + e);
}
```

To select your system's look and feel, use getSystemLookAndFeelClassName(), which is inside the setLookAndFeel() method call in the preceding example. This produces different results on different operating systems. A Windows 95 or 98 user would get that platform's look and feel by using getSystemLookAndFeelClassName(). A UNIX user would get the Motif look and feel.

19

Standard Dialog Boxes

The JOptionPane class offers several methods that can be used to create standard dialog boxes: small windows that ask a question, warn a user, or provide a brief, important message. Figure 19.4 shows a dialog box with the Metal look and feel.

FIGURE 19.4.

A standard dialog box.

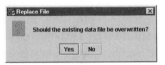

You have doubtlessly seen dialog boxes of this kind. When your system crashes, a dialog box appears and breaks the bad news. When you delete files, a dialog box might pop up to make sure you really want to do that. These windows are an effective way to communicate with a user without the overhead of creating a new class to represent the window, adding components to it, and writing event-handling methods to take input. All of these things are handled automatically when one of the standard dialog boxes offered by JOptionPane is used.

There are four standard dialog boxes:

- ConfirmDialog—Asks a question, with buttons for Yes, No, and Cancel responses.
- InputDialog—Prompts for text input.
- MessageDialog—Displays a message.
- OptionDialog—Comprises all three of the other dialog box types.

Each of these dialog boxes has its own method in the JOptionPane class.

Confirm Dialog Boxes

The easiest way to create a Yes/No/Cancel dialog box is with the showConfirmDialog(*Component*, *Object*) method call. The *Component* argument specifies the container that should be considered the parent of the dialog box, and this information is used to determine where on the screen the dialog window should be displayed. If null is used instead of a container, or if the container is not a Frame object, the dialog box will be centered onscreen.

The second argument, *Object*, can be a string, a component, or an Icon object. If it's a string, that text will be displayed in the dialog box. If it's a component or an icon, that object will be displayed in place of a text message.

This method returns one of three possible integer values, each a class variable of JOptionPane: YES_OPTION, NO_OPTION, and CANCEL_OPTION.

The following example uses a confirm dialog box with a text message and stores the response in the `response` variable:

```
int response;
response = JOptionPane.showConfirmDialog(null,
    "Should I delete all of your irreplaceable personal files");
```

Another method offers more options for the confirm dialog:
`showConfirmDialog(Component, Object, String, int, int)`. The first two arguments are the same as those in other `showConfirmDialog()` methods. The last three arguments are the following:

- A string that will be displayed in the dialog box's title bar.
- An integer that indicates which option buttons will be shown. It should be equal to the class variables `YES_NO_CANCEL_OPTION` or `YES_NO_OPTION`.
- An integer that describes the kind of dialog box it is, using the class variables `ERROR_MESSAGE`, `INFORMATION_MESSAGE`, `PLAIN_MESSAGE`, `QUESTION_MESSAGE`, or `WARNING_MESSAGE`. This argument is used to determine which icon to draw in the dialog box along with the message.

For Example:

```
int response = JOptionPane.showConfirmDialog(null,
    "Error reading file. Want to try again?",
    "File Input Error",
    JOptionPane.YES_NO_OPTION,
    JOptionPane.ERROR_MESSAGE);
```

Figure 19.5 shows the resulting dialog box with the Windows look and feel.

19

FIGURE 19.5.

A confirm dialog box.

Input Dialog Boxes

An input dialog box asks a question and uses a text field to store the response. Figure 19.6 shows an example with the Motif look and feel.

FIGURE 19.6.

An input dialog box.

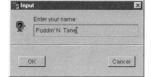

The easiest way to create an input dialog is with a call to the
showInputDialog(*Component*, *Object*) method. The arguments are the parent component and the string, component, or icon to display in the box.

The input dialog method call returns a string that represents the user's response. The following statement creates the input dialog box shown in Figure 19.6:

```
String response = JOptionPane.showInputDialog(null,
    "Enter your name:");
```

You also can create an input dialog box with the showInputDialog(*Component*,
Object, *String*, *int*) method. The first two arguments are the same as the shorter
method call, and the last two are the following:

- The title to display in the dialog box title bar.
- One of five class variables describing the type of dialog box: ERROR_MESSAGE,
  INFORMATION_MESSAGE, PLAIN_MESSAGE, QUESTION_MESSAGE, or WARNING_MESSAGE.

The following statement creates an input dialog box using this method:

```
String response = JOptionPane.showInputDialog(null,
    "What is your ZIP code?",
    "Enter ZIP Code",
    JOptionPane.QUESTION_MESSAGE);
```

Message Dialog Boxes

A message dialog box is a simple window that displays information. Figure 19.7 shows
an example with the Metal look and feel.

FIGURE 19.7.

A message dialog box.

A message dialog box can be created with a call to the showMessageDialog(*Component*,
Object) method. As with other dialog boxes, the arguments are the parent component
and the string, component, or icon to display.

Unlike the other dialog boxes, message dialog boxes do not return any kind of response
value. The following statement creates the message dialog shown in Figure 19.7:

```
JOptionPane.showMessageDialog(null,
    "The program has been uninstalled.");
```

You also can create a message input dialog box with the
showMessageDialog(*Component*, *Object*, *String*, *int*) method. The use is identical

to the showInputDialog() method, with the same arguments, except that showMessageDialog() does not return a value.

The following statement creates a message dialog box using this method:

```
String response = JOptionPane.showMessageDialog(null,
    "An asteroid has destroyed the Earth.",
    "Asteroid Destruction Alert",
    JOptionPane.WARNING_MESSAGE);
```

Option Dialog Boxes

The most complex of the dialog boxes is the option dialog box, which combines the features of all the other dialogs. It can be created with the showOptionDialog(*Component*, *Object*, *String*, *int*, *int*, *Icon*, *Object[]*, *Object*) method.

The arguments to this method are as follows:

- The parent component of the dialog.
- The text, icon, or component to display.
- A string to display in the title bar.
- The type of box, using the class variables YES_NO_OPTION or YES_NO_CANCEL_OPTION, or the literal 0 if other buttons will be used instead.
- The icon to display, using the class variables ERROR_MESSAGE, INFORMATION_ MESSAGE, PLAIN_MESSAGE, QUESTION_MESSAGE, or WARNING_MESSAGE, or the literal 0 if none of these should be used.
- An Icon object to display instead of one of the icons in the preceding argument.
- An array of objects holding the components or other objects that represent the choices in the dialog box, if YES_NO_OPTION and YES_NO_CANCEL_OPTION are not being used.
- The object representing the default selection if YES_NO_OPTION and YES_NO_CANCEL option are not being used.

The last two arguments enable you to create a wide range of choices for the dialog box. You can create an array of buttons, labels, text fields, or even a mixture of different components as an object array. These components are displayed using the flow layout manager—there's no way to specify a different manager within the dialog.

The following example creates an option dialog box that uses an array of JButton objects for the options in the box and the gender[2] element as the default selection:

```
JButton[] gender = new JButton[3];
gender[0] = new JButton("Male");
```

19

```
gender[1] = new JButton("Female");
gender[2] = new JButton("None of Your Business");
int response = JOptionPane.showOptionDialog(null,
    "What is your gender?",
    "Gender",
    0,
    JOptionPane.INFORMATION_MESSAGE,
    null,
    gender,
    gender[2]);
```

Figure 19.8 shows the resulting dialog box with the Motif look and feel.

FIGURE 19.8.

An option dialog box.

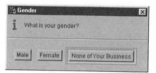

An Example: The `Info` Application

The next project shows a series of dialog boxes in a working program. The `Info` application uses dialogs to get information from the user, which is then placed into text fields on the application's main window.

Enter Listing 19.4 and compile the result.

TYPE   **LISTING 19.4.** THE FULL TEXT OF INFO.JAVA.

```
 1: import java.awt.GridLayout;
 2: import java.awt.event.*;
 3: import javax.swing.*;
 4:
 5: public class Info extends JFrame {
 6:     private JLabel titleLabel = new JLabel("Title: ",
 7:         SwingConstants.RIGHT);
 8:     private JTextField title;
 9:     private JLabel addressLabel = new JLabel("Address: ",
10:         SwingConstants.RIGHT);
11:     private JTextField address;
12:     private JLabel typeLabel = new JLabel("Type: ",
13:         SwingConstants.RIGHT);
14:     private JTextField type;
15:
16:     public Info() {
17:         super("Site Information");
18:
19:         // Site name
20:         String response1 = JOptionPane.showInputDialog(null,
21:             "Enter the site title:");
```

```
22:            title = new JTextField(response1, 20);
23:
24:            // Site address
25:            String response2 = JOptionPane.showInputDialog(null,
26:                "Enter the site address:");
27:            address = new JTextField(response2, 20);
28:
29:            // Site type
30:            String[] choices = { "Personal", "Commercial", "Unknown" };
31:            int response3 = JOptionPane.showOptionDialog(null,
32:                "What type of site is it?",
33:                "Site Type",
34:                0,
35:                JOptionPane.QUESTION_MESSAGE,
36:                null,
37:                choices,
38:                choices[0]);
39:            type = new JTextField(choices[response3], 20);
40:
41:            JPanel pane = new JPanel();
42:            pane.setLayout(new GridLayout(3, 2));
43:            pane.add(titleLabel);
44:            pane.add(title);
45:            pane.add(addressLabel);
46:            pane.add(address);
47:            pane.add(typeLabel);
48:            pane.add(type);
49:
50:            setContentPane(pane);
51:        }
52:
53:        public static void main(String[] args) {
54:            try {
55:                UIManager.setLookAndFeel(
56:                    UIManager.getSystemLookAndFeelClassName());
57:            } catch (Exception e) {
58:                System.err.println("Couldn't use the system "
59:                            + "look and feel: " + e);
60:            }
61:
62:            JFrame frame = new Info();
63:
64:            WindowListener l = new WindowAdapter() {
65:                public void windowClosing(WindowEvent e) {
66:                    System.exit(0);
67:                }
68:            };
69:            frame.addWindowListener(l);
70:
71:            frame.pack();
72:            frame.setVisible(true);
73:        }
74: }
```

19

Figure 19.9 shows this application's main window with the Window look and feel after it's been run with the Java interpreter. Three text fields have values supplied by dialog boxes.

FIGURE 19.9.

The main window of the Info application.

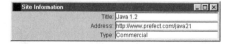

Much of this application is boilerplate code that can be used with any Swing application. The following lines relate to the dialog boxes:

- Lines 19–22—An input dialog asks the user to enter a site title. This title is used in the constructor for a JTextField object, which puts the title in the text field.
- Lines 24–27—A similar input dialog asks for a site address, which is used in the constructor for another JTextField object.
- Line 30—An array of String objects called choices is created, and three elements are given values.
- Lines 31–38—An option dialog box asks for the site type. The choices array is the seventh argument, which sets up three buttons on the dialog with the strings in the array: Personal, Commercial, and Unknown. The last argument, choices[0], designates the first array element as the default selection in the dialog. Figure 19.10 shows this option dialog box.
- Line 39—The response to the option dialog, an integer identifying the array element that was selected, is stored in a JTextField component called type.

FIGURE 19.10.

The site type option dialog box.

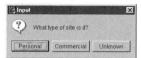

Summary

After several hundred thousand programmers had a chance to use the first versions of Java, one of the main complaints was about the AWT. Although it allows a functional interface to be created, there were some problems with making all interfaces work across different platforms, and some elements of a graphical user interface were not supported by the AWT.

Swing is an effective answer to this criticism, offering a sophisticated windowing system that's suitable for many different types of Java programs. If you take a look at the documentation included with Swing, you'll find more than 30 different components.

Tomorrow you'll take a "swing" at turning an interface into a full application.

Q&A

Q Can an application be created without Swing?

A Certainly. Swing is just an expansion on the AWT, and you can continue to use the AWT for applications with Java 2. The event-handling techniques you learned for Java 1.02 applets can be used with applications as well. Whether you should create an application without Swing is another issue. There's no comparison between Swing's capabilities and those offered by the AWT. With Swing, you can use many more components and control them in more sophisticated ways.

19

DAY **20**

Handling User Events with Swing

In order to turn a working Java interface into a working Java program, you must make the interface receptive to user events.

You've dealt with events before, learning how to handle mouse clicks and other user input with the Abstract Windowing Toolkit. You used this knowledge to create Java 2–compatible applets.

NEW TERM Swing handles events differently with a set of classes called *event listeners*. Today you learn how to add listeners of all kinds to your Swing programs, including those that handle action events, mouse events, and other interaction.

When you're done, you'll celebrate the event by completing a full Java application using the Swing set of classes.

The Main Event

Under the event-handling system you learned about last week, events were dealt with via a set of methods that are available to all components. Methods such as `mouseDown()`, `keyDown()`, and `action()` can be overridden by any AWT program that wants to handle those events.

This event-handling system applies only to Java 2 because a greatly improved solution for events was offered in subsequent versions of the language.

You use the new system to create Swing applications.

Event Listeners

If a class wants to respond to a user event under the Java 2 event-handling system, it must implement the interface that deals with the events. These interfaces are called event listeners.

Each listener handles a specific kind of event, and a class can implement as many of them as needed.

NEW TERM   The following event listeners are available:

* `ActionListener`   *Action events*, which are generated by a user taking an action on a component, such as a click on a button.

* `AdjustmentListener`   *Adjustment events*, which are generated when a component is adjusted, such as when a scrollbar is moved.

* `FocusListener`   *Keyboard focus events*, which are generated when a component such as a text field gains or loses the focus.

* `ItemListener`   *Item events*, which are generated when an item such as a check box is changed.

* `KeyListener`   *Keyboard events*, which occur when a user enters text on the keyboard.

* `MouseListener`   *Mouse events*, which are generated by mouse clicks, a mouse entering a component's area, and a mouse leaving a component's area.

* `MouseMotionListener`   *Mouse movement events*, which track all movement by a mouse over a component.

* `WindowListener`   *Window events*, which are generated by a window (such as the main application window) being maximized, minimized, moved, or closed.

The following class is declared so that it can handle both action and text events:

```
public class Suspense extends JFrame implements ActionListener,
    TextListener {
    // ...
}
```

The `java.awt.event` package contains all of the basic event listeners as well as the objects that represent specific events. In order to use these classes in your programs, you can import them individually or use a statement like the following:

```
import java.awt.event.*;
```

Setting Up Components

When you make a class an event listener you have set up a specific type of event to be heard by that class. This will never happen if you don't follow up with a second step: A matching listener must be added to the component. That listener generates the events when the component is used.

After a component is created, you can call one of the following methods on the component to associate a listener with it:

- `addActionListener()` `JButton`, `JCheckBox`, `JComboBox`, `JTextField`, and `JRadioButton` components
- `addAdjustmentListener()` `JScrollBar` components
- `addFocusListener()` All Swing components
- `addItemListener()` `JButton`, `JCheckBox`, `JComboBox`, and `JRadioButton` components
- `addKeyListener()` All Swing components
- `addMouseListener()` All Swing components
- `addMouseMotionListener()` All Swing components
- `addWindowListener()` All `JWindow` and `JFrame` components

Caution

> Modifying a component after adding it to a container is an easy mistake to make in a Java program. You must add listeners to a component and handle any other configuration before it is added to any containers; otherwise these settings are disregarded when the program is run.

20

The following example creates a `JButton` object and associates an action event listener with it:

```
JButton zap = new JButton("Zap");
zap.addActionListener(this);
```

All of the different add methods take one argument: the object that is listening for events of that kind. Using `this` indicates that the current class is the event listener. You could specify a different object, as long as its class implements the right listener interface.

Event-Handling Methods

When you associate an interface with a class, the class must handle all of the methods contained in the interface.

In the case of event listeners, each of the methods is called automatically by the windowing system when the corresponding user event takes place.

The `ActionListener` interface has only one method: `actionPerformed()`. All classes that implement `ActionListener` must have a method with a structure like the following:

```
public void actionPerformed(ActionEvent evt) {
    // handle event here
}
```

If only one component in your program's graphical user interface has a listener for action events, this `actionPerformed()` method can be used to respond to an event generated by that component.

If more than one component has an action event listener, you must use the method to figure out which component was used and act accordingly in your program.

In the `actionPerformed()` method, you might have noticed that an `ActionEvent` object is sent as an argument when the method is called. This object can be used to discover details about the component that generated the event.

`ActionEvent` and all other event objects are part of the `java.awt.event` package, and they are subclasses of the `EventObject` class.

Every event-handling method is sent an event object of some kind. The object's `getSource()` method can be used to determine the component that sent the event, as in the following example:

```
public void actionPerformed(ActionEvent evt) {
    Object src = evt.getSource();
}
```

The object returned by the `getSource()` method can be compared to components by using the == operator. The following statements can be used inside the preceding `actionPerformed()` example:

```
if (src == quitButton)
    quitProgram();
else if (src == sortRecords)
    sortRecords();
```

This example calls the `quitProgram()` method if the `quitButton` object generated the event; it calls the `sortRecords()` method if the `sortRecords` button generated the event.

Many event-handling methods call a different method for each different kind of event or component. This makes the event-handling method easier to read. In addition, if there is more than one event-handling method in a class, each can call the same methods to get work done.

Using the `instanceof` keyword inside an event-handling method is another useful technique for checking what kind of component generated the event. The following example can be used in a program with one button and one text field, each of which generates an action event:

```
void actionPerformed(ActionEvent evt) {
    Object src = evt.getSource();
    if (src instanceof JTextField)
        calculateScore();
    else if (src instanceof JButton)
        quitProgram();
}
```

The program in Listing 20.1 uses the application framework to create a JFrame and add components to it. The program itself sports two JButton components , which are used to change the text on the frame's title bar.

TYPE **LISTING 20.1.** THE FULL TEXT OF CHANGETITLE.JAVA.

```
 1: import java.awt.event.*;
 2: import javax.swing.*;
 3: import java.awt.*;
 4:
 5: public class ChangeTitle extends JFrame implements ActionListener {
 6:     JButton b1 = new JButton("Rosencrantz");
 7:     JButton b2 = new JButton("Guildenstern");
 8:
 9:     public ChangeTitle() {
10:         super("Title Bar");
11:
12:         b1.addActionListener(this);
13:         b2.addActionListener(this);
14:         JPanel pane = new JPanel();
15:         pane.add(b1);
16:         pane.add(b2);
17:
18:         setContentPane(pane);
19:     }
20:
21:     public static void main(String[] args) {
22:         JFrame frame = new ChangeTitle();
23:
24:         WindowListener l = new WindowAdapter() {
```

20

continues

LISTING 20.1. CONTINUED

```
25:                    public void windowClosing(WindowEvent e) {
26:                        System.exit(0);
27:                    }
28:                };
29:                frame.addWindowListener(l);
30:
31:                frame.pack();
32:                frame.setVisible(true);
33:            }
34:
35:            public void actionPerformed(ActionEvent evt) {
36:                Object source = evt.getSource();
37:                if (source == b1)
38:                    setTitle("Rosencrantz");
39:                else if (source == b2)
40:                    setTitle("Guildenstern");
41:                repaint();
42:            }
43: }
```

After you run this application with the Java interpreter, the program's interface should resemble Figure 20.1.

FIGURE 20.1.

The ChangeTitle
application.

Only 12 lines were needed to respond to action events in this application:

- Line 1 imports the java.awt.event package.

- Lines 12 and 13 add action listeners to both JButton objects.

- Lines 35–42 respond to action events that occur from the two JButton objects. The evt object's getSource() method determines the source of the event. If it is equal to the b1 button, the title of the frame is set to Rosencrantz; if it is equal to b2, the title is set to Guildenstern. A call to repaint() is needed so that the frame is redrawn after any title change that might have occurred in the method.

Working with Methods

The following sections detail the structure of each event-handling method and the methods that can be used within them.

In addition to the methods described, the getSource() method can be used on any event object to determine the object that generated the event.

Action Events

Action events occur when a user completes an action using one of the following components: JButton, JCheckBox, JComboBox, JTextField, or JRadioButton.

A class must implement the ActionListener interface in order to handle these events. In addition, the addActionListener() method must be called on each component that should generate an action event—unless you want to ignore that component's action events.

There is only one method in the ActionListener interface: actionPerformed(*ActionEvent*). It takes the following form:

```
public void actionPerformed(ActionEvent evt) {
    // ...
}
```

In addition to the getSource() method, you can use the getActionCommand() method on the ActionEvent object to discover more information about the event's source.

The action command, by default, is the text associated with the component, such as the label on a JButton. You also can set a different action command for a component by calling its setActionCommand(*String*) method. The string argument should be the action command's desired text.

For example, the following statements create a JButton and a JTextField and give both of them the action command "Sort Files":

```
JButton sort = new JButton("Sort");
JTextField name = new JTextField();
sort.setActionCommand("Sort Files");
name.setActionCommand("Sort Files");
```

20

Note

Action commands become exceptionally useful when you're writing a program in which more than one component should cause the same thing to happen. A program with a Quit button and a Quit option on a pull-down menu is an example of this. By giving both components the same action command, you can handle them with the same code in an event-handling method.

Adjustment Events

Adjustment events occur when a JScrollBar component is moved by using the arrows on the bar or on the box, or by clicking anywhere on the bar. To handle these events, a class must implement the AdjustmentListener interface.

There is only one method in the AdjustmentListener interface: adjustmentValueChanged(*AdjustmentEvent*). It takes the following form:

```
public void adjustmentValueChanged(AdjustmentEvent evt) {
    // ...
}
```

To see what the current value of the JScrollBar is within this event-handling method, the getValue() method can be called on the AdjustmentEvent object. This method returns an integer representing the scrollbar's value.

You also can determine the way the user moved the scrollbar by using the AdjustmentEvent object's getAdjustmentType() method. This returns one of five values, each of which is a class variable of the Adjustment class:

- UNIT_INCREMENT   A value increase of 1, which can be caused by clicking a scrollbar arrow or using a cursor key.

- UNIT_DECREMENT   A value decrease of 1.

- BLOCK_INCREMENT   A larger value increase, caused by clicking the scrollbar in the area between the box and the arrow.

- BLOCK_DECREMENT   A larger value decrease.

- TRACK   A value change caused by moving the box.

The program in Listing 20.2 illustrates the use of the AdjustmentListener interface. A scrollbar and an uneditable text field are added to a frame, and messages are displayed in the field whenever the scrollbar is moved.

TYPE   **LISTING 20.2.** THE FULL TEXT OF WELLADJUSTED.JAVA.

```
1: import java.awt.event.*;
2: import javax.swing.*;
3: import java.awt.*;
4:
5: public class WellAdjusted extends JFrame implements AdjustmentListener {
6:     BorderLayout bord = new BorderLayout();
7:     JTextField value = new JTextField();
8:     JScrollBar bar = new JScrollBar(SwingConstants.HORIZONTAL,
9:         50, 10, 0, 100);
```

```
10:
11:    public WellAdjusted() {
12:        super("Well Adjusted");
13:
14:        bar.addAdjustmentListener(this);
15:        value.setHorizontalAlignment(SwingConstants.CENTER);
16:        value.setEditable(false);
17:        JPanel pane = new JPanel();
18:        pane.setLayout(bord);
19:        pane.add(value, "South");
20:        pane.add(bar, "Center");
21:
22:        setContentPane(pane);
23:    }
24:
25:    public static void main(String[] args) {
26:        JFrame frame = new WellAdjusted();
27:
28:        WindowListener l = new WindowAdapter() {
29:            public void windowClosing(WindowEvent e) {
30:                System.exit(0);
31:            }
32:        };
33:        frame.addWindowListener(l);
34:
35:        frame.pack();
36:        frame.setVisible(true);
37:    }
38:
39:    public void adjustmentValueChanged(AdjustmentEvent evt) {
40:        Object source = evt.getSource();
41:        if (source == bar) {
42:            int newValue = bar.getValue();
43:            value.setText("" + newValue);
44:        }
45:        repaint();
46:    }
47: }
```

20

Figure 20.2 shows a screen capture of the application after you run it with the Java interpreter.

FIGURE 20.2.

The output of the WellAdjusted *application.*

Tip

NEW TERM	You might be wondering why there's an empty set of quotation marks in the call to setText() in line 43 of this program. The empty quotation is called a null *string*, and it is concatenated to the newValue integer to turn the argument into a string. As you might recall, if a string and non-string are concatenated, Java always treats the result as a string. The null string is a shortcut when you want to display something that isn't already a string.

Focus Events

Focus events occur when any component gains or loses input focus on a graphical user interface. *Focus* describes the component that is currently active for keyboard input. If one of the fields has the focus (in a user interface with several editable text fields), a cursor will be blinking in the field. Any text entered goes into this component.

Focus applies to all components that can receive input. In a JButton object, a dotted outline appears on the button that has the focus.

To handle a focus event, a class must implement the FocusListener interface. There are two methods in the interface: focusGained(*FocusEvent*) and focusLost(*FocusEvent*). They take the following form:

```
public void focusGained(FocusEvent evt) {
    // ...
}

public void focusLost(FocusEvent evt) {
    // ...
}
```

To determine which object gained or lost the focus, the getSource() method can be called on the FocusEvent object sent as an argument to the focusGained() and focusLost() methods.

Item Events

Item events occur when an item is selected or deselected on any of the following components: JButton, JCheckBox, JComboBox, or JRadioButton. A class must implement the ItemListener interface in order to handle these events.

There is only one method in the ItemListener interface: itemStateChanged(*ItemEvent*). It takes the following form:

```
void itemStateChanged(ItemEvent evt) {
    // ...
}
```

To determine the item where the event occurred, the getItem() method can be called on the ItemEvent object.

You also can determine whether the item was selected or deselected by using the getStateChange() method. This method returns an integer that will equal either the class variable ItemEvent.DESELECTED or ItemEvent.SELECTED.

The use of item events is illustrated in Listing 20.3. The SelectItem application displays the choice from a combo box in a text field.

TYPE **LISTING 20.3.** THE FULL TEXT OF SELECTITEM.JAVA.

```
 1: import java.awt.event.*;
 2: import javax.swing.*;
 3: import java.awt.*;
 4:
 5: public class SelectItem extends JFrame implements ItemListener {
 6:     BorderLayout bord = new BorderLayout();
 7:     JTextField result = new JTextField(27);
 8:     JComboBox pick = new JComboBox();
 9:
10:     public SelectItem() {
11:         super("Select Item");
12:
13:         pick.addItemListener(this);
14:         pick.addItem("Navigator");
15:         pick.addItem("Internet Explorer");
16:         pick.addItem("Opera");
17:         pick.setEditable(false);
18:         result.setHorizontalAlignment(SwingConstants.CENTER);
19:         result.setEditable(false);
20:         JPanel pane = new JPanel();
21:         pane.setLayout(bord);
22:         pane.add(result, "South");
23:         pane.add(pick, "Center");
24:
25:         setContentPane(pane);
26:     }
27:
28:     public static void main(String[] args) {
29:         JFrame frame = new SelectItem();
30:
31:         WindowListener l = new WindowAdapter() {
32:             public void windowClosing(WindowEvent e) {
33:                 System.exit(0);
34:             }
35:         };
36:         frame.addWindowListener(l);
37:
```

20

continues

LISTING 20.3. CONTINUED

```
38:            frame.pack();
39:            frame.setVisible(true);
40:       }
41:
42:       public void itemStateChanged(ItemEvent evt) {
43:           Object source = evt.getSource();
44:           if (source == pick) {
45:               Object newPick = evt.getItem();
46:               result.setText(newPick.toString() + " is the selection.");
47:           }
48:           repaint();
49:       }
50: }
```

Figure 20.3 shows this application with the Opera item as the current selection in the combo box. The object's toString() method is used to retrieve the object's text returned by getItem().

FIGURE 20.3.

The output of the SelectItem application.

Key Events

Key events occur when a key is pressed on the keyboard. Any component can generate these events, and a class must implement the KeyListener interface to support them.

There are three methods in the KeyListener interface: keyPressed(*KeyEvent*), keyReleased(*KeyEvent*), and keyTyped(*KeyEvent*). They take the following form:

```
public void keyPressed(KeyEvent evt) {
    // ...
}

public void keyReleased(KeyEvent evt) {
    // ...
}

public void keyTyped(KeyEvent evt) {
    // ...
}
```

KeyEvent's getKeyChar() method returns the character of the key associated with the event. If there is no Unicode character that can be represented by the key, getKeyChar() returns a character value equal to the class variable KeyEvent.CHAR_UNDEFINED.

Mouse Events

Mouse events are generated by several different types of user interaction:

- A mouse click
- A mouse entering a component's area
- A mouse leaving a component's area

Any component can generate these events, which are implemented by a class through the `MouseListener` interface. This interface has five methods:

```
mouseClicked(MouseEvent)

mouseEntered(MouseEvent)

mouseExited(MouseEvent)

mousePressed(MouseEvent)

mouseReleased(MouseEvent)
```

Each takes the same basic form as `mouseReleased(MouseEvent)`:

```
public void mouseReleased(MouseEvent evt) {
    // ...
}
```

The following methods can be used on `MouseEvent` objects:

- `getClickCount()`   Returns the number of times the mouse was clicked as an integer.
- `getPoint()`   Returns the x,y coordinates within the component where the mouse was clicked as a `Point` object.
- `getX()`   Returns the x position.
- `getY()`   Returns the y position

Mouse Motion Events

Mouse motion events occur when a mouse is moved over a component. As with other mouse events, any component can generate mouse-motion events. A class must implement the `MouseMotionListener` interface in order to support them.

There are two methods in the `MouseMotionListener` interface:
`mouseDragged(MouseMotionEvent)` and `mouseMoved(MouseMotionEvent)`. They take the following form:

20

```
public void mouseDragged(MouseEvent evt) {
    // ...
}

public void mouseMoved(MouseEvent evt) {
    // ...
}
```

Unlike the other event listener interfaces you have dealt with to this point, MouseMotionListener does not have its own event type. Instead, MouseEvent objects are used.

Because of this, you can call the same methods you would for mouse events: getClick(), getPoint(), getX(), and getY().

Window Events

Window events occur when a user opens or closes a window object such as a JFrame or a JWindow. Any component can generate these events, and a class must implement the WindowListener interface in order to support them.

There are seven methods in the WindowListener interface:

windowActivated(*WindowEvent*)

windowClosed(*WindowEvent*)

windowClosing(*WindowEvent*)

windowDeactivated(*WindowEvent*)

windowDeiconified(*WindowEvent*)

windowIconified(*WindowEvent*)

windowOpened(*WindowEvent*)

They all take the same form as the windowOpened() method:

```
public void windowOpened(WindowEvent evt) {
    // ...
}
```

The windowClosing() and windowClosed() methods are similar, but one is called as the window is closing and the other is called after it is closed. You can take action in a windowClosing() method to stop the window from being closed, in fact.

An Example: The `SwingColorTest` Application

Yesterday you created a graphical user interface for the RGB-to-HSB conversion program using Swing components.

You turn the `SwingColorTest` interface into a working program to get more experience working with the event-handling model in place for Swing.

Two classes were created for this project yesterday: `SwingColorTest` and `SwingColorControls`. `SwingColorTest` contains the application window and the `main()` method that is used to set up the window. `SwingColorControls`, a helper class, is a panel that holds three labels and three text fields used to choose a color.

All of the user input in this program takes place on the color controls—the text fields are used to define RGB or HSB values.

Because of this, all of the event-handling behaviors are added to the `SwingColorControls` class.

The first thing to do is make the `SwingColorControls` class handle two kinds of events: action events and focus events. The `extends` clause should be added to the `class` declaration statement so that the `ActionListener` and `FocusListener` interfaces are implemented. It is shown here:

```
class SwingColorControls extends JPanel
    implements ActionListener, FocusListener {
```

Action and focus listeners must next be added to the three text fields in the class: `tfield1`, `tfield2`, and `tfield3`. These listeners must be added after the text fields are created but before they are added to a container. The following statements can be used:

```
tfield1.addFocusListener(this);
tfield2.addFocusListener(this);
tfield3.addFocusListener(this);
tfield1.addActionListener(this);
tfield2.addActionListener(this);
tfield3.addActionListener(this);
```

Finally, you must add all of the methods that are defined in the two interfaces this class implements: `actionPerformed(ActionEvent)`, `focusLost(FocusEvent)`, and `focusGained(FocusEvent)`.

The color controls enter a numeric value for a color, and this causes the color to be drawn on a panel. It also causes the other color controls to be updated to reflect the color change.

20

There are two ways a user can finalize a new color choice—by pressing Enter inside a text field, which generates an action event, and by leaving the field to edit a different field, which generates a focus event.

The following statements compose the `actionPerformed()` and `focusLost()` methods that should be added to the class:

```
public void actionPerformed(ActionEvent evt) {
    if (evt.getSource() instanceof TextField)
        frame.update(this);
}
public void focusLost(FocusEvent evt) {
    frame.update(this);
}
```

One of these, `focusGained()`, doesn't need to be handled. Because of this, an empty method definition should be added:

```
public void focusGained(FocusEvent evt) { }
```

The event-handling methods added to `SwingColorControls` call a method in its parent class, `update(SwingColorControls)`.

This method doesn't contain any event-handling behavior—it updates the color swatch and all of the color controls to reflect a color change. It's identical to the version created during Day 14, "Developing Advanced User Interfaces with the AWT."

Listing 20.4 contains the application, including both the `SwingColorTest` and `SwingColorControls` classes.

TYPE **LISTING 20.4.** THE FULL TEXT OF SWINGCOLORTEST.JAVA.

```
1: import java.awt.*;
2: import java.awt.event.*;
3: import javax.swing.*;
4:
5: public class SwingColorTest extends JFrame {
6:     SwingColorControls RGBcontrols, HSBcontrols;
7:     JPanel swatch;
8:
9:     public SwingColorTest() {
10:         super("Color Test");
11:
12:         JPanel pane = new JPanel();
13:         pane.setLayout(new GridLayout(1, 3, 5, 15));
14:         swatch = new JPanel();
15:         swatch.setBackground(Color.black);
16:         RGBcontrols = new SwingColorControls(this, "Red",
```

```
17:                    "Green", "Blue");
18:           HSBcontrols = new SwingColorControls(this, "Hue",
19:               "Saturation", "Brightness");
20:           pane.add(swatch);
21:           pane.add(RGBcontrols);
22:           pane.add(HSBcontrols);
23:
24:           setContentPane(pane);
25:       }
26:
27:       public static void main(String[] args) {
28:           JFrame frame = new SwingColorTest();
29:
30:           WindowListener l = new WindowAdapter() {
31:               public void windowClosing(WindowEvent e) {
32:                   System.exit(0);
33:               }
34:           };
35:           frame.addWindowListener(l);
36:
37:           frame.pack();
38:           frame.setVisible(true);
39:       }
40:
41:       public Insets getInsets() {
42:           return new Insets(10, 10, 10, 10);
43:       }
44:
45:       void update(SwingColorControls controlPanel) {
46:           Color c;
47:           // get string values from text fields, convert to ints
48:           int value1 = Integer.parseInt(controlPanel.tfield1.getText());
49:           int value2 = Integer.parseInt(controlPanel.tfield2.getText());
50:           int value3 = Integer.parseInt(controlPanel.tfield3.getText());
51:
52:           if (controlPanel == RGBcontrols) {
53:               // RGB has changed, update HSB
54:               c = new Color(value1, value2, value3);
55:
56:               // convert RGB values to HSB values
57:               float[] HSB = Color.RGBtoHSB(value1, value2, value3,
58:                   (new float[3]));
59:               HSB[0] *= 360;
60:               HSB[1] *= 100;
61:               HSB[2] *= 100;
62:
63:               // reset HSB fields
64:               HSBcontrols.tfield1.setText(String.valueOf((int)HSB[0]));
65:               HSBcontrols.tfield2.setText(String.valueOf((int)HSB[1]));
66:               HSBcontrols.tfield3.setText(String.valueOf((int)HSB[2]));
67:
```

20

continues

LISTING 20.4. CONTINUED

```
68:            } else {
69:                // HSB has changed, update RGB
70:                c = Color.getHSBColor((float)value1 / 360,
71:                    (float)value2 / 100, (float)value3 / 100);
72:
73:                // reset RGB fields
74:                RGBcontrols.tfield1.setText(String.valueOf(c.getRed()));
75:                RGBcontrols.tfield2.setText(String.valueOf(c.getGreen()));
76:                RGBcontrols.tfield3.setText(String.valueOf(c.getBlue()));
77:            }
78:
79:            // update swatch
80:            swatch.setBackground(c);
81:            swatch.repaint();
82:        }
83: }
84:
85: class SwingColorControls extends JPanel
86:        implements ActionListener, FocusListener {
87:
88:        SwingColorTest frame;
89:        JTextField tfield1, tfield2, tfield3;
90:
91:        SwingColorControls(SwingColorTest parent,
92:            String l1, String l2, String l3) {
93:
94:            frame = parent;
95:            setLayout(new GridLayout(3,2,10,10));
96:            tfield1 = new JTextField("0");
97:            tfield2 = new JTextField("0");
98:            tfield3 = new JTextField("0");
99:            tfield1.addFocusListener(this);
100:            tfield2.addFocusListener(this);
101:            tfield3.addFocusListener(this);
102:            tfield1.addActionListener(this);
103:            tfield2.addActionListener(this);
104:            tfield3.addActionListener(this);
105:            add(new JLabel(l1, JLabel.RIGHT));
106:            add(tfield1);
107:            add(new JLabel(l2, JLabel.RIGHT));
108:            add(tfield2);
109:            add(new JLabel(l3, JLabel.RIGHT));
110:            add(tfield3);
111:        }
112:
113:        public Insets getInsets() {
114:            return new Insets(10, 10, 0, 0);
```

```
115:        }
116:
117:        public void actionPerformed(ActionEvent evt) {
118:            if (evt.getSource() instanceof TextField)
119:                frame.update(this);
120:        }
121:
122:        public void focusLost(FocusEvent evt) {
123:            frame.update(this);
124:        }
125:
126:        public void focusGained(FocusEvent evt) { }
127: }
```

Figure 20.4 shows the finished product.

FIGURE 20.4.

The SwingColorTest *application.*

Summary

Internally, the event-handling system used with Swing is much more robust and more easily extended to handle new types of user interaction.

Externally, the new system also should make more sense from a programming stand-point. Event handling is added to a program through the same steps:

- A listener interface is added to the class that will contain the event-handling meth-ods.

- A listener is added to each component that will generate the events to handle.

- The methods are added, each with an EventObject class as the only argument to the method.

- Methods of that EventObject class, such as getSource(), are used to learn which component generated the event and what kind of event it was.

Once you know these steps, you can work with each of the different listener interfaces and event classes. You also can learn about new listeners as they are added to Swing with new components.

20

Q&A

Q **Can a program's event-handling behavior be put into its own class instead of including it with the code that creates the interface?**

A It can, and many programmers will tell you that it's a good way to design your programs. Separating interface design from your event-handling code enables the two to be developed separately—the SwingColorTest application today shows the alternative approach. This makes it easier to maintain the project; related behavior is grouped and isolated from unrelated behavior.

WEEK 3

DAY 21

Advanced Swing Programming

Working with Swing

The four weeks in this book provide a thorough introduction to the Swing class library, the most extensive improvement to the Java language introduced in version 2.

The term *introduction* may be discouraging, given the amount of Swing-related material that has been covered up to this point—not to mention what lies ahead today and during Week 4.

However, the term is appropriate, given the complexity and sophistication of Swing's windowing toolkit. There are more than 110 classes in the `javax.swing` package, just 1 of 10 packages in Java 2 that compose the Swing class library.

By comparison, version 1.0 of the Java language contained slightly more than 200 classes in its entire library.

Today you learn about several new Swing components and event-handling techniques, including the following:

- Setting numeric values via sliders
- Combining several components into a toolbar
- Enabling users to move a toolbar to a different part of a user interface
- Tracking a task's progress toward completion with a progress bar
- Using scrollbars with any component by placing it into a scroll pane container

As you learn to use these components and containers, you'll be working with several fairly extensive projects that employ them. You'll also become more accustomed to working with the Swing library.

Swing User-Interface Improvements

During Day 19, "Designing a User Interface with Swing," you learned about the user-interface elements that make up the bulk of most Swing programs—the same group of elements that were offered by the Abstract Windowing Toolkit for prior versions of the language: buttons, text fields, labels, and the like.

Swing also offers a huge number of different new components, including sliders, toolbars, and progress bars.

All of these new components are part of the `javax.swing` package, the Swing library's basic package.

As you are introduced today to new components, containers, and event-handling methods, you'll discover that they use many of the same techniques that the projects on Day 19 use. Most Swing components share the same method calls, such as `setText()` and `getText()` for text components, `setValue()` and `getValue()` for components that store a numeric value, and `setEnabled()` and `getEnabled()` to control user interaction with a component.

Because of these similarities, you can extend your knowledge of new components by focusing on the new features they introduce.

Sliders

Sliders, which are implemented in Swing with the `JSlider` class, enable a number to be set by sliding a control within the range of a minimum and maximum value. In many cases, a slider can be used for numeric input instead of a text field, and it has the advantage of restricting input to a range of acceptable values.

Figure 21.1 shows an example of a JSlider component.

FIGURE 21.1.

A JSlider component.

Sliders are horizontal by default. The orientation can be explicitly set by using two class variables of the SwingConstants class: HORIZONTAL or VERTICAL.

You can use the following constructor methods:

- JSlider(*int*, *int*)   A slider with the specified minimum value and maximum value.

- JSlider(*int*, *int*, *int*)   A slider with the specified minimum value, maximum value, and starting value.

- JSlider(*int*, *int*, *int*, *int*)   A slider with the specified orientation, minimum value, maximum value, and starting value.

Slider components have an optional label that can be used to indicate the minimum value, maximum value, and two different sets of tick marks ranging between the values.

The elements of this label are established by calling several methods of JSlider:

- setMajorTickSpacing(*int*)   Separate major tick marks by the specified distance. The distance is not in pixels, but in value between the minimum and maximum values represented by the slider.

- setMinorTickSpacing(*int*)   Separate minor tick marks by the specified distance. Minor ticks are displayed half as tall as major ticks.

- setPaintTicks(*boolean*)   Determine whether the tick marks should be displayed (a true argument) or not (a false argument).

- setPaintLabels(*boolean*)   Determine whether the numeric label of the slider should be displayed (true) or not (false).

These methods should be called on the slider before it is added to a container.

Listing 21.1 contains the Slider.java source code; the application is shown in Figure 21.1.

21

LISTING 21.1. THE FULL TEXT OF SLIDER.JAVA.

```
 1: import java.awt.event.*;
 2: import javax.swing.*;
 3:
 4: public class Slider extends JFrame {
 5:
 6:     public Slider() {
 7:         super("Slider");
 8:
 9:         JSlider pickNum = new JSlider(JSlider.HORIZONTAL, 0, 30, 5);
10:         pickNum.setMajorTickSpacing(10);
11:         pickNum.setMinorTickSpacing(1);
12:         pickNum.setPaintTicks(true);
13:         pickNum.setPaintLabels(true);
14:         JPanel pane = new JPanel();
15:         pane.add(pickNum);
16:
17:         setContentPane(pane);
18:     }
19:
20:     public static void main(String[] args) {
21:         Slider frame = new Slider();
22:
23:         WindowListener l = new WindowAdapter() {
24:             public void windowClosing(WindowEvent e) {
25:                 System.exit(0);
26:             }
27:         };
28:         frame.addWindowListener(l);
29:
30:         frame.pack();
31:         frame.setVisible(true);
32:     }
33: }
```

Lines 9–17 contain the code that's used to create a JSlider component, set up its tick marks to be displayed, and add the component to a container. The rest of the program is a basic framework for an application that consists of a main JFrame container with no menus.

Change Listeners

Slider movement is represented in Swing by the ChangeEvent class, which like other new event-handling classes introduced with Swing, is part of the javax.swing.event package.

In order to make a component generate change events, a listener must be added by calling the component's addChangeListener(*Object*) method. The argument to the method is the object that will handle the change event. The keyword this can be used if the same object is being used to send the event and to receive it.

The class that receives a ChangeEvent must implement the ChangeListener interface. This interface includes only one method—stateChanged(*ChangeEvent*)—which takes the following format:

```
public void stateChanged(ChangeEvent evt) {
    // method code here
}
```

The event's getSource() method can be used to find out which component generated the change event.

An important thing to note about change events and sliders is the frequency at which they are generated. When a user moves a slider from one value to another, change events are generated throughout the move, even as the slider is being dragged.

The component's getValueIsAdjusting() method can be used to test whether the slider is still being moved. This returns true while the slider is moving and false otherwise.

The following is an example of a stateChanged() for two slider components:

```
public void stateChanged(ChangeEvent evt) {
    int value1, value2;
    Object source = evt.getSource();
    if (source == slider1)
        value1 = slider1.getValue();
    else
        value2 = slider2.getValue();
}
```

Scroll Panes

In versions of Java prior to 2, some components (such as text areas) had a built-in scrollbar. The bar could be used when the text in the component took up more space than the component could display. Scrollbars could be used in either the vertical or horizontal direction to scroll through the text.

One of the most common examples of scrolling is in a Web browser, where a scrollbar can be used on any page that is bigger than the browser's display area.

Swing changes the rules for scrollbars to the following:

- In order for a component to be able to scroll, it must be added to a JScrollPane container.

- This JScrollPane container is added to a container in place of the scrollable component.

21

Scroll panes can be created by using the ScrollPane(*Object*) constructor, where *Object* represents the component that can be scrolled.

The following example creates a text area in a scroll pane and adds it to a container called mainPane:

```
textBox = new JTextArea(7, 30);
JScrollPane scroller = new JScrollPane(textBox);
mainPane.add(scroller);
```

As you're working with scroll panes, it can often be useful to indicate the size you would like it to occupy on the interface. This is done by calling the setPreferredSize(*Dimension*) method of the scroll pane before it is added to a container. The Dimension object represents the width and height of the preferred size represented in pixels.

The following code builds on the previous example by setting the preferred size of the scroller object:

```
Dimension pref = new Dimension(350, 100);
scroller.setPreferredSize(pref);
```

This should be handled before the scroller object is added to a container.

By default, a scroll pane does not display scrollbars unless they are needed. If the component inside the pane is no larger than the pane itself, the bars won't appear. In the case of components such as text areas, where the component size may increase as the program is used, the bars automatically appear when they're needed and disappear otherwise.

To override this behavior, you can set a policy when the JScrollBar component is created by using several ScrollPaneConstants class variables:

- HORIZONTAL_SCROLLBAR_ALWAYS
- HORIZONTAL_SCROLLBAR_AS_NEEDED
- HORIZONTAL_SCROLLBAR_NEVER
- VERTICAL_SCROLLBAR_ALWAYS
- VERTICAL_SCROLLBAR_AS_NEEDED
- VERTICAL_SCROLLBAR_NEVER

These class variables are used with the ScrollPane(*Object, int, int*) constructor, which specifies the component in the pane, the vertical scrollbar policy, and the horizontal scrollbar policy.

Toolbars

A *toolbar*, created in Swing with the JToolBar class, is a container that groups several components into a row or column. These components most often are buttons.

If you have used software such as Microsoft Word, Netscape Navigator, or Lotus WordPro, you probably are familiar with the concept of toolbars. In these programs and many others, the most commonly used program options are grouped together as a series of buttons. You can click these buttons as an alternative to using pull-down menus or shortcut keys.

Toolbars are horizontal by default, but the orientation is explicitly set with the HORIZON-TAL or VERTICAL class variables of the SwingConstants class.

Constructor methods include the following:

- JToolBar()   Create a new toolbar.
- JToolBar(*int*)   Create a new toolbar with the specified orientation.

Once you have created a toolbar, you can add components to it by using the toolbar's add(*Object*) method, where *Object* represents the component to place on the toolbar.

Many programs that use toolbars allow the user to move the bars. These are called *dockable toolbars* because you can dock them along an edge of the screen like a boat being brought to dock. Swing toolbars also can be docked into a new window, separate from the original.

A dockable JToolBar component must be laid out using the BorderLayout manager. As you may recall, a border layout divides a container into five areas: north, south, east, west, and center. Each of the directional components takes up whatever space it needs, and the rest is allocated to the center.

The toolbar should be placed in one of the directional areas of the border layout. The only other area of the layout that can be filled is the center.

Figure 21.2 shows a dockable toolbar occupying the north area of a border layout. A text area has been placed in the center.

FIGURE 21.2.

A dockable toolbar and a text area.

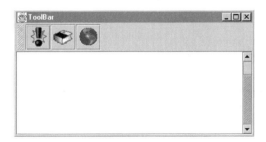

21

Listing 21.2 contains the source code used to produce this application.

LISTING 21.2. THE FULL TEXT OF TOOLBAR.JAVA.

```
 1: import java.awt.*;
 2: import java.awt.event.*;
 3: import javax.swing.*;
 4:
 5: public class ToolBar extends JFrame {
 6:
 7:     public ToolBar() {
 8:         super("ToolBar");
 9:
10:         ImageIcon image1 = new ImageIcon("button1.gif");
11:         JButton button1 = new JButton(image1);
12:         ImageIcon image2 = new ImageIcon("button2.gif");
13:         JButton button2 = new JButton(image2);
14:         ImageIcon image3 = new ImageIcon("button3.gif");
15:         JButton button3 = new JButton(image3);
16:         JToolBar bar = new JToolBar();
17:         bar.add(button1);
18:         bar.add(button2);
19:         bar.add(button3);
20:         JTextArea edit = new JTextArea(8,40);
21:         JScrollPane scroll = new JScrollPane(edit);
22:         JPanel pane = new JPanel();
23:         BorderLayout bord = new BorderLayout();
24:         pane.setLayout(bord);
25:         pane.add("North", bar);
26:         pane.add("Center", scroll);
27:
28:         setContentPane(pane);
29:     }
30:
31:     public static void main(String[] args) {
32:         ToolBar frame = new ToolBar();
33:
34:         WindowListener l = new WindowAdapter() {
35:             public void windowClosing(WindowEvent e) {
36:                 System.exit(0);
37:             }
38:         };
39:         frame.addWindowListener(l);
40:
41:         frame.pack();
42:         frame.setVisible(true);
43:     }
44: }
```

This application uses three images to represent the graphics on the buttons: button1.gif, button2.gif, and button3.gif. You can find these on the book's CD-ROM or the book's official World Wide Web site at http://www.prefect.com/java21pre. You also can use graphics from your own system, though they must be in GIF format and reasonably small.

The toolbar in this application can be grabbed by its handle—the area immediately to the left of the exclamation button in Figure 21.2. If you drag it within the window, you can dock it along different edges of the application window. When you release the toolbar, the application is rearranged using the border layout manager. You also can drag the toolbar out of the application window entirely.

Although toolbars are most commonly used with graphical buttons, they can contain textual buttons, combo boxes, and other components.

Progress Bars

If you have ever installed computer software, you're familiar with *progress bars*. These components are most commonly used with a long task to show the user how much time is left before the task is complete.

Progress bars are implemented in Swing through the JProgressBar class. An example of a Java program that makes use of this component is shown in Figure 21.3.

FIGURE 21.3.

The progress bar is above a text area and button.

Progress bars are used to track the progress of a task that can be represented numerically. They are created by specifying a minimum and a maximum value that represent the points at which the task is beginning and ending.

A software installation that consists of 335 different files is an example. The number of files transferred can be used to monitor the progress of the task. The minimum value is 0 and the maximum value 335.

21

Constructor methods include the following:

- JProgressBar()   Create a new progress bar.

- JProgressBar(*int*, *int*)   Create a new progress bar with the specified minimum value and maximum value.

- JProgressBar(*int*, *int*, *int*)   Create a new progress bar with the specified orientation, minimum value, and maximum value.

The orientation of a progress bar can be established with the SwingConstants.VERTICAL and SwingConstants.HORIZONTAL class variables. Progress bars are horizontal by default.

The minimum and maximum values also can be set up by calling the progress bar's setMinimum(*int*) and setMaximum(*int*) values with the indicated values.

To update a progress bar, you call its setValue(*int*) method with a value indicating how far along the task is at that moment. This value should be somewhere between the minimum and maximum values established for the bar. The following example tells the install progress bar in the preceding example of a software installation how many files have been uploaded thus far:

```
int filesDone = getNumberOfFiles();
install.setValue(filesDone);
```

In this example, the getNumberOfFiles() method represents some code that would be used to keep track of how many files have been copied so far during the installation. When this value is passed to the progress bar by the setValue() method, the bar is immediately updated to represent the percentage of the task that has been completed.

Progress bars often include a text label in addition to the graphic of an empty box filling up. This label displays the percentage of the task that has become completed, and you can set it up for a bar by calling the setStringPainted(*boolean*) method with a value of true. A false argument turns this label off.

Listing 21.3 contains Progress, the application shown at the beginning of this section in Figure 21.3.

LISTING 21.3. THE FULL TEXT OF PROGRESS.JAVA.

```
1: import java.awt.*;
2: import java.awt.event.*;
3: import javax.swing.*;
4:
5: public class Progress extends JFrame
6:     implements Runnable, ActionListener {
```

```
 7:
 8:        JProgressBar current;
 9:        JTextArea out;
10:        JButton find;
11:        Thread runner;
12:        int currentVal;
13:        static int GOAL = 2000;
14:
15:        public Progress() {
16:            super("Progress");
17:
18:            JPanel top = new JPanel();
19:            top.setLayout(new FlowLayout());
20:            current = new JProgressBar(0, GOAL);
21:            current.setValue(0);
22:            current.setStringPainted(true);
23:            top.add(current);
24:
25:            out = new JTextArea(8, 30);
26:            out.setLineWrap(true);
27:            JScrollPane scroller = new JScrollPane(out);
28:            JPanel bottom = new JPanel();
29:            bottom.setLayout(new FlowLayout());
30:            find = new JButton("Find First " + GOAL + " Primes");
31:            find.addActionListener(this);
32:            bottom.add(find);
33:
34:            JPanel pane = new JPanel();
35:            pane.setLayout(new BorderLayout());
36:            pane.add("North", top);
37:            pane.add("Center", scroller);
38:            pane.add("South", bottom);
39:
40:            setContentPane(pane);
41:        }
42:
43:
44:        public void run() {
45:            find.setEnabled(false);
46:            int numPrimes = 0;
47:            int candidate = 2;
48:            out.setText("");
49:            while (numPrimes < GOAL) {
50:                if (isPrime(candidate)) {
51:                    numPrimes++;
52:                    current.setValue(numPrimes);
53:                    out.append(candidate + " ");
54:                }
55:                candidate++;
56:            }
57:            find.setEnabled(true);
```

continues

LISTING 21.3. CONTINUED

```
58:     }
59:
60:     boolean isPrime(int checkNumber) {
61:         double root = Math.sqrt(checkNumber);
62:         for (int i = 2; i <= root; i++) {
63:             if (checkNumber % i == 0)
64:                 return false;
65:         }
66:         return true;
67:     }
68:
69:     public void actionPerformed(ActionEvent evt) {
70:         Object source = evt.getSource();
71:         if (source == find) {
72:             Thread runner = new Thread(this);
73:             runner.start();
74:         }
75:     }
76:
77:     public static void main(String[] args) {
78:         Progress frame = new Progress();
79:
80:         WindowListener l = new WindowAdapter() {
81:             public void windowClosing(WindowEvent e) {
82:                 System.exit(0);
83:             }
84:         };
85:         frame.addWindowListener(l);
86:
87:         frame.pack();
88:         frame.setVisible(true);
89:     }
90: }
```

The Progress application is used to find the first 2,000 prime numbers and display their values in a text area. This task can take up to a minute to complete, depending on the speed of your system and other factors.

Using a progress bar is a way to make the program more user friendly when a computer program is going to be busy for more than a few seconds. Software users like progress bars because they indicate how much more time something's going to take, and this information can be a deciding factor in whether to wait at the computer, launch an expedition for something to drink, or take advantage of the company's lax policy in regard to personal long-distance calls. (If the task is especially time consuming, a progress bar is essential—artists who create 3D computer scenes have become accustomed to tasks that take 12 hours or more to complete).

Progress bars also provide another essential piece of information: proof that the program is still running and has not crashed.

The Progress program keeps track of the number of primes that have been found, a variable that makes it possible to track the task with a progress bar.

In line 20, a JProgressBar object is created with a minimum value of 0 and a maximum value of 2000—the starting and ending totals for the task of finding 2,000 prime numbers.

When the Find button is clicked, a new thread that handles the task of finding the prime numbers is created. When this thread begins with a call to its start() method in line 73, the run() method in lines 44–58 is called.

In this method, the numPrimes integer is used to track how many primes have been found. This is used in line 52 as the argument to the progress bar's setValue() method.

A Swing Image Viewer Applet

The conclusion to your three-day swing through Java's new windowing classes is a more sophisticated project. The Viewer applet is an image viewer that displays images that are larger than the applet's display area through the use of a scroll pane.

In addition, you can use a slider to set the reproduction size of the image, which can range from 1 to 150 percent.

The Viewer applet takes a single parameter—IMAGE—which is used to specify a GIF or JPEG graphic to display in the applet's viewing area.

If the image is larger than the area that has been allotted to it on the applet window, scrollbars can be used to display different parts of the image.

Listing 21.4 contains the applet's full source code.

LISTING 21.4. THE FULL TEXT OF VIEWER.JAVA.

```
 1: import java.awt.*;
 2: import javax.swing.event.*;
 3: import javax.swing.*;
 4:
 5: public class Viewer extends javax.swing.JApplet
 6:     implements ChangeListener {
 7:
 8:     JLabel pictLabel;
 9:     JSlider size;
10:     JScrollPane scroller;
```

21

continues

LISTING 21.4. CONTINUED

```
11:
12:     Image lookSee, newLook;
13:
14:     public void init() {
15:         JPanel top = new JPanel();
16:         top.setLayout(new BorderLayout());
17:         JLabel sizeLabel = new JLabel
                ("Display Size (as a %)", JLabel.CENTER);
18:         size = new JSlider(JSlider.HORIZONTAL, 0, 150, 100);
19:         size.setMajorTickSpacing(50);
20:         size.setMinorTickSpacing(10);
21:         size.setPaintTicks(true);
22:         size.setPaintLabels(true);
23:         size.addChangeListener(this);
24:         top.add("North", sizeLabel);
25:         top.add("Center", size);
26:
27:         String source = getParameter("IMAGE");
28:         if (source != null) {
29:             lookSee = getImage(getCodeBase(), source);
30:             ImageIcon lookIcon = new ImageIcon(lookSee);
31:             pictLabel = new JLabel(lookIcon);
32:             pictLabel.setVerticalAlignment(SwingConstants.TOP);
33:             pictLabel.setHorizontalAlignment(SwingConstants.LEFT);
34:         } else
35:             pictLabel = new JLabel();
36:         scroller = new JScrollPane(pictLabel,
37:             ScrollPaneConstants.VERTICAL_SCROLLBAR_ALWAYS,
38:             ScrollPaneConstants.HORIZONTAL_SCROLLBAR_ALWAYS);
39:
40:         JPanel pane = new JPanel();
41:         pane.setLayout(new BorderLayout());
42:         pane.add("North", top);
43:         pane.add("Center", scroller);
44:
45:         setContentPane(pane);
46:     }
47:
48:     public void stateChanged(ChangeEvent evt) {
49:         if (size.getValueIsAdjusting() != true) {
50:             float scale = (float)size.getValue() / 100;
51:             int width = lookSee.getWidth(this);
52:             int height = lookSee.getHeight(this);
53:             newLook = lookSee.getScaledInstance(
54:                 (int)(scale*width),
55:                 (int)(scale*height),
56:                 Image.SCALE_FAST);
57:             pictLabel.setIcon(new ImageIcon(newLook));
58:             scroller.validate();
59:         }
60:     }
61: }
```

This applet requires the use of the `appletviewer` or a Web browser that fully supports Java 1.2; there wasn't one available at the time of this writing.

The HTML code of a Web page that can be used to display the applet is shown in Listing 21.5.

LISTING 21.5. THE FULL TEXT OF VIEWER.HTML.

```
1: <applet code="Viewer.class" height=400 width=400>
2: <param name="IMAGE" value="highway.jpg">
3: </applet>
```

Because this program takes the image from an `<APPLET>` parameter, it can be used to display any image that's stored on your hard drive. If you're trying this out on the World Wide Web, you can use it to display any image that's stored on the same Web server as the applet itself. (The graphics files stored on other servers can't be loaded from an applet due to the default security restrictions in place for an applet.)

Listing 21.5 refers to a graphic called `highway.jpg` that can be found on this book's CD-ROM or its Web site at `http://www.prefect.com/java21pre`.

> **Caution**
>
> This applet can be fairly memory-intensive if you're working with an extremely large image. As you're testing the program, you may want to use a smaller image or close all applications other than the one that's loading the applet.

An example of this applet running is shown in Figure 21.4.

As you'll see when running this applet, rescaling the image to a new size can take a few seconds (or more), depending on your system, the image, and the memory available to the Java interpreter.

This applet contains one event-handling method, `stateChanged()`, which is part of the `ChangeListener` interface. Because `ChangeListener` is part of the new `javax.swing.event` package, this package is imported in line 2 of the program.

The `stateChanged()` method is called every time the slider is moved, even if it is still being dragged. To prevent this from causing constant image rescaling, the slider's `getValueIsAdjusting()` method is checked every time that `stateChanged()` is called. This method returns a `true` value while a slider is being dragged from one value to another, and only returns `false` when it has been released.

21

FIGURE 21.4.

The Viewer applet.

Lines 53–57 of the `stateChanged()` method are used to create a new `Image` object, which is a scaled version of the `lookSee` image; the `lookSee` image holds the graphics file being viewed.

The `getScaledInstance()` method of the `lookSee` object is called to create the scaled image. This method takes three arguments: the new width of the object, the new height of the object, and the rules under which the scaling should be processed. The class variable `SCALE_FAST` indicates that image quality should be sacrificed in an effort to scale the image as quickly as possible.

The other class variables that could have been used are as follows:

- `SCALE_AREA_AVERAGING`   Scale using the area-averaging method.
- `SCALE_REPLICATE`   Scale using the `ReplicateScaleFilter` class's scaling method.
- `SCALE_SMOOTH`   Scale with a preference for image quality at the expense of scaling speed.
- `SCALE_DEFAULT`   Scale use the default scaling method.

Line 58 of the Viewer applet contains a call to the scroll pane's `validate()` method. This can be called on any container, and it tells the Java windowing system that the contents of the container may need to be updated due to a change in the container's contents. The call to `validate()` makes sure that the scroll pane is updated to reflect the size change of `pictLabel`.

Summary

Java programmers who have worked with the language since the introduction of 1.0 often decried the limitations of the Abstract Windowing Toolkit, the class library used to implement a graphical user interface in Java programs.

During the past three years, many companies and individuals have introduced new user-interface components and class libraries. Some supplemented the Abstract Windowing Toolkit, while others sought to replace it entirely.

The Swing class library represents a huge effort by Sun to supplement and extend the Abstract Windowing Toolkit. Swing makes it possible to create a graphical user interface with Java that's comparable to those possible with more established languages such as Visual C++, Visual Basic, and Borland Delphi.

In the bonus week to this book you have the opportunity to work with additional aspects of Swing, including the Accessibility library, a package of classes that offer support for computer users with various abilities.

Q&A

Q In the Progress application, why is the GOAL variable declared with the static modifier and named with all capital letters?

A The GOAL variable is used to represent the number of prime numbers being searched for in the program. This number would not change during the run of the program, so it can be a constant—a variable that keeps the same value. Constants are normally declared static variables so that each object of that class does not need to redundantly store its own copy of the same value.

The capitalization of the variable name is a programming convention to differentiate constants from other variables. This makes it easier to replace a constant with the value it stores if the programmer decides later that this will speed the execution of the program.

Q If scroll panes adjust themselves dynamically based on their contents, why would there be a reason to configure scrollbars to always be visible?

A Aside from aesthetic considerations, there shouldn't be a reason for always-displayed scrollbars other than a means of avoiding user confusion.

However, bugs in beta versions of the Java Development Kit caused the scrollbars to disappear after a scroll pane's contents shrank and then were expanded later. Keeping the scroll bars visible is a way to ensure that a user always will be able to use them when needed.

21

Q **How can I find out more about the entire Swing class library—more specifically, about the methods and constructors for each of these components?**

A The most up-to-date and extensive source of information is Sun's official documentation for Java 2's class library. It is available for free on the World Wide Web at `http://java.sun.com/products/jdk/1.2/docs/api`.

You also ought to check out the *Swing Connection*, a Web magazine that Sun publishes currently at `http://java.sun.com/products/jfc/tsc/index.html`. The site includes announcements related to Swing and tutorials for different aspects of the library, including component-specific projects like the ones you've tackled today.

BONUS WEEK

Expanding Your Knowledge of Java

22

23

24

25

26

27

28

BONUS WEEK

DAY 22

The Java Development Kit

The Java Development Kit (JDK) has been used throughout this book to create, compile, and run Java programs. Because of this, you might think you're already an expert in its use.

This chapter, the first of seven that focus on advanced topics, should poke a hole in that belief fairly quickly. The tools that make up the JDK contain numerous features that many programmers don't explore at all, and some of the tools themselves may be new to you.

Today, you'll learn about many of these tools and about features you can use to create more reliable, better-tested, and faster-running Java programs.

The following topics will be covered:

- Running Java applications with the interpreter.
- Compiling programs with the compiler.
- Running Java applets with the appletviewer.
- Creating documentation with the documentation tool.
- Finding bugs in your program and learning more about its performance with the debugger.
- Setting system properties with the interpreter and applet viewer.

An Overview of the JDK

Although there are several dozen software packages that you can use to create Java programs, the most widely used is the Java Development Kit (JDK) from Sun Microsystems. It's a set of command-line tools that are used to develop software with the Java language.

There are two main reasons for the popularity of the JDK:

- It's free. You can download a copy at no cost from Sun's official Java World Wide Web site at `http://java.sun.com`.
- It's first. Whenever Sun releases a new version of the language, the first tools that support this version are in the JDK.

The JDK uses the command line—also called the MS-DOS prompt on Windows 95/98 systems and the console on Windows NT. Commands are entered using the keyboard, as in the following example:

```
javac BeanieBase.java
```

This command compiles a Java program called `BeanieBase.java` using the JDK compiler. There are two elements to the command: the name of the JDK compiler, `javac`, followed by the name of the program to compile, `BeanieBase.java`. The two elements are separated by a space character.

Each JDK command follows the same format: the name of the tool to use, followed by one or more elements indicating what the tool should do. These elements are called *arguments*.

The following illustrates the use of command-line arguments:

```
java BeanieBase add Blizzard "white tiger"
```

This command tells the Java interpreter to run a class file called `BeanieBase` with three command-line arguments: the strings `add`, `Blizzard`, and `white tiger`.

 Note

You might think there are four command-line arguments because of the space between the words `white` and `tiger`. The quote marks around `"white tiger"` cause it to be considered one command-line argument rather than two. This makes it possible to include a space character.

Some arguments used with the JDK modify how a tool will function. These arguments are preceded by a hyphen character and are called *options*.

22

The following command shows the use of an option:

```
java -version
```

This command tells the Java interpreter to display its version number rather than trying to run a class file. It's a good way to find out if the JDK is configured to run Java programs correctly on your system. Here's an example of the output if you're running JDK 1.2:

```
java version "1.2"
Classic VM (build JDK-1.2-v, native threads)
```

In some instances, you can combine options with other arguments. If you compile a Java class that uses deprecated methods, you can see more information on these methods by compiling the class with a -deprecation option, as in the following:

```
javac -deprecation OldBeanieBase.java
```

The java Interpreter

java, the Java interpreter, is used to run Java applications from the command line. It takes as an argument the name of a class file to run, as in the following example:

```
java BuyBeanie
```

Although Java class files end with the .class extension, this extension is not specified when using the interpreter.

The class loaded by the Java interpreter must contain a main() method that takes the following form:

```
public static void main(String[] arguments) {
    // Method here
}
```

Some simple Java programs may use only one class—the one containing the main() method. In other cases, the interpreter automatically loads any other classes that are needed.

The Java interpreter runs bytecode—the compiled instructions that are executed by a Java virtual machine. Once a Java program is in bytecode form as a .class file, it can be run by different interpreters without modification. If you have compiled a Java 2 program, it should be compatible with any interpreter that fully supports Java 2.

Note

Interestingly enough, Java is no longer the only language that you can use to create Java bytecode. NetRexx, JPython, and several other languages will compile into .class files of executable bytecode through the use of compilers specific to those languages. A list of these languages is currently available from the Web page at http://grunge.cs.tu-berlin.de/~tolk/vmlanguages.html.

There are two different ways to specify the class file that should be run by the Java interpreter. If the class is not part of any package, you can run it by specifying the name of the class, as in the preceding java BuyBeanie example and all the examples in prior chapters of this book. If the class is part of a package, you must specify the class by using its full package and class name.

For example, consider a SellBeanie class that is part of the com.prefect.beanies package. To run this application, the following command would be used:

```
java com.prefect.beanies.SellBeanie
```

Each element of the package name corresponds to its own subfolder, so the Java interpreter will look for the SellBeanie.class file in several different places:

- The com\prefect\ subfolder of the folder where the java command was entered. (If the command was made from the C:\J21work folder, for example, the SellBeanie.class file could be run successfully if it was in the C:\J21work\com\prefect folder.)
- The com\prefect\ subfolder of any folder in your CLASSPATH setting.

If you're creating your own packages, an easy way to manage them is to add a folder to your CLASSPATH that's the root folder for any packages you create. After creating subfolders based on your package names, you can compile the Java source files within these subfolders and run them from any folder on your system.

The javac Compiler

javac, the Java compiler, converts Java source code into one or more class files of bytecode that can be run by a Java interpreter.

Java source code is stored in a file with the .java file extension. This file can be created with any text editor or word processor that can save a document without any special formatting codes. The terminology varies depending on the text editing software being used, but these files are often called plain text, ASCII text, DOS text, or something similar.

22

A Java source code file can contain more than one class, but only one of the classes can be declared to be public. A class can contain no public classes at all if desired, although this isn't possible with applets because of the rules of inheritance.

If a source code file contains a class that has been declared to be public, the name of the file must match the name of that class. For example, the source code for a public class called DeleteBeanie must be stored in a file called DeleteBeanie.java.

To compile a file, the javac tool is run with the name of the file as an argument, as in the following:

```
javac BuyBeanie.java
```

You can compile more than one source file by including each separate filename as a command-line argument, such as this command:

```
javac BuyBeanie.java SellBeanie.java
```

You also can use wildcard characters such as * and ?. Use the following command to compile all .java files in a folder:

```
javac *.java
```

When you compile one or more Java source code files, a separate .class file will be created for each Java class that compiles successfully.

Caution

> An easy mistake to make when you're putting a Java applet on the Web is to forget some of the .class files that make up the applet. You can combine several files into a single archive using the jar tool, which you learned about on Day 8, "Putting Interactive Programs on the Web." jar enables all files associated with an applet to be grouped together into a single file.

One of the javac tool's options is -deprecation, which you can use to find out more about the deprecated methods being employed in a Java program. Normally, the compiler will issue a single warning if it finds any deprecated methods in a program. The -deprecation option causes the compiler to list each method that has been deprecated, as in the following command:

```
javac -deprecation SellBeanie.java
```

If you're more concerned with the speed of a Java program than the size of its class files, you can compile its source code with the -O option. This creates class files that have been optimized for faster performance. Methods that are static, final, or private may be compiled *inline*, a technique that makes the class file larger but causes the methods to be executed more quickly.

Normally, the Java compiler doesn't provide a lot of information. In fact, if all of the source code compiles successfully and no deprecated methods are employed, you won't see any output from the compiler at all. No news is good news in this case.

If you'd like to see more information on what the `javac` tool is doing as it compiles source code, use the `-verbose` option. The more verbose compiler will describe the time it takes to complete different functions, the classes that are being loaded, and the overall time required.

The `appletviewer` Browser

`appletviewer`, the Java applet viewer, is used to run Java programs that require a Web browser and are presented as part of a Web page.

`appletviewer` takes a Web page as a command-line argument, as in the following example:

```
appletviewer BeanieSearch.html
```

When a page is loaded by `appletviewer`, every applet on that page will begin running in its own window. The size of these windows depends on the HEIGHT and WIDTH attributes that were set in the applet's HTML tag.

Unlike a Web browser, `appletviewer` cannot be used to view the Web page itself. If you want to see how the applet(s) is laid out in relation to the other contents of the page, you must use a Java-capable Web browser such as Netscape Navigator or Microsoft Internet Explorer.

 Note

At the time of this writing, neither Navigator nor Internet Explorer supports Java 2 applets. Sun has developed a Java plug-in that can be used to run version 2 applets with either browser. It is available from Sun's Web site at `http://java.sun.com/products/plugin`. This plug-in is also part of the JDK 1.2 as well as the JRE 1.2.

Using `appletviewer` is reasonably straightforward, but you may not be familiar with some of the menu options that are available as the viewer runs an applet. Figure 22.1 shows the options on the `appletviewer` tool's Applet pull-down menu.

FIGURE 22.1.

The Applet pull-down menu of `appletviewer`.

The following menu options are available:

- The Restart and Reload options are used to restart the execution of the applet. The difference between these two options is that Restart does not unload the applet before restarting it, while Reload does. The Reload option is equivalent to closing the applet viewer and opening it up again on the same Web page.

- The Start and Stop options are used to directly call the `start()` and `stop()` methods of the applet.

- The Clone option creates a second copy of the same applet running in its own window.

- The Tag option displays the program's <APPLET> tag, along with the HTML for any <PARAM> tags that configure the applet.

Another option on the Applet pull-down menu is Info, which calls the `getAppletInfo()` and `getParameterInfo()` methods of the applet. A programmer can implement these methods to provide more information about the applet and the parameters that it can handle. The `getAppletInfo()` method should return a string that describes the applet. The `getParameterInfo()` method should return an array of string arrays that specify the name, type, and description of each parameter.

Listing 22.1 contains an applet that demonstrates the use of these methods.

LISTING 22.1. THE FULL TEXT OF APPINFO.JAVA.

```
 1: import java.awt.Graphics;
 2:
 3: public class AppInfo extends java.applet.Applet {
 4:     String name, date;
 5:     int version;
 6:
 7:     public String getAppletInfo() {
 8:         String response = "This applet demonstrates the "
 9:             + "use of the Applet's Info feature.";
10:         return response;
11:     }
12:
13:     public String[][] getParameterInfo() {
14:         String[] p1 = { "Name", "String", "Programmer's name" };
15:         String[] p2 = { "Date", "String", "Today's date" };
16:         String[] p3 = { "Version", "int", "Version number" };
17:         String[][] response = { p1, p2, p3 };
18:         return response;
19:     }
20:
21:     public void init() {
22:         name = getParameter("Name");
23:         date = getParameter("Date");
24:         String versText = getParameter("Version");
25:         if (versText != null)
26:             version = Integer.parseInt(versText);
28:     }
29:
30:     public void paint(Graphics screen) {
31:         screen.drawString("Name: " + name, 5, 50);
32:         screen.drawString("Date: " + date, 5, 100);
33:         screen.drawString("Version: " + version, 5, 150);
34:     }
35: }
```

The main function of this applet is to display the value of three parameters: Name, Date, and Version. The getAppletInfo() method returns the following string:

This applet demonstrates the use of the Applet's Info feature.

The getParameterInfo() method is a bit more complicated if you haven't worked with multi-dimensional arrays. The following things are taking place:

- Line 13 defines the return type of the method as a two-dimensional array of String objects.

- Line 14 creates an array of String objects with three elements: "Name", "String", and "Programmer's Name". These elements describe one of the parameters that can be defined for the AppInfo applet. They describe the name of the parameter (Name in this case), the type of data that the parameter should hold (a string), and a description of the parameter ("Programmer's Name"). The three-element array is stored in the p1 object.

- Lines 15 and 16 define two more String arrays for the Date and Version parameters.

- Line 17 uses the response object to store an array that contains three string arrays: p1, p2, and p3.

- Line 18 uses the response object as the method's return value.

Listing 22.2 contains a Web page that can be used to load the AppInfo applet.

LISTING 22.2. THE FULL TEXT OF APPINFO.HTML.

```
1: <applet code="AppInfo.class" height=200 width=170>
2: <param name="Name" value="Rogers Cadenhead">
3: <param name="Date" value="12/05/98">
4: <param name="Version" value="1">
5: </applet>
```

Figure 22.2 shows the applet running with the applet viewer, and Figure 22.3 is a screen capture of the dialog box that opens when the viewer's Info menu option is selected.

FIGURE 22.2.

The AppInfo applet running in appletviewer.

FIGURE 22.3.

The Info dialog box of the AppInfo applet.

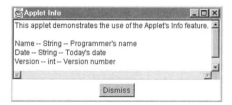

These features require a browser that makes this information available to users. The `appletviewer` handles this through the Info menu option, but browsers such as Internet Explorer 4.0 do not offer anything like it at this time.

The `javadoc` Documentation Tool

`javadoc`, the Java documentation creator, takes a `.java` source code file or package name as input and generates detailed documentation in HTML format.

In order for `javadoc` to create full documentation for a program, a special type of comment statement must be used in the program's source code. On previous days, you have used `//`, `/*` and `*/` in source code to create *comments*—information for people who are trying to make sense of the program.

Java also has a more structured type of comment that can be read by the `javadoc` tool. This comment is used to describe program elements such as classes, variables, objects, and methods. It takes the following format:

```
/** A descriptive sentence or paragraph.
  * @tag1 Description of this tag.
  * @tag2 Description of this tag.
  */
```

A Java documentation comment should be placed immediately above the program element it is documenting and should succinctly explain what the program element is. For example, if the comment precedes a `class` statement, it should describe the purpose of the class.

In addition to the descriptive text, different items can be used to further document the program element. These items, called *tags,* are preceded by an @ sign and are followed by a space and a descriptive sentence or paragraph.

Listing 22.3 contains a thoroughly documented version of the AppInfo applet called AppInfo2. The following tags are used in this program:

- `@author`—The program's author. This tag can be used only when documenting a class, and it will be ignored unless the `-author` option is used when `javadoc` is run.

- `@version text`—The program's version number. This also is restricted to class documentation, and it requires the `-version` option when you're running `javadoc` or the tag will be ignored.

- `@return text`—The variable or object returned by the method being documented.

- @serial *text*—A description of the data type and possible values for a variable or object that can be serialized. You'll learn more about serialization during Day 25, "Advanced Object Programming."

LISTING 22.3. THE FULL TEXT OF APPINFO2.JAVA.

```
 1: import java.awt.Graphics;
 2:
 3: /** This class creates displays the values of three parameters:
 4:  * Name, Date and Version.
 5:  * @author <a href="http://www.prefect.com/java21pre">
         Rogers Cadenhead</a>
 6:  * @version 1.0
 7:  */
 8: public class AppInfo2 extends java.applet.Applet {
 9:     /**
10:      * @serial The programmer's name.
11:      */
12:     String name;
13:     /**
14:      * @serial The current date.
15:      */
16:     String date;
17:     /**
18:      * @serial The program's version number.
19:      */
20:     int version;
21:
22:     /**
23:      * This method describes the applet for any browsing tool that
24:      * request information out the program.
25:      * @return A String describing the applet.
26:      */
27:     public String getAppletInfo() {
28:         String response = "This applet demonstrates the "
29:             + "use of the Applet's Info feature.";
30:         return response;
31:     }
32:
33:     /**
34:      * This method describes the parameters that the applet can take
35:      * for any browsing tool that requests this information.
36:      * @return An array of String[] objects for each parameter.
37:      */
38:     public String[][] getParameterInfo() {
39:         String[] p1 = { "Name", "String", "Programmer's name" };
40:         String[] p2 = { "Date", "String", "Today's date" };
41:         String[] p3 = { "Version", "int", "Version number" };
42:         String[][] response = { p1, p2, p3 };
```

continues

LISTING 22.3. CONTINUED

```
43:          return response;
44:     }
45:
46:     /**
47:      * This method is called when the applet is first initialized.
48:      */
49:     public void init() {
50:         name = getParameter("Name");
51:         date = getParameter("Date");
52:         String versText = getParameter("Version");
53:         if (versText != null)
54:             version = Integer.parseInt(versText);
55:     }
56:
57:     /**
58:      * This method is called when the applet's display window is
59:      * being repainted.
60:      */
61:     public void paint(Graphics screen) {
62:         screen.drawString("Name: " + name, 5, 50);
63:         screen.drawString("Date: " + date, 5, 100);
64:         screen.drawString("Version: " + version, 5, 150);
65:     }
66: }
```

The following command would be used to create HTML documentation from the source code file AppInfo2.java:

```
javadoc -author -version AppInfo2.java
```

The Java documentation tool will create several different Web pages in the same folder as AppInfo2.java. These pages will document the program in the same manner as Sun's official documentation for the Java language.

Tip

To see the official documentation for Java 2, the JDK, and the Java 2 class libraries, visit http://java.sun.com/products/jdk/1.2/docs/.

To see the documentation that javadoc has created for AppInfo2, load the newly created Web page index.html on your Web browser. Figure 22.4 shows this page loaded with Internet Explorer.

FIGURE 22.4.

Java documentation for the AppInfo2 program.

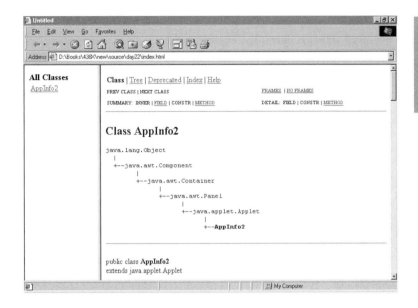

The `javadoc` tool produces extensively hyperlinked Web pages. Navigate through the pages to see where the information in your documentation comments and tags shows up.

If you're familiar with HTML programming, you can use HTML tags such as `<A>`, `<TT>`, and `<B>` within your documentation comments. Line 5 of the AppInfo2 program uses an `<A>` tag to turn the text "Rogers Cadenhead" into a hyperlink to this book's Web site.

The `javadoc` tool also can be used to document an entire package by specifying the package name as a command-line argument. HTML files will be created for each `.java` file in the package, along with an HTML file indexing the package.

If you would like the Java documentation to be produced in a different folder than the default, use the `-d` option followed by a space and the folder name.

The following command creates Java documentation for AppInfo2 in a folder called `C:\JavaDocs\`:

```
javadoc -author -version -d C:\JavaDocs\ AppInfo2.java
```

The following list details the other tags you can use in Java documentation comments:

- `@deprecated` *text*—A note that this class, method, object, or variable has been deprecated. This causes the `javac` compiler to issue a deprecation warning when the feature is used in a program that's being compiled.

- @exception *class description*—Used with methods that throw exceptions, this tag documents the exception's class name and its description.
- @param *name description*—Used with methods, this tag documents the name of an argument and a description of the values the argument can hold.
- @see *class*—The name of another class, which will be turned into a hyperlink to the Java documentation of that class. This can be used without restriction in comments.
- @see *class#method*—The name of a method of another class, which will be used for a hyperlink directly to the documentation of that method. Usable without restriction.
- @since *text*—A note describing when a method or feature was added to its class library.

The jdb Debugger

jdb, the Java debugger, is a sophisticated tool that helps you find and fix bugs in Java programs. You can also use it to better understand what is taking place behind the scenes in the Java interpreter as a program is running. It has a large number of features, including some that might be beyond the expertise of a Java programmer who is new to the language.

You don't need to use the debugger to debug Java programs. This is fairly obvious, especially if you've been creating your own Java programs during the first three weeks of this book. After the Java compiler generates an error, the most common response is to load the source code into an editor, find the line cited in the error message, and try to spot the problem. This dreaded compile-curse-find-fix cycle is repeated until the program compiles without complaint.

After using this debugging method for a while, you might think that the debugger isn't necessary to the programming process because it's such a complicated tool to master. This reasoning makes sense when you're fixing problems that cause compiler errors. Many of these problems are simple things like a misplaced semicolon, unmatched { and } brackets, or the use of the wrong type of data as a method argument. However, when you start looking for logic errors—more subtle bugs that don't stop the program from compiling and running—a debugger is an invaluable tool.

The Java debugger has two features that are extremely useful when you're searching for a bug that can't be found by other means: single-step execution and breakpoints. Single-step execution pauses a Java program after every line of code is executed. Breakpoints

22

are points where execution of the program will pause. Using the Java debugger, these breakpoints can be triggered by specific lines of code, method calls, or caught exceptions.

The Java debugger works by running a program using a version of the Java interpreter that it has complete control over.

Before you use the Java debugger, you should compile the program with the -g option, which causes extra information to be included in the class file. This information greatly aids in debugging. Also, you shouldn't use the -O option because its optimization techniques may produce a class file that does not directly correspond with the program's source code.

Debugging Applications

If you're debugging an application, the jdb tool can be run with a Java class as an argument. This is shown in the following:

```
jdb WriteBytes
```

This example runs the debugger with WriteBytes.class, an application you created during Day 17, "Handling Data Through Java Streams." For the upcoming project, make sure that the WriteBytes.class and WriteBytes.java files are in the same folder that you run the debugger from.

The WriteBytes application writes a series of bytes to disk to produce the file pic.gif.

The debugger loads this program but does not begin running it, displaying the following output:

```
Initializing jdb...
0x9e:class(WriteBytes)
>
```

The debugger is controlled by typing commands at the > prompt.

To set a breakpoint in a program, the stop in or stop at commands are used. The stop in command sets a breakpoint at the first line of a specific method in a class. You specify the class and method name as an argument to the command, as in the following example:

```
stop in SpaceWar.SaveScore
```

This command sets a breakpoint at the first line of the SaveScore method. Note that no arguments or parentheses are needed after the method name.

The stop at command sets a breakpoint at a specific line number within a class. You specify the class and number as an argument to the command, as in the following example:

```
stop at WriteBytes:14
```

If you're trying this with the `WriteBytes` class, you'll see the following output after entering this command:

```
breakpoint set at WriteBytes:14
```

You can set as many breakpoints as desired within a class. To see the breakpoints that are currently set, use the `clear` command without any arguments. The `clear` command lists all current breakpoints by line number rather than method name, even if they were set using the `stop in` command.

By using `clear` with a class name and line number as an argument, you can remove a breakpoint. If the hypothetical `SpaceWar.SaveScore` method was located at line 1960 of `SpaceWar`, you could clear this breakpoint with the following command:

```
clear SpaceWar:1960
```

Within the debugger, you can begin executing a program with the `run` command. The following output shows what the debugger displays after you begin running the `WriteBytes` class:

```
run WriteBytes
running...
main[1]
Breakpoint hit: WriteBytes.main(WriteBytes:14)
```

Once you have reached a breakpoint in the `WriteBytes` class, experiment with the following commands:

- `list`—At the point where execution stopped, this displays the source code of the line and several lines around it. This requires access to the `.java` file of the class where the breakpoint has been hit, so you must have `WriteBytes.java` in either the current folder or one of the folders in your `CLASSPATH`.
- `locals`—Lists the values for local variables that are currently in use or will soon be defined.
- `print text`—Displays the value of the variable, object, or array element specified by `text`.
- `step`—Executes the next line and stops again.
- `cont`—Continues running the program at the point it was halted.
- `!!` —Repeats the previous debugger command.

After trying out these commands within the application, you can resume running the program by clearing the breakpoint and using the `cont` command. Use the `exit` command to end the debugging session.

The `WriteBytes` application creates a file called `pic.gif`. You can verify that this file ran successfully by loading it with a Web browser or image editing software. You'll see a small letter *J* in black and white.

After you have finished debugging a program, you should remember to recompile it without the `-g` option.

Debugging Applets

You can't debug an applet by loading it using the `jdb` tool. Instead, use the `-debug` option of the `appletviewer`, as in the following example:

```
appletviewer -debug AppInfo.html
```

This will load the Java debugger, and when you use a command such as `run`, the `appletviewer` will begin running also. Try out this example to see how these tools interact with each other.

Before you use the `run` command to execute the applet, set a breakpoint in the program at the first line of the `getAppletInfo` method. Use the following command:

```
stop in AppInfo.getAppletInfo
```

After you begin running the applet, the breakpoint won't be hit until you cause the `getAppletInfo()` method to be called. This is accomplished by selecting Applet, Info from the `appletviewer`'s menu.

Advanced Debugging Commands

With the features you have learned about so far, you can use the debugger to stop execution of a program and learn more about what's taking place. This may be sufficient for many of your debugging tasks, but the debugger also offers many other commands. These include the following:

- `up`—Moves up the stack frame so that you can use `locals` and `print` to examine the program at the point before the current method was called.
- `down`—Moves down the stack frame to examine the program after the method call.

In a Java program, often there are places where a chain of methods is called. One method calls another method, which calls another method, and so on. At each point where a method is being called, Java keeps track of all the objects and variables within that scope by grouping them together. This grouping is called a *stack*, as if you were stacking these objects like a deck of cards. The various stacks in existence as a program runs are called the *stack frame*.

By using up and down along with commands such as `locals`, you can better understand how the code that calls a method interacts with that method.

You can also use the following commands within a debugging session:

- `classes`—Lists the classes currently loaded into memory.
- `methods`—Lists the methods of a class.
- `memory`—Lists the total memory and the amount that isn't currently in use.
- `threads`—Lists the threads that are executing.

The `threads` command numbers all of the threads, which enables you to use the `suspend` command followed by that number to pause the thread, as in `suspend 1`. You can resume a thread by using the `resume` command followed by its number.

Another convenient way to set a breakpoint in a Java program is to use the `catch` *text* command, which pauses execution when the `Exception` class named by *text* is caught.

You can also cause an exception to be ignored by using the `ignore` *text* command with the `Exception` class named by *text*.

Using System Properties

One obscure feature of the JDK is that the command-line option `-D` can modify the performance of the Java class library.

If you have used other programming languages prior to learning Java, you may be familiar with environment variables, which provide information about the operating system in which a program is running. An example is the `CLASSPATH` setting, which indicates the folders in which the Java interpreter should look for a class file.

Because different operating systems have different names for their environment variables, they cannot be read directly by a Java program. Instead, Java includes a number of different system properties that are available on any platform with a Java implementation.

Some properties are used only to get information. The following system properties are among those that should be available on any Java implementation:

- `java.version`—The version number of the Java interpreter.
- `java.vendor`—A string identifying the vendor associated with the Java interpreter.
- `os.name`—The operating system in use.
- `os.version`—The version number of that operating system.

Other properties can affect how the Java class library performs when being used inside a Java program. An example of this is the `java2d.font.usePlatformFont` property. If this property has a value of `true`, a Java program will use the Java 1.1 style of font rendering rather than the system introduced with version 2. This property became useful with JDK 1.2 Beta 4, which had some bugs in how the `appletviewer` tool handled fonts.

A property can be set at the command line by using the `-D` option followed by the property name, an equals sign, and the new value of the property, as in this command:

```
java -Djava2d.font.usePlatformFont=true Beanie
```

The use of the system property in this example will cause the `Beanie` application to use 1.1-style fonts.

You also can create your own properties and read them using the `getProperty()` method of the `System` class, which is part of the `java.lang` package.

Listing 22.4 contains the source code of a simple program that displays the value of a user-created property.

LISTING 22.4. THE FULL TEXT OF BEANIEPROP.JAVA.

```
1: class BeanieProp {
2:     public static void main(String[] arguments) {
3:         String n = System.getProperty("beanie.name");
4:         System.out.println("The property equals " + n);
5:     }
6: }
```

If this program is run without setting the `beanie.name` property on the command line, the output is the following:

```
The property equals null
```

The `beanie.name` property can be set using the `-D` option, as in this command:

```
java -Dbeanie.name=Seaweed BeanieProp
```

The output is the following:

```
The property equals Seaweed
```

The `-D` option is used with the Java interpreter. To use it with the `appletviewer` as well, all you have to do differently is precede the `-D` with `-J`. The following command shows how this can be done:

```
appletviewer -J-Djava2d.font.usePlatformFont=true BeaniePage.html
```

This example causes `appletviewer` to use Java 1.1-style fonts with all applets on `BeaniePage.html`.

Summary

Today you explored several features of the JDK that weren't required for your programming projects during the first three weeks. These features included the following:

- Using the Java debugger with applets and applications.
- Creating an optimized version of a compiled class.
- Writing applet methods that provide information to a browser upon request.
- Using the Java documentation creation tool to fully describe a class, its methods, and other aspects of the program.

These JDK features weren't previously required because of the relative simplicity of the tutorial programs in this book. Although it can be complicated to develop a Swing application or to work with threads and streams for the first time, your biggest challenge lies ahead: integrating concepts like these into more sophisticated Java programs.

Tools such as `javadoc` and the debugger really come into their own on complex projects.

When a bug occurs because of how two classes interact with each other, or similar subtle logic errors creep into your code, a debugger is the best way to identify and repair the problems.

As you create an entire library of classes, `javadoc` can easily document these classes and show how they are interrelated.

Two days from now, you'll learn about `javakey`, a tool that's used to establish digital signatures and other aspects of Java security.

Q&A

Q **The official Java documentation is filled with long paragraphs that describe classes and methods. How can these be produced using `javadoc`?**

A In the Java documentation creator, there's no limit to the length of a description. Although they're often as brief as a sentence or two, they can be longer if necessary. End the description with a period, immediately followed by a new line with a tag of some kind or the end of the comment.

Q **Do I have to document everything in my Java classes if I'm planning to use the `javadoc` tool?**

A The Java documentation creator will work fine no matter how many or how few comments you use. Deciding which elements of the program need to be documented is up to you. You probably should describe the class and all methods, variables, and objects that aren't hidden from other classes.

The javadoc tool will display a warning each time a serializable object or variable is defined in a program without a corresponding Java documentation comment.

22

BONUS WEEK

DAY 23

Accessibility

Of the enhancements introduced with Java's version 2, the improvements to the user interface are the most extensive. The introduction of Swing, Java 2D, and related class libraries enable more sophisticated interaction between a user and a Java program.

One of the most dramatic changes involves how Java programs work for people who need assistive technology in order to interact with their computers.

The Accessibility classes included as a standard part of Java 2 make it possible for Java programs to work in conjunction with products such as Braille terminals, screen readers, and speech recognition systems.

These classes also offer features that benefit everyone who uses a Swing-developed interface in a Java program.

The following topics are covered today:

- Using keyboard shortcut keys in a program
- Setting up ToolTip text to document what an interface component is used for
- Associating a label with the component it describes

- Describing a component's name and purpose
- Implementing the `Accessible` Interface

Making Programs More Accessible

The Java Accessibility classes enable Java programs to be controlled with a range of input devices wider than a mouse and keyboard.

These devices include the following:

- Screen readers that use a speech synthesizer to read the contents of a screen aloud
- Screen magnifiers that enlarge elements of a monitor's display area up to 16 times regular size
- Software keyboards that use speech recognition and word prediction features for people who can't type on a keyboard

In order for these devices to function, software must either work directly with them (such as a Web browser designed specifically for visually impaired users) or must include features that are compatible with assistive technology.

A Java program that uses the Accessibility classes does not require the use of assistive devices in order to function. Instead, the program has additional capabilities for those who need them.

These capabilities offer support for computing in environments away from the desktop, which is becoming more important as Java is included in embedded devices such as smart cards, personal information managers, and kiosks.

One of the examples on Sun's Accessibility home page is a dashboard computer on a car. Accessibility could be used to check email by using voice input and output to control the device. Anyone who has watched someone apply makeup or eat a four-course meal while driving should understand the need for alternative-input devices in this case.

Note   The Accessibility home page is currently available at
`http://java.sun.com/products/jfc/accessibility/doc`. In addition to
documentation on the Accessibility classes and a list of frequently asked
questions, the Web site describes the company's overall approach to the
technology and provides a set of Accessibility utilities you can run.

The Accessibility classes are part of the Java Foundation Class library, so you work with Swing as you develop accessible programs.

One of the Swing features included in Java's approach to accessibility is pluggable look-and-feel, which is covered during Day 19, "Designing a User Interface with Swing."

Pluggable look-and-feel makes it possible for a Java interface to adopt a different look (and feel) without any required changes to the program. Although this is used for cosmetic purposes on Day 19, when interface components changed in appearance to achieve a Windows or Metal look and feel, this can be extended. For example, an interface's entire appearance and functionality would require changes in order to adapt to a screen reader.

The Accessibility Classes

Java Accessibility is offered in three distinct areas:

- The `javax.accessibility` package
- Methods in Swing classes that provide accessible features
- A set of Accessibility utilities that can be used by assistive technology providers

The `javax.accessibility` package is used to define the way a Java interface component communicates with an assistive device. Swing components already implement this functionality, so you don't have to work directly with the Accessibility classes when you're working with the standard user-interface components.

When you're creating new user-interface components, you'll be working with this package to make the component accessible.

The main class in the `javax.accessibility` package is the `Accessible` interface. A user-interface component must implement `Accessible` in order to be compatible with assistive devices.

This interface has one method: `getAccessibleContext()`. This method returns an `AccessibleContext` object.

The `AccessibleContext` class describes the information that an accessible object provides to other classes that need the information. This includes the object's name, a description of its purpose, the role it plays in an interface, and its current state.

Accessing a Swing Component

Figure 23.1 shows a Java applet that contains a combo box used to select a profession from a list of six choices.

FIGURE 23.1.

The Combo applet.

This applet uses the JComboBox standard Swing component, so it contains some built-in support for accessibility. The role of the component is as a combo box and an action that can be taken with the component is to toggle the pop-up state of the box. If it has popped up, the list of six choices is visible, as shown in Figure 23.1. If it isn't up, only the current selection is visible.

Listing 23.1 contains the Combo applet, a simple program that displays a Swing combo box that's used to select a profession from a list of six choices.

LISTING 23.1. THE FULL TEXT OF COMBO.JAVA.

```
 1: import java.awt.*;
 2: import javax.swing.*;
 3: import javax.accessibility.*;
 4:
 5: public class Combo extends JApplet {
 6:     JComboBox job = new JComboBox();
 7:
 8:     public void init() {
 9:         FlowLayout flo = new FlowLayout();
10:         Container pane = getContentPane();
11:         job.addItem("Butcher");
12:         job.addItem("Baker");
13:         job.addItem("Candlestick maker");
14:         job.addItem("Fletcher");
15:         job.addItem("Fighter");
16:         job.addItem("Technical writer");
17:         job.setEditable(true);
18:         AccessibleContext ac = job.getAccessibleContext();
19:         ac.setAccessibleDescription(
20:             "Select a profession from a combo box.");
21:         ac.setAccessibleName("Profession");
22:         pane.setLayout(flo);
23:         pane.add(job);
24:         setContentPane(pane);
25:         ComboSpy spy = new ComboSpy(job);
26:     }
27: }
```

All JComboBox objects provide information to the Accessibility classes regarding the role and actions the object can take. Two other items that an accessible object should provide? A name and a description.

These two things can't be provided by default for all combo boxes because they depend on the purpose of the component and what it is used for in a program.

Providing a textual description of a Swing component is accomplished via a two-step process:

23

1. Get the AccessibleContext object associated with the component by calling the component's getAccessibleContext() method.

2. Call the setAccessibleDescription()>(String) method on that AccessibleContext object. The string argument should be the component's text description.

For example, the following example sets the description of a JButton object:

```
JButton quit = new JButton("Quit");
quit.getAccessibleContext().setAccessibleDescription(
    "When you click this button, the program terminates.");
```

The setAccessibleName()>(String) method works the same way setAccessibleDescription(String) works. It can be used to give a name to the component that succinctly describes its purpose. Quit Button is an appropriate name for the quit object in the previous example. The next example sets the name for a text field called nm to "Name Field":

```
JTextField nm = new JTextField();
nm.getAccessibleContext().setAccessibleName("Name Field");
```

In order to support assistive devices, an accessible name should be established for any component that isn't already labeled with a string. JButton components usually have a text label that describes the button, and this is used as its name unless setAccessibleName() gives it a different one.

Along the same lines, a description should be set up for any component that doesn't have a ToolTip associated with it. *ToolTips* are text that appears over a component when the mouse hovers over it for a moment. You learn more about them in the next section.

The accessible name and description in the Combo applet are set in lines 18–21.

Line 25 of the applet contains the following code:

```
ComboSpy spy = new ComboSpy(job);
```

This creates a new `ComboSpy` object. This class's source code is in Listing 23.2. The class spies on the Combo applet, uses different `AccessibleContext` methods to discover more about the applet's combo box, and actually manipulates the combo box.

LISTING 23.2. THE FULL TEXT OF COMBOSPY.JAVA.

```
 1: import java.awt.*;
 2: import javax.swing.*;
 3: import javax.accessibility.*;
 4:
 5: public class ComboSpy implements Runnable {
 6:     Thread runner;
 7:     JComboBox profession;
 8:
 9:     ComboSpy(JComboBox pro) {
10:         profession = pro;
11:         if (runner == null) {
12:             runner = new Thread(this);
13:             runner.start();
14:         }
15:     }
16:
17:     public void run() {
18:         AccessibleContext ac =
19:             profession.getAccessibleContext();
20:         System.out.println("\nName: " +
21:             ac.getAccessibleName());
22:         System.out.println("Description: " +
23:             ac.getAccessibleDescription());
24:         System.out.println("Role: " +
25:             ac.getAccessibleRole());
26:         while (runner != null) {
27:             try {
28:                 Thread.sleep(1500);
29:             } catch (InterruptedException e) { }
30:             AccessibleAction aa =
31:                 ac.getAccessibleAction();
32:             int count = aa.getAccessibleActionCount();
33:             for (int i = 0; i < count; i++)
34:                 System.out.println("ActionDescription: " +
35:                     aa.getAccessibleActionDescription(i));
36:             try {
37:                 aa.doAccessibleAction(0);
38:             } catch (IllegalComponentStateException e) { }
39:         }
40:     }
41: }
```

The following HTML can be used on a Web page to test the Combo applet:

```
<applet code="Combo.class" height=160 width=160>
</applet>
```

The ComboSpy class implements the Runnable interface and runs in its own thread, separate from the Combo class.

In lines 18–19, ComboSpy creates an AccessibleContext object associated with profession, an object that refers to the Combo applet's combo box. This AccessibleContext object contains all of the accessible information about the component.

The name and description of the combo box are available as strings returned by the getAccessibleName() and getAccessibleDescription() methods of the AccessibleContext class.

Swing combo boxes also support the AccessibleAction interface, which is used to determine the actions that can take place when the combo box is manipulated.

Lines 30–31 create an AccessibleAction object associated with the combo box.

Before you can find out what actions are associated with an Accessible component, the getAccessibleActionCount() method must be used to find out how many actions there are. This method returns that value as an integer, as shown in line 32.

The getAccessibleActionDescription(*int*) method determines the textual description of each action that can be taken. Lines 33–35 loop through the combo box's possible actions and display each description.

Up to this point in the program, all communication has been one way: Information about the combo box was received by the ComboSpy class.

You also can use Accessibility features to control a user-interface component.

Every user-interface component that supports accessible actions can be manipulated via the doAccessibleAction(*int*) method. The integer argument represents the action that should be performed.

Line 37 uses doAccessibleAction() to perform the first action that the combo box can perform. A try...catch block is used to catch an IllegalComponentStateException, which occurs if an accessible action is performed on a component that is no longer visible.

When you load the Combo applet with the appletviewer tool, the ComboSpy class displays output that should be similar to the following:

```
Name: Profession
Description: Select a profession from a combo box.
Role: Combo box
ActionDescription: togglePopup
ActionDescription: togglePopup
ActionDescription: togglePopup
ActionDescription: togglePopup
ActionDescription: togglePopup
ActionDescription: togglePopup
```

The last line of the output repeats each time `ComboSpy` causes the combo box's `togglePopup` action to be performed.

When you run the Combo applet, you will discover that the combo box brings up a list of six professions that can be selected. The applet closes and the selection is displayed when a choice is selected.

By calling the `togglePopup` action repeatedly, the `ComboSpy` class causes the combo box list to appear and disappear on its own. If you know a Java programmer who isn't familiar with Accessibility yet, this technique is a good way to make them believe in ghosts.

Note

This technique has use beyond the realm of the supernatural as well. Accessibility can be used to create programs that test a graphical user interface by simulating its use and selecting all available options.

Many Swing components have standard features that are used by an `Accessible` class to discover more information about the component.

You already made a component more accessible if you did any of the following:

- Used the `super(String)` method in a window or frame class to put text in the component's title bar
- Placed text on a button or label
- Employed other features that make a component's purpose more self-explanatory

Using Accessibility Features

Accessibility support is built into `JButton`, `JLabel`, `JFrame`, and all other Swing components, so a lot of the work supporting assistive devices is done automatically.

There are other things that make your programs more accessible, both to users with various abilities and others who are trying to make sense of a user interface with the standard mouse and keyboard.

These include the following:

- Use ToolTips. Text that appears over a component whenever a mouse hovers over it for a moment.
- Use keyboard mnemonics. Shortcut keys that can be pressed to simulate a mouse click on a component.
- Whenever a label is used to describe another component, use the component's `setLabelFor(object)` method to indicate this relationship.
- If a component is identified by an `ImageIcon` object rather than a textual label, use the component's `setDescription()` method to provide an assistive text description.

Another thing you can do is use containers to group components that logically belong with each other. If three buttons are used to start, stop, and pause an animation applet, for instance, they can be associated with each other by placing them within the same `JPanel` container.

Keyboard Mnemonics

A *keyboard mnemonic*, also called a *key accelerator* or *shortcut key*, is a keyboard sequence that can be used to control a user-interface component.

Keyboard mnemonics simulate a mouse action when they are used, and the method of use varies depending on the platform being used. A keyboard mnemonic on a computer running Windows 95 or 98 is available by holding down the Alt key in combination with another key.

Keyboard mnemonics are set by calling the `setMnemonic(char)` method on the component the mnemonic can control. The `char` argument is the key that should be used as part of the mnemonic. The following example creates a `JButton` object and associates the character `'i'` with the button:

```
JButton infoButton = new JButton("Information");
infoButton.setMnemonic('i');
```

Pressing Alt+I causes the `infoButton` component to be clicked.

When a keyboard mnemonic has been set for a component that has a textual label, the key used should be one of the characters on that label whenever possible. This causes the selected character to be underlined on the label.

Figure 23.2 shows several command buttons that have keyboard mnemonics associated with them.

FIGURE 23.2.

Several command buttons with keyboard mnemonics identified by underlining.

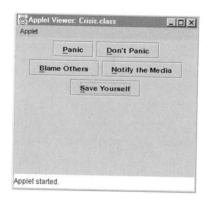

ToolTips

Another way to make a program more user friendly is to associate ToolTips with components on an interface. You might already be familiar with ToolTips—text captions that appear in some programs if your mouse lingers for a few seconds over a component.

ToolTips describe the component's purpose. When you're learning to use a program for the first time, ToolTips are an excellent learning resource.

Call the setToolTipText(*String*) method of the component to set up a ToolTip for a component. The string should be a concise description of the component's purpose.

The following example creates a JScrollBar component and associates a ToolTip with it:

```
JScrollBar speed = new JScrollBar();
speed.setToolTipText("Move to set animation speed");
```

The ToolTip's text can only be one line long, so you cannot use the newline character ('\n') to break the text over multiple lines.

If a keyboard mnemonic has been established for a component that has a ToolTip, the mnemonic is displayed along with the tip.

Figure 23.3 shows several command buttons that have keyboard mnemonics associated with them.

setLabelFor()

Some components in a user interface have a fairly obvious use. A clickable button labeled Quit Program is used to quit a program (unless the program is being used to torment someone, of course).

FIGURE 23.3.

A ToolTip for a command button.

23

Others are less obvious, such as a JTextField or JTextArea component. These usually require a text or image label that identifies the text input component's purpose.

The setLabelFor(*Object*) method makes the relationship between a label and component known to assistive devices.

This method is called on the component that is being labeled. The single Object argument should be the component that serves as its label.

When you use the setLabelFor() method to establish this relationship, a keyboard mnemonic for the label works on the component it identifies.

The following example creates a labeled text field:

```
JTextField name = new JTextField(20);
JLabel nameLabel = new JLabel("Enter Your Name:");
nameLabel.setMnemonic('n');
name.setLabelFor(nameLabel);
```

An Accessible Application: PageData

Today's last hands-on project is PageData, a Java application that includes support for several of the Accessibility features that have been described today.

Although this is a fairly extensive program, most of it utilizes Swing and Java networking features that were introduced during the previous week.

PageData is an application that enables you to enter a Web page address and discover information about that document and the Web server that provided it.

One new concept introduced in the application is the use of the getHeaderField(*String*) method of the java.net.URLConnection class.

This method retrieves information from the Web server that is sending information through the URLConnection object. HTTP protocol, which determines how a server communicates with other programs, includes a number of items that describe the server, the document it is serving, and other, related information. Each of these items is called a *header*, and the term relates to how a printed document's header can be used to describe the document.

An example of an HTTP header is Server, which is used to identify the software used to run the Web server. This information can be requested using a call to getHeaderField("Server"). The following example requests this information from an URLConnection object called pipe and stores it in a string called serv:

```
String serv = pipe.getHeaderField("Server");
```

If the server has been configured to provide this information, it is returned as a string. Otherwise, the return value is null.

The PageData program is made accessible to assistive technology in several ways:

- The super() method gives the application's main frame the title Page Data.
- Each button is labeled with text that identifies its purpose.
- Labels are associated with text fields using the setLabelFor() method.
- ToolTips and keyboard mnemonics are associated with each command button.

Listing 23.3 contains the full source code for this project.

LISTING 23.3. THE FULL TEXT OF PAGEDATA.JAVA.

```
1: import java.awt.*;
2: import java.awt.event.*;
3: import java.net.*;
4: import java.io.*;
5: import javax.swing.*;
6:
7: public class PageData extends JFrame implements ActionListener,
8:     Runnable {
9:
10:     Thread runner;
11:     String[] headers = { "Content-Length", "Content-Type",
12:         "Date", "Public", "Expires", "Last-Modified",
13:         "Server" };
14:
15:     URL page;
16:     JTextField url;
17:     JLabel[] headerLabel = new JLabel[7];
18:     JTextField[] header = new JTextField[7];
```

```
19:     JButton readPage, clearPage, quitLoading;
20:     JLabel status;
21:
22:     public PageData() {
23:         super("Page Data");
24:
25:         JPanel pane = new JPanel();
26:         pane.setLayout(new GridLayout(10, 1));
27:
28:         JPanel first = new JPanel();
29:         first.setLayout(new FlowLayout(FlowLayout.RIGHT));
30:         JLabel urlLabel = new JLabel("URL:");
31:         url = new JTextField(22);
32:         urlLabel.setLabelFor(url);
33:         first.add(urlLabel);
34:         first.add(url);
35:         pane.add(first);
36:
37:         JPanel second = new JPanel();
38:         second.setLayout(new FlowLayout());
39:         readPage = new JButton("Read Page");
40:         clearPage = new JButton("Clear Fields");
41:         quitLoading = new JButton("Quit Loading");
42:         readPage.setMnemonic('r');
43:         clearPage.setMnemonic('c');
44:         quitLoading.setMnemonic('q');
45:         readPage.setToolTipText("Begin Loading the Web Page");
46:         clearPage.setToolTipText("Clear All Header Fields Below");
47:         quitLoading.setToolTipText("Quit Trying to Load the Web
                Page");
48:         readPage.setEnabled(true);
49:         clearPage.setEnabled(false);
50:         quitLoading.setEnabled(false);
51:         readPage.addActionListener(this);
52:         clearPage.addActionListener(this);
53:         quitLoading.addActionListener(this);
54:         second.add(readPage);
55:         second.add(clearPage);
56:         second.add(quitLoading);
57:         pane.add(second);
58:
59:         JPanel[] row = new JPanel[7];
60:         for (int i = 0; i < 7; i++) {
61:             row[i] = new JPanel();
62:             row[i].setLayout(new FlowLayout(FlowLayout.RIGHT));
63:             headerLabel[i] = new JLabel(headers[i]+":");
64:             header[i] = new JTextField(22);
65:             headerLabel[i].setLabelFor(header[i]);
66:             row[i].add(headerLabel[i]);
67:             row[i].add(header[i]);
68:             pane.add(row[i]);
```

23

continues

LISTING 23.3. CONTINUED

```
69:          }
70:
71:          JPanel last = new JPanel();
72:          last.setLayout(new FlowLayout(FlowLayout.LEFT));
73:          status = new JLabel("Enter a URL address to check.");
74:          last.add(status);
75:          pane.add(last);
76:
77:          setContentPane(pane);
78:      }
79:
80:      public void actionPerformed(ActionEvent evt) {
81:          Object source = evt.getSource();
82:          if (source == readPage) {
83:              try {
84:                  page = new URL(url.getText());
85:                  if (runner == null) {
86:                      runner = new Thread(this);
87:                      runner.start();
88:                  }
89:                  quitLoading.setEnabled(true);
90:                  readPage.setEnabled(false);
91:              }
92:              catch (MalformedURLException e) {
93:                  status.setText("Bad URL: " + page);
94:              }
95:          } else if (source == clearPage) {
96:              for (int i = 0; i < 7; i++)
97:                  header[i].setText("");
98:              quitLoading.setEnabled(false);
99:              readPage.setEnabled(true);
100:             clearPage.setEnabled(false);
101:         } else if (source == quitLoading) {
102:             runner = null;
103:             url.setText("");
104:             quitLoading.setEnabled(false);
105:             readPage.setEnabled(true);
106:             clearPage.setEnabled(false);
107:         }
108:     }
109:
110:     public void run() {
111:         URLConnection conn = null;
112:         try {
```

```
113:            conn = this.page.openConnection();
114:            conn.connect();
115:            status.setText("Connection opened ...");
116:            for (int i = 0; i < 7; i++)
117:                header[i].setText(conn.getHeaderField(headers[i]));
118:            quitLoading.setEnabled(false);
119:            clearPage.setEnabled(true);
120:            status.setText("Done");
121:            runner = null;
122:        }
123:    catch (IOException e) {
124:            status.setText("IO Error:" + e.getMessage());
125:    }
126:    }
127:
128:    public static void main(String[] arguments) {
129:        PageData frame = new PageData();
130:
131:        WindowListener l = new WindowAdapter() {
132:            public void windowClosing(WindowEvent e) {
133:                System.exit(0);
134:            }
135:        };
136:        frame.addWindowListener(l);
137:        frame.pack();
138:        frame.setVisible(true);
139:    }
140: }
```

23

This program requires an active Internet connection, so you should log into your service provider before running it with the Java interpreter.

The ToolTips, selective enabled components, and other features should make using this program a quick learn. If the Web address you entered isn't being loaded, you should use the Quit Loading button to stop attempting to connect—the program is doggedly persistent as designed and won't give up unless you tell it to.

Figure 23.4 shows the PageData application after it has been used to load information about a Web page.

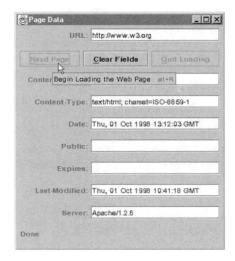

Summary

During the last 15 years, the standard for a computer interface has progressed from type-and-read to point-and-click. The all-text environment of an operating system such as MS-DOS has been replaced with windowing platforms from Microsoft, Apple, Be, and other companies.

This change has been a great benefit for most computer users, who find today's software easier to learn and use because of the ubiquitous graphical user interface. (Some of us holdouts have an Amish-like love for the era when DOS, CP/M, UNIX, and the like were king, but we're definitely in the minority.)

The push to windowing environments has created a greater challenge for developers who want their programs to be useful for the widest possible audience. As Sun states on its Accessibility home page, there are more than 40 million people with various disabilities in the United States alone.

Swing and the Accessibility classes make Java 2 the most accessible version of the language. By using ToolTips, keyboard mnemonics, textual components, and the classes of the `javax.accessibility` package, you can make Java programs that work with assistive technologies such as screen readers, Braille terminals, and voice-driven input and output systems.

These features have benefits for everyone who uses your programs because they make a user interface easier to learn and use.

Q&A

Q **What's the difference between Sun's Accessibility classes and those offered by Microsoft in its Active Accessibility technology?**

A Although Microsoft participated in early planning for Sun's Accessibility classes, the company elected to implement its own accessibility solution before the release of Java 2. The primary difference between the two is compatibility. Sun's Accessibility features are implemented entirely in Java and can work with any platform that supports Java. Active Accessibility supports only the Win32 platform and provides hooks into Windows features that have no analogue on other operating systems, such as online Help files.

Q **How can I find out more about assistive technology devices and pluggable look-and-feel that supports Accessibility?**

A At the time of this writing, Sun is actively maintaining an Accessibility home page at `http://java.sun.com/products/jfc/accessibility/doc`. In addition to supporting the classes and featured described today, this page describes technology that is related to the concept of assistive computing as a whole. It appears to be the best place to start if you're trying to keep up with developments in this area of programming.

23

BONUS WEEK

DAY **24**

Signed Applets and Security

When the Java language was introduced in late 1995, security was arguably the biggest hurdle to its widespread adoption. At that time, Web pages contained text, image files, and other types of static information that was transferred from a Web server to a Web user.

Java was the first programming language that could be used to send interactive programs over the World Wide Web. Because these programs run on the user's system, rather than running on a Web server like a CGI program, there are serious security issues to consider. Java requires highly restrictive security to prevent a malicious programmer from using the language to wreak havoc on the systems of anyone who runs programs from a Web page.

Three years after Java's public launch, the core security features of the language have been well established. Applets are restricted from doing such things as writing to a user's disk or connecting to Web servers other than the one they have been stored on. Java applications, on the other hand, can do anything without restriction.

Java 2 introduces a middle ground between the "no can do" policy towards applets and the "anything goes" policy towards applications.

Today you'll learn how this is implemented as you cover the following topics:

- How digital signatures are used to sign applets.
- What certificates and certificate authorities can do.
- How public keys and private keys are used to protect data.
- Using the `keytool` program to create and manage key pairs and certificates.
- Using the `jarsigner` program to digitally sign a Java archive.
- How Netscape Navigator and Microsoft Internet Explorer support digitally signed applets.

Using Digital Signatures to Identify Applets

One of the fundamental assumptions of Java's applet security strategy is that you can't trust anyone on the Web. Such thinking might sound cynical, but what it means in practice is this: Java security assumes that someone might try to write malicious applets, so it has to prevent them from trying. As a result, any language feature that has the potential for abuse has been blocked from use in applets. The prohibited features include the following:

- Reading files from the system the applet is running on.
- Writing files to the system the applet is running on.
- Getting information about a file on the system.
- Deleting a file on the system.
- Making a network connection to any machine other than the one that delivered the Web page containing the applet.
- Displaying a window that does not include the standard "Java applet window" warning.

Java 2 makes it possible for applets to do everything that a Java application can do—but only if they come from a trusted applet provider and are digitally signed to verify their authenticity. A *digital signature* is an encrypted file or files that accompany a program, indicating exactly from whom the file(s) came. The document that represents this digital signature is called a *certificate*.

In order to establish trust, an applet provider must verify its identity using a group called a *certificate authority*. Ideally, a certificate authority should not be affiliated with the applet developer in any way, and should have an established reputation as a reliable company. At present, the following companies offer certificate authentication services in some form:

- VeriSign—The first and most widely established certificate authority, offering both Microsoft- and Netscape-specific authorization (`http://www.verisign.com`).
- Thawte Certification—A newer authority for Microsoft, Netscape, and test certificates (`http://www.thawte.com`).

Other companies offer certification for clients in specific geographic areas. Netscape lists the certificate authorities it works with at the following Web address:

`https://certs.netscape.com/client.html`

Users who know who produced a program can decide whether that group or individual should be trusted. People who are familiar with ActiveX controls will recognize this system. It's similar to how ActiveX programs are made available on Web pages.

 Note

> The general security model described here is the official one created by Sun for use in its own HotJava browser and any browsers that fully support Java 2. Netscape and Microsoft have introduced their own security models for use in their browsers. Therefore, at the time of this writing, an applet must implement different systems for each browser it should run in. Fortunately, the systems are similar, so mastering one makes it much easier to learn the others.

You also can establish levels of security other than complete trust (an applet can do anything) or no trust (an applet can't do anything that might be damaging). Java 2 enables this with a set of classes called *permissions*.

For now, every applet will be fully restricted unless the developer digitally signs the applet and a user establishes that the developer is trustworthy.

A Digital Signature Example

You might better understand the applet-trusting process if you use three fictional entities: an applet developer called Fishhead Software, a Java industry group called Signatures 'R' Us, and a Web user named Gilbert.

Fishhead Software offers a game applet on its Web site that saves high scores and other information on the user's hard drive. This capability isn't normally possible with an applet—disk access is a definite no-no. For the game to be playable, Fishhead must digitally sign the applet and enable users to establish Fishhead as a trusted programmer.

This process has five steps:

1. Fishhead Software uses `keytool`, a tool that comes with the JDK, to create two encrypted files called a *public key* and a *private key*. Together, these keys form an electronic ID card that fully identifies the company. Fishhead makes sure its private key is hidden from everyone else. It can—and should—make its public key available to everyone as a partial form of ID.

2. Fishhead needs an entity that can verify who it is. It sends its public key and a descriptive file about itself to an independent group that Java users are likely to trust—Signatures 'R' Us.

3. Signatures 'R' Us verifies that Fishhead is a legitimate group with the same public key that was sent to Signatures 'R' Us. When Fishhead passes muster, Signatures 'R' Us creates a new encrypted file called a *certificate*. This is sent back to Fishhead.

4. Fishhead creates a Java archive file that contains its game applet and all related files. With a public key, private key, and certificate, Fishhead can now use the `jar` tool to digitally sign the archive file.

5. Fishhead puts the signed archive on the Web site, along with a way to download its public key.

This is all Fishhead needs to do to make the applet available to anyone who trusts the company enough to run the applet over the Web. One of the people who decides to trust Fishhead is a Web user named Gilbert, who has a Java 2–enabled browser.

His process is simpler:

1. Gilbert realizes that he can't run Fishhead's new game applet without establishing the company as a trustworthy programmer. He downloads Fishhead's public key.

2. Deciding that Fishhead is an organization he can trust, Gilbert uses another JDK security tool, `jarsigner`, in conjunction with Fishhead's public key to add the company to his system's list of trusted programmers.

Now Gilbert can play Fishhead's game applet to his heart's content. Depending on how the security permissions are established within the applet, it could possibly read and write files and open other network connections on Gilbert's system, as well as perform other unsafe tasks. Malicious or unintentionally damaging code could be executed on Gilbert's system, but this is also true of any other software that he installs and runs on his computer. The advantage of a digital signature is that the programmers are clearly identified. Ask yourself how many virus writers would distribute their work under a system that provided a trail of digital "crumbs" leading straight to them.

Why do you have both a public key *and* a private key? If they are used together to identify someone, how can the public key alone be used as an ID for Fishhead?

The public key and the private key are a matched set. Because they fully identify Fishhead Software, that company is the only one that has access to both keys. Otherwise, someone else could pretend to be Fishhead and no one could tell the difference. If Fishhead protects its private key, it protects its identity and reputation.

When Signatures 'R' Us uses a public key to verify Fishhead's identity, its main function is to make sure the public key really belongs to that company. Because public keys can be given to anyone, Fishhead can make its public key available on its Web site. As part of its certification process, Signatures 'R' Us downloads this public key and compares it to the one it received. It acts as a substitute of sorts for the private key, verifying that the public key is legitimate. The certificate that is issued is linked to the public key, which can be used only with Fishhead's private key.

Anyone can issue a certificate for a public key using the keytool program—Fishhead could even certify itself. However, doing so would make it much harder for users to trust the company than if a well established, independent certification group were used. Working together, the public key, private key, and certificate can create a reliable digital signature for a Java archive.

JDK Security Tools

If you're going to offer an applet that bypasses Java's default security, you'll need to take steps to establish your identity and digitally sign your applet.

To use Sun's method for signed applets, you'll need to use three tools included in the Java Development Kit (JDK): jar, jarsigner, and keytool.

 Caution | The keytool and jarsigner tools replace javakey, a command-line program introduced in JDK 1.1. The new tools greatly extend the functionality that was available with javakey, and you must use the new tools when you're implementing the security policies in place for Java 2.

keytool

keytool, the Java security key tool, is used to create and manage public keys, private keys, and security certificates. It can be used to do the following:

- Manage your own public key/private key pairs.
- Store the public keys of people and groups you communicate with.

- Use the certificates associated with these keys to authenticate yourself to others.
- Authenticate the source and integrity of data.

All of the information managed by `keytool` is stored in a database called a *key store*. The `keytool` utility works with any key store that is stored as a file.

Sun includes a default key store that uses a new file format called *JKS* (which presumably is an acronym for *Java Key Store*). To see if you have a key store on your system that's using this format, enter the following at a command line:

```
keytool -list
```

If you don't have anything in your key store (which is probably the case if you're working with Java security for the first time), you'll see an error message like the following:

```
keytool error: Keystore file does not exist: C:\Windows\.keystore
```

In the preceding example, the JDK looked for the main key store in the `C:\Windows\` folder, a common location for important system files on a Windows 95, 98, or NT system. The place that `keytool` looks for this file is established by the Java system property `user.home`.

`keytool` can work with different key stores through the use of the `-keystore` option, as in the following example:

```
keytool -list -keystore C:\java\keys\mainstore
```

This would look for a key store in a file called `mainstore` in the `C:\java\keys\mainstore` folder. If the file could not be found, a "keystore file does not exist" error would occur.

Working With Public and Private Key Pairs

The `-genkey` option of `keytool` is used to create a new public key/private key pair. There are many configuration options that can be used to generate a key pair. Here's one of the simplest:

```
keytool -genkey -alias aliasName
```

The `-alias` option provides a name for this key pair; `aliasName` should be replaced with a short descriptive name for the public and private key pair. This name can be used to retrieve, replace, or delete the pair. Key store aliases aren't case sensitive, so `ThisKey`, `Thiskey`, and `thiskey` all refer to the same thing.

If the `-keystore` option is not used, the key pair will be stored in the default key store on your system. To add a pair to this key store, enter the following command:

```
keytool -genkey -alias samplekey
```

When you're working with keys, the security of the private key is essential. This key is necessary to prove the identity of a person, company, or other entity. If its security is compromised, the key pair can't be used reliably any longer.

There are two passwords involved in adding a key pair to a key store. The first is the key store password, which must be used to access any keys that it contains. If you're adding a key to a new key store, you'll be asked to give the key store a password.

The second password is for the private key, which you'll also have a chance to set up as you create a key pair. If you're planning to use a key store for more than one key pair, you should give the key store and each private key different passwords.

After entering a command to create a new key pair for a new key store, you'll be asked to enter a password for the key store.

24

Caution	For private keys, key stores, and other information that must remain private, a password should mix capital letters, lowercase letters, punctuation, and numerals. This makes it much harder for someone else to guess the password or discover it through cracking.

When you're creating a new key pair, the key tool will ask a number of questions about you and your organization:

- Your first and last name (also called your *common name* by the key tool).
- Your organizational unit.
- Your organization.
- Your city or locality.
- Your state or province.
- Your two-letter country code.

As a group, these answers are called the *X.500 distinguished name* of the source. Every group or individual on the Internet should have a unique distinguished name.

The answers to these questions don't matter for test examples such as those you're working with today. But if you're using `keytool` to sign applets or authenticate yourself, these answers provide important information for users who are determining whether to establish you as a trusted source. Once you have created a key and added it to a key store, you can use `keytool`'s `-list` option to see whether it is in the key store.

If you added a key pair to the default key store, you can use `keytool -list` to look for it. Otherwise, add the `-keystore` option, followed by the folder location and filename of the key store you added it to.

Tip

> `keytool` can output a verbose listing of the contents of a key store. To see this, add a `-v` option to the command, as in `keytool -list -v`.

To delete a key pair from this database, use a command in the following format:

```
keytool -delete -alias aliasName
```

aliasName represents the name of the key to delete. As with other `keytool` features, this can be used with the `-keystore` option to specify a different key store.

`keytool` includes numerous command-line options to configure how a key pair is created. In addition to the ones that have been covered already, these options include the following:

- `-dname text`—Sets the X.500 distinguished name of the pair using the specified text.
- `-storepass text`—If the key store does not exist, sets its password to the specified text. If it does exist, uses this password when `keytool` tries to access the store.
- `-keypass text`—As with `-storepass`, either creates or uses the specified password, depending on whether the key pair existed prior to the use of this command.
- `-validity value`—Makes this key valid for the specified number of days, after which it expires and cannot be used.

The text indicated with the `-dname` option must follow a specific format: `CN=commonName`, `OU=organizationUnit`, `O=organizationName`, `L=localityName`, `S=stateName`, `C=country`. Each of the italicized items should be replaced with the pertinent information. You don't need to specify all of these for a distinguished name, but if you omit one or more items, the remaining items should remain in the same order.

Note

> Because commas are used to separate the elements in a distinguished name, you can't normally include a comma in an item of that name. If one of the items needs a comma, precede the comma with a backslash character (\\).

For use in a subsequent example, create a key pair with the following information:

- Alias: snettkey
- Common name: Sam Snett
- Organizational unit: Sams Publishing

- Organization: Macmillan Computer Publishing
- City: Indianapolis
- State: IN
- Country code: US
- Key password: huN67t

If you have established a password for your system's default key store, you'll need it to add snettkey to the store.

After you create this key pair in your system's default key store, use the keylist -list -v -alias snettkey command to produce the following verbose description of the pair:

```
Alias name: snettkey
Creation date: Thu Oct 08 16:42:31 EDT 1998
Entry type: keyEntry
Certificate chain length: 1
Certificate[1]:
Owner: CN=Sam Snett, OU=Sams Publishing, O=Macmillan Computer
Publishing, L=Indianapolis, ST=IN, C=US
Issuer: CN=Sam Snett, OU=Sams Publishing, O=Macmillan Computer
Publishing, L=Indianapolis, ST=IN, C=US
Serial number: 361d237a
Valid from: Thu Oct 08 16:41:30 EDT 1998 until: Wed Jan 06
15:41:30 EST 1999
Certificate fingerprints:
     MD5:  8B:86:47:49:69:2D:7A:1B:70:75:C1:94:91:B4:12:C6
     SHA1: 62:FC:53:54:D5:CD:5F:12:1A:A0:82:7E:CA:A5:91:35:
     5F:5F:78:DD
```

24

Working with Certificates

When an entity such as an applet programmer seeks to establish a trusted relationship with a user, it sends a digitally signed certificate along with the information that should be trusted. If a user accepts this certificate, the trusting relationship is established. In the case of an applet, perhaps the trust was needed before the applet could save data to the user's hard drive.

The keytool utility can display, import, and export certificates in addition to key pairs. These certificates are called X.509 certificates because they follow the X.509 standard, the only one presently supported by keytool.

X.509 certificates contain a digital signature and the following information:

- The version of the X.509 standard used by the certificate. At the time of this writing, keytool can read versions v1, v2, and v3 of the standard and write version v1.
- The entity that issued the certificate—also called a certification authority. Normally this is an established group such as VeriSign or Thawte.

- A unique serial number generated by the certification authority, which distinguishes this certificate from all others that it has issued.

- An identifier indicating the algorithm used by the authority to create the certificate.

- The start date and end date of the certificate's validity. For this period, the authority vouches for the authenticity of the certificate unless the private key associated with it has not remained secret.

- The distinguished name of the individual or group identified by the certificate.

- The public key of this individual or group.

Certification

The first step in acquiring a certificate is to use the key tool to create a new public/private key pair. This automatically bundles the new public key with a new certificate that is signed by the same entity that created the public key. These are called *self-signed certificates*. A self-signed certificate isn't a reliable certification of identity, but it's needed to create a certificate signing request.

This request is created using `keytool` with the `-certreq` option. The following command can be used to create a request for the `snettkey` key pair:

```
keytool -alias snettkey -certreq -file snettreq.txt
```

The `-file` option is used to specify a file where the certificate signing request should be saved. The output for a certificate request should resemble that of `snettkey`, which follows:

```
-----BEGIN NEW CERTIFICATE REQUEST-----
MIICjDCCAkoCAQAwgYcxCzAJBgNVBAYTAlVTMQswCQYDVQQIEwJJTjEVMBMGA1UEBxMMSW5ka
WFuYXBvbGlzMSYwJAYDVQQKEx1NYWNtaWxsYW4gQ29tcHV0ZXIgUHVibGlzaGluZzEYMBYGA1
UECxMPU2FtcyBQdWJsaXNoaW5nMRIwEAYDVQQDEwlTYW0gU251dHQwggG3MIIBLAYHKoZIzjg
EATCCAR8CgYEA/X9TgR11EilS30qcLuzk5/YRt1I870QAwx4/gLZRJmlFXUAiUftZPY1Y+r/F
9bow9subVWzXgTuAHTRv8mZgt2uZUKWkn5/oBHsQIsJPu6nX/rfGG/g7V+fGqKYVDwT7g/bTx
R7DAjVUE1oWkTL2dfOuK2HXKu/yIgMZndFIAccCFQCXYFCPFSMLzLKSuYKi64QL8Fgc9QKBgQ
D34aCF1ps93su8q1w2uFe5eZSvu/o66oL5V0wLPQeCZ1FZV4661FlP5nEHEIGAtEkWcSPoTCg
WE7fPCTKMyKbhPBZ6i1R8jSjgo64eK7OmdZFuo38L+iE1YvH7YnoBJDvMpPG+qFGQiaiD3+Fa
5Z8GkotmXoB7VSVkAUw7/s9JKgOBhAACgYBuK3i82Z8LtAjv5TSoSTCQdPupjro0ikpXwPTbX
lTSgUiaqRRITUZ8nQfoyEa65L7gQWYXXS0WQajn6CYAzMKaVWExF0tGua7mHmWL5hBBMRfG8X
aYlV9UbGaalljubfcuSQitQGcn0iVDFaoBN1e2qbJuWmqyWPrqIst9cK+fD6AAMAsGByqGSM4
4BAMFAAMvADAsAhQ7/D4GLZdbs8VXdUKj
G/mC+8/4OwIUJuzg49xlSQISQV3c6rrhMYE8x0o=
-----END NEW CERTIFICATE REQUEST-----
```

The certificate signing request is simply a means of encoding the information needed by a certification authority. Specific submission guidelines will be provided by groups that will authenticate Java applets, but the request should provide the primary information that's needed.

Note

> Note that certification authorities are businesses. A developer can expect some kind of fee based on the information being certified, the amount of time the certificate must be valid, and other factors. For more information on fees, visit the Web sites of the certification authorities.

After it receives an authentication request, a certificate authority will follow its own procedures for verifying the identity of the person or group seeking its services. This is often a manual process: Someone employed by the authority must use documentary evidence such as newspapers, Web sites, and other databases to verify the identity. For an individual developer, some certificate authorities will attempt to match the name, address, and other information with the same information in a credit database such as TRW or Equifax.

If everything passes muster, the certificate authority will send back a certificate that can be used as proof of identity. This certificate actually may be composed of a chain of different certificates. In such a chain, each certificate verifies the next in the chain. This could be used by the certificate authority to verify the certificate authority identity at the same time it verifies yours.

When you receive a certificate from an authority, it can be imported into a key store by using the `-import` option of `keytool`. For example, if `snettkey` was sent to Signatures 'R' Us for authentication, Signatures 'R' Us could check Sam Snett out and then send back a file called `snettok.cer` that contains the certificate he needs. This certificate would be imported into the main database file with the following command:

```
keytool -alias snettkey -import snettok.cer
```

Trusted Certificates

The `-import` option also can be used to establish a trust relationship on your system with an entity such as an applet programmer. This requires more caution than when you're establishing your own certificates because once you establish this relationship, you have granted this entity the right to violate security provisions that protect your system from malicious code.

If you receive a certificate from a group or individual for use with Java 2 and need to know whether to approve it, the first step is to use the `-printcert` option of `keytool` to take a look at the certificate. This displays information about the certificate without granting any trust on your system.

24

The -printcert option should be used in conjunction with the -file option, as in the following command:

```
keytool -printcert -file schmoe.cer
```

The output of the -printcert option is substantially the same as the verbose listing for a public/private key pair. If the information appears to be legitimate, you can import the certificate with the -import option. Once this has been done, anything signed by the entity associated with the certificate will be trusted on your system for the duration of the certificate.

The jar Archival Tool and jarsigner

The Java archival tool jar is used to package into a single archive file a Java program and all resource files that it requires.

The most common use of the jar tool is to speed up the loading time for an applet on the Web, especially when the applet needs a group of other files in order to function. A good example would be an animation applet that must load a series of GIF files before it can display them in sequence. The use of the jar tool for this purpose is covered on Day 8, "Putting Interactive Programs on the Web."

jar is also necessary to create a digitally signed Java program. Before a Java program can be signed, it must be packaged into an archive file with all class files and other files the program needs. This is accomplished by the same means as packaging a Java applet for speedier download on the Web.

When you have a jar archive containing the program that should be signed, you're ready to use jarsigner, the JDK tool that is used for the following security tasks:

- Digitally signing a Java archive file.
- Verifying the digital signature and contents of a Java archive.

To digitally sign a Java archive, you must specify the name of the jar archive and the name of the private key to sign it with. Under most circumstances, this key should have gone through an authentication process prior to being used for a signature.

The following command uses a key called snettkey to sign a Java archive called SnettApplet.jar:

```
jarsigner SnettApplet.jar snettkey
```

The jarsigner tool has several command-line options that are identical to those offered by keytool, including -keystore, which is used to specify the folder and file location of a key store.

When you're using the `jar` tool to authenticate an archive, you will be prompted for the key store's password and the password associated with the private key.

The `jar` tool also can be used to verify a digitally signed archive by adding the `-verify` option to the command. If the private key matches the Java archive and the archive's contents didn't change after it was signed, it will be verified by `jarsigner`.

Additional documentation on the JDK's security tools, permissions, and other new security features are available from

`http://java.sun.com/products/JDK/1.2/docs/guide/security.`

Browser-Specific Signatures

At the time of this writing, the only way to digitally sign an applet is to use the procedures set up by the developers at Netscape and Microsoft for their own Web browsers. You have to use their tools and sign an applet using both procedures if you want to reach the users of both browsers.

Signing an applet for use on Microsoft Internet Explorer requires the following:

- A Microsoft Authenticode digital ID from a certificate authority such as VeriSign or Thawte.
- Internet Explorer 4.0 or higher.
- The following tools from the Microsoft Java Software Development Kit: `cabarc.exe, chktrust.exe, signcode.exe,` and the DLL files `javasign.dll` and `signer.dll`. This kit is available for download from Microsoft at `http://www.microsoft.com/java/download.htm.`

Signing an applet for use on Netscape Navigator browsers requires the following:

- A Netscape Object Signing software publishing digital ID, which can be acquired from one of the companies listed at `https://certs.netscape.com/client.html.`
- The Netscape Signing Tool, which is available at `http://developer.netscape.com/software/signedobj/jarpack.html.` The Signing Tool has a feature for using a test certificate before you have acquired a digital ID.

Note

Documentation for these tools is available from Microsoft's and Netscape's respective Web sites. In addition, Daniel Griscom of Suitable Systems has compiled an excellent Java code signing resource at the following Web address:

`http://www.suitable.com/Doc_CodeSigning.shtml`

24

Security Policies

Prior to Java 2, there was a built-in assumption that all applications should be completely trusted and allowed to use all features of the language. To make it easier to create applications that are more limited, applications now are held under the same security scrutiny as applets.

In general practice, this will not change how applications are written or run. Those you have created during this book should not have encountered any security exceptions as they ran on your system. This is because the security policy set up during the JDK installation is the most liberal possible, allowing all of the features available to applications.

The security policy is stored in a file called `java.policy`, which can be found in the `lib\security\` subfolder of the main JDK installation folder. This file can be edited with any text editor, although you shouldn't alter it unless you're well versed in how it is established. You also can use a graphical policy-editing tool included with the JDK called `policytool`.

An overview of the security features implemented in Java 2 is available from Sun at `http://java.sun.com/products/jdk/1.2/docs/guide/security/spec/security-spec.doc.html`.

Summary

Today you learned the basics of how Java 2's security model is being implemented, including the use of digital signatures, certificates, and security tools such as `keytool`, `jarsigner`, and the `jar` archival tool.

Java 2's security model is a marked departure from the way the subject has been approached in previous versions of the language. It's now possible to offer digitally signed applets that have none of the restrictions previously applied to Web-executable Java programs.

At this point, some Microsoft Internet Explorer users will be very familiar with the way ActiveX controls run on a Web page. ActiveX uses a security model that is similar to how digitally signed applets can be offered as of Java 2. Before an ActiveX control runs on a user's system, the user must look over a digitally signed certificate that identifies the ActiveX control's source and the certificate authority that verified this information.

It is expected that Java's security procedures will eventually be integrated into a Web browser the way that ActiveX control usage is integrated into Internet Explorer. Until then, you'll be using the tools that were covered today as you create, manage, and evaluate digital signatures and digitally signed code.

Q&A

Q **What encryption standards are supported by `keytool` and the other security tools?**

A By default, key pair generation algorithm uses the DSA cryptographic algorithm, which generates the SHA1withDSA signature algorithm. `keytool` also can be used to generate RSA key pairs and MD5withRSA signatures.

If this sounds like alphabet soup to you, you'll need more exposure to the process of digital signing before you can evaluate which security standard suits your purposes. For an overview of Java 2's security implementation, visit Sun's Web site at `http://java.sun.com/products/jdk/1.2/docs/guide/security/index.html`.

Q **What's to stop me from creating an applet and verifying its authenticity with a separate entity that I also control?**

A Aside from scruples, nothing. The system of trusted signatures and certification authorities depends on companies that can be trusted to reliably authenticate executable content and users who can discern between these companies and unreliable ones.

Anyone can hang out a shingle and call themselves a certificate authenticator. However, companies that exist only to verify their own code or to produce malicious programs will be fairly easy to spot in comparison to established organizations like VeriSign and Thawte.

Make note of any authentication procedures that you're asked to undertake as you load a Web site for the first time. If you're an Internet Explorer user, you doubtlessly will run into some ActiveX controls that must be trusted before they are executed. The best policy is to reject a digital signature if you have any doubts about its reliability.

24

BONUS WEEK

DAY 25

Advanced Object Programming

An essential concept of object-oriented programming is the way it represents data. In an object-oriented language such as Java, an object represents two things:

- Behavior—The things an object can do.
- Attributes—The data that differentiates the object from other objects.

Combining behavior and attributes is a departure from many other programming languages. A program has typically been defined as a set of instructions that manipulate data. The data itself is a separate thing, as in the example of word-processing software. Most word processors are considered programs that are used to create and edit textual documents.

Object-oriented programming and other techniques are blurring the line between program and data. Current word processors such as Microsoft Word and Lotus WordPro may include programming instructions that affect how the document is formatted, edited, and displayed. These instructions are saved with a document, along with the text and formatting codes that compose its data.

Along the same lines, an object in a language such as Java encapsulates both instructions (behavior) and data (attributes).

Today you discover two ways a Java program can take advantage of this representation:

- Object serialization—The capability to read and write an object using streams.
- Remote method invocation—The capability to query another object in order to investigate its features and call its methods.

Object Serialization

Java handles access to external data via the use of a class of objects called streams. A *stream* is an object that carries data from one place to another. Some streams carry information from a source into a Java program. Others go the opposite direction and take data from a program to a destination.

A stream that reads a Web page's data into an array in a Java program is an example of the former. A stream that writes a `String` array to a disk file is an example of the latter.

Two types of streams were introduced during Day 17, "Handling Data Through Java Streams."

- *Byte streams*, which read and write a series of integer values ranging from `0` to `255`
- *Character streams*, which read and write textual data

These streams separate the data from the Java class that works with it. To use the data at a later time, you must read it in through a stream and convert it into a form the class can use, such as a series of variables or objects.

A third type of stream, *object streams*, make it possible for data to be represented as part of an object rather than something external to it.

Object streams, like byte and character streams, are part of the `java.io` package. Working with them requires many of the same techniques you used during Day 17.

In order for an object to be saved to a destination such as a disk file, it must be converted to serial form.

Note

Serial data is sent one element at a time, like a line of cars on an assembly line. You may be familiar with the *serial port* on a computer, which is used to send information as a series of bits one after the other. Another way to send data is in *parallel*, where more than one element is transferred simultaneously.

An object indicates that it can be used with streams by implementing the `Serializable` interface. This interface, which is part of the `java.io` package, differs from other interfaces you have worked with—it does not contain a single method that must be included in the classes that implement it. The sole purpose of `Serializable` is to indicate that objects of that class can be stored and retrieved in serial form.

Objects can be serialized to disk on a single machine or across a network such as the Internet, even in a case where different operating systems are involved. You can create an object on a Windows machine, serialize it to a UNIX machine, and load it back into the original Windows machine without any errors being introduced. Java transparently works with the different formats for saving data on these systems when objects are serialized.

A programming concept involved in object serialization is *persistence*, the capability of an object to exist and function outside the program that created it.

Normally, an object that is not serialized is not persistent. When the program that uses the object stops running, the object ceases to exist.

Serialization enables object persistence because the stored object continues to serve a purpose even when no Java program is running. It contains information that can be restored in a program so that it can resume functioning.

When an object is saved to a stream in serial form, all objects that it contains are saved also. This makes it easier to work with serialization; you can create one object stream that takes care of numerous objects at the same time.

You also can exclude some of an object's variables from serialization, which may be necessary in order to save disk space or prevent information that presents a security risk from being saved. As you see later today, this requires the use of the `transient` modifier.

Object Output Streams

An object is written to a stream via the `ObjectOutputStream` class.

An object output stream is created with the `ObjectOutputStream(OutputStream)` constructor. The argument to this constructor can be either of the following:

- An output stream representing the where the object should be stored in serial form
- A filter that is associated with the output stream leading to the destination

As with other streams, you can chain more than one filter between the output stream and the object output stream.

The following code creates an output stream and an associated object output stream:

```
FileOutputStream disk = new FileOutputStream(
    "SavedObject.dat");
ObjectOutputStream obj = new ObjectOutputStream(disk);
```

The object output stream created in this example is called `obj`. Methods of the `obj` class can be used to write serializable objects and other information to a file called `SavedObject.dat`.

Once you have created an object output stream, you can write an object to it by calling the stream's `writeObject(Object)` method.

The following statement calls this method on `disk`, the stream created in the previous example:

```
disk.writeObject(userData);
```

This statement writes an object called `userData` to the `disk` object output stream. The class represented by `userData` must be serializable in order for it to work.

An object output stream also can be used to write other types of information with the following methods:

- `write(int)`—Write the specified integer to the stream.
- `write(byte[])`—Write the specified byte array.
- `write(byte[], int, int)`—Write a subset of the specified byte array. The second argument specifies the first array element to write and the last argument represents the number of subsequent elements to write.
- `writeBoolean(boolean)`—Write the specified `boolean`.
- `writeByte(int)`—Write the specified integer as a byte value.
- `writeBytes(String)`—Write the specified string as a series of bytes.
- `writeChar(int)`—Write the specified character.
- `writeChars(String)`—Write the specified string as a series of characters.
- `writeDouble(double)`—Write the specified `double`.
- `writeFloat(float)`—Write the specified `float`.
- `writeInt(int)`—Write the specified int.
- `writeLong(long)`—Write the specified `long`.
- `writeShort(short)`—Write the specified `short`.

The `ObjectOutputStream` constructor and all methods that write data to an object output stream throw `IOException` objects. These must be accounted for using a `try...catch` block or a `throws` clause.

Listing 25.1 contains a Java application that consists of two classes: ObjectToDisk and Message. The Message class represents a message that one person could send to another, perhaps as electronic mail or a short note in a private chat. This class has from and to objects that store the names of the sender and recipient, a now object that holds a Date value representing the time it was sent, and a text array of String objects that holds the message itself. There also is an int called lineCount that keeps track of the number of lines in the message.

When designing a program that transmits and receives electronic messages, it makes sense to use some kind of stream to save these messages to disk. The information that constitutes the message must be saved in some form as it is transmitted from one place to another; it also may need to be saved until the recipient is able to read it.

Messages can be preserved by saving each message element separately to a byte or character stream. In the example of the Message class, the from and to objects could be written to a stream as strings and the text object could be written as an array of strings. The now object is a little trickier, since there isn't a way to write a Date object to a character stream. However, it could be converted into a series of integer values representing each part of a date: hour, minute, seconds, and so on. Those could be written to the stream.

Using an object output stream makes it possible to save Message objects without first translating them into another form.

The ObjectToDisk class in Listing 25.1 creates a Message object, sets up values for its variables, and saves it to a file called Message.obj via an object output stream.

LISTING 25.1. THE FULL TEXT OF OBJECTTODISK.JAVA.

```
 1: import java.io.*;
 2: import java.util.*;
 3:
 4: public class ObjectToDisk {
 5:     public static void main(String[] arguments) {
 6:         Message mess = new Message();
 7:         String author = "Your son Scott";
 8:         String recipient = "Mom and Dad";
 9:         String[] letter = { "Hi, mom and dad!",
10:             "Things are going OK here at college. I could",
11:             "always use more money, but I don't blame you for",
12:             "sticking to our original agreement. If I eat less",
13:             "food at each meal, I can make it to the end of the",
14:             "term. I also can get a job — my plan to give 8",
15:             "hours a week to save the spotted owl can wait",
16:             "another semester I guess. With any luck, there",
17:             "will be some owls left to save when that time",
```

continues

25

LISTING 25.1. CONTINUED

```
18:                    "comes. Gotta go. Feeling light-headed. Gave too",
19:                    "much at the blood bank this morning. Thinking of",
20:                    "you always." };
21:            Date now = new Date();
22:            mess.writeMessage(author, recipient, now, letter);
23:            try {
24:                FileOutputStream fo = new FileOutputStream(
25:                    "Message.obj");
26:                ObjectOutputStream oo = new ObjectOutputStream(fo);
27:                oo.writeObject(mess);
28:                oo.close();
29:                System.out.println("Object created successfully.");
30:            } catch (IOException e) {
31:                System.out.println("Error - " + e.toString());
32:            }
33:        }
34: }
35:
36: class Message implements Serializable {
37:     int lineCount;
38:     String from, to;
39:     Date when;
40:     String[] text;
41:
42:     void writeMessage(String inFrom,
43:         String inTo,
44:         Date inWhen,
45:         String[] inText) {
46:
47:         text = new String[inText.length];
48:         for (int i = 0; i < inText.length; i++)
49:             text[i] = inText[i];
50:         lineCount = inText.length;
51:         to = inTo;
52:         from = inFrom;
53:         when = inWhen;
54:     }
55: }
```

You should see the following output after you compile and run the ObjectToDisk application:

```
Object created successfully.
```

Object Input Streams

An object is read from a stream using the `ObjectInputStream` class. As with other streams, working with an object input stream is very similar to working with an object output stream. The primary difference is the change in the data's direction.

An object input stream is created with the `ObjectInputStream(InputStream)` constructor. There are two exceptions thrown by this constructor: `IOException`and `StreamCorruptionException`. `IOException`, common to stream classes, occurs whenever any kind of input/output error occurs during the data transfer. `StreamCorruptionException` is specific to object streams, and it indicates that the data in the stream is not a serialized object.

An object input stream can be constructed from an input stream or a filtered stream.

The following code creates an input stream and an object input stream to go along with it:

```
try {
    FileInputStream disk = new FileInputStream(
        "SavedObject.dat");
    ObjectInputStream obj = new ObjectInputStream();
} catch (IOException ie) {
    System.out.println("IO error -- " + ie.toString());
} catch (StreamCorruptionException se) {
    System.out.println("Error - data not an object.");
}
```

This object input stream is set up to read from an object that is stored in a file called `SavedObject.dat`. If the file does not exist or cannot be read from disk for some reason, an `IOException` is thrown. If the file isn't a serialized object, a thrown `StreamCorruptionException` indicates this problem.

An object can be read from an object input stream by using the `readObject()` method, which returns an `Object`. This object can be immediately cast into the class it belongs to, as in the following example:

```
WorkData dd = (WorkData)disk.readObject();
```

This statement reads an object from the `disk` object stream and casts it into an object of the class `WorkData`. In addition to `IOException`, this method throws `OptionalDataException` and `ClassNotFoundException` errors.

`OptionalDataException` indicates that the stream contains data other than serialized object data, which makes it impossible to read an object from the stream.

`ClassNotFoundException` occurs when the object retrieved from the stream belongs to a class that could not be found. When objects are serialized, the class itself is not saved to the stream. Instead, the name of the class is saved to the stream and the class is loaded when the object is loaded from a stream.

Other types of information can be read from an object input stream with the following methods:

- `read()`—Read the next byte from the stream, which is returned as an `int`.
- `read(byte[], int, int)`—Read bytes into the specified byte array. The second argument specifies the first array element where a byte should be stored. The last argument represents the number of subsequent elements to read and store in the array.
- `readBoolean()`—Read a `boolean` value from the stream.
- `readByte()`—Read a `byte` value from the stream.
- `readChar()`—Read a `char` value from the stream.
- `readDouble()`—Read a `double` value from the stream.
- `readFloat()`—Read a `float` value from the stream.
- `readInt()`—Read an `int` value from the stream.
- `readLine()`—Read a `String` from the stream.
- `readLong()`—Read a `long` value from the stream.
- `readShort()`—Read a `short` value from the stream.
- `readUnsignedByte()`—Read an unsigned byte value and return it as an `int`.
- `readUnsignedShort()`—Read an unsigned short value and return it as an `int`.

Each of these methods throws an `IOException` if an input/output error occurs as the stream is being read.

When an object is created by reading an object stream, it is created entirely from the variable and object information stored in that stream. No constructor method is called to create variables and set them up with initial values.

Listing 25.2 contains a Java application that reads an object from a stream and displays its variables to standard output. The `ObjectFromDisk` application loads the object that was serialized to the file `message.obj`.

This class must be run from the same folder that contains the file `message.obj`. In addition, the `Message` class must either be in the same folder or in a folder that is accessible from the `CLASSPATH` folders on your system.

LISTING 25.2. THE FULL TEXT OF OBJECTFROMDISK.JAVA.

```
 1: import java.io.*;
 2: import java.util.*;
 3:
 4: public class ObjectFromDisk {
 5:     public static void main(String[] arguments) {
 6:         try {
 7:             FileInputStream fi = new FileInputStream(
 8:                 "message.obj");
 9:             ObjectInputStream oi = new ObjectInputStream(fi);
10:             Message mess = (Message) oi.readObject();
11:             System.out.println("Message:\n");
12:             System.out.println("From: " + mess.from);
13:             System.out.println("To: " + mess.to);
14:             System.out.println("Date: " + mess.when + "\n");
15:             for (int i = 0; i < mess.lineCount; i++)
16:                 System.out.println(mess.text[i]);
17:             oi.close();
18:         } catch (Exception e) {
19:             System.out.println("Error — " + e.toString());
20:         }
21:     }
22: }
```

25

The output of this program is as follows:

```
Message:
From: Your son Scott
To: Mom and Dad
Date: Sat Oct 10 16:58:29 EDT 1998

Hi, mom and dad!
Things are going OK here at college. I could
always use more money, but I don't blame you for
sticking to our original agreement. If I eat less
food at each meal, I can make it to the end of the
term. I also can get a job — my plan to give 8
hours a week to save the spotted owl can wait
another semester I guess. With any luck, there
will be some owls left to save when that time
comes. Gotta go. Feeling light-headed. Gave too
much at the blood bank this morning. Thinking of
you always.
```

Transient Variables

When creating an object that can be serialized, one design consideration is whether all of
the object's instance variables should be saved.

In some cases, an instance variable must be created from scratch each time the object is restored. A good example is an object referring to a file or input stream. This object must be created anew when it is part of a serialized object loaded from an object stream, so it doesn't make sense to save this information when serializing the object.

It's a good idea to exclude a variable that contains sensitive information from serialization. If an object stores the password needed to gain access to a resource, that password is more at risk if serialized into a file. It also might be detected if part of an object that was being restored over a stream that exists on a network.

A third reason not to serialize a variable is to save space on the storage file that holds the object. If its values can be established without serialization, you might want to omit the variable from the process.

To prevent an instance variable from being included in serialization, the `transient` modifier is used.

This modifier is included in the statement that creates the variable, preceding the class or data type of the variable. The following statement creates a transient variable called `limit`:

```
public transient int limit = 55;
```

Remote Method Invocation

Remote method invocation (RMI) creates Java applications that can talk to other Java applications over a network. To be more specific, RMI allows an application to call methods and access variables inside another application, which may be running in different Java environments or different operating systems altogether, and to pass objects back and forth over a network connection. RMI is a more sophisticated mechanism for communicating between distributed Java objects than a simple socket connection is; the mechanisms and protocols by which you communicate between objects are defined and standardized. You can talk to another Java program using RMI without having to know beforehand what protocol to speak to or how to speak it.

Note

Another form of communicating between objects is called RPC (*remote procedure calls*), where you can call methods or execute procedures in other programs over a network connection. While RPC and RMI have a lot in common, the major difference is that RPC sends only procedure calls over the wire, with the arguments either passed along or described in such a way that they can be reconstructed at the other end. RMI actually passes whole objects back and forth over the Internet, and is therefore better suited for a fully object-oriented distributed object model.

While the concept of RMI may bring up visions of objects all over the world merrily communicating with each other, RMI is most commonly used in a more traditional client/server situation: A single server application receives connections and requests from a number of clients. RMI is simply the mechanism by which the client and server communicate.

The RMI Architecture

The goals for RMI were to integrate a distributed object model into Java without disrupting the language or the existing object model, and to make interacting with a remote object as easy as interacting with a local one. A programmer should be able to do the following:

- Use remote objects in precisely the same ways as local objects (assign them to variables, pass them as arguments to methods, and so on).
- Call methods in remote objects the same way local calls are accomplished.

In addition, RMI includes more sophisticated mechanisms for calling methods on remote objects to pass whole objects or parts of objects either by reference or by value; it also includes additional exceptions for handling network errors that may occur while a remote operation is occurring.

RMI has several layers in order to accomplish all these goals, and a single method call crosses many of these layers to get where it's going (see Figure 25.1). There are actually three layers:

FIGURE 25.1.

RMI layers.

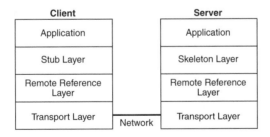

- The Stubs and Skeletons Layers on the client and server, respectively. These layers behave as surrogate objects on each side, hiding the remoteness of the method call from the actual implementation classes. For example, in your client application you can call remote methods in precisely the same way you call local methods; the stub object is a local surrogate for the remote object.
- The Remote Reference Layer, which handles packaging of a method call and its parameters and return values for transport over the network.

25

- The Transport Layer, which is the actual network connection from one system to another.

Having three layers for RMI allows each layer to be independently controlled or implemented. Stubs and skeletons allow the client and server classes to behave as if the objects they were dealing with were local, and to use exactly the same Java language features to access those objects. The Remote Reference Layer separates the remote object processing into its own layer, which can then be optimized or reimplemented independently of the applications that depend on it. Finally, the network transport layer is used independently of the other two so that you can use different kinds of socket connections for RMI (TCP, UDP, or TCP with some other protocol, such as SSL).

When a client application makes a remote method call, the call passes to the stub and then onto the Reference Layer, which packages the arguments if necessary; it then passes it via the Network Layer to the server, where the reference later, on the server side, unpackages the arguments and passes them to the skeleton and then to the server implementation. The return values for the method call then take the reverse trip back to the client side.

NEW TERM   The packaging and passing of method arguments is one of the more interesting aspects of RMI, as objects have to be converted into something that can be passed over the network using serialization. As long as an object can be serialized, RMI can use it as a method parameter or a return value.

Remote Java objects used as method parameters or return values are passed by reference, just as they would be locally. Other objects, however, are copied. Note that this behavior affects how you write your Java programs when they use remote method calls—you cannot, for example, pass an array as an argument to a remote method, have the remote object change that array, and expect the local copy to be modified. This is not how local objects behave, where all objects are passed as references.

Creating RMI Applications

To create an application that uses RMI, you use the classes and interfaces defined by the `java.rmi` packages, which include the following:

- `java.rmi.server`—For server-side classes.
- `java.rmi.registry`—Which contains the classes for locating and registering RMI servers on a local system.
- `java.rmi.dgc`—For garbage collection of distributed objects.

The `java.rmi` package itself contains the general RMI interfaces, classes, and exceptions.

To implement an RMI-based client/server application, you first define an interface that contains all the methods your remote object will support. The methods in that interface must all include a throws RemoteException statement, which handles potential network problems; this may prevent the client and server from communicating.

Listing 25.3 contains a simple interface that can be used with a remote object.

LISTING 25.3. THE FULL TEXT OF PIREMOTE.JAVA.

```
1: package com.prefect.pi;
2:
3: import java.rmi.*;
4:
5: interface PiRemote extends Remote {
6:     double getPi() throws RemoteException;
7: }
```

An RMI interface like this must be part of a package in order for it to be accessible from a remote client program.

Caution	Using a package name causes the Java compiler and interpreter to be more picky about where a program's Java and class files are located. A package's root folder should be a folder in your system's CLASSPATH, and each part of a package name is used to create a subfolder. If the folder C:\java is on your system, the PiRemote.java file could be saved in a folder called C:\java\com\prefect\pi. If you don't have a folder matching the package name, you should create it.

This interface doesn't do anything, requiring a class to implement it. For now, you can compile it by entering the following command from the folder where PiRemote is located:

```
javac PiRemote.java
```

Although the package name is required when compiling the file, it isn't needed when compiling the interface.

The next step is to implement the remote interface in a server-side application, which usually extends the UnicastRemoteObject class. You implement the methods in the remote interface inside that class, and you also create and install a security manager for that server (to prevent random clients from connecting and making unauthorized method calls). You can, of course, configure the security manager to allow or disallow various operations. The Java class library includes a class called RMISecurityManager, which can be used for this purpose.

In the server application you also register the remote application, which binds it to a host and port.

Listing 25.4 contains a Java server application that implements the PiRemote interface:

LISTING 25.4. THE FULL TEXT OF PI.JAVA.

```
 1: package com.prefect.pi;
 2:
 3: import java.net.*;
 4: import java.rmi.*;
 5: import java.rmi.registry.*;
 6: import java.rmi.server.*;
 7:
 8: public class Pi extends UnicastRemoteObject
 9:     implements PiRemote {
10:
11:     public double getPi() throws RemoteException {
12:         return Math.PI;
13:     }
14:
15:     public Pi() throws RemoteException {
16:     }
17:
18:     public static void main(String[] arguments) {
19:         System.setSecurityManager(new
20:             RMISecurityManager());
21:         try {
22:             Pi p = new Pi();
23:             Naming.bind("//Default:1010/Pi", p);
24:         } catch (Exception e) {
25:             System.out.println("Error — " +
26:                 e.toString());
27:                 e.printStackTrace();
28:         }
29:     }
30: }
```

In the call to the bind() method in line 23, the text Default:1010 identifies the machine name and port for the RMI registry. If you were running this application from a Web server of some kind, the name Default would be replaced with an URL. The name Default should be changed to your machine's real name. On a Windows 95 or 98 system, you can find your system's name by selecting Control Panel, Settings, Network. Click the Identification tag to see the machine name, which is located in the Computer Name field, as shown in Figure 25.2.

FIGURE 25.2.

The Network dialog box's Identification tab.

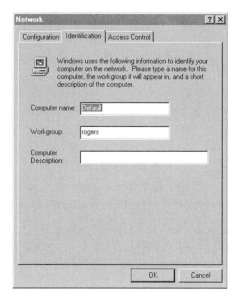

On the client side, you implement a simple application that uses the remote interface and calls methods in that interface. A Naming class (in java.rmi) allows the client to transparently connect to the server. Listing 25.5 contains OutputPi.java.

LISTING 25.5. THE FULL TEXT OF OUTPUTPI.JAVA.

```
 1: package com.prefect.pi;
 2:
 3: import java.rmi.*;
 4: import java.rmi.registry.*;
 5:
 6: public class OutputPi {
 7:     public static void main(String[] arguments) {
 8:         System.setSecurityManager(
 9:             new RMISecurityManager());
10:         try {
11:             PiRemote pr =
12:                 (PiRemote)Naming.lookup(
13:                     "//Default:1010/Pi");
14:             for (int i = 0; i < 10; i++)
15:                 System.out.println("Pi = " + pr.getPi());
16:         } catch (Exception e) {
17:             System.out.println("Error — " + e.toString());
18:             e.printStackTrace();
19:         }
20:     }
21: }
```

25

At this point you can compile these programs using the standard Java compiler. Before you can use these programs, you must use the `rmic` command-line program to generate the Stubs and Skeletons Layers so that RMI can actually work between the two sides of the process.

To create the stubs and skeletons files for the current project, go to the folder that contains the file `Pi.class` and enter the following command:

```
rmic com.prefect.pi.Pi
```

Two files are created: `Pi_Stub.class` and `Pi_Skel.class`.

Finally, the `rmiregistry` program connects the server application to the network itself and binds it to a port so that remote connections can be made.

The `rmiregistry` program does not work correctly if the `Pi_Stub.class` and `Pi_Skel.class` files are located on your system's CLASSPATH. This is because the program assumes you don't need remote implementations of these files if they can be found locally.

The easiest way to avoid this problem is to run `rmiregistry` after temporarily disabling your CLASSPATH. This can be done on a Windows 95 or 98 system by opening a new MS-DOS window and entering the following command:

```
set CLASSPATH=
```

Because the client and server applications use port 1010, you should start the `rmiregistry` program with the following command:

```
start rmiregistry 1010
```

After starting the RMI registry, you should run the server program `Pi`. Because this application is part of a package, you must include its full package name when running the application with the Java interpreter.

You also must indicate where all of the class files associated with the application can be found, including `Pi_Stub.class` and `Pi_Skel.class`. This is done by setting the `java.rmi.server.codebase` property.

If the application's class files were stored at `http://www.prefect.com/java21pre/java/`, the following command could be used to run the application from the same folder that contains `Pi.class`:

```
java -Djava.rmi.server.codebase=http://www.prefect.com/java21pre/
java/ com.prefect.pi.Pi
```

The last step is to run the client program `OutputPi`. Switch to the folder that contains `OutputPi.class` and enter the following:

```
java com.prefect.pi.OutputPi
```

This program produces the following output:

```
Pi = 3.141592653589793
Pi = 3.141592653589793
Pi = 3.141592653589793
Pi = 3.141592653589793
Pi = 3.141592653589793
Pi = 3.141592653589793
Pi = 3.141592653589793
Pi = 3.141592653589793
Pi = 3.141592653589793
Pi = 3.141592653589793
```

RMI and Security

RMI generates security errors when you attempt to run the `Pi` and `OutputPi` programs on some systems.

If you get `AccessControlException` error messages associated with calls to the `Naming.bind()` and `Naming.lookup()` methods, your system needs to be configured so that these RMI calls can execute successfully.

One way to do this is to set up a simple file that contains the most lax security policy possible for Java and use this file to set the `java.security.policy` property when you run `Pi` and `OutputPi`.

Listing 25.6 contains a text file that can be used for this purpose. Create this file using a text editor and save it as `policy.txt` in the same folder as `OutputPi.class` and `Pi.class`.

LISTING 25.6. THE FULL TEXT OF `POLICY.TXT`.

```
1: grant {
2:     permission java.security.AllPermission;
3:     // Allow everything for now
4: };
```

Security policy files of this kind are used to grant and deny access to system resources. In this example all permissions are granted, which prevents the `AccessControlException` error from occurring as you run the RMI client and server programs.

The `-Djava.security.policy=policy.txt` option can be used with the Java interpreter. The following examples show how this can be done:

```
java -Djava.rmi.server.codebase=http://www.prefect.com/java21pre/
java/ -Djava.security.policy=policy.txt com.prefect.pi.Pi

java -Djava.security.policy=policy.txt com.prefect.pi.OutputPi
```

 Note

> More information on RMI and how to use the RMI classes is available from Sun's guide to RMI on its official Java site:
> `http://java.sun.com/products/JDK/1.2/docs/guide/rmi/index.html`.

Summary

Although Java has always been a network-centric language, with applets running on Web browsers since version 1.0, the topics covered today show how the language is extending in two directions.

Object serialization shows how objects created with Java have a lifespan beyond that of a Java program itself. You can create objects in a program that are saved to a storage device such as a hard drive and re-created later, long after the original program has ceased to run.

RMI shows how Java's method calls have a reach beyond that of a single machine. By using RMI's techniques and command-line tools, you can create Java programs that can work with other programs no matter where they're located, whether in another room or another continent.

Although both of these features can be used to create sophisticated networked applications, object serialization is suitable for many other tasks. You may see a need for it in some of the first programs that you create; persistence is an effective way to save elements of a program for later use.

Q&A

Q Are object streams associated with the Writer and Reader classes that are used to work with character streams?

A The ObjectInputStream and ObjectOutputStream classes are independent of the byte stream and character stream superclasses in the java.io package, although they function similarly to many of the byte classes.

There shouldn't be a need to use Writer or Reader classes in conjunction with object streams because you can accomplish the same things via the object stream classes and their superclasses (InputStream and OutputStream).

Q Are `private` variables and objects saved when they are part of an object that's being serialized?

A They are saved. As you may recall from today's chapter, no constructor methods are called when an object is loaded into a program using serialization. Because of this, all variables and objects that are not declared `transient` are saved to prevent the object from losing something that might be necessary to its function.

Saving `private` variables and objects may present a security risk in some cases, especially when the variable is being used to store a password or some other sensitive data. Using `transient` prevents a variable or object from being serialized.

25

Bonus Week

Day 26

Data Structures

Few programs can be developed without using data structures, which are responsible for storing and maintaining information used by a program. Whether you develop your own data structures from scratch or rely on those developed and tested by others, you will undoubtedly need to use data structures at some point in your Java programming.

Today's lesson takes a look at data structures as they relate to Java. It covers the following topics:

- Data structure basics
- The standard Java data structures
- Building your own data structures

By the end of today's lesson, you'll have a good idea of which data structures are readily available in the standard Java packages, along with some data structures you can implement yourself without too much pain.

Data Structure Fundamentals

Like algorithms, data structures are one of the general concepts in computer science that can be applied to many different areas of software development. A solid understanding of data structures and when to use them will be applicable throughout your Java programming efforts. Many Java programs that you create will rely on a solid means of storing and manipulating data.

Almost every Java applet works with information to some extent. Even very simple animation applets that display a series of images must somehow store the images in such a way that they can be referenced quickly. In this example, an elementary data structure such as an array might be the best solution because all that is required is the storage of multiple images. Even so, remember that every program has its own set of data requirements that greatly affect the applicability of different data structures.

If you don't understand the full range of programming options in terms of data structures, you'll find yourself trying to use an array in every program you write. Relying on one solution for all your programming problems will end up getting you into trouble. By understanding how to use a wide variety of data structures, you'll be better able to meet new programming challenges.

Outside of primitive data types, arrays are the simplest data structures supported by Java. An array is simply a series of data elements of the same type. It's treated as a single entity, just like a primitive data type. However, it actually contains multiple elements that can be accessed independently. Arrays are useful whenever you need to store and access information that is all of the same type. For example, you could store the height achieved in a series of high jumps using an array of floating-point values.

The glaring limitation of arrays is that they can't change in size to accommodate more or fewer elements. This means that you can't add new elements to an array that's already full.

The data requirements for many practical programs reach far beyond what arrays can provide. In other languages, it's often necessary to develop custom data structures whenever the requirements go beyond arrays.

However, the Java class library provides a set of data structures in the `java.util` package that give you more flexibility in approaching the organization and manipulation of data. There still may be situations in which these standard data structures don't fit your needs, in which case you'll have to write your own. You'll learn how to implement your own custom data structures later in today's lesson.

> **Note**
>
> Unlike the data structures provided by the `java.util` package, arrays are considered such a core component of Java that they are implemented in the language itself. Therefore, you can use arrays in Java without importing any packages.

The Standard Java Data Structures

The data structures provided by the `java.util` package are very powerful and perform a wide range of functions. These data structures consist of the `Enumeration` interface and the following five classes:

- `BitSet`
- `Vector`
- `Stack`
- `Dictionary`
- `Hashtable`

The `Enumeration` interface isn't itself a data structure, but it is very important within the context of the data structures. It defines a means to retrieve successive elements from a data structure. For example, `Enumeration` defines a method called `nextElement()` that gets the next element in a data structure that contains multiple elements.

The `BitSet` class implements a group of bits, or flags, that can be set and cleared individually. This class is very useful when you need to keep up with a set of boolean values; you just assign a bit to each value and set or clear it as appropriate.

NEW TERM   A *flag* is a boolean value that represents one of a group of on/off type states in a program.

The `Vector` class is similar to a traditional Java array, except that it can grow as necessary to accommodate new elements. Like an array, elements of a `Vector` object can be accessed via an index into the vector. The nice thing about using the `Vector` class is that you don't have to worry about setting it to a specific size upon creation; it shrinks and grows automatically when necessary.

The `Stack` class implements a last-in-first-out stack of elements. You can think of a stack literally as a vertical stack of objects; when you add a new element, it's stacked on top of the others. When you pull an element off the stack, it comes off the top. In other words, the last element you added to the stack is the first one to come back off.

26

The `Dictionary` class is an abstract class that defines a data structure for mapping keys to values. This is useful when you want to access data through a particular key rather than an integer index. Because the `Dictionary` class is abstract, it provides only the framework for a key-mapped data structure rather than a specific implementation.

NEW TERM A *key* is an identifier used to reference, or look up, a value in a data structure.

An actual implementation of a key-mapped data structure is provided by the `Hashtable` class, which organizes data based on some user-defined key structure. For example, in an address list hash table, you could store and sort data based on a key such as ZIP code rather than on a person's name. The specific meaning of keys in a hash table is totally dependent on how the table is used and the data it contains.

The next section looks at the data structures provided by the `java.util` package in more detail to show how they work.

Enumerations

The `Enumeration` interface provides a standard means of iterating through a list of sequentially stored elements, which is a common task for many data structures. Even though you can't use the interface outside a particular data structure, understanding how it works will help you understand other Java data structures.

With that in mind, take a look at the only two methods defined by the `Enumeration` interface:

```
public abstract boolean hasMoreElements();

public abstract Object nextElement();
```

The `hasMoreElements()` method determines if the enumeration contains any more elements. You will typically call this method to see if you can continue iterating through an enumeration. An example of this is calling `hasMoreElements()` in the conditional clause of a `while` loop that is iterating through an enumeration.

The `nextElement()` method actually retrieves the next element in an enumeration. If no more elements are in the enumeration, `nextElement()` will throw a `NoSuchElementException` exception. To avoid generating this exception, use `hasMoreElements()` in conjunction with `nextElement()` to make sure there is another element to retrieve.

The following is a `while` loop that uses these two methods to iterate through a data structure object that implements the `Enumeration` interface:

```
// en is an object that implements the Enumeration interface
while (en.hasMoreElements()) {
    Object o = en.nextElement();
    System.out.println(o);
}
```

This sample code prints out the contents of an enumeration using the `hasMoreElements()` and `nextElement()` methods.

> **Note**
>
> Because Enumeration is an interface, you'll never use it directly as a data structure. Rather, you'll use the methods defined by Enumeration within the context of other data structures. The significance of this architecture is that it provides a consistent interface for many of the standard data structures, which makes them easier to learn and use.

Bit Sets

The `BitSet` class is useful whenever you need to represent a group of boolean flags. The nice thing about using the `BitSet` class is that you can use individual bits to store boolean values without the mess of extracting bit values by using bitwise operations. You simply refer to each bit using an index. Another nice feature is that it automatically grows to represent the number of bits required by a program. Figure 26.1 shows the logical organization of a bit set data structure.

FIGURE 26.1.

The logical organization of a bit set data structure.

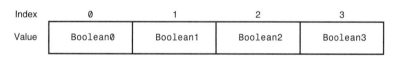

26

For example, you can use `BitSet` as an object with a number of attributes that can easily be modeled by boolean values. Because the individual bits in a bit set are accessed via an index, you can define each attribute as a constant index value:

```
class SomeBits {
    public static final int readable = 0;
    public static final int writeable = 1;
    public static final int streamable = 2;
    public static final int flexible = 3;
}
```

Notice that the attributes are assigned increasing values, beginning with 0. You can use these values to get and set the appropriate bits in a bit set. But first, you need to create a `BitSet` object:

```
BitSet bits = new BitSet();
```

This constructor creates a bit set with no specified size. You can also create a bit set with a specific size:

```
BitSet bits = new BitSet(4);
```

This creates a bit set containing four boolean bit fields. Regardless of the constructor used, all bits in new bit sets are initially set to `false`. Once you have a bit set created, you can easily set and clear the bits using the `set` and `clear` methods along with the bit constants you defined:

```
bits.set(SomeBits.writeable);
bits.set(SomeBits.streamable);
bits.set(SomeBits.flexible);
bits.clear(SomeBits.writeable);
```

In this code, the `writeable`, `streamable`, and `flexible` attributes are set and then the `writeable` bit is cleared. Notice that the fully qualified name is used for each attribute because the attributes are declared as static in the `SomeBits` class.

You can get the value of individual bits in a bit set by using the `get` method:

```
boolean canIWrite = bits.get(SomeBits.writeable);
```

You can find out how many bits are being represented by a bit set by using the `size` method:

```
int numBits = bits.size();
```

The `BitSet` class also provides other methods for performing comparisons and bitwise operations on bit sets such as `AND`, `OR`, and `XOR`. All these methods take a `BitSet` object as their only argument.

Vectors

The `Vector` class implements an expandable array of objects. Because the `Vector` class is responsible for expanding as necessary to support more elements, it has to decide when and how much to grow as new elements are added. You can easily control this aspect of vectors upon creation.

Before getting into that, take a look at how to create a basic vector:

```
Vector v = new Vector();
```

That's about as simple as it gets! This constructor creates a default vector containing no elements. Actually, all vectors are empty upon creation. One of the attributes that determines how a vector sizes itself is its initial capacity, or the number of elements it allocates memory for, by default.

NEW TERM The *size* of a vector is the number of elements currently stored in it.

NEW TERM The *capacity* of a vector is the amount of memory allocated to hold elements, and is always greater than or equal to the size.

The following code shows how to create a vector with a specified capacity:

```
Vector v = new Vector(25);
```

This vector will allocate enough memory to support 25 elements. Once 25 elements have been added, however, the vector must decide how to expand to accept more elements. You can specify the value by which a vector grows using another Vector constructor:

```
Vector v = new Vector(25, 5);
```

This vector has an initial size of 25 elements, and will expand in increments of five elements when more than 25 elements are added to it. This means that the vector will jump to 30 elements in size, then 35, and so on. A smaller grow value results in greater memory management efficiency at the cost of more execution overhead because more memory allocations are taking place. A larger grow value results in fewer memory allocations, but sometimes memory may be wasted if you don't use all the extra space created.

You can't just use square brackets ([]) to access the elements in a vector, as you can in an array. You must use methods defined in the Vector class. Use the addElement() method to add an element to a vector, as in the following example:

```
v.addElement("Watson");
v.addElement("Palmer");
v.addElement("Nicklaus");
```

This code shows how to add some strings to a vector. To retrieve the last string added to the vector, you can use the lastElement method:

```
String s = (String)v.lastElement();
```

Notice that you have to cast the return value of lastElement() because the Vector class is designed to work with the Object class. Although lastElement() certainly has its usefulness, you will probably find more value in the elementAt() method, which allows you to retrieve a vector element using an index.

The following is an example of the elementAt() method:

```
String s1 = (String)v.elementAt(0);
String s2 = (String)v.elementAt(2);
```

Because vectors are zero-based, the first call to elementAt() retrieves the "Watson" string and the second call retrieves the "Palmer" string. Just as you can retrieve an

26

element at a particular index, you can also add and remove elements at an index by using the `insertElementAt()` and `removeElementAt()` methods:

```
v.insertElementAt("Hogan", 1);
v.insertElementAt("Jones", 0);
v.removeElementAt(3);
```

The first call to `insertElementAt()` inserts an element at index 1, between the `"Watson"` and `"Palmer"` strings. The `"Palmer"` and `"Nicklaus"` strings are moved up an element in the vector to accommodate the inserted `"Hogan"` string. The second call to `insertElementAt()` inserts an element at index 0, which is the beginning of the vector. All existing elements are moved up one space in the vector to accommodate the inserted `"Jones"` string. At this point, the contents of the vector look like this:

- `"Jones"`
- `"Watson"`
- `"Hogan"`
- `"Palmer"`
- `"Nicklaus"`

The call to `removeElementAt()` removes the element at index 3, which is the `"Palmer"` string. The resulting vector consists of the following strings:

- `"Jones"`
- `"Watson"`
- `"Hogan"`
- `"Nicklaus"`

You can use the `setElementAt()` method to change a specific element:

```
v.setElementAt("Woods", 1);
```

This method replaces the `"Watson"` string with the `"Woods"` string, resulting in the following vector:

- `"Jones"`
- `"Woods"`
- `"Hogan"`
- `"Nicklaus"`

If you want to clear out the vector completely, you can remove all the elements with the `removeAllElements()` method:

```
v.removeAllElements();
```

The `Vector` class also provides some methods for working with elements without using indexes. These methods actually search through the vector for a particular element. The first of these methods is the `contains()` method, which simply checks if an element is in the vector:

```
boolean isThere = v.contains("O'Meara");
```

Another method that works in this manner is the `indexOf()` method, which finds the index of an element based on the element itself:

```
int i = v.indexOf("Nicklaus");
```

The `indexOf()` method returns the index of the element in question if it is in the vector, or -1 if not. The `removeElement()` method works similarly, removing an element based on the element itself rather than on an index:

```
v.removeElement("Woods");
```

If you're interested in working with all the elements in a vector sequentially, you can use the `elements()` method, which returns an enumeration of the elements:

```
Enumeration e = v.elements();
```

As you learned earlier today, you can use an enumeration to step through elements sequentially. In this example, you can work with the enumeration e using the methods defined by the `Enumeration` interface.

At some point you might want to work with the size of a vector. Fortunately, the `Vector` class provides a few methods for determining and manipulating a vector's size. First, the `size` method determines the number of elements in the vector:

```
int size = v.size();
```

If you want to explicitly set the size of the vector, you can use the `setSize()` method:

```
v.setSize(10);
```

The `setSize()` method expands or truncates the vector to the size specified. If the vector is expanded, null elements are inserted as the newly added elements. If the vector is truncated, any elements at indexes beyond the specified size are discarded.

Recall that vectors have two different attributes relating to size: size and capacity. The size is the number of elements in the vector, and the capacity is the amount of memory allocated to hold all the elements. The capacity is always greater than or equal to the size. You can force the capacity to exactly match the size by using the `trimToSize()` method:

```
v.trimToSize();
```

26

You can also check to see what the capacity is by using the `capacity()` method:

```
int capacity = v.capacity();
```

You'll find that the `Vector` class is one of the most useful data structures in the Java class library.

Stacks

Stacks are a classic data structure used to model information that is accessed in a specific order. The `Stack` class in Java is implemented as a last-in-first-out (LIFO) stack, which means that the last item added to the stack is the first one to be removed. Figure 26.2 shows the logical organization of a stack.

FIGURE 26.2.

The logical organiza-tion of a stack data structure.

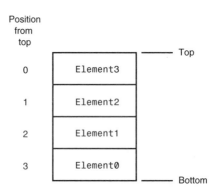

You may wonder why the numbers of the elements don't match their position from the top of the stack. Keep in mind that elements are added to the top, so `Element0`, which is on the bottom, was the first element added to the stack. Likewise, `Element3`, which is on top, was the last element added. Also, because `Element3` is at the top of the stack, it will be the first to be removed.

The `Stack` class defines only one constructor, which is a default constructor that creates an empty stack. You use this constructor to create a stack like this:

```
Stack s = new Stack();
```

You add new elements to a stack by using the `push()` method, which pushes an element onto the top of the stack:

```
s.push("One");
s.push("Two");
s.push("Three");
s.push("Four");
s.push("Five");
s.push("Six");
```

This code pushes six strings onto the stack, with the last string ("Six") remaining on top. You pop elements back off the stack by using the pop() method:

```
String s1 = (String)s.pop();
String s2 = (String)s.pop();
```

This code pops the last two strings off the stack, leaving the first four strings. This code results in the s1 variable containing the "Six" string and the s2 variable containing the "Five" string.

If you want to get the top element on the stack without actually popping it off the stack, you can use the peek() method:

```
String s3 = (String)s.peek();
```

This call to peek() returns the "Four" string but leaves the string on the stack. You can search for an element on the stack using the search() method:

```
int i = s.search("Two");
```

The search() method returns the distance from the top of the stack of the element if it is found, or -1 if not. In this case, the "Two" string is the third element from the top, so the search() method returns 2 (zero-based).

Note

As in all Java data structures that deal with indexes or lists, the Stack class reports element position in a zero-based fashion. This means that the top element in a stack has a location of 0, and the fourth element down has a location of 3.

26

The only other method defined in the Stack class is empty, which determines whether a stack is empty:

```
boolean isEmpty = s.empty();
```

Although the Stack class isn't quite as useful as the Vector class, it provides the functionality for a very common and established data structure.

Dictionaries

The Dictionary class defines a framework for implementing a basic key-mapped data structure. Although you can't actually create Dictionary objects because the class is abstract, you can still learn a lot about key-mapped data modeling by learning how the Dictionary class works. You can put the key-mapped approach to work by using the Hashtable class, which is derived from Dictionary, or by deriving your own class from Dictionary. You'll learn about the Hashtable class in the next section.

The Dictionary class defines a means of storing information based on a key. This is similar in some ways to the Vector class, in which elements are accessed through an index, which is a specific type of key. However, keys in the Dictionary class can be just about anything. You can create your own classes to use as the keys for accessing and manipulating data in a dictionary. Figure 26.3 shows how keys map to data in a dictionary.

FIGURE 26.3.

The logical organization of a dictionary's data structure.

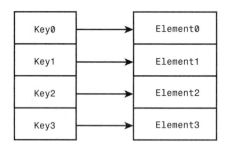

The Dictionary class defines a variety of methods for working with the data stored in a dictionary. All these methods are defined as abstract, meaning that derived classes will have to implement all of them to actually be useful. The put and get methods are used to put objects in the dictionary and get them back. Assuming dict is a Dictionary-derived class that implements these methods, the following code shows how to use the put method to add elements to a dictionary:

```
dict.put("small", new Rectangle(0, 0, 5, 5));
dict.put("medium", new Rectangle(0, 0, 15, 15));
dict.put("large", new Rectangle(0, 0, 25, 25));
```

This code adds three rectangles to the dictionary, using strings as the keys. To get an element from the dictionary, use the get method and specify the appropriate key:

```
Rectangle r = (Rectangle)dict.get("medium");
```

You can also remove an element from the dictionary with a key by using the remove() method:

```
dict.remove("large");
```

You can find out how many elements are in the dictionary by using the size() method, much as you did with the Vector class:

```
int size = dict.size();
```

You can also check whether the dictionary is empty by using the isEmpty() method:

```
boolean isEmpty = dict.isEmpty();
```

Finally, the `Dictionary` class includes two methods for enumerating the keys and values contained within: `keys()` and `elements()`. The `keys()` method returns an enumeration containing all the keys contained in a dictionary, while the `elements()` method returns an enumeration of all the key-mapped values contained. The following is an example of retrieving both enumerations:

```
Enumeration keys = dict.keys();
Enumeration elements = dict.elements();
```

Note that because keys are mapped to elements on a one-to-one basis, these enumerations are of equal length.

Hash Tables

The `Hashtable` class is derived from `Dictionary` and provides a complete implementation of a key-mapped data structure. Similar to dictionaries, hash tables allow you to store data based on some type of key. Unlike dictionaries, hash tables have an efficiency associated with them that's defined by the load factor of the table. The *load factor* is a number between 0.0 and 1.0 that determines how and when the hash table allocates space for more elements.

Like vectors, hash tables have a capacity, or the amount of allocated memory. Hash tables allocate memory by comparing the current size of the table with the product of the capacity and the load factor. If the size of the hash table exceeds this product, the table increases its capacity by rehashing itself.

Load factors closer to 1.0 result in a more efficient use of memory at the expense of a longer lookup time for each element. Similarly, load factors closer to 0.0 result in more efficient lookups but also tend to be more wasteful with memory. Determining the load factor for your own hash tables is dependent on how you use each hash table and whether your priority is performance or memory efficiency.

26

You can create hash tables in any one of three ways. The first constructor creates a default hash table:

```
Hashtable hash = new Hashtable();
```

The second constructor creates a hash table with the specified initial capacity:

```
Hashtable hash = new Hashtable(20);
```

Finally, the third constructor creates a hash table with the specified initial capacity and load factor:

```
Hashtable hash = new Hashtable(20, 0.75);
```

All the abstract methods defined in `Dictionary` are implemented in the `Hashtable` class. Because these methods perform the same functions in `Hashtable`, there's no need to cover them again. However, they are listed here so you'll have an idea of the support `Hashtable` provides:

- `elements()`
- `get()`
- `isEmpty()`
- `keys()`
- `put()`
- `remove()`
- `size()`

In addition to these methods, the `Hashtable` class implements a few others that perform functions specific to supporting hash tables. One of these is the `clear()` method, which clears a hash table of all its keys and elements:

```
hash.clear();
```

The `contains()` method checks if an object is stored in the hash table. This method searches for an object value in the hash table rather than a key. The following code shows how to use the `contains()` method:

```
boolean isThere = hash.contains(new Rectangle(0, 0, 5, 5));
```

Similar to `contains()`, the `containsKey()` method searches a hash table, but based on a key rather than a value:

```
boolean isThere = hash.containsKey("Small");
```

As mentioned earlier, a hash table will rehash itself when it determines that it must increase its capacity. You can force a rehash yourself by calling the `rehash()` method:

```
hash.rehash();
```

That pretty much sums up the important methods implemented by the `Hashtable` class. Even though you've seen all the methods, you still may be wondering exactly how the `Hashtable` class is useful. The practical use of a hash table is actually in representing data that is too time-consuming to search or reference by value. In other words, hash tables often come in handy when you're working with complex data and it's much more efficient to access the data by using a key rather than comparing the data objects themselves.

Furthermore, hash tables typically compute a key for elements, which is called a hash code. For example, a string can have an integer hash code computed for it that uniquely represents the string. When a bunch of strings are stored in a hash table, the table can access the strings by using integer hash codes as opposed to using the contents of the strings themselves. This results in much more efficient searching and retrieving capabilities.

New Term   A *hash code* is a computed key that uniquely identifies each element in a hash table.

This technique of computing and using hash codes for object storage and reference is exploited heavily throughout the Java system. The parent of all classes, `Object`, defines a `hashCode()` method that is overridden in most standard Java classes. Any class that defines a `hashCode()` method can be efficiently stored and accessed in a hash table. A class that wants to be hashed must also implement the `equals()` method, which defines a way of telling if two objects are equal. The `equals()` method usually just performs a straight comparison of all the member variables defined in a class.

Hash tables are an extremely powerful data structure that should probably be integrated into some of your programs that manipulate large amounts of data. The fact that they are so widely supported in the Java class library via the `Object` class should give you a clue as to their importance in Java programming.

Building Your Own Data Structures

Even though the `java.util` package provides some very powerful and useful data structures, there may be situations in which you need something a little different. You are encouraged to make the most of the standard Java data structures whenever possible. Reusing stable code is always a smarter solution than writing your own code. However, when the standard data structures just don't seem to fit, you may need to turn your attention to other options.

Throughout the rest of today's lesson, you'll learn all about one of these other options. As an exercise in creating a custom data structure, you'll see how to create a linked list class that you can reuse in your own Java programs. Building custom structures isn't as difficult as it might sound.

Linked List Basics

Like vectors and arrays, linked lists are used to store a sequential list of objects. The primary difference between these data structures is that arrays and vectors are better at referencing elements via a numeric index, whereas linked lists are better at accessing data in a purely sequential manner. In other words, linked lists aren't suited for the type of random access provided by arrays and vectors. This may seem like a limitation, but it is

26

in fact what makes linked lists unique as a data structure; they are much more efficient at adding, inserting, and removing elements.

To get a better idea of why linked lists have the properties mentioned, take a look at the logical organization of linked lists shown in Figure 26.4.

FIGURE 26.4.

The logical organization of a doubly linked list data structure.

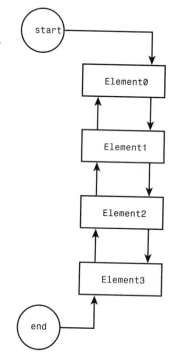

The figure shows that the linked list has a distinct start and end, which is somewhat different from arrays and vectors. Sure, arrays and vectors have a first element and a last element, but these elements have no more significance than any other elements. The start and end of linked lists are a strict requirement because linked lists don't hold elements in a fixed amount of memory.

This actually touches on the biggest difference between linked lists and vectors/arrays. Linked lists simply hold references to the start and end elements contained within, whereas vectors and arrays contain references to all of their elements.

Another key point to note from Figure 26.4 is that each element in a linked list contains a reference to both the element before it and the element after it. This is how elements in linked lists are accessed: by traversing the list through the references to successive elements. In other words, to get the third element in a linked list, you have to start with the first element and follow its reference to the second element, and then repeat the process to get to the third element. This may seem like a tedious process, but it actually works quite well in some situations.

So far, we've glossed over the two types of linked lists. The type shown in Figure 26.4 is called a *doubly linked list* because it contains references to both the element following a particular element and the element preceding it. Another popular type of linked list is the *singly linked list*, where each element contains only a reference to the element following it. Figure 26.5 shows the logical organization of a singly linked list.

FIGURE 26.5.

The logical organization of a singly linked list data structure.

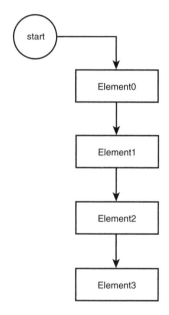

Because doubly linked lists tend to be more general and therefore have a wider range of application, you'll focus on them in today's lesson. Besides, a doubly linked list is really just a singly linked list with more features, which means you can use it just like a singly linked list if you want.

Implementing a Linked List

Now that you have an idea of what a linked list is, let's take a stab at developing a fully functioning linked list class.

Before jumping into the details, however, consider the fact that the linked list class you're developing is actually an extension of the standard Java data structures you learned about earlier today. This means that you should design the class to fit well with the design of the existing data structures.

26

A good approach, then, would be to model the linked list class around the Vector class, at least in regard to some of the basic techniques of manipulating elements through methods. This is so anyone else using your linked list class can easily see how to use the class based on their understanding of other standard Java classes, such as Vector. Extending the standard Java classes is very important when it comes to writing reusable code.

Even though the linked list implementation has been described in terms of a single class, it takes a few classes to build a complete linked list. These classes consist of a linked list class, a linked list entry class, and a linked list enumeration class.

The linked list class models the list itself and is the only class anyone using the linked list will come into contact with. The other two classes are helper classes that provide some type of behind-the-scenes functionality for the linked list class. The linked list entry class models an individual element within the linked list, and the linked list enumerator class provides support for the Enumeration interface.

Because it is by far the most simple of the three classes, let's start by looking at the linked list entry class, which is called LinkedListEntry:

```java
import java.util.*;

class LinkedListEntry {
    protected Object val = null;
    protected LinkedListEntry next = null;
    protected LinkedListEntry prev = null;

    public LinkedListEntry(Object obj) {
        // Make sure the object is valid
        if (obj == null)
            throw new NullPointerException();

        val = obj;
    }
}
```

The LinkedListEntry class contains three member variables, which keep up with the value of the entry (the element being stored) and reference the next and previous elements. This class has a single constructor defined, which simply checks the validity of the object being stored in the entry and assigns it to the entry's val member variable.

Most of the functionality of the linked list is provided by the main linked list class. This class is called LinkedList and contains a few member variables:

```java
protected LinkedListEntry start = null;
protected LinkedListEntry end = null;
protected int numElements;
```

The start and end member variables hold references to the beginning and end elements in the list, while the numElements member keeps up with the size of the list. There are also a variety of methods defined in the LinkedList class that resemble methods in the Vector class. One of the most important methods is addElement(), which adds a new element to the end of the list. The source code for addElement() is shown in Listing 26.1.

LISTING 26.1. THE LinkedList CLASS'S ADDELEMENT() METHOD.

```
 1: public void addElement(Object obj) {
 2:     // Make sure the object is valid
 3:     if (obj == null)
 4:         throw new NullPointerException();
 5:
 6:     // Create the new entry
 7:     LinkedListEntry newElement = new LinkedListEntry(obj);
 8:     numElements++;
 9:
10:     // See if the new element is the start of the list
11:     if (start == null) {
12:         start = newElement;
13:         end = newElement;
14:     }
15:     else {
16:         end.next = newElement;
17:         newElement.prev = end;
18:         end = newElement;
19:     }
20: }
```

26

The addElement() method first makes sure the new object is valid. It then creates an entry to hold the object and checks if the new element will be placed at the start of the list. addElement() then adjusts the references of elements related to the new element so the list's structure is maintained.

Just as the addElement() method is important for adding a new element to the end of the list, the insertElementAt() method is useful for inserting a new element at any point in the list. Listing 26.2 contains the source code for insertElementAt().

LISTING 26.2. THE LinkedList CLASS'S INSERTELEMENTAT() METHOD.

```
 1: public void insertElementAt(Object obj, Object pos) {
 2:     // Make sure the objects are valid
 3:     if (obj == null || pos == null)
 4:         throw new NullPointerException();
```

continues

LISTING 26.2. CONTINUED

```
 5:
 6:     // Make sure the position object is in the list
 7:     LinkedListEntry posEntry = find(pos);
 8:     if (posEntry == null)
 9:         throw new NullPointerException();
10:
11:     // Create the new entry
12:     LinkedListEntry newElement = new LinkedListEntry(obj);
13:     numElements++;
14:
15:     // Link in the new entry
16:     newElement.next = posEntry;
17:     newElement.prev = posEntry.prev;
18:     if (posEntry == start)
19:         start = newElement;
20:     else
21:         posEntry.prev.next = newElement;
22:     posEntry.prev = newElement;
23: }
```

The insertElementAt() method takes two arguments that specify the new object to be
added to the list, along with the object at the position where the new object is to be
inserted. insertElementAt() first makes sure both objects are valid, and then it checks if
the position object is in the list. If things are okay at this point, a new entry is created to
hold the new object and the references in adjacent elements are adjusted to reflect the
insertion.

You now have two methods that allow you to add and insert elements to the linked list.
However, you still can't remove elements from the list. Listing 26.3 contains the source
code for removeElement(), a method that allows you to remove an element by specifying the object itself.

LISTING 26.3. THE LinkedList CLASS'S REMOVEELEMENT() METHOD.

```
 1: public boolean removeElement(Object obj) {
 2:     // Make sure the object is valid
 3:     if (obj == null)
 4:         throw new NullPointerException();
 5:
 6:     // Make sure the object is in the list
 7:     LinkedListEntry delEntry = find(obj);
 8:     if (delEntry == null)
 9:         return false;
10:
```

```
11:        // Unlink the entry
12:        numElements--;
13:        if (delEntry == start)
14:            start = delEntry.next;
15:        else
16:        delEntry.prev.next = delEntry.next;
17:        if (delEntry == end)
18:            end = delEntry.prev;
19:        else
20:            delEntry.next.prev = delEntry.prev;
21:        return true;
22: }
```

The removeElement() method first checks if the object passed in is valid, and then it searches for the object in the list. It performs this search by calling the find method, which is a private method you'll learn about in just a moment. When removeElement() finds the entry in the list, it unlinks the entry by adjusting the references in adjacent entries.

The find() method is a private method used internally by the LinkedList class to find entries in the list based on the object they store. The following is the source code for the find() method:

```
private LinkedListEntry find(Object obj) {
    // Make sure the list isn't empty and the object is valid
    if (isEmpty() || obj == null)
        return null;

    // Search the list for the object
    LinkedListEntry tmp = start;
    while (tmp != null) {
        if (tmp.val == obj)
            return tmp;
        tmp = tmp.next;
    }
    return null;
}
```

26

The find() method first makes sure that the list isn't empty and that the object in question is valid. It then traverses the list using a while loop, checking the val member variable of each entry against the object passed in. If there is a match, the entry holding the object is returned; otherwise, null is returned.

The find() method isn't public because you don't want users of the LinkedList class to know anything about the LinkedListEntry class. In other words, the LinkedListEntry class is a purely internal helper class, so the LinkedListEntry object returned from find() wouldn't make any sense to a user of LinkedList.

Even though `find()` is private, there is a public method that you can use to see if an object is in the list. This method is called `contains()`, and its source code follows:

```
public boolean contains(Object obj) {
    return (find(obj) != null);
}
```

As you can see, all the `contains()` method does is call `find()` and compare the return value to `null`. Because `find()` only returns a non-`null` value if an object is found, this little trick works perfectly!

You may have noticed earlier that the `find()` method made a call to the `isEmpty()` method to see if the list was empty. The code for this method follows:

```
public boolean isEmpty() {
    return (start == null);
}
```

Because the `start` reference in `LinkedList` only contains a `null` value if the list is empty, the `isEmpty()` method simply makes sure it is in fact set to `null`. This is a very simple and effective way to see if the list is empty.

That pretty much sums up the `LinkedList` class, except for how it supports the `Enumeration` interface. Your best bet is to look to the `Vector` class. The `Vector` class supports the `Enumeration` interface through a method called `elements`, which returns an object of type `Enumeration` that can be used to enumerate the elements in a vector.

Let's use this same approach to add enumeration capabilities to the linked list. The following is the source code for the `elements()` method in the `LinkedList` class:

```
public Enumeration elements() {
    return new LinkedListEnumerator(this);
}
```

The `elements()` method is probably a lot simpler than you expected. That's because the work of actually supporting the `Enumeration` interface is left to the `LinkedListEnumerator` class. Listing 26.4 contains the source code for the `LinkedListEnumerator` class.

LISTING 26.4. THE FULL TEXT OF LINKEDLISTENUMERATOR.JAVA.

```
1: import java.util.*;
2:
3: class LinkedListEnumerator implements Enumeration {
4:     protected LinkedListEntry pos;
5:
6:     public LinkedListEnumerator(LinkedList list) {
7:         pos = list.start;
```

```
 8:     }
 9:
10:     public boolean hasMoreElements() {
11:         return (pos != null);
12:     }
13:
14:     public Object nextElement() {
15:         // Make sure the current object is valid
16:         if (pos == null)
17:             throw new NoSuchElementException();
18:
19:         // Increment the list and return the object
20:         LinkedListEntry tmp = pos;
21:         pos = pos.next;
22:         return tmp.val;
23:     }
24: }
```

Notice that the LinkedListEnumerator class implements the Enumeration interface, which is evident in the class definition. The LinkedListEnumerator class contains one member variable, pos, which keeps up with the current entry in the enumeration. The constructor simply sets the pos member to the start of the list.

Other than saying so in the class definition, implementing the Enumeration interface involves supporting two methods: hasMoreElements() and nextElement(). The hasMoreElements() method simply checks if the pos member is non-null, in which case there are more elements to enumerate. The nextElement() method makes sure the current entry is valid and then returns the object stored in this entry. That's all there is to the LinkedListEnumerator class.

You now have a complete linked list class that you can put to use in a practical Java program.

 Note   All of the source code for these linked list classes is located on this book's CD-ROM and on its official Web site at http://www.prefect.com/java21pre.

Summary

In today's lesson, you have learned all about data structures and their relevance to Java programming.

You began the lesson with a brief overview of data structures and why it is important to have a solid understanding of them. You then learned about the standard data structures provided in the Java utility package.

These standard data structures provide a range of options that cover many practical programming scenarios. However, in case you need something a little different to hold data, you also learned about a type of data structure that isn't provided by the Java utility package: linked lists.

You implemented a linked list class that you can reuse in your own Java programs. This knowledge, combined with an understanding of the standard Java data structures, should help you handle data in practical programming scenarios.

Q&A

Q If Java arrays are data structures, why aren't they implemented as classes?

A Actually, Java arrays are implemented as classes; they just aren't used as classes in the traditional sense of calling methods and so on. Even though you won't find a class called Array in the Java class library documentation, you can rest assured that Java has an array class that is at least vaguely similar to the Vector class.

Q Do all of the standard Java data structures implement the Enumeration interface?

A No, because the design of the Enumeration interface is based on a sequential data structure. For example, the Vector class is sequential and fits in perfectly with supporting the Enumeration interface. However, the BitSet class is nonsequential, so supporting the Enumeration interface wouldn't make any sense.

Q What is the importance of using a hash table?

A Calculating a hash code for a complex piece of data is important because you can lessen the overhead involved in searching for the data. The hash code allows you to home in on a particular point in a large set of data before you begin the arduous task of searching based on the data itself. This can greatly improve performance.

Q How are linked lists different from vectors in the storage of individual elements?

A Vectors manage the memory requirements of all elements by allocating a certain amount of memory upon creation. When a vector is required to grow, it will allocate enough memory to hold the existing data and the new data and will then copy everything to it. Even if a vector only holds references to objects, it must still manage the memory that holds the references. Linked lists don't manage any of the memory for the elements contained in the list, except for references to the start and end elements.

BONUS WEEK

DAY 27

JavaBeans

As you have learned, one of the primary advantages of object-oriented programming is the capability to reuse an object in different programs. If you have created a spellchecker object that works great with your word processing program, you should be able to use the same object with an email program also.

Sun has extended this principle with the introduction of JavaBeans. A *JavaBean*, also called a *bean*, is a software object that interacts with other objects according to a strict set of guidelines. By following these guidelines, the bean can most easily be used with other objects. Once you know how to work with one JavaBean according to these rules, you know how to work with all of them.

Another advantage of JavaBeans occurs when you're using a programming tool that has been developed with beans in mind. These environments, including Sun's own free JavaBeans Development Kit, make it possible to develop Java programs quickly by using existing beans and establishing the relationships between them.

Today, you'll explore the following subjects:

- Creating reusable software objects in Java
- How JavaBeans relates to the Java class library
- The JavaBeans API
- JavaBeans development tools
- The JavaBeans Development Kit
- Working with JavaBeans
- Creating an applet with JavaBeans

Reusable Software Components

A growing trend in the field of software development is the use of *reusable components*—elements of a program that can be used with more than one software package.

 A *software component* is a piece of software isolated into a discrete, easily reusable structure.

If you develop parts of a program so that they are completely self-contained, it should be possible for these components to be assembled into programs with much greater development efficiency. This notion of reusing carefully packaged software was borrowed, to some extent, from the assembly-line approach that became so popular in the United States during the Industrial Revolution. This idea, as applied to software, is to build small, reusable components once and then reuse them as much as possible, thereby streamlining the entire development process.

Perhaps the greatest difficulty that component software has had to face is the wide range of disparate microprocessors and operating systems in use today. There have been several reasonable attempts at component software, but they've always been limited to a specific operating system. Microsoft's VBX and OCX component architectures have had great success in the Intel PC world, but they've done little to bridge the gap between PCs and other operating systems.

Note Microsoft's ActiveX technology, which is based on its OCX technology, aims to provide an all-purpose component technology that's compatible across a wide range of platforms. However, considering the dependency of ActiveX on 32-bit Windows code, it remains to be seen how Microsoft will solve the platform-dependency issue.

Some existing component technologies also suffer from having been developed in a particular programming language or for a particular development environment. Just as platform-dependency cripples components at runtime, limiting component development to a particular programming language or development environment cripples components at the development end. Software developers want to decide for themselves which language is the most appropriate for a particular task. Likewise, they want to select the development environment that best fits their needs, rather than being forced to use one based on a component technology. Therefore, any realistic long-term component technology must deal with both—platform-dependency and language-dependency.

Java has been a major factor in making truly platform-independent software development a reality, and it offers software component development through JavaBeans.

JavaBeans is an architecture- and platform-independent set of classes for creating and using Java software components. It picks up where other component technologies have left off, using the portable Java platform to provide a complete component software solution.

The Goal of JavaBeans

JavaBeans was designed to be compact because components will often be used in distributed environments where entire components are transferred across a low-bandwidth Internet connection. The second part of this goal relates to the ease with which the components are built and used. It's not such a stretch to imagine components that are easy to use, but creating a component architecture that makes it easy to build components is a different issue altogether.

JavaBeans components are largely based on the class structure already in use with traditional Java applet programming, and applets designed around the Abstract Windowing Toolkit (AWT) can easily scale to new JavaBeans components. This also has the positive side effect of making JavaBeans components very compact because Java applets are already very efficient in terms of file size.

JavaBeans's second major goal is to be fully portable. As a result, developers will not need to worry about including platform-specific libraries with their Java applets.

The existing Java architecture already offers a wide range of benefits that are easily applied to components. One of the more important (but rarely mentioned) features of Java is its built-in class discovery mechanism, which allows objects to interact with each other dynamically. This results in a system where objects can be integrated with each other independently of their respective origins or development history. The class discovery mechanism is not just a neat Java feature; it is a necessary requirement in any component architecture.

27

NEW TERM Another example of JavaBeans inheriting existing Java functionality is *persistence*, which is the capability of an object to store and retrieve its internal state. Persistence is handled automatically in JavaBeans by using the serialization mechanism already present in Java. *Serialization* is the process of storing or retrieving information through a standard protocol. Alternatively, developers can create customized persistence solutions whenever necessary.

Although support for distributed computing is not a core element of the JavaBeans architecture, it is provided. JavaBeans component developers can select the distributed computing approach that best fits their needs. Sun provides a distributed computing solution in its Remote Method Invocation (RMI) technology, but JavaBeans developers are in no way handcuffed to this solution. Other options include CORBA (Common Object Request Broker Architecture) and Microsoft's DCOM (Distributed Component Object Model), among others.

Distributed computing has been cleanly abstracted from JavaBeans to keep things tight while still giving developers who require distributed support a wide range of options. JavaBeans's final design goal deals with design-time issues and how developers build applications using JavaBeans components.

The JavaBeans architecture includes support for specifying design-time properties and editing mechanisms to better facilitate visual editing of JavaBeans components. The result is that developers will be able to use visual tools to assemble and modify JavaBeans components in a seamless fashion, much the way existing PC visual tools work with components such as VBX or OCX controls. In this way, component developers specify the way in which the components are to be used and manipulated in a development environment.

How JavaBeans Relates to Java

Although Java's object-oriented nature provides a means for objects to work in conjunction with each other, there are a few rules or standards governing how object interactions are conducted. These rules are needed for a robust component software solution, and they are provided through JavaBeans.

JavaBeans specifies a rich set of mechanisms for interaction between objects, along with common actions most objects will need to support, such as persistence and event handling. It also provides the framework by which this component communication can take place. Even more important is the fact that JavaBeans components can be easily tweaked via a standard set of well-defined properties. JavaBeans merges the power of full-blown Java applets with the compactness and reusability of Java windowing components such as buttons.

JavaBeans components aren't limited to user-interface objects such as buttons, however. You can just as easily develop nonvisual JavaBeans components that perform some background function in concert with other components. In this way, JavaBeans merges the power of visual Java applets with nonvisual Java applications under a consistent component framework.

Note

> **NEW TERM** A *nonvisual component* is any component that doesn't have a visible output. If you think of components in terms of AWT objects like buttons and menus, this may seem a little strange. However, keep in mind that a component is simply a tightly packaged program and doesn't need to be visual. A good example is a timer component, which fires timing events at specified intervals and is nonvisual. Timer components are very popular in other component development environments, such as Microsoft Visual Basic.

With visual tools, you can use a variety of JavaBeans components together without necessarily writing any code. JavaBeans components expose their own interfaces visually, providing a means to edit their properties without programming. Furthermore, by using a visual editor, you can drop a JavaBeans component directly into an application without writing any code. This is an entirely new level of flexibility and reusability that was impossible in Java alone.

The JavaBeans API

JavaBeans is ultimately a programming interface, meaning that all its features are implemented as extensions to the standard Java class library. All the functionality provided by JavaBeans is actually implemented in the JavaBeans API, a suite of smaller APIs devoted to specific functions (services). The following is a list of the main component services in the JavaBeans API that are necessary for all the features you've been learning about today:

- Graphical user interface merging
- Persistence
- Event handling
- Introspection
- Application builder support

If you understand these services and how they work, you'll have much more insight into exactly what type of technology JavaBeans is. These services are implemented as smaller APIs contained within the larger JavaBeans API.

27

The user-interface–merging APIs enable a component to merge its elements with a container. Most containers have menus and toolbars that display any special features provided by the component. The interface-merging APIs allow the component to add features to the container document's menu and toolbar. These APIs also define the mechanism that facilitates interface layout between components and their containers.

The persistent APIs specify the mechanism by which components can be stored and retrieved within the context of a containing document. By default, components inherit the automatic serialization mechanism provided by Java. Developers are also free to design more elaborate persistence solutions based on the specific needs of their components.

The event-handling APIs specify an event-driven architecture that defines how components interact with each other. The Java AWT already includes a powerful event-handling model, which serves as the basis for the event-handling component APIs. These APIs are critical in giving components the freedom to interact with each other in a consistent fashion.

The introspection APIs define the techniques by which components make their internal structure readily available at design time. These APIs allow development tools to query a component for its internal state, including the interfaces, methods, and member variables of which the component is composed.

These APIs are divided into two distinct sections, based on the level at which they are being used. For example, the low-level introspection APIs give development tools direct access to component internals, which is a function you wouldn't necessarily want in the hands of component users. This brings us to the high-level APIs, which use the low-level APIs to determine which parts of a component are exported for user modification. Although development tools will undoubtedly use both APIs, they will use the high-level APIs only when providing component information to the user.

The application builder support APIs provide the overhead necessary for editing and manipulating components at design time. These APIs are used largely by visual development tools to visually lay out and edit components while constructing an application. The section of a component that provides visual editing capabilities is specifically designed to be physically separate from the component itself. This is because standalone runtime components should be as compact as possible. In a purely runtime environment, components are transferred with only the necessary runtime component. Developers who only want to use the design-time portion of the component can do so.

The JavaBeans specifications are available at the Java Web site at
`http://java.sun.com/products/jdk/1.2/docs/guide/beans/index.html`.

Development Tools

The best way to understand JavaBeans is to work with them in a programming environment that supports bean development.

Bean programming requires an environment with a fairly sophisticated graphical user interface because much of the development work is done visually. In an integrated development environment such as Symantec Visual Café, you can establish a relationship between two beans in an interface by dragging a line between them with your mouse.

The tools in the Java Development Kit are almost exclusively used from the command line without a graphical interface. Because of this, you need a different programming tool to develop JavaBeans when using the JDK tools. Most of the commercially available Java development tools support JavaBeans, including Visual Café, Metrowerks CodeWarrior, IBM VisualAge for Java, Inprise Borland JBuilder, and SunSoft Java WorkShop.

 Caution
At the time of this writing, only a few of these commercial tools support Java 2 in any form, although most have Java 2 upgrades under development. If you're shopping for a Java integrated development environment that supports JavaBeans, an important thing to note is whether it supports Java 1.1 or 2.

If you don't have a development tool that supports JavaBeans programming, you can use the free JavaBeans Development Kit from Sun.

JavaBeans Development Kit

Sun's JavaBeans Development Kit, also called the BDK, is a free tool that can be used if no other bean-enabled programming environment is available.

If this sounds like damning the BDK with faint praise, it is. Sun makes the following recommendation on its Java Web site: "The BDK is not intended for use by application developers, nor is it intended to be a full-fledged application development environment. Instead, application developers should consider the various Java application development environments supporting JavaBeans."

When the BDK was released, it served a similar purpose to the original Java Development Kit, enabling programmers to work with a new technology when no other alternatives were available. With the arrival of numerous JavaBeans-capable programming tools, Sun has not focused its efforts on extending the functionality of the BDK and

27

improving its performance. The BDK is now useful primarily as an introduction to JavaBeans development. That's what it will be used for today.

The BDK is available for Windows 95, 98, and NT, and Solaris 2.4 and 2.5. It was developed using the Java language, so it also can be run on other Java-enabled operating systems. It currently can be downloaded from

`http://java.sun.com/beans/software/bdk_download.html`.

 Caution

> If this page is not available, visit the main page at Sun's Java site at `http://java.sun.com`. The BDK and other programming tools are available in the "Products & APIs" section of the site.

The BDK is almost 4MB in size, requiring up to 30 minutes to download on a 28,800-baud Internet connection. While you're waiting for the file transfer to finish, be sure to read the installation instructions and last-minute notes on the BDK download page. You may need to make changes to your system's CLASSPATH setting for the BDK to function properly.

The BDK is transferred as a single executable file that must be run to install the software. During the installation, you will select the Java virtual machine that the BDK will use. Choose the Java interpreter that you've been using to run Java 2 programs.

The following things are included in the BDK:

- The BeanBox, a JavaBean container that can be used to manipulate sample beans and work with those of your own creation.
- More than a dozen sample beans, including a Juggler bean that displays a juggling animation, a Molecule bean that displays a 3D molecule, and OrangeButton, a user interface component.
- The complete Java source code of the BeanBox.
- Makefiles, configuration scripts that can be used to re-create the BDK.
- A tutorial from Sun on JavaBeans and the BeanBox.

Working with JavaBeans

As you work with JavaBeans in a development environment such as the BDK, you'll quickly discover how different they are from Java classes that weren't designed to be beans.

JavaBeans differ from other classes in a fairly major way: They can interact with a development environment, running inside it as if they were being run by a user. The development environment also can interact directly with the JavaBean, calling its methods and setting up values for its variables.

If you have installed the BDK, you can use it in the following sections to work with existing JavaBeans and create a new one. If not, you'll still learn more about how JavaBeans are used in conjunction with a development environment.

Bean Containers

The AWT and Swing use *containers*—user interface components that hold other components.

JavaBeans development takes place within a bean container. The BDK includes the BeanBox, a rudimentary container that can be used to do the following:

- Save a bean
- Load a saved bean
- Drop beans into a window where they can be laid out
- Move and resize beans
- Edit a bean's properties
- Configure a bean
- Associate a bean that generates an event with an event-handler
- Associate the properties of different beans with each other
- Convert a bean into an applet
- Add new beans from a Java archive (jar files)

To run the BeanBox application, go to the folder where the BDK was installed and open the beanbox subfolder. This subfolder contains two batch-command files that can be used to run the BeanBox: run.bat for Windows systems, and run.sh for Solaris systems.

These batch files load the BeanBox application using the Java interpreter you selected during BDK installation, which is probably the Java 2 interpreter. Three windows will open, as shown in Figure 27.1.

27

FIGURE 27.1.

The three windows that make up the BeanBox application.

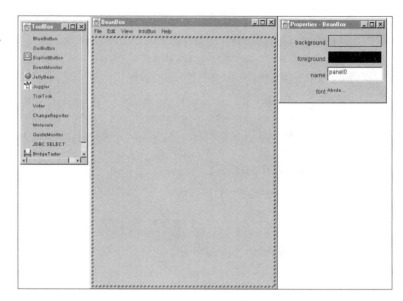

> **Caution**
>
> If you associate the BeanBox with a beta version of Java Development Kit 1.2 during BDK installation, you may experience problems displaying fonts and colored text in the BeanBox. To fix this, edit the `run` batch file used to run the BeanBox so that it sets the Java system property `java2d.font.usePlatformFont`, as in the following:
>
> ```
> java -Djava2d.font.usePlatformFont=true sun.beanbox.BeanBoxFrame
> ```

The largest window is the BeanBox composition window, which arranges beans and creates their associations with each other.

The other two windows are the Toolbox window, which lists several JavaBeans that can be selected for placement in the composition window, and a Properties window, which is used to configure the bean.

Most of the work will be done within the composition window, which is comparable to the main window of a drawing program such as Adobe Illustrator. All beans are placed, rearranged, lined up, and selected for editing within this window.

Placing a Bean

The first step in placing a bean in the BeanBox is to select it in the Toolbox window. When you do this, your cursor will switch to a crosshairs symbol. With the crosshairs, you can click anywhere in the main composition window to place the selected type of bean in it. When you place a bean, it's best to choose someplace near the middle of the composition window. You can use the Edit, Cut and Edit, Paste menu commands to move the bean if needed. You also can move a bean by placing your cursor over the edge of the bean until the cursor becomes a set of compass-direction arrows, dragging the bean to a new location, and releasing the mouse.

Try this out by clicking the Juggler label in the Toolbox window and then clicking somewhere in the middle of the main composition window. An animation of a juggling bicuspid will appear in the main window (see Figure 27.2). You'll probably recognize the juggler—rather than a tooth, he's Duke, the official mascot of the Java language. Appropriately enough, the objects he's tossing around are giant beans.

FIGURE 27.2.

Duke juggles some giant beans in the main BeanBox window.

In Figure 27.2, the striped line around the Juggler bean indicates that it is currently selected for editing. You can select the BeanBox window itself by clicking anywhere other than the Juggler bean, and you can select the Juggler bean again by clicking it. You can edit, copy, cut, and paste a bean only if it has been selected for editing.

Adjusting a Bean's Properties

When a bean has been selected in the main composition window of the BeanBox, its editable properties, if any, are displayed in the Properties window. This window for the current project is shown in Figure 27.3.

27

FIGURE 27.3.

*Editable properties of
a bean, shown in the
Properties window.*

As shown in Figure 27.3, the Juggler bean has five editable properties: `background`, `animationRate`, `foreground`, `name`, and `font`.

Changes to a JavaBean's properties will be reflected in the bean. If you give the Juggler bean's `animationRate` property a higher integer value, there'll be a longer pause between each frame of the animation. If you decrease the property, the animation will speed up.

After you change the `animationRate` property, the bean will change accordingly once you skip to a different property by either hitting the Tab key or clicking on a different property's value. Try entering extreme values such as 1 and 1000 for the animation speed to see the response in the Juggler bean itself.

A JavaBean's editable properties are established by public methods within the bean itself. Each property that can be set has a `set()` method whose full name matches the name of the property in the Properties window of the BeanBox. Likewise, each property whose value can be read has a corresponding `get()` method.

For example, the `animationRate` property of the Juggler bean could have two methods like the following:

```
public int getAnimationRate(){
    return animRate;
}

public void setAnimationRate(int newRate) {
    animRate = newRate;
}
```

In these two methods, `animRate` is a private variable that determines the pause between frames of the juggling animation.

By using the prefixes `set` and `get` for these method names, the Juggler bean developer indicates that the `animationRate` property can be altered from within a JavaBean development environment such as the BeanBox.

The BeanBox, like all bean development tools that follow the standards established by Sun, calls the public `get()` methods of the bean to determine which properties to include in the Properties window. When one of the properties is changed, a set() method is called with the changed value as an argument.

Tip

> Keeping a variable private and using get() and set() methods to read and change it is a good principle in all object-oriented programming, even when you're not trying to develop a JavaBean. This practice is called *encapsulation*, and it is used to control how an object can be accessed by other objects. The more encapsulated an object is, the harder it becomes for other objects to use it incorrectly.

Creating Interactions Between Beans

Another purpose of the BeanBox is to establish interactions between different beans.

To see how this works, first place two ExplicitButton beans anywhere in the main composition window of the BeanBox. If they overlap with the Juggler bean or with each other, move the beans further away from each other. Figure 27.4 shows two buttons along the bottom edge of the Juggler bean.

FIGURE 27.4.

Two ExplicitButton beans and a Juggler bean in the main BeanBox window.

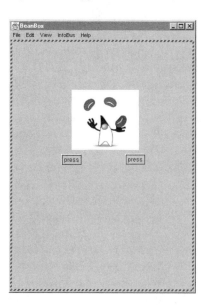

ExplicitButton beans are similar to the Button and JButton components that you have used in graphical user interfaces. They have a background color, foreground color, and text labels with configurable fonts.

27

After placing the buttons, give one the label "Stop!" and change its background color to red. Give the other the label "Go!" and change the background color to green.

At this point, the purpose of these buttons should be fairly obvious: One will stop the animation, and the other will start it. In order for these things to take place, you must establish a relationship between the buttons and the Juggler bean.

The first step is to select the bean that is causing something to take place. In the current example, that bean would be either of the ExplicitButton beans. Clicking one of these causes something to happen to the Juggler bean.

After selecting the bean, choose the menu command Edit, Events, button push, actionPerformed. A red line will connect the button and the cursor, as shown in Figure 27.5.

FIGURE 27.5.

Establishing an event association between two beans.

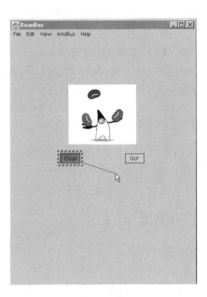

This red line should connect the ExplicitButton bean with the Juggler bean. Clicking on the Juggler bean will establish the association between the two beans.

When this association has been established, you'll see an EventTargetDialog window that lists different methods in the target bean, as shown in Figure 27.6. The method that is chosen will be called automatically when the specified ExplicitButton bean fires an actionPerformed event. (This event occurs when the button is clicked or the Enter key is pressed while the button has the input focus on the interface.)

FIGURE 27.6.

Choosing a method to call in the EventTargetDialog window.

The Juggler bean contains two methods that are used to either stop or start the juggling animation. These are called `stopJuggling()` and `startJuggling()`, respectively. By separating behavior like this into its own method, the Juggler developer enables these methods to be useful in an interaction between different beans. Organizing a bean's methods in this way, offering as many different interactions as necessary, is one of the biggest tasks in JavaBeans development.

The Stop! button should be associated with the Juggler bean's `stopJuggling()` method, and the Go! button should be associated with `startJuggling()`.

By establishing this interaction between three JavaBeans, you have created a simple, functional Java program that can display, start, and stop an animation.

Creating a JavaBeans Program

Once you have placed one or more JavaBeans on a shared interface, set up their properties, and established interactions between them, you have created a Java program.

To save a project in the BeanBox, use the File, Save menu command. This enables you to save the following information to a file:

- The beans as they are currently configured.
- The arrangement of the beans.
- The size of the window they occupy.
- The interactions between the beans.

27

This does not save the project as a Java program that you can run outside of the BeanBox. To save a project in a form that you can run, use the File, MakeApplet command. This command requires two things: the name to give the applet's main class file, and the name of the `jar` archive that will hold all files needed to run the applet, including class files and other data.

Once you specify these items, an applet will be created with an example HTML page that loads it. The HTML file will be placed in the same folder that contains the applet's jar archive. You can load this page using appletviewer or any Web browser that supports Java 1.2.

These applets are distributed using jar archives for the applet itself and any beans in it. Listing 27.1 contains the applet tag generated by BeanBox for the applet, which was named JugglingFool.

LISTING 27.1. THE APPLET TAG GENERATED BY BEANBOX.

```
 1: <applet
 2:     archive="./JugglingFool.jar,./support.jar
 3:          ,./juggler.jar
 4:          ,./buttons.jar
 5:     "
 6:     code="JugglingFool"
 7:     width=220
 8:     height=182
 9: >
10: Trouble instantiating applet JugglingFool!!
11: </applet>
```

Figure 27.7 shows the Juggler animation applet running in the appletviewer tool.

FIGURE 27.7.

A JavaBeans applet running in Appletviewer.

 Note

The size of the applet's window will be determined by the size of the main composition window in the BeanBox. To resize the window, select it by clicking outside all JavaBeans inside the window and then resize it like you would a bean.

Working with Other JavaBeans

Developing software by using prepackaged components like this is a form of *rapid application development*. Unlike many of the terms you have learned in this book, rapid application development, also called RAD, is self-explanatory jargon. It's often used to quickly create a working version of software for demonstration or prototype purposes.

A common example of RAD is using Microsoft Visual Basic to create a prototype of a Visual C++ program. One of the strengths of Visual Basic is its speedy graphical user interface design, which makes it a more effective solution for prototyping than the more complex Visual C++.

JavaBeans make RAD development more commonplace in Java software development. A programmer can swiftly cobble together a working program using existing JavaBeans components.

There are hundreds of JavaBeans available from Sun and other developers, including those at the following sites:

- Gamelan, Developer.Com's directory of Java-related resources: `http://www.developer.com/directories/pages/dir.java.html/`.
- *JavaWorld* Magazine's Developer Tools Guide: `http://www.javaworld.com/javaworld/tools/jw-tools-index.html`.
- Sun's JavaBeans home page: `http://java.sun.com/beans/index.html`.

Beans are packaged into jar archives. If you have downloaded a bean and would like it to show up in the Toolbox window of the BeanBox, save the bean's jar archive in BDK's jars folder. This folder can be found in the folder where the BDK was installed on your system.

Summary

When combined with an integrated development environment that supports them, JavaBeans enable rapid application development of Java programs.

Today, you learned about the underlying principles of reusable software components and how these principles are realized in Java. Putting these ideas into practice, you saw how Sun's JavaBeans Development Kit (BDK) can be used to work with existing beans, establish relationships between them, and create full Java programs.

Although you should seek a more capable development tool than the BDK for developing your own programs with JavaBeans, you can use the BDK to evaluate the applicability of beans to your own programming tasks.

27

You also should use the JavaBeans resources on the World Wide Web. Many of the beans that are available over the Web already accomplish tasks you'll try to handle in your own programs. By using beans, you can reduce the number of things you must create from scratch.

Q&A

Q Will the JavaBeans Development Kit be upgraded into a fully featured bean programming tool?

A At the time of this writing, Sun continues to state that the BDK is intended for testing beans and providing a reference version of how beans should be used inside development environments. It appears that professional programming tools, such as Visual Café and others, are going to remain the best choice for JavaBeans development.

Q In the Juggler example, the `animationRate` property has a different capitalization in the `setAnimationRate()` and `getAnimationRate()` methods. What accounts for this difference?

A The capitalization is different because of the following naming conventions for Java programs: All variables and method names begin with a lowercase letter, and all words but the first in a variable name begin with a single uppercase letter.

The first-letter-lowercase rule differentiates variable and method names from class names. The subsequent-word-capitalized rule differentiates between words in a variable name.

DAY **28**

Connecting to Databases Through JDBC

Java Database Connectivity, or JDBC, is a class library that is used to work with different relational databases from within Java, including proprietary data formats from Microsoft, Sybase, Oracle, Informix, and many others.

After 27 days of hard work exploring the Java 2 class library, you deserve some good news: Today's subject is one of the easier ones to implement in your Java programs. The JDBC library has only a small set of methods and classes that are needed to read and write database records.

Unfortunately, there's a catch.

Before you can use the JDBC class library, you must configure a data source so that it can be reached from within Java. This is often the most difficult part of the process.

Today you'll learn how to make this chore easier, and you'll be introduced to the following subjects:

- Working with Java Database Connectivity (JDBC)
- Using drivers to work with different relational databases
- Accessing a database with Structured Query Language (SQL)
- Moving through the records that result from an SQL database operation
- Establishing ODBC data sources that work in conjunction with JDBC
- Finding JDBC drivers
- Setting up a JDBC data source

Java Database Connectivity

Java Database Connectivity (JDBC) is a set of classes that can be used to develop client/server database applications using Java. Client/server software connects a user of information with a provider of that information, and it's one of the most commonplace forms of programming. You use it every time you surf the Web: A client program called a Web browser requests Web pages, image files, and other documents using a Uniform Resource Locator or URL. Different server programs provide the requested information, if it can be found, for the client.

One of the biggest obstacles faced by database programmers is the wide variety of database formats in use, each with its own proprietary method of accessing data. To simplify using relational database programs, a standard language called SQL (Structured Query Language) has been introduced. This language supplants the need to learn different database-querying languages for each database format.

In database programming, a request for records in a database is called a *query*. Using SQL, you can send complex queries to a database and get the records you're looking for in any order you specify.

Consider the example of a database programmer at a student loan company who has been asked to prepare a report on the most delinquent loan recipients. The programmer could use SQL to query a database for all records in which the last payment was more than 180 days ago and the amount due is more than $0.00. SQL also can be used to control the order in which records are returned, so the programmer can get the records in the order of Social Security Number, recipient name, amount owed, or another field in the loan database.

All of this is possible with SQL, and the programmer hasn't used any of the proprietary languages associated with popular database formats.

Caution SQL is strongly supported by many database formats, so in theory you should be able to use the same SQL commands for each database tool that supports the language. However, you still may need to learn some idiosyncrasies of a specific database format when accessing it through SQL.

SQL is the industry-standard approach to accessing relational databases. JDBC supports SQL, enabling developers to use a wide range of database formats without knowing the specifics of the underlying database. It also enables the use of database queries that are specific to a database format.

The JDBC class library's approach to accessing databases with SQL is comparable to existing database development techniques, so interacting with an SQL database using JDBC isn't much different than it is using traditional database tools. Java programmers who already have some database experience can hit the ground running with JDBC. The JDBC API has already been widely endorsed by industry leaders, including some development-tool vendors who have announced future support for JDBC in their development products.

The JDBC library includes classes for each of the tasks that are commonly associated with database usage:

- Making a connection to a database.
- Creating a statement using SQL.
- Executing that SQL query in the database.
- Viewing the resulting records.

These JDBC classes are all part of the `java.sql` in Java 2.

Database Drivers

Java programs that use JDBC classes can follow the familiar programming model of issuing SQL statements and processing the resulting data. The format of the database and the platform it was prepared on don't matter.

This platform- and database-independence is made possible in a Java program by a driver manager. The classes of the JDBC class library are largely dependent on driver managers, which keep track of the drivers required to access database records. You'll need a different driver for each database format that's being used in a program.

JDBC database drivers can be either written entirely in Java or implemented using native methods to bridge Java applications to existing database access libraries.

28

JDBC also includes a driver that bridges JDBC and another database connectivity standard, called ODBC.

The JDBC-ODBC Bridge

ODBC, Microsoft's common interface for accessing SQL databases, is managed on a Windows system by the ODBC Data Source Administrator. This is run from the Control Panel on a Windows 95 or 98 system by clicking the Start button and then Settings, Control Panel. The administrator adds ODBC drivers, configures drivers to work with specific database files, and logs SQL use. Figure 28.1 shows the ODBC-32 administrator on a Windows system.

FIGURE 28.1.

The ODBC-32 administrator on a Windows 98 system.

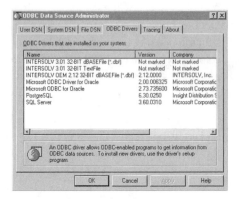

In Figure 28.1, a tabbed dialog box lists all of the ODBC drivers that are present on the system. Some of the drivers are specific to a database company's format, including the Microsoft ODBC Driver for Oracle. Others work with a server that is centered around SQL itself, including PostgreSQL and the Microsoft SQL Server.

Note

The Microsoft SQL Server is Windows NT software that manages relational databases that are queried using SQL. You can find more information at Microsoft's Web site at http://www.microsoft.com/sql.

The JDBC-ODBC bridge allows JDBC drivers to be used as ODBC drivers by converting JDBC method calls into ODBC function calls.

Using the JDBC-ODBC bridge requires three things:

- The JDBC-ODBC bridge driver included with Java 2:
  `sun.jdbc.odbc.JdbcOdbcDriver`.

- An ODBC driver.
- An ODBC data source that has been associated with the driver using software such as the ODBC Data Source Administrator.

ODBC data sources can be set up from within some database programs. For example, when a new database file is created in Lotus Approach, users have the option of associating it with an ODBC driver.

All ODBC data sources must be given a short descriptive name. This name will be used inside Java programs when a connection is made to the database that the source refers to.

On a Windows 95 or 98 system, once an ODBC driver is selected and the database is created, they will show up in the ODBC Data Source Administrator. Figure 28.2 shows an example of this for a data source named `FavoriteSites`.

FIGURE 28.2.

A listing of data sources in the ODBC-32 administrator.

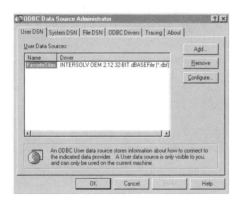

The data source `FavoriteSites` is associated with a 32-bit INTERSOLV dBase driver, according to Figure 28.2.

Note

That INTERSOLV driver is one of many ODBC drivers that is commercially available for Windows 95, 98, and NT users. INTERSOLV merged with Micro Focus after this driver was released, and the company currently does business at `http://www.microfocus.com`.

Connecting to an ODBC Data Source

28

Your first project today is a Java application that uses a JDBC-ODBC bridge to connect to a dBase file. dBase, a database format of the Ashton-Tate Corp., is one of the oldest databases still in popular use. Many database development programs can create dBase files, including Microsoft Access and Lotus Approach.

The dBase file for this project is `favsites.dbf`, a database of favorite Web sites. This database has four fields:

- `URL`—The Web address of the site.
- `SITENAME`—A descriptive name for the site.
- `CATEGORY`—A short string describing the type of site, which is one of the following: `News`, `Technology`, `Humor`, `Politics`, or `Personal`.
- `DATEADDED`—The date that this site was added to the database.

The database used during the preparation of this project contains more than a dozen different records, most coming from the `News` category. It's included on this book's CD-ROM and the official Web site at `http://www.prefect.com/java21pre`.

To use this database, you must have an ODBC driver on your system that supports 32-bit dBase files. Using the ODBC Data Source Administrator (or a similar program if you're on a non-Windows system), you must create a new ODBC data source that is associated with `favsites.dbf`.

It may be easier to create a new database on your system that can be associated with an ODBC driver during creation. Some drivers support formats such as `.dbf`, while others, called ODBC text drivers, can handle comma-separated text files.

If you have a driver that supports this kind of text database, enter Listing 28.1 using a text editor and save the file as `favsites.txt`. Make sure to save it as a text-only file with no special formatting.

LISTING 28.1. THE FULL TEXT OF FAVSITES.TXT.

```
 1: "SITETITLE","URL","CATEGORY","DATEADDED"
 2: "Slashdot","http://www.slashdot.org","News","1998-10-18."
 3: "The Obscure Store","http://www.obscurestore.com","News","1998-10-18."
 4: "Request Line","http://www.requestline.com/mbd","News","1998-10-18."
 5: "Salon","http://www.salon1999.com","News","1998-10-18."
 6: "Drudge Retort","http://www.drudge.com","News","1998-10-18."
 7: "Wall Street Journal","http://interactive.wsj.com","News","1998-10-
    18."
 8: "Stating the Obvious","http://www.theobvious.com","News","1998-10-18."
 9: "Java News","http://www.intelligence.com/java","News","1998-10-18."
10: "CNN","http://www.cnn.com","News","1998-10-18."
11: "Variety","http://www.variety.com","News","1998-10-18."
12: "Need to Know","http://www.ntk.net","News","1998-10-18."
13: "Christian Science Monitor","http://www.csmonitor.com","News","1998-
    10-18."
14: "Mercury Center","http://www.sjmercury.com","News","1998-10-18."
15: "Fort Worth Star-Telegram","http://www.startext.com","News","1998-10-
    18."
```

```
16: "MSNBC","http://www.msnbc.com","News","1998-10-18."
17: "News.Com","http://www.news.com","News","1998-10-18."
18: "The Onion","http://www.theonion.com","News","1998-10-18."
19: "Wired News","http://www.wired.com/news","News","1998-10-18."
```

A comma-separated text file is just about the simplest form a database can take. It is structured according to a few simple rules:

- Each record in the database is on its own line.
- Quote marks are used around each field in a record.
- Commas separate fields from each other.
- The first record provides the names for each field.

The favsites.txt file should be saved in its own subfolder on your system. When you associate an ODBC driver with this file, you indicate the folder where favsites.txt can be found. Many database creation programs can import a comma-separated file like this and turn it into a database file.

Other setup work may be needed depending on the ODBC drivers that are present on your system, if any. Consult the documentation included with the ODBC driver.

Caution

This aspect of JDBC-ODBC bridge programming often can be more difficult than using the JDBC class library in a program. You may need to install an ODBC driver and learn more about its use before you try to create a JDBC-ODBC application.

For the project as it is described here, the first step in the process is to create favsites.dbf using Lotus Approach 97, a database development program from IBM that is bundled with the SmartSuite productivity suite. Lotus Approach 97 can create database files in several different formats: dBase III+, dBase IV, Foxpro, and Paradox. If ODBC drivers are installed on a system, Approach also enables you to create a database that is immediately associated with this driver.

Choosing an ODBC driver causes a database development tool like Approach to follow the rules of that driver. In the example of favsites.dbf and the INTERSOLV 32-bit dBase driver, all fields are limited to 10 characters and can't include any spaces. Using Approach, the database is created with the same fields shown in Listing 28.1: SITETITLE, URL, CATEGORY, and DATEADDED. The database is then filled with each of the records and saved.

28

Note

Lotus Approach is not required for this project—it is described to give you some insight into the process of creating a database and associating it with an ODBC driver. There are many other database programs you can use to either create a database like favsites.dbf or use an ODBC driver directly with the favsites.txt file.

The final step in getting favsites.dbf ready for JDBC-ODBC is to create a data source associated with favsites.dbf. Unlike other input-output classes in Java, JDBC doesn't use a filename to identify a data file and use its contents. Instead, a tool such as the ODBC Data Source Administrator is used to name the ODBC source and indicate the file folder where it can be found.

Figure 28.3 shows the dialog box used to set up favsites.dbf as a data source in the Windows ODBC administrator. In addition to the name, a short description, and the folder that contains the database, its database format is designated as dBASE5.

FIGURE 28.3.

The ODBC dBase Driver Setup dialog box.

Once a database has been associated with an ODBC data source, working with it in a Java program is relatively easy if you are conversant with SQL.

The first task in a JDBC program is to load the driver (or drivers) that will be used to connect to a data source. A driver is loaded with the Class.forName(*String*) method. Class, part of the java.lang package, can be used to load classes into the Java interpreter. The forName(*String*) method loads the class named by the specified string. A ClassNotFoundException may be thrown by this method.

All programs that use an ODBC data source will use sun.jdbc.odbc.JdbcOdbcDriver, the JDBC-ODBC bridge driver that is included with Java 2. Loading this class into a Java interpreter requires the following statement:

```
Class.forName("sun.jdbc.odbc.JdbcOdbcDriver");
```

Once the driver has been loaded, you can establish a connection to the data source using the DriverManager class in the java.sql package.

The getConnection(*String*, *String*, *String*) method of DriverManager can be used to set up the connection. It returns a Connection object representing an active data connection.

The three arguments of this method are as follows:

- A name identifying the data source and the type of database connectivity used to reach it
- A username
- A password

The last two items are needed only if the data source is secured with a username and a password. If not, these arguments can be null strings (`""`).

The name of the data source is preceded by the text `jdbc:odbc:` when using the JDBC-ODBC bridge, which indicates the type of database connectivity in use.

The following statements could be used to connect to a data source called `Payroll` with a username of `Doc` and a password of `Notnow`:

```
Connection payday = DriverManager.getConnection(
    "jdbc:odbc:Payroll", "Doc", "Notnow");
```

The `getConnection()` method and all others called on a data source will throw `SQLException` errors if something goes wrong as the data source is being used. SQL has its own error messages, and they will be passed along as part of `SQLException` objects.

An SQL statement is represented in Java by a `Statement` object. `Statement` is an interface, so it can't be instantiated directly. However, it is returned by the `createStatement()` method of a `Connection` object, as in the following example:

```
Statement lookSee = payday.CreateStatement();
```

Once you have a `Statement` object, you can use it to conduct an SQL query by calling the object's `executeQuery(String)` method. The `String` argument should be an SQL query that follows the syntax of that language. Although you need to learn SQL to do any extensive work with it, a lot of the language is easy to pick up from any examples you can find.

The following is an example of an SQL query that could be used on the `favsites.dbf` database:

```
SELECT SITENAME, URL FROM favsites.dbf WHERE (SITENAME Is Not Null) ORDER
BY URL
```

This SQL query retrieves the `SITENAME` and `URL` fields for each record in the database where the `SITENAME` field is not equal to null. The records that are returned are sorted according to their `URL` field, so `http://www.cnn.com` would precede `http://www.news.com`.

28

If the SQL query has been phrased correctly, the executeQuery() method will return a ResultSet object holding all of the records that have been retrieved from the data source.

When a ResultSet is returned from executeQuery(), it is positioned at the first record that has been retrieved. The following methods of ResultSet can be used to pull information out of the current record:

- getDate(*String*)—Returns the Date value stored in the specified field name.
- getDouble(*String*)—Returns the double value stored in the specified field name.
- getFloat(*String*)—Returns the float value stored in the specified field name.
- getInt(*String*)—Returns the int value stored in the specified field name.
- getLong(*String*)—Returns the long value stored in the specified field name.
- getString(*String*)—Returns the String stored in the specified field name.

These are just the simplest methods that are available in the ResultSet interface. The ones you should use depend on the form that the field data took when the database was created, although methods such as getString() and getInt() can be more flexible in the information they retrieve from a record. An SQLException will be thrown if a database error occurs as you try to retrieve information from a result set.

After you have pulled the information you need from a record, you can move to the next record by calling the next() method of the ResultSet object. This method returns a false boolean value when it tries to move past the end of a result set.

You also can move through the records in a result set with these other methods:

- afterLast()—Moves to a place immediately after the last record in the set.
- beforeFirst()—Moves to a place immediately before the first record in the set.
- first()—Moves to the first record in the set.
- last()—Moves to the last record in the set.
- previous()—Moves to the previous record in the set.

With the exception of afterLast() and beforeFirst(), these methods return a false boolean value if no record is available at that position in the set.

When you're done using a connection to a data source, you can close it by calling the connection's close() method with no arguments.

Listing 28.2 contains the Favorites application, which uses the JDBC-ODBC bridge and an SQL statement to retrieve some records from a database of favorite Web sites. Four fields are retrieved from each record indicated by the SQL statement: SITENAME, URL,

CATEGORY, and DATEADDED. The result set is sorted according to the SITENAME field, and these fields are displayed to standard output.

LISTING 28.2. THE FULL TEXT OF FAVORITES.JAVA.

```
 1: import java.sql.*;
 2:
 3: public class Favorites {
 4:     public static void main(String[] arguments) {
 5:         String data = "jdbc:odbc:FavoriteSites";
 6:         try {
 7:             Class.forName("sun.jdbc.odbc.JdbcOdbcDriver");
 8:             Connection conn = DriverManager.getConnection(
 9:                 data, "", "");
10:             Statement st = conn.createStatement();
11:             ResultSet rec = st.executeQuery(
12:                 "SELECT SITENAME, URL, CATEGORY, DATEADDED " +
13:                 "FROM favsites.dbf " +
14:                 "WHERE " +
15:                 "(CATEGORY='" + arguments[0] + "') " +
16:                 "ORDER BY SITENAME");
17:             while(rec.next()) {
18:                 System.out.println(rec.getString("SITENAME") + ", "
19:                         + rec.getString("URL") + ", "
20:                         + rec.getString("CATEGORY") + ", "
21:                         + rec.getString("DATEADDED") + ".");
22:             }
23:             st.close();
24:         } catch (Exception e) {
25:             System.out.println("Error — " + e.toString());
26:         }
27:     }
28: }
```

This program must be run with a single argument specifying the CATEGORY field in the database to pull records from. If the application was run with an argument of News, the output from the example database would be the following:

```
CNN                      , http://www.cnn.com              , News
          , 1998-10-18.
Christian Science Monitor, http://www.csmonitor.com        , News
          , 1998-10-18.
Drudge Retort            , http://www.drudge.com           , News
          , 1998-10-18.
Fort Worth Star-Telegram , http://www.startext.com         , News
          , 1998-10-18.
Java News                , http://www.intelligence.com/java , News
          , 1998-10-18.
```

28

MSNBC	, http://www.msnbc.com	, News
, 1998-10-18.		
Mercury Center	, http://www.sjmercury.com	, News
, 1998-10-18.		
Need to Know	, http://www.ntk.net	, News
, 1998-10-18.		
News.Com	, http://www.news.com	, News
, 1998-10-18.		
Request Line	, http://www.requestline.com/mbd	, News
, 1998-10-18.		
Salon	, http://www.salon1999.com	, News
, 1998-10-18.		
Slashdot	, http://www.slashdot.org	, News
, 1998-10-18.		
Stating the Obvious	, http://www.theobvious.com	, News
, 1998-10-18.		
The Obscure Store	, http://www.obscurestore.com	, News
, 1998-10-18.		
The Onion	, http://www.theonion.com	, News
, 1998-10-18.		
Variety	, http://www.variety.com	, News
, 1998-10-18.		
Wall Street Journal	, http://interactive.wsj.com	, News
, 1998-10-18.		
Wired News	, http://www.wired.com/news	, News
, 1998-10-18.		

JDBC Drivers

Creating a Java program that uses a JDBC driver is substantially similar to creating one that uses the JDBC-ODBC bridge.

The first step is to acquire and install a JDBC driver. Sun does not include one with Java 1.2, but more than a dozen companies now sell them or package them with commercial products, including Informix, Oracle, Symantec, IBM, and Sybase. A list of JDBC drivers that are currently available can be found on Sun's JDBC site at http://java.sun.com/products/jdbc/jdbc.drivers.html.

Some of these drivers are available to download for evaluation. You'll use one of them, Symantec's dbAnywhere Server, for today's next project. The dbAnywhere Server is currently available for trial download from http://www.symantec.com/dba/.

The steps for setting up a data source for JDBC are the same as with JDBC-ODBC:

- Create the database.
- Associate the database with a JDBC driver.
- Establish a data source, which may include selecting a database format, database server, username, and password.

Symantec dbAnywhere Server includes a Java application called Configure DataSources that serves the same function as the ODBC Data Source Administrator. Figure 28.4 shows the Configure DataSources program being used to set up a source for a Microsoft Access database that will be named `Presidents`.

FIGURE 28.4.

The dbAnywhere Configure DataSources utility.

Listing 28.3 is a Java application that uses a dbAnywhere JDBC driver to access a database file called `People.mdb`. This database is a Microsoft Access file with contact information for all living U.S. presidents.

LISTING 28.3. THE FULL TEXT OF PRESIDENTS.JAVA.

```
 1: import java.sql.*;
 2:
 3: public class Presidents {
 4:     public static void main(String[] arguments) {
 6:         String data = "jdbc:dbaw://localhost:8889/MS_Access/"
 7:             + "Presidents/Presidents";
 8:         try {
 9:             Class.forName("symantec.itools.db.jdbc.Driver");
10:             Connection conn = DriverManager.getConnection(
11:                 data, "", "");
12:             Statement st = conn.createStatement();
13:             ResultSet rec = st.executeQuery(
14:                 "SELECT NAME, ADDRESS1, ADDRESS2, PHONE, E-MAIL " +
15:                 "FROM People.mdb Contacts " +
16:                 "WHERE " +
17:                 "ORDER BY NAME");
18:             while(rec.next()) {
19:                 System.out.println(rec.getString("NAME") +  "\n"
20:                     + rec.getString("ADDRESS1") + "\n"
```

28

continues

LISTING 28.3. CONTINUED

```
21:                          + rec.getString("ADDRESS2") + "\n"
22:                          + rec.getString("PHONE") + "\n"
23:                          + rec.getString("E-MAIL") + "\n");
24:                }
25:            st.close();
26:        } catch (Exception e) {
27:            System.out.println("Error — " + e.toString());
28:        }
29:    }
30: }
```

Before this program will run successfully, the dbAnywhere Server must be started. The reference to `localhost:8889` in Line 6 refers to this server—`localhost` is a substitute for the name of your own machine, and `8889` is the default port number that dbAnywhere runs on.

The dbAnywhere Server can be used to connect remotely to servers on the Internet, so `localhost` could be replaced in an Internet address, such as `db.prefect.com:8889`, if a dbAnywhere Server was running at that location and port.

Lines 6–7 create the database address that will be used when creating a `Connection` object representing the connection to the `Presidents` data source. This address includes more information than the one used with the JDBC-ODBC bridge driver, as shown:

```
jdbc:dbaw://localhost:8889/MS_Access/Presidents/Presidents
```

Line 9 of the `Presidents` application loads the JDBC driver included with Symantec dbAnywhere Server:

```
symantec.itools.db.jdbc.Driver
```

Configuration information for the data source and driver will be provided by the company that developed the JDBC driver. The database address can vary widely from one JDBC driver implementation to another, although there should always be a reference to a server, a database format, and the name of the data source.

If the `People.mdb` database exists and the JDBC driver has been set up correctly, the output of the `Presidents` application should be similar to the following (depending on the records in the database):

```
Gerald Ford
Box 927
Rancho Mirage, CA 92270
(734) 741-2218
library@fordlib.nara.gov
```

```
Jimmy Carter
Carter Presidential Center
1 Copenhill, Atlanta, GA 30307
(404) 727-7611
carterweb@emory.edu

Ronald Reagan
11000 Wilshire Blvd.
Los Angeles, CA 90024
library@reagan.nara.gov

George Bush
Box 79798
Houston, TX 77279
(409) 260-9552


Bill Clinton
White House, 1600 Pennsylvania Ave.
Washington, DC 20500
(202) 456-1414
president@whitehouse.gov
```

Sun's Java site contains extensive information and specification about JDBC at `http://java.sun.com/products/JDK/1.2/docs/guide/jdbc/index.html`.

Summary

This brings us to the main event: the conclusion of your four-week trip through the Java language. Now that you've had a chance to work with the syntax and the core classes that make up Java, you're ready to tackle the really hard stuff: your own programs.

This book has an official Web site at `http://www.prefect.com/java21pre`. It features answers to frequently asked questions, all of the book's source code, and, in the unlikely event that an error or typo appears in this book, an errata page where corrections can be errored.

Congratulations! Now that you've been introduced to the most remarkable programming language of the last decade, it's your job to do more remarkable things with it.

As you put long hours into your own programs, learning new features and extending Java classes into your own packages, you'll learn another reason why the name of the language was an inspired one:

Java, like its caffeinated counterpart, can be habit-forming.

28

Note   "Don't let it end like this. Tell them I said something."
—The last words of Pancho Villa (1877-1923)

Q&A

Q **Can the JDBC-ODBC bridge driver be used in an applet?**

A The default security in place for applets does not allow the JDBC-ODBC bridge to be used because the ODBC side of the bridge driver employs native code rather than Java. Native code can't be held to the security restrictions in place for Java, so there's no way to ensure that this code is secure.

JDBC drivers that are implemented entirely in Java can be used in applets, and they have the advantage of requiring no configuration on the client computer.

Q **With the exception of `next()`, none of the other methods for moving through a result set are working in my application. What's the problem?**

A You might be using a version of Sun's JDBC-ODBC driver that doesn't support JDBC 2.0, the version of the connectivity standard that was incorporated into Java 2.

Prior to JDBC 2.0, the only navigational method supported by the JDBC-ODBC bridge driver was `next()`. The JDBC-ODBC driver that was shipped with beta versions of Java 2 did not yet support JDBC 2.0. Visit Sun's JDBC Web site at `http://java.sun.com/products/jdbc` to download an upgraded JDBC-ODBC driver if one has become available.

Appendixes

APPENDIX A

Java Resources on the Internet

This appendix lists books, Web sites, Internet discussion forums, and other resources you can use to expand your knowledge of Java.

This Book's Web Site

Rogers Cadenhead, this book's coauthor, maintains the official Web site for the book at the following address:

```
http://www.prefect.com/java21pre
```

Visit the site for the source code of all projects in the book, the current errata and clarifications list, updated links, and other information.

Other Books to Consider

Sams Publishing is the leader in Java programming books, and there are numerous books you should consider reading as you develop your skills. The following list includes ISBN numbers, which bookstores need if they don't currently carry the book you're looking for:

- *Developing Intranet Applications with Java* by Jerry Ablan, Rogers Cadenhead, et al. ISBN: 1-57521-166-1.
- *Java Unleashed* by Jamie Jaworski. ISBN: 1-57521-389-3.
- *Developing Professional Java Applets* by K.C. Hopson and Stephen E. Ingram. ISBN: 1-57521-083-5.
- *Tricks of the Java Programming Gurus* by Glenn Vanderburg, et al. ISBN: 1-57521-102-5.
- *Creating Web Applets with Java* by David Gulbransen and Ben Rawlings. ISBN: 1-57521-070-3.
- Sams' *Teach Yourself Internet Game Programming with Java in 21 Days* by Michael Morrison. ISBN: 1-57521-148-3.

Several of these books are available in their entirety on the Web at the Macmillan Computer Publishing site:

```
http://www.mcp.com
```

The site includes the Macmillan Online Bookstore and links to author Web sites.

Sun's Java Site

As you learned during Day 1, "A Fistful of Java," Sun maintains a comprehensive Web site at the following address:

```
http://java.sun.com
```

The Java division of Sun Microsystems produces new versions of the JDK, Java class library, and other products. This site is the first place to look for language-related information. New versions of the JDK and many other programming resources are available from this site.

At the time of this writing, the Java site is broken down into the following areas:

- **What's New?**   Announcements related to upcoming product releases and events, such as JavaOne, the semiyearly conference for Java programmers. This area also contains Sun press releases and schedules for training sessions offered by the company.

- **Read About Java**   Articles about the language, aimed at people who are discovering it for the first time. This is a good place to check out because it introduces topics with beginners in mind.

- **Products & APIs**   All products and documentation that can be downloaded from Sun, including the JDK, language documentation, and other files.

- **Applets**   A showcase for Java programs running on the Web, including more than two dozen offered by Sun that can be adapted for use on your own Web pages. There also are links to several Internet applet directories, including Developer.Com's Gamelan at `http://www.gamelan.com` and the Java Applet Rating Service (JARS) at `http://www.jars.com`.

- **For Developers**   Jumping-off point to the Java Developer Connection, a consolidated resource for official support from Sun and documentation for the Java language in HTML format. You can find information on language conferences, official Java books, and other resources.

- **Java in the Real World**   Features and timelines on Java "success stories" in settings as diverse as the U.S. Postal Service, UCLA Medical Center, Ergon Informatik, and the Mars Pathfinder mission.

- **Business & Licensing**   Provides licensing and trademark guidelines for using Java products.

- **Support & Services**   Listings for technical support, customer support, and sales services.

- **Marketing**   Details on the "100 Percent Pure Java" program, Java Solutions Guide, and other marketing and support efforts related to the language.

- **Employment**   Current job listings at Sun's Java division in Engineering, Technical Writing, Marketing/Sales, and other departments.

- **Java Store**   A catalog of official Java merchandise that can be ordered over the Web, including denim shirts, coffee mugs, T-shirts, and baseball caps.

This site is continually updated with free resources of use to Java programmers. One thing you might want to take advantage of immediately is the documentation page at the following address:

`http://java.sun.com/docs/index.html`

Other Java Web Sites

Because so much of the Java phenomenon has been inspired by its use on Web pages, a large number of Web sites focus on Java and Java programming.

The Java Books Page

As a way to sort through the hundreds of books that have been published about Java, several review sites have been compiled with listings of new, current, and out-of-print books.

JavaWorld, an online magazine that covers the language and related technology, maintains a list of current and upcoming Java books. You can find it at the following address:

```
http://www.javaworld.com/javaworld/books/jw-books-index.html
```

Another rundown of Java-related books is presented by Elliotte Rusty Harold, the author of several of the books described on the preceding Web page. Harold's list, with reviews of many of the books, is available at the following page:

```
http://sunsite.unc.edu/javafaq/books.html
```

Developer.Com's Gamelan Java Directory

Because Java is an object-oriented programming language, it is easy to use resources created by other programmers in your own programs. Before you start a Java project of any significance, you should scan the Web for resources that you might be able to use.

The place to start is Developer.Com's Gamelan, the Web site that catalogs Java programs, programming resources, and other information. Visit the following address:

```
http://www.gamelan.com
```

Gamelan is the most comprehensive directory of its kind on the Web, surpassing even Sun's own site in the depth of its coverage. It has become the first place that a Java programmer registers information about a program when it is completed. Staff members update this site on a daily basis. Gamelan also highlights the best submissions to its directory at the following page:

```
http://www.developer.com/directories/pages/cool.html
```

Java Applet Rating Service

To access another directory that rates Java applets, direct your Web browser to the following address:

```
http://www.jars.com
```

A

The logo of the Java Applet Rating Service (JARS) can be seen on numerous Java applets offered on Web pages. The JARS site has been expanded recently to include news about the language and related developments, reviews of Java development tools, and other useful information.

JavaWorld Magazine

One of the best magazines that has sprung up to serve the Java programming community is also the cheapest. *JavaWorld* is available for free on the Web at the following address:

```
http://www.javaworld.com
```

JavaWorld publishes frequent tutorial articles, along with Java development news and other features that are updated monthly. The Web-only format provides an advantage over some of its print competitors (such as *Java Report*) in the area of how-to articles. As an article discusses a particular concept or type of programming, *JavaWorld* can offer a Java applet that demonstrates the lesson.

Java Frequently Asked Questions

As a complement to the Java frequently asked questions (FAQ) lists that are available on Sun's Java Web site, Java programmers using Internet discussion groups have collaborated on their own list of questions and answers.

Elliotte Rusty Harold, one of the keepers of the Java books' Web pages, also offers the current Java FAQ list at the following address:

```
http://sunsite.unc.edu/javafaq/javafaq.html
```

Another similar resource, the Unofficial Obscure Java FAQ, was begun to answer some less frequently asked questions. It's at the following site:

```
http://k2.scl.cwru.edu/~gaunt/java/java-faq.html
```

Java Newsgroups

One of the best resources for both novice and experienced Java programmers is Usenet, the international network of discussion groups that is available to most Internet users. The following are descriptions of some of the Java discussion groups available on Usenet:

- `comp.lang.java.help` This group is good for all subjects that don't belong in one of the other groups, especially for people who have just begun to use the language.

- `comp.lang.java.advocacy`   This group is devoted to any Java discussions that are likely to inspire heated or comparative debate. If you want to argue the merits of Java against another language, this is the place for it. Consult this group if you want to see whether Java is the right choice for a project you're working on.

- `comp.lang.java.announce`   This group posts announcements, advertisements, and press releases of interest to the Java development community. It is moderated, so all postings must be submitted for approval before they are posted to the group.

- `comp.lang.java.api`   This group discusses the Java language's Application Programming Interface (API), the full library of class programs that comes with the JDK, as well as other implementations of the language.

- `comp.lang.java.programmer`   This group contains questions and answers related to Java programming, which makes it another good place for new programmers to frequent.

- `comp.lang.java.security`   This discussion group is devoted to security issues related to Java, especially running Java programs and other executable content on the Web.

- `comp.lang.java.setup`   This group provides a place to discuss installation problems related to Java programming tools and similar issues.

- `comp.lang.java.tech`   The most advanced of the Java discussion groups, this group is devoted to discussing the implementation of the language, issues with porting it to new machines, the specifics of the Java Virtual Machine, and similar subjects.

Job Opportunities

If you're learning Java as a means of finding a job, you should check out some of the Java-related job listings that are presented on the Web. Several of the resources listed in this appendix have a section devoted to job opportunities.

If you're interested in joining Sun's Java division itself, visit the following Web page:

`http://java.sun.com/jobs/index.html`

JavaWorld offers a Career Opportunities page that sometimes lists openings for Java developers:

`http://www.javaworld.com/javaworld/common/jw-jobop.html`

One thing you can do to make Java employers aware of your skills is register yourself as a resource for the Gamelan directory. Gamelan will add you to its site, and this listing could result in email about Java-related job assignments. To find out about registering yourself, head to the following address in the Add a Resource section of Gamelan:

```
http://www.gamelan.com/submit/submit_person.shtml
```

Although this Web page isn't specifically a Java employment resource, the Career Path Web site enables you to search the job classifieds of more than two dozen U.S. newspapers. You have to register to use the site, but it's free and there are more than 100,000 classifieds that you can search using keywords such as Java or Internet. Visit the following address:

```
http://www.careerpath.com
```

A

APPENDIX **B**

Configuring the Java Development Kit

The Java Development Kit (JDK) is a set of command-line utilities that are used to create, compile, and run Java programs. The JDK requires a command prompt because you run each of its programs by typing in its name along with any arguments that are needed.

Windows 95 and Windows NT Configuration

Windows 95 and Windows NT users can get to a command prompt by using the MS-DOS `Prompt` command, available as Start, Programs, MS-DOS Prompt from the taskbar.

When you use the MS-DOS `Prompt` command, a window opens in which you can type commands and use MS-DOS commands to navigate through the folders on your system. The starting folder will be the `\WINDOWS` folder on your primary hard drive (usually `C:\WINDOWS`).

Here's an example of a command you can enter once you have installed the JDK:

```
java -version
```

This command runs `java.exe`, the Java interpreter that is part of the JDK. The argument, `-version`, causes the interpreter to display its version number.

Try this command yourself. If you're using JDK 1.2—the version of the JDK that currently is used in Java 2— the following message should be displayed in response:

```
java version "1.2"
```

Later versions of JDK 1.2 will respond with a slightly different version number.

If you get an error such as the wrong version number or a `File not found` message, your system is having trouble finding the Java interpreter. You need to make some changes to your system's configuration to correct this.

The first thing to do when tackling a JDK configuration problem in Windows is find out where `java.exe` is located on your system. Use the `Find Files` command (Start, Find, Files or Folders from the taskbar) to search for `java.exe` on the hard drive where you installed the JDK.

If you don't find `java.exe`, you need to reinstall the JDK and make sure that the installation file is the right size before you run it again.

If you find `java.exe`, you may find more than one version of it. Look at the Find window's `In Folder` column to determine the names of the folders that contain versions of `java.exe`. One of these should include a reference to the folder where you installed JDK 1.2.

In Figure B.1, there are three versions of `java.exe` listed in the Find window. The one referring to the current JDK installation in this example is `C:\jdk1.2\bin`.

FIGURE B.1.

The result of a Find Files search for `java.exe`.

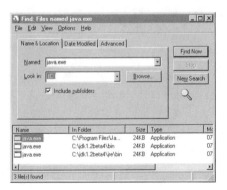

Make a note of this folder exactly as it is listed under the In folder. It's the JDK Path folder, and you'll be using it soon.

Checking the PATH Statement

To make sure that your system is looking in the right place for JDK 1.2 files, you need to look at the PATH setting for your system. PATH indicates where to find a program when you enter its name at an MS-DOS prompt (such as `java -version`).

To display the current setting for PATH, enter the following at a command prompt:

INPUT   `path`

You will see a listing of all folders where Windows looks for MS-DOS programs; they're separated by semicolons. Here's an example:

```
PATH=C:\WINDOWS;C:\WINDOWS\COMMAND;C:\JDK1.2\BIN
```

In this PATH listing, `C:\JDK1.2\BIN` refers to the JDK Path folder, which is where the system will look for the file `java.exe`. There are also two other folders listed in the PATH—`C:\WINDOWS` and `C:\WINDOWS\COMMAND`.

Your PATH setting should include a reference to the JDK Path folder. (Capitalization is not important in this instance—`C:\JDK1.2\BIN` would be the same as `C:\jdk1.2\bin`.)

If PATH doesn't include the JDK Path folder, you need to edit your PATH setting and add it.

Changing Your PATH Setting

The PATH setting must be changed by editing `autoexec.bat`, a text file in the root folder of your system's primary hard drive (usually the C drive).

On a Windows NT system, you don't have to load a text file to alter the PATH setting. Instead, you can change it from the Environment tab in the System Control Panel.

Note

To change any environmental variable in Windows NT (including the path), you must be logged in as Administrator or possess Administrator privileges.

To change PATH on a Windows 95 system, right-click `autoexec.bat` and select the Edit command to load it into Notepad.

The `autoexec.bat` file will contain a lot of technical-looking stuff that will be incomprehensible to the MS-DOS novice. Look for a line that begins with the text PATH=, SET PATH=, or PATH followed by a blank space.

Problem: No PATH Statement

If you don't find a PATH statement, you should add one to the `autoexec.bat` file. Scroll down to the bottom of the text file and add a blank line. On this line, enter **PATH=** followed by the JDK Path folder. The following line could be used if your JDK is located in the `C:\jdk1.2` folder on your system:

```
PATH=C:\jdk1.2\bin
```

After making this change, save the file. You must reboot your system before the change takes effect. If the `java.exe` file is in the folder you've indicated in the PATH statement, you should be able to run `java -version` successfully.

Problem: No JDK 1.2 Folder in the PATH Statement

If you find a PATH statement in the `autoexec.bat` file that doesn't contain any reference to the JDK Path folder, look for %JAVA_HOME% on that line followed by text such as \bin.

If you find %JAVA_HOME%, delete it and the text that follows it up to, but not including, the next semicolon. Replace this text with the JDK Path folder. Make sure not to delete any of the semicolons that are used to separate folder names.

If you do not find %JAVA_HOME% in the PATH statement, place your cursor at the end of that line and add a semicolon followed by the JDK Path folder. If your JDK Path folder is `C:\jdk1.2\bin`, the PATH statement should look like the following:

```
PATH=C:\WINDOWS;C:\WINDOWS\COMMAND;C:\jdk12\bin
```

No other version of the JDK should be referred to in the PATH statement. If you see a folder that refers to a previous version of the JDK on the PATH line, delete the reference to that folder. If this results in a PATH line that contains two semicolon characters in a row (;;), delete one of them.

Save the file after making these changes. You must reboot your system before the new PATH statement takes effect. If the `java.exe` file is in the folder you've indicated in the PATH statement, you should be able to run `java -version` successfully.

Fixing Class Not Found Errors

Java programs are compiled with the JDK by running the Java compiler `javac` with the name of the source file as an argument. For example, if you were in the same folder as the source file `HelloDan.java`, you could compile it with the following command:

```
javac HelloDan.java
```

Tip

> If you haven't yet tried to compile a Java program to test the JDK, you can use the HelloDan.java file from this book's Web site at http://www.prefect.com/java21pre.

If you get a Class not found error when using the Java compiler on a source file, the first thing to check is whether you have spelled and capitalized the name correctly. Make sure you're in the folder that contains the source file you're trying to compile, and double-check the filename.

Windows users can use the dir command at an MS-DOS prompt to list all of the files in a folder. Each file's full name is displayed in the rightmost column, as shown in Figure B.2. The abbreviated filenames down the left side of the listing should be ignored—they are used internally by Windows to manage the files.

FIGURE B.2.

A listing of files in an MS-DOS window.

```
MS-DOS Prompt

Microsoft(R) Windows 95
    (C)Copyright Microsoft Corp 1931-1996.

C:\WINDOWS>cd \j21work

C:\J21work>dir

 Volume in drive C has no label
 Volume Serial Number is D845-2F2F
 Directory of C:\J21work

.            <DIR>        01-24-98  2:39a .
..           <DIR>        01-24-98  2:39a ..
HELLOD~1 JAV          143 01-24-98  2:28a HelloDan.java
HELLOD~1 CLA          486 01-24-98  2:49a HelloDan.class
         2 file(s)              629 bytes
         2 dir(s)        61,931,520 bytes free

C:\J21work>_
```

If the name of the source file is correct and there are no errors in the Java source code itself, your system is having trouble finding tools.jar, a file that contains all of the Java class files needed to successfully compile and run Java 1.2 programs.

The JDK looks for tools.jar in two ways. First, it uses the CLASSPATH setting for the system (if one has been set up). Second, it looks for java.exe and uses that file's location to determine where tools.jar can be found.

Most Class not found errors can be fixed by using the CLASSPATH setting to indicate the location of tools.jar. One way to find tools.jar is to open the folder where you installed the JDK (such as \jdk1.2). There should be a subfolder called lib that contains tools.jar.

In Windows 95 or Windows NT, use the Find Files command (Start, Find, Files or Folders from the taskbar) to search for tools.jar on the same drive where you installed the JDK (as shown in Figure B.3).

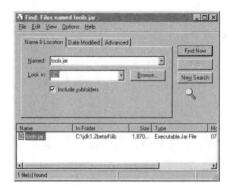

FIGURE B.3.

The result of a Find Files search for tools.jar.

Sometimes there will be more than one file named tools.jar on your system. Some of them might be from past versions of the JDK and other Java development tools, and others could be used by Web browsers that support Java.

Look in the In Folder column to see the full folder name (including hard-drive letter) of each folder that contains a file named tools.jar. Find the one that includes a reference to the folder where you installed JDK 1.2. (In Figure B.3, it's C:\jdk1.2beta4\lib.) Make a note of this folder, which, followed by \tools.jar, should be in your CLASSPATH setting.

Checking the CLASSPATH Statement

To make sure that your system is looking in the right place for the JDK 1.2 version of tools.jar, you need to look at your system's CLASSPATH setting.

Windows users can display the current setting for CLASSPATH by entering the following at an MS-DOS prompt:

INPUT   echo %CLASSPATH%

Make sure to include a percentage mark (%) before and after CLASSPATH. If your system has CLASSPATH set up, you'll see a listing of all folders and files in which JDK tools will look for Java classes. Each folder and filename is separated by a semicolon. Here's an example:

```
.;C:\jdk1.2\lib\tools.jar
```

In this CLASSPATH listing, C:\jdk1.2\lib\tools.jar is one place from which Java classes will be loaded. There's also a period (.) listed as the first item—this reference ensures that JDK utilities will also look in the current folder for any classes that cannot be found.

If CLASSPATH doesn't include the reference to the copy of JDK 1.2's tools.jar, you need add it.

Changing Your CLASSPATH Setting

The CLASSPATH setting must be changed by editing autoexec.bat, a text file in the root folder of your system's primary hard drive (usually the C drive).

On a Windows NT system, you don't have to load a text file to change the CLASSPATH setting. Instead, choose Control Panel, Settings from the taskbar.

To change CLASSPATH on a Windows 95 system, right-click autoexec.bat and select the Edit command to load it into Notepad.

The autoexec.bat file will contain a lot of technical-looking stuff that will be incomprehensible to the MS-DOS novice. Look for a line that begins with CLASSPATH=, SET CLASSPATH=, or CLASSPATH, followed by a blank space.

Problem: No CLASSPATH Statement

If you don't find a CLASSPATH statement, you should add one to the autoexec.bat file. Scroll down to the bottom of the text file and add a blank line. On this line, enter **CLASSPATH=** followed by the JDK Path folder, as in the following:

```
CLASSPATH=.;C:\jdk1.2\lib\tools.jar
```

Save the file after making this change. You must reboot your system before the change takes effect. If the tools.jar file is in the folder you've indicated in the CLASSPATH statement, you should be able to compile programs successfully.

Problem: No JDK 1.2 Folder in CLASSPATH Statement

If you find a CLASSPATH statement in the autoexec.bat file that doesn't contain any reference to the correct location of tools.jar, look for %JAVA_HOME% on that line.

You may find %JAVA_HOME% followed by \lib\tools.jar, as in
CLASSPATH=%JAVA_HOME%\lib\tools.jar or
CLASSPATH=%JAVA_HOME%\..\lib\tools.jar.

If you find %JAVA_HOME%, delete it and any text that follows it all the way to the next semicolon. Replace it with the correct location of tools.jar. Make sure not to delete any of the semicolons that are used to separate folder names.

If you do not find %JAVA_HOME% in the CLASSPATH statement, place your cursor at the end of the line containing the CLASSPATH statement and add a semicolon followed by the correct location of tools.jar. If that's C:\jdk1.2\lib\tools.jar, the CLASSPATH statement should look like the following line:

```
CLASSPATH=.;C:\DEV\CHATSERVER\;C:\jdk1.2\lib\tools.jar
```

B

No other version of the JDK should be referred to in the CLASSPATH statement. If you see a folder that refers to a previous version of the JDK on the CLASSPATH line, delete the reference to this folder. If this results in a CLASSPATH line that contains two semicolons in a row (; ;), delete one of them.

Save the file after making these changes. You must reboot your system before the new CLASSPATH statement takes effect. If the correct tools.jar file is in the folder you've indicated in the PATH statement, you should be able to compile and run example programs such as HelloDan successfully.

UNIX Configuration

To configure the JDK on a Solaris system, add the java/bin or jdk/bin directory to your execution path. You can usually do this by adding a line like the following to your .profile, .cshrc, or .login file:

```
set path= (~/java/bin/ $path)
```

This line assumes that you've installed the JDK into the directory java in your home directory. An installation elsewhere will require a change to the directory added to your execution path.

These changes will not take effect until you log out and back in again, or use the source command with the name of the file you changed. If you altered the .login file, the source command would be as follows:

```
source ~/.login
```

Fixing Class Not Found Errors on Other Platforms

To correct any Class not found errors on Solaris systems, the best thing to do is make sure that the CLASSPATH environment variable is not being set automatically at login.

To see if CLASSPATH is being set, enter the following at a command prompt:

INPUT   `echo $CLASSPATH`

If a CLASSPATH value has been set, you can unset it by entering the following command:

```
unsetenv CLASSPATH
```

To make this change permanent, you should remove the command that sets up CLASS-PATH from your .profile, .cshrc, or .login file.

These changes will not take effect until you log out and back in again, or use the source command with the name of the file you changed. If you altered the .login file, the source command would be as follows:

```
source ~/.login
```

APPENDIX C

Using a Text Editor with the JDK

Unlike Java development tools such as Visual Café and SunSoft Java WorkShop, the Java Development Kit (JDK) does not come with a text editor to use when you create source files.

In this appendix you'll learn how to select an editor for use with the JDK and how to configure your system to work with that editor.

Choosing a Text Editor

In order for an editor or word processor to work with the JDK, it must be able to save text files with no formatting.

This feature has different names in different editors. Look for a format option such as the following when you save a document or set the properties for a document:

- Plain text
- ASCII text

- DOS text
- Text-only

If you're using Windows 95, there are several editors included with the operating system. Windows Notepad, available at Programs, Accessories, Notepad from the Start button, is a no-frills text editor that only works with plain-text files. It can only handle one document at a time.

Windows WordPad (Programs, Accessories, WordPad from the Start button) is a step above Notepad. It can handle more than one document at a time and can handle both plain text and Microsoft Word formats. It also remembers the last several documents it has worked on and makes them available from the File pull-down menu.

DOS Edit, which can be run from an MS-DOS prompt with the command `edit`, is another simple editor that handles plain-text documents. It will seem crude to a Windows 95 user who isn't familiar with MS-DOS, but it and some other text editors do have one feature that Notepad and WordPad lack: They show you the number of the line you're currently editing. Numbering begins with `1` at the topmost line in the file and increases as you move downward. Figure C.1 shows Edit; the line number is indicated in the lower-right corner of the program window.

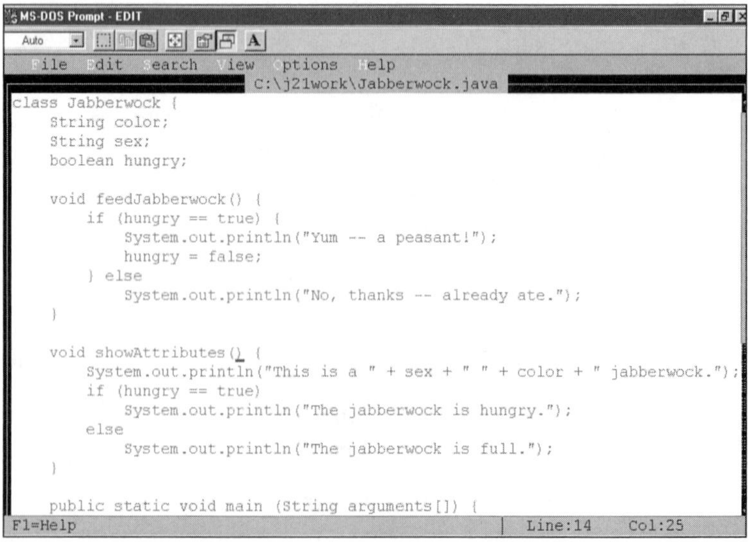
MS-DOS Prompt - EDIT
Auto
File Edit Search View Options Help
C:\j21work\Jabberwock.java
class Jabberwock {
String color;
String sex;
boolean hungry;
void feedJabberwock() {
if (hungry == true) {
System.out.println("Yum -- a peasant!");
hungry = false;
} else
System.out.println("No, thanks -- already ate.");
}
void showAttributes() {
System.out.println("This is a " + sex + " " + color + " jabberwock.");
if (hungry == true)
System.out.println("The jabberwock is hungry.");
else
System.out.println("The jabberwock is full.");
}
public static void main (String arguments[]) {
F1=Help
Line:14 Col:25

FIGURE C.1.

A Java source file loaded in DOS Edit.

Seeing the line number helps in Java programming because many Java compilers indicate the line number at which an error occurred. Take a look at the following error generated by the JDK compiler:

```
Palindrome.java:2: Class Font not found in type declaration.
```

The number 2 after the name of the Java source file indicates the line that triggered the compiler error. With a text editor that supports numbering, you can go directly to that line and start looking for the error.

Usually there are better ways to debug a program with a commercial Java programming package, but JDK users must search for compiler-generated errors using the line number indicated by the `javac` tool. Because of this, it's best to use a text editor that supports numbering.

Creating a File Association in Windows 95

After a text editor has been selected, Windows 95 users should associate that editor with the `.java` file extension. This makes it possible to open a `.java` source file by clicking its name in a folder. It also prevents editors, such as Windows Notepad, from incorrectly adding the `.txt` file extension to `.java` source files.

To create a file association, you first must have a file to work on. Open a folder in Windows 95 and create a new text document by selecting File, New, Text Document from the folder's menu bar (see Figure C.2).

FIGURE C.2.

Creating a new text document in a Windows 95 folder.

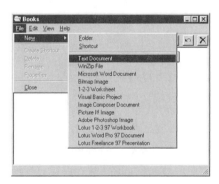

A new text document called `New Text Document.txt` is created, and you have a chance to immediately rename it. Change the name to `Anything.java` and confirm this new name when Windows 95 asks if you really want to change the file extension.

Double-click `Anything.java`. If your system does not associate the `.java` file extension with any program, you'll see an Open With window. You can use this to associate the

.java file extension with your chosen editor. Skip to "Creating a New Association" later in this appendix.

If anything else happens, you must delete the existing .java association before you can create a new one.

Deleting an Existing File Association

If your system already has something associated with the .java file extension, you can remove this association from any Windows 95 folder. Select View, Options from a folder's menu bar; an Options window with three tabbed dialog boxes opens. Select the File Types tab to see that dialog box (see Figure C.3).

FIGURE C.3.

The File Types tabbed dialog box.

The Registered File Types list box in this window shows all the file extensions that are associated with programs on your system. Highlight a file type in the list box to see two other fields that provide information about it:

- The Extension field displays all file extensions that work with this file type.
- The Opens With field displays the program that is used to open this file type.

The file type 1-2-3 Worksheets in Figure C.3 has four file extensions: WK4, WT4, WK1, and WK3. Any file with these extensions can be opened with the program 123W (which is the Lotus 1-2-3 spreadsheet application).

Scroll through the Registered File Types list until you find one that includes JAVA in its Extension field. The most likely place to find it is under a heading such as "Java files" or "Java programs," but that might not be the case on your system.

When you find the right file type, you need to delete the existing association so you can replace it with a new one. Select Remove to delete the existing association, and click Yes to confirm that you want to remove it. Once you do this, you can create a new association for the .java file extension.

Creating a New Association

An Open With window opens when you double-click a file that has no known association for its file extension. This is shown in Figure C.4.

FIGURE C.4.

Associating a file extension with a program.

Use the following steps to create a .java file association:

- In the Description of .java Files text box, enter **Java source file** or something similar.
- In the Choose the Program You Want to Use list box, find the text editor or word processor you want to use with Java source files. If you don't find it, click the Other button and find the program manually. If you're using DOS Edit, on most systems it can be found in the \Windows\Command folder with the filename edit or edit.exe.
- Make sure that the Always Use This Program to Open This File option is checked.

When you click OK to confirm these settings, your chosen editor opens the Anything.java file and any other files that have the .java file extension.

Associating an Icon with a File Type

After you have associated .java files with your chosen editor, an icon is assigned by default to all .java files on your system.

If you want to change this icon, select View, Options, File Types from a folder's menu bar to see the File Types dialog box. Scroll through the registered file types to find the one associated with the JAVA file extension.

When this file type is highlighted, select Edit to open an Edit File Type window, which is shown in Figure C.5.

FIGURE C.5.

The Edit File Type window.

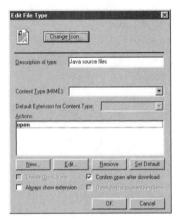

Select Change Icon from the Edit File Type window and choose a different icon to display for all .java files. If you like one of the icons displayed in the Current Icon window, highlight that icon and click OK to make the change. If you would like to look at other icons, select Browse to look inside files on your system to see the icons they contain. You can open any icon file, Windows 95 program, or .DLL file to see what icons it contains. They are displayed in the Current Icon window after you select a file.

Once you find an icon that you like, highlight it and click OK to select it.

APPENDIX D

by Jamie Jaworski

Java 2 API Description

This appendix describes the packages of the Java 2 API in terms of their interfaces, classes, exceptions, and errors. Also, hierarchical relationships between package elements are identified.

`java.applet`	`java.awt.image.renderable`
`java.awt`	`java.awt.print`
`java.awt.color`	`javax.swing`
`java.awt.datatransfer`	`javax.swing.border`
`java.awt.dnd`	`javax.swing.colorchooser`
`java.awt.event`	`javax.swing.event`
`java.awt.font`	`javax.swing.table`
`java.awt.geom`	`javax.swing.text`
`java.awt.im`	`javax.swing.text.html`
`java.awt.image`	`javax.swing.text.rtf`

javax.swing.tree	java.util.zip
javax.swing.undo	javax.accessibility
java.beans	javax.swing
java.beans.beancontext	javax.swing.border
java.io	javax.swing.colorchooser
java.lang	javax.swing.event
java.lang.ref	javax.swing.filechooser
java.lang.reflect	javax.swing.plaf
java.math	javax.swing.plaf.basic
java.net	javax.swing.plaf.metal
java.rmi	javax.swing.plaf.multi
java.rmi.activation	javax.swing.table
java.rmi.dgc	javax.swing.text
java.rmi.registry	javax.swing.text.html
java.rmi.server	javax.swing.tree
java.security	javax.swing.undo
java.security.acl	org.omg.CORBA
java.security.cert	org.omg.CORBA.DynAnyPackage
java.security.interfaces	org.omg.CORBA.ORBPackage
java.security.spec	org.omg.CORBA.portable
java.sql	org.omg.CORBA.TypeCodePackage
java.text	org.omg.CosNaming
java.util	org.omg.CosNaming. NamingContextPackage
java.util.jar	

Package `java.applet`

The `java.applet` package is one of the smallest packages in the Core API. It consists of one class and three interfaces that provide the basic functionality needed to implement applets.

Interfaces

AppletContext

The `AppletContext` interface defines methods that allow an applet to access the context in which it is being run.

AppletStub

The `AppletStub` interface supports communication between an applet and its browser environment, and is used to develop custom applet viewers.

AudioClip

The `AudioClip` interface provides methods that support the playing of audio clips.

Classes

Applet

The `Applet` class is the superclass of all applets. It provides methods for displaying images, playing audio files, responding to events, and obtaining information about an applet's execution environment. The `Applet` class is a subclass of `java.awt.panel`.

Exceptions and Errors

None.

Package `java.awt`

The `java.awt` package implements the core classes and interfaces of the Abstract Windowing Toolkit (AWT). It is a large package, containing 64 classes and 14 interfaces. These classes and interfaces provide the standard AWT GUI controls, as well as drawing, printing, and other capabilities.

Interfaces

ActiveEvent

The `ActiveEvent` interface defines methods that are implemented by self-dispatching event classes.

Adjustable

The Adjustable interface is implemented by classes such as sliders and scrollbars, which allow a value to be selected from a range of values.

Composite

The Composite interface defines methods that are implemented by classes that allow drawing to be composed with an underlying graphics area.

CompositeContext

The CompositeContext interface defines methods for classes that provide a context for compositing drawing operations.

ItemSelectable

The ItemSelectable interface is implemented by classes whose objects, such as choices or lists, may contain selectable items.

LayoutManager

The LayoutManager interface is implemented by classes that can lay out Container objects.

LayoutManager2

The LayoutManager2 interface extends the LayoutManager interface to provide support for layout constraints.

MenuContainer

The MenuContainer interface defines methods for classes that may contain Menu objects.

Paint

The Paint interface extends the Transparency interface, providing support for defining color patterns for use in graphics operations.

PaintContext

The PaintContext interface provides methods that define the context for paint operations.

PrintGraphics

The PrintGraphics interface defines a graphics context for printing a single page.

Shape

The Shape interface defines methods that are implemented by classes that encapsulate geometric shapes.

Stroke

The Stroke interface provides methods that are implemented by classes that define pen strokes.

Transparency

The Transparency interface defines methods for classes that support transparency-related graphics operations.

Classes

AlphaComposite

The AlphaComposite class is a subclass of Object that implements alpha compositing rules for combining source and destination image pixels. It implements the Composite interface.

AWTEvent

The AWTEvent class is a subclass of java.util.EventObject that serves as the base class for all AWT-related events.

AWTEventMulticaster

The AWTEventMulticaster class is a subclass of Object that provides thread-safe, multi-cast event-dispatching capabilities. It implements the following interfaces of the java.awt.event package: ActionListener, AdjustmentListener, ComponentListener, ContainerListener, FocusListener, InputMethodListener, ItemListener, KeyListener, MouseListener, MouseMotionListener, TextListener, and WindowListener.

AWTPermission

The AWTPermission class is a subclass of java.security.BasicPermission that implements security permissions for a variety of AWT-related operations.

BasicStroke

The BasicStroke class is a subclass of Object that provides a set of properties for a basic implementation of the Stroke interface.

BorderLayout

The BorderLayout class is a subclass of Object that is used to lay out the components of a container along the container's border. It implements the LayoutManager2 and java.lang.Serializable interfaces.

Button

The Button class is a subclass of Component that encapsulates a GUI text-labeled push-button.

Canvas

The Canvas class is a subclass of Component that provides a rectangular drawing area.

CardLayout

The CardLayout class is a subclass of Object that provides the capability to lay out a Container object in a card-like fashion. It implements the LayoutManager2 and java.io.Serializable interfaces.

Checkbox

The Checkbox class is a subclass of Container that provides the capability to display and work with check box and radio button GUI controls. It implements the ItemSelectable interface.

CheckboxGroup

The CheckboxGroup class is a subclass of Object that is used to group Checkbox objects together as a set of radio buttons. It implements the java.io.Serializable interface.

CheckboxMenuItem

The CheckboxMenuItem class is a subclass of MenuItem that is used to create a menu item that may be in an on or off state. It implements the ItemSelectable interface.

Choice

The Choice class is a subclass of Component that provides a pop-up menu of choices. It implements the ItemSelectable interface.

Color

The Color class is a subclass of Object that is used to define colors within a particular color space. It implements the Paint and java.io.Serializable interfaces.

Component

The Component class is a subclass of Object that provides the base class for the development of GUI components. It implements the MenuContainer, java.awt.imaga.ImageObserver, and java.io.Serializable interfaces.

ComponentOrientation

The ComponentOrientation class is a subclass of Object that implements the Serializable interface. It is used to specify the language-specific orientation of text.

Container

The Container class is a subclass of Component that acts as a container for other GUI components.

Cursor

The Cursor class is a subclass of Object that encapsulates a changeable cursor associated with a pointing device. It implements the java.io.Serializable interface.

Dialog

The Dialog class is a subclass of Window that provides a base class for the development of dialog boxes.

Dimension

The Dimension class is a subclass of java.awt.geom.Dimension2D that provides the capability to specify the height and width of an object. It implements the java.io.Serializable interface.

Event

The Event class is a subclass of Object that provides the base class for implementing events in the JDK 1.0 event model. It implements the java.io.Serializable interface.

EventQueue

The EventQueue class is a subclass of Object that implements the system event queue.

FileDialog

The FileDialog class is a subclass of Dialog that encapsulates a file system dialog box.

FlowLayout

The FlowLayout class is a subclass of Object that is used to lay out Container objects in a left-to-right and top-to-bottom fashion. It implements the LayoutManager and java.io.Serializable interfaces.

Font

The Font class is a subclass of Object that encapsulates text fonts. It implements the java.io.Serializable interface.

FontMetrics

The FontMetrics class is a subclass of Object that provides information about the properties of a font. It implements the java.io.Serializable interface.

D

Frame

The Frame class is a subclass of Window that provides a top-level application window. It implements the MenuContainer interface.

GradientPaint

The GradientPaint class is a subclass of Object that provides the capability to fill a drawing area with a linear gradient color fill. It implements the Paint interface.

Graphics

The Graphics class is a subclass of Object that is the base class for the development of graphics drawing contexts.

Graphics2D

The Graphics2D class is a subclass of Graphics that serves as the basic graphics context for the Java 2D API.

GraphicsConfigTemplate

The GraphicsConfigTemplate class is a subclass of Object that is used as a template for the creation of GraphicsConfiguration objects. It implements the java.io.Serializable interface.

GraphicsConfiguration

The GraphicsConfiguration class is a subclass of Object that specifies the physical characteristics of a graphics display device.

GraphicsDevice

The GraphicsDevice class is a subclass of Object that describes the graphics display devices available to the system.

GraphicsEnvironment

The GraphicsEnvironment class is a subclass of Object that describes the entire graphics environment available to the system, including all of the accessible GraphicsDevice objects.

GridBagConstraints

The GridBagConstraints class is a subclass of Object that is used to specify how containers are to be laid out using GridBagLayout objects. It implements the java.lang.Cloneable and java.io.Serializable interfaces.

GridBagLayout

The GridBagLayout class is a subclass of Object that is used to lay out a container according to the properties of a GridBagConstraints object. It implements the LayoutManager2 and java.io.Serializable interfaces.

GridLayout

The GridLayout class is a subclass of Object that is used to lay out a container in a grid-like fashion. It implements the LayoutManager and java.io.Serializable interfaces.

Image

The Image class is a subclass of Object that encapsulates a displayable image.

Insets

The Insets class is a subclass of Object that specifies the border of a GUI component. It implements the java.lang.Cloneable and java.io.Serializable interfaces.

Label

The Label class is a subclass of Component that implements a GUI text label.

List

The List class is a subclass of Component that encapsulates a scrollable list GUI control. It implements the ItemSelectable interface.

D

MediaTracker

The MediaTracker class is a subclass of Object that is used to track the loading status of multimedia objects. It implements the java.io.Serializable interface.

Menu

The Menu class is a subclass of MenuItem that encapsulates a pull-down menu. It implements the MenuContainer interface.

MenuBar

The MenuBar class is a subclass of MenuComponent that provides the capability to attach a menu bar to a Frame object. It implements the MenuContainer interface.

MenuComponent

The MenuComponent class is a subclass of Object that is the base class for all other AWT menu-related classes. It implements the java.io.Serializable interface.

MenuItem

The MenuItem class is a subclass of MenuComponent that implements a menu item value that is selectable from a Menu object.

MenuShortcut

The MenuShortcut class is a subclass of Object that provides the capability to associate a keyboard accelerator with a MenuItem object. It implements the java.io.Serializable interface.

Panel

The Panel class is a subclass of Container that provides a rectangular container for other GUI components.

Point

The Point class is a subclass of java.awt.geom.Point2D that encapsulates a point in the xy-plane. It implements the java.io.Serializable interface.

Polygon

The Polygon class is a subclass of Object that is used to describe a mathematical polygon. It implements the Shape and java.io.Serializable interfaces.

PopupMenu

The PopupMenu class is a subclass of Menu that provides a menu that can be popped up at a specific location within a component.

PrintJob

The PrintJob class is a subclass of Object that is used to implement a system-specific printing request.

Rectangle

The Rectangle class is a subclass of java.awt.geom.Rectangle2D that encapsulates a mathematical rectangle. It implements the Shape and java.io.Serializable interfaces.

RenderingHints

The RenderingHints class is a subclass of Object that implements the Map and Cloneable interfaces. It is used to provide information for rendering objects for display.

RenderingHints.Key

The RenderingHints.Key class is an inner class of RenderingHints that provides a base class for specifying keys used in the rendering process.

Scrollbar

The Scrollbar class is a subclass of Component that provides a GUI scrollbar component. It implements the Adjustable interface.

ScrollPane

The ScrollPane class is a subclass of Container that provides a combination of a panel and vertical and horizontal scrollbars.

SystemColor

The SystemColor class is a subclass of Color that is used to specify the color scheme used with GUI components. It implements the java.io.Serializable interface.

TextArea

The TextArea class is a subclass of TextComponent that provides a GUI text area control.

TextComponent

The TextComponent class is a subclass of Component that is the base class for TextField and TextArea.

TextField

The TextField class is a subclass of TextComponent that implements a GUI text input field.

TexturePaint

The TexturePaint class is a subclass of Object that provides the capability to fill a geometrical shape with a texture image. It implements the Paint interface.

Toolkit

The Toolkit class is a subclass of Object that provides access to implementation-specific AWT resources.

Window

The Window class is a subclass of Container that provides a basic window object.

Exceptions and Errors

AWTError

The AWTError class is a subclass of java.lang.Error that is thrown when a fundamental error occurs in the AWT operation.

AWTException

The AWTException class is a subclass of java.lang.Exception that signals the occurrence of an AWT-specific exception.

IllegalComponentStateException

The IllegalComponentStateException class is a subclass of java.lang.IllegalStateException that identifies that an AWT component is in the wrong state for a particular operation.

Package java.awt.color

The java.awt.color package is part of the Java 2D API. It provides five classes that support the capability to work with different color models.

Interfaces

None.

Classes

ColorSpace

The ColorSpace class is an abstract subclass of Object that specifies the color space used with other objects. It provides constants that define popular color spaces and methods for converting colors between color spaces.

ICC_ColorSpace

The ICC_ColorSpace class is a subclass of ColorSpace that provides a non-abstract implementation of the ColorSpace methods. It represents color spaces in accordance with the ICC Profile Format Specification, Version 3.4, August 15, 1997, from the International Color Consortium. For more information, refer to http://www.color.org.

ICC_Profile

The ICC_Profile class is a subclass of Object that provides a representation of color profile data for color spaces based on the ICC Profile Format Specification. Color profiles represent transformations from the color space of a device, such as a monitor, to a profile connection space, as defined by the ICC Profile Format Specification.

ICC_ProfileGray

The ICC_ProfileGray class is a subclass of ICC_Profile that supports color conversion to monochrome color spaces.

ICC_ProfileRGB

The ICC_ProfileRGB class is a subclass of ICC_Profile that supports color conversion between RGB and CIEXYZ color spaces.

Exceptions and Errors

CMMException

The CMMException class is a subclass of java.lang.RuntimeException that defines an exception that is thrown when the color model manager returns an error.

ProfileDataException

The ProfileDataException class is a subclass of java.lang.RuntimeException that defines an exception that is thrown when an error occurs in accessing or processing an ICC_Profile object.

Package java.awt.datatransfer

The java.awt.datatransfer package provides four classes and three interfaces that support clipboard operations.

Interfaces

ClipboardOwner

The ClipboardOwner interface defines the lostOwnership() method, which is invoked to notify an object that it has lost ownership of a clipboard. This interface is implemented by classes that copy data to a clipboard.

FlavorMap

The FlavorMap interface maps MIME types to Java data flavors.

Transferable

The Transferable interface defines methods that support the transfer of data via the clipboard or other mechanisms. It is implemented by classes that support clipboard-related data transfers.

Classes

Clipboard

The Clipboard class is a subclass of Object that provides access to system- and user-defined clipboards. It provides methods for getting and setting the contents of a clipboard and retrieving the name of a clipboard.

D

DataFlavor

The DataFlavor class is a subclass of Object that defines the types of data available for a transfer operation (such as those that take place via a clipboard). Flavors are implemented as MIME types. The DataFlavor class provides methods for reading and writing objects to be transferred and for accessing MIME type information. It implements the java.io.Serializable and java.lang.Cloneable interfaces.

StringSelection

The StringSelection class is a subclass of Object that supports the transfer of String objects as plain text. It provides methods for working with string-related data flavors, and it implements the Transferable and ClipboardOwner interfaces.

SystemFlavorMap

The SystemFlavorMap class extends the Object class and provides a default implementation of the FlavorMap interface.

Exceptions and Errors

UnsupportedFlavorException

The UnsupportedFlavorException class is a subclass of java.lang.Exception that is used to signal that transferable data is not supported in a particular flavor.

Package java.awt.dnd

The java.awt.dnd package supports the new Java 2 drag-and-drop capability. It contains 12 classes and four interfaces.

Interfaces

Autoscroll

The Autoscroll interface provides methods that support automatic scrolling through GUI components in support of drag-and-drop operations.

DragGestureListener

The DragGestureListener interface extends the EventListener interface to allow for the handling of the DragGestureEvent event.

DragSourceListener

The DragSourceListener interface extends the java.util.EventListener interface to define methods that are implemented by objects that originate drag-and-drop operations.

These methods track the state of drag-and-drop operations and enable feedback to be provided to the user.

DropTargetListener

The DropTargetListener interface extends the java.util.EventListener interface to define methods that are implemented by objects that are the target of drag-and-drop operations.

Classes

DnDConstants

The DnDConstants class is a subclass of Object that defines constants that are used in drag-and-drop operations.

DragGestureEvent

The DragGestureEvent class extends the EventObject class to define an event signaling that a user has initiated a drag-and-drop operation.

DragGestureRecognizer

The DragGestureRecognizer class extends Object to provide an abstract class for the development of platform-dependent event listeners for drag-and-drop operations.

DragSource

The DragSource class is a subclass of Object that implements the source originator of a drag-and-drop operation. It defines several java.awt.Cursor objects that define the cursor state during drag-and-drop. Its startDrag() method is used to initiate drag-and-drop.

DragSourceContext

The DragSourceContext class is a subclass of Object that is used to manage the source side of drag-and-drop operations. It manages events associated with the drag source and implements the DragSourceListener interface.

DragSourceDragEvent

The DragSourceDragEvent class is a subclass of DragSourceEvent. It implements the event that is handled by a DragSourceListener during the dragging stage of a drag-and-drop operation.

DragSourceDropEvent

The DragSourceDropEvent class is a subclass of DragSourceEvent. It implements the event that is handled by a DragSourceListener during the dropping stage of a drag-and-drop operation.

DragSourceEvent

The DragSourceEvent class is a subclass of java.util.EventObject that is used as the base class for DragSourceDragEvent and DragSourceDropEvent.

DropTarget

The DropTarget class is a subclass of Object that is used to implement the target of a drag-and-drop operation. Objects of DropTarget are associated with components that function as drop targets. These objects are typically GUI components. DropTarget implements the DropTargetListener and java.io.Serializable interfaces.

DropTarget.DropTargetAutoScroller

The DropTarget.DropTargetAutoScroller class is an inner class of DropTarget that supports scrolling operations.

DropTargetContext

The DropTargetContext class is a subclass of Object that is used to implement the context of a drop operation. Objects of this class are dynamically created when an object is dragged over a potential drop target. This class is used by the drop target to provide feedback to the user and to initiate the data transfer associated with the drag-and-drop operation.

DropTargetDragEvent

The DropTargetDragEvent class is a subclass of DropTargetEvent that informs DropTargetListener objects of the dragging state of a drag-and-drop operation.

DropTargetDropEvent

The DropTargetDropEvent class is a subclass of DropTargetEvent that informs DropTargetListener objects of the dropping state of a drag-and-drop operation.

DropTargetEvent

The DropTargetEvent class is a subclass of java.util.EventObject that serves as the base class for DropTargetDragEvent and DropTargetDropEvent.

MouseDragGestureRecognizer

The MouseDragGestureRecognizer class extends DragGestureRecognizer and implements the MouseListener and MouseMotionListener interfaces. This class provides support for mouse-based drag-and-drop listeners.

Exceptions and Errors

InvalidDnDOperationException

The InvalidDnDOperationException class is a subclass of java.lang.IllegalStateException that signals that a drag-and-drop operation cannot be carried out.

Package java.awt.event

The java.awt.event package provides the foundation for JDK 1.1-style event processing. It contains 21 classes and 13 interfaces.

Interfaces

ActionListener

The ActionListener interface extends the java.util.EventListener interface and defines methods that are implemented by classes that handle ActionEvent events.

AdjustmentListener

The AdjustmentListener interface extends the java.util.EventListener interface and defines methods that are implemented by classes that handle AdjustmentEvent events.

AWTEventListener

The AWTEventListener interface extends the java.util.EventListener interface and defines methods that are implemented by classes that handle the AWTEvent.

ComponentListener

The ComponentListener interface extends the java.util.EventListener interface and defines methods that are implemented by classes that handle ComponentEvent events.

ContainerListener

The ContainerListener interface extends the java.util.EventListener interface and defines methods that are implemented by classes that handle ContainerEvent events.

FocusListener

The FocusListener interface extends the java.util.EventListener interface and defines methods that are implemented by classes that handle FocusEvent events.

D

InputMethodListener

The InputMethodListener interface extends the java.util.EventListener interface and defines methods that are implemented by classes that handle InputMethodEvent events.

ItemListener

The ItemListener interface extends the java.util.EventListener interface and defines methods that are implemented by classes that handle Item events.

KeyListener

The KeyListener interface extends the java.util.EventListener interface and defines methods that are implemented by classes that handle KeyEvent events.

MouseListener

The MouseListener interface extends the java.util.EventListener interface and defines methods that are implemented by classes that handle MouseEvent events.

MouseMotionListener

The MouseMotionListener interface extends the java.util.EventListener interface and defines methods that are implemented by classes that handle MouseEvent events.

TextListener

The TextListener interface extends the java.util.EventListener interface and defines methods that are implemented by classes that handle TextEvent events.

WindowListener

The WindowListener interface extends the java.util.EventListener interface and defines methods that are implemented by classes that handle WindowEvent events.

Classes

ActionEvent

The ActionEvent class is a subclass of java.awt.AWTEvent that implements an event generated by user interface actions, such as clicking on a button or selecting a menu item.

AdjustmentEvent

The AdjustmentEvent class is a subclass of java.awt.AWTEvent that implements an event generated by scrolling actions.

ComponentAdapter

The `ComponentAdapter` class is a subclass of `Object` that provides a basic implementation of the `ComponentListener` interface.

ComponentEvent

The `ComponentEvent` class is a subclass of `java.awt.AWTEvent` that implements an event generated either by changes to the position, focus, or sizing of a window component, or by a keyboard input or other mouse action.

ContainerAdapter

The `ContainerAdapter` class is a subclass of `Object` that provides a basic implementation of the `ContainerListener` interface.

ContainerEvent

The `ContainerEvent` class is a subclass of `java.awt.ComponentEvent` that implements an event generated by adding and removing components from a container.

FocusAdapter

The `FocusAdapter` class is a subclass of `Object` that provides a basic implementation of the `FocusListener` interface.

FocusEvent

The `FocusEvent` class is a subclass of `ComponentEvent` that implements an event generated by a change in the status of a component's input focus.

InputEvent

The `InputEvent` class is a subclass of `ComponentEvent` that is the base class for defining events generated by user keyboard and mouse actions.

InputMethodEvent

The `InputMethodEvent` class is a subclass of `java.awt.AWTEvent` that implements an event generated by changes to the text being entered via an input method.

InvocationEvent

The `InvocationEvent` class extends the `java.awt.AWTEvent` class and implements the `java.awt.ActiveEvent` interface. It signals the invocation of a `Runnable` object.

ItemEvent

The `ItemEvent` class is a subclass of `AWTEvent` that implements an event generated by a component state change, such as selecting an item from a list.

KeyAdapter

The KeyAdapter class is a subclass of Object that provides a basic implementation of the KeyListener interface.

KeyEvent

The KeyEvent class is a subclass of InputEvent that implements an event generated by user keyboard actions.

MouseAdapter

The MouseAdapter class is a subclass of Object that provides a basic implementation of the MouseListener interface.

MouseEvent

The MouseEvent class is a subclass of InputEvent that implements an event generated by low-level mouse actions.

MouseMotionAdapter

The MouseMotionAdapter class is a subclass of Object that provides a basic implementation of the MouseMotionListener interface.

PaintEvent

The PaintEvent class is a subclass of ComponentEvent that implements an event generated by the painting/repainting of a window.

TextEvent

The TextEvent class is a subclass of java.awt.AWTEvent that implements an event generated by text-related events, such as changing the value of a text field.

WindowAdapter

The WindowAdapter class is a subclass of Object that provides a basic implementation of the WindowListener interface.

WindowEvent

The WindowEvent class is a subclass of ComponentEvent that implements an event generated by events such as the opening, closing, and minimizing of a window.

Exceptions and Errors

None.

Package `java.awt.font`

The `java.awt.font` package is new to Java 2. It provides 13 classes and two interfaces that support advanced font capabilities.

Interfaces

MultipleMaster

The `MultipleMaster` interface defines methods that are implemented by classes that support Type 1 Multiple Master fonts.

OpenType

The `OpenType` interface defines methods that are implemented by classes that support Open Type and True Type fonts.

Classes

FontRendererContext

The `FontRendererContext` class extends the `Object` class to provide a container for the information needed to correctly measure text.

GlyphJustificationInfo

The `GlyphJustificationInfo` class is a subclass of `Object` that provides information about the justification of a glyph.

GlyphMetrics

The `GlyphMetrics` class is a subclass of `Object` that defines the properties of a single glyph.

GlyphVector

The `GlyphVector` class is a subclass of `Object` that represents text as a sequence of integer glyph codes. It implements the `java.lang.Cloneable` interface.

GraphicAttribute

The `GraphicAttribute` class is a subclass of `Object` that is used to identify a graphic that is embedded in text.

ImageGraphicAttribute

The `ImageGraphicAttribute` class is a subclass of `GraphicAttribute` that is used to identify an image that is embedded in text.

LineBreakMeasurer

The LineBreakMeasurer class is a subclass of Object that organizes lines of text according to a wrapping width.

LineMetrics

The LineMetrics class extends the Object class to provide access to line-oriented text metrics.

ShapeGraphicAttribute

The ShapeGraphicAttribute class is a subclass of GraphicAttribute that is used to identify a Shape object that is embedded in text.

TextAttribute

The TextAttribute class is a subclass of java.text.AttributedCharacterIterator.Attribute that maintains a set of attributes for rendering text.

TextHitInfo

The TextHitInfo class is a subclass of Object that is used to specify a position within text.

TextLayout

The TextLayout class is a subclass of Object that provides support for laying out styled text. It implements the java.lang.Cloneable interface.

TextLayout.CaretPolicy

The TextLayout.CaretPolicy class is an inner class of TextLayout that specifies how the caret should be used with a TextLayout object. It is a subclass of Object.

TextLine.TextLineMetrics

The TextLine.TextLineMetrics class extends Object to provide basic metrics for working with text.

TransformAttribute

The TransformAttribute class extends Object and implements the Serializable interface. It allows transforms to be used as attributes.

Exceptions and Errors

None.

Package `java.awt.geom`

The `java.awt.geom` package is a new Java 2 package that is part of the Java 2D API. It provides 30 classes and one interface that support standard geometrical objects and transformations.

Interfaces

PathIterator

The `PathIterator` interface provides constants and methods for iterating over the points in a path.

Classes

AffineTransform

The `AffineTransform` class is a subclass of `Object` that provides the capability to compute two-dimensional affine transformations. It implements the `java.lang.Cloneable` interface.

Arc2D

The `Arc2D` class is a subclass of `RectangularShape` that defines an arc within a bounding rectangle.

Arc2D.Double

The `Arc2D.Double` class is an inner class of `Arc2D` that specifies the arc in `double` precision.

Arc2D.Float

The `Arc2D.Float` class is an inner class of `Arc2D` that specifies the arc in `float` precision.

Area

The `Area` class is a subclass of `Object` that encapsulates an arbitrary 2D area. It implements the `java.awt.Shape` and `java.lang.Cloneable` interfaces.

CubicCurve2D

The `CubicCurve2D` class is a subclass of `Object` that encapsulates a cubic curve.

CubicCurve2D.Double

The `CubicCurve2D.Double` class is an inner class of `CubicCurve2D` that specifies the curve in `double` precision.

D

CubicCurve2D.Float

The CubicCurve2D.Float class is an inner class of CubicCurve2D that specifies the curve in float precision.

Dimension2D

The Dimension2D class is a subclass of Object that encapsulates width and height dimensions. It implements the java.lang.Cloneable interface.

Ellipse2D

The Ellipse2D class is a subclass of RectangularShape that represents an ellipse.

Ellipse2D.Double

The Ellipse2D.Double class is an inner class of Ellipse2D that specifies the ellipse in double precision.

Ellipse2D.Float

The Ellipse2D.Float class is an inner class of Ellipse2D that specifies the ellipse in float precision.

FlatteningPathIterator

The FlatteningPathIterator class is a subclass of Object that is used to flatten a path. It implements the PathIterator interface.

GeneralPath

The GeneralPath class is a subclass of Object that represents a general 2D path. It implements the java.awt.Shape and java.lang.Cloneable interfaces.

Line2D

The Line2D class is a subclass of Object that encapsulates a 2D line. It implements the java.awt.Shape and java.lang.Cloneable interfaces.

Line2D.Double

The Line2D.Double class is an inner class of Line2D that specifies the line in double precision.

Line2D.Float

The Line2D.Float class is an inner class of Line2D that specifies the line in float precision.

Point2D

The Point2D class is a subclass of Object that represents a 2D point. It implements the java.lang.Cloneable interface.

Point2D.Double

The Point2D.Double class is an inner class of Point2D that specifies the point in double precision.

Point2D.Float

The Point2D.Float class is an inner class of Point2D that specifies the point in float precision.

QuadCurve2D

The QuadCurve2D class is a subclass of Object that encapsulates a 2D quadratic curve. It implements the java.awt.Shape and java.lang.Cloneable interfaces.

QuadCurve2D.Double

The QuadCurve2D.Double class is an inner class of QuadCurve2D that specifies the curve using a double value.

QuadCurve2D.Float

The QuadCurve2D.Float class is an inner class of QuadCurve2D that specifies the curve using a float value.

Rectangle2D

The Rectangle2D class is a subclass of RectangularShape that encapsulates a 2D rectangle.

Rectangle2D.Double

The Rectangle2D.Double class is an inner class of Rectangle2D that specifies the rectangle using double values.

Rectangle2D.Float

The Rectangle2D.Float class is an inner class of Rectangle2D that specifies the rectangle using float values.

RectangularShape

The RectangularShape class is a subclass of Object that is the base class for other rectangular shapes. It implements the java.awt.Shape and java.lang.Cloneable interfaces.

RoundRectangle2D

The `RoundRectangle2D` class is a subclass of `RectangularShape` that defines a rectangle with rounded corners.

RoundRectangle2D.Double

The `RoundRectangle2D.Double` class is an inner class of `RoundRectangle2D` that specifies the rectangle using `double` values.

RoundRectangle2D.Float

The `RoundRectangle2D.Float` class is an inner class of `RoundRectangle2D` that specifies the rectangle using `float` values.

Exceptions and Errors

IllegalPathStateException

The `IllegalPathStateException` class is a subclass of `java.lang.RuntimeException` that signals an attempt to perform an operation on a path when it is in the incorrect state for that operation.

NoninvertibleTransformException

The `NoninvertibleTransformException` class is a subclass of `java.lang.Exception` indicating that an operation requiring an invertible transform was performed using a non-invertible transform.

Package `java.awt.im`

The `java.awt.im` package is a new package that supports the Input Method API. It contains three classes and one interface.

Interfaces

InputMethodRequests

The `InputMethodRequests` interface defines methods that must be implemented by an input handling class in order to function within the Input Method API. These methods are used to obtain information about the text being entered by the user.

Classes

InputContext

The `InputContext` class is a subclass of `Object` that is used to implement the connection between text editing components and input methods. It does this by generating events that are handled by the text editing components and input methods.

InputMethodHighlight

The InputMethodHighlight class is a subclass of Object that supports the highlighting and conversion of text that is input via an input method.

InputSubset

The InputSubset class extends java.lang.Character.Subset to provide Unicode support for input methods.

Exceptions and Errors

None.

Package `java.awt.image`

The java.awt.image package is a Java 2D API package that supports image processing. It provides 38 classes and 8 interfaces that support common image filters.

Interfaces

BufferedImageOp

The BufferedImageOp interface defines methods for classes that perform operations on BufferedImage objects.

ImageConsumer

The ImageConsumer interface defines methods for classes that receive image data from ImageProducer objects.

ImageObserver

The ImageObserver interface defines methods for classes that observe the loading/construction of Image objects.

ImageProducer

The ImageProducer interface defines methods for classes that produce image data for use by ImageConsumer objects.

RasterOp

The RasterOp interface is implemented by classes that support operations on Raster objects.

RenderedImage

The RenderedImage interface is implemented by classes that produce image data in the form of Raster objects.

D

TileObserver

The TileObserver interface defines methods for handling events generated by changes to tiles of an image.

WritableRenderedImage

The WritableRenderedImage interface defines methods for classes that implement images that can be overwritten.

Classes

AffineTransformOp

The AffineTransformOp class is a subclass of Object that performs a 2D affine transform between two images. It implements the BufferedImageOp and RasterOp interfaces.

AreaAveragingScaleFilter

The AreaAveragingScaleFilter class is a subclass of ReplicateScaleFilter that supports image resizing using an area-averaging algorithm.

BandCombineOp

The BandCombineOp class is a subclass of Object that performs operations that combine bands in a Raster object. It implements the RasterOp interface.

BandedSampleModel

The BandedSampleModel class is a subclass of SampleModel that provides advanced band control.

BufferedImage

The BufferedImage class is a subclass of Image that provides access to buffered image data. It implements the WritableRenderedImage interface.

BufferedImageFilter

The BufferedImageFilter class is a subclass of ImageFilter that supports BufferedImage objects. It implements the RasterImageConsumer and java.lang.Cloneable interfaces.

ByteLookupTable

The ByteLookupTable class is a subclass of LookupTable that supports byte data.

ColorConvertOp

The ColorConvertOp class is a subclass of Object that supports pixel-by-pixel color conversions. It implements the BufferedImageOp and RasterOp interfaces.

ColorModel

The ColorModel class is a subclass of Object that provides the base class for the development of a variety of color models. It implements the Transparency interface.

ComponentColorModel

The ComponentColorModel class is a subclass of ColorModel that provides support for a variety of color spaces.

ComponentSampleModel

The ComponentSampleModel class is a subclass of SampleModel that supports the separate storage of color component data.

ConvolveOp

The ConvolveOp class is a subclass of Object that supports convolution operations on image data. It implements the BufferedImageOp and RasterOp interfaces.

CropImageFilter

The CropImageFilter class is a subclass of ImageFilter that supports image cropping.

DataBuffer

The DataBuffer class is a subclass of Object that supports the buffering of image data.

DataBufferByte

The DataBufferByte class is a subclass of DataBuffer that supports byte-oriented image buffering.

DataBufferInt

The DataBufferInt class is a subclass of DataBuffer that supports int-oriented image buffering.

DataBufferShort

The DataBufferShort class is a subclass of DataBuffer that supports short-oriented image buffering.

DataBufferUShort

The DataBufferUShort class is a subclass of DataBuffer that supports unsigned short-oriented image buffering.

DirectColorModel

The DirectColorModel class is a subclass of PackedColorModel that supports direct RGB pixel colors.

FilteredImageSource

The FilteredImageSource class is a subclass of Object that combines an ImageProducer with an ImageFilter. It implements the ImageProducer interface.

ImageFilter

The ImageFilter class is a subclass of Object that supports general image-filtering operations. It implements the ImageConsumer and java.lang.Cloneable interfaces.

IndexColorModel

The IndexColorModel class is a subclass of ColorModel that represents pixels as indices into a color map.

Kernel

The Kernel class is a subclass of Object that defines matrices for filtering operations.

LookupOp

The LookupOp class is a subclass of Object that supports image lookup operations. It implements the BufferedImageOp and RasterOp interfaces.

LookupTable

The LookupTable class is a subclass of Object that defines a lookup table for use in imaging operations.

MemoryImageSource

The MemoryImageSource class is a subclass of Object that provides image data from a memory source. It implements the ImageProducer interface.

MultiPixelPackedSampleModel

The MultiPixelPackedSampleModel class is a subclass of SampleModel that supports the processing of multiple one-sample pixels.

PackedColorModel

The PackedColorModel class is a subclass of ColorModel that represents color values directly within pixel data.

PixelGrabber

The PixelGrabber class is a subclass of Object that is used to retrieve a subset of the pixels of an image. It implements the ImageConsumer interface.

PixelInterleavedSampleModel

The `PixelInterleavedSampleModel` class extends `ComponentSampleModel` to provide the capability to store interleaved pixel image data.

RGBImageFilter

The `RGBImageFilter` class is a subclass of `ImageFilter` that supports the filtering of RGB color values.

Raster

The `Raster` class is a subclass of `Object` that implements a rectangular array of pixels.

ReplicateScaleFilter

The `ReplicateScaleFilter` class is a subclass of `ImageFilter` that implements a simple scaling algorithm.

RescaleOp

The `RescaleOp` class is a subclass of `Object` that supports image-rescaling operations. It implements the `BufferedImageOp` and `RasterOp` interfaces.

SampleModel

The `SampleModel` class is a subclass of `Object` that provides a base class for developing approaches to sampling image data.

ShortLookupTable

The `ShortLookupTable` class is a subclass of `LookupTable` that supports short-valued data.

SinglePixelPackedSampleModel

The `SinglePixelPackedSampleModel` class is a subclass of `SampleModel` that packs single-pixel samples in a single data element.

WritableRaster

The `WritableRaster` class is a subclass of `Raster` that provides support for image updating.

Exceptions and Errors

ImagingOpException

The `ImagingOpException` class is a subclass of `java.lang.RuntimeException` that indicates errors encountered during filtering operations.

RasterFormatException

The RasterFormatException class is a subclass of java.lang.RuntimeException that indicates format errors in Raster objects.

Package java.awt.image.renderable

The java.awt.image.renderable package provides four classes and three interfaces that support image rendering.

Interfaces

ContextualRenderedImageFactory

The ContextualRenderedImageFactory interface extends the RenderedImageFactory interface to provide methods that support rendering-independent operations. It is implemented by subclasses of RenderableImageOp.

RenderableImage

The RenderableImage interface provides a common set of methods for rendering-independent images. These methods support image operations that are independent of any specific image rendering.

RenderedImageFactory

The RenderedImageFactory interface defines the create() method for use by classes that provide different image renderings, depending on a particular set of rendering parameters.

Classes

ParameterBlock

The ParameterBlock class is a subclass of Object that provides a common set of parameters for use with RenderableImageOp objects. It implements the java.lang.Cloneable and java.io.Serializable interfaces.

RenderContext

The RenderContext class is a subclass of Object that specifies contextual information for rendering a RenderableImage object. This contextual information includes the area of interest, transforms, and rendering hints. It implements the java.lang.Cloneable interface.

RenderableImageOp

The RenderableImageOp class is a subclass of Object that supports context-specific image rendering. It implements the RenderableImage interface.

RenderableImageProducer

The RenderableImageProducer class is a subclass of Object that supports the asynchronous production of a RenderableImage object. It implements the java.awt.image.ImageProducer and java.lang.Runnable interfaces.

Exceptions and Errors

None.

Package java.awt.print

The java.awt.print package is a Java 2D API package that supports the printing of text and graphics. It contains eight classes and three interfaces.

Interfaces

PrinterGraphics

The PrinterGraphics interface provides access to a PrinterJob object.

Pageable

The Pageable interface specifies methods used for objects that represent a set of pages to be printed. These methods retrieve the number of pages to be printed and a specific page from within the page list.

Printable

The Printable interface defines the print() method for printing a page on a Graphics object.

Classes

Book

The Book class is a subclass of Object that maintains a list of pages to be printed. It provides methods for adding and managing pages. It implements the Pageable interface.

D

PageFormat

The PageFormat class is a subclass of Object that specifies the size and orientation of a page to be printed. It provides methods for setting the Paper object to be used and the page orientation. It also provides methods for switching the drawing space between portrait and landscape mode and for retrieving the characteristics of the drawing area. It implements the java.lang.Cloneable interface.

Paper

The Paper class is a subclass of Object that specifies the physical characteristics of the paper used for printing. It provides methods for getting and setting the paper size and the drawing area.

PrinterJob

The PrinterJob class is a subclass of Object that initiates, manages, and controls a printing request. Provides methods for printing Pageable objects and specifying print properties.

Exceptions and Errors

PrinterAbortException

The PrinterAbortException class is a subclass of PrinterException that indicates a print job has been aborted.

PrinterException

The PrinterException class extends java.lang.Exception to provide a base class for printing-related exceptions.

PrinterIOException

The PrinterIOException class extends PrinterException to indicate a printing I/O error.

Package java.beans

The java.beans package contains 15 classes and eight interfaces that provide the basic JavaBeans functionality.

Interfaces

AppletInitializer

The AppletInitializer interface provides support for initializing beans that are also applets.

BeanInfo

The BeanInfo interface is used to provide explicit information about a bean.

Customizer

The Customizer interface provides methods for customizing a bean's GUI.

DesignMode

The DesignMode interface is used to signal that a bean is in design (as opposed to execution) mode.

PropertyChangeListener

The PropertyChangeListener interface defines methods for handling events that result from changes to bound bean properties. It extends java.util.EventListener.

PropertyEditor

The PropertyEditor interface provides support for changing the properties of a bean.

VetoableChangeListener

The VetoableChangeListener interface extends java.util.EventListener to provide support for handing constrained property change events.

Visibility

The Visibility interface is used to signal whether a bean needs a GUI to perform its processing.

Classes

BeanDescriptor

The BeanDescriptor class is a subclass of FeatureDescriptor that provides global information about a bean.

Beans

The Beans class is a subclass of Object that provides general-purpose bean support.

EventSetDescriptor

The EventSetDescriptor class is a subclass of FeatureDescriptor that describes the events supported by a bean.

FeatureDescriptor

The FeatureDescriptor class is a subclass of Object that serves as a base class for explicit bean descriptions.

IndexedPropertyDescriptor

The IndexedPropertyDescriptor class is a subclass of PropertyDescriptor that supports indexed property descriptions.

Introspector

The Introspector class is a subclass of Object that provides static methods for obtaining information about a bean.

MethodDescriptor

The MethodDescriptor class is a subclass of FeatureDescriptor that provides information about a bean's methods.

ParameterDescriptor

The ParameterDescriptor class is a subclass of FeatureDescriptor that describes the parameters supported by a bean method.

PropertyChangeEvent

The PropertyChangeEvent class is a subclass of java.util.EventObject that signals a change in a bean's properties.

PropertyChangeSupport

The PropertyChangeSupport class is a subclass of Object that provides support for PropertyChangeEvent handling. It implements the java.io.Serializable interface.

PropertyDescriptor

The PropertyDescriptor class is a subclass of FeatureDescriptor that describes a bean property.

PropertyEditorManager

The PropertyEditorManager class is a subclass of Object that is used to access bean property editors.

PropertyEditorSupport

The PropertyEditorSupport class is a subclass of Object that provides a basic implementation of the PropertyEditor interface.

SimpleBeanInfo

The SimpleBeanInfo class is a subclass of Object that provides a basic implementation of the BeanInfo interface.

VetoableChangeSupport

The VetoableChangeSupport class is a subclass of Object that provides support for property change event handling. It implements the java.io.Serializable interface.

Exceptions and Errors

IntrospectionException

The IntrospectionException class is a subclass of java.lang.Exception that indicates that an exception occurred during introspection.

PropertyVetoException

The PropertyVetoException class is a subclass of java.lang.Exception that indicates an invalid property change.

Package java.beans.beancontext

The java.beans.beancontext package provides nine classes and 11 interfaces that implement an execution context for beans.

Interfaces

BeanContext

The BeanContext interface is implemented by classes that act as containers for other beans. It extends the BeanContextChild, java.util.Collection, java.beans.DesignMode, and java.beans.Visibility interfaces.

BeanContextChild

The BeanContextChild interface defines methods that allow classes to access their execution environment.

BeanContextChildComponentProxy

The BeanContextChildComponentProxy interface provides access to the AWT component associated with a BeanContextChildren object.

BeanContextContainerProxy

The BeanContextContainerProxy interface provides access to the AWT container associated with a BeanContext object.

BeanContextMembershipListener

The `BeanContextMembershipListener` interface defines methods for handling events associated with changes in membership in a bean context. It extends the `java.util.EventListener` interface.

BeanContextProxy

The `BeanContextProxy` interface is implemented by beans that use the context of other beans.

BeanContextServiceProvider

The `BeanContextServiceProvider` interface defines methods that are used to provide services to a bean context.

BeanContextServiceProviderBeanInfo

The `BeanContextServiceProviderBeanInfo` interface extends the `BeanInfo` interface to provide explicit information about the services of an interface.

BeanContextServiceRevokedListener

The `BeanContextServiceRevokedListener` interface supports the handling of events associated with revocation of a service to a bean context. It extends the `java.util.EventListener` interface.

BeanContextServices

The `BeanContextServices` interface defines methods that allow a `BeanContext` object to make services available to its contained `BeanContextChild` objects. It extends the `BeanContext` and `BeanContextServicesListener` interfaces.

BeanContextServicesListener

The `BeanContextServicesListener` interface defines methods for handling events associated with a service becoming available to a bean context. It extends the `BeanContextServiceRevokedListener` interface.

Classes

BeanContextChildSupport

The `BeanContextChildSupport` class is a subclass of `Object` that provides a basic implementation of the `BeanContextChild` interface. It also implements the `BeanContextServicesListener` and `java.io.Serializable` interfaces.

BeanContextEvent

The BeanContextEvent class is a subclass of java.util.EventObject that serves as the base class for bean context-related events.

BeanContextMembershipEvent

The BeanContextMembershipEvent class is a subclass of BeanContextEvent that is used to signal a change in the set of beans that is contained in a bean context.

BeanContextServiceAvailableEvent

The BeanContextServiceAvailableEvent class is a subclass of BeanContextEvent that indicates that a service has been made available to a bean context.

BeanContextServiceRevokedEvent

The BeanContextServiceRevokedEvent class is a subclass of BeanContextEvent that indicates that a service is no longer available to a bean context.

BeanContextServicesSupport

The BeanContextServicesSupport class is a subclass of BeanContextSupport that provides a basic implementation of the BeanContextServices interface.

BeanContextServicesSupport.BCSSChild

The BeanContextServicesSupport.BCSSChild class is an inner class of BeanContextServicesSupport that is inherited from BeanContextSupport. It is a subclass of BeanContextSupport.BCSChild.

BeanContextSupport

The BeanContextSupport class is a subclass of BeanContextChildSupport that provides a basic implementation of the BeanContext interface. It also implements the java.beans.PropertyChangeListener, java.beans.VetoableChangeListener, and java.io.Serializable interfaces.

BeanContextSupport.BCSIterator

The BeanContextSupport.BCSIterator class is an inner class of BeanContextSupport that is used as an iterator within its parent. It is a subclass of Object that implements the java.util.Iterator interface.

Exceptions and Errors

None.

D

Package `java.io`

The `java.io` package provides 50 classes and 10 interfaces that implement stream-based input and output.

Interfaces

DataInput

The `DataInput` interface provides methods for reading primitive types from a byte stream.

DataOutput

The `DataOutput` interface provides methods for writing primitive types to a byte stream.

Externalizable

The `Externalizable` interface extends the `Serializable` interface to provide methods for writing objects to a stream and for reading them back from a stream.

FileFilter

The `FileFilter` interface provides the capability to filter path names.

FilenameFilter

The `FilenameFilter` interface provides the capability to filter file names during file name selection.

ObjectInput

The `ObjectInput` interface extends the `DataInput` interface to support the reading of objects from input streams.

ObjectInputValidation

The `ObjectInputValidation` interface supports the validation of objects within a graph.

ObjectOutput

The `ObjectOutput` interface extends the `DataOutput` interface to support the writing of objects to output streams.

ObjectStreamConstants

The `ObjectStreamConstants` interface provides constants that are used to perform object-based input and output.

Serializable

The Serializable interface identifies an object as being capable of being written to and read from a stream.

Classes

BufferedInputStream

The BufferedInputStream class is a subclass of FilterInputStream that supports input buffering.

BufferedOutputStream

The BufferedOutputStream class is a subclass of FilterOutputStream that supports output buffering.

BufferedReader

The BufferedReader class is a subclass of Reader that supports input buffering.

BufferedWriter

The BufferedWriter class is a subclass of Writer that supports output buffering.

ByteArrayInputStream

The ByteArrayInputStream class is a subclass of InputStream that supports input from a byte array.

ByteArrayOutputStream

The ByteArrayOutputStream class is a subclass of OutputStream that supports output to a byte array.

CharArrayReader

The CharArrayReader class is a subclass of Reader that supports input from a character array.

CharArrayWriter

The CharArrayWriter class is a subclass of Writer that supports output to a character array.

DataInputStream

The DataInputStream class is a subclass of FilterInputStream that allows primitive types to be read from an input stream. It implements the DataInput interface.

D

DataOutputStream

The DataOutputStream class is a subclass of FilterOutputStream that allows primitive types to be written to an output stream. It implements the DataOutput interface.

File

The File class is a subclass of Object that encapsulates a disk file. It implements the Serializabe and java.lang.Comparable interfaces.

FileDescriptor

The FileDescriptor class is a subclass of Object that encapsulates a file descriptor.

FileInputStream

The FileInputStream class is a subclass of InputStream that supports file-based input.

FileOutputStream

The FileOutputStream class is a subclass of OutputStream that supports file-based output.

FilePermission

The FilePermission class is a subclass of java.security.Permission that is used to control access to files. It implements the Serializable interface.

FileReader

The FileReader class is a subclass of InputStreamReader that supports file-based input.

FileWriter

The FileWriter class is a subclass of OutputStreamWriter that supports file-based output.

FilterInputStream

The FilterInputStream class is a subclass of InputStream that is used to filter data that is being read from a stream.

FilterOutputStream

The FilterOutputStream class is a subclass of OutputStream that is used to filter data that is being written to a stream.

FilterReader

The FilterReader class is a subclass of Reader that allows filtering of data that is being read.

FilterWriter

The FilterWriter class is a subclass of Writer that allows filtering of data that is being written.

InputStream

The InputStream class is a subclass of Object that provides the base class for all stream-based input.

InputStreamReader

The InputStreamReader class is a subclass of Reader that is used to read a stream using a Reader object.

LineNumberInputStream

The LineNumberInputStream class is a subclass of FilterInputStream that supports line number identification.

LineNumberReader

The LineNumberReader class is a subclass of BufferedReader that supports line number identification.

ObjectInputStream

The ObjectInputStream class is a subclass of InputStream that supports the reading of objects from streams. It implements the ObjectInput and ObjectStreamConstants interfaces.

ObjectInputStream.GetField

The ObjectInputStream.GetField class is an inner class of ObjectInputStream that provides support for the reading of individual object fields. It is a subclass of Object.

ObjectOutputStream

The ObjectOutputStream class is a subclass of OutputStream that supports the writing of objects to streams. It implements the ObjectOutput and ObjectStreamConstants interfaces.

ObjectOutputStream.PutField

The ObjectOutputStream.PutField class is an inner class of ObjectOutputStream that allows individual object fields to be accessed. It is a subclass of Object.

ObjectStreamClass

The ObjectStreamClass class is a subclass of Object that describes a serialized class. It implements the Serializable interface.

ObjectStreamField

The ObjectStreamField class is a subclass of Object that describes a field of a serialized class. It implements the java.lang.Comparable interface.

OutputStream

The OutputStream class is a subclass of Object that provides the basis for stream-based output.

OutputStreamWriter

The OutputStreamWriter class is a subclass of Writer that allows output streams to be accessed as Writer objects.

PipedInputStream

The PipedInputStream class is a subclass of InputStream that supports communication between threads.

PipedOutputStream

The PipedOutputStream class is a subclass of OutputStream that supports communication between threads.

PipedReader

The PipedReader class is a subclass of Reader that supports communication between threads.

PipedWriter

The PipedWriter class is a subclass of Writer that supports communication between threads.

PrintStream

The PrintStream class is a subclass of FilterOutputStream that supports printing to the standard output stream.

PrintWriter

The PrintWriter class is a subclass of Writer that supports printing to the standard output stream.

PushbackInputStream

The PushbackInputStream class is a subclass of FilterInputStream that allows data that is read in to be pushed back onto the input stream.

PushbackReader

The PushbackReader class is a subclass of FilterReader that allows data that is read in to be pushed back onto the input source.

RandomAccessFile

The RandomAccessFile class is a subclass of Object that supports random file input and output. It implements the DataInput and DataOutput interfaces.

Reader

The Reader class is a subclass of Object that provides the basis for Unicode character input.

SequenceInputStream

The SequenceInputStream class is a subclass of InputStream that supports the concatenation of two or more input streams.

SerializablePermission

The SerializablePermission class is a subclass of java.security.BasicPermission that controls access to object serialization.

StreamTokenizer

The StreamTokenizer class is a subclass of Object that supports input stream parsing.

StringBufferInputStream

The StringBufferInputStream class is a subclass of InputStream that supports input from String objects.

StringReader

The StringReader class is a subclass of Reader that supports input from String objects.

StringWriter

The StringWriter class is a subclass of Writer that supports output to String objects.

Writer

The Writer class is a subclass of Object that provides the basis for Unicode character-based output.

D

Exceptions and Errors

CharConversionException

The CharConversionException class is a subclass of IOException that signals that an error occurred during character conversion.

EOFException

The EOFException class is a subclass of IOException that signals that the end of a file has been encountered.

FileNotFoundException

The FileNotFoundException class is a subclass of IOException that signals that a file cannot be located.

IOException

The IOException class is a subclass of java.lang.Exception that serves as the base class for defining I/O-based exceptions.

InterruptedIOException

The InterruptedIOException class is a subclass of IOException that signals an I/O operation has been interrupted.

InvalidClassException

The InvalidClassException class is a subclass of ObjectStreamException that signals that an invalid class was encountered during object serialization.

InvalidObjectException

The InvalidObjectException class is a subclass of ObjectStreamException that signals that an invalid object was encountered during object serialization.

NotActiveException

The NotActiveException class is a subclass of ObjectStreamException that signals that serialization is not active.

NotSerializableException

The NotSerializableException class is a subclass of ObjectStreamException that signals that an object is not serializable.

ObjectStreamException

The ObjectStreamException class is a subclass of IOException that serves as a base class for defining exceptions that occur during object I/O.

OptionalDataException

The OptionalDataException class is a subclass of ObjectStreamException that signals that additional data was encountered when reading an object from an input stream.

StreamCorruptedException

The StreamCorruptedException class is a subclass of ObjectStreamException that signals that an object stream contains errors.

SyncFailedException

The SyncFailedException class is a subclass of IOException that signals that synchronization of I/O could not take place.

UTFDataFormatException

The UTFDataFormatException class is a subclass of IOException that signals that an invalid UTF-8 string was read.

UnsupportedEncodingException

The UnsupportedEncodingException class is a subclass of IOException that identifies the use of unsupported data encoding.

WriteAbortedException

The WriteAbortedException class is a subclass of ObjectStreamException indicating that the writing of an object was aborted.

Package `java.lang`

The java.lang package provides 30 classes and three interfaces that implement fundamental Java objects. Because of its importance, the java.lang package is included with all Java platforms, ranging from EmbeddedJava to the full-blown JDK.

Interfaces

Cloneable

The Cloneable interface identifies a class as being cloneable by the clone() method of the Object class.

Comparable

The Comparable interface provides the compareTo() method for ordering the objects of a class.

Runnable

The Runnable interface identifies a class as being runnable as a separate thread.

Classes

Boolean

The Boolean class is a subclass of Object that wraps the primitive boolean type as a class. It implements the java.io.Serializable interface.

Byte

The Byte class is a subclass of Number that encapsulates a byte value. It implements the Comparable interface.

Character

The Character class is a subclass of Object that encapsulates a two-byte Unicode character value. It implements the Comparable and java.io.Serializable interfaces.

Character.Subset

The Character.Subset class is an inner class of Character that defines Unicode constants. It is a subclass of Object.

Character.UnicodeBlock

The Character.UnicodeBlock class extends Character.Subset to provide Unicode support.

Class

The Class class is a subclass of Object that is used to refer to classes as objects. It implements the java.io.Serializable interface.

ClassLoader

The ClassLoader class is a subclass of Object that is the base class for implementing custom class loaders for use with the runtime system.

Compiler

The Compiler class is a subclass of Object that is used to implement Just-In-Time (JIT) compilation.

Double

The Double class is a subclass of Number that encapsulates the double primitive type. It implements the Comparable interface.

Float

The Float class is a subclass of Number that encapsulates the float primitive type. It implements the Comparable interface.

InheritableThreadLocal

The InheritableThreadLocal class extends ThreadLocal to provide support for inheritance of thread values.

Integer

The Integer class is a subclass of Number that encapsulates the int primitive type. It implements the Comparable interface.

Long

The Math class is a subclass of Number that encapsulates the long primitive type. It implements the Comparable interface.

Math

The Math class is a subclass of Object that provides access to mathematical constants and functions.

Number

The Number class is a subclass of Object that is used as the base class for the wrapping of primitive numerical types. It implements the java.io.Serializable interface.

Object

The Object class is the highest class in the Java class hierarchy. It provides methods that are inherited by all Java classes.

Package

The Package class is a subclass of Object that is used to provide version information about a Java package.

Process

The Process class is a subclass of Object that is used to control external processes that are executed from within the Java runtime environment.

Runtime

The Runtime class is a subclass of Object that provides access to the Java runtime environment.

D

RuntimePermission

The RuntimePermission class is a subclass of java.security.BasicPermission that is used to control access to the runtime environment.

SecurityManager

The SecurityManager class is a subclass of Object that is used to implement a Java security policy.

Short

The Short class is a subclass of Number that encapsulates a short integer value. It implements the Comparable interface.

String

The String class is a subclass of Object that encapsulates a growable Unicode text string. It implements the Comparable and java.io.Serializable interfaces.

StringBuffer

The StringBuffer class is a subclass of Object that provides a buffer for the implementation of String objects. It implements the java.io.Serializable interface.

System

The System class is a subclass of Object that provides access to operating system-specific resources.

Thread

The Thread class is a subclass of Object that provides the capability to create objects that run as separate threads. It implements the Runnable interface.

ThreadGroup

The ThreadGroup class is a subclass of Object that represents a collection of Thread objects.

ThreadLocal

The ThreadLocal class is a subclass of Object that provides variables that are local to a specific thread instance.

Throwable

The Throwable class is a subclass of Object that is the base class for all Java errors and exceptions. It implements the java.io.Serializable interface.

Void

The `ArithmeticException` class is a subclass of `Object` that represents the class of the void primitive type.

Exceptions and Errors

AbstractMethodError

The `AbstractMethodError` class is a subclass of `IncompatibleClassChangeError` that indicates an attempt to invoke an abstract method.

ArithmeticException

The `ArithmeticException` class is a subclass of `RuntimeException` that is used to signal an arithmetic error, such as divide by zero.

ArrayIndexOutOfBoundsException

The `ArrayIndexOutOfBoundsException` class is a subclass of `IndexOutOfBoundsException` that indicates that an array index has exceeded its legal range.

ArrayStoreException

The `ArrayStoreException` class is a subclass of `RuntimeException` that indicates an attempt to store the wrong type of object in an array.

ClassCastException

The `ClassCastException` class is a subclass of `RuntimeException` that indicates an attempt to perform an illegal object cast.

ClassCircularityError

The `ClassCircularityError` class is a subclass of `LinkageError` that indicates a circularity in a class definition.

ClassFormatError

The `ClassFormatError` class is a subclass of `LinkageError` that indicates an error in the format of a class's bytecode file.

ClassNotFoundException

The `ClassNotFoundException` class is a subclass of `Exception` that signals that the class loader is unable to locate a particular class.

D

CloneNotSupportedException

The CloneNotSupportedException class is a subclass of Exception that signals an attempt to clone an object that does not implement the Cloneable interface.

Error

The Error class is a subclass of Throwable that is the base class of all Java error classes.

Exception

The Exception class is a subclass of Throwable that is the base class of all Java exception classes.

ExceptionInInitializerError

The ExceptionInInitializerError class is a subclass of LinkageError that indicates the occurrence of an unexpected exception.

IllegalAccessError

The IllegalAccessError class is a subclass of IncompatibleClassChangeError that indicates an attempt to access a field or method that violates the access modifier assigned to the field or method.

IllegalAccessException

The IllegalAccessException class is a subclass of Exception that signals an illegal attempt to load a class.

IllegalArgumentException

The IllegalArgumentException class is a subclass of RuntimeException that indicates an illegal attempt to pass an argument.

IllegalMonitorStateException

The IllegalMonitorStateException class is a subclass of RuntimeException that signals an attempt to use a monitor without owning it.

IllegalStateException

The IllegalStateException class is a subclass of RuntimeException that signals that a method invocation occurred while the runtime environment was not in an appropriate state for the method invocation.

IllegalThreadStateException

The IllegalThreadStateException class is a subclass of IllegalArgumentException that signals that a thread is not in an appropriate state for a requested operation.

IncompatibleClassChangeError

The IncompatibleClassChangeError class is a subclass of LinkageError that indicates an incompatible change to a class definition has occurred.

IndexOutOfBoundsException

The IndexOutOfBoundsException class is a subclass of RuntimeException that indicates an index has exceeded its range.

InstantiationError

The InstantiationError class is a subclass of IncompatibleClassChangeError indicating that an attempt to instantiate an abstract class or interface has occurred.

InstantiationException

The InstantiationException class is a subclass of Exception that indicates an attempt to instantiate an abstract class or interface.

InternalError

The InternalError class is a subclass of VirtualMachineError that indicates an unexpected internal error has occurred in the virtual machine.

InterruptedException

The InterruptedException class is a subclass of Exception that is thrown when a thread is interrupted.

LinkageError

The LinkageError class is a subclass of Error that indicates a class has changed in such a way that dependencies on that class are no longer valid.

NegativeArraySizeException

The NegativeArraySizeException class is a subclass of RuntimeException that is thrown as the result of attempting to allocate an array of negative size.

NoClassDefFoundError

The NoClassDefFoundError class is a subclass of LinkageError that indicates that a class definition cannot be found.

NoSuchFieldError

The NoSuchFieldError class is a subclass of IncompatibleClassChangeError that indicates an attempt to access a field that no longer exists.

D

NoSuchFieldException

The NoSuchFieldException class is a subclass of Exception that indicates that a referenced field name does not exist.

NoSuchMethodError

The NoSuchMethodError class is a subclass of IncompatibleClassChangeError that indicates an attempt to access a method that no longer exists.

NoSuchMethodException

The NoSuchMethodException class is a subclass of Exception indicating that a referenced method name does not exist.

NullPointerException

The NullPointerException class is a subclass of RuntimeException that is thrown by the use of a null reference.

NumberFormatException

The NumberFormatException class is a subclass of IllegalArgumentException that is thrown when an attempt is made to convert a String object to a number and the object does not have a valid numeric representation.

OutOfMemoryError

The OutOfMemoryError class is a subclass of VirtualMachineError that indicates that the JVM is out of memory and no memory could be made available.

RuntimeException

The RuntimeException class is a subclass of Exception that serves as the base class for defining exceptions that occur at runtime during normal JVM operation.

SecurityException

The SecurityException class is a subclass of RuntimeException that is thrown by a security policy violation.

StackOverflowError

The StackOverflowError class is a subclass of VirtualMachineError that indicates that a stack overflow has occurred.

StringIndexOutOfBoundsException

The StringIndexOutOfBoundsException class is a subclass of IndexOutOfBoundsException that indicates an attempt to access an element of a String object that is outside the string's bounds.

ThreadDeath

The ThreadDeath class is a subclass of Error that is thrown after a thread is stopped.

UnknownError

The UnknownError class is a subclass of VirtualMachineError that indicates that an unknown error occurred in the JVM.

UnsatisfiedLinkError

The UnsatisfiedLinkError class is a subclass of LinkageError that signals an attempt to access a nonexistent native method.

UnsupportedClassVersionError

The UnsupportedClassVersionError class extends ClassFormatError to identify situations where the JVM does not support the version of Java used by a class file.

UnsupportedOperationException

The UnsupportedOperationException class is a subclass of RuntimeException that is thrown by an object to indicate that it does not support a particular method.

VerifyError

The VerifyError class is a subclass of LinkageError that is thrown when the verifier encounters an inconsistency in a class file that it is verifying.

VirtualMachineError

The VirtualMachineError class is a subclass of Error that indicates that the virtual machine is incapable of further processing.

Package `java.lang.ref`

The java.lang.ref package provides five classes that implement the new Java 2 reference object capability. Reference objects are objects that are used to refer to other objects. They are similar to C and C++ pointers.

Interfaces

None.

Classes

PhantomReference

The PhantomReference class is a subclass of Reference. When the referent of a registered PhantomReference object is no longer strongly, guardedly, or weakly reachable, the PhantomReference object is cleared and added to the ReferenceQueue to which it is registered.

Reference

The Reference class is a subclass of Object that implements a reference to another object.

ReferenceQueue

The ReferenceQueue class is a subclass of Object that is used to collect Reference objects whose reachability has changed.

SoftReference

The SoftReference class is a subclass of Reference. An instance of this class is automatically cleared when memory is low and its referent is reachable only via soft references.

WeakReference

The WeakReference class is a subclass of Reference. When the referent of a registered WeakReference object is no longer strongly or guardedly reachable, the WeakReference object is cleared and added to the ReferenceQueue to which it is registered. The referent is then subject to finalization.

Exceptions and Errors

None.

Package `java.lang.reflect`

The java.lang.reflect package contains seven classes and one interface that provide the capability to implement runtime discovery of information about an object's class.

Interfaces

Member

The Member interface is used to provide information that is reflected about a Field, Constructor, or Method.

Classes

AccessibleObject

The AccessibleObject class is a subclass of Object that is the superclass of the Constructor, Field, and Method classes. It was added to the class hierarchy in Java 2 to provide the capability to specify whether an object suppresses reflection access control checks.

Array

The Array class is a subclass of Object that is used to obtain information about, create, and manipulate arrays.

Constructor

The Constructor class is a subclass of AccessibleObject that is used to obtain information about class constructors. It implements the Member interface.

Field

The Field class is a subclass of AccessibleObject that is used to obtain information about and access the field variables of a class. It implements the Member interface.

Method

The Method class is a subclass of Object that is used to obtain information about and access the methods of a class. It implements the Member interface.

Modifier

The Modifier class is a subclass of Object that is used to decode integers that represent the modifiers of classes, interfaces, field variables, constructors, and methods.

ReflectPermission

The ReflectPermission class is a subclass of java.security.BasicPermission that is used to specify whether the default language access checks should be suppressed for reflected objects.

Exceptions and Errors

InvocationTargetException

The InvocationTargetException class is a subclass of java.lang.Exception that wraps an exception thrown by an invoked method or constructor.

Package `java.math`

The `java.math` package provides two classes, `BigDecimal` and `BigInteger`, that provide the capability to perform arbitrary-precision arithmetic.

Interfaces

None.

Classes

BigDecimal

The `BigDecimal` class is a subclass of `java.lang.Number` that provides the capability to perform arbitrary-precision decimal arithmetic. It implements the `java.lang.Comparable` interface.

BigInteger

The `BigInteger` class is a subclass of `java.lang.Number` that provides the capability to perform arbitrary-length integer arithmetic. It implements the `java.lang.Comparable` interface.

Exceptions and Errors

None.

Package `java.net`

The `java.net` package provides 21 classes and five interfaces for TCP/IP network programming. Six new classes are introduced with Java 2.

Interfaces

ContentHandlerFactory

The `ContentHandlerFactory` interface is implemented by classes that create `ContentHandler` objects.

FileNameMap

The `FileNameMap` interface is implemented by classes that map file names to MIME types.

SocketImplFactory

The `SocketImplFactory` interface is implemented by classes that create `SocketImpl` objects.

SocketOptions

The SocketOptions interface defines constants that can be used to tailor a socket configuration.

URLStreamHandlerFactory

The URLStreamHandlerFactory interface is implemented by classes that create URLStreamHandler objects.

Classes

Authenticator

The Authenticator class is a subclass of Object that is used to authenticate a network connection.

ContentHandler

The ContentHandler class is a subclass of Object that is used to handle downloaded content based on its MIME type.

DatagramPacket

The DatagramPacket class is a subclass of Object that is used to implement UDP socket communication.

DatagramSocket

The DatagramSocket class is a subclass of Object that is used for UDP communication.

DatagramSocketImpl

The DatagramSocketImpl class is a subclass of Object that is a base class for implementing connectionless socket-based communication.

HttpURLConnection

The HttpURLConnection class is a subclass of URLConnection that supports the Hypertext Transfer Protocol (HTTP).

InetAddress

The InetAddress class is a subclass of Object that encapsulates an IP address.

JarURLConnection

The JarURLConnection class is a subclass of URLConnection that is used to access a JAR file via a network connection.

D

MulticastSocket

The MulticastSocket class is a subclass of DatagramSocket that supports multicast communication.

NetPermission

The NetPermission class is a subclass of java.security.BasicPermission that supports network security policy implementation.

PasswordAuthentication

The PasswordAuthentication class is a subclass of Object that supports network authentication by password.

ServerSocket

The ServerSocket class is a subclass of Object that is used to implement the server side of client-server applications.

Socket

The Socket class is a subclass of Object that provides an encapsulation of the client side of TCP and UDP sockets.

SocketImpl

The SocketImpl class is a subclass of Object that is used to create custom socket implementations.

SocketPermission

The SocketPermission class is a subclass of java.security.Permission that is used to define socket-level access controls. It implements the java.io.Serializable interface.

URL

The URL class is a subclass of Object that encapsulates a Universal Resource Locator (URL). It implements the java.lang.Comparable and java.io.Serializable interfaces.

URLClassLoader

The URLClassLoader class is a subclass of java.security.SecureClassLoader that is used to load classes from a location specified by a URL.

URLConnection

The URLConnection class is a subclass of Object that is used as a base class for implementing TCP connections to a URL-referenced resource.

URLDecoder

The URLDecoder class extends Object to support x-www-form-urlencoded decoding.

URLEncoder

The URLEncoder class is a subclass of Object that supports x-www-form-urlencoded encoding.

URLStreamHandler

The URLStreamHandler class is a subclass of Object that is used to support the development of stream-based protocol handlers.

Exceptions and Errors

BindException

The BindException class is a subclass of SocketException that indicates that an error occurred during socket binding.

ConnectException

The ConnectException class is a subclass of SocketException that indicates that an error occurred during socket connection.

MalformedURLException

The MalformedURLException class is a subclass of java.io.IOException that identifies the use of an incorrectly formed URL.

NoRouteToHostException

The NoRouteToHostException class is a subclass of SocketException that indicates that the network was not able to establish a route to a remote host.

ProtocolException

The ProtocolException class is a subclass of java.io.IOException indicating that an error occurred in the protocol stack.

SocketException

The SocketException class is a subclass of java.io.IOException that indicates that an error occurred in the underlying socket implementation.

UnknownHostException

The UnknownHostException class is a subclass of java.io.IOException that is thrown by a reference to a host whose IP address could not be resolved.

UnknownServiceException

The UnknownServiceException class is a subclass of java.io.IOException that is thrown by an attempt to use a network service that is unknown to the requestor.

Package java.rmi

The java.rmi package provides three classes and one interface that support basic remote method invocation (RMI) capabilities.

Interfaces

Remote

The Remote interface is used to identify an object as being remotely accessible. It does not define any constants or methods.

Classes

MarshalledObject

The MarshalledObject class is a subclass of Object that supports object persistence for remote object activation by representing method arguments and return values as serialized byte streams. It implements the java.io.Serializable interface.

Naming

The Naming class is a subclass of Object that provides static methods for accessing remote objects via RMI URLs. It is used to bind object names to the remote objects they represent.

RMISecurityManager

The RMISecurityManager class is a subclass of java.lang.SecurityManager that defines the default security policy used with remote objects. This class can be extended to implement custom RMI security policies.

Exceptions and Errors

AccessException

The AccessException class is a subclass of RemoteException that is used to signal an access violation.

AlreadyBoundException

The AlreadyBoundException class is a subclass of java.lang.Exception that is used to signal that a name has already been bound.

ConnectException

The ConnectException class is a subclass of RemoteException that signals that a connection was refused by the remote host.

ConnectIOException

The ConnectIOException class is a subclass of RemoteException that signals that an I/O error occurred during connection establishment.

MarshalException

The MarshalException class is a subclass of RemoteException that identifies that an error in object marshalling occurred.

NoSuchObjectException

The NoSuchObjectException class is a subclass of RemoteException that identifies an attempt to invoke a method on an object that is no longer available.

NotBoundException

The NotBoundException class is a subclass of java.lang.Exception that identifies an attempt to look up a name that has not been bound.

RMISecurityException

The RMISecurityException class is a subclass of java.lang.SecurityException that identifies that a security exception has occurred during RMI.

RemoteException

The RemoteException class is a subclass of java.io.IOException that serves as a base class for RMI-related exceptions.

ServerError

The ServerError class is a subclass of RemoteException that identifies that an error occurred on a remote server as the result of processing a method invocation.

ServerException

The ServerException class is a subclass of RemoteException that identifies that an exception occurred on a remote server as the result of processing a method invocation.

ServerRuntimeException

The ServerRuntimeException class is a subclass of RemoteException that identifies that a runtime exception occurred on a remote server as the result of processing a method invocation.

StubNotFoundException

The `StubNotFoundException` class is a subclass of `RemoteException` that identifies that the stub of a requested remote object has not been exported.

UnexpectedException

The `UnexpectedException` class is a subclass of `RemoteException` that identifies that an exception occurred during a remote method invocation that was not specified in the method's signature.

UnknownHostException

The `UnknownHostException` class is a subclass of `RemoteException` that identifies an attempt to access the registry of an unknown host.

UnmarshalException

The `UnmarshalException` class is a subclass of `RemoteException` that identifies that an error occurred in the unmarshalling of a marshalled object.

Package `java.rmi.activation`

The `java.rmi.activation` package supports persistent object references and remote object activation. It contains seven classes and four interfaces.

Interfaces

ActivationInstantiator

The `ActivationInstantiator` interface is implemented by classes that create remotely activatable objects. It extends the `Remote` interface.

ActivationMonitor

The `ActivationMonitor` interface is implemented by classes that monitor the activation status of an `ActivationGroup` object. The `ActivationGroup` object notifies its `ActivationMonitor` when objects in the group change their activation status or when the group as a whole becomes inactive. `ActivationMonitor` extends the `Remote` interface.

ActivationSystem

The `ActivationSystem` interface is implemented by classes that support the registration of activatable objects and `ActivationGroup` objects. It extends the `Remote` interface.

Activator

The `Activator` interface is implemented by a class that activates classes whose objects are remotely activatable. The system `Activator` object is invoked by a faulting remote reference. It then initiates the activation of the object needed to complete the remote reference. It extends the `Remote` interface.

Classes

Activatable

The `Activatable` class is a subclass of `RemoteServer` that is the base class for developing remotely activatable classes. It is extended by classes that require remote activation or object persistence.

ActivationDesc

The `ActivationDesc` class is a subclass of `Object` that encapsulates the information needed to activate a remotely activatable object. This information includes the object's class name, activation group, code location, and initialization data. The `ActivationDesc` class implements the `java.io.Serializable` interface.

ActivationGroup

The `ActivationGroup` class is a subclass of `UnicastRemoteObject` that is used to manage a group of activatable objects. It implements the `ActivationInstantiator` interface.

ActivationGroupDesc

The `ActivationGroupDesc` class is a subclass of `Object` that encapsulates the information needed to activate an `ActivationGroup` object. This information includes the object's class name, code location, and initialization data. The `ActivationGroupDesc` class implements the `java.io.Serializable` interface.

ActivationGroupDesc.CommandEnvironment

The `ActivationGroupDesc.CommandEnvironment` class is an inner class of `ActivationGroupDesc` that supports the implementation of startup options for `ActivationGroup` objects.

ActivationGroupID

The `ActivationGroupID` class is a subclass of `Object` that uniquely identifies an `ActivationGroup` object as well as its `ActivationSystem` object. It implements the `java.io.Serializable` interface.

ActivationID

The `ActivationID` class is a subclass of `Object` that uniquely identifies a remotely activatable object as well as its `Activator` object. It implements the `java.io.Serializable` interface.

Exceptions and Errors

ActivateFailedException

The `ActivateFailedException` class is a subclass of `java.rmi.RemoteException` that identifies the failure to activate a remotely activatable object.

ActivationException

The `ActivationException` class is a subclass of `java.lang.Exception` that is the superclass of `UnknownGroupException` and `UnknownObjectException`.

UnknownGroupException

The `UnknownGroupException` class is a subclass of `ActivationException` that is generated by an attempt to activate an object from an unknown `ActivationGroup` object.

UnknownObjectException

The `UnknownObjectException` class is a subclass of `ActivationException` that is generated by an attempt to activate an object that is unknown to an `Activator` object.

Package `java.rmi.dgc`

The `java.rmi.dgc` package supports distributed garbage collection. It contains two classes and one interface.

Interfaces

DGC

The `DGC` interface is implemented by the server side of the distributed garbage collector. It defines the `clean()` and `dirty()` methods for keeping track of which objects should be garbage-collected.

Classes

Lease

The `Lease` class is a subclass of `Object` that creates objects that are used to keep track of object references. It implements the `java.io.Serializable` interface.

VMID

The `VMID` class is a subclass of `Object` that implements an ID that uniquely identifies a Java virtual machine on a particular host. It implements the `java.io.Serializable` interface.

Exceptions and Errors

None.

Package `java.rmi.registry`

The `java.rmi.registry` package supports distributed registry operations. It contains one class and two interfaces.

Interfaces

Registry

The `Registry` interface provides methods for associating names with remotely accessible objects. It is implemented by classes that provide the RMI registry. It extends the `Remote` interface.

RegistryHandler

The `RegistryHandler` interface provides methods for accessing a `Registry` implementation. These methods have been deprecated in Java 2.

Classes

LocateRegistry

The `LocateRegistry` class is a subclass of `Object` that provides methods for accessing the RMI registry on a particular host.

Exceptions and Errors

None.

D

Package `java.rmi.server`

The `java.rmi.server` package provides the low-level classes and interfaces that implement RMI. It contains 10 classes and nine interfaces.

Interfaces

LoaderHandler

The `LoaderHandler` interface provides methods for working with RMI class loaders.

RMIFailureHandler

The `RMIFailureHandler` interface defines methods for handling RMI failure events.

RMIClientSocketFactory

The RMIClientSocketFactory interface provides access to client sockets for RMI calls.

RMIServerSocketFactory

The RMIServerSocketFactory interface provides access to server sockets for RMI calls.

RemoteCall

The RemoteCall interface defines methods for supporting a remote method invocation.

RemoteRef

The RemoteRef interface extends the java.io.Externalizable interface and provides methods for implementing a reference to a remote object.

ServerRef

The ServerRef interface extends the RemoteRef interface to provide a server-side reference to a remote object.

Skeleton

The Skeleton interface provides methods that are implemented by server-side skeletons.

Unreferenced

The Unreferenced interface provides methods that are implemented by a remote object to determine when the object is no longer remotely referenced.

Classes

LogStream

The LogStream class is a subclass of java.io.PrintStream that supports the logging of RMI errors.

ObjID

The ObjID class is a subclass of Object that uniquely identifies a remote object. It implements the java.io.Serializable interface.

Operation

The Operation class is a subclass of Object that encapsulates a remote method.

RMIClassLoader

The RMIClassLoader class is a subclass of Object that supports class loading during RMI.

RMISocketFactory

The RMISocketFactory class is a subclass of Object that is used to load custom RMI socket implementations.

RemoteObject

The RemoteObject class is a subclass of Object that is the base class for developing remote objects. It implements the Remote and java.io.Serializable interfaces.

RemoteServer

The RemoteServer class is a subclass of RemoteObject that is the base class for implementing an RMI server.

RemoteStub

The RemoteStub class is a subclass of RemoteObject that is the base class of all RMI stubs.

UID

The UID class is a subclass of Object that uniquely identifies an object on a particular host. It implements the java.io.Serializable interface.

UnicastRemoteObject

The UnicastRemoteObject class is a subclass of RemoteServer that provides a default RMI server implementation.

Exceptions and Errors

ExportException

The ExportException class is a subclass of java.rmi.RemoteException indicating that an error occurred during object export.

ServerCloneException

The ServerCloneException class is a subclass of java.rmi.RemoteException that indicates an attempt to clone a non-cloneable remote object.

ServerNotActiveException

The ServerNotActiveException class is a subclass of java.lang.Exception that indicates that the remote server is not currently active.

SkeletonMismatchException

The SkeletonMismatchException class is a subclass of java.rmi.RemoteException indicating that the skeleton of a remote object is inappropriate for the object being referenced.

SkeletonNotFoundException

The SkeletonNotFoundException class is a subclass of java.rmi.RemoteException that signals that the skeleton of a remote object cannot be located.

SocketSecurityException

The SocketSecurityException class is a subclass of ExportException that signals a socket operation that violates the current security policy.

Package java.security

The java.security package provides 39 classes and eight interfaces that provide the foundation for the Security API.

Interfaces

Certificate

The Certificate interface is a deprecated interface that provides support for digital certificates.

Guard

The Guard interface defines methods for objects that protect other objects.

Key

The Key interface extends the java.io.Serializable interface to encapsulate a cryptographic key.

Principal

The Principal interface provides methods for a subject that may have an identity.

PrivateKey

The PrivateKey interface extends the Key interface to provide support for a private key.

PrivilegedAction

The PrivilegedAction interface is used to perform privileged actions that do not throw checked exceptions.

PrivilegedExceptionAction

The PrivilegedExceptionAction interface is used to perform privileged actions that do throw checked exceptions.

PublicKey

The PublicKey interface extends the Key interface to provide support for a public key.

Classes

AccessControlContext

The AccessControlContext class is a subclass of Object that is used to make access control decisions.

AccessController

The AccessController class is a subclass of Object that implements security access controls.

AlgorithmParameterGenerator

The AlgorithmParameterGenerator class is a subclass of Object that generates parameters for use with cryptographic algorithms.

AlgorithmParameterGeneratorSpi

The AlgorithmParameterGeneratorSpi class is a subclass of Object that defines a service provider interface for an AlgorithmParameterGenerator class.

AlgorithmParameters

The AlgorithmParameters class is a subclass of Object that encapsulates parameters used with cryptographic algorithms.

AlgorithmParametersSpi

The AlgorithmParametersSpi class is a subclass of Object that provides a service provider interface for an AlgorithmParameters class.

AllPermission

The AllPermission class is a subclass of Permission that implies all other permissions.

BasicPermission

The BasicPermission class is a subclass of Permission that provides a base class for implementing permissions that use the same naming approach. It implements the java.io.Serializable interface.

CodeSource

The CodeSource class is a subclass of Object that identifies the location from which code is loaded. It implements the java.io.Serializable interface.

D

DigestInputStream

The DigestInputStream class is a subclass of java.io.FilterInputStream that is used to read a message digest.

DigestOutputStream

The DigestOutputStream class is a subclass of java.io.FilterOutputStream that is used to write a message digest.

GuardedObject

The GuardedObject class is a subclass of Object that is used to protect other objects. It implements the java.io.Serializable interface.

Identity

The Identity class is a subclass of Object that implements an identity used for making access control decisions. It implements the Principal and java.io.Serializable interfaces.

IdentityScope

The IdentityScope class is a subclass of Identity that defines the scope of an identity.

KeyFactory

The KeyFactory class is a subclass of Object that is used to create Key objects.

KeyFactorySpi

The KeyFactorySpi class is a subclass of Object that provides a service provider interface to a KeyFactory class.

KeyPair

The KeyPair class is a subclass of Object that encapsulates a public-private key pair.

KeyPairGenerator

The KeyPairGenerator class is a subclass of KeyPairGeneratorSpi that is used to create key pairs.

KeyPairGeneratorSpi

The KeyPairGeneratorSpi class is a subclass of Object that provides a service provider interface to a KeyPairGenerator object.

KeyStore

The KeyStore class is a subclass of Object that supports the management of cryptographic keys.

KeyStoreSpi

The KeyStoreSpi class extends Object to provide a service provider interface for the KeyStore class.

MessageDigest

The MessageDigest class is a subclass of MessageDigestSpi that implements a message digest.

MessageDigestSpi

The MessageDigestSpi class is a subclass of Object that provides a service provider interface to a MessageDigest class.

Permission

The Permission class is a subclass of Object that defines a permission to a protected resource. It implements the Guard and java.io.Serializable interfaces.

PermissionCollection

The PermissionCollection class is a subclass of Object that implements a collection of Permission objects. It implements the java.io.Serializable interface.

Permissions

The Permissions class is a subclass of PermissionCollection that supports a mixed collection of Permission objects. It implements the java.io.Serializable interface.

Policy

The Policy class is a subclass of Object that implements a Java security policy.

ProtectionDomain

The ProtectionDomain class is a subclass of Object that identifies a set of classes with the same permissions.

Provider

The Provider class is a subclass of java.util.Properties that implements a service provider.

SecureClassLoader

The SecureClassLoader class is a subclass of java.lang.ClassLoader that supports secure class loading.

D

SecureRandom

The SecureRandom class is a subclass of java.util.Random that provides secure random-number-generation capabilities.

SecureRandomSpi

The SecureRandomSpi class extends Object and implements Serializable to provide a service provider interface for the SecureRandom class.

Security

The Security class is a subclass of Object that provides common access to security-related objects.

SecurityPermission

The SecurityPermission class is a subclass of BasicPermission that defines security-related permissions.

Signature

The Signature class is a subclass of SignatureSpi that provides digital signature support.

SignatureSpi

The SignatureSpi class is a subclass of Object that provides a service provider interface to a Signature class.

SignedObject

The SignedObject class is a subclass of Object that represents an object that has been signed. It implements the java.io.Serializable interface.

Signer

The Signer class is a subclass of Identity that is capable of signing a signature-related object.

UnresolvedPermission

The UnresolvedPermission class is a subclass of Permission that does not have an accessible permission class. It implements the java.io.Serializable interface.

Exceptions and Errors

AccessControlException

The AccessControlException class is a subclass of SecurityException that indicates a violation of security access controls.

DigestException

The DigestException class is a subclass of GeneralSecurityException that is thrown by errors in message digest calculation.

GeneralSecurityException

The GeneralSecurityException class is a subclass of java.lang.Exception that is used as the base class for defining the security-related exceptions.

InvalidAlgorithmParameterException

The InvalidAlgorithmParameterException class is a subclass of GeneralSecurityException that indicates that an invalid parameter was supplied to a cryptographic algorithm.

InvalidKeyException

The InvalidKeyException class is a subclass of KeyException that indicates that an invalid key was supplied to a cryptographic algorithm.

InvalidParameterException

The InvalidParameterException class is a subclass of IllegalArgumentException indicating that an invalid parameter was supplied to a cryptographic algorithm.

D

KeyException

The KeyException class is a subclass of GeneralSecurityException that identifies an exception related to a cryptographic key.

KeyManagementException

The KeyManagementException class is a subclass of KeyException that identifies an exception in the management of keys.

KeyStoreException

The KeyStoreException class is a subclass of GeneralSecurityException that identifies an exception in the storage of keys.

NoSuchAlgorithmException

The NoSuchAlgorithmException class is a subclass of GeneralSecurityException indicating that a requested algorithm does not exist.

NoSuchProviderException

The NoSuchProviderException class is a subclass of GeneralSecurityException indicating that a requested service provider does not exist.

PrivilegedActionException

The `PrivilegedActionException` class extends `Exception` to indicate that the performance of a privileged action resulted in a checked exception.

ProviderException

The `ProviderException` class is a subclass of `java.lang.RuntimeException` that is generated by a service provider.

SignatureException

The `SignatureException` class is a subclass of `GeneralSecurityException` that identifies an exception occurring during signature calculation.

UnrecoverableKeyException

The `UnrecoverableKeyException` class is a subclass of `GeneralSecurityException` that signals that a key cannot be recovered from a keystore.

Package `java.security.acl`

The `java.security.acl` package provides five interfaces that provide the basic elements for implementing security access controls.

Interfaces

Acl

The `Acl` interface extends the `Owner` interface to define methods for classes that implement access control lists. An `Acl` object consists of zero or more `AclEntry` objects.

AclEntry

The `AclEntry` interface defines methods for an entry in an access control list. It identifies a set of permissions for a `Principal`. It extends the `java.lang.Cloneable` interface.

Group

The `Group` interface extends the `java.security.Principal` interface to provide methods for working with a group of `Principal` objects. A `Group` object may also contain other `Group` objects.

Owner

The `Owner` interface defines methods for working with the owners of an access control list.

Permission

The Permission interface defines methods for implementing permissions to access-protected resources.

Classes

None.

Exceptions and Errors

AclNotFoundException

The AclNotFoundException class is a subclass of java.lang.Exception that signals a reference to a nonexistent access control list.

LastOwnerException

The LastOwnerException class is a subclass of java.lang.Exception that signals an attempt to delete the last owner of an access control list.

NotOwnerException

The NotOwnerException class is a subclass of java.lang.Exception that signals an attempt to modify an access control list by an object that is not its owner.

Package java.security.cert

The java.security.cert package provides seven classes and one interface that implement digital certificates.

Interfaces

X509Extension

The X509Extension interface provides methods that encapsulate extensions defined for X.509 v3 certificates and v2 certificate revocation lists.

Classes

Certificate

The Certificate class is a subclass of Object that provides an abstract base class for implementing identity certificates.

CertificateFactory

The CertificateFactory class extends Object to provide a factory for creating certificates and certificate revocation lists.

CertificateFactorySpi

The CertificateFactorySpi class extends Object to provide a security provider interface for the CertificateFactory class.

CRL

The CRL class extends Object to provide an abstract implementation of a certificate revocation list.

X509CRLEntry

The X509CRLEntry class extends Object and implements the X509Extension interface to provide an abstract class for a revoked certificate in a CRL.

X509CRL

The X509CRL class is a subclass of Object that implements an X.509 certificate revocation list. It implements the X509Extension interface.

X509Certificate

The X509Certificate class is a subclass of Certificate that provides an abstract base class for implementing X.509 digital certificates.

Exceptions and Errors

CRLException

The CRLException class is a subclass of java.security.GeneralSecurityException that identifies an exception occurring in the processing of a certificate revocation list.

CertificateEncodingException

The CertificateEncodingException class is a subclass of CertificateException that identifies that an exception occurred during the encoding of a certificate.

CertificateException

The CertificateException class is a subclass of java.security.GeneralSecurityException that acts as a base class for other certificate-related exceptions.

CertificateExpiredException

The CertificateExpiredException class is a subclass of CertificateException that identifies that an expired certificate has been encountered.

CertificateNotYetValidException

The `CertificateNotYetValidException` class is a subclass of `CertificateException` that identifies that a certificate has been processed before its valid date range.

CertificateParsingException

The `CertificateParsingException` class is a subclass of `CertificateException` that indicates that an error occurred in the parsing of a certificate.

Package `java.security.interfaces`

The `java.security.interfaces` package provides eight interfaces that support implementation of the NIST digital signature algorithm.

Interfaces

DSAKey

The `DSAKey` interface defines the `getParams()` method for accessing a Digital Signature Algorithm (DSA) public or private key.

DSAKeyPairGenerator

The `DSAKeyPairGenerator` interface is implemented by objects that can generate DSA key pairs.

DSAParams

The `DSAParams` interface defines methods for accessing a set of DSA key parameters.

DSAPrivateKey

The `DSAPrivateKey` interface extends the `DSAKey` and `java.security.PrivateKey` interfaces to provide access to a DSA private key.

DSAPublicKey

The `DSAPublicKey` interface extends the `DSAKey` and `java.security.PublicKey` interfaces to provide access to a DSA public key.

RSAPrivateCrtKey

The `RSAPrivateCrtKey` interface extends `RSAPrivateKey` with support for the Chinese Remainder Theorem.

RSAPrivateKey

The `RSAPrivateKey` interface extends `PrivateKey` to provide support for RSA private keys.

D

RSAPublicKey

The RSAPublicKey interface extends PublicKey to provide support for RSA public keys.

Classes

None.

Exceptions and Errors

None.

Package java.security.spec

The java.security.spec package provides nine classes and two interfaces that provide specifications for cryptographic keys.

Interfaces

AlgorithmParameterSpec

The AlgorithmParameterSpec interface provides no constants or methods. It is used to identify an object that provides cryptographic algorithm parameters.

KeySpec

The KeySpec interface provides no constants or methods. It is used to identify an object that is a key for a cryptographic algorithm.

Classes

DSAParameterSpec

The DSAParameterSpec class is a subclass of Object that provides parameters for a Digital Signature Algorithm (DSA) implementation. It implements the AlgorithmParameterSpec and java.security.interfaces.DSAParams interfaces.

DSAPrivateKeySpec

The DSAPrivateKeySpec class is a subclass of Object that implements a private DSA key. It implements the KeySpec interface.

DSAPublicKeySpec

The DSAPublicKeySpec class is a subclass of Object that implements a public DSA key. It implements the KeySpec interface.

EncodedKeySpec

The EncodedKeySpec class is a subclass of Object that implements an encoded public or private key. It implements the KeySpec interface.

PKCS8EncodedKeySpec

The PKCS8EncodedKeySpec class is a subclass of EncodedKeySpec that represents the PKCS #8 standard encoding of a private key.

RSAPrivateCrtKeySpec

The RSAPrivateCrtKeySpec class extends RSAPrivateKeySpec to specify an RSA private key using Chinese Remainder Theorem values.

RSAPrivateKeySpec

The RSAPrivateKeySpec class extends Object and implements KeySpec to provide support for RSA private keys.

RSAPublicKeySpec

The RSAPublicKeySpec class extends Object and implements KeySpec to provide support for RSA public keys.

X509EncodedKeySpec

The X509EncodedKeySpec class is a subclass of EncodedKeySpec that represents the X.509 standard encoding of a public or private key.

Exceptions and Errors

InvalidKeySpecException

The InvalidKeySpecException class is a subclass of java.security.GeneralSecurityException that identifies an invalid key specification.

InvalidParameterSpecException

The InvalidParameterSpecException class is a subclass of java.security.GeneralSecurityException that identifies an invalid parameter specification.

Package java.sql

The java.sql package provides six classes and 16 interfaces that provide Java database connectivity.

Interfaces

Array

The Array interface provides a reference to an array that is stored by the database server.

Blob

The Blob interface provides a reference to a binary large object that is stored by the database server.

CallableStatement

The CallableStatement interface extends the PreparedStatement interface to provide support for stored procedures.

Clob

The Clob interface provides a reference to a character large object that is stored by the database server.

Connection

The Connection interface encapsulates a database connection.

DatabaseMetaData

The DatabaseMetaData interface provides access to information about the database itself.

Driver

The Driver interface encapsulates a database driver.

PreparedStatement

The PreparedStatement interface provides access to precompiled, stored SQL statements.

Ref

The Ref interface provides a reference to a stored SQL value.

ResultSet

The ResultSet interface encapsulates the results of a database query.

ResultSetMetaData

The ResultSetMetaData interface provides information about a ResultSet object.

SQLData

The SQLData interface provides support for mapping SQL and Java data types.

SQLInput

The SQLInput interface represents an input stream of a SQL UDT instance.

SQLOutput

The SQLOutput interface represents a SQL UDT output stream.

Statement

The Statement interface provides support for executing SQL statements.

Struct

The Struct interface encapsulates a SQL structured type.

Classes

Date

The Date class is a subclass of java.util.Date that supports SQL date objects.

DriverManager

The DriverManager class is a subclass of Object that is used to manage database drivers.

DriverPropertyInfo

The DriverPropertyInfo class is a subclass of Object that provides information about a database driver.

Time

The Time class is a subclass of java.util.Time that supports SQL time objects.

Timestamp

The Timestamp class is a subclass of Object that encapsulates a SQL time stamp.

Types

The Types class is a subclass of Object that defines constants for use with SQL types.

Exceptions and Errors

BatchUpdateException

The BatchUpdateException class is a subclass of SQLException that signals the occurrence of errors during batch update operations.

DataTruncation

The DataTruncation class is a subclass of SQLWarning that indicates that a date value has been truncated.

D

SQLException

The SQLException class is a subclass of java.lang.Exception that serves as a base class for database exceptions.

SQLWarning

The SQLWarning class is a subclass of SQLException that signals warnings about database operations.

Package java.text

The java.text package provides 20 classes and two interfaces that support internationalization.

Interfaces

AttributedCharacterIterator

The AttributedCharacterIterator interface extends the CharacterIterator interface to provide support for iterating through text that is associated with style, internationalization, or other attributes.

CharacterIterator

The CharacterIterator interface provides internationalization support for bidirectional text iteration.

Classes

Annotation

The Annotation class is a subclass of Object that is used to work with text attribute values.

AttributedCharacterIterator.Attribute

The AttributedCharacterIterator.Attribute class extends Object and implements Serializable to define attribute keys that are used to identify text attributes.

AttributedString

The AttributedString class is a subclass of Object that encapsulates text and related attribute information.

BreakIterator

The `BreakIterator` class is a subclass of `Object` that provides support for identifying text-break boundaries. It implements the `java.lang.Cloneable` and `java.io.Serializable` interfaces.

ChoiceFormat

The `ChoiceFormat` class is a subclass of `NumberFormat` that allows number formatting to be associated with a range of numbers.

CollationElementIterator

The `CollationElementIterator` class is a subclass of `Object` that is used to iterate through international text strings.

CollationKey

The `CollationKey` class is a subclass of `Object` that is used to compare two `Collator` objects. It implements the `java.lang.Comparable` interface.

Collator

The `Collator` class is a subclass of `Object` that supports locale-specific string comparisons. It implements the `java.lang.Comparable`, `java.lang.Cloneable`, and `java.io.Serializable` interfaces.

DateFormat

The `DateFormat` class is a subclass of `Format` that provides international date formatting support.

DateFormatSymbols

The `DateFormatSymbols` class is a subclass of `Object` that provides support for locale-specific date formatting information. It implements the `java.lang.Cloneable` and `java.io.Serializable` interfaces.

DecimalFormat

The `DecimalFormat` class is a subclass of `Object` that provides international decimal point formatting support.

DecimalFormatSymbols

The `DecimalFormatSymbols` class is a subclass of `Object` that provides locale-specific decimal formatting information. It implements the `java.lang.Cloneable` and `java.io.Serializable` interfaces.

FieldPosition

The FieldPosition class is a subclass of Object that is used to identify fields in formatted output.

Format

The Format class is a subclass of Object that is the base class for international formatting support. It implements the java.lang.Cloneable and java.io.Serializable interfaces.

MessageFormat

The MessageFormat class is a subclass of Format that supports international message concatenation.

NumberFormat

The NumberFormat class is a subclass of Format that provides international number formatting support.

ParsePosition

The ParsePosition class is a subclass of Object that is used to keep track of the current parsing position.

RuleBasedCollator

The RuleBasedCollator class is a subclass of Collator that supports rule-based sorting.

SimpleDateFormat

The SimpleDateFormat class is a subclass of DateFormat that supports basic international date formatting.

StringCharacterIterator

The StringCharacterIterator class is a subclass of Object that provides a basic implementation of the CharacterIterator interface. It also implements the java.io.Serializable interface.

Exceptions and Errors

ParseException

The ParseException class is a subclass of java.lang.Exception that signals a parsing error.

Package `java.util`

The `java.util` package, like `java.lang` and `java.io`, is fundamental to any Java platform. It provides 34 classes and 13 interfaces that cover a wide variety of common programming needs. Most of the new classes and interfaces support the Collections API.

Interfaces

Collection

The `Collection` interface defines methods for working with arbitrary collections of objects.

Comparator

The `Comparator` interface defines methods for implementing a comparison function.

Enumeration

The `Enumeration` interface defines methods for working with an ordered collection of objects.

EventListener

The `EventListener` interface provides the basic interface to support Java event handling.

Iterator

The `Iterator` interface defines methods for iterating through an ordered collection.

List

The `List` interface extends the `Collection` interface to an ordered list of objects.

ListIterator

The `ListIterator` interface extends the `Iterator` interface to support iteration through a `List` object.

Map

The `Map` interface provides methods for mapping between two object sets.

Map.Entry

The `Map.Entry` interface defines methods for a single mapping element.

Observer

The `Observer` interface defines methods for observing the occurrence of an event, action, or processing.

D

Set

The Set interface extends the Collection interface to implement a collection in which each element occurs only once.

SortedMap

The SortedMap interface extends the Map interface to identify an ordering between the map elements.

SortedSet

The SortedSet interface extends the Set interface to order the collection of set elements.

Classes

AbstractCollection

The AbstractCollection class is a subclass of Object that provides an abstract implementation of the Collection interface.

AbstractList

The AbstractList class is a subclass of AbstractCollection that provides an abstract implementation of the List interface.

AbstractMap

The AbstractMap class is a subclass of Object that provides an abstract implementation of the Map interface.

AbstractSequentialList

The AbstractSequentialList class is a subclass of AbstractList that provides a sequential access data store.

AbstractSet

The AbstractSet class is a subclass of AbstractCollection that provides an abstract implementation of the Set interface.

ArrayList

The ArrayList class is a subclass of AbstractList that is implemented in terms of an array. It implements the List, java.lang.Cloneable, and java.io.Serializable interfaces.

Arrays

The Arrays class is a subclass of Object that provides support for array manipulation.

BitSet

The BitSet class is a subclass of Object that provides a growable vector of bits. It implements the java.lang.Cloneable and java.io.Serializable interfaces.

Calendar

The Calendar class is a subclass of Object that provides basic support for date, time, and calendar functions. It implements the java.lang.Cloneable and java.io.Serializable interfaces.

Collections

The Collections class is a subclass of Object that provides static methods for working with collections of objects.

Date

The Date class is a subclass of Object that provides basic date/time support. It implements the java.lang.Comparable, java.lang.Cloneable, and java.io.Serializable interfaces.

Dictionary

The Dictionary class is a subclass of Object that maps names to values.

EventObject

The EventObject class is a subclass of Object that provides the basic class from which most Java events are derived. It implements the java.io.Serializable interface.

GregorianCalendar

The GregorianCalendar class is a subclass of Calendar that implements a Gregorian calendar.

HashMap

The HashMap class is a subclass of AbstractMap that provides an implementation of the Map interface using a hash table. It implements the Map, java.lang.Cloneable, and java.io.Serializable interfaces.

HashSet

The HashSet class is a subclass of AbstractSet that implements the Set interface using a hash table. It implements the Set, java.lang.Cloneable, and java.io.Serializable interfaces.

D

Hashtable

The Hashtable class is a subclass of Dictionary that maps keys to their values. It implements the Map, java.lang.Cloneable, and java.io.Serializable interfaces.

LinkedList

The LinkedList class is a subclass of AbstractSequentialList that encapsulates a linked list data structure. It implements the List, java.lang.Cloneable, and java.io.Serializable interfaces.

ListResourceBundle

The ListResourceBundle class is a subclass of ResourceBundle that provides internationalization in the form of a list.

Locale

The Locale class is a subclass of Object that encapsulates a local region for internationalization purposes. It implements the java.lang.Cloneable and java.io.Serializable interfaces.

Observable

The Observable class is a subclass of Object that represents observable data in the model-view paradigm.

Properties

The Properties class is a subclass of Hashtable that represents a set of properties and property values.

PropertyPermission

The PropertyPermission class is a subclass of java.security.BasicPermission that implements access controls on system properties.

PropertyResourceBundle

The PropertyResourceBundle class is a subclass of ResourceBundle that manages internationalization resources using properties.

Random

The Random class is a subclass of Object that provides random-number generation capabilities. It implements the java.io.Serializable interface.

ResourceBundle

The ResourceBundle class is a subclass of Object that is used to manage internationalization resources.

SimpleTimeZone

The SimpleTimeZone class is a subclass of TimeZone that provides basic time zone information.

Stack

The Stack class is a subclass of Vector that implements a stack data structure.

StringTokenizer

The StringTokenizer class is a subclass of Object that supports the parsing of strings. It implements the Enumeration interface.

TimeZone

The TimeZone class is a subclass of Object that encapsulates the notion of a time zone. It implements the java.lang.Cloneable and java.io.Serializable interfaces.

TreeMap

The TreeMap class is a subclass of AbstractMap that provides a tree-based implementation of the Map interface. It implements the SortedMap, java.lang.Cloneable, and java.io.Serializable interfaces.

TreeSet

The TreeSet class is a subclass of AbstractSet that provides a tree-based implementation of the Set interface. It implements the SortedSet, java.lang.Cloneable, and java.io.Serializable interfaces.

Vector

The Vector class is a subclass of AbstractList that provides a growable array of objects. It implements the List, java.lang.Cloneable, and java.io.Serializable interfaces.

WeakHashMap

The WeakHashMap class extends AbstractMap and implements the Map interface to provide a hashtable-based Map implementation with weak keys.

Exceptions and Errors

ConcurrentModificationException

The ConcurrentModificationException class is a subclass of java.lang.RuntimeException that identifies invalid concurrent accesses to collections objects.

EmptyStackException

The EmptyStackException class is a subclass of java.lang.RuntimeException that signals an attempt to pop an object from an empty stack.

MissingResourceException

The MissingResourceException class is a subclass of java.lang.RuntimeException that signals an access to a missing resource.

NoSuchElementException

The NoSuchElementException class is a subclass of java.lang.RuntimeException indicating that an Enumeration contains no more elements.

TooManyListenersException

The TooManyListenersException class is a subclass of java.lang.Exception indicating that too many event listeners are associated with an event.

Package java.util.jar

The java.util.jar package provides seven classes for working with JAR files.

Interfaces

None.

Classes

Attributes

The Attributes class is a subclass of Object that maps manifest attribute names to string values. It implements the java.util.Map and java.lang.Cloneable interfaces.

Attributes.Name

The Attributes.Name class is an inner class of Attributes that represents a specific attribute name of the Attributes map. It is a subclass of Object.

JarEntry

The JarEntry class is a subclass of java.util.zip.ZipEntry that represents an entry in a JAR file. It provides methods for reading the attributes and identities of JAR file entries.

JarFile

The JarFile class is a subclass of java.util.zip.ZipFile that is used to read JAR files. It supports reading of the manifest as well as individual JAR file entries.

JarInputStream

The JarInputStream class is a subclass of java.util.zip.ZipInputStream that is used to read a JAR file from an input stream.

JarOutputStream

The JarOutputStream class is a subclass of java.util.zip.ZipOutputStream that is used to write the contents of a JAR file to an output stream.

Manifest

The Manifest class is a subclass of Object that implements a JAR file manifest. It provides methods for accessing manifest names and their attributes. It implements the java.lang.Cloneable interface.

Exceptions and Errors

JarException

The JarException class is a subclass of java.util.zip.ZipException that is used to report errors that occur in the reading or writing of a JAR file.

Package java.util.zip

The java.util.zip package provides 14 classes and one interface for working with compressed files.

Interfaces

Checksum

The Checksum interface provides a common set of methods for classes that compute a checksum.

Classes

Adler32

The Adler32 class is a subclass of Object that computes an Adler-32 checksum on an input stream. It implements the Checksum interface.

CRC32

The CRC32 class is a subclass of Object that computes an CRC-32 checksum on an input stream. It implements the Checksum interface.

CheckedInputStream

The CheckedInputStream class is a subclass of java.io.FilterInputStream that computes a checksum of the data being read.

CheckedOutputStream

The CheckedOutputStream class is a subclass of java.io.FilterOutputStream that computes a checksum of the data being written.

Deflater

The Deflater class is a subclass of Object that supports compression using the ZLIB compression library.

DeflaterOutputStream

The DeflaterOutputStream class is a subclass of java.io.FilterOutputStream that compresses stream output using the deflate format of the ZLIB compression library.

GZIPInputStream

The GZIPInputStream class is a subclass of InflatorInputStream that supports the reading of GZIP-compressed data.

GZIPOutputStream

The GZIPOutputStream class is a subclass of DeflatorOutputStream that supports the writing of GZIP-compressed data.

Inflater

The Inflater class is a subclass of Object that supports decompression using the ZLIB compression library.

InflaterInputStream

The InflaterInputStream class is a subclass of java.io.FilterIntputStream that decompresses stream input using the inflate format of the ZLIB compression library.

ZipEntry

The ZipEntry class is a subclass of Object that encapsulates a ZIP file entry. It implements the java.lang.Cloneable interface.

ZipFile

The ZipFile class is a subclass of Object that supports the reading of ZipEntry objects from ZIP files.

ZipInputStream

The ZipInputStream class is a subclass of InflaterInputStream that is used for reading streams that are in the compressed or uncompressed ZIP format.

ZipOutputStream

The ZipOutputStream class is a subclass of DeflaterOutputStream that is used to write compressed and uncompressed ZIP file entries to an output stream.

Exceptions and Errors

DataFormatException

The DataFormatException class is a subclass of java.lang.Exception that is used to identify the occurrence of a data format error during compression or decompression.

ZipException

The ZipException class is a subclass of java.io.IOException that signals an error in the reading or writing of a ZIP file or stream.

Package javax.accessibility

The javax.accessibility package provides seven classes and seven interfaces that support the use of assistive technologies for disabled users.

Interfaces

Accessible

The Accessible interface is implemented by all components that support accessibility. It defines the single getAccessibleContext() method to return an object that implements the AccessibleContext interface.

AccessibleAction

The AccessibleAction interface defines methods that can be used to determine which actions are supported by a component. It also provides methods for accessing these actions.

AccessibleComponent

The AccessibleComponent interface defines methods for controlling the behavior and display of GUI components that support assistive technologies.

AccessibleHypertext

The AccessibleHypertext interface is implemented by GUI components that display hypertext. It supports assistive technologies for hypertext display.

AccessibleSelection

The AccessibleSelection interface provides support for determining which subcomponents of a GUI component have been selected, and for controlling the selection status of those components.

AccessibleText

The AccessibleText interface provides constants and methods for use with GUI components that display text. It allows assistive technologies to control the content, attributes, and layout of displayed text.

AccessibleValue

The AccessibleValue interface is implemented by GUI components that support the selection of a numerical value from a range of values, such as a scrollbar. This interface provides methods for getting and setting the numerical value and for determining the range of values.

Classes

AccessibleBundle

The AccessibleBundle class is a subclass of Object that provides access to resource bundles and supports string conversions.

AccessibleContext

The AccessibleContext class is a core accessibility API class and provides access to other assistive technology objects. It defines the information that is used by all accessible objects and is subclassed by objects that implement assistive technologies. It is a subclass of Object.

AccessibleHyperlink

The AccessibleHyperlink extends Object to provide accessibility support for a hyperlink or set of hyperlinks.

AccessibleResourceBundle

The AccessibleResourceBundle class is a subclass of java.util.ListResourceBundle that implements a resource bundle for assistive technology applications. It provides localized accessibility properties for a particular locale.

AccessibleRole

The AccessibleRole class is a subclass of AccessibleBundle that provides constants that describe the role of an accessibility GUI component, such as LIST, MENU, and CHECK_BOX.

AccessibleState

The AccessibleState class is a subclass of AccessibleBundle that describes the state of an accessibility object. AccessibleState objects are contained in AccessibleStateSet objects. The AccessibleState class provides constants that define common object states, such as BUSY, CHECKED, and ENABLED.

AccessibleStateSet

The AccessibleStateSet class is a subclass of Object that implements a collection of AccessibleState objects. AccessibleStateSet objects are used to define the overall state of an accessibility object.

Exceptions and Errors

None.

Package `javax.swing`

The javax.swing package is the core Swing package. It contains 90 classes and 22 interfaces that provide the foundation for the Swing API.

Interfaces

Action

The Action interface extends the java.awt.ActionListener interface and defines methods for defining, enabling, and disabling a unit of program operation.

BoundedRangeModel

The BoundedRangeModel interface defines a data model used for range-bounded components, such as sliders and progress bars.

ButtonModel

The ButtonModel interface extends the java.awt.ItemSelectable interface to provide methods that define the state of a button.

CellEditor

The CellEditor interface defines methods that are used to edit the cell values of GUI components, such as tables.

ComboBoxEditor

The ComboBoxEditor interface defines methods for editing combo boxes.

ComboBoxModel

The ComboBoxModel interface extends the ListModel interface and defines methods for supporting the data model of a combo box.

DesktopManager

The DesktopManager interface provides methods that are implemented by classes that support a Java-based desktop.

Icon

The Icon interface defines methods that are implemented by classes that provide desktop and application icons.

JComboBox.KeySelectionManager

The JComboBox.KeySelectionManager interface defines a key for selecting items from a combo box.

ListCellRenderer

The ListCellRenderer interface defines methods for painting the cells in a JList object.

ListModel

The ListModel interface defines methods that support the data model for a list.

ListSelectionModel

The ListSelectionModel interface defines methods for selecting elements from a list.

MenuElement

The MenuElement interface defines methods that are implemented by items that are placed in a menu.

MutableComboBoxModel

The MutableComboBoxModel interface extends the ComboBoxModel interface to provide update support.

Renderer

The Renderer interface defines methods for obtaining access to and setting the value of GUI components.

RootPaneContainer

The RootPaneContainer interface defines methods that are implemented by top-level window components.

ScrollPaneConstants

The ScrollPaneConstants interface defines constants that are used by scrollable pane classes.

Scrollable

The Scrollable interface defines methods that are implemented by scrollable container classes.

SingleSelectionModel

The SingleSelectionModel interface defines methods for selecting a single item from a list of items.

SwingConstants

The SwingConstants interface defines constants for laying out GUI components.

UIDefaults.ActiveValue

The UIDefaults.ActiveValue interface supports an active (preset) approach to defining user interface default values.

UIDefaults.LazyValue

The UIDefaults.LazyValue interface supports a lazy (as-needed) approach to defining user interface default values.

WindowConstants

The WindowConstants interface defines constants that are used in window operations.

Classes

AbstractAction

The AbstractAction class is a subclass of Object that provides a default implementation of the Action interface. It also implements the java.lang.Cloneable and java.io.Serializable interfaces.

AbstractButton

The AbstractButton class is a subclass of JComponent that serves as a base class for developing other JFC buttons. It implements the SwingConstants and java.awt.ItemSelectable interfaces.

AbstractListModel

The AbstractListModel class is a subclass of Object that provides an abstract data model for list-related classes. It implements the ListModel and java.io.Serializable interfaces.

BorderFactory

The BorderFactory class is a subclass of Object that provides support for creating Border objects.

Box

The Box class is a subclass of java.awt.Container that lays out components in a BoxLayout. It implements the java.awt.accessibility.Accessible interface.

Box.Filler

The Box.Filler class is an inner class of Box that supports the layout of Box objects. It is a subclass of java.awt.Component.

BoxLayout

The BoxLayout class is a subclass of Object that supports the layout of containers in a box-like, top-to-bottom, left-to-right fashion. It implements the java.awt.LayoutManager2 and java.io.Serializable interfaces.

ButtonGroup

The ButtonGroup class is a subclass of Object that supports the development of radio button-like button groups in which only one button can be selected at a time. It implements the java.io.Serializable interface.

CellRendererPane

The CellRendererPane class is a subclass of java.awt.Container that supports the organization of cell-oriented components, such as lists and tables. It implements the java.awt.accessibility.Accessible interface.

DebugGraphics

The DebugGraphics class is a subclass of java.awt.Graphics that provides debugging support.

DefaultBoundedRangeModel

The DefaultBoundedRangeModel class is a subclass of Object that provides a default implementation of the BoundedRangeModel interface. It also implements the java.io.Serializable interface.

DefaultButtonModel

The DefaultButtonModel class is a subclass of Object that provides a default implementation of the ButtonModel interface. It also implements the java.io.Serializable interface.

DefaultCellEditor

The DefaultCellEditor class is a subclass of Object that provides a default implementation of the javax.swing.table.TableCellEditor and javax.swing.tree.TreeCellEditor interfaces. It also implements the java.io.Serializable interface.

DefaultComboBoxModel

The DefaultComboBoxModel class is a subclass of AbstractListModel and implements the MutableComboBoxModel and java.io.Serializable interfaces. It provides a default model for combo boxes.

D

DefaultDesktopManager

The DefaultDesktopManager class is a subclass of Object that provides a default implementation of the DesktopManager interface.

DefaultFocusManager

The DefaultFocusManager class is a subclass of FocusManager that provides support for accessing the components governed by the focus manager.

DefaultListCellRenderer

The DefaultListCellRenderer class extends JLabel and implements the ListCellRenderer and Serializable interfaces to provide a default rendering for a list cell.

DefaultListCellRenderer.UIResource

The DefaultListCellRenderer.UIResource class is an inner class of DefaultListCellRenderer that implements the UIResource interface.

DefaultListModel

The DefaultListModel class is a subclass of AbstractListModel that provides support for managing the addition and deletion of list elements.

DefaultListSelectionModel

The DefaultListSelectionModel class is a subclass of Object that provides a default implementation of the ListSelectionModel interface. It also implements the java.lang.Cloneable and java.io.Serializable interfaces.

DefaultSingleSelectionModel

The DefaultSingleSelectionModel class is a subclass of Object that provides a default implementation of the SingleSelectionModel interface. It also implements the java.io.Serializable interface.

FocusManager

The FocusManager class is a subclass of Object that is used to manage the current input focus.

GrayFilter

The GrayFilter class is a subclass of java.awt.image.RGBImageFilter that provides a grayscale rendering of an image.

ImageIcon

The ImageIcon class is a subclass of Object that provides a default implementation of the Icon interface. It also implements the java.io.Serializable interface.

JApplet

The JApplet class is a subclass of java.applet.Applet that provides Swing support. It implements the java.awt.accessibility.Accessible and RootPaneContainer interfaces.

JButton

The JButton class is a subclass of AbstractButton that provides a Swing pushbutton. It implements the java.awt.accessibility.Accessible interface.

JCheckBox

The JCheckBox class is a subclass of JToggleButton that provides a Swing check box. It implements the java.awt.accessibility.Accessible interface.

JCheckBoxMenuItem

The JCheckBoxMenuItem class is a subclass of JMenuItem that implements a check box that can be used as a menu item. It implements the SwingConstants and java.awt.accessibility.Accessible interfaces.

JColorChooser

The JColorChooser class extends JComponent and implements the Accessible interface. It enables users to select a color from a color selection panel.

JComboBox

The JComboBox class is a subclass of JComponent that provides a combo box GUI component. It implements the java.awt.ItemSelectable, java.awt.event.ActionListener, javax.swing.event.ListDataListener, and java.awt.accessibility.Accessible interfaces.

JComponent

The JComponent class is a subclass of java.awt.Container that is the base class for all Swing components. It implements the java.io.Serializable interface.

JDesktopPane

The JDesktopPane class is a subclass of JLayeredPane that supports the implementation of a desktop manager. It implements the java.awt.accessibility.Accessible interface.

JDialog

The JDialog class is a subclass of java.awt.Dialog that provides a Swing dialog box. It implements the RootPaneContainer, WindowConstants, and java.awt.accessibility.Accessible interface.

JEditorPane

The JEditorPane class is a subclass of JTextComponent that supports text editing.

JFileChooser

The JFileChooser class extends JComponent and implements the Accessible interface. It allows a user to select a file from a file chooser panel.

JFrame

The JFrame class is a subclass of java.awt.Frame that adds Swing support. It implements the RootPaneContainer, WindowConstants, and java.awt.accessibility.Accessible interfaces.

JInternalFrame

The JInternalFrame class is a subclass of JComponent that provides a frame that can be used within a JDesktopPane object. It implements the RootPaneContainer, WindowConstants, java.awt.accessibility.Accessible,

D

java.awt.event.ComponentListener, java.awt.event.MouseListener, and java.awt.event.MouseMotionListener interfaces.

JInternalFrame.JDesktopIcon

The JInternalFrame.JDesktopIcon class is an inner class of JInternalFrame that provides an icon for use with the JInternalFrame object. It is a subclass of JComponent and implements the java.awt.accessibility.Accessible interface.

JLabel

The JLabel class is a subclass of JComponent that provides a Swing label (text or image). It implements the SwingConstants and java.awt.accessibility.Accessible interfaces.

JLayeredPane

The JLayeredPane class is a subclass of JComponent that provides a multilayer pane. It implements the java.awt.accessibility.Accessible interface.

JList

The JList class is a subclass of JComponent that provides a basic list component. It implements the Scrollable and java.awt.accessibility.Accessible interfaces.

JMenu

The JMenu class is a subclass of JMenuItem that provides a Swing menu. It implements the MenuElement and java.awt.accessibility.Accessible interfaces.

JMenuBar

The JMenuBar class is a subclass of JComponent that provides a Swing menu bar. It implements the MenuElement and java.awt.accessibility.Accessible interfaces.

JMenuItem

The JMenuItem class is a subclass of AbstractButton that provides a Swing menu item. It implements the MenuElement and java.awt.accessibility.Accessible interfaces.

JOptionPane

The JOptionPane class is a subclass of JComponent that provides support for option dialog boxes.

JPanel

The JPanel class is a subclass of JComponent that provides a generic Swing panel. It implements the java.awt.accessibility.Accessible interface.

JPasswordField

The JPasswordField class is a subclass of JTextField that provides the capability to enter a password without it being displayed.

JPopupMenu

The JPopupMenu class is a subclass of JComponent that provides a pop-up menu capability. It implements the java.awt.accessibility.Accessible and MenuElement interfaces.

JPopupMenu.Separator

The JPopupMenu.Separator class is an inner class of JPopupMenu that provides accessibility support. It implements a menu separator.

JProgressBar

The JProgressBar class is a subclass of JComponent that provides a vertical or horizontal progress bar. It implements the SwingConstants and java.awt.accessibility.Accessible interfaces.

JRadioButton

The JRadioButton class is a subclass of JToggleButton that provides a basic radio button. It implements the java.awt.accessibility.Accessible interface.

JRadioButtonMenuItem

The JRadioButtonMenuItem class is a subclass of JMenuItemu that can be used as a menu item. It implements the java.awt.accessibility.Accessible interface.

JRootPane

The JRootPane class is a subclass of JComponent that provides the root pane for window container operations. It implements the java.awt.accessibility.Accessible interface.

JScrollBar

The JScrollBar class is a subclass of JComponent that provides a basic scrollbar. It implements the java.awt.Adjustible and java.awt.accessibility.Accessible interfaces.

JScrollPane

The JScrollPane class is a subclass of JComponent that provides a scrollable panel. It implements the ScrollPaneConstants and java.awt.accessibility.Accessible interfaces.

D

JSeparator

The JSeparator class is a subclass of JComponent that provides a menu separator. It implements the java.awt.accessibility.Accessible interface.

JSlider

The JSlider class is a subclass of JComponent that provides a slider control. It implements the SwingConstants and java.awt.accessibility.Accessible interfaces.

JSplitPane

The JSplitPane class is a subclass of JComponent that is used to split exactly two components. It implements the java.awt.accessibility.Accessible interface.

JTabbedPane

The JTabbedPane class is a subclass of JComponent that provides a tabbed multilayer pane. It implements the SwingConstants, java.io.Serializable, and java.awt.accessibility.Accessible interfaces.

JTable

The JTable class is a subclass of JComponent that provides a basic table implementation. It implements the Scrollable, java.awt.accessibility.Accessible, javax.swing.event.TableModelListener, javax.swing.event.TableColumnModelListener, javax.swing.event.ListSelectionListener, and javax.swing.event.CellEditorListener interfaces.

JTextArea

The JTextArea class is a subclass of JTextComponent that provides a Swing text area component.

JTextField

The JTextField class is a subclass of JTextComponent that provides a Swing text field. It implements the SwingConstants interface.

JTextPane

The JTextPane class is a subclass of JEditorPane that supports styled text.

JToggleButton

The JToggleButton class is a subclass of AbstractButton that supports a two-state button. It implements the java.awt.accessibility.Accessible interface.

JToggleButton.ToggleButtonModel

The `JToggleButton.ToggleButtonModel` class is an inner class of `JToggleButton` that supports button configuration. It is a subclass of `DefaultButtonModel`.

JToolBar

The `JToolBar` class is a subclass of `JComponent` that provides a basic toolbar. It implements the `java.awt.accessibility.Accessible` interface.

JToolBar.Separator

The `JToolBar.Separator` class is an inner class of `JToolBar` that acts as a toolbar separator. It is a subclass of `java.awt.Component`.

JToolTip

The `JToolTip` class is a subclass of `JComponent` that provides a pop-up ToolTip. It implements the `java.awt.accessibility.Accessible` interface.

JTree

The `JTree` class is a subclass of `JComponent` that provides a basic tree component. It implements the `Scrollable` and `java.awt.accessibility.Accessible` interfaces.

JTree.DynamicUtilTreeNode

The `JTree.DynamicUtilTreeNode` class is an inner class of `JTree` that supports dynamic tree node management. It is a subclass of `DefaultMutableTreeNode`.

JTree.EmptySelectionModel

The `JTree.EmptySelectionModel` class is an inner class of `JTree` that supports tree selection. It is a subclass of `DefaultTreeSelectionModel`.

JViewport

The `JViewport` class is a subclass of `JComponent` that acts as a porthole for viewing displayed information. It implements the `java.awt.accessibility.Accessible` interface.

JWindow

The `JWindow` class is a subclass of `java.awt.Window` that provides Swing support. It implements the `RootPaneContainer` and `java.awt.accessibility.Accessible` interfaces.

KeyStroke

The `KeyStroke` class is a subclass of `Object` that implements a user-typed keystroke. It implements the `java.io.Serializable` interface.

LookAndFeel

The LookAndFeel class is a subclass of Object that supports pluggable look and feel.

MenuSelectionManager

The MenuSelectionManager class is a subclass of Object that supports the management of menu selections.

OverlayLayout

The OverlayLayout class is a subclass of Object that supports overlay-type container layout. It implements the java.awt.LayoutManager2 and java.io.Serializable interfaces.

ProgressMonitor

The ProgressMonitor class is a subclass of Object that supports the monitoring of an operation in progress.

ProgressMonitorInputStream

The ProgressMonitorInputStream class is a subclass of java.io.FilterInputStream that supports the monitoring of data that is read from an input stream.

RepaintManager

The RepaintManager class is a subclass of Object that supports the repainting of JComponent objects.

ScrollPaneLayout

The ScrollPaneLayout class is a subclass of Object that is used to lay out a JScrollPane object. It implements the ScrollPaneConstants, java.awt.LayoutManager, and java.io.Serializable interfaces.

ScrollPaneLayout.UIResource

The ScrollPaneLayout.UIResource class is an inner class of ScrollPaneLayout that provides access to a UIResource.

SizeRequirements

The SizeRequirements class is a subclass of Object that provides information used by layout managers. It implements the java.io.Serializable interface.

SwingUtilities

The SwingUtilities class is a subclass of Object that provides general static methods that are used by Swing components. It implements the SwingConstants interface.

Timer

The Timer class is a subclass of Object that provides a timer/event generator. It implements the java.io.Serializable interface.

ToolTipManager

The ToolTipManager class is a subclass of java.awt.event.MouseAdapter that is used to provide ToolTip support. It implements the java.awt.event.MouseMotionListener interface.

UIDefaults

The UIDefaults class is a subclass of java.util.Hashtable that supports the storage of user interface parameter information.

UIManager

The UIManager class is a subclass of Object that supports look and feel management. It implements the java.io.Serializable interface.

UIManager.LookAndFeelInfo

The UIManager.LookAndFeelInfo class is an inner class of UIManager that supports the storage of look and feel information. It is a subclass of Object.

ViewportLayout

The ViewportLayout class is a subclass of Object that supports the layout of JViewport objects. It implements the java.awt.LayoutManager and java.io.Serializable interfaces.

Exceptions and Errors

UnsupportedLookAndFeelException

The UnsupportedLookAndFeelException class is a subclass of java.lang.Exception that signals that an unsupported look and feel has been selected.

Package javax.swing.border

The javax.swing.border package provides nine classes and one interface that implement borders and border styles.

Interfaces

Border

The Border interface provides methods for rendering a border around a Swing component.

Classes

AbstractBorder

The AbstractBorder class is a subclass of Object that provides an abstract base class used to implement other javax.swing.border classes. It implements the Border and java.io.Serializable interfaces.

BevelBorder

The BevelBorder class is a subclass of AbstractBorder that implements a two-line bevel border.

CompoundBorder

The CompoundBorder class is a subclass of AbstractBorder that combines two Border objects into a single border.

EmptyBorder

The EmptyBorder class is a subclass of AbstractBorder that implements an empty, spaceless border. It implements the java.io.Serializable interface.

EtchedBorder

The EtchedBorder class is a subclass of AbstractBorder that implements an etched border. The border can be etched either in or out.

LineBorder

The LineBorder class is a subclass of AbstractBorder that draws a line border around an object. The line thickness and color of the border may be specified.

MatteBorder

The MatteBorder class is a subclass of EmptyBorder that implements a matte-like border. The border can consist of a specified color or a javax.swing.Icon object.

SoftBevelBorder

The SoftBevelBorder class is a subclass of BevelBorder that implements a bevel border with softened (rounded) corners. The beveling may be raised or lowered.

TitledBorder

The TitledBorder class is a subclass of AbstractBorder that specifies a text tile at a specified position on the border.

Exceptions and Errors

None.

Package `javax.swing.colorchooser`

The `javax.swing.colorchooser` package provides three classes and one interface that support color selection.

Interfaces

ColorSelectionModel

The `ColorSelectionModel` interface defines methods that support the selection of colors.

Classes

AbstractColorChooserPanel

The `AbstractColorChooserPanel` class extends `JPanel` to provide an abstract class for the implementation of color choosers.

ColorChooserComponentFactory

The `ColorChooserComponentFactory` class extends `Object` to provide a factory for the generation of components used in color choosers.

DefaultColorSelectionModel

The `DefaultColorSelectionModel` class extends `Object` and implements the `ColorSelectionModel` and `Serializable` interfaces. It provides a base class for the implementation of color selection models.

Exceptions and Errors

None.

Package `javax.swing.event`

The `javax.swing.event` package provides 23 classes and 23 interfaces that implement Swing events and event listeners.

Interfaces

AncestorListener

The `AncestorListener` interface extends the `java.util.EventListener` interface to support handling of the `AncestorEvent`.

CaretListener

The `CaretListener` interface extends the `java.util.EventListener` interface to support handling of the `CaretEvent`.

CellEditorListener

The CellEditorListener interface extends the java.util.EventListener interface to support table cell editing by the handling of the ChangeEvent.

ChangeListener

The ChangeListener interface extends the java.util.EventListener interface to support general handling of the ChangeEvent.

DocumentEvent

The DocumentEvent interface provides methods for handling document change notifications.

DocumentEvent.ElementChange

The DocumentEvent.ElementChange interface provides methods for handling changes made to a document element.

DocumentListener

The DocumentListener interface extends the java.util.EventListener interface to support handling of the DocumentEvent.

HyperlinkListener

The HyperlinkListener interface extends the java.util.EventListener interface to support handling of the HyperlinkEvent.

InternalFrameListener

The InternalFrameListener interface extends the java.util.EventListener interface to support handling of the InternalFrameEvent.

ListDataListener

The Listener interface extends the java.util.EventListener interface to support handling of the ListDataEvent.

ListSelectionListener

The ListSelectionListener interface extends the java.util.EventListener interface to support handling of the ListSelectionEvent.

MenuDragMouseListener

The MenuDragMouseListener interface extends EventListener to provide support for the MenuDragMouseEvent.

MenuKeyListener

The MenuKeyListener interface extends EventListener to provide support for the MenuKeyEvent.

MenuListener

The MenuListener interface extends the java.util.EventListener interface to support handling of the MenuEvent.

MouseInputListener

The MouseInputListener interface extends MouseListener and MouseMotionListener to support a combined mouse event handler.

PopupMenuListener

The PopupMenuListener interface extends the java.util.EventListener interface to support handling of the PopupMenuEvent.

TableColumnModelListener

The TableColumnModelListener interface extends the java.util.EventListener interface to support handling of the TableColumnModelEvent.

TableModelListener

The TableModelListener interface extends the java.util.EventListener interface to support handling of the TableModelEvent.

TreeExpansionListener

The TreeExpansionListener interface extends the java.util.EventListener interface to support handling of the TreeExpansionEvent.

TreeModelListener

The TreeModelListener interface extends the java.util.EventListener interface to support handling of the TreeModelEvent.

TreeSelectionListener

The TreeSelectionListener interface extends the java.util.EventListener interface to support handling of the TreeSelectionEvent.

TreeWillExpandListener

The TreeWillExpandListener interface extends the java.util.EventListener interface to support handling of the TreeExpansionEvent.

D

UndoableEditListener

The UndoableEditListener interface extends the java.util.EventListener interface to support handling of the UndoableEditEvent.

Classes

AncestorEvent

The AncestorEvent class is a subclass of java.AWT.AWTEvent that indicates changes in a component's ancestor.

CaretEvent

The CaretEvent class is a subclass of java.util.EventObject that indicates a change in the text caret.

ChangeEvent

The ChangeEvent class is a subclass of java.util.EventObject that indicates a change in the state of a component.

DocumentEvent.EventType

The DocumentEvent.EventType class is a subclass of Object that is used to enumerate the types of document events.

EventListenerList

The EventListenerList class is a subclass of Object that provides a list of EventListener objects. It implements the java.io.Serializable interface.

HyperlinkEvent

The HyperlinkEvent class is a subclass of java.util.EventObject that indicates an action with respect to a hypertext link.

HyperlinkEvent.EventType

The HyperlinkEvent.EventType class is an inner class of HyperlinkEvent that enumerates the types of hyperlink events.

InternalFrameAdapter

The InternalFrameAdapter class is a subclass of Object that provides a default implementation of the InternalFrameListener interface.

InternalFrameEvent

The InternalFrameEvent class is a subclass of java.awt.AWTEvent that provides events related to javax.swing.JInternalFrame objects.

ListDataEvent

The ListDataEvent class is a subclass of java.util.EventObject that identifies changes in list-type components.

ListSelectionEvent

The ListSelectionEvent class is a subclass of java.util.EventObject that identifies changes in the current list selection.

MenuDragMouseEvent

The MenuDragMouseEvent class extends MouseEvent to provide support for menu-related drag-and-drop operations.

MenuEvent

The MenuEvent class is a subclass of java.util.EventObject that is used to signal menu-related events.

MenuKeyEvent

The MenuKeyEvent class is a subclass of KeyEvent that supports menu-related key actions.

MouseInputAdapter

The MouseInputAdapter class is a subclass of Object that provides a default implementation of the MouseInputListener interface.

PopupMenuEvent

The PopupMenuEvent class is a subclass of java.util.EventObject that is used to signal pop-up menu-related events.

SwingPropertyChangeSupport

The SwingPropertyChangeSupport class extends java.beans.PropertyChangeSupport to provide Swing support.

TableColumnModelEvent

The TableColumnModelEvent class is a subclass of java.util.EventObject that is used to identify changes in a table column model.

TableModelEvent

The TableModelEvent class is a subclass of java.util.EventObject that is used to identify changes in a table model.

D

TreeExpansionEvent

The TreeExpansionEvent class is a subclass of java.util.EventObject that indicates that a tree has been expanded.

TreeModelEvent

The TreeModelEvent class is a subclass of java.util.EventObject that is used to signal a change in a tree model.

TreeSelectionEvent

The TreeSelectionEvent class is a subclass of java.util.EventObject that is used to signal a change in the current tree selection. It implements the java.lang.Cloneable interface.

UndoableEditEvent

The UndoableEditEvent class is a subclass of java.util.EventObject indicating that an operation that can be undone has been performed.

Exceptions and Errors

None.

Package javax.swing.filechooser

The javax.swing.filechooser package provides three classes that support basic file system operations.

Interfaces

None.

Classes

FileFilter

The FileFilter class extends Object to provide an abstract class for file filtering operations.

FileSystemView

The FileSystemView class extends Object to provide a default file system view.

FileView

The FileView class extends Object to provide a default information about a file.

Exceptions and Errors

None.

Package `javax.swing.plaf`

The `javax.swing.plaf` package provides 42 classes and one interface that support pluggable look and feel.

Interfaces

UIResource

The `UIResource` interface is used to identify an object as supporting pluggable look and feel.

Classes

BorderUIResource

The `BorderUIResource` class extends `Object` and implements the `Border`, `UIResource`, and `Serializable` interfaces to define a `UIResource` for `Border` objects.

BorderUIResource.BevelBorderUIResource

The `BorderUIResource.BevelBorderUIResource` class extends `BevelBorder` and implements `UIResource` to support pluggable look and feel.

BorderUIResource.CompoundBorderUIResource

The `BorderUIResource.CompoundBorderUIResource` class extends `CompoundBorder` and implements `UIResource` to support pluggable look and feel.

BorderUIResource.EmptyBorderUIResource

The `BorderUIResource.EmptyBorderUIResource` class extends `EmptyBorder` and implements `UIResource` to support pluggable look and feel.

BorderUIResource.EtchedBorderUIResource

The `BorderUIResource.EtchedBorderUIResource` class extends `EtchedBorder` and implements `UIResource` to support pluggable look and feel.

BorderUIResource.LineBorderUIResource

The `BorderUIResource.LineBorderUIResource` class extends `LineBorder` and implements `UIResource` to support pluggable look and feel.

D

BorderUIResource.MatteBorderUIResource

The BorderUIResource.MatteBorderUIResource class extends MatteBorder and implements UIResource to support pluggable look and feel.

BorderUIResource.TitledBorderUIResource

The BorderUIResource.TitledBorderUIResource class extends TitledBorder and implements UIResource to support pluggable look and feel.

ButtonUI

The ButtonUI class extends ComponentUI to support pluggable look and feel for JButtonUI objects.

ColorChooserUI

The ColorChooserUI class extends ComponentUI to support pluggable look and feel for JColorChooser objects.

ColorUIResource

The ColorUIResource class extends Color and implements UIResource to support pluggable look and feel for Color objects.

ComboBoxUI

The ComboBoxUI class extends ComponentUI to support pluggable look and feel for JComboBoxUI objects.

ComponentUI

The ComponentUI class extends Object to support pluggable look and feel for Swing component objects.

DesktopIconUI

The DesktopIconUI class extends ComponentUI to support pluggable look and feel for JDesktopIcon objects.

DesktopPaneUI

The DesktopPaneUI class extends ComponentUI to support pluggable look and feel for JDesktopPane objects.

DimensionUIResource

The DimensionUIResource class extends Dimension and implements UIResource to support pluggable look and feel for Dimension objects.

FileChooserUI

The FileChooserUI class extends ComponentUI to support pluggable look and feel for JFileChooser objects.

FontUIResource

The FontUIResource class extends Font and implements UIResource to support pluggable look and feel for Font objects.

IconUIResource

The IconUIResource class extends Object and implements UIResource, Icon and Serializable to support pluggable look and feel for Icon objects.

InsetsUIResource

The InsetsUIResource class extends Insets and implements UIResource to support pluggable look and feel for Insets objects.

InternalFrameUI

The InternalFrameUI class extends ComponentUI to support pluggable look and feel for JInternalFrame objects.

LabelUI

The LabelUI class extends ComponentUI to support pluggable look and feel for JLabel objects.

ListUI

The ListUI class extends ComponentUI to support pluggable look and feel for JList objects.

MenuBarUI

The MenuBarUI class extends ComponentUI to support pluggable look and feel for JMenuBar objects.

MenuItemUI

The MenuItemUI class extends ButtonUI to support pluggable look and feel for JMenuItem objects.

OptionPaneUI

The OptionPaneUI class extends ComponentUI to support pluggable look and feel for JOptionPane objects.

PanelUI

The PanelUI class extends ComponentUI to support pluggable look and feel for JPanel objects.

PopupMenuUI

The PopupMenuUI class extends ComponentUI to support pluggable look and feel for JPopupMenu objects.

ProgressBarUI

The ProgressBarUI class extends ComponentUI to support pluggable look and feel for JProgressBar objects.

ScrollBarUI

The ScrollBarUI class extends ComponentUI to support pluggable look and feel for JScrollBar objects.

ScrollPaneUI

The ScrollPaneUI class extends ComponentUI to support pluggable look and feel for JScrollPane objects.

SeparatorUI

The SeparatorUI class extends ComponentUI to support pluggable look and feel for JSeparator objects.

SliderUI

The SliderUI class extends ComponentUI to support pluggable look and feel for JSlider objects.

SplitPaneUI

The SplitPaneUI class extends ComponentUI to support pluggable look and feel for JSplitPane objects.

TabbedPaneUI

The TabbedPaneUI class extends ComponentUI to support pluggable look and feel for JTabbedPane objects.

TableHeaderUI

The TableHeaderUI class extends ComponentUI to support pluggable look and feel for JTableHeader objects.

TableUI

The TableUI class extends ComponentUI to support pluggable look and feel for JTable objects.

TextUI

The TextUI class extends ComponentUI to support pluggable look and feel for JText objects.

ToolBarUI

The ToolBarUI class extends ComponentUI to support pluggable look and feel for JToolBar objects.

ToolTipUI

The ToolTipUI class extends ComponentUI to support pluggable look and feel for JToolTip objects.

TreeUI

The TreeUI class extends ComponentUI to support pluggable look and feel for JTree objects.

ViewportUI

The ViewportUI class extends ComponentUI to support pluggable look and feel for JViewport objects.

Exceptions and Errors

None.

Package javax.swing.plaf.basic

The javax.swing.plaf.basic package provides 65 classes and one interface that support the basic look and feel.

Interfaces

ComboPopup

The ComboPopup interface defines methods required to implement a BasicComboBoxUI.

Classes

BasicArrowButton

The BasicArrowButton class extends JButton and implements the SwingConstants interface to support an arrow button with the basic look and feel.

BasicBorders

The BasicBorders class extends Object to provide a border factory for the basic look and feel.

BasicBorders.ButtonBorder

The BasicBorders.ButtonBorder class extends AbstractBorder and implements UIResource to provide a button border with the basic look and feel.

BasicBorders.FieldBorder

The BasicBorders.FieldBorder class extends AbstractBorder and implements UIResource to provide a field border with the basic look and feel.

BasicBorders.MarginBorder

The BasicBorders.MarginBorder class extends AbstractBorder and implements UIResource to provide a margin border with the basic look and feel.

BasicBorders.MenuBarBorder

The BasicBorders.MenuBarBorder class extends AbstractBorder and implements UIResource to provide a menu bar border with the basic look and feel.

BasicBorders.RadioButtonBorder

The BasicBorders.RadioButtonBorder class extends BasicBorders.ButtonBorder to provide a border with the basic look and feel.

BasicBorders.SplitPaneBorder

The BasicBorders.SplitPaneBorder class extends Object and implements the Border and UIResource interfaces to provide a split pane border with the basic look and feel.

BasicBorders.ToggleButtonBorder

The BasicBorders.ToggleButtonBorder class extends BasicBorders.ButtonBorder to provide a border with the basic look and feel.

BasicButtonListener

The BasicButtonListener class extends Object and implements the MouseListener, MouseMotionListener, FocusListener, ChangeListener, and PropertyChangeListener interfaces to handle button-related events for the basic look and feel.

BasicButtonUI

The BasicButtonUI class extends ButtonUI to support the basic look and feel.

BasicCheckBoxMenuItemUI

The BasicCheckBoxMenuItemUI class extends BasicMenuItemUI to support the basic look and feel for check box menu items.

BasicCheckBoxUI

The BasicCheckBoxUI class extends BasicRadioButtonUI to support the basic look and feel for check boxes.

BasicColorChooserUI

The BasicColorChooserUI class extends ColorChooserUI to support the basic look and feel.

BasicComboBoxEditor

The BasicComboBoxEditor class extends Object and implements the ComboBoxEditor and FocusListener interfaces to provide a default editor for editable combo boxes.

BasicComboBoxEditor.UIResource

The BasicComboBoxEditor.UIResource class extends BasicComboBoxEditor and implements UIResource to provide a UIResource for the BasicComboBoxEditor class.

BasicComboBoxRenderer

The BasicComboBoxRenderer class extends JLabel and implements the ListCellRenderer and Serializable interfaces to support the rendering of combo boxes with the basic look and feel.

BasicComboBoxRenderer.UIResource

The BasicComboBoxRenderer.UIResource class extends BasicComboBoxRenderer and implements UIResource to provide a UIResource for the BasicComboBoxRenderer class.

BasicComboBoxUI

The BasicComboBoxUI class extends ComboBoxUI to support the basic look and feel.

D

BasicComboPopup

The BasicComboPopup class extends JPopupMenu and implements ComboPopup to provide a combo pop-up component for the basic look and feel.

BasicDesktopIconUI

The BasicDesktopIconUI class extends DesktopIconUI to support the basic look and feel.

BasicDesktopPaneUI

The BasicDesktopPaneUI class extends DesktopPaneUI to support the basic look and feel.

BasicDirectoryModel

The BasicDirectoryModel class extends AbstractListModel and implements the PropertyChangeListener interface to implement a file list with the basic look and feel.

BasicEditorPaneUI

The BasicEditorPaneUI class extends BasicTextUI to support the basic look and feel.

BasicFileChooserUI

The BasicFileChooserUI class extends FileChooserUI to support the basic look and feel.

BasicGraphicsUtils

The BasicGraphicsUtils class extends Object to provide graphic utilities used with the basic look and feel.

BasicIconFactory

The BasicIconFactory class extends Object and implements Serializable to provide a factory for the creation of icons with the basic look and feel.

BasicInternalFrameTitlePane

The BasicInternalFrameTitlePane class extends JComponent to provide a basic look-and-feel implementation of a title bar.

BasicInternalFrameUI

The BasicInternalFrameUI class extends InternalFrameUI to support the basic look and feel.

BasicLabelUI

The BasicLabelUI class extends LabelUI and implements the PropertyChangeListener interface to support the basic look and feel.

BasicListUI

The BasicListUI class extends ListUI to support the basic look and feel.

BasicLookAndFeel

The BasicLookAndFeel class extends Object and implements Serializable to provide the basic look-and-feel specification.

BasicMenuBarUI

The BasicMenuBarUI class extends MenuBarUI to support the basic look and feel.

BasicMenuItemUI

The BasicMenuItemUI class extends MenuItemUI to support the basic look and feel.

BasicMenuUI

The BasicMenuUI class extends BasicMenuItemUI to support the basic look and feel for menus.

BasicOptionPaneUI

The BasicOptionPaneUI class extends OptionPaneUI to support the basic look and feel.

BasicOptionPaneUI.ButtonAreaLayout

The BasicOptionPaneUI.ButtonAreaLayout class extends Object and implements LayoutManager to support the layout of option panes with the basic look and feel.

BasicPanelUI

The BasicPanelUI class extends PanelUI to support the basic look and feel.

BasicPasswordFieldUI

The BasicPasswordFieldUI class extends BasicTextFieldUI to support the basic look and feel for password fields.

BasicPopupMenuSeparatorUI

The BasicPopupMenuSeparatorUI class extends BasicSeparatorUI to support the basic look and feel for menu separators.

D

BasicPopupMenuUI

The BasicPopupMenuUI class extends PopupMenuUI to support the basic look and feel.

BasicProgressBarUI

The BasicProgressBarUI class extends ProgressBarUI to support the basic look and feel.

BasicRadioButtonMenuItemUI

The BasicRadioButtonMenuItemUI class extends BasicMenuItemUI to support the basic look and feel for radio button menu items.

BasicRadioButtonUI

The BasicRadioButtonUI class extends BasicToggleButtonUI to support the basic look and feel for radio buttons.

BasicScrollBarUI

The BasicScrollBarUI class extends ScrollBarUI and implements the LayoutManager and SwingConstants interfaces to support the basic look and feel.

BasicScrollPaneUI

The BasicScrollPaneUI class extends ScrollPaneUI and implements the ScrollPaneConstants interface to support the basic look and feel.

BasicSeparatorUI

The BasicSeparatorUI class extends SeparatorUI to support the basic look and feel.

BasicSliderUI

The BasicSliderUI class extends SliderUI to support the basic look and feel.

BasicSplitPaneDivider

The BasicSplitPaneDivider class extends Container and implements PropertyChangeListener to provide a divider used by BasicSplitPaneUI.

BasicSplitPaneUI

The BasicSplitPaneUI class extends SplitPaneUI to support the basic look and feel.

BasicTabbedPaneUI

The BasicTabbedPaneUI class extends TabbedPaneUI and implements the SwingConstants interface to support the basic look and feel.

BasicTableHeaderUI

The BasicTableHeaderUI class extends TableHeaderUI to support the basic look and feel.

BasicTableUI

The BasicTableUI class extends TableUI to support the basic look and feel.

BasicTextAreaUI

The BasicTextAreaUI class extends BasicTextUI to support the basic look and feel.

BasicTextFieldUI

The BasicTextFieldUI class extends BasicTextUI to support the basic look and feel.

BasicTextPaneUI

The BasicTextPaneUI class extends BasicEditorPaneUI to support the basic look and feel.

BasicTextUI

The BasicTextUI class extends TextUI and implements the ViewFactory interface to support the basic look and feel.

BasicTextUI.BasicCaret

The BasicTextUI.BasicCaret class extends DefaultCaret and implements UIResource to provide a text caret with the basic look and feel.

BasicTextUI.BasicHighlighter

The BasicTextUI.BasicHighlighter class extends DefaultHighlighter and implements UIResource to provide a text highlighter with the basic look and feel.

BasicToggleButtonUI

The BasicToggleButtonUI class extends BasicButtonUI to support the basic look and feel.

BasicToolBarSeparatorUI

The BasicToolBarSeparatorUI class extends BasicSeparatorUI to support the basic look and feel.

BasicToolBarUI

The BasicToolBarUI class extends ToolBarUI and implements SwingConstants to support the basic look and feel.

D

BasicToolTipUI

The BasicToolTipUI class extends ToolTipUI to support the basic look and feel.

BasicTreeUI

The BasicTreeUI class extends TreeUI to support the basic look and feel.

BasicViewportUI

The BasicViewportUI class extends ViewportUI to support the basic look and feel.

DefaultMenuLayout

The DefaultMenuLayout class extends BoxLayout and implements UIResource to provide a menu layout manager with the basic look and feel.

Exceptions and Errors

None.

Package javax.swing.plaf.metal

The javax.swing.plaf.metal package provides 47 classes that support the Metal look and feel.

Interfaces

None.

Classes

DefaultMetalTheme

The DefaultMetalTheme class extends the Object class to provide a default implementation of the Metal look and feel.

MetalBorders

The MetalBorders class extends the Object class to provide a border with the Metal look and feel.

MetalBorders.ButtonBorder

The MetalBorders.ButtonBorder class extends the AbstractBorder class and implements the UIResource interface to create a border class with the Metal look and feel.

MetalBorders.Flush3DBorder

The MetalBorders.Flush3DBorder class extends the AbstractBorder class and implements the UIResource interface to create a border class with the Metal look and feel.

MetalBorders.InternalFrameBorder

The `MetalBorders.InternalFrameBorder` class extends the `AbstractBorder` class and implements the `UIResource` interface to create a border class with the Metal look and feel.

MetalBorders.MenuBarBorder

The `MetalBorders.MenuBarBorder` class extends the `AbstractBorder` class and implements the `UIResource` interface to create a border class with the Metal look and feel.

MetalBorders.MenuItemBorder

The `MetalBorders.MenuItemBorder` class extends the `AbstractBorder` class and implements the `UIResource` interface to create a border class with the Metal look and feel.

MetalBorders.PopupMenuBorder

The `MetalBorders.PopupMenuBorder` class extends the `AbstractBorder` class and implements the `UIResource` interface to create a border class with the Metal look and feel.

MetalBorders.RolloverButtonBorder

The `MetalBorders.RolloverButtonBorder` class extends the `AbstractBorder` class and implements the `UIResource` interface to create a border class with the Metal look and feel.

MetalBorders.ScrollPaneBorder

The `MetalBorders.ScrollPaneBorder` class extends the `AbstractBorder` class and implements the `UIResource` interface to create a border class with the Metal look and feel.

MetalBorders.TextFieldBorder

The `MetalBorders.TextFieldBorder` class extends the `AbstractBorder` class and implements the `UIResource` interface to create a border class with the Metal look and feel.

MetalBorders.ToolBarBorder

The `MetalBorders.ToolBarBorder` class extends the `AbstractBorder` class and implements the `UIResource` interface to create a border class with the Metal look and feel.

MetalButtonUI

The `MetalButtonUI` class extends the `BasicButtonUI` class with the Metal look and feel.

MetalCheckBoxIcon

The MetalCheckBoxIcon class extends the Object class and implements the Icon, UIResource, and Serializable interfaces to create a check box icon with the Metal look and feel.

MetalCheckBoxUI

The MetalCheckBoxUI class extends the MetalRadioButtonUI class to create a metal check box.

MetalComboBoxButton

The MetalComboBoxButton class extends the JButton class with the Metal look and feel.

MetalComboBoxEditor

The MetalComboBoxEditor class extends the BasicComboBoxEditor class with the Metal look and feel.

MetalComboBoxEditor.UIResource

The MetalComboBoxEditor.UIResource class is an inner class of the MetalComboBoxEditor class that implements the UIResource interface to provide a UIResource for the MetalComboBoxEditor class.

MetalComboBoxIcon

The MetalComboBoxIcon class extends the Object class and implements the Icon and Serializable interfaces to create a combo box icon with the Metal look and feel.

MetalComboBoxUI

The MetalComboBoxUI class extends the BasicComboBoxUI class with the Metal look and feel.

MetalDesktopIconUI

The MetalDesktopIconUI class extends the BasicDesktopIconUI class with the Metal look and feel.

MetalFileChooserUI

The MetalFileChooserUI class extends the BasicFileChooserUI class with the Metal look and feel.

MetalIconFactory

The MetalIconFactory class extends the Object class and implements the Serializable interface to create an icon factory with the Metal look and feel.

MetalIconFactory.FileIcon16

The `MetalIconFactory.FileIcon16` class extends the `Object` class and implements the `Icon` and `Serializable` interfaces to provide a file icon with the Metal look and feel.

MetalIconFactory.FolderIcon16

The `MetalIconFactory.FolderIcon16` class extends the `Object` class and implements the `Icon` and `Serializable` interfaces to provide a folder icon with the Metal look and feel.

MetalIconFactory.TreeControlIcon

The `MetalIconFactory.TreeControlIcon` class extends the `Object` class and implements the `Icon` and `Serializable` interfaces to provide a tree control icon with the Metal look and feel.

MetalIconFactory.TreeFolderIcon

The `MetalIconFactory.TreeFolderIcon` class extends the `MetalIconFactory.FolderIcon16` class to create a tree folder icon with the Metal look and feel.

MetalIconFactory.TreeLeafIcon

The `MetalIconFactory.TreeLeafIcon` class extends the `MetalIconFactory.FileIcon16` class to create a tree file icon with the Metal look and feel.

MetalInternalFrameUI

The `MetalInternalFrameUI` class extends the `BasicInternalFrameUI` class with the Metal look and feel.

MetalLabelUI

The `MetalLabelUI` class extends the `BasicLabelUI` class with the Metal look and feel.

MetalLookAndFeel

The `MetalLookAndFeel` class extends the `BasicLookAndFeel` class with the Metal look and feel.

MetalPopupMenuSeparatorUI

The `MetalPopupMenuSeparatorUI` class extends the `MenuSeparatorUI` class to create a pop-up menu separator with the Metal look and feel.

MetalProgressBarUI

The `MetalProgressBarUI` class extends the `BasicProgressBarUI` class with the Metal look and feel.

D

MetalRadioButtonUI

The `MetalRadioButtonUI` class extends the `BasicRadioButtonUI` class with the Metal look and feel.

MetalScrollBarUI

The `MetalScrollBarUI` class extends the `BasicScrollBarUI` class with the Metal look and feel.

MetalScrollButton

The `MetalScrollButton` class extends the `BasicArrowButton` class with the Metal look and feel.

MetalScrollPaneUI

The `MetalScrollPaneUI` class extends the `BasicScrollPaneUI` class with the Metal look and feel.

MetalSeparatorUI

The `MetalSeparatorUI` class extends the `BasicSeparatorUI` class with the Metal look and feel.

MetalSliderUI

The `MetalSliderUI` class extends the `BasicSliderUI` class with the Metal look and feel.

MetalSplitPaneUI

The `MetalSplitPaneUI` class extends the `BasicSplitPaneUI` class with the Metal look and feel.

MetalTabbedPaneUI

The `MetalTabbedPaneUI` class extends the `BasicTabbedPaneUI` class with the Metal look and feel.

MetalTextFieldUI

The `MetalTextFieldUI` class extends the `BasicTextFieldUI` class with the Metal look and feel.

MetalTheme

The `MetalTheme` class extends the `Object` class to provide a general description of the Metal look and feel.

MetalToggleButtonUI

The MetalToggleButtonUI class extends the BasicToggleButtonUI class with the Metal look and feel.

MetalToolBarUI

The MetalToolBarUI class extends the BasicToolBarUI class with the Metal look and feel.

MetalToolTipUI

The MetalToolTipUI class extends the BasicToolTipUI class with the Metal look and feel.

MetalTreeUI

The MetalTreeUI class extends the BasicTreeUI class with the Metal look and feel.

Exceptions and Errors

None.

Package javax.swing.plaf.multi

The javax.swing.plaf.multi package provides 29 classes that support the multiplexing look and feel.

Interfaces

None.

Classes

MultiButtonUI

The MultiButtonUI class extends the ButtonUI class with the multiplexing look and feel.

MultiColorChooserUI

The MultiColorChooserUI class extends the ColorChooserUI class with the multiplexing look and feel.

MultiComboBoxUI

The MultiComboBoxUI class extends the ComboBoxUI class with the multiplexing look and feel.

MultiDesktopIconUI

The MultiDesktopIconUI class extends the DesktopIconUI class with the multiplexing look and feel.

MultiDesktopPaneUI

The MultiDesktopPaneUI class extends the DesktopPaneUI class with the multiplexing look and feel.

MultiFileChooserUI

The MultiFileChooserUI class extends the FileChooserUI class with the multiplexing look and feel.

MultiInternalFrameUI

The MultiInternalFrameUI class extends the InternalFrameUI class with the multiplexing look and feel.

MultiLabelUI

The MultiLabelUI class extends the LabelUI class with the multiplexing look and feel.

MultiListUI

The MultiListUI class extends the ListUI class with the multiplexing look and feel.

MultiLookAndFeel

The MultiLookAndFeel class extends the LookAndFeel class with the multiplexing look and feel.

MultiMenuBarUI

The MultiMenuBarUI class extends the MenuBarUI class with the multiplexing look and feel.

MultiMenuItemUI

The MultiMenuItemUI class extends the MenuItemUI class with the multiplexing look and feel.

MultiOptionPaneUI

The MultiOptionPaneUI class extends the OptionPaneUI class with the multiplexing look and feel.

MultiPanelUI

The MultiPanelUI class extends the PanelUI class with the multiplexing look and feel.

MultiPopupMenuUI

The `MultiPopupMenuUI` class extends the `PopupMenuUI` class with the multiplexing look and feel.

MultiProgressBarUI

The `MultiProgressBarUI` class extends the `ProgressBarUI` class with the multiplexing look and feel.

MultiScrollBarUI

The `MultiScrollBarUI` class extends the `ScrollBarUI` class with the multiplexing look and feel.

MultiScrollPaneUI

The `MultiScrollPaneUI` class extends the `ScrollPaneUI` class with the multiplexing look and feel.

MultiSeparatorUI

The `MultiSeparatorUI` class extends the `SeparatorUI` class with the multiplexing look and feel.

MultiSliderUI

The `MultiSliderUI` class extends the `SliderUI` class with the multiplexing look and feel.

MultiSplitPaneUI

The `MultiSplitPaneUI` class extends the `SplitPaneUI` class with the multiplexing look and feel.

MultiTabbedPaneUI

The `MultiTabbedPaneUI` class extends the `TabbedPaneUI` class with the multiplexing look and feel.

MultiTableHeaderUI

The `MultiTableHeaderUI` class extends the `TableHeaderUI` class with the multiplexing look and feel.

MultiTableUI

The `MultiTableUI` class extends the `TableUI` class with the multiplexing look and feel.

MultiTextUI

The `MultiTextUI` class extends the `TextUI` class with the multiplexing look and feel.

MultiToolBarUI

The MultiToolBarUI class extends the ToolBarUI class with the multiplexing look and feel.

MultiToolTipUI

The MultiToolTipUI class extends the ToolTipUI class with the multiplexing look and feel.

MultiTreeUI

The MultiTreeUI class extends the TreeUI class with the multiplexing look and feel.

MultiViewportUI

The MultiViewportUI class extends the ViewportUI class with the multiplexing look and feel.

Exceptions and Errors

None.

Package javax.swing.table

The javax.swing.table package provides seven classes and four interfaces that implement the Swing table component.

Interfaces

TableCellEditor

The TableCellEditor interface extends the javax.swing.CellEditor interface to provide support for the text editing of table cells.

TableCellRenderer

The TableCellRenderer interface defines methods for rendering the cells of JTable objects.

TableColumnModel

The TableColumnModel interface defines methods for manipulating the rows of a table.

TableModel

The TableModel interface defines methods that are implemented by a data model that provides data for a JTable object.

Classes

AbstractTableModel

The `AbstractTableModel` class is a subclass of `Object` that provides an abstract implementation of the `TableModel` interface. It also implements the `java.io.Serializable` interface.

DefaultTableCellRenderer

The `DefaultTableCellRenderer` class is a subclass of `javax.swing.JLabel` that is used to render the individual cells of a table. It implements the `TableCellRenderer` and `java.io.Serializable` interfaces.

DefaultTableCellRenderer.UIResource

The `DefaultTableCellRenderer.UIResource` class is an inner class of `DefaultTableCellRenderer` that provides support for cell rendering.

DefaultTableColumnModel

The `DefaultTableColumnModel` class is a subclass of `Object` that provides a default implementation to the `TableColumnModel` interface. It also implements the `java.beans.PropertyChangeListener`, `javax.swing.event.ListSelectionListener`, and `java.io.Serializable` interfaces.

DefaultTableModel

The `DefaultTableModel` class is a subclass of `AbstractTableModel` that organizes its data using `java.util.Vector` objects. It implements the `java.io.Serializable` interface.

JTableHeader

The `JTableHeader` class is a subclass of `javax.swing.JComponent` that encapsulates the column header of a `JTable` object. It implements the `TableColumnModelListener` and `java.awt.accessibility.Accessible` interfaces.

TableColumn

The `TableColumn` class is a subclass of `Object` that defines the properties of a column in a `JTable` object. It implements the `java.io.Serializable` interface.

Exceptions and Errors

None.

D

Package `javax.swing.text`

The `javax.swing.text` package provides 63 classes and 21 interfaces that implement text-processing components.

Interfaces

AbstractDocument.AttributeContext

The `AbstractDocument.AttributeContext` interface supports attribute compression.

AbstractDocument.Content

The `AbstractDocument.Content` interface describes a sequence of editable content.

AttributeSet

The `AttributeSet` interface defines a read-only set of text attributes.

AttributeSet.CharacterAttribute

The `AttributeSet.CharacterAttribute` interface defines an attribute type signature.

AttributeSet.ColorAttribute

The `AttributeSet.ColorAttribute` interface defines a color type signature.

AttributeSet.FontAttribute

The `AttributeSet.FontAttribute` interface defines a font type signature.

AttributeSet.ParagraphAttribute

The `AttributeSet.ParagraphAttribute` interface defines a paragraph type signature.

Caret

The `Caret` interface defines a document insertion point caret.

Document

The `Document` interface defines a container for editable text.

Element

The `Element` interface defines a structural piece of a `Document` object.

Highlighter

The `Highlighter` interface provides support for highlighted text.

Highlighter.Highlight

The `Highlighter.Highlight` interface defines the location of highlighted text.

Highlighter.HighlightPainter

The `Highlighter.HighlightPainter` interface defines the manner in which highlighted text is to be painted.

Keymap

The `Keymap` interface binds keystrokes to actions.

MutableAttributeSet

The `MutableAttributeSet` interface extends the `AttributeSet` interface to provide methods for updating the set of attributes.

Position

The `Position` interface defines a location within a `Document` object.

Style

The `Style` interface defines text, paragraph, and other document-related styles.

StyledDocument

The `StyledDocument` interface extends the `Document` interface to provide style support.

TabExpander

The `TabExpander` interface provides support for tab settings.

TabableView

The `TabableView` interface provides support for viewing expanded tabs within a document.

ViewFactory

The `ViewFactory` interface provides support for creating different views of a document.

Classes

AbstractDocument

The `AbstractDocument` class is a subclass of `Object` that provides a basic implementation of the `Document` interface. It also implements the `java.io.Serializable` interface.

AbstractDocument.ElementEdit

The `AbstractDocument.ElementEdit` class is an inner class of `AbstractDocument` that provides undo/redo support. It is a subclass of `javax.swing.undo.AbstractUndoableEdit`.

AbstractWriter

The AbstractWriter class is an subclass of Object that supports the display of text.

BoxView

The BoxView class is a subclass of CompositeView that provides a box-like organization of document content.

ComponentView

The ComponentView class is a subclass of View that provides a view of a single document component.

CompositeView

The CompositeView class is a subclass of View that provides a view of multiple document components.

DefaultCaret

The DefaultCaret class is a subclass of Object that provides a default implementation of the Caret interface. It also implements the java.awt.event.FocusListener, java.awt.event.MouseListener, java.awt.event.MouseMotionListener, and java.io.Serializable interfaces.

DefaultEditorKit

The DefaultEditorKit class is a subclass of EditorKit that provides a basic text editing capability.

DefaultEditorKit.BeepAction

The DefaultEditorKit.BeepAction class is an inner class of DefaultEditorKit that creates a beep sound. It is a subclass of Object.

DefaultEditorKit.CopyAction

The DefaultEditorKit.CopyAction class is an inner class of DefaultEditorKit that copies data to the clipboard. It is a subclass of Object.

DefaultEditorKit.CutAction

The DefaultEditorKit.CutAction class is an inner class of DefaultEditorKit that cuts data to the clipboard. It is a subclass of Object.

DefaultEditorKit.DefaultKeyTypedAction

The DefaultEditorKit.DefaultKeyTypedAction class is an inner class of DefaultEditorKit that handles key presses. It is a subclass of Object.

DefaultEditorKit.InsertBreakAction

The DefaultEditorKit.InsertBreakAction class is an inner class of DefaultEditorKit that inserts a line break into a document. It is a subclass of Object.

DefaultEditorKit.InsertContentAction

The DefaultEditorKit.InsertContentAction class is an inner class of DefaultEditorKit that inserts content into a document. It is a subclass of Object.

DefaultEditorKit.InsertTabAction

The DefaultEditorKit.InsertTabAction class is an inner class of DefaultEditorKit that inserts a tab into a document. It is a subclass of Object.

DefaultEditorKit.PasteAction

The DefaultEditorKit.PasteAction class is an inner class of DefaultEditorKit that pastes content into a document from the clipboard. It is a subclass of Object.

DefaultHighlighter

The DefaultHighlighter class is a subclass of Object that provides a default implementation of the Highlighter interface.

DefaultHighlighter.DefaultHighlightPainter

The DefaultHighlighter.DefaultHighlightPainter class is an inner class of DefaultHighlighter that implements the Highlighter.HighlightPainter interface. It is a subclass of Object.

D

DefaultStyledDocument

The DefaultStyledDocument class is a subclass of AbstractDocument and implements the StyledDocument interface.

DefaultStyledDocument.AttributeUndoableEdit

The DefaultStyledDocument.AttributeUndoableEdit class is an inner class of DefaultStyledDocument that supports undoable edit operations.

DefaultStyledDocument.ElementSpec

The DefaultStyledDocument.ElementSpec class is an inner class of DefaultStyledDocument that supports the building of document elements. It is a subclass of Object.

DefaultTextUI

The DefaultTextUI class is a subclass of javax.swing.plaf.TextUI that provides a default implementation of the ViewFactory interface. It also implements the java.io.Serializable interface.

EditorKit

The EditorKit class is a subclass of Object that provides a base class for developing a text editor. It implements the java.lang.Cloneable and java.io.Serializable interfaces.

ElementIterator

The ElementIterator class extends Object and implements the Cloneable interface. It is used to iterate through the elements of a document.

FieldView

The FieldView class is a subclass of PlainView that supports a single-line editing view.

GapContent

The GapContent class extends Object and implements the AbstractDocument.Content and Serializable interfaces to provide an encapsulation of a gap buffer.

IconView

The IconView class is a subclass of View that provides support for viewing an icon.

JTextComponent

The JTextComponent class is a subclass of javax.swing.JComponent that provides the base class for Swing text components. It implements the javax.swing.Scrollable and java.awt.accessibility.Accessible interfaces.

JTextComponent.KeyBinding

The JTextComponent.KeyBinding class is an inner class of JTextComponent that provides key binding support. It is a subclass of Object.

LabelView

The LabelView class is a subclass of View that implements the TabableView interface.

LabelView2D

The LabelView2D class extends View to provide the capability to render a 2D label.

LayeredHighlighter

The LayeredHighlighter class is a subclass of Object that implements the Highlighter interface.

LayeredHighlighter.LayerPainter

The LayeredHighlighter.LayerPainter class is an inner class of LayeredHighlighter that supports layered highlight rendering.

ParagraphView

The ParagraphView class is a subclass of BoxView that provides the capability to display styled paragraphs. It implements the TabExpander interface.

PasswordView

The PasswordView class is a subclass of FieldView that provides password-hiding support.

PlainDocument

The PlainDocument class is a subclass of AbstractDocument that supports one text font and color.

PlainView

The PlainView class is a subclass of View that supports the display of one font and one color. It implements the TabExpander interface.

Position.Bias

The Position.Bias class extends Object to provide the capability to specify a bias in a character position.

Segment

The Segment class is a subclass of Object that represents a text fragment.

SimpleAttributeSet

The SimpleAttributeSet class is a subclass of Object that provides a default implementation of the MutableAttributeSet interface. It also implements the java.io.Serializable interface.

StringContent

The StringContent class is a subclass of Object that provides a default implementation of the AbstractDocument.Content interface. It also implements the java.io.Serializable interface.

D

StyleConstants

The StyleConstants class is a subclass of Object that provides constants and methods for implementing text, paragraph, and document styles.

StyleConstants.CharacterConstants

The StyleConstants.CharacterConstants class is an inner class of StyleConstants that supports character styles. It is a subclass of Object and implements the AttributeSet.CharacterAttribute interface.

StyleConstants.ColorConstants

The StyleConstants.ColorConstants class is an inner class of StyleConstants that supports text colors. It is a subclass of Object and implements the AttributeSet.ColorAttribute and AttributeSet.CharacterAttribute interfaces.

StyleConstants.FontConstants

The StyleConstants.FontConstants class is an inner class of StyleConstants that supports fonts. It is a subclass of Object and implements the AttributeSet.FontAttribute and AttributeSet.CharacterAttribute interfaces.

StyleConstants.ParagraphConstants

The StyleConstants.ParagraphConstants class is an inner class of StyleConstants that supports paragraph styles. It is a subclass of Object and implements the AttributeSet.ParagraphAttribute interface.

StyleContext

The StyleContext class is a subclass of Object that provides style constants and resources. It implements the java.io.Serializable and AbstractDocument.AttributeContext interfaces.

StyledEditorKit

The StyledEditorKit class is a subclass of DefaultEditorKit that provides a text editor that supports text styles.

StyledEditorKit.AlignmentAction

The StyledEditorKit.AlignmentAction class is an inner class of StyledEditorKit that supports paragraph alignment. It is a subclass of StyledEditorKit.StyledTextAction.

StyledEditorKit.BoldAction

The StyledEditorKit.BoldAction class is an inner class of StyledEditorKit that supports text bolding. It is a subclass of StyledEditorKit.StyledTextAction.

StyledEditorKit.FontFamilyAction

The `StyledEditorKit.FontFamilyAction` class is an inner class of `StyledEditorKit` that supports the use of fonts. It is a subclass of `StyledEditorKit.StyledTextAction`.

StyledEditorKit.FontSizeAction

The `StyledEditorKit.FontSizeAction` class is an inner class of `StyledEditorKit` that supports the control of text font size. It is a subclass of `StyledEditorKit.StyledTextAction`.

StyledEditorKit.ForegroundAction

The `StyledEditorKit.ForegroundAction` class is an inner class of `StyledEditorKit` that supports the setting of text foreground color. It is a subclass of `StyledEditorKit.StyledTextAction`.

StyledEditorKit.ItalicAction

The `StyledEditorKit.ItalicAction` class is an inner class of `StyledEditorKit` that supports the use of italics. It is a subclass of `StyledEditorKit.StyledTextAction`.

StyledEditorKit.StyledTextAction

The `StyledEditorKit.StyledTextAction` class is an inner class of `StyledEditorKit` that supports text operations. It is a subclass of `TextAction`.

StyledEditorKit.UnderlineAction

The `StyledEditorKit.UnderlineAction` class is an inner class of `StyledEditorKit` that supports underlining. It is a subclass of `StyledEditorKit.StyledTextAction`.

TabSet

The `TabSet` class is a subclass of `Object` that defines a set of tab stops. It implements the `java.io.Serializable` interface.

TabStop

The `TabStop` class is a subclass of `Object` that encapsulates a single tab stop. It implements the `java.io.Serializable` interface.

TableView

The `TableView` class is a subclass of `BoxView` that provides table support.

TextAction

The `TextAction` class is a subclass of `AbstractAction` that is used to define key mappings for text operations.

Utilities

The Utilities class is a subclass of Object that provides utility methods for text operations.

View

The View class is a subclass of Object that defines a view of part of a document.

WrappedPlainView

The WrappedPlainView class is a subclass of BoxView that supports wrapped plain text. It implements the TabExpander interface.

Exceptions and Errors

BadLocationException

The BadLocationException class is a subclass of java.lang.Exception that identifies errors in Document objects.

ChangedCharSetException

The ChangedCharSetException class extends java.io.IOException to signal a change from one character set to another.

Package javax.swing.text.html

The javax.swing.text.html package consists of 28 classes that provide basic HTML editing capabilities.

Interfaces

None.

Classes

BlockView

The BlockView class extends BoxView to provide the capability to display and HTML block with CSS attributes.

CSS

The CSS class extends Object to define an enumeration of CSS attributes.

CSS.Attribute

The CSS.Attribute class extends Object to define keys for CSS-related attribute sets.

FormView

The FormView class extends ComponentView and implements the ActionListener interface to provide a view implementation for HTML form elements.

HTML

The HTML class extends Object to define constants used in HTML documents.

HTML.Attribute

The HTML.Attribute class extends Object to provide an enumeration of HTML attributes.

HTML.Tag

The HTML.Tag class extends Object to provide an enumeration of HTML tags.

HTML.UnknownTag

The HTML.UnknownTag class extends Object and implements the Serializable interface to identify an unknown HTML tag.

HTMLDocument

The HTMLDocument class extends DefaultStyledDocument to encapsulate an HTML document.

HTMLDocument.Iterator

The HTMLDocument.Iterator class extends Object to provide the capability to iterate over HTML tags.

HTMLEditorKit

The HTMLEditorKit class is a subclass of javax.swing.text.StyledEditorKit that provides a basic HTML editing capability.

HTMLEditorKit.HTMLFactory

The HTMLEditorKit.HTMLFactory class extends Object and implements the ViewFactory interface to provide the capability to build HTML views.

HTMLEditorKit.HTMLTextAction

The HTMLEditorKit.HTMLTextAction class extends StyledEditorKit.StyledTextAction to provide basic support for HTML text editing.

HTMLEditorKit.InsertHTMLTextAction

The HTMLEditorKit.InsertHTMLTextAction class extends Object to allow the insertion of HTML into an existing HTML document.

D

HTMLEditorKit.LinkController

The HTMLEditorKit.LinkController class is an inner class of HTMLWriter that provides basic mouse event-handling support. It is a subclass of java.awt.event.MouseAdapter.

HTMLEditorKit.Parser

The HTMLEditorKit.Parser class extends HTMLEditorKit.HTMLTextAction to provide the capability to insert HTML into an existing document.

HTMLEditorKit.ParserCallback

The HTMLEditorKit.ParserCallback class extends Object to support HTML parsing.

HTMLFrameHyperlinkEvent

The HTMLFrameHyperlinkEvent class extends HyperlinkEvent to signal that an HTML link is activated.

HTMLWriter

The HTMLWriter class extends AbstractWriter to provide a basic Writer object for HTML documents.

InlineView

The InlineView class extends LabelView to display inline HTML elements with CSS attributes.

ListView

The ListView class extends BlockView to provide the capability to display an HTML list.

MinimalHTMLWriter

The MinimalHTMLWriter class extends AbstractWriter to provide an HTML Writer that displays HTML that is not produced by the HTML editor kit API.

ObjectView

The ObjectView class extends ComponentView to support the <OBJECT> tag.

Option

The Option class extends Object to provide support for the <OPTION> tag.

ParagraphView

The ParagraphView class extends javax.swing.text.ParagraphView to display an HTML paragraph with CSS attributes.

StyleSheet

The StyleSheet class extends StyleContext to provide CSS support.

StyleSheet.BoxPainter

The StyleSheet.BoxPainter class extends Object and implements the Serializable interface to support CSS box-like formatting.

StyleSheet.ListPainter

The StyleSheet.ListPainter class extends Object and implements the Serializable interface to support CSS list-like formatting.

Exceptions and Errors

None.

Package javax.swing.tree

The javax.swing.tree package provides 10 classes and seven interfaces that provide the capability to work with javax.swing.JTree components. The JTree component is a GUI component that displays a set of hierarchical data as an outline.

Interfaces

MutableTreeNode

The MutableTreeNode interface extends the TreeNode interface to provide methods for modifying the properties of a TreeNode object.

RowMapper

The RowMapper interface is used to identify the row corresponding to a TreeNode object.

TreeCellEditor

The TreeCellEditor interface extends the javax.swing.CellEditor interface to support the editing of tree elements.

TreeCellRenderer

The TreeCellRenderer interface is used to render the nodes of a tree.

TreeModel

The TreeModel interface is used to model the data used to build a tree.

TreeNode

The TreeNode interface defines methods for classes that implement the nodes of a tree.

TreeSelectionModel

The TreeSelectionModel interface defines constants and methods for working with the current selection state of the nodes of a tree.

Classes

AbstractLayoutCache

The AbstractLayoutCache class extends Object and implements the RowMapper interface to support layout development.

AbstractLayoutCache.NodeDimensions

The AbstractLayoutCache.NodeDimensions class is an inner class of AbstractLayoutCache that provides support for size and positioning in support of layout development.

DefaultMutableTreeNode

The DefaultMutableTreeNode class is a subclass of Object that provides a default, modifiable tree node. It implements the MutableTreeNode, java.lang.Cloneable, and java.io.Serializable interfaces.

DefaultTreeCellEditor

The DefaultTreeCellEditor class extends Object and implements the ActionListener, TreeCellEditor, and TreeSelectionListener interfaces. It provides a basic capability to edit tree cells.

DefaultTreeCellRenderer

The DefaultTreeCellRenderer class extends JLabel and implements the TreeCellRenderer interface to provide the capability to render a tree cell.

DefaultTreeModel

The DefaultTreeModel class is a subclass of Object that provides a default TreeModel implementation. It also implements the java.io.Serializable interface.

DefaultTreeSelectionModel

The DefaultTreeSelectionModel class is a subclass of Object that provides a default TreeSelectionModel implementation. It also implements the java.lang.Cloneable and java.io.Serializable interfaces.

FixedHeightLayoutCache

The FixedHeightLayoutCache class extends AbstractLayoutCache to support fixed height layout.

TreePath

The TreePath class is a subclass of Object that identifies a path to a node of a tree. It implements the java.io.Serializable interface.

VariableHeightLayoutCache

The VariableHeightLayoutCache class extends AbstractLayoutCache to support variable height layout.

Exceptions and Errors

ExpandVetoException

The ExpandVetoException class extends java.lang.Exception to provide the capability to veto the expanding or collapsing of a tree.

Package `javax.swing.undo`

The javax.swing.undo package provides five classes and two interfaces that support the implementation of undo and redo capabilities.

Interfaces

StateEditable

The StateEditable interface is implemented by classes whose state can be undone or redone by the StateEdit class.

UndoableEdit

The UndoableEdit interface is implemented by classes that support the undoing or redoing of edit operations.

Classes

AbstractUndoableEdit

The AbstractUndoableEdit class is a subclass of Object that provides an abstract implementation of the UndoableEdit interface.

CompoundEdit

The CompoundEdit class is a subclass of AbstractUndoableEdit that provides the capability to implement compound undo/redo operations.

D

StateEdit

The StateEdit class is a subclass of AbstractUndoableEdit that supports undo/redo operations on objects that change state.

UndoManager

The UndoManager class is a subclass of CompoundEdit that provides for thread-safe undo/redo operations. It implements the javax.swing.event.UndoableEditListener interface.

UndoableEditSupport

The UndoableEditSupport class is a subclass of Object that supports the management of undoable editing operations.

Exceptions and Errors

CannotRedoException

The CannotRedoException class is a subclass of RuntimeException that indicates a redo operation cannot be performed.

CannotUndoException

The CannotUndoException class is a subclass of RuntimeException that indicates an undo operation cannot be performed.

Package org.omg.CORBA

The org.omg.CORBA package consists of 40 classes and 29 interfaces that implement the foundation for supporting Java-CORBA integration.

Interfaces

ARG_IN

The ARG_IN interface identifies a method input argument.

ARG_INOUT

The ARG_INOUT interface identifies an argument that may be used as both an input and an output in a method invocation.

ARG_OUT

The ARG_OUT interface identifies a method output argument.

BAD_POLICY

The BAD_POLICY interface is used to indicate a bad policy.

BAD_POLICY_TYPE

The BAD_POLICY_TYPE interface is used to indicate a bad policy type.

BAD_POLICY_VALUE

The BAD_POLICY_VALUE interface is used to indicate a bad policy value.

CTX_RESTRICT_SCOPE

The CTX_RESTRICT_SCOPE interface is used as a flag to restrict the search scope of the get_values() method.

Current

The Current interface extends the Object interface to provide the capability to access information associated with a particular thread of execution.

DomainManager

The DomainManager interface extends the Object interface to provide the capability to manage the policy associated with a particular domain.

DynAny

The DynAny interface extends the Object interface to support the dynamic traversal of CORBA Any values.

DynArray

The DynArray interface extends the Object and DynAny interfaces to support arrays.

DynEnum

The DynEnum interface extends the Object and DynAny interfaces to support IDL enum types.

DynFixed

The DynFixed interface extends the Object and DynAny interfaces to support IDL fixed types.

DynSequence

The DynSequence interface extends the Object and DynAny interfaces to support IDL sequence types.

D

DynStruct

The DynStruct interface extends the Object and DynAny interfaces to support IDL structs.

DynUnion

The DynUnion interface extends the Object and DynAny interfaces to support IDL union types.

DynValue

The DynValue interface extends the Object and DynAny interfaces to support name value pairs.

IDLType

The IDLType interface encapsulates an IDL IDLType. It extends the Object and IRObject interfaces.

IRObject

The IRObject interface encapsulates an interface repository object. It extends the Object interface.

Object

The Object interface represents a CORBA object reference.

Policy

The Policy interface extends the Object interface to provide a basic mechanism for policy implementation.

PRIVATE_MEMBER

The PRIVATE_MEMBER interface extends the Object interface to support the implementation of private members.

PUBLIC_MEMBER

The PUBLIC_MEMBER interface extends the Object interface to support the implementation of public members.

UNSUPPORTED_POLICY

The UNSUPPORTED_POLICY interface extends the Object interface to support the specification of unsupported policy.

UNSUPPORTED_POLICY_VALUE

The UNSUPPORTED_POLICY_VALUE interface extends the Object interface to support the specification of unsupported policy.

VM_ABSTRACT

The VM_ABSTRACT interface extends the Object interface to support the specification of an abstract virtual machine.

VM_CUSTOM

The VM_CUSTOM interface extends the Object interface to support the specification of a custom virtual machine.

VM_NONE

The VM_NONE interface extends the Object interface to support the specification of a nonexistent virtual machine.

VM_TRUNCATABLE

The VM_TRUNCATABLE interface extends the Object interface to support the specification of a truncatable virtual machine.

Classes

Any

The Any class is a subclass of Object that acts as a container for data of any primitive IDL type.

AnyHolder

The AnyHolder class is a subclass of Object that acts as a holder for Any objects used as INOUT and OUT method parameters.

BooleanHolder

The BooleanHolder class is a subclass of Object that is used to hold boolean values for use as INOUT and OUT arguments.

ByteHolder

The ByteHolder class is a subclass of Object that is used to hold byte values for use as INOUT and OUT arguments.

CharHolder

The CharHolder class is a subclass of Object that is used to hold char values for use as INOUT and OUT arguments.

CompletionStatus

The CompletionStatus class is a subclass of Object that identifies the completion status of a method that throws a SystemException.

Context

The Context class is a subclass of Object that provides information about the context in which a method invocation request takes place.

ContextList

The ContextList class is a subclass of Object that specifies properties associated with a Context object.

DefinitionKind

The DefinitionKind class is a subclass of Object that is used to hold Boolean types for use as INOUT and OUT arguments.

DoubleHolder

The DoubleHolder class is a subclass of Object that is used to hold double values for use as INOUT and OUT arguments.

DynamicImplementation

The DynamicImplementation class is a subclass of org.omg.CORBA.portable.ObjectImpl that provides support for the dynamic servant interface.

Environment

The Environment class is a subclass of Object that is used to make exceptions available to the client that requested a method invocation.

ExceptionList

The ExceptionList class is a subclass of Object that lists the exceptions that can be thrown by a method.

FixedHolder

The FixedHolder class is a subclass of Object that is used to hold fixed IDL type values for use as INOUT and OUT arguments.

FloatHolder

The FloatHolder class is a subclass of Object that is used to hold float values for use as INOUT and OUT arguments.

IntHolder

The IntHolder class is a subclass of Object that is used to hold int values for use as INOUT and OUT arguments.

LongHolder

The LongHolder class is a subclass of Object that is used to hold long values for use as INOUT and OUT arguments.

NVList

The NVList class is a subclass of Object that provides a list of NamedValue objects.

NamedValue

The NamedValue class is a subclass of Object that is used to describe method arguments and return values.

NameValuePair

The NameValuePair class extends Object to hold names and values of IDL structs in the DynStruct API.

ORB

The ORB class is a subclass of Object that serves as the CORBA object request broker.

ObjectHolder

The ObjectHolder class is a subclass of Object that is used to hold object references for use as INOUT and OUT arguments.

Principal

The Principal class is a subclass of Object that identifies a client making a remote method invocation request.

PrincipalHolder

The PrincipalHolder class is a subclass of Object that is used to hold Principal objects for use as INOUT and OUT arguments.

Request

The Request class is a subclass of Object that encapsulates a client request to invoke a remote method.

ServerRequest

The ServerRequest class is a subclass of Object that encapsulates a dynamic skeleton interface request.

ServiceDetail

The ServiceDetail class extends Object that implements the IDLEntity interface. It is used to provide service information.

ServiceDetailHelper

The ServiceDetailHelper class extends Object to provide helper support for service detail information.

ServiceInformation

The ServiceInformation class extends Object to provide information to a service information IDL struct.

ServiceInformationHelper

The ServiceInformationHelper class extends Object to provide helper support for the service information IDL struct.

ServiceInformationHolder

The ServiceInformationHolder class extends Object to provide holder support for the service information IDL struct.

SetOverrideType

The SetOverrideType class extends Object and implements the IDLEntity interface to provide support for the override type.

ShortHolder

The ShortHolder class is a subclass of Object that is used to hold short values for use as INOUT and OUT arguments.

StringHolder

The StringHolder class is a subclass of Object that is used to hold String objects for use as INOUT and OUT arguments.

StructMember

The StructMember class is a subclass of Object that describes a member of a CORBA data structure.

TCKind

The TCKind class is a subclass of Object that encapsulates the IDL TCKind object.

TypeCode

The TypeCode class is a subclass of Object that is used to identify a primitive IDL value type.

TypeCodeHolder

The TypeCodeHolder class is a subclass of Object that is used to hold TypeCode objects for use as INOUT and OUT arguments.

UnionMember

The UnionMember class is a subclass of Object that provides support for IDL union constructs.

ValueMember

The ValueMember class extends Object and implements the IDLEntity interface to provide an interface repository description of the value object.

Exceptions and Errors

BAD_CONTEXT

The BAD_CONTEXT class is a subclass of SystemException that supports the CORBA BAD_CONTEXT exception.

BAD_INV_ORDER

The BAD_INV_ORDER class is a subclass of SystemException that supports the CORBA BAD_INV_ORDER exception.

BAD_OPERATION

The BAD_OPERATION class is a subclass of SystemException that supports the CORBA BAD_OPERATION exception.

BAD_PARAM

The BAD_PARAM class is a subclass of SystemException that supports the CORBA BAD_PARAM exception.

BAD_TYPECODE

The BAD_TYPECODE class is a subclass of SystemException that supports the CORBA BAD_TYPECODE exception.

Bounds

The Bounds class is a subclass of UserException that provides support for the user-defined bounds exception.

D

COMM_FAILURE

The `COMM_FAILURE` class is a subclass of `SystemException` that supports the CORBA `COMM_FAILURE` exception.

DATA_CONVERSION

The `DATA_CONVERSION` class is a subclass of `SystemException` that supports the CORBA `DATA_CONVERSION` exception.

FREE_MEM

The `FREE_MEM` class is a subclass of `SystemException` that supports the CORBA `FREE_MEM` exception.

IMP_LIMIT

The `IMP_LIMIT` class is a subclass of `SystemException` that supports the CORBA `IMP_LIMIT` exception.

INITIALIZE

The `INITIALIZE` class is a subclass of `SystemException` that supports the CORBA `INITIALIZE` exception.

INTERNAL

The `INTERNAL` class is a subclass of `SystemException` that supports the CORBA `INTERNAL` exception.

INTF_REPOS

The `INTF_REPOS` class is a subclass of `SystemException` that supports the CORBA `INTF_REPOS` exception.

INVALID_TRANSACTION

The `INVALID_TRANSACTION` class is a subclass of `SystemException` that supports the CORBA `INVALID_TRANSACTION` exception.

INV_FLAG

The `INV_FLAG` class is a subclass of `SystemException` that supports the CORBA `INV_FLAG` exception.

INV_IDENT

The `INV_IDENT` class is a subclass of `SystemException` that supports the CORBA `INV_IDENT` exception.

INV_OBJREF

The INV_OBJREF class is a subclass of SystemException that supports the CORBA INV_OBJREF exception.

INV_POLICY

The INV_POLICY class is a subclass of SystemException that supports the CORBA INV_POLICY exception.

MARSHAL

The MARSHAL class is a subclass of SystemException that supports the CORBA MARSHAL exception.

NO_IMPLEMENT

The NO_IMPLEMENT class is a subclass of SystemException that supports the CORBA NO_IMPLEMENT exception.

NO_MEMORY

The NO_MEMORY class is a subclass of SystemException that supports the CORBA NO_MEMORY exception.

NO_PERMISSION

The NO_PERMISSION class is a subclass of SystemException that supports the CORBA NO_PERMISSION exception.

NO_RESOURCES

The NO_RESOURCES class is a subclass of SystemException that supports the CORBA NO_RESOURCES exception.

NO_RESPONSE

The NO_RESPONSE class is a subclass of SystemException that supports the CORBA NO_RESPONSE exception.

OBJECT_NOT_EXIST

The OBJECT_NOT_EXIST class is a subclass of SystemException that supports the CORBA OBJECT_NOT_EXIST exception.

OBJ_ADAPTER

The OBJ_ADAPTER class is a subclass of SystemException that supports the CORBA OBJ_ADAPTER exception.

D

PERSIST_STORE

The PERSIST_STORE class is a subclass of SystemException that supports the CORBA PERSIST_STORE exception.

PolicyError

The PolicyError class extends UserException to provide support for identifying policy-related errors.

SystemException

The SystemException class is a subclass of java.lang.RuntimeException that serves as the base class for implementing CORBA exceptions.

TRANSACTION_REQUIRED

The TRANSACTION_REQUIRED class is a subclass of SystemException that supports the CORBA TRANSACTION_REQUIRED exception.

TRANSACTION_ROLLEDBACK

The TRANSACTION_ROLLEDBACK class is a subclass of SystemException that supports the CORBA TRANSACTION_ROLLEDBACK exception.

TRANSIENT

The TRANSIENT class is a subclass of SystemException that supports the CORBA TRANSIENT exception.

UNKNOWN

The UNKNOWN class is a subclass of SystemException that supports the CORBA UNKNOWN exception.

UnknownUserException

The UnknownUserException class is a subclass of UserException that identifies an unknown user exception returned by the remote server.

UserException

The UserException class is a subclass of java.lang.Exception that supports the implementation of IDL-defined user exceptions.

WrongTransaction

The WrongTransaction class is a subclass of UserException that identifies a requested transaction as being from an incorrect transaction scope.

Package `org.omg.CORBA.DynAnyPackage`

The `org.omg.CORBA.DynAnyPackage` package defines four exceptions, which are used to support the `DynAny` interface.

Interfaces

None.

Classes

None.

Exceptions and Errors

Invalid

The `Invalid` class extends `UserException` to indicate that a bad `DynAny` or `Any` is passed as a parameter.

InvalidSeq

The `InvalidSeq` class extends `UserException` to indicate an invalid array sequence.

InvalidValue

The `InvalidValue` class extends `UserException` to a bad `DynAny` value was encountered.

TypeMismatch

The `TypeMismatch` class extends `UserException` to indicate that the type of an object does not match the type being accessed.

Package `org.omg.CORBA.ORBPackage`

The `org.omg.CORBA.ORBPackage` package defines the `InconsistentTypeCode` and `InvalidName` exceptions.

Interfaces

None.

Classes

None.

Exceptions and Errors

InconsistentTypeCode

The InconsistentTypeCode class is a subclass of org.omg.CORBA.UserException that indicates an attempt to create a dynamic Any with a type code that does not match the particular subclass of DynAny.

InvalidName

The InvalidName class is a subclass of org.omg.CORBA.UserException that indicates that the ORB was passed a name for which there is no initial reference.

Package org.omg.CORBA.TypeCodePackage

The org.omg.CORBA.TypeCodePackage package defines the BadKind and Bounds exceptions, which are used to signal exceptions related to type usage and constraints.

Interfaces

None.

Classes

None.

Exceptions and Errors

BadKind

The BadKind class is a subclass of org.omg.CORBA.UserException that indicates that an inappropriate operation was attempted on an org.omg.CORBA.TypeCode object.

Bounds

The Bounds class is a subclass of org.omg.CORBA.UserException that indicates that an out-of-bounds exception occurred as the result of an operation on an org.omg.CORBA.TypeCode object.

Package org.omg.CORBA.portable

The org.omg.CORBA.portable package consists of five classes and four interfaces that are used to support vendor-specific CORBA implementations.

Interfaces

IDLEntity

The IDLEntity interface extends the Serializable interface to indicate that an implementing class is a Java value type from IDL that has a corresponding helper class.

InvokeHandler

The InvokeHandler interface provides the capability to invoke a ResponseHandler object.

ResponseHandler

The ResponseHandler interface provides the capability to respond to a method invocation.

Streamable

The Streamable interface provides methods for marshalling and unmarshalling holders to and from streams.

Classes

Delegate

The Delegate class is a subclass of Object that specifies a portable API for ORB-vendor-specific implementation of the org.omg.CORBA.Object methods.

InputStream

The InputStream class is a subclass of Object that provides methods for reading IDL types from streams.

ObjectImpl

The ObjectImpl class is a subclass of Object that provides a default implementation of the org.omg.CORBA.Object interface.

OutputStream

The OutputStream class is a subclass of Object that provides methods for writing IDL types to streams.

ServantObject

The ServantObject class extends Object to encapsulate a CORBA servant.

D

Exceptions and Errors

ApplicationException

The `ApplicationException` class extends `java.lang.Exception` to indicate that an exception occurred in the current application.

RemarshalException

The `RemarshalException` class extends `java.lang.Exception` to indicate that an exception occurred while remarshalling a method invocation.

Package `org.omg.CosNaming`

The `org.omg.CosNaming` package consists of 22 classes and two interfaces that implement a tree-structured naming service.

Interfaces

BindingIterator

The `BindingIterator` interface extends the `org.omg.CORBA.Object` interface and provides the capability to iterate through a list of name-object bindings.

NamingContext

The `NamingContext` interface extends the `org.omg.CORBA.Object` interface and provides access to the naming service.

Classes

Binding

The `Binding` class is a subclass of `Object` that associates a name with an object.

BindingHelper

The `BindingHelper` class is a subclass of `Object` that provides static methods for manipulating bindings.

BindingHolder

The `BindingHolder` class is a subclass of `Object` that holds the value of a `Binding` object.

BindingIteratorHelper

The `BindingIteratorHelper` class is a subclass of `Object` that provides static methods for manipulating binding iterators.

BindingIteratorHolder

The BindingIteratorHolder class is a subclass of Object that holds the value of a binding iterator.

BindingListHelper

The BindingListHelper class is a subclass of Object that provides static methods for manipulating binding lists.

BindingListHolder

The BindingListHolder class is a subclass of Object that holds the value of a binding list.

BindingType

The BindingType class is a subclass of Object that identifies the type of a Binding object.

BindingTypeHelper

The BindingTypeHelper class is a subclass of Object that provides static methods for manipulating binding types.

BindingTypeHolder

The BindingTypeHolder class is a subclass of Object that holds the value of a binding type.

IstringHelper

The IstringHelper class is a subclass of Object that provides static methods for manipulating strings.

NameComponent

The NameComponent class is a subclass of Object that is used to build hierarchical names.

NameComponentHelper

The NameComponentHelper class is a subclass of Object that provides static methods for manipulating name components.

NameComponentHolder

The NameComponentHolder class is a subclass of Object that holds the value of a name component. It implements the org.omg.CORBA.portable.Streamable interface.

D

NameHelper

The NameHelper class is a subclass of Object that provides static methods for manipulating names.

NameHolder

The NameHolder class is a subclass of Object that holds the value of a name. It implements the org.omg.CORBA.portable.Streamable interface.

NamingContextHelper

The NamingContextHelper class is a subclass of Object that provides static methods for manipulating name contexts.

NamingContextHolder

The NamingContextHolder class is a subclass of Object that holds the value of a naming context. It implements the org.omg.CORBA.portable.Streamable interface.

_BindingIteratorImplBase

The _BindingIteratorImplBase class is a subclass of org.omg.CORBA.DynamicImplementation that supports the implementation of binding iterators. It implements the BindingIterator interface.

_BindingIteratorStub

The BindingIteratorStub class is a subclass of org.omg.CORBA.portable.ObjectImpl that supports the implementation of a binding iterator stub.

_NamingContextImplBase

The _NamingContextImplBase class is a subclass of org.omg.CORBA.DynamicImplementation that supports the implementation of naming contexts. It implements the NamingContext interface.

_NamingContextStub

The NamingContextStub class is a subclass of org.omg.CORBA.portable.ObjectImpl that supports the implementation of a naming context stub.

Exceptions and Errors

None.

Package
org.omg.CosNaming.NamingContextPackage

The org.omg.CosNaming.NamingContextPackage package consists of 13 classes that implement aspects of the naming service's name context. The name context implements nodes within the tree-structured naming scheme.

Interfaces

None.

Classes

AlreadyBoundHelper

The AlreadyBoundHelper class is a subclass of Object that provides support for the AlreadyBound exception.

AlreadyBoundHolder

The AlreadyBoundHolder class is a subclass of Object that provides support for the AlreadyBound exception. It implements the org.omg.CORBA.portable.Streamable interface.

CannotProceedHelper

The CannotProceedHelper class is a subclass of Object that provides support for the CannotProceed exception.

CannotProceedHolder

The CannotProceedHolder class is a subclass of Object that provides support for the CannotProceed exception. It implements the org.omg.CORBA.portable.Streamable interface.

InvalidNameHelper

The InvalidNameHelper class is a subclass of Object that provides support for the InvalidName exception.

InvalidNameHolder

The InvalidNameHolder class is a subclass of Object that provides support for the InvalidName exception. It implements the org.omg.CORBA.portable.Streamable interface.

D

NotEmptyHelper

The NotEmptyHelper class is a subclass of Object that provides support for the NotEmpty exception.

NotEmptyHolder

The NotEmptyHolder class is a subclass of Object that provides support for the NotEmpty exception. It implements the org.omg.CORBA.portable.Streamable interface.

NotFoundHelper

The NotFoundHelper class is a subclass of Object that provides support for the NotFound exception.

NotFoundHolder

The NotFoundHolder class is a subclass of Object that provides support for the NotFound exception.

NotFoundReason

The NotFoundReason class is a subclass of Object that provides support for the NotFound exception.

NotFoundReasonHelper

The NotFoundReasonHelper class is a subclass of Object that provides support for the NotFoundReason object.

NotFoundReasonHolder

The NotFoundReasonHolder class is a subclass of Object that provides storage for a NotFoundReason object. It implements the org.omg.CORBA.portable.Streamable interface.

Exceptions and Errors

AlreadyBound

The AlreadyBound class is a subclass of org.omg.CORBA.UserException that identifies a name as being already bound with an object.

CannotProceed

The CannotProceed class is a subclass of org.omg.CORBA.UserException that signals that the CORBA implementation has come to a standstill.

InvalidName

The InvalidName class is a subclass of org.omg.CORBA.UserException that indicates that an invalid name has been used.

NotEmpty

The NotEmpty class is a subclass of org.omg.CORBA.UserException that signals that a non-empty reference was encountered when one was not expected.

NotFound

The NotFound class is a subclass of org.omg.CORBA.UserException that signals that a referenced name cannot be found.

D

INDEX

E

X-Z

Sun Microsystems, Inc.
Binary Code License Agreement

READ THE TERMS OF THIS AGREEMENT AND ANY PROVIDED SUPPLEMEN-
TAL LICENSE TERMS (COLLECTIVELY "AGREEMENT") CAREFULLY BEFORE
OPENING THE SOFTWARE MEDIA PACKAGE. BY OPENING THE SOFTWARE
MEDIA PACKAGE, YOU AGREE TO THE TERMS OF THIS AGREEMENT. IF YOU
ARE ACCESSING THE SOFTWARE ELECTRONICALLY, INDICATE YOUR
ACCEPTANCE OF THESE TERMS BY SELECTING THE "ACCEPT" BUTTON AT
THE END OF THIS AGREEMENT. IF YOU DO NOT AGREE TO ALL THESE
TERMS, PROMPTLY RETURN THE UNUSED SOFTWARE TO YOUR PLACE OF
PURCHASE FOR A REFUND OR, IF THE SOFTWARE IS ACCESSED ELECTRONI-
CALLY, SELECT THE "DECLINE" BUTTON AT THE END OF THIS AGREEMENT.

1. **LICENSE TO USE.** Sun grants you a non-exclusive and non-transferable
   license for the internal use only of the accompanying software and documentation
   and any error corrections provided by Sun (collectively "Software"), by the number
   of users and the class of computer hardware for which the corresponding fee has
   been paid.

2. **RESTRICTIONS.** Software is confidential and copyrighted. Title to Software and
   all associated intellectual property rights is retained by Sun and/or its licensors.
   Except as specifically authorized in any Supplemental License Terms, you may not
   make copies of Software, other than a single copy of Software for archival purposes. Unless enforcement is prohibited by applicable law, you may not modify,
   decompile, reverse engineer Software. Software is not designed or licensed for use
   in on-line control of aircraft, air traffic, aircraft navigation or aircraft communications; or in the design, construction, operation or maintenance of any nuclear facility. You warrant that you will not use Software for these purposes. You may not
   publish or provide the results of any benchmark or comparison tests run on
   Software to any third party without the prior written consent of Sun. No right, title
   or interest in or to any trademark, service mark, logo or trade name of Sun or its
   licensors is granted under this Agreement.

3. **LIMITED WARRANTY.** Sun warrants to you that for a period of ninety (90)
   days from the date of purchase, as evidenced by a copy of the receipt, the media on
   which Software is furnished (if any) will be free of defects in materials and work-
   manship under normal use. Except for the foregoing, Software is provided "AS
   IS". Your exclusive remedy and Sun's entire liability under this limited warranty
   will be at Sun's option to replace Software media or refund the fee paid for
   Software.

4. **DISCLAIMER OF WARRANTY.** UNLESS SPECIFIED IN THIS AGREE-
MENT, ALL EXPRESS OR IMPLIED CONDITIONS, REPRESENTATIONS
AND WARRANTIES, INCLUDING ANY IMPLIED WARRANTY OF MER-
CHANTABILITY, FITNESS FOR A PARTICULAR PURPOSE, OR NON-
INFRINGEMENT, ARE DISCLAIMED, EXCEPT TO THE EXTENT THAT
THESE DISCLAIMERS ARE HELD TO BE LEGALLY INVALID.

5. **LIMITATION OF LIABILITY.** TO THE EXTENT NOT PROHIBITED BY
LAW, IN NO EVENT WILL SUN OR ITS LICENSORS BE LIABLE FOR ANY
LOST REVENUE, PROFIT OR DATA, OR FOR SPECIAL, INDIRECT, CONSE-
QUENTIAL, INCIDENTAL OR PUNITIVE DAMAGES, HOWEVER CAUSED
REGARDLESS OF THE THEORY OF LIABILITY, ARISING OUT OF OR
RELATED TO THE USE OF OR INABILITY TO USE SOFTWARE, EVEN IF
SUN HAS BEEN ADVISED OF THE POSSIBILITY OF SUCH DAMAGES. In
no event will Sun's liability to you, whether in contract, tort (including negli-
gence), or otherwise, exceed the amount paid by you for Software under this
Agreement. The foregoing limitations will apply even if the above stated warranty
fails of its essential purpose.

6. **Termination.** This Agreement is effective until terminated. You may terminate this
Agreement at any time by destroying all copies of Software. This Agreement will
terminate immediately without notice from Sun if you fail to comply with any provision of this Agreement. Upon Termination, you must destroy all copies of
Software.

7. **Export Regulations.** All Software and technical data delivered under this
Agreement are subject to US export control laws and may be subject to export or
import regulations in other countries. You agree to comply strictly with all such
laws and regulations and acknowledge that you have the responsibility to obtain
such licenses to export, re-export, or import as may be required after delivery to
you.

8. **U.S. Government Restricted Rights.** Use, duplication, or disclosure by the U.S.
Government is subject to restrictions set forth in this Agreement and as provided in
DFARS 227.7202-1 (a) and 227.7202-3(a) (1995), DFARS 252.227-7013
(c)(1)(ii)(Oct 1988), FAR 12.212 (a) (1995), FAR 52.227-19 (June 1987), or FAR
52.227-14(ALT III) (June 1987), as applicable.

9. **Governing Law.** Any action related to this Agreement will be governed by
California law and controlling U.S. federal law. No choice of law rules of any
jurisdiction will apply.

10. **Severability.** If any provision of this Agreement is held to be unenforceable, This Agreement will remain in effect with the provision omitted, unless omission would frustrate the intent of the parties, in which case this Agreement will immediately terminate.

11. **Integration.** This Agreement is the entire agreement between you and Sun relating to its subject matter. It supersedes all prior or contemporaneous oral or written communications, proposals, representations and warranties and prevails over any conflicting or additional terms of any quote, order, acknowledgment, or other communication between the parties relating to its subject matter during the term of this Agreement. No modification of this Agreement will be binding, unless in writing and signed by an authorized representative of each party.

For inquiries please contact: Sun Microsystems, Inc., 901 San Antonio Road, Palo Alto, California 94303

JAVA™ DEVELOPMENT KIT VERSION 1.2 SUPPLEMENTAL LICENSE TERMS

These supplemental terms ("Supplement") add to the terms of the Binary Code License Agreement ("Agreement"). Capitalized terms not defined herein shall have the same meanings ascribed to them in the Agreement. The Supplement terms shall supersede any inconsistent or conflicting terms in the Agreement.

1. **Limited License Grant.** Sun grants to you a non-exclusive, non-transferable limited license to use the Software without fee for evaluation of the Software and for development of Java(TM) applets and applications provided that you: (i) may not re-distribute the Software in whole or in part, either separately or included with a product. (ii) may not create, or authorize your licensees to create additional classes, interfaces, or subpackages that are contained in the "java" or "sun" packages or similar as specified by Sun in any class file naming convention; and (iii) agree to the extent Programs are developed which utilize the Windows 95/98 style graphical user interface or components contained therein, such applets or applications may only be developed to run on a Windows 95/98 or Windows NT platform. Refer to the Java Runtime Environment Version 1.2 binary code license (http://java.sun.com/products/JDK/1.2/index.html) for the availability of runtime code which may be distributed with Java applets and applications.

2. **Java Platform Interface.** In the event that Licensee creates an additional API(s) which: (i) extends the functionality of a Java Environment; and, (ii) is exposed to

third party software developers for the purpose of developing additional software which invokes such additional API, Licensee must promptly publish broadly an accurate specification for such API for free use by all developers.

3. **Trademarks and Logos.** This Agreement does not authorize Licensee to use any Sun name, trademark or logo. Licensee acknowledges as between it and Sun that Sun owns the Java trademark and all Java-related trademarks, logos and icons including the Coffee Cup and Duke ("Java Marks") and agrees to comply with the Java Trademark Guidelines at http://java.sun.com/trademarks.html.

4. **High Risk Activities.** Notwithstanding Section 2, with respect to high risk activities, the following language shall apply: the Software is not designed or intended for use in on-line control of aircraft, air traffic, aircraft navigation or aircraft communications; or in the design, construction, operation or maintenance of any nuclear facility. Sun disclaims any express or implied warranty of fitness for such uses.

SAMS
Teach Yourself
in 21 Days

Sams Teach Yourself in 21 Days *teaches you all the skills you need to master the basics and then moves on to the more advanced features and concepts. This series is designed for the way you learn. Go chapter by chapter through the step-by-step lessons or just choose those lessons that interest you the most.*

Sams Teach Yourself Borland JBuilder 2 in 21 Days
Don Doherty
ISBN: 0-672-31318-9
$39.99 US/$57.95 CAN

Sams Teach Yourself Visual J++ 6 in 21 Days
Rick Leinecker
ISBN: 0-672-31351-0
$29.99 US/$42.95 CAN

Sams Teach Yourself Visual InterDev 6 in 21 Days
Michael Van hoozer
ISBN: 0-672-31251-4
$34.99 US/$50.95 CAN

SAMS

www.*samspublishing*.com

All prices are subject to change.

What's on the CD-ROM

This book's CD-ROM is a hybrid that works on Windows 95/98, Windows NT, and UNIX operating systems. The CD includes the source code from the book, sample applets, the official Java Development Kit from Sun Microsystems, and additional Java development tools.

Source Code

All the code listings in the book can be found on the CD, organized by chapter number.

Java Development Tools

- Sun Microsystems' Java Development Kit (JDK) 1.2 (Windows 95/98/NT and Solaris)
- Borland JBuilder™ 2 Publisher's Edition (Windows)
- Tek-Tools' Kawa (Windows)
- Java Gamelet Toolkit (Windows)

Licensing Agreement

Use of this software is subject to the Binary Code License terms and conditions on page 945. Read the license carefully. By opening this package, you are agreeing to be bound by the terms and conditions of this license from Sun Microsystems, Inc.

By opening this package, you are also agreeing to be bound by the following agreement:

Some of the software included with this product might be copyrighted, in which case all rights are reserved by the respective copyright holder. You are licensed to use software copyrighted by the publisher and its licensors on a single computer. You may copy and/or modify the software as needed to facilitate your use of it on a single computer. Making copies of the software for any other purpose is a violation of United States copyright laws.

This software is sold as-is, without warranty of any kind, either expressed or implied, including but not limited to the implied warranties of merchantability and fitness for a particular purpose. Neither the publisher nor its dealers or distributors assumes any liability for any alleged or actual damages arising from the use of this program. (Some states do not allow for the exclusion of implied warranties, so the exclusion might not apply to you.)